Compiler Design

Compiler Design

Manoj B Chandak
Professor & Head, Department of Computer Science and Engineering,
Shri Ramdeobaba College of Engineering and Management,
Nagpur, Maharashtra

Khushboo P Khurana
Assistant Professor, Department of Computer Science and Engineering,
Shri Ramdeobaba College of Engineering and Management,
Nagpur, Maharashtra

Universities Press

COMPILER DESIGN

UNIVERSITIES PRESS (INDIA) PRIVATE LIMITED

Registered Office
3-6-747/1/A & 3-6-754/1, Himayatnagar, Hyderabad 500 029, Telangana, India
info@universitiespress.com; www.universitiespress.com

Distributed by
Orient Blackswan Private Limited

Registered Office
3-6-752 Himayatnagar, Hyderabad 500 029, Telangana, India

Other Offices
Bengaluru / Bhopal / Chennai / Guwahati / Hyderabad / Jaipur
Kolkata / Lucknow / Mumbai / New Delhi / Noida / Patna / Vijayawada

501467

ISBN 978-93-86235-64-0

Typeset in Times New Roman 10 points *by*
MacroTex Solutions, Chennai 600 091, Tamil Nadu, India

Printed at
Yash Printographics, Noida

Published by
Universities Press (India) Private Limited
3-6-747/1/A & 3-6-754/1, Himayatnagar, Hyderabad 500 029, Telangana, India

Preface

In today's era of technology, the course on Compiler Design plays a major role in understanding the mathematical and computing aspects of other courses such as Natural Language Processing, Machine Learning, Data Analytics, and so on. This course can be considered as the basis of design systems, similar to human beings. The main objective of the book is to present the role of the various phases of compiler design by explaining the mathematical and numerical components related to each phase.

The computer is capable of executing simple programs written in the language of 0s and 1s. As writing programs in this language is a tedious and error-prone task, they are written in high-level language. Machine-independent high-level languages require conversion to low-level language programs that can be executed by a machine. The compiler is a program that converts a high-level language program to a low-level one. The code generated by the compiler may not be very efficient and may require optimisation. This book focuses on explaining the basic concepts involved in designing a compiler and the optimisation of the code that is generated. It is intended to be a basic reading material for compiler design and has many solved examples to explain the concepts in depth.

The first chapter is an introductory one, discussing the front-end and back-end phases of the compiler. The front-end phases are discussed in detail in chapters 2, 3, 4 and 5, while the back-end phases are discussed in chapters 6 and 7. The run-time environment, error handling and symbol table management, which are related to all the phases, are elaborated in chapters 8 and 9. Chapters 11 and 12 deal with the compiling concepts of functional languages and parallel programming, respectively. The remaining chapters focus on programming.

Chapter Organisation

The book is organised as follows:

Chapter 1 introduces the subject and the different phases of the compiler. These phases are discussed in detail in the remaining chapters. It also relates the phases of the compiler to formal systems that can be used with each phase of the compiler.

Chapter 2 describes the first phase of compilation – lexical analysis. The use of regular expressions is described, along with their implementation using finite automata.

Chapter 3 presents the syntax analysis phase of the compiler. Various techniques of parsing (syntax analysis) are discussed in detail, ranging from recursive descent parser, which is a top-down parser, to bottom-up LR techniques. Operator precedence parsers are also discussed.

Chapter 4 describes the semantic analysis phase of the compiler and elaborates the type systems and type checking.

Chapter 5 explains the intermediate code generation phase. The intermediate representation of the three-address code is used in this chapter.

Chapter 6 discusses machine-dependent and machine-independent code optimisation techniques.

Chapter 7 discusses the techniques of target code generation.

Chapter 8 details the run-time environment required for the execution of a program. The aspects to be handled in the run-time environment such as memory organisation, activation of procedures, activation records, procedure calls and returns, and parameter passing are explained.

Chapter 9 provides an introduction to the errors that can be encountered during each phase of compilation, and how these errors can be handled.
Chapter 10 discusses various compiler construction tools that help in the auto-generation of code for some phases of the compiler.
Chapter 11 provides an introduction to the main concepts in functional languages and describes the compilation process in functional languages.
Chapter 12 provides an overview of concepts in parallel programming and discusses the parallel compiler.
Chapter 13 concentrates on programming. Programs related to each phase of the compiler are presented in this chapter.
Chapter 14 includes solved questions related to compiler design from previous GATE exams.

Each chapter contains review questions, practice questions and programming questions to help students get hands-on practice and to check their understanding of the concepts covered in that chapter. A summary is also included after each chapter to provide a quick recap of the topics discussed in the chapter.

Manoj B Chandak
Khushboo P Khurana

Acknowledgements

We are indebted to a number of people, and take this opportunity to acknowledge and extend our deep sense of gratitude to all of them. Firstly, we would like to express our sincere thanks to our institute – Shri Ramdeobaba College of Engineering and Management, Nagpur – and the Honorable Management for providing constant support and encouragement.

We wholeheartedly appreciate the efforts of Universities Press in helping us at different stages of the book. Their creativity, assistance and patience during the production of this book are truly appreciated. We would like to thank Ms Madhavi Sethupathi, Senior Editor, for her constant support during the editing of the book. The entire team deserves a special thanks for the timely publication of the book. We would also like to thank Mr Thomas Mathew Rajesh, Vice-President, and Mr Kallol Das, Acquisitions Editor.

The book could not have been completed without the support of our family members. We would like to thank our parents for their teachings and blessings. The valuable advice and motivation from our family helped us work to the best of our abilities.

Finally, we would like to express our heartfelt thanks to all those who have directly and indirectly helped us in making the book a reality.

Manoj B Chandak
Khushboo P Khurana

Contents

To my beloved parents

Manoj B Chandak

To my parents and mother-in-law

Khushboo P Khurana

1 Introduction to Compilers

Objectives

- To introduce the basic concepts of interpreter and compiler
- To introduce the language processing system
- To introduce the phases of compilation and relate them to language constructs
- To describe T-diagrams
- To discuss cross-compiler and bootstrapping

1.1 Introduction

Machine language is a set of instructions that can be directly executed by the central processing unit (CPU). It is the lowest level programming language and is written using the binary number system. This number system has only two values: 0 and 1. Programs in machine language are thus streams of 0s and 1s.

Consider the example of the letter 'A'. At machine level, it is represented as a stream of 8 binary numbers, 01000001. A simple word like 'COMPUTER' is represented in machine language as, 010000 11010011110100110101010000010101010101000100010101010010. A total of 64 digits represent an 8-letter word, i.e., 8 bits are used for each alphabet.

If a complete program is written using this language of 0s and 1s, it would be very difficult to understand the code and find errors in the program. Even if a single digit was mistyped or was left out while typing, the meaning of the program would change and this may create errors. However, programmers can easily understand languages like English. This is why high-level languages (HLLs) were developed to write programs to be executed by the CPU. However, HLLs are not easily understood by computers. In the early days, assembly language – a low-level programming language that uses mnemonics to represent each machine instruction and operands to specify data – was used, but later on, high-level programming languages became popular. Hence, compilers were developed to convert HLLs to a form that could be understood by the computer.

A **compiler** is a program that translates the source code written in a high-level language to its equivalent target program in a low-level language. The output of compilation has traditionally been called the **object code**. The object code is machine code that the processor can process or execute, one instruction at a time. Some compilers provide output in assembly language, which is then converted to machine language by an assembler. A compiler works on the complete source program. A typical compiler is shown in Fig. 1.1.

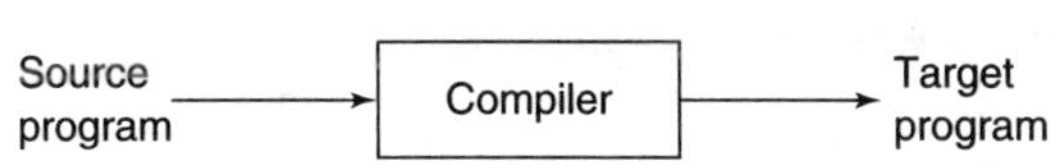

Figure 1.1 Compiler function

The **C compiler** accepts C programs with a '.c' extension as the source program and converts it into object code. Object files usually have a '.o' extension, but on Windows operating systems, they often have a '.obj' extension. The object code consists of function definitions in binary form; however, they cannot be executed directly. One or more object files are given to the linker, which produces a binary file called the **binary executable** that can be executed directly. Binary executable files have a '.exe' extension on the Windows platform.

The **Java compiler** produces bytecode as output. This can be run on any computer platform that has been provided with a Java virtual machine (JVM) or bytecode interpreter to convert the bytecode into instructions that can be executed by the hardware of the system. Using this virtual machine, the bytecode can optionally be recompiled on the execution platform by a just-in-time compiler.

Compiled languages like C and C++ perform translation before execution. This saves time at execution and is one reason why most operating system code and application code is written in a compiled language like C.

1.2 History of Compiler

The term compiler was coined in the early 1950s by Grace Hopper, and the first compiler was written for the A-0 system (Arithmetic Language version 0) language. It functioned more as a loader or linker than the modern idea of a compiler. One of the first true compilers was the FORTRAN compiler of the late 1950s. It enabled a programmer to use a problem-oriented source language. AUTOCODER, written in 1952, was the first primitive compiler. The first ALGOL 58 compiler was completed in 1958 by Friedrich L Bauer, Hermann Bottenbruch, Heinz Rutishauser and Klaus Samelson for the Z22 computer. By 1960, an extended Fortran compiler called ALTAC was available on the Philco 2000, so it is likely that a Fortran program was compiled for both the IBM and Philco computer architectures in the mid-1960s. The first known cross-platform, high-level language was COBOL. COBOL programs were compiled and executed on the UNIVAC II and RCA 501 in 1960. The COBOL compiler for UNIVAC II was probably the first to be written in a high-level language, namely, FLOW-MATIC, by a team led by Grace Hopper.

When the very first compiler was developed, no other compilers were available, and so it was written in assembly language. Similarly, when a completely new language is implemented, the compiler or interpreter must be written in another language. For example, Y Niklaus wrote the first Pascal compiler in Fortran. If, however, a compiler for that language had been available and a compiler was required for a superset of that language or for a new architecture, then another technique, called bootstrapping, may be used. After that, the compiler may be rewritten in its own language and become a self-hosting compiler. Bootstrapping is further explained in Section 1.9.

1.2.1 C Compiler

In the 1960s, Digital Equipment Corporation (DEC) introduced the PDP series of minicomputers that featured magnetic core memories and a variety of other advanced technologies. The first version of Unix was written in the low-level assembly language of PDP-7. TMG (TransMoGrifier) language was created for PDP-7 and this was used by Ken Thompson to develop a FORTRAN compiler. FORTRAN is a programming language that was developed in the 1950s and which is still widely used for scientific and numerical applications. Though Ken Thompson's aim was to develop a compiler for FORTAN, he ended up creating one for a new high-level language called B. B language was influenced by an earlier language called Basic Common Programming Language (BCPL). BCPL required a huge amount of assembly code to accomplish a given task. B was designed to perform the same functionality in just a few lines of code.

C language can be thought of as a descendant of B language. It was written when the PDP-11 computer arrived at Bell Labs. Dennis Ritchie used B to create a new language, called NB or NewB. NB was created because of deficiencies that had been detected when code written in B was moved to the PDP-11. NB was later refined and gave rise to C.

Hence, the first C compiler created by Dennis Ritchie was written in the short-lived language NB. C itself was refined many times. The latest versions of GCC (GNU Compiler Collection) distribution containing C and C++ compilers that were written in C are moving towards C++.

1.2.2 Java Compiler

The first Java compiler created by Sun Microsystems was written in C and used some libraries from C++. Today, the Java compiler is written in Java while the Java Runtime Environment (JRE) is written in C.

Initially, the Java compiler was written as a program in Java and was compiled using a Java compiler written in C. Thus, a bootstrap compiler was created, which was written in Java and which could compile Java programs. The concept of bootstrapping is explained in Section 1.9.

1.3 Language Processing System

The output of the compiler may not be directly executable by the target machine. Figure 1.2 shows a compiler that accepts a preprocessed source program and produces assembly code. The assembly code is then used as input for the assembler, which produces relocatable machine code. This relocatable code and the required library files are given to the linker, which produces executable machine code. The loader then loads the executable file into memory and executes it.

1.3.1 Preprocessor

The preprocessor produces input for the compiler. The preprocessor commands written in a high-level language are processed by the preprocessor before the compiler takes over. A source program may be divided into modules and stored in separate files. The task of collecting the source program is performed by the preprocessor.

Some of the functions performed by the preprocessor are given below:

- **Macro expansion**: Some languages allow the user to use a macro for bigger language constructs or a set of logically cohesive code constructs. A macro is a fragment of code that is given a name. Whenever the name is used, the preprocessor replaces it with the contents of the macro.
- **File inclusion**: The preprocessor includes header files in the program. Both user-defined and standard header files may be included.
- **Language extensions**: Preprocessors attempt to add capabilities to the language with built-in macros. For example, extensions are added to the standard C language to enable the user to perform actions that are cumbersome in standard, portable C.
- **Rational preprocessors (Augmentation)**: Preprocessors augment older languages with modern control flow and data structures. For example, control flow statements such as if-then, while, do-while and for, which are missing from a language can be provided in the form of built-in macros.

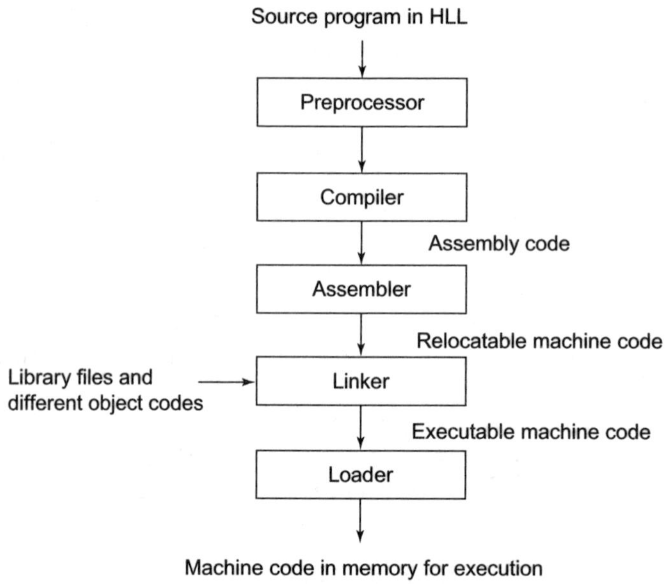

Figure 1.2 Language processing system

1.3.2 Assembler

Some compilers (Fig. 1.2) produce assembly code as output, which is then given to assemblers for further processing, whereas other compilers perform the job of the assembler and directly produce relocatable machine code that can be passed to the linker/loader. The **assembler** is a translator that converts an assembly language program to machine language. Assemblers need to translate assembly instructions and pseudo-instructions into machine instructions and convert the characters, decimal numbers, etc., specified by the programmer, into binary form.

Assembly code is a mnemonic form of machine code, in which names are used instead of binary codes, for operations. Memory addresses are also given names. An example of an assembly code to add 1 to a number stored in memory location 'a' is as follows:

```
Mov a, R1
Add #1, R1
Mov R1, a
```

Earlier assemblers were simple assemble-go systems – they could only assemble code directly in memory and start execution. The concept of a routine library was then developed, and assemblers were required to locate library routines, load them into memory, and link them to the main program. This task of locating, loading and linking – of assembling a single working program from individual pieces – led to the name, assembler. Today, assemblers are translators and they work on one program at a time. The tasks of locating, loading and linking (as well as many other tasks) are performed by the linker and loader.

Assemblers are of two types:

- **Single-pass assembler**: The job of the assembler is to perform a collection of substitutions, such as replacing mnemonics with machine operation code (op-code), character representation by its corresponding numeric encoding, etc. If all these substitutions are performed in a single sequential pass over the source text, then it is called a single-pass assembler. References to instructions that have not been scanned by the assembler (forward reference) may be required. In the case of the two-pass assembler, this is easy to handle. However, in a one-pass assembler, certain limitations are to be imposed on handling forward reference. One-pass assemblers are particularly attractive when secondary storage is either slow or missing entirely, as on many small machines.

- **Two-pass assembler**: Assemblers that perform substitutions in two passes over the source text are called two-pass assemblers. Mnemonic op-code and operational fields are separated, the storage requirements for every assembly language statement are determined, location counter is updated and the symbol table is built to store labels and their value in the first pass. In the second pass over the source code, object code is generated.

A compiler can be distinguished from an assembler by the fact that each input statement does not correspond to a single machine instruction or fixed sequence of instructions. A compiler may support features such as automatic allocation of variables, arithmetic expressions, control structures such as for and while loops, etc.

1.3.3 Linker

A linker is a computer program that merges the object files produced by separate compilation or assembly and creates an executable file. The main tasks of the linker are as follows:

- Search the program to find library routines such as `printf()`, math routines, etc.
- Determine the memory locations that the code from each module will occupy and relocate its instructions by adjusting the absolute references
- Resolve references among files

The linker carries out some relocation and produces a load module that can later be loaded by a simple relocating loader. If more than one object module is to be run at the same time and they cross-reference each other's instruction sequences or data, then an additional step may be required after compilation to resolve the relative location of instructions and data. This is also called **linkage editing** and the output module is called the **load module**.

1.3.4 Loader

A loader is a computer program that loads an executable file from a disk into memory and starts its execution. The main tasks of the loader are as follows:

- Read the executable file's header to determine the size of the text and data segments
- Create a new address space for the program
- Copy instructions and data into the address space
- Copy arguments passed to the program on the stack
- Initialise the machine registers, including the stack pointer
- Jump to a start-up routine that copies the program's arguments from the stack to the registers and calls the program's main routine

Some types of loaders are given below:

- **Absolute loader**: It can only load absolute object files, i.e., only programs starting from a fixed location in memory.

- **Relocatable loader**: It can load relocatable object files, thus loading the same program starting at any location. This loader allows for delay in binding time. The relocatable loader accepts as input a sequence of segments, each in a special relocatable load format, and loads these segments into memory. The addresses into which segments are loaded are determined by the relocatable loader, not by the assembler or programmer.
- **Bootstrap loader**: It uses its first few instructions to either load the rest of itself or to load another loader, into memory. It is typically stored in ROM.
- **Linking loader**: It can link programs that were assembled separately, and load them as a single module.

1.4 Interpreter and Compiler

Programs written in a high-level language are either directly executed by an interpreter or converted into machine code by a compiler (and assembler and linker) for the CPU to execute.

1.4.1 Interpreter

An interpreter reads an executable source program, written in a high-level programming language, as well as the data for this program, and runs the program against the data to produce results. It generally uses one of the following strategies for program execution:

- Parse the source code and execute it directly. Examples: Early versions of the Lisp programming language and BASIC
- Translate source code into an efficient intermediate representation and immediately execute this. Examples: Perl, Python, MATLAB and Ruby
- Explicitly execute stored precompiled code created by a compiler that is part of the interpreter system. Example: Pascal

In some languages, the second and third strategies are combined. Source programs are compiled ahead of time and stored as machine-independent code. This is then linked at run-time and executed by an interpreter and/or compiler. Java is the best example of this.

1.4.2 Compiler

Compilers (or compilers with assemblers) either produce machine code that is directly executable by hardware or an intermediate form called object code. Object code is machine-specific code that is augmented with a symbol table containing names and tags that make executable code identifiable and relocatable. A linker is used to combine library files with the object file(s) of the application to form a single executable file.

1.4.3 Interpreter vs Compiler

Both compilers and interpreters convert source code into tokens. These tokens may be grouped to generate a parse tree, which is converted to intermediate code. The basic difference is that the compiler generates stand-alone machine code, which can then be executed; whereas, the interpreter executes the actions specified in the source program. The compiler translates HLL code to intermediate code and then into machine code. The interpreter translates HLL code into an intermediate form and executes it. The interpreter can avoid the time-consuming compilation stage during which machine instructions are generated. However, generally, compiled programs run faster than interpreted programs. Since the interpreter can immediately execute the high-level program, it can be used during the development of a program, when small codes are to be added and tested quickly.

Also, an interpreter is generally slower than a compiler because it processes and interprets each statement in a program as many times as the number of evaluations of this statement. For example, when a `for`-loop is interpreted, the statements inside the `for`-loop body will be analysed and evaluated on every loop step.

Both interpreters and compilers are available for most HLLs. However, BASIC and Lisp are specifically designed to be executed by an interpreter. In addition, page description languages, such as PostScript, use an interpreter. Every PostScript printer, for example, has a built-in interpreter that executes PostScript instructions. The Unix shell interpreter runs operating system commands interactively. Some languages, such as Java and Lisp, come with an interpreter and a compiler. Java source programs (Java classes with a .java extension) are translated by the javac compiler into bytecode (with a .class extension). The Java interpreter, called the JVM, may actually interpret bytecode directly or may internally compile them to machine code and then execute that code (JIT or just-in-time compilation).

Some of the main differences between interpreters and compilers are given in Table 1.1.

Table 1.1 Differences between interpreters and compilers

Interpreter	Compiler
It works line by line. It translates programs one statement at a time.	It scans the entire program and translates it as a whole into assembly code or machine code.
It takes less time to analyse the source code, but overall execution is slower than with the compiler.	It takes more time to analyse the source code but overall execution is faster than with the interpreter.
No intermediate code is generated as output. It directly executes the instructions.	The compiler may generate intermediate object code, which requires linking.
Interpreted programs are memory efficient.	It requires more memory as the complete object code must be stored in memory.
Interpreted programs are interpreted line by line every time they are run.	Compilation is carried out once and the compiled program can be run anytime.
Error is reported as soon as the first error is encountered. The rest of the program is not checked until the first error is removed.	Errors are reported only after scanning the complete program.
Debugging is easy, as the interpreter stops and reports errors as soon as it encounters them.	Debugging is comparatively hard in compiled language.
Programming languages like Python, Ruby and MATLAB use interpreters.	Programming languages like C and C++ use compilers.

1.5 Phases of Compiler

Compiling is a complex process that cannot be carried out in a single step. For this reason, it is customary to partition the process into a series of sub-processes, called phases. Each phase takes its input from the previous stage, has its own representation of the source program, and feeds its output to the next phase of the compiler. The phases of compiler are shown in Fig. 1.3.

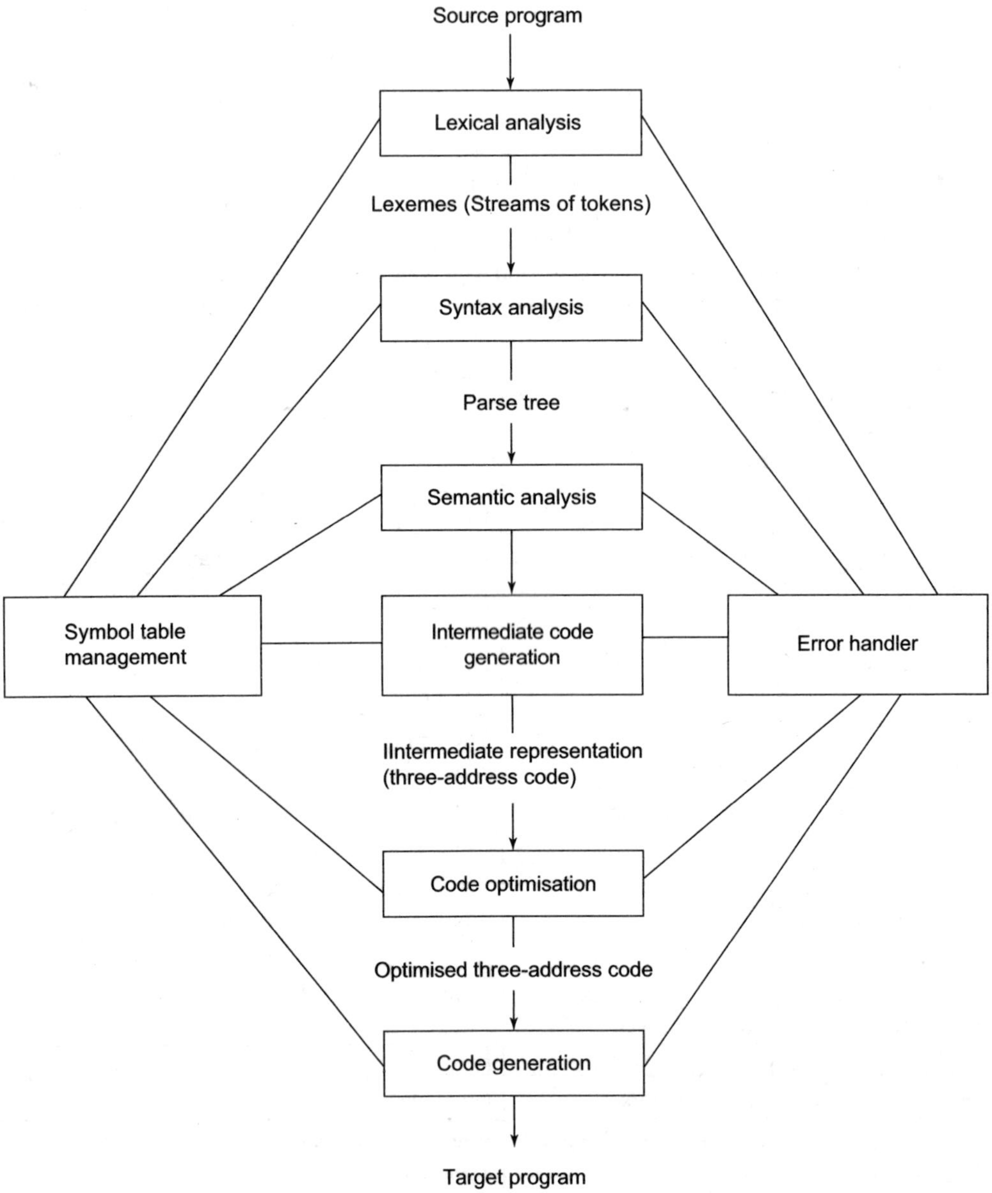

Figure 1.3 Phases of compiler

1.5.1 Lexical Analysis

The first phase of the compilation process is called lexical analysis, or scanning. Here, the compiler accepts the source language program and separates the characters of the source language into streams of tokens, in which each token represents a logically cohesive sequence of characters. These sequences of tokens are referred as **lexemes**. Hence, the name lexical analysis. What a token is depends on the language that is considered. Common examples of tokens are:

- Keywords
- Identifiers
- Constants
- Operators
- Symbols
- Strings

Lexical analysis breaks up a program into tokens by:

- Grouping characters into non-separatable units (tokens)
- Changing a stream of characters to a stream of tokens

Consider the following C code, which prints numbers from 1 to 10, as the source program.

```
void main( )
{
int count;
for(count = 1; count <= 10; count ++)
printf("%d", count);
printf("\n");
}
```

The tokens that will be identified are as follows:

```
void   main    (   )
{
int    count   ;
for        (   count    =   1   ;   count    <=    10   ;   count    ++    )
printf     (   "%d"     ,   count   )   ;
printf     (   "\n"     )   ;
}
```

In total, 34 tokens will be identified in the above program segment. In C, strings are also identified as tokens. All characters inside quotation marks are considered as strings. Multi-character operators such as <= are also recognised. In order to find the next token, the lexical analyser examines successive characters in the source program, starting from the first character not yet grouped into a token. It may be required to search many characters beyond the next token in order to determine what the next token actually is.

After detecting the tokens, the type of token and its value (if any) are entered in the symbol table. If the lexical analyser finds an invalid token, it generates an error. The symbol table stores <token-type, attribute value> pairs for all the tokens identified.

Consider the statement: int count = 1;

It contains the following tokens:

Token	Token type	Symbol table entry
int	keyword	<keyword, int>
count	identifier	<id, pointer to symbol table entry of count>

(Cont'd)

Table (Continued)

Token	Token type	Symbol table entry
=	operator	<assign_op, >
1	constant	<constant, 1>
;	symbol	<symbol, ;>

If the identifiers are allocated values, they will be entered in the symbol table in the subsequent phases. Other phases can refer to the symbol table values entered by the lexical analysis phase and also update the values, if needed.

When the lexical analyser reads the source code, it scans it letter by letter; and when it encounters a whitespace, operator symbol or special symbol, it decides that a word is completed.

For example: int intval;

While scanning both lexemes till 'int', the lexical analyser cannot determine whether it is a keyword `int` or the initials of identifier `intval`. The lexical analyser uses the Longest Match Rule, which states that the lexeme scanned should be determined based on the longest match among all the tokens available.

The analyser also follows rule priority, where a reserved word, such as a keyword, of a language is given priority over user input. That is, if the lexical analyser finds a lexeme that matches any existing reserved word, it should generate an error.

1.5.2 Syntax Analysis

This phase accepts tokens from the lexical analysis phase and checks if they appear in the patterns that are permitted by the specification for the source language. If the tokens are in proper syntax, it imposes a hierarchical structure on the token stream, referred to as the **parse tree**. If the tokens are not specified as per the language specification, the error routine is invoked. This phase is also referred as the **parser**.

Consider the statement in C language: A=B+C

After lexical analysis, this expression might appear to the syntax analyser as

id = id + id

The expression will be converted into a parse tree, as shown in Fig. 1.4.

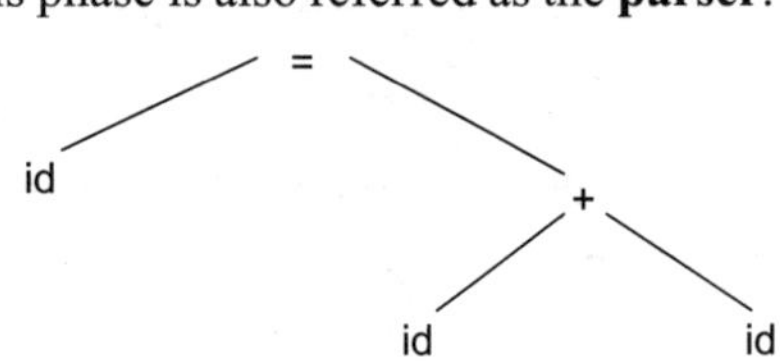

Figure 1.4 Parse tree for A=B+C

1.5.3 Semantic Analysis

This phase checks the source program for semantic errors and gathers type information for the subsequent phases. The parse tree generated in the previous phase is used to determine the operator and its operands. Type checking is one of the important functions of the semantic analyser. In type checking, the compiler checks if the operator has operands that are permitted by the source language specification. It checks if the token is declared before its use, whether identifiers are used in the appropriate context, and checks subroutine call arguments and labels.

Dynamic semantic checks are also performed at run-time. The compiler produces code that performs these checks, such as array index within bounds; arithmetic errors such as division by zero; pointers not de-referenced unless pointing to valid objects and that there is no un-initialised variable.

1.5.4 Intermediate Code Generation

This phase transforms the parse tree into an intermediate language representation of the source program. The three-address form of intermediate representation is used in this section. This form can contain a sequence of instructions, each of which has at most three operands. The parse tree in Fig. 1.4 might appear in the three-address form as

$$T1 = B + C \qquad (1.1)$$

$$A = T1$$

1.5.5 Code Optimisation

Certain compilers have within them a phase that tries to apply transformations to the output of the intermediate code generator, in an attempt to generate faster or smaller object language programs. There is variation in the amount of compilation that compilers perform. An optimising compiler spends a lot of time on this phase and improves the speed of the target program by a factor of two. However, simple optimisations can significantly improve the running time of the target program without slowing down the compilation time. Some of these optimising techniques are as follows:

- Local optimisation
- Loop optimisation
- Dead code elimination
- Copy propagation
- Common sub-expression elimination

1.5.6 Code Generation

This phase converts intermediate code into a sequence of machine instructions. Expression (1.1) might be appear in machine code as:

Load B
Add C
Store A

This is a straightforward machine code generation which may include many redundant load and store operations. Code optimisation can be applied after the code generation phase. This is called **machine-dependent code optimisation**, and it takes advantage of the special features of the target machine. It involves CPU registers and may have absolute memory references rather than relative references. Machine-dependent optimisers attempt to take maximum advantage of memory hierarchy.

1.5.7 Symbol Table and Error Handling

Each phase uses a symbol table and error handler. The symbol table stores information about the occurrence of various entities such as variable names, function names, objects, classes and interfaces. Phases may store information or use the information from the symbol table. The error handler can be invoked by any phase if an error has occurred. It reports error once compilation is performed. It may also carry out error correction.

1.6 Overview of Compiler Design

The compiler is designed in two phases: analysis and synthesis. The analysis phase is also known as the front end of the compiler, while the synthesis phase is known as the back end of the compiler. Figure 1.5 shows the front and back end arrangement of a compiler.

The main objective of the analysis phase is to break the source code into parts. It then arranges these pieces into a meaningful structure (or grammar of the language). The analysis phase generates an intermediate representation of the source program and symbol table, which should be fed to the synthesis phase as input.

The following phases of compiler design constitute the front end of the compiler:

- Lexical analysis
- Syntax analysis
- Semantic analysis

The synthesis phase generates the target program with the help of intermediate source code representation and the symbol table.

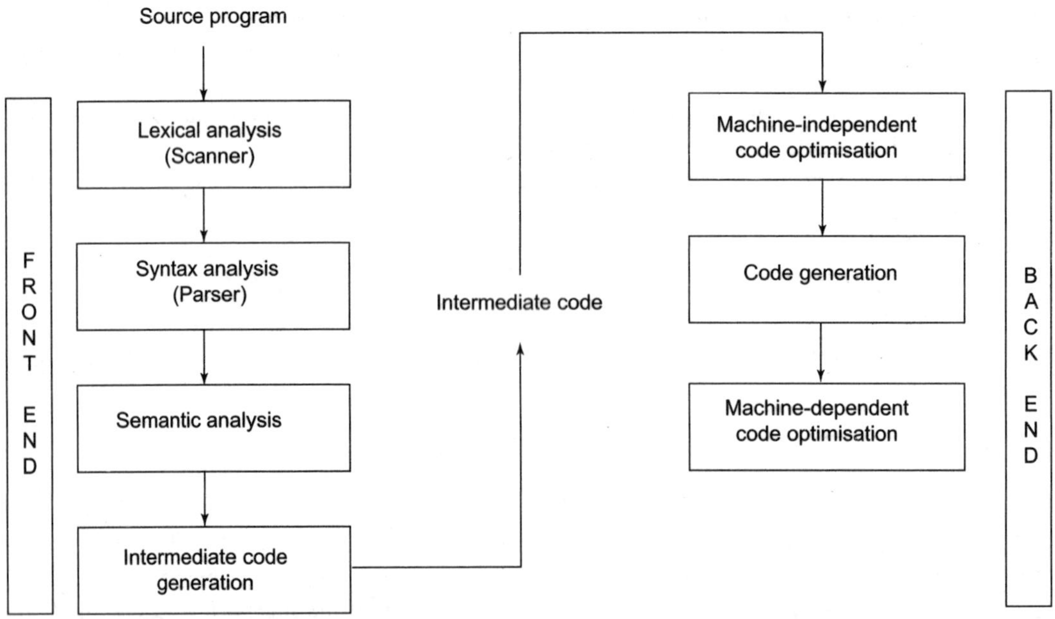

Figure 1.5 Front end and back end of a compiler

1.6.1 Pass and Phase

A compiler can have many phases and passes:

- A **phase** is a logically cohesive operation, which takes input from the previous stage, processes the data and yields output that can be used as input for the next phase.
- A **pass** refers to the traversal of a compiler through the entire program. A pass reads the source program or output of the previous pass, makes transformations specified by its phases and writes the output in an intermediate file, which may be read by subsequent passes.

The structure of the source language has a strong effect on the number of passes performed. Certain languages require at least two phases to generate code. A multi-pass compiler uses less space than a single-pass compiler, as the space occupied by the computer program for one pass can be reused by the other passes. However, a multi-pass compiler is slower than a single-pass compiler, because each pass reads and writes an intermediate file. Thus, compilers running on computers with less memory use several passes, while on a computer with large memory, a compiler with fewer passes would be possible.

Certain compilers produce code in a single pass, using a technique called **backpatching**. In this, the code is generated and the part which cannot be computed is left blank; whenever that part is computed, the compiler backpatches to the incomplete statement of the code and generates the remaining code. In a compiler, most of the backpatching is carried out over a relatively short distance.

Passes and phases can be distinguished, as shown in Table 1.2.

Table 1.2 Differences between pass and phase

Pass	Phase
It is a physical scan over a source program, i.e., how many times the source code will be scanned.	It logically accepts input in one representation of the source program and produces output in another representation.
It scans the source program, processes it and stores it in an intermediate file.	It passes the processed information from one phase to the next.
An intermediate file is required between passes.	No such file is required between phases.
Splitting into more number of passes reduces memory.	Splitting into more number of phases reduces complexity, not memory.
A single-pass compiler is faster than a multi-pass compiler.	Reduction in number of phases increases complexity.

1.7 Application of Techniques Used in Compiler Design

The techniques used in compiler design can also be applied to other domains of computer science:

- Techniques used in the lexical analyser can be used in text editors, information retrieval systems, query languages, etc.
- Parser techniques can be used in query processing systems like SQL and in pattern recognition systems.
- Most of the techniques can be applied to natural language processing.

1.8 Tombstone Diagram

Tombstone diagrams or T-diagrams are used to represent compilers and other language processing programs using small puzzle pieces. The puzzle pieces (symbols) that can be used to represent a program, machine, interpreter or compiler are shown in Table 1.3.

A program can run on a machine only if it is expressed in the correct machine language. For example, M must be the same, as shown here.

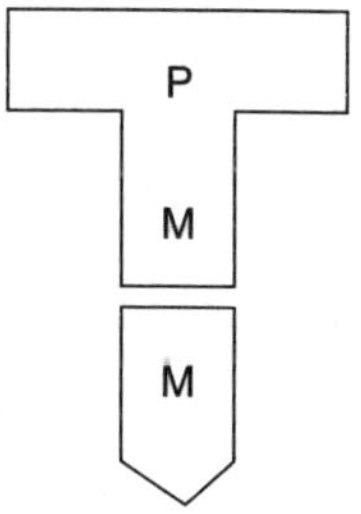

A compiler may be characterised by three languages: source S, target T and implementation L. The source language is the language being compiled. For example, in a C compiler, the source language is C. The target language is the language produced by the compiler. The implementation language is the language in which the compiler is written. Alternatively, the following notation can be used: ${}^{S}C_{L}^{T}$

These individual symbols can be combined to understand the process of changing the implementation language, pipelining, cross-compiling and bootstrapping.

Change of implementation (host) language is performed for portability. Suppose a program S is written in language L and the target language is T. The T-diagram to change the host language to Z can be represented as

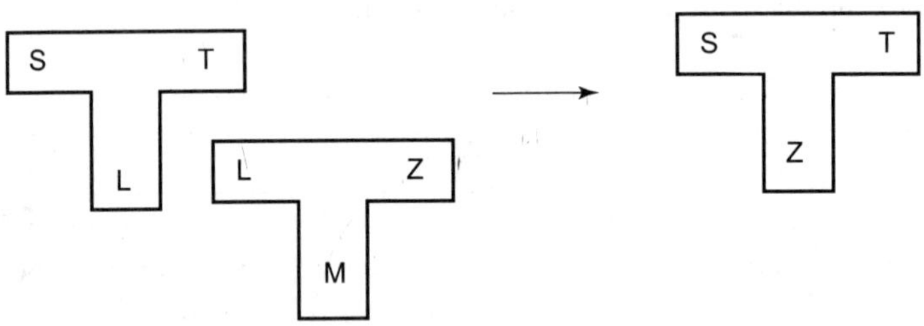

In pipelining of a compiler, the output of the first compiler is provided as input to the second compiler. The representation is as follows:

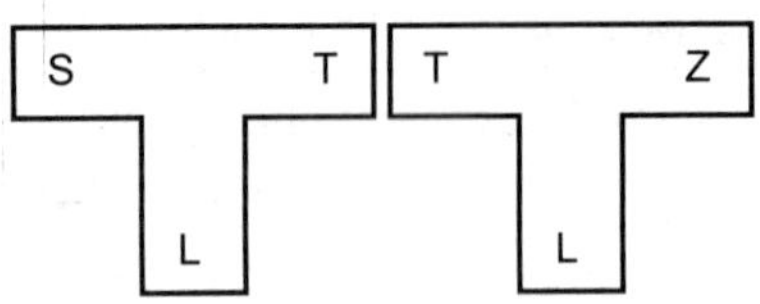

Table 1.3 T-diagram symbols

Symbol	Represents	Details
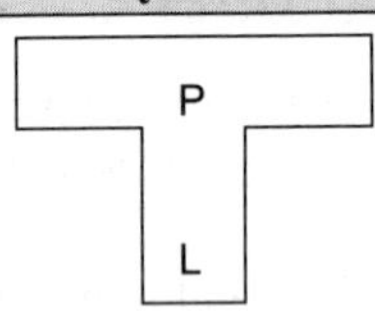	Program	Program P written in language L
	Machine	
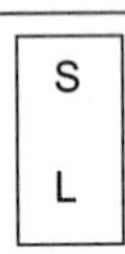	Interpreter	Interpreter executing language S written in language L
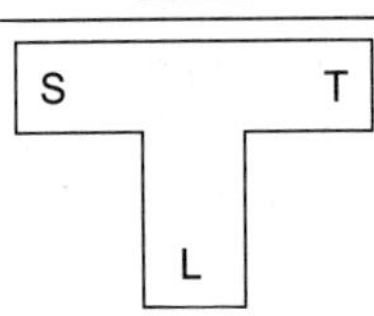	Compiler	A compiler with source language S, producing code for T, written in language L

Example 1.1 Represent using a T-diagram

(a) Program Sort written in C language

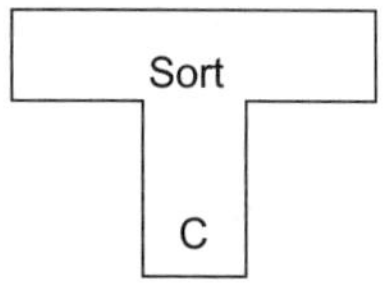

(b) A Java program P is compiled by the Java compiler to generate Java bytecode for JVM

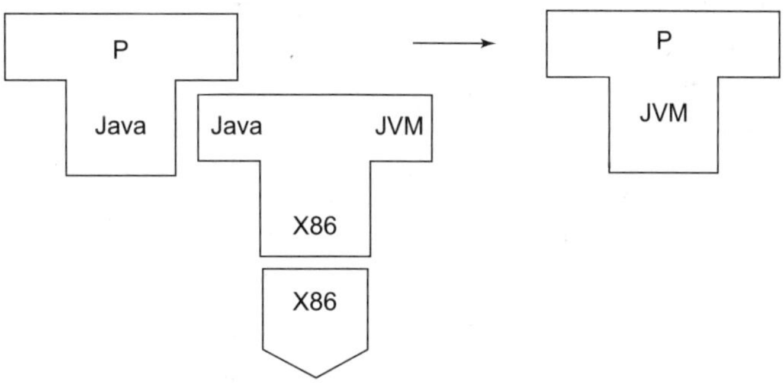

(c) A minimum cost-spanning tree program MST is written in high-level C++. The C++ compiler runs on SPARC (Scalable Process Architecture) from Sun Microsystems, which produces object code for it. Show how the code is compiled.

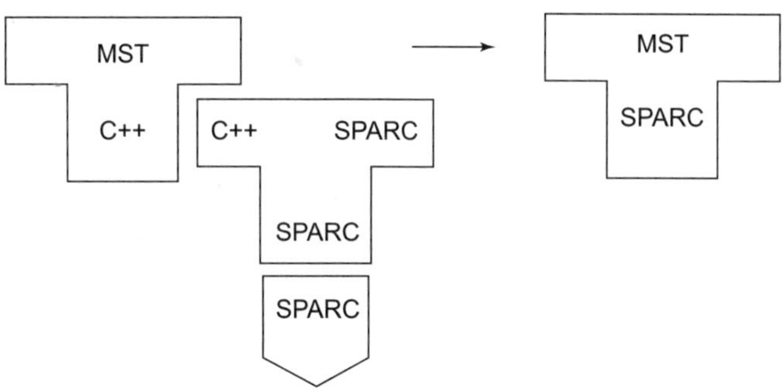

1.9 Cross-compiler and Bootstrapping

A **cross-compiler** is a compiler that runs on one machine and produces object code for another type of machine. Cross-compilers are used to generate software that can run on computers with a new architecture or on special-purpose devices that cannot host their own compilers. The fundamental use of a cross-compiler is to separate the build environment from the target environment.

Embedded computers, where a device has extremely limited resources, might use cross-compilation. For example, a microwave oven will have an extremely small computer to read its touchpad, perform a task and provide output to a digital display. This is not powerful enough to run a compiler, and cross-compilation can be a better option than native compilation. Cross-compilers can be used to implement bootstrapping.

Bootstrapping is the process of writing a compiler in the source programming language that it intends to compile, which leads to a self-hosting compiler. An early self-hosting compiler was written for Lisp by Tim Hart and Mike Levin at MIT in 1962. They wrote a Lisp compiler in Lisp, testing it inside an existing Lisp interpreter. Later the compiler was improved to compile its own source code and it became self-hosting.

The process of implementing a new language is given below:

1. Devise a minimal subset of a language.
2. Write a compiler for that minimal subset in the language of that minimal subset.
3. Hand-translate this minimal subset source code into assembly language and assemble it, producing a working compiler for a subset of the target language.
4. Write a new compiler in the language of the working compiler to accept more source features that are missing from the language of the working compiler.
5. Use the working compiler to compile this new compiler, producing a new working compiler which accepts a superset of the language under which it was compiled.
6. Repeat the last two steps until the working compiler realises all the features in the source language.

Suppose there is a new language L, which has to be made available on machine A.

1. As the first step, create ${}^{S}C_{A}^{A}$, a compiler for a subset S, of the desired language L, using language A, which runs on machine A. (Language A may be the assembly language.)

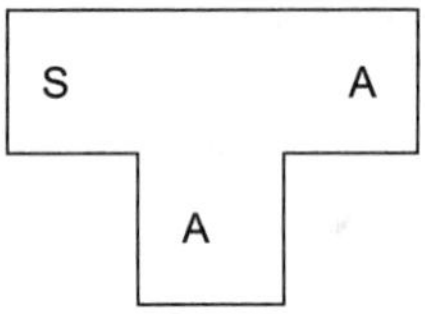

2. Then create ${}^{L}C_{S}^{A}$, a compiler for language L, written in its subset S, running on machine A.

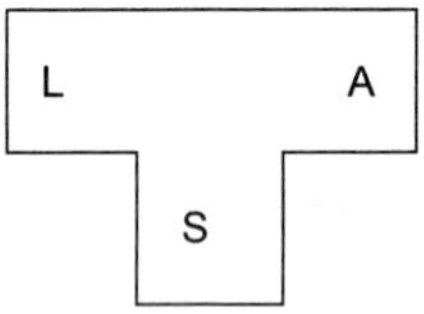

3. Compile ${}^{L}C_{S}^{A}$ using ${}^{S}C_{A}^{A}$ to obtain ${}^{L}C_{A}^{A}$, a compiler for language L, written in A and running on A. The T-diagrams show the process (Figs 1.6 and 1.7).

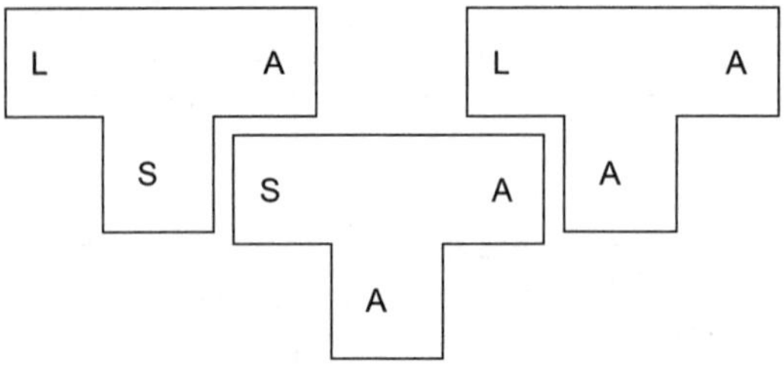

$${}^{L}C_{S}^{A} \rightarrow {}^{S}C_{A}^{A} \rightarrow {}^{L}C_{A}^{A}$$

Figure 1.6 Bootstrapping compiler

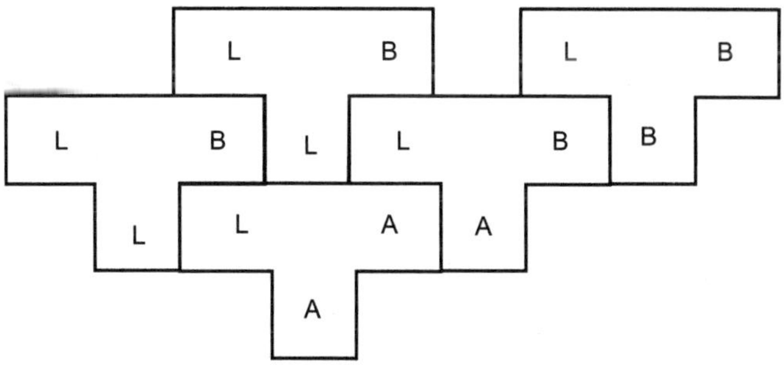

$$ {}^{L}C_S^A \rightarrow {}^{L}C_A^A \rightarrow {}^{L}C_A^B $$

$$ {}^{L}C_L^B \rightarrow {}^{L}C_A^B \rightarrow {}^{L}C_B^B $$

Figure 1.7 Bootstrapping a compiler using the cross-compiler

To produce a compiler for a different machine B:

1. Convert ${}^{L}C_S^A$ into ${}^{L}C_L^B$. (Language S is a subset of language L).
2. Compile ${}^{L}C_L^B$ to produce ${}^{L}C_A^B$, a cross-compiler for L which runs on machine A and produces code for machine B.
3. Compile ${}^{L}C_L^B$ with the cross-compiler to produce ${}^{L}C_B^B$, a compiler for language L which runs on machine B.

1.10 Relating Compilation Phases with Formal Systems

The source language is accepted by the first phase – lexical analysis. To recognise valid tokens of the specified language, a recogniser is required. Programming language tokens can be described by **regular languages** (a language defined by regular expressions is called a regular language). Thus, regular expression notations are used to describe the token identification pattern. A **regular expression (RE)** expresses finite languages by defining a pattern for finite strings of symbols; for example, keywords of the language. A **finite automata (FA)** is a state machine that accepts a string of input and changes its state to recognise a regular expression. FA can be constructed using the regular expression. Hence, they are used by the lexical analyser to recognise valid tokens of a language, as shown in Fig. 1.8.

Figure 1.8 Scanner using finite automata

A parser (syntax analyser) recognises whether the tokens are grouped according to the language under consideration. A **context-free grammar (CFG)** is used to specify the rules of the language. Figure 1.9 shows that the parser is a recogniser that takes as input a string or token along with grammatical rules in CFG to conclude whether the input is valid or invalid. A CFG can be converted to **PDA (pushdown automata)** to implement the CFG to recognise valid language constructs. PDA can remember an infinite amount of information. It is a finite state machine along with a stack.

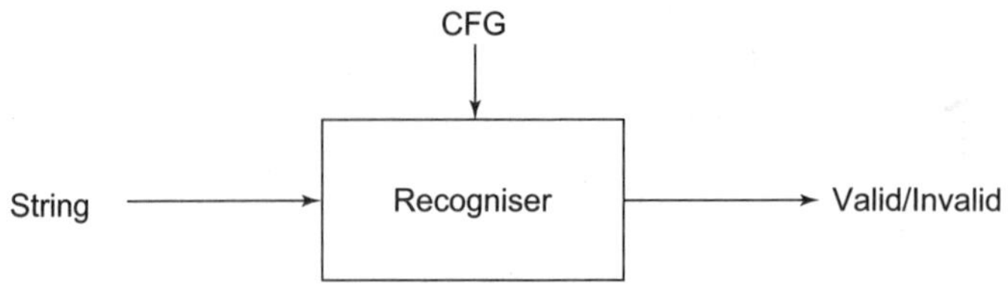

Figure 1.9 Parser

The intermediate code generator receives input from its previous phase, in the form of an annotated syntax tree. This tree then can be converted into a linear representation, for example, postfix notation. Intermediate code tends to be machine independent. Therefore, the code generator assumes that it has unlimited memory storage (register) to generate code. Intermediate code can be represented using quadruple, triple or indirect triple notation (see Chapter 5, Section 5.2). Various data structures are available to implement this representation in an efficient manner.

Data flow analysis in code optimisation uses fixed-point algorithms. Dead code elimination uses graph algorithms. Computer architecture is used for machine code generation. Greedy algorithms and graph-based algorithms can be used for register allocation. Dynamic programming techniques can be used for instruction selection. Complex data structures are utilised by symbol tables, parse trees and data-dependence graphs.

1.11 Compiler Construction Tools

Compiler writers can make use of software tools such as debuggers, version managers, profilers and so on. In addition, various other tools are available that can help in the development of individual phases of the compiler. Some of the compiler construction tools used to enhance compiler performance are given below:

- **Scanner generators**: These generators automatically generate a lexical analyser from a specification based on regular expression. Lex is an example of a scanner generator. Flex generates scanners for use with C++. JFlex is the fastest scanner generator for Java.
- **Parser generators**: These generators produce syntax analysers from input based on CFG. In old compilers, syntax analysis consumed not only a fraction of the running time of a compiler, but a large fraction of the intellectual effort of writing a compiler. Many parser generators utilise powerful algorithms that are too complex to be carried out by hand. A **compiler-compiler** is a compiler generator that can generate the parser whose input is the Backus Normal Form (BNF) and whose generated output is the source code of a parser often used as a component of the compiler. BNF is a notation for context-free grammars, often used to describe the syntax of languages.
  Examples are Yacc, Bison and LEMON parser generators. LEMON is an LALR(1) open source parser generator that produces C program as output and is faster than Yacc and Bison. ANTLR (ANother Tool for Language Recognition) is a powerful parser generator for reading, processing, executing or translating structured text or binary files.
- **Syntax-directed translation engines**: These engines produce intermediate code in the three-address format, from input that is based on the parse tree.
- **Automatic code generators**: These take a collection of rules that define the translation of each operation of the intermediate language for the target machine. The input specification of the system may contain a description of the lexical and syntactic structure of the given source language, of the output to be generated for each source language and the target machine.

- **Data flow engines**: Normally, much more information is required for good code optimisation. It involves data flow analysis, the gathering of information about how values are transmitted from one part of a program to another.

For more information on compiler construction tools, please see Chapter 10.

Summary

- A compiler is a program that translates source code written in a high-level language to its equivalent target program in a low-level language.
- The compiler produces as output either assembly code or machine code directly executable by computer hardware, or an intermediate code in the form of object code.
- An interpreter reads an executable source program written in a high-level programming language along with input data and runs the program against the data to produce results.
- Phases of compilation: lexical analyser, syntax analyser, semantic analyser, intermediate code generator, code optimiser and code generator.
- Error handling and symbol table management are handled by the compiler.
- Compilation takes place in two main phases: analysis and synthesis.
- The analysis phase is also known as the front end of the compiler, and consists of lexical analysis, syntax analysis, semantic analysis and intermediate code generation.
- The synthesis phase is known as the back end of the compiler, and consists of code optimisation and generation.
- A pass refers to the traversal of a compiler through the entire program. A pass reads the source program or the output of the previous pass, makes transformations specified by its phases and writes the output in an intermediate file, which may be read by subsequent passes.
- T-diagrams are used to represent compilers and other language processing programs using small puzzle pieces.
- T-diagrams specify three languages: source language S, target language T and implementation language L.
- A cross-compiler is a compiler that runs on one machine and produces object code for another type of machine.
- Bootstrapping is the process of writing a compiler in the source programming language that it intends to compile, which leads to a self-hosting compiler.
- Regular expressions are used to specify patterns to identify tokens. Finite automata are used to recognise regular expressions.
- The parser uses context-free grammar. Pushdown automata are used to implement CFG to recognise valid language constructs.

Exercises

Review Questions

Fill in the blanks with appropriate answers:

1. __________ is input to the code generator.
2. A compiler for a high-level language that runs on one machine and produces code for a different machine is called __________.

3. __________ is a technique for building cross-compilers for other machines.
4. __________ was developed from the beginning as a cross-compiler.
5. The output of the lexical analyser is __________.
6. The concept of grammar is used in the __________ phase of a compiler.
7. Parsing is also known as __________.
8. A compiler program written in a high-level language is called __________.
9. System programs, such as compilers, are designed so that they are __________ (serially usable or re-enterable).
10. A system program that brings together separately compiled modules of a program into a form language that is suitable for execution is __________.

Answers: 1. Intermediate code 2. Cross compiler 3. Canadian Cross 4. Free Pascal 5. Tokens 6. Parser 7. Syntax analysis 8. Source program 9. Re-enterable 10. Linker loader

State whether true or false:

1. Cross-compiler is used in bootstrapping.
2. GCC is a cross-compiler.
3. Identifiers, keywords and operators are lexemes.
4. A programmer, by mistake, writes a program to multiply two numbers instead of dividing them; this error is detected by syntax analysis.
5. Pass 1 assigns addresses to all statements, saves the values assigned to all labels for use in pass 2 and performs some processing.
6. The functions performed by the loader are to allocate memory for the programs and resolve symbolic references between object decks; address dependent locations, such as address constants, to correspond to the allocated space; and physically place the machine instructions and data into memory.
7. Machine language specifies the sequence of instructions to run a program.
8. Finite automata recognise context-free grammar.
9. Null string can be accepted by finite automata.
10. Lex is a parser generator.
11. A lexical analyser may be required to search many characters beyond the next token in order to determine what the next token actually is.

Answers: 1. True 2. True 3. True 4. False 5. True 6. True 7. False 8. False 9. True 10. False

Practice Questions

1. How is a one-pass compiler different from a two-pass compiler?
2. A multi-pass compiler uses less space than a single-pass compiler. Justify.
3. Explain the T-diagram:

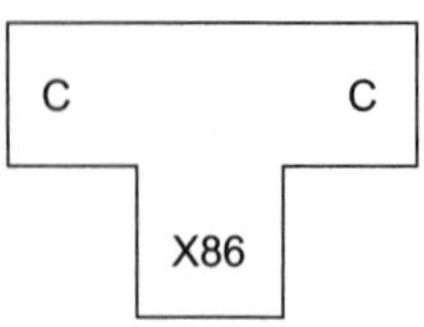

4. What are the phases in a Pascal compiler?
5. Explain the working of a C compiler.

2 Lexical Analysis

Objectives

- To introduce the lexical analysis phase of the compiler
- To understand the process of input buffering
- To introduce the concepts of tokens, patterns and lexemes
- To discuss the use of the symbol table in lexical analysis
- To discuss the need for regular expression and finite automata
- To describe the methods of conversion of regular expressions to deterministic finite automata

2.1 Lexical Analysis and Tokens

Lexical analysis is the first phase of the compilation process. In this phase, the source code of a language is accepted as input. It is the process where the stream of characters that make up the source program is read from left to right and grouped into tokens, by removing any whitespace or comments, resulting in a token stream. If the lexical analyser or scanner finds an invalid token, it generates an error. The lexical analyser works closely with the syntax analyser. It reads character streams from the source code, checks for legal tokens and passes the data to the syntax analyser, as shown in Fig. 2.1. The functions of the lexical analyser are to tokenise the source language and pass it to the syntax analyser, to store information in the symbol table and to invoke the error handler, when required.

The source code is scanned one character at a time, and when the scanner encounters a whitespace, operator symbol or special symbol, it decides that a word has been completed. To declare a word as a token, the scanner follows the Longest Match Rule and applies rule priority by granting priority to a reserved word over a user declared identifier. If the lexical analyser finds the name of an identifier that matches any existing reserved word, it should generate an error.

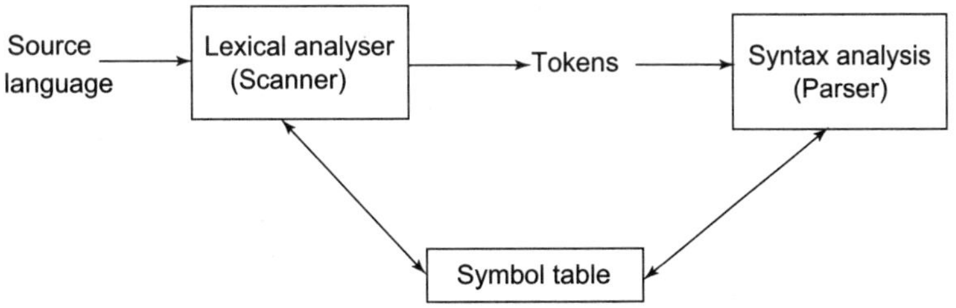

Figure 2.1 Lexical analysis process

The lexical analyser collects information about tokens and their associated attributes. The tokens influence parsing decisions; the attributes influence the translation of tokens. A token usually has only one attribute – a pointer to the symbol table entry in which information about the token is stored; the pointer becomes the attribute for the token. The symbol table stores the token type and its associated attribute, which can be referred to by other phases of compilation. The main functions of the lexical analyser are as follows:

- Stripping out comments and whitespace in the form of blank, tab and newline characters from the source program
- Finding and sending streams of tokens as output
- Generating the symbol table by storing information about identifiers and constants
- Generating errors and correlating error messages with the proper line number of the source program

Sometimes, the lexical analyser is divided into two phases: scanning and lexical analysis. The scanner is responsible for scanning the input string. This is done using input buffering, and the lexical analyser then finds the tokens of the language.

2.2 Input Buffering

The input program is read only in the first phase, namely, lexical analysis. The source program is read character by character, so there is a need to speed up the process. For many source languages, there are times when the lexical analyser needs to look ahead several characters beyond the lexeme for a pattern before a match can be announced. A two-buffer scheme for buffering the input in order to speed up input access is discussed below.

2.2.1 Two-buffer Input Scheme Using Buffer Pair

In this scheme, there are two buffers that can hold the input. The buffer is divided into two N-character halves, where N is the number of characters on one disk block; for example, 1024 or 4096. Instead of reading one character at a time, N characters are read into each half of the buffer with one system *read* command. If fewer than N characters remain in the input, then a special character eof is placed into the buffer after the input characters.

Two pointers are used, a forward pointer (FP) and a lexeme_begin pointer (LP). The string of characters between the two pointers is the current lexeme. Initially, both pointers point to the first character of buffer-1. The forward pointer then moves forward and scans ahead until a match for a pattern is found. After the lexeme is identified, both pointers are set to the next character immediately after the current recognised lexeme. If the forward pointer reaches the end of buffer-1, then data is loaded into buffer-2 and the forward pointer is advanced to point to the start of buffer-2. The algorithm describing the movement of pointers is given below:

Algorithm Input Buffering

```
LP=FP= start of buffer-1              // initially

If FP reaches end of the first buffer
Begin
        Reload second buffer;
        FP=FP+1;                      // FP points to start of buffer-2
End
Else if FP reaches end of the second buffer
Begin
        Reload first buffer;
```

```
        FP=start of buffer1;
End
Else
        FP=FP+1;
```

```
If a pattern is recognised, then
Begin
        String of characters between LP and FP = Current Lexeme (including the characters pointed at
        by LP and FP)
        Set LP=FP= FP +1
End
```

Sentinels: In the two-buffer input scheme, the amount of look-ahead is limited. This may make it impossible to recognise tokens in situations where the distance that the forward pointer must travel is more than the length of the buffer. Also, it must be checked each time, if the forward pointer should be moved off the first half of the buffer. Except at the ends of each half, this technique requires two tests for each advance of the forward pointer:

- To check the end of buffer
- To determine what character is read

The two tests can be reduced to one if a special sentinel character is added at the end of each buffer half, as shown below:

Buffer-1						**Buffer-2**					
......	.....	.....	.....	....	eof	....	....	....	.....	.....	eof

The sentinel eof is added to the first buffer and also to the second buffer. The eof at the end indicates end of input. The algorithm that describes the movement of the forward pointer is given below:

Algorithm FPSentinel

```
FP=FP+1;

If FP=eof, then
Begin
        If FP is at end of buffer-1, then
        Begin
                Reload second half;
                FP=FP+1;                        // FP points to start of buffer-2
        End
        Else if FP is at end of second buffer, then
        Begin
                Reload first buffer;
                FP=start of Buffer1;
        End
        Else
```

```
        // eof within a buffer signifying end of input
        Terminate lexical analysis;
End
```

Most of the time, only one test is performed to check whether the forward pointer points to eof. Only when the pointer reaches the end of the buffer half or eof does it perform more tests. Since there are N input characters encountered between eofs, the average number of tests per input character is close to 1.

Example 2.1 Working of input buffer in lexical analyser using buffer pair scheme

Let the input to the lexical analyser be

`int newNo =12;`

Let us assume that each buffer can hold 6 characters. Initially

Buffer-1						Buffer-2					
i	n	t	n	e	w						

↑

LP = FP

FP and LP are initially pointed to the start of buffer-1. FP moves forward from i, n, t and n. When it reaches n, the keyword *int* is recognised.

Buffer-1						Buffer-2					
i	n	t	n	e	w						

↑ ↑

LP LP

Then, LP and FP are set to the next character, n.

Buffer-1						Buffer-2					
i	n	t	n	e	w						

↑

LP = FP

FP moves further till the end of buffer-1. After FP reaches end of buffer-1, the second buffer is loaded and FP is incremented to point to the start of buffer-2 (as shown below). It then moves forward. When it reaches =, the identifier *newNo* is recognised. More than one character may be required in the look-ahead to determine the token.

Buffer-1						Buffer-2					
i	n	t	n	e	w	N	o	=	1	2	eof

↑ ↑

LP FP he

The process stops when the pointers reach the eof symbol. The tokens identified are: int, newNo, = and 12. Entries of the tokens are made in the symbol table.

Example 2.2 Input buffering using the sentinel method

Consider the input sentence

`int a = 12,`

Initially

Buffer-1						Buffer-2					
i	n	t	a	=	eof						

↑

LP = FP

FP and LP are initially pointed to the start of buffer-1. FP moves forward to i, n, t, a and a new token *int* is recognised. This movement of FP past *int* is required to confirm if the token is the keyword *int* or the beginning of any user-defined identifier. Then, LP and FP are set to a.

Buffer-1						Buffer-2					
i	n	t	a	=	eof						

↑

LP = FP

FP moves forward to = and token *a* is recognised as an identifier. Next, LP and FP point to = and FP moves forward to eof.

Buffer-1						Buffer-2					
i	n	t	a	=	eof						

↑ ↑

LP FP

The eof symbol marks the end of buffer-1. Hence, buffer 2 is loaded and FP moves forward to the start of buffer-2.

Buffer-1						Buffer-2					
i	n	t	a	=	eof	1	2	eof			eof

↑ ↑

LP FP

After FP points to 1, the lexeme = is recognised as a token and LP = FP is set at 1. Then, FP moves forward to point to eof and 12 is recognised as a token. The eof symbol denotes the end of the statement. The last eof indicates the end of input.

2.3 Separation of Lexical Analysis and Syntax Analysis

There are many reasons for separating the lexical analysis and syntax analysis phases of the compilation process:

- It often allows us to simplify one or the other of these phases.
- A parser is more complicated than a lexical analyser. Shrinking the grammar makes the parser faster.

- Lexical analysers are implemented using finite automata (FA) and are more efficient to implement than pushdown automata (PDA), which are used for implementing parsers.
- Input/Output and related issues can be handled only by a lexical analyser.
- A parser that takes care of the conventions for space, tab and comments along with parsing is significantly more complex than one which assumes that whitespaces and comments have already been removed by lexical analysis. Hence, space, tab and comments need not be handled by the parser.
- A separate lexical analyser allows the construction of a specialised and potentially more efficient processor. A large amount of time is spent in reading the source program and partitioning it into tokens. Specialised buffering techniques and processing of tokens can speed up the performance of a compiler. Moreover, the system is split into two smaller parts, which may be smaller than the combined system of lexical analyser and parser.
- No rules for numbers, names, comments, etc. are needed in the parser.
- Compiler portability is enhanced.

Specialised tools have been designed to automate the construction of separate lexical analyser and syntax analyser.

2.4 Specification of Tokens

In this section, the concepts related to language are described. An **alphabet** is a finite set of symbols. Typical examples of symbols are letters, characters and numbers. The binary alphabet set is {0, 1}. An alphabet is denoted by Σ.

A **string** over some alphabet is a sequence of symbols from the alphabet set. For example, 01100010 is a string of length 8 using binary alphabets. ε is considered as an empty string having length 0. A set of all strings over Σ is denoted by Σ^*.

A **language** is a set of strings over some fixed alphabet. It may contain a finite or an infinite number of strings. For example, ∅ and {ε} are languages. The set of strings {01, 10, 111} over {0,1} is a finite language. The set of palindromes over {0,1} is an infinite language. Each subset of Σ^* is a language.

Regular expressions (type 3 or regular languages), context-free grammars (type 2 or context-free languages), context-sensitive grammars (type 1 or context-sensitive languages), and type 0 grammars are finite representations of the respective languages.

For example, let $\Sigma = \{a,b,c\}$
L1= $\{a^m b^n \mid m,n >=0\}$ is a regular language
L2= $\{a^n b^n \mid n>=0\}$ is a context-free language but not regular
L3=$\{a^n b^n c^n \mid n>=0\}$ is a context-sensitive language but is neither regular nor context-free

To recognise a language, **automata** are constructed. **Finite automata** accept the regular language specified by regular expressions. **Pushdown automata** accept context-free language, specified using context-free grammar. **Linear bounded automata** accept context-sensitive language specified by context-sensitive grammar. The **Turing machine** accepts type 0 languages specified using type 0 grammar.

Operations on languages

- **Union**: If L and M are two languages, then their union, denoted by L ∪ M, is the language containing every string in L and every string in M (any string that is in both L and M appears only once).
- **Concatenation**: If L and M are two languages, then their concatenation, denoted by L ∩ M, is the language containing every string that appears in both L and M.

- **Kleene closure (Kleene Star):** Kleene closure of a language L is denoted by L*; it is a unary operation, either on sets of strings or on sets of symbols or characters. It is used to characterise certain automata, where it means 'zero or more'.
  $L^* = \{\varepsilon\} \cup L1 \cup L2 \cup L3 \cup \ldots.$
  where Li is the set of alphabet combinations over the alphabet. For example, if L = {a, b}, then
  $L^* = \{ \varepsilon$, a, b, aa, ab, ba, bb, aaa, aba, baa, bba, aab, abb, bab, bbb, ... }
  It is an infinite set of all possible strings over the alphabet {a,b}.
- **Positive closure (Kleene Plus):** Kleene Plus of a language L is denoted by L^+
  $L^+ = L1 \cup L2 \cup L3 \cup L4 \cup \ldots$
  It is used to characterise certain automata, where it means 'one or more'. So, there is no ε. For example, if L = {a, b}, then
  L^+= {a, b, aa, ab, ba, bb, aaa, aba, baa, bba, aab, abb, bab, bbb, ... }.

Example 2.3 Perform operations on the given language
Let L = {A, B, ... , Z, a, b, ..., z} be the set of all capital and lowercase letters and D = {0, 1, 2, 3, 4, 5, 6, 7, 8, 9} be the set of all digits. The results after performing various operations on the given language are shown in Table 2.1.

Table 2.1 Various operations on the language

Representation	Result
L ∪ D	Set of all letters and digits
LD	Set of strings consisting of a letter followed by a digit
L3	Set of all three-letter strings
L*	Set of all possible string combinations of letters including the empty string ε
L(L ∪ D)*	Set of all strings containing letters and digits that begin with a letter
L+	Set of all possible string combinations of letters
D+	Set of all possible string combinations of digits
D*	Set of all possible string combinations of digits and letters, including the empty string ε

2.5 Tokens, Patterns and Lexemes

There is a set of strings in the input for which the same token is produced as output. This set of strings is described by a rule called a **pattern** associated with the token. The pattern is said to match each string in the set. A **lexeme** is a sequence of characters in the source program that is matched by the pattern for a token. A string of characters, which logically belong together, is called a **token**.

A token, containing a sequence of characters, must have a collective meaning. There are some predefined rules for every lexeme to be identified as a valid token. These rules are defined by grammar rules, by means of a pattern. A pattern explains what can be a token, and these patterns are defined by means of regular expressions.

For example, int a = 12;

The substring *int* is a lexeme for the token 'keyword'. The substring *a* is a lexeme for the token 'identifier'. Usually, there are only a small number of tokens for a programming language: keywords, identifiers, constants, strings, operators and punctuation symbols. The various types of tokens are discussed below.

Keywords: Keywords are predefined words in a programming language. Each keyword is meant to perform a specific function. As keywords are reserved words used by the compiler to perform a predefined task, they cannot be used as variable names. C language has 32 keywords (examples: auto, double, int, struct, case, void, if and static), whereas Java contains 60 keywords.

Identifiers: Identifiers are user-defined names given to identify entities of a programming language such as variables, functions, arrays, etc. An identifier must have a unique name to identify it during the execution of a program. The rules for constructing an identifier name in C are as follows:

- The first character should be an alphabet or underscore.
- Succeeding characters may be digits or letters.
- Punctuation and special characters are not allowed, except underscore.
- Identifiers should not be keywords.

Constants: A constant is a value or an identifier whose value cannot be altered in a program. An identifier can also be defined as a constant. For example, const double PI = 3.14, where PI is a constant. Some types of constants in C are integer constants, real or floating point constants, octal constants, hexadecimal constants, character constants and backslash character constants.

String literals: String literals are also a type of constant, enclosed in double quotes "". A string contains characters that are similar to character literals: plain characters, escape sequences and universal characters.

Operators: An operator is a symbol that tells the compiler to perform specific mathematical or logical functions. A high-level language typically contains operators such as arithmetic operators, relational operators, logical operators, bitwise operators and assignment operators.
For example, the following operators are available in Java:

Arithmetic operators	+ - / *
Relational operators	< , <=, ==, !=, > and >=
Logical operator	&&(logical and), || (logical OR) and !(logical not)
Bitwise operator	&, |, ^,~, <<, >>
Assignment operators	=, +=, -=, *=,/=,%=, <<=, >>=, &=, ^= and |=

Symbols: Various symbols like punctuations and special symbols exist, such as comma (,), semicolon (;), dot (.), arrow (→), #, $, etc.

Example 2.4 To find tokens in the given code
Consider the high level code

```
int a, b,sum;
printf("\n Enter two numbers:");
scanf("%d %d",&a,&b);
sum=a+b;
printf("sum: %d", sum);
```

The lexical analyser accepts the above source code as input and eliminates any spaces, comments and tab characters. Then, it recognises the tokens corresponding to the lexemes (Table 2.2). Here, only distinct lexemes are considered. For example, `printf` appears twice.

Table 2.2 Lexemes and corresponding tokens

Lexeme	Token
int	Keyword
a	Identifier
b	Identifier
c	Identifier
sum	Identifier
;	Symbol
printf	Keyword
(	Symbol
)	Symbol
scanf	Keyword
"\n Enter two numbers:"	String
"%d %d"	String
&	Symbol
=	Operator
+	Operator
"sum: %d"	String
,	Symbol

Example 2.5 To find the total number of tokens and distinct number of tokens in a given code fragment

Consider the given code fragment in C

```
int i;
printf("Number is %d & incremented number is %d", i , ++i);
```

The different tokens corresponding to lexemes are shown in Table 2.3.

Table 2.3 Lexemes and token types

Lexeme	Token types
int	Keyword
i	Identifier
;	Symbol
printf	Identifier/ C Function

(Cont'd)

Table 2.3 (Continued)

Lexeme	Token types
(	Symbol
"Number is %d & incremented number is %d"	String
,	Symbol
i	Identifier
++	Operator
i	Identifier
)	Symbol
;	Symbol

Therefore, the total number of lexemes is 12 and the total number of tokens is also 12.
Distinct token are int, i, comma (,), semicolon (;), printf (,), text inside quotes, ++
So, there are 9 distinct tokens in total.

2.6 Attributes for Tokens

When more than one pattern matches a lexeme, the lexical analyser must provide additional information about the particular lexeme that was matched, so that subsequent phases of the compiler can recognise the proper token. For example, the pattern for a digit is [0–9]. All the numbers from 0 to 9 will match the pattern for digit. However, it is essential for the code generator to know what number was actually matched.

The lexical analyser stores information about tokens and their associated attributes. A token usually has only a single attribute that is a pointer to the symbol table entry in which the information about the token is kept. The pointer becomes the attribute for the token. The lexeme for an identifier and the line number on which it was first seen are stored in the symbol table entry for the identifier.

For example, in an expression E=a+1, the corresponding token and associated attribute values will be

<id, pointer to symbol table entry for E>
<assign_op, >
< id, pointer to symbol table entry for a>
<add_op, >
<digit, integer value 1>

2.7 Lexical Analyser and Symbol Table

A symbol table stores information for subsequent phases in the compilation process. It keeps track of information about various tokens:

- The **identifiers** that the source program is using – names of scalars, arrays, variable, functions, etc.

- **Constants** are included in the symbol table because their values must be stored somewhere. Rather than creating a separate structure, the symbol table is used as it is easier to create.
- **Keywords** of the language such as if, while, do, etc. are also stored in the symbol table as their lexemes look like the lexemes of identifiers. The keywords are pre-loaded into the symbol table before the source program is read so that the first time the source program uses a keyword, it will be assigned the proper token type.

Other lexemes like operators and symbols are pre-loaded into the symbol table.

Example 2.6 Find the total number of tokens in the given C statement

```
printf(" String % d" , ++ i ++ &&& i ** a);
```

The tokens are

printf ("String % d" , ++ i ++ && & i * * a) ;

So, there are 15 tokens in total.

Example 2.7 Specify the <token, attribute> set for the C statement, a = (b + c) * 2 ;

<id , 100> <=, > <(, > <id , 101> <+, > <id , 102> <), > <*, > <Constant, 103> <;, >

The numbers after the comma (,) represent the pointer to the symbol table entry. The symbol table entry at memory location 100 stores the identifier 'a', 101 stores 'b' and 102 stores 'c'. A constant value 2 is stored at location 103.

Example 2.8 Find the lexemes and the < token type, attribute> set for the C expression, a=(b+c−d)/f;

The lexemes are

a = (b + c − d) / f ;

The tokens along with their associated attributes are

< id, 1> <=> <(> <b , 2> <+> <c , 3> <−> <d , 4> <)> <f , 5> <;>

The number after the comma (,) is the attribute pointing to the symbol table entry for that identifier. A part of symbol table is shown below:

Location	Token type	Value
1	Identifier	a
2	Identifier	b
3	Identifier	c
4	Identifier	d
5	Identifier	f

Example 2.9 Assume that the symbol table contains entries for some keywords, operators and symbols pre-loaded, as in Table 2.4, and having two entries: token types and variables. Consider the C code fragment and generate the <token type, attribute> set.

```
int a , b , c ;
a = ( b + c ) * 2 ;
```

Table 2.4 Existing symbol table

Location	Token type	Value	Location	Token type	Value
1000	Keyword	int	1008	Operators	*
1001	Keyword	float	1009	Operators	=
1002	Keyword	double	1010	Operators	++
1003	Keyword	char	1011	Symbol	(
1004	Keyword	for	1012	Symbol	)
1005	Operators	+	1013	Symbol	;
1006	Operators	–	1014	Symbol	,
1007	Operators	/	1015	Symbol	&

The token set generated for the given C fragment is shown in Table 2.5, and the entries added to the symbol table (Table 2.4) are shown in Table 2.6.

Table 2.5 The <token, attribute> set

Lexeme	<token, attribute > pair	Lexeme	<token, attribute > pair
int	<keyword, 1000>	(	<Symbol , 1011>
a	<id , 1016>	b	<id , 1017>
,	<Symbol , 1014>	+	<operator , 1005>
b	<id , 1017>	c	<id , 1018>
,	<Symbol , 1014>	)	<Symbol , 1012>
c	<id , 1018>	*	<Symbol , 1008>
;	<Symbol , 1013>	2	<Constant , 1019>
a	<id , 1016>	;	<Symbol , 1013>
=	<operator , 1009>		

In the case of the lexeme *int*, the entry is already present in the symbol table, and hence, the attribute points to the symbol table entry of int at location 1000. If the entry is not in the symbol table, then an entry is added, as in the case of identifier *a*.

Table 2.6 Symbol table entries added to Table 2.4

Location	Token type	Value
1016	Identifier	a
1017	Identifier	b
1018	Identifier	c
1019	Constant	d

2.8 Regular Expression

The lexical analyser needs to identify a finite set of valid tokens of a programming language. Regular expressions have the ability to express finite languages by defining a pattern for finite strings of symbols. The grammar defined by regular expressions is known as regular grammar. The language defined by regular grammar is known as regular language, specifying the regular set.

Regular expression is a notation for specifying patterns. Each pattern matches a set of strings, so regular expressions serve as names for a set of strings. Programming language tokens can be described by regular languages.

Regular languages are easy to understand and have efficient implementation. Hence, the lexical analyser uses regular expressions to identify the tokens of a language. Regular expressions are an important notation for specifying patterns. Each pattern matches a set of strings, so regular expressions serve as names for sets of strings. Regular expressions are then converted to finite automata, which are capable of recognising the patterns.

Notations used to represent regular expressions: There are rules that define the regular expressions over the alphabet Σ. Associated with each rule is a specification of the language denoted by the regular expression being defined. These rules are as follows:

1. ε is a regular expression that denotes language $\{\varepsilon\}$, the set containing the empty string.
2. If a is a symbol in Σ, then a is a regular expression that denotes $\{a\}$, the set containing string a.
3. If r and s are regular expressions denoting languages L(r) and L(s), then
   - (r) | (s) is a regular expression denoting $L(r) \cup L(s)$
   - (r) (s) is a regular expression denoting L(r) L(s)
   - (r)* is a regular expression denoting (L(r))*
   - (r) is a regular expression denoting L(r)

Parentheses can be avoided in regular expressions if:

- The unary operator * has the highest precedence and is left associative
- Concatenation has the second highest precedence and is left associative
- | has the lowest precedence and is left associative

The notations given in Table 2.7 can also be used along with these rules. These notations are called a shorthand (they are more convenient to use). For example, digits can be described by the regular expression (0 | 1| 2 | 3| 4 | 5 | 6 | 7 | 8 | 9)+. Instead of writing all the numbers, use shorthand notations; regular expressions for digit can also be written as [0–9]+. The specification of a regular expression is an example of a recursive definition. Rules (1) and (2) form the basis of the definition, while Rule (3) is the inductive step.

Table 2.7 Regular expression notations

Notation	Description	Example
{ }+	One or more repetitions	{a}+ String contains a repeated one or more times
[ ]	Optional (called character class)	[abc] String can contain a or b or c
–	Range	[a–z] String can contain any character between a and z

(Cont'd)

Table 2.7 (Continued)

Notation	Description	Example
?	Zero or one instance	
( )	Grouping	(a | b)
^	Except	[^a] a is not included

Algebraic laws for regular expressions: A number of algebraic laws are obeyed by regular expressions, and they can be used to manipulate them into equivalent forms. Some algebraic laws for regular expressions r, s and t are as follows:

- | is commutative. For example, r | s = s | r
- | is associative. For example, r|(s|t) = (r|s)|t
- Concatenation is associative. For example, (rs)t = r(st)
- Concatenation distributes over |. For example, r(s|t) = rs | rt
- ε is to identify the element. For example, εr = r
- r*=(ε|r)*
- * is idempotent. For example, r** = r*

Examples of regular expressions

- Regular expression for strings of 0s and 1s not accepting an empty string is [01]+
- Regular expression for a string abc is abc
- Regular expression for a string containing substring ab and any letters before and after is [a–z]+ab[a–z]+
- Regular expression for a string containing small letters and capital letters separated by @ is ([a–z]@[A–Z] | [A–Z]@[a–z])+

2.9 Transition Diagram

Lexical analysis uses transition diagrams to keep track of information about characters that are identified as the forward pointer scans the input. Positions in a transition diagram are drawn as circles and are called states. The states are connected by arrows called edges. A double circle indicates an accepting state, a state in which a token is found. a* indicates that input retraction must take place. FA are used to represent the transition diagram.

Finite automata (FA): FA is a recogniser for regular expressions. It is a state machine that takes a string of symbols as input and changes its state accordingly. If the input string is successfully processed and the automata reach their final state, the string fed as input is accepted and considered to be a valid token of the language. When a regular expression string is fed into FA, it changes its state for each literal. The mathematical model of FA consists of:

- Finite set of input symbols (Σ)
- Finite set of states (Q)
- One start state (q0)
- One or more final states (qf)
- Transition function (δ)

The transition function (δ) maps the finite set of state (Q) to a finite set of input symbols (Σ), $Q \times \Sigma \rightarrow Q$

FA construction: Once all the tokens are defined using regular expressions, a finite automaton can be created for recognising them. Let L(r) be a regular language recognised by some FA. The FA is constructed as follows:

1. Represent the states of FA as circles and write the state names inside the circles.
   - **Start state:** The state from which the automaton starts. This state has an arrow pointed towards it, to mark it as the start state.
   - **Intermediate states:** All intermediate states have at least two arrows, one pointing towards and another pointing out from them.
   - **Final state:** This is represented by double circles. If the input string is successfully parsed, the automaton is expected to be in this state. It can have an odd number of arrows pointing towards it and and even number of arrows pointing out from it. The number of odd arrows is one greater than the number of even arrows, i.e., odd = even + 1.
2. **Transition:** The transition from one state to another happens when a desired symbol in the input is found. Upon transition, automata can either move to the next state or stay in the same state. Movement from one state to another is shown by a directed arrow, where the arrows points to the destination state.

For example, Fig. 2.2 shows the FA that accepts a string starting with a and ending with b and having any number of b. The regular expression corresponding to FA is ab+

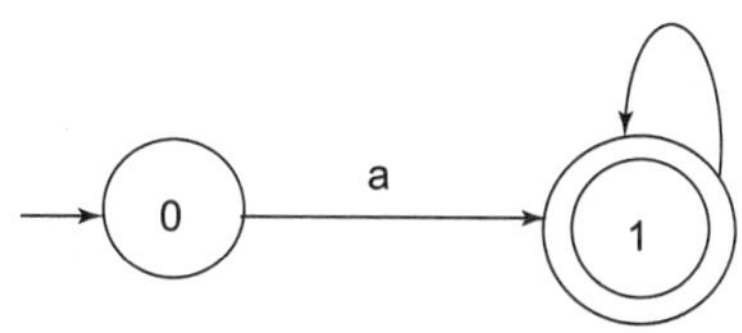

Figure 2.2 FA that accepts a string starting with a and ending with b, and having any number of b

Example 2.10 Transition diagram for relational operators in Java

Java has six relational operators: <, <=, ==, !=, > and >=. One way to recognise a token is with a finite state automaton following a particular transition diagram. The transition diagram for the RELOP token is shown in Fig. 2.3.

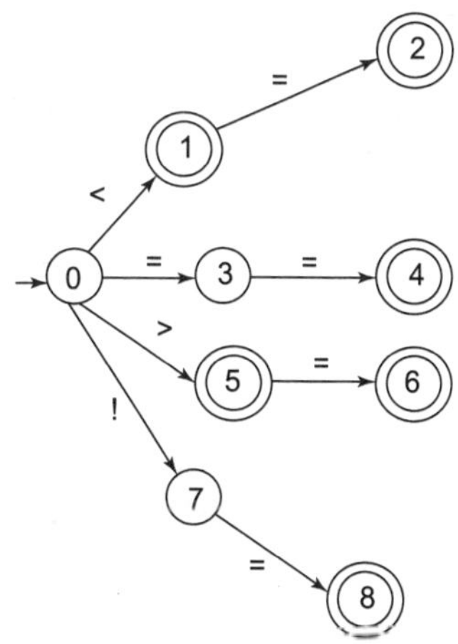

Figure 2.3 Transition diagram for relational operators in Java

Example 2.11 Transition diagram for identifiers of C

A name is an identifier if:

1. It starts with a letter or underscore
2. The characters that follow are digits or letters or underscore (zero or more times)
3. No punctuation and special characters are allowed, except underscore

The regular expression for identifier uses letters and digits, as

letter → a | A | b | B | c | C | ....
digit →0 | 1 | 2 | 3 | 4 | 5 |6 | 7 | 8 | 9

According to the rules of identifier, the regular expression for an identifier will be

identifier → (_ | letter)$^+$ (letter | digit | _)*

(_ | letter)$^+$ denotes that the identifier can start with _ or a letter. At least one _ or letter must be present. This is shown by a + sign, denoting one or more occurrences. This is followed by a letter or digit or underscore (_), zero or more times.

Some of the permissible identifiers are as follows:

- Underscore (_), underscore followed by underscore (__), underscore followed by two underscores (___), and so on.
- Any single letter, for example, A, B, p, q, and so on.
- _num, nu_m, num_ , etc.

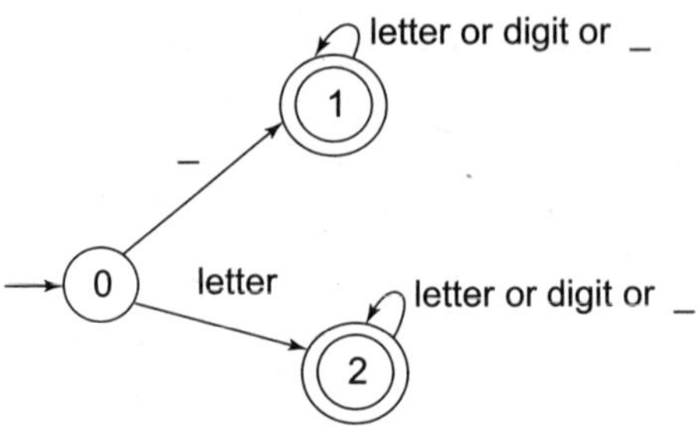

Figure 2.4 Transition diagram for identifiers of C language

The transition diagram for identifiers is shown in Fig. 2.4.

Example 2.12 Transition diagram for numeric constants

The transition diagram of some unsigned numeric constants using the regular expression is expressed as

digit →0 | 1 | 2 | 3 | 4 | 5 |6 | 7 | 8 | 9

Integers: They are represented by the regular expression

Int → digit (digit)*

The transition diagram corresponding to integers is shown in Fig. 2.5 (a).

Floating point constant: They are represented by the regular expression

Fconst → digit+ (. digit+)*

The transition diagram corresponding to floating point numbers is shown in Fig. 2.5 (b).

Exponential numbers: They are represented by the regular expression

exp → digit+ (. digit+)? E ('+' | '-')? digit+

The transition diagram corresponding to exponential numbers is shown in Fig. 2.5 (c).

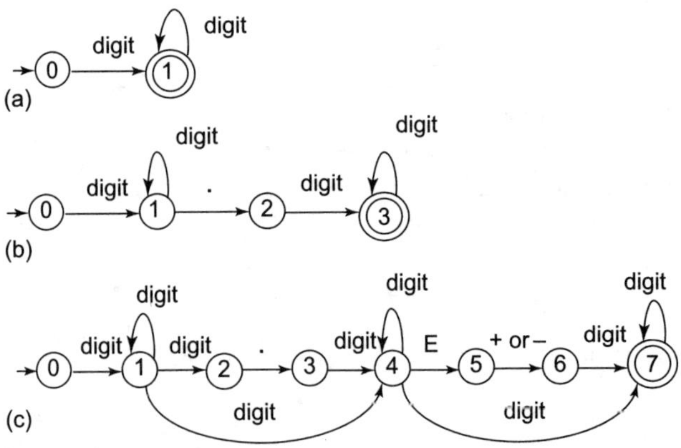

Figure 2.5 Transition diagram for numeric constants

2.10 Recognition of Tokens

In this section, tokens for a sample grammar are specified and their recognition is explained.
Let us consider a grammar

stmt → if *expr* then *stmt*
  | if *expr* then *stmt* else *stmt*
  | ε
expr → *term* relop *term*
  | *term*
term → id
  | num

Assumption: Identifiers cannot contain underscore or any special character and only integer numbers are accepted.

The regular definitions for tokens are as follows:

if → if
then → then
else → else
relop → < | <= | = | <> | > | >=
id → letter (letter|digit)*
num → digit$^+$
delim → blank | tab | newline
ws → delim$^+$

Let us construct an analyser that will return <token, attribute> pairs as output. The analyser must identify the if, then and else keywords, and lexemes denoted by relop, id and num. Let us understand the recognition of tokens using the regular definitions:

- The first step of the lexical analyser is to strip out whitespaces and comments. For our example, the regular definition of ws is used to strip out the whitespaces. If a match to ws is found, then no token is returned; instead, the parser proceeds to find the next token.

  The lexical analyser will return a <token, attribute> pair corresponding to each token found. Table 2.8 shows the attribute values used in this example. The transition diagram for the sample grammar is shown in Fig. 2.6.

Table 2.8 Attribute values for tokens

Regular expression	Token	Attribute value
ws	-	-
if	if	-
then	then	-
else	else	-
id	id	Pointer to symbol table entry
num	num	Pointer to symbol table entry

(*Cont'd*)

Table 2.8 (Continued)

Regular expression	Token	Attribute value
<	relop	LT
<=	relop	LE
=	relop	EQ
<>	relop	NE
>	relop	GT
>=	relop	GE

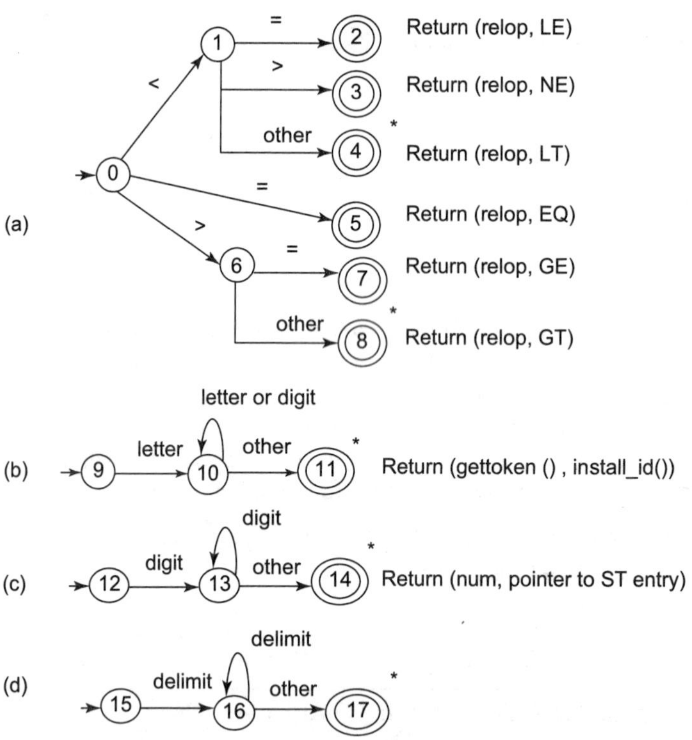

Figure 2.6 Transition diagrams using Method 2

Relational operators: Consider that the process starts at state 0. Read the next input character and follow the edge with label < to reach state 1. If the next input character is =, follow the edge labelled = to reach state 2, which is an accepting state, recognising token "<=". Else, if the next input character is >, follow the edge labelled > to reach state 3, which is also an accepting state that recognises token "< >". Else, state 4 is reached.

Notice that for character <, extra characters are read as we follow the sequence of edges from the start state to accepting state 4. As the extra characters (= or >) are not part of the relational operator, retract the forward pointer one character. a * is used on the state to indicate that input retraction must take place. The <token, attribute> pair returned by the lexical analyser is specified beside the state in Fig. 2.6. State 2 recognises <= lexeme, which is a relop. As per Table 2.8, state 2 will return the pair <relop, LE>.

Identifiers and keywords: States 9, 10 and 11 are used in the transition diagram to represent the identifiers. Keywords are sequences of letters; they are exceptions to the rule that a sequence of letters and digits starting with a letter is an identifier. Separate transition diagrams can be generated for identifiers and keywords or the same diagram can be used with added functions. Both the methods are discussed in this section.

Method 1: Different diagrams for identifier and keyword
Different transition diagrams can be generated for identifiers and keywords. The transition diagram for identifiers is shown in Fig. 2.6 (b) and that corresponding to keywords in the example is shown in Fig. 2.7. However, this will work only for the specified keywords and is not generalised.

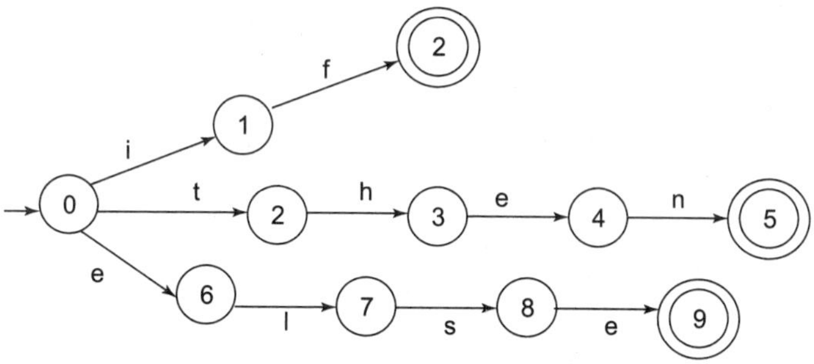

Figure 2.7 Transition diagram using Method 1

Method 2: Using the same diagram for identifier and keyword
Rather than creating different transition diagram for keywords, some code is executed to determine if the lexeme leading to the accepting state is a keyword or an identifier when accepting state 11 is reached. A simple technique for separating keywords from identifiers is to initialise the symbol table in which information about identifiers is saved, with keywords. We need to enter the strings of keywords into the symbol table before any characters in the input are scanned. The symbol table should be updated with the token to be returned when one of these strings is recognised. As shown in Fig. 2.6(b), the return statement uses two functions: *gettoken()* and *install_id()*.

gettoken(): This function is used to obtain the token. It searches for the lexeme in the symbol table. If the lexeme is a keyword, the corresponding token is returned; otherwise, the token ID is returned.

install_id(): This function is used to obtain the attribute value corresponding to the token. It can access the buffer, where the identifier lexeme is located. The symbol table is examined and if the lexeme is found, it is marked as a keyword. The function returns 0, if the lexeme is found and it is a program variable or identifier. The pointer to the symbol table entry is returned. If the lexeme is not found in the symbol table, it is installed as an identifier and a pointer to the newly created entry is returned.

num: The token is num and the value is entered in the symbol table and its pointer is returned.

ws: Nothing is returned. Revert to the start state and begin looking for a new pattern.

Implementing the transition diagram: Transition diagrams can be easily converted into programs to look for tokens specified by the diagrams. Separate cases can be considered for initialising the start states.

Variable *state* is used to keep track of the state, and variable *start* to specify the start state. *lexical_value* is used to return the second component of a token. The function *nextchar*() is used to read the next character from the input buffer, advance the forward pointer at each call, and return the character read. If there is an edge labelled by the character read or labelled by a character class containing the character read, then control is transferred to the code for the state pointed to by that edge. If there is no such edge, and the current state is not one that indicates that a token has been found, then a routine *fail()* is invoked to retract the forward pointer to the position of the beginning pointer and to initiate a search for a token specified by the next transition diagram. The C program code for some states of transition diagrams shown in Fig. 2.6 is given below:

```
int state=0, start=0;
int lexical_value;
int fail()
{
      forward = token_beginning;
      switch(start)
      {
      case 0: start = 9 ; break;
      case 9: start = 12; break;
      case 12: start = 15; break;
      case 15: recover( ); break;
      default:    // error
      }
return start;
}
token nexttoken()
{
while(1) {
switch(state) {
      case 0: c=nextchar( );
            if(c==blank || c==tab || c==newline) {
            state=0;
            lexeme_beginning++;
            }
            else if (c== '<') state =1;
            else if (c== '=') state =5;
            else if (c== '>') state =6;
            else state = fail();
            break;
      case 9: c=nextchar( );
            if(isletter(c)) state =10;
            else state = fail();
```

```
            break;
        case 10: c=nextchar();
            if(isletter(c)) state=10;
            elseif (isdigit(c)) state=10;
            else state=11;
            break;
        case 11: retract (1); install_id( );
            return(gettoken() );
        case 12: c=nextchar();
            if(isdigit(c)) state = 13 ;
            else state= fail ();
            break;
        case 17: retract(1); install_num;
            return(num);
        }
}
}
```

Example 2.13 Transition diagram for accepting the data needed by a company for the given employees

Consider a company that wants to accept data from employees. The data is described as follows:

- Name of the employee: Can have only letters. Name can start with a capital letter.
- Employee ID: It must have the format EMP_<number>.
- Address: The address must start with a digit (one or more). Then, a separator comma is allowed, followed by letters.
- E-mail: Letters followed by @ followed by mail provider (like gmail, yahoo); then . and domain name (like com, org).
- Salary: Floating point number is allowed.

The regular definition for the new language to be designed is as follows:

sletter → [a–z]
cletter→[A–Z]
digit→[0–9]
underscore→ _
provider→ gmail | yahoo | rediffmail | hotmail
domain→com |org | edu
name→cletter sletter+
empid→ EMP underscore (digit)+
address→digit+, sletter // cletter and combination with sletter is also valid
email→ sletter+@provider.domain
salary→(digit)+[.]?(digit)+

The transition diagram is shown in Fig. 2.8.

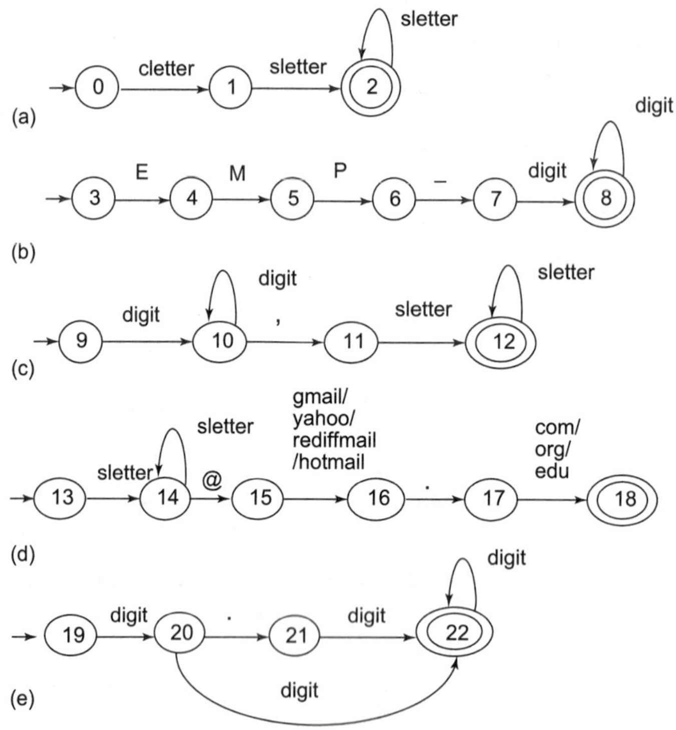

Figure 2.8 Transition diagram for Example 2.13

2.11 Lexical Errors

Errors are detected at every phase of the compilation process. However, a few errors become evident only at lexical analysis phase, as the lexical analyser is the only phase where the source code is read. For example, consider a code fragment in C

```
if(a>b)
     pintf("a is greater");
esle
     printf("b is greater");
```

In the above fragment, proper tokens are found until the lexical analyser encounters 'esle'. The lexical analyser encounters esle and cannot judge if it is a misspelling of the keyword else or an identifier. However, esle is a valid identifier, so the lexical analyser must return the token for an identifier and let the latter phases handle any error.

However, if the lexical analyser is unable to proceed, then error detection and handling must be performed. A lexical analyser finds an error when it is unable to proceed because none of the patterns match the prefix of the remaining input. Some of the error recovery strategies are given below:

- **Panic mode error recovery:** The simplest recovery strategy is the 'panic mode'. In this strategy, successive characters from the remaining input are deleted until the lexical analyser can find a token. This may even give rise to other errors and confuse the parser. It is a good strategy only in an interactive environment.

- Deleting an extraneous character
- Inserting a missing character
- Replacing an incorrect character with the correct character
- Transposing two adjacent characters

These error recovery methods attempt to transform the input code to repair it. The simplest strategy is to determine if a prefix of the remaining input can be transformed into a valid lexeme by a single error transformation. This strategy assumes that most lexical errors are the result of a single transformation. However, this may not always be the case.

2.12 NFA and DFA for Lexical Analysis

Finite automata are of two types: non-deterministic finite automata (NFA) and deterministic finite automata (DFA). NFA and DFA can be described by mathematical models consisting of input symbols (Σ), set of states (Q), one start state (q0), one or more final states (qf) and a transition function (δ).

In NFA, there can be more than one option for transition with the same symbol. Also, there may be transition with ε or any other symbol. So there are choices at each step, and the action or transition cannot be determined based on the current state and input. NFA accepts an input string if there exist some transitions that lead to the accepting state. Thus, even if there is one path leading to the accepting state and all other paths rejecting the string, the string is accepted. However, every path must reject for the overall NFA to reject any input string. For example, Fig. 2.9 shows an NFA for a string that ends with 001.

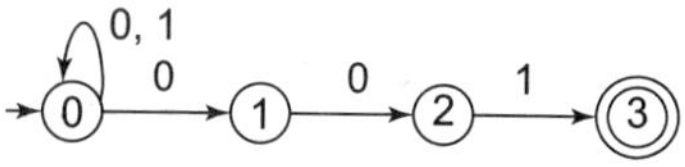

Figure 2.9 NFA for string ending with 001

Two transitions are possible with input 0 from state 0. One path leads to state-1 and another to state-0. Let us consider the input string 001001 and its transitions.

$0 \xrightarrow{0} 0 \xrightarrow{0} 1 \xrightarrow{1}$ No path. Try another path.

$0 \xrightarrow{0} 1 \xrightarrow{0} 2 \xrightarrow{1}$ No path. Try another path.

$0 \xrightarrow{0} 0 \xrightarrow{0} 0 \xrightarrow{1} 0 \xrightarrow{0} 1 \xrightarrow{0} 2 \xrightarrow{1} 3$

The paths are attempted until all the possible paths are exhausted. Even if a single path accepts the string, the input is accepted. In our example, the third try results in state-3, at the end of which is an accepting state. Hence, the input 001001 is accepted. All the possible paths can be tried in parallel or separately. The method for finding paths is as follows:

- *Guess method*: Guess the next state and try.
- *Compute tree*: A tree is constructed for all possible paths. If there is any leaf labelled 'accept', the input is accepted. In Example 2.14, the compute tree method is used.

The non-deterministic nature of NFA is not close to real machines. They have to be transformed into DFA, which are easy to implement and execute. The non-determinism is removed in DFA. Every state of DFA always has exactly one exiting transition arrow for each symbol in the alphabet. So, DFA is mostly used for implementation of the lexical analyser. The token specification in the regular expression form must be converted to DFA. The regular expressions can be converted into DFA directly or by first converting RE to NFA and then NFA to DFA. Both the methods are discussed later in this chapter.

Example 2.14 Draw the compute tree for the given NFA and input string. State if the string is accepted or rejected.

The given NFA: 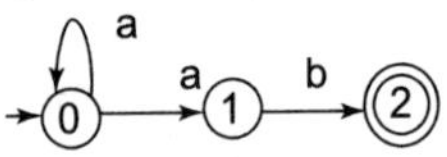

Let us consider the input string as, 'aaab'. The compute tree shows the possible paths to process an input string. Even if a single path leads to an accept state, the NFA accepts the input string. The compute tree for the given NFA is shown in Fig. 2.10. As there is a path that leads to the accept state, the NFA is said to accept the input string.

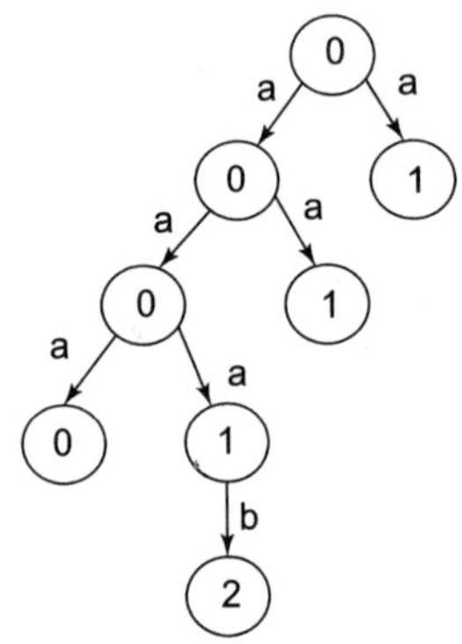

Figure 2.10 Compute tree for Example 2.14

2.12.1 Combining NFAs of Different Patterns into a Single NFA

Different NFAs recognising different patterns can be combined into a single NFA. The NFA in Fig. 2.11 (a) recognises string a, the NFA of Fig. 2.11 (b) recognises string ba and the NFA of Fig. 2.11 (c) recognises string b*aa*. These NFAs are combined, as shown in Fig. 2.12. The process of recognising string 'bbaa' in the combined NFA is shown with the help of states that can be reached, in Fig. 2.13.

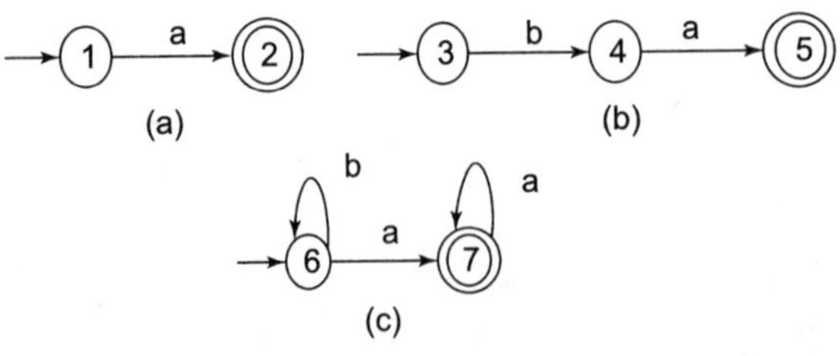

Figure 2.11 Different NFAs recognising different patterns

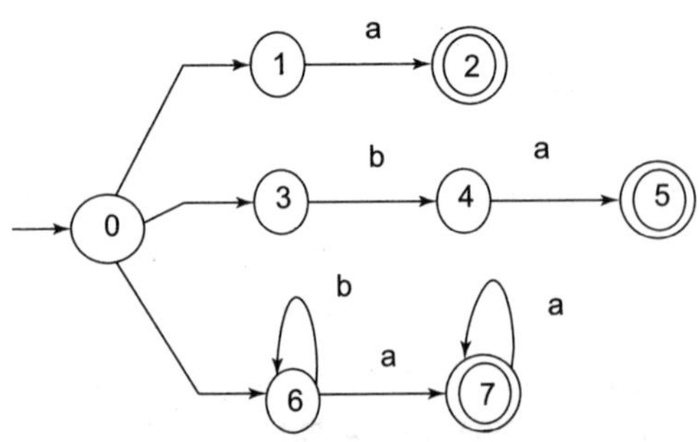

Figure 2.12 Combined NFA for different patterns

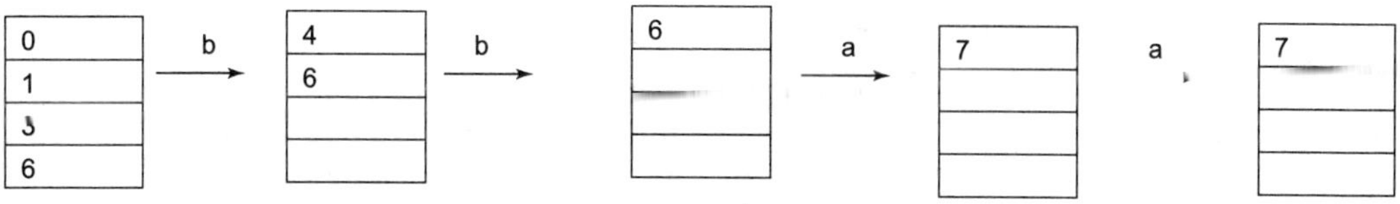

Figure 2.13 Processing of input string 'bbaa' in the combined NFA

2.13 Regular Expression to NFA

The rules for converting a regular expression to NFA are given below. In this method, each component of a regular expression is considered as one finite state machine and the components are connected using the ε operator.

Rule 1: For any sub-expression a, the NFA is created as 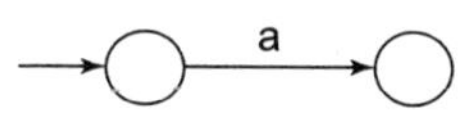

Rule 2: For an empty string 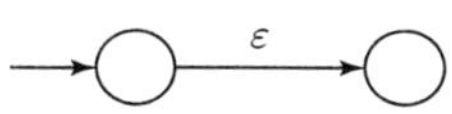

Rule 3: For a union operation denoted by r = r1 + r2 or r = r1| r2, the NFA is 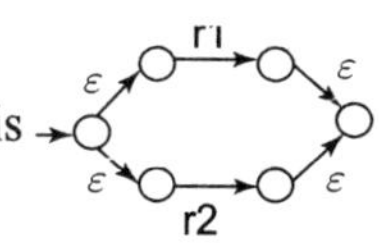

Rule4: For a concatenation operation denoted by r=r1 r2, the NFA is 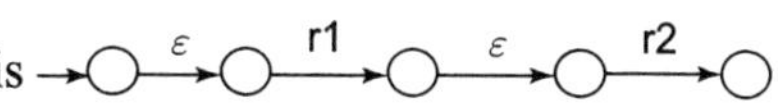

Rule 5: For a closure operation denoted by r = r1*, the NFA will be 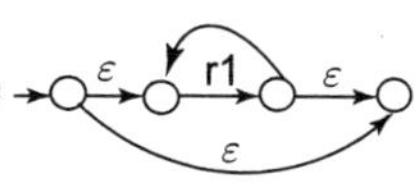

Example 2.15 Convert RE to NFA

NFA for the regular expression ab*(a|b) is computed as follows.

NFA for sub-expression a 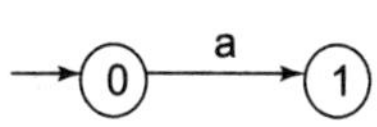

NFA for sub-expression b* 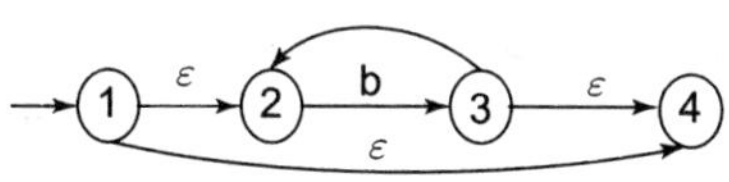

NFA for sub-expression a|b 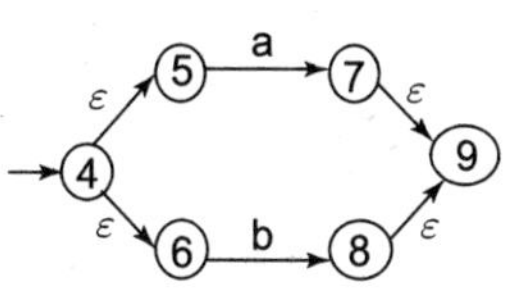

Hence the NFA for ab*(a|b) is shown in Fig. 2.14.

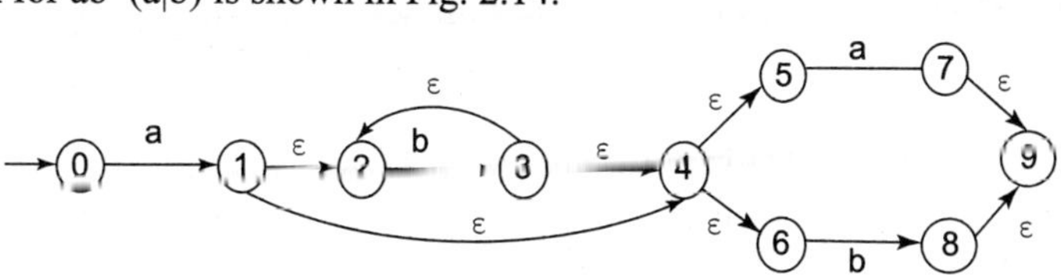

Figure 2.14 NFA for ab*(alb)

2.14 NFA to DFA Conversion

After an NFA is obtained from a regular expression, it can be converted to a DFA. Conversion of NFA to DFA is also called **subset construction**. The task is to convert the input NFA *N* to DFA *D*, accepting the same language. Let us assume that *s* represents the state in NFA and *T* represents a set of NFA states.

Construct *Dstates*, the set of states of *D*, and *Dtran*, the transition table for *D*. Each state of *D* corresponds to a set of NFA states that *N* could be in after reading some sequence of input symbols including all possible ε-transitions before or after the symbols are read. The start state of *D* is ε-closure(s0). A state of *D* is an accepting state if it is a set of NFA states containing at least one accepting state of *N*.

The algorithm for subset construction is given below:

```
initially, ε-closure(s0) is the only state in Dstates and it is unmarked;
while there is an unmarked state T in Dstates do begin
        mark T;
        for each input symbol a do begin
        U = ε-closure(move(T,a));
        if U is not in Dstates then
                add U as an unmarked state to Dstates;
        Dtran[T,a]=U;
    end
    end
```

The operations used in the algorithms are as follows:

- ε-closure(s): Set of NFA states reachable from NFA state s on ε-transitions alone
- ε-closure(T): Set of NFA states reachable from NFA state s in T on ε-transitions alone
- *move*(T,a)): Set of NFA states to which there is a transition on input symbol a from some NFA state s in T.

The simplified explanation of the procedure for conversion from NFA to DFA is as follows:

1. Alphabets of DFA are the same as alphabets of NFA. Also, the start state remains the same. DFA(Σ)=NFA(Σ) and DFA(q0)=NFA(q0)
2. The states permitted in DFA are a subset of the power set of states of NFA. The power set contains the combinations of states of NFA; there can be 2^Q states in the power set.
3. Transitions are found for DFA by processing each state created on input symbols. The process starts with the start state. The created state is added to Q if it is available in the power set. The transition process ends when there is no new state left unprocessed.
4. Final state for DFA contains all states that contain components of NFA final states.

This procedure is valid for NFA if there is no ε. If there is ε in the NFA, it is first converted to NFA without ε and then to DFA. The ε-closure of a state is the set of all states, including the state itself and all states which are reachable using ε-transitions. The procedure to convert NFA with ε to NFA without ε is as follows:

1. Find the ε-closure of all states in NFA.
2. Remove ε and find transitions for NFA without ε. The transitions from a state s on input a are δ'(s,a)= ε-closure(δ(δ^(s, ε),a), where delta cap δ^(s, ε) is the ε-closure(s).

The algorithm to find ε-closure is as follows:

```
Push all states in T onto stack;
Initialise ε-closure (T) to T;
While stack is not empty, do begin
    Pop t, the top element, off the stack
    For each state u with an edge from t to u labelled ε do
    If u is not in ε-closure (T), do begin
        Add u to ε-closure (T);
        Push u onto the stack
    End
End
```

The process to find the transitions from each state using each input symbol is explained with an example. Consider the NFA

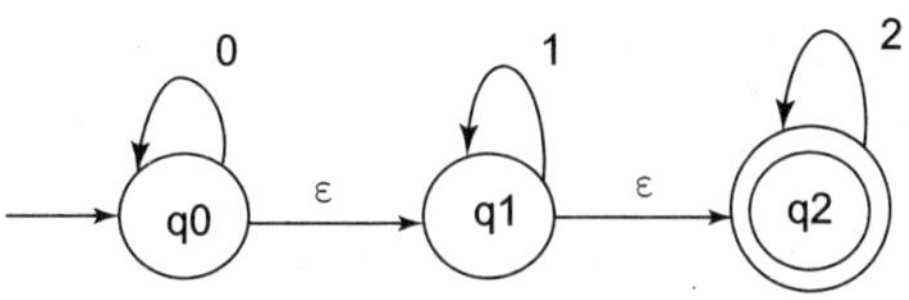

ε-closure(q0)={q0,q1,q2}
ε-closure(q1)={q1,q2}
ε-closure(q2)={q2}

To find the transitions of NFA without ε, start with start state q0 and process it on input symbols 0,1 and 2

$\delta'(q0,0) = \varepsilon\text{-closure}(\delta(\hat{\delta}(q0, \varepsilon),0)$ // $\hat{\delta}(q0, \varepsilon) = \varepsilon\text{-closure}(q0) = \{q0,q1,q2\}$
$= \varepsilon\text{-closure}(\delta(q0,q1,q2,0))$ // operating q0 on input 0 we get q0, operating q1 and q2 on input 0 we get ∅. Taking union q0 is obtained
$= \varepsilon\text{-closure}(q0)$ // ε-closure(q0)= {q0,q1,q2}
$= \{q0,q1,q2\}$

$\delta'(q0,1) = \varepsilon\text{-closure}(\delta(\hat{\delta}(q0, \varepsilon),1)$
$= \varepsilon\text{-closure}(\delta(q0,q1,q2,1))$
$= \varepsilon\text{-closure}(q1)$
$= \{q1,q2\}$

$\delta'(q0,2) = \varepsilon\text{-closure}(\delta(\hat{\delta}(q0, \varepsilon),2)$
$= \varepsilon\text{-closure}(\delta(q0,q1,q2,2))$
$= \varepsilon\text{-closure}(q2)$
$= \{q2\}$

Similarly

$\delta'(q1,0) = \varepsilon\text{-closure}(\delta(\hat{\delta}(q1, \varepsilon),0)$
$= \varepsilon\text{-closure}(\delta(q1,q2,0))$
$= \varepsilon\text{-closure}(\varnothing)$
$= \{\varnothing\}$

$\delta'(q1,1) = \varepsilon\text{-closure}(\delta(\hat{\delta}(q1, \varepsilon),1)$
$= \varepsilon\text{-closure}(\delta(q1,q2,1))$
$= \varepsilon\text{-closure}(q1)$
$= \{q1,q2\}$

$\delta'(q1,2) = \varepsilon\text{-closure}(\delta(\hat{\delta}(q1, \varepsilon),2)$
$= \varepsilon\text{-closure}(\delta(q1,q2,2))$
$= \varepsilon\text{-closure}(q2)$
$= \{q2\}$

And

δ'(q2,0)= {∅}
δ'(q2,1)= {∅}
δ'(q2,2) ={q2}

Therefore, the transition table for NFA without ε is shown on the right.

State	0	1	2
→q0	q0,q1,q2	q1,q2	q2
q1	∅	q1,q2	q2
*q2	∅	∅	q2

Example 2.16 NFA without ε to DFA conversion

Consider NFA having Q={p,q,r,s} Σ={0,1},δ,q0=p,qf={q,s}

The transition table for the NFA is given below:

State	0	1
→ p	q ,s	q
* q	r	q, r
r	s	p
* s	ϕ	p

Conversion of NFA without ε to DFA

DFA(Σ) = NFA(Σ)
DFA(q0) = NFA(q 0)
Q' for DFA is power set of Q
Q={p,q,r,s}
$Q'=2^Q = 16$
Q'= {φ,p,q,r,s,pq,pr,ps,qr,qs,rs,pqr,pqs,qrs,pqrs}

The transitions for DFA are computed as follows:

Transitions	Q for DFA	Action
	Empty.	Add p to Q, as it is the start state of NFA and find transitions of p with input symbols.
δ'(p,0) = [q s] δ'(p,1) = [q]	p = A	New Q is generated [q s]. Add it to Q and process transitions from qs.
δ'(qs,0) = [r] δ'(qs,1) = [pqr]	q s = B	Find transitions from r and then from pqr.
δ'(q,0) = [r] δ'(q,1) = [qr]	q = C	q is processed and generates r and qr.
δ'(r,0) = [s] δ'(r,1) = [p]	r = D	r is processed.
δ'(pqr,0) = [qrs] δ'(pqr,1) = [pqr]	pqr=E	pqr is processed.
δ'(qr,0) = [rs] δ'(qr,1) = [pqr]	qr=F	qr is processed.
δ'(s,0) = [ϕ] δ'(s,1) = [p]	s=G	s is processed.

(Cont'd)

Table (Continued)

Transitions	Q for DFA	Action
δ'(qrs,0) = [rs] δ'(qrs,1) = [pqr]	qrs=H	qrs is processed.
δ'(rs,0) = [s] δ'(rs,1) = [p]	rs=I	rs is processed.

The final states of DFA will be the states that contain the final states of NFA. The final states of NFA are q and s. So the final states of DFA will be C, B, E, F, G, H, I.

The transition table for DFA is as follows:

State/ Σ	0	1
→ A	B	C
* B	D	E
* C	D	F
* D	G	A
* E	H	E
* F	I	E
* G	ϕ	A
* H	I	E
* I	G	A

Many states have the same transition for input symbols. So the DFA must be optimised. Minimum-DFA is discussed in Section 2.16.

Example 2.17 Consider the transition diagram of NFA and convert NFA with ε to DFA

The transition table for the given NFA will be as follows:

State/ Σ	A	b	C
→ q0	q1,q2	-	q1
* q1	q1	q3	-
q2	-	-	q3
q3	q0,q3	Q2	-

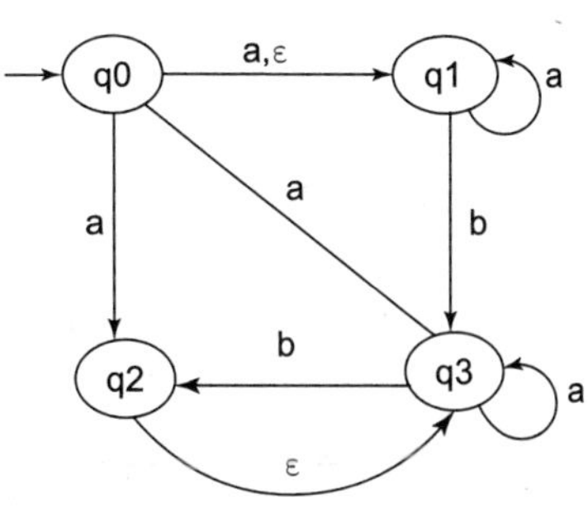

Step 1: NFA with ε to NFA without e

Find the ε closure for all NFA states

ε-closure (q0) = {q0,q1}

ε-closure (q1) = {q1}

ε-closure (q2) = {q2,q1}

ε-closure (q3) = {q3}

Remove ε and find the transition for each input symbol to obtain NFA without ε

δ'(q0,a) = ε-closure (δ (δ^ (q0, ε),a))
= ε-closure (δ (q0,q1,a))
=ε-closure(q1,q2)
={q1,q2,q3}

δ'(q0,b) = ε-closure (δ (q0,q1,b))
= ε-closure (q3)
= {q3}

Similarly, the transitions are
δ'(q1,a)= ε-closure (δ (q1,a))
= ε-closure (q1)
= {q1}

δ'(q1,b)= {q3}

δ'(q2,a) = {q0,q1,q3}
δ'(q2,b) = {q2,q3}

δ'(q3,a) = {q0,q1,q3}
δ'(q3,b) = {q2,q3}

NFA without ε will be as shown on the right.

State/ Σ	a	B
→ q0	q1,q2,q3	q3
* q1	q1	q3
q2	q0,q1,q3	q2,q3
q3	q0,q1,q3	q2q3

Step 2: Conversion from NFA to DFA

1. δ' (q0,a) = [q1,q2,q3] A=q0
   δ' (q0,b) = [q3]
2. δ' (q1q2q3,a) = [q0q1q3] B=q1q2q3
   δ' (q1q2q3,b) = [q2q3]
3. δ' (q3,a) = [q0q1q3] C=q3
   δ' (q3,b) = [q2q3]
4. δ'(q1q2q3,a) = [q0q1q2q3] D=q1q2q3
   δ'(q1q2q3,b) = [q2q3]
5. δ' (q2q3,a) = [q0q1q3] E=q2q3
   δ' (q2q3,b) = [q2q3]
6. δ' (q0q1q2q3,a) = [q0q1q2q3] F=q0q1q2q3
   δ' (q0q1q2q3,b) = [q2q3]

State/ Σ	A	b
→ A	B	C
* B	D	E
C	D	E
* D	F	E
E	D	E
* F	F	E

The final states of DFA will be B, D and F. The transition table for DFA is given above and the DFA is shown in Fig. 2.15. The DFA in Fig. 2.15 is not optimised. The optimised DFA is shown in Fig. 2.16. The optimisation process is discussed in Section 2.16.

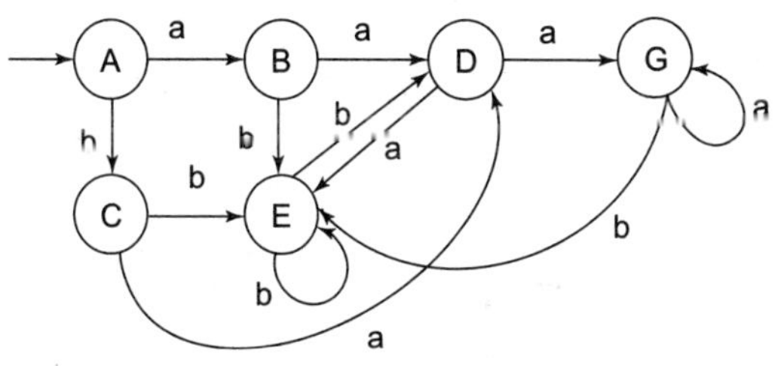

Figure 2.15 DFA for Example 2.17

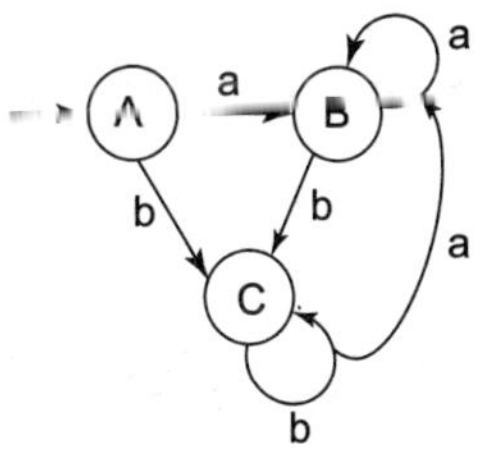

Figure 2.16 Optimised DFA for Example 2.17

Example 2.18 Convert regular expression to NFA

Consider the regular expression (a|b)*a. The NFA corresponding to the given RE is shown in Fig. 2.17. Now, find the ε-closure of all the NFA states

ε-closure (0)= {0,1,2,4,7}
ε-closure (1)= {0,1}
ε-closure (2)= {2}
ε-closure (3)= {3,6,1,7,2,4}
ε-closure (4)= {4}
ε-closure (5)= {5,6,7,1,2,4}
ε-closure (6)= {1,6,7}
ε-closure (7)= {7}
ε-closure (8)= {8}

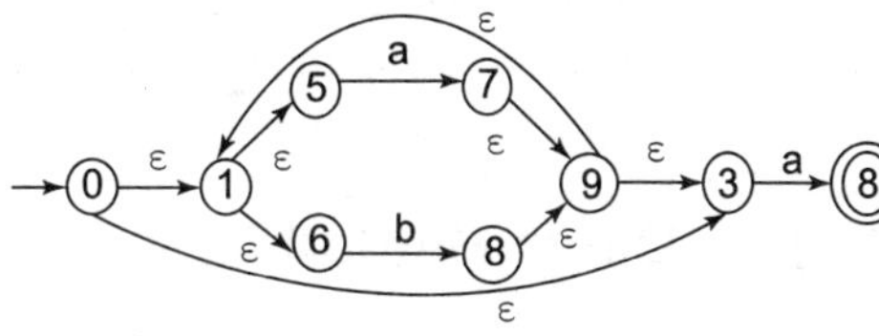

Figure 2.17 NFA for Example 2.18

Let {0,1,2,4,7} = A
Find the transitions using input symbols a and b.

δ'(A,a)= ε-closure(δ(δ^(A, ε),a)
=ε-closure(δ(0,1,2,4,7,a))
=ε-closure(3,8) = {3,6,1,7,2,4,8} = B

δ'(A,b)= ε-closure(δ(δ^(A, ε),b)
=ε-closure(δ(0,1,2,4,7,b))
=ε-closure(5) = {5,6,7,1,2,4} = C

δ'(B,a)= ε-closure(δ(δ^(B, ε),a)
=ε-closure(δ(3,6,1,7,2,4,8,a))
=ε-closure(3,8) = {3,6,1,7,2,4,8} = B

δ'(B,b)= ε-closure(δ(δ^(B, ε),b)
=ε-closure(δ(3,6,1,7,2,4,8, b))
=ε-closure(5) = {5,6,7,1,2,4} = C

δ'(C,a)= ε-closure(δ(δ^(C, ε),a)
=ε-closure(δ(5,6,7,1,2,4, a))
=ε-closure(3,8) = {3,6,1,7,2,4,8} = B

δ'(C,b)= ε-closure(δ(δ^(C, ε),b)
=ε-closure(δ(5,6,7,1,2,4,b))
=ε-closure(5) = {5,6,7,1,2,4} = C
The DFA is shown in Fig. 2.18.

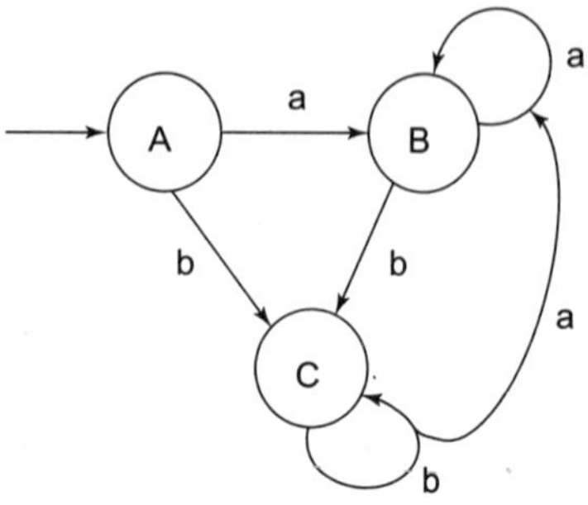

Figure 2.18 DFA for given RE

2.15 Regular Expression to DFA

DFA are mostly used to implement regular expressions in the lexical analyser. Regular expressions can be converted into DFA using the following methods:

- **Thompson's subset construction**
  - The given regular expression is converted into NFA.
  - The resultant NFA is converted into DFA.

  Conversion of a regular expression to NFA is discussed in Section 2.13 and conversion of NFA to DFA is discussed in Section 2.14.
- **Direct method:** Here, the given regular expression is converted directly into DFA. This method is discussed in detail below.

2.15.1 Direct Method for Conversion of RE to DFA

The direct method is used to convert the given regular expression directly into DFA. It uses augmented regular expression (r)#. The steps for conversion are as follows:

1. Represent the regular expression as a syntax tree.
2. Construct the DFA directly from the regular expression by computing the functions *nullable*(n), *firstpos*(n), *lastpos*(n) and *followpos*(i) from the syntax tree.

Syntax tree construction: The syntax tree T is constructed from the regular expression (r)#, where interior nodes correspond to operators representing the union, concatenation and closure operations and leaf nodes correspond to the input symbols. The syntax tree representation is given below:

- Leaves correspond to operands
  - Leaves are labelled ε or by an alphabet symbol.
  - Attach a unique integer that corresponds to the position of the leaf, to the node that is labelled by the alphabet of the language or the operands.
- Interior nodes correspond to operators
  - cat-node – Concatenation operator (dot represented as 0 in further examples)
  - or-node – Union operator (|)
  - star-node – Star operator (*)

DFA construction using the syntax tree: The construction of DFA from a syntax tree is a two-step process:

1. Computation of the functions *nullable*, *firstpos*, *lastpos*, *followpos*
2. Building the set of DFA states

These steps are explained below

1. Function computation: The functions *nullable*, *firstpos* and *lastpos* are computed first. The rules for computing these functions are given in Table 2.9. After computing these three functions, *follopos* is computed. The functions are described below:

- *nullable* (n): It is true for * node and nodes labelled ε. For other nodes, it is false.
- *firstpos* (n): Set of positions at node ti that corresponds to the first symbol of the sub-expression rooted at n.
- *lastpos* (n): Set of positions at node ti that corresponds to the last symbol of the sub-expression rooted at n.
- *followpos* (i): Set of positions that follows the given position by matching the first or last symbol of a string generated by the sub-expression of the given regular expression.

Table 2.9 Rules for computing functions: nullable, firstpos and lastpos

Node n	nullable (n)	firstpos (n)	lastpos (n)
A leaf labelled n	True	Ø	Ø
A leaf with position i	False	{i}	{i}
An or-node n = c1 | c2	nullable (c1) or nullable (c2)	firstpos (c1) ∪ firstpos (c2)	lastpos (c1) U lastpos (c2)

A cat-node
n = c1 0 c2
	nullable (c1) and
	nullable (c2)
		If (nullable (c1))
		firstpos (c1) ∪
		firstpos (c2)
		else
		firstpos (c1)
			If (nullable (c2))
			lastpos (c1) ∪
			lastpos (c2)
			else
			lastpos (c2)

A star-node n = c1*	True	firstpos (c1)	lastpos (c1)

Computation of followpos: After computing *nullable*, *firstpos* and *lastpos* for each node, *followpos* can be computed by making a depth-first traversal of the syntax tree. *followpos*(i) reveals what positions can follow position i in the syntax tree. The rules to find *followpos(i)* are as follows:

Rule 1: If n is a cat-node with left child c1 and right child c2, and I is a position in *lastpos*(c1), then all positions in *firstpos*(c2) are in *followpos*(i). In other words, for a cat-node, for each position i in *lastpos* of its left child, the *firstpos* of its right child will be in *followpos(i)*.

Rule 2: If n is a star-node and i is a position in *lastpos*(n), then all the positions in *firstpos*(n) are in *followpos*(i). In other words, for a star-node, the *firstpos* of that node is in the *followpos* of all positions in the *lastpos* of that node.

2. Building a set of DFA states: Construct *Dstates*, the set of states of *D* and *Dtran*, the transition table for *D*. The states in *Dstates* are sets of positions; initially, each state is 'unmarked', and a state becomes 'marked' just before its transitions are considered. The start state of *D* is *firstpos*(root), and the accepting states are those containing the position associated with the endmarker #. The algorithm is given below:

Initialise *Dstates* to contain only the unmarked state *firstpos*(n0), where n0 is the root of syntax tree *T* for (r)#;

```
While(there is an unmarked state S in Dstates)
{
    Mark S;
    For(each input symbol a)
    {
```

```
        Let U be the union of followpos(p) for all p in S that correspond to a;
              If(U is not in Dstates)
                    Add U as unmarked state to Dstates;
              Dtran[S,a]=U;
        }
}
```

Example 2.19 Convert the regular expression (a|b)*abb to DFA

Step 1: Syntax tree construction for the given regular expression.

The syntax tree for the given regular expression is shown in Fig. 2.19. The tree after adding position numbers is shown in Fig. 2.20. All the leaf nodes are given unique integer numbers. Also, the end marker is added at the end of the regular expression.

The position numbers of alphabets in the expression are:

Expression:	(a	|	b)	*	a	b	b	#
Position Numbers:	1		2		3	4	5	6

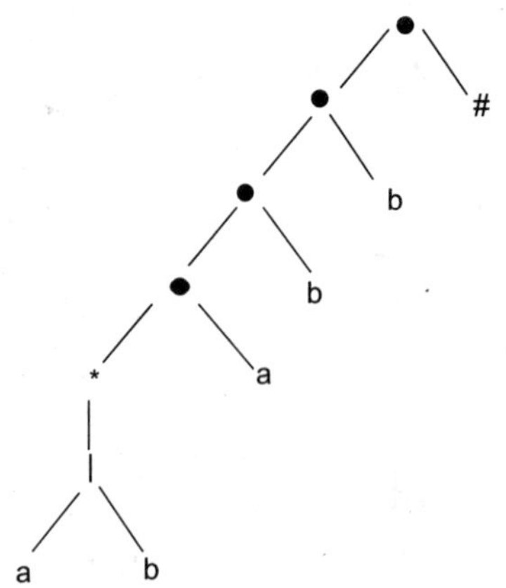

Figure 2.19 Syntax tree for RE, (a|b)*abb#

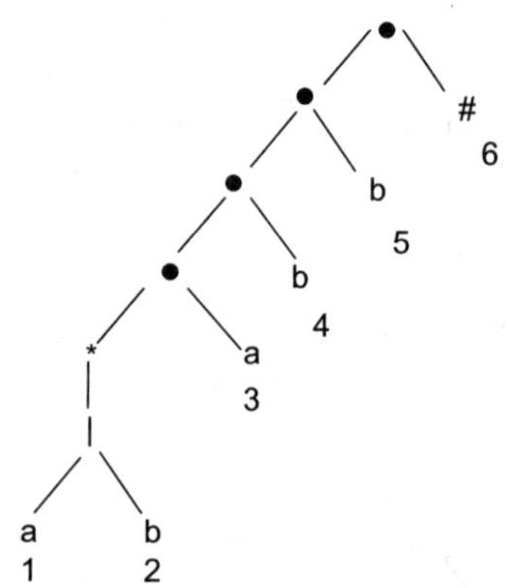

Figure 2.20 Syntax tree for RE, (a|b)*abb# with position numbers

Step 2: Function computation: nullable, firstpos and lastpos.

- *nullable* is true only for the star-node (*) as there is no ε node in the syntax tree.
- **Sample *firstpos* computation**: As per Table 2.9, the *firstpos* of leaf node having position i is {i}. The same symbol may have more than one position. The *firstpos* of all leaf nodes given from bottom to top, left to right will be

  firstpos(a) = {1}, *firstpos*(b)={2}, *firstpos*(a)={3}, *firstpos*(b)={4}, *firstpos*(b)={5} and *firstpos*(#)={6}.

  firstpos for union node (|) is *firstpos* (c1) ∪ *firstpos* (c2), where c1 and c2 are the left and right children of the node |.

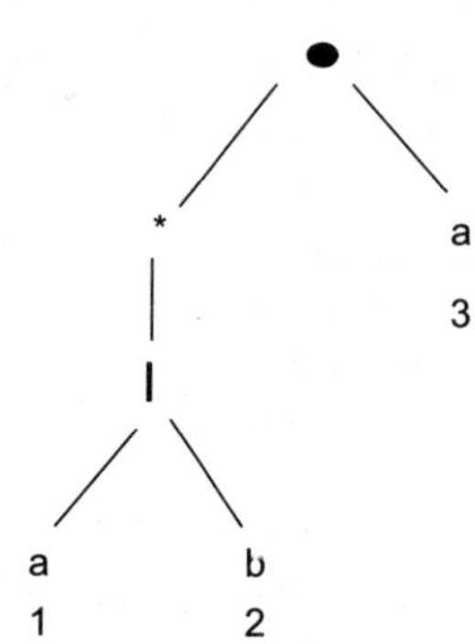

Hence, for our example, *firstpos*(|)= {1} ∪ {2} = {1,2}

firstpos for star-node (*) is *firstpos* (c1) , where c1 is the left child of the node *

For our example, *firstpos*(*)=*firstpos* (c1) = {1,2}

firstpos for cat-node (0) is *firstpos* (c1) ∪ *firstpos* (c2) if (*nullable* (c1)) *else firstpos* (c1)

For the cat-node as shown on the previous page, the *firstpos* will be
firstpos(0) = *firstpos* (c1) ∪ *firstpos* (c2)   (since c1 is * it is nullable=true)
      = {1,2} ∪ {3} = {1,2,3}

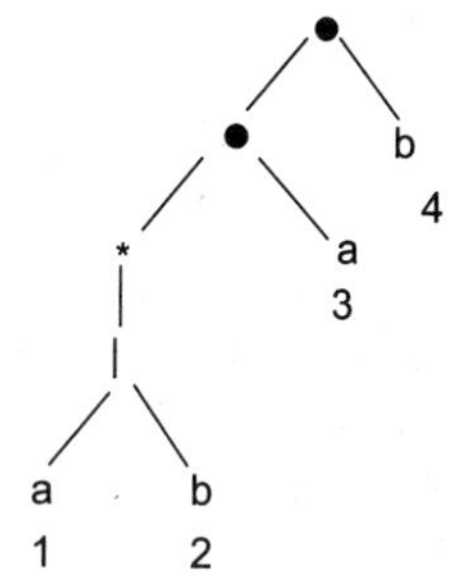

For the cat-node as below, the *firstpos* will be
firstpos(0) = *firstpos (c1)*   (since c1 has nullable=false)
      = {1,2,3}
The *firstpos* for all the nodes of the syntax tree are shown in Fig. 2.21.

Sample lastpos computation: As per Table 2.9, the *lastpos* of the leaf node having position i is {i}. The same symbol may have more than one position. The lastpos of all leaf nodes given from bottom to top, left to right will be

lastpos (a) = {1}, *lastpos*(b)={2}, *lastpos*(a)={3}, *lastpos*(b)={4}, *lastpos*(b)={5} and *lastpos*(#)={6}.

lastpos for union node (|) is *lastpos*(c1) ∪ *lastpos*(c2), where c1 and c2 are the left and right children of the node |.
Hence, for our example, *lastpos*(|)= {1} ∪ {2} = {1,2}

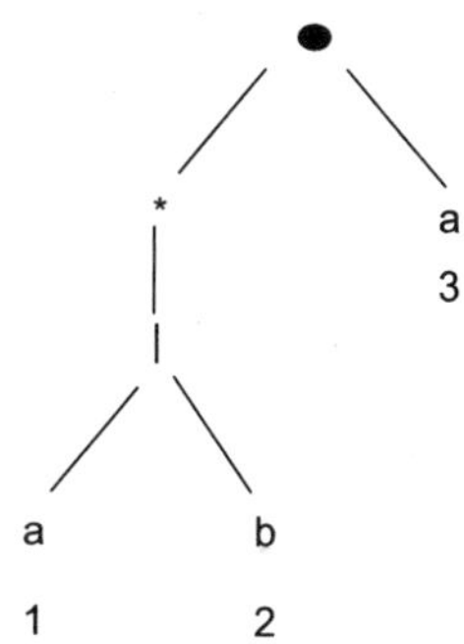

lastpos for star-node (*) is *lastpos* (c1), where c1 is the left child of the node *
For our example, *lastpos*(*)=*lastpos*(c1) = {1,2}

lastpos for cat-node (0) is *lastpos* (c1) ∪ *lastpos* (c2) if (nullable (c2)) else *lastpos* (c2), where c1 is the left child of the node 0 and c2 is the right child
For the cat-node as shown on the right, the *lastpos* will be
lastpos(0) = lastpos(c2)   (since c2 has nullable=false)
      = {3}

The *lastpos* for all the nodes of the syntax tree are shown in Fig. 2.21.

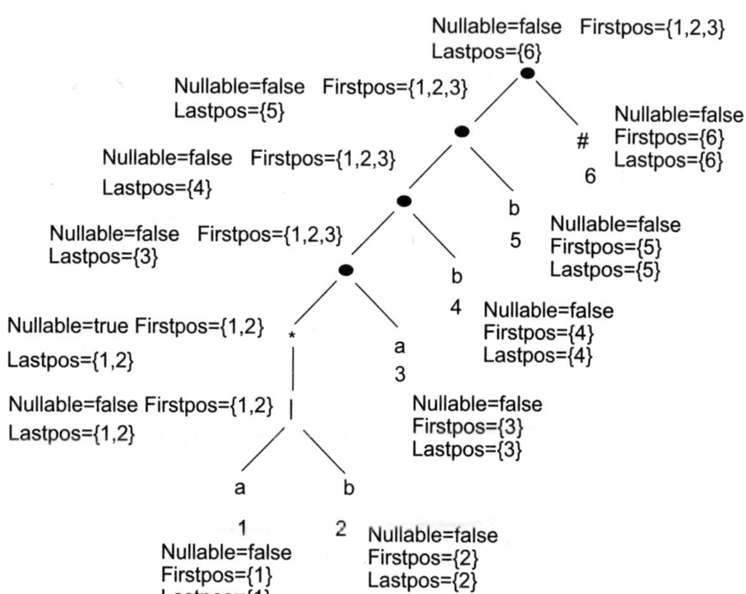

Figure 2.21 Nullable, firstpos and lastpos for all nodes of the syntax tree

Step 3: Computing followpos.

Applying Rule 1, for cat-node, for each position i in *lastpos* of its left child, the *firstpos* of its right child will be in *followpos*(i).

Hence

followpos(1)= {3}
followpos(2)= {3}
followpos(3)= {4}
followpos(4)= {5}
followpos(5)= {6}

Applying Rule 2, for star node, the *firstpos* of that node is in the *followpos* of all positions in the *lastpos* of that node.

Hence

followpos(1)= {1,2}
followpos(2)= {1,2}

Hence, the *followpos* of all nodes of the syntax tree is given in the table below. *followpos* shows the successor node for any node. The transition diagram for *followpos* information is shown in Fig. 2.22.

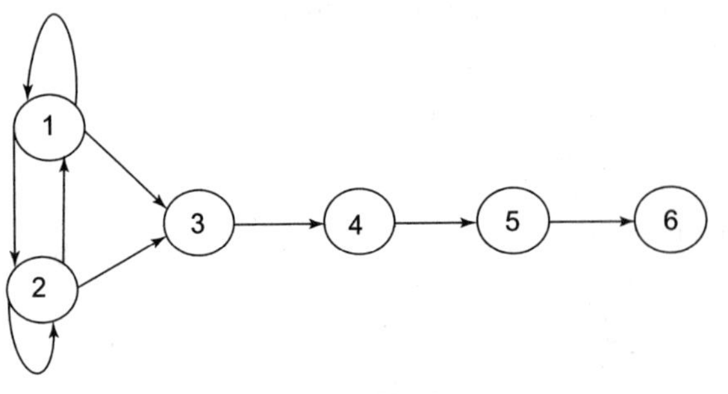

Figure 2.22 Transition diagram for followpos

Node n	Followpos(n)
1	{1,2,3}
2	{1,2,3}
3	{4}
4	{5}
5	{6}
6	Ø

Step 4: DFA construction.

Start with the *firstpos* of the root node and find the transition with each alphabet.

firstpos (n_0)= *firstpos* (root)= {1,2,3} = A. Now a is added in *Dstates.*

Finding transitions in *Dtran:* For *Dtran*[A,a] union the *followpos*(i) where i is the position number of symbol a in A. Position numbers of symbol a are 1 and 3. Both 1 and 3 are in A. Hence
Dtran[A,a]= *followpos*(1) ∪ *followpos*(3)= {1,2,3,4}=B

Now, find transition of symbol b from A.

Dtran[A,b]= *followpos*(2) = {1,2,3}=A

The next state is B

Dtran[B,a]= *followpos*(1) ∪ *followpos*(3)=B
Dtran[B,b]= *followpos*(2) ∪ *followpos*(4)={1,2,3,5}=C

The next state is C

Dtran[C,a]=*followpos*(1) ∪ *followpos*(3)= {1,2,3,4}=B
Dtran[C,b]=*followpos*(2) ∪ *followpos*(5)={1,2,3,6}=D

The next state is D

Dtran[D,a]=*followpos*(1) ∪ *followpos*(3)= {1,2,3,4}=B
Dtran[D,b]=*followpos*(2) = {1,2,3}=A

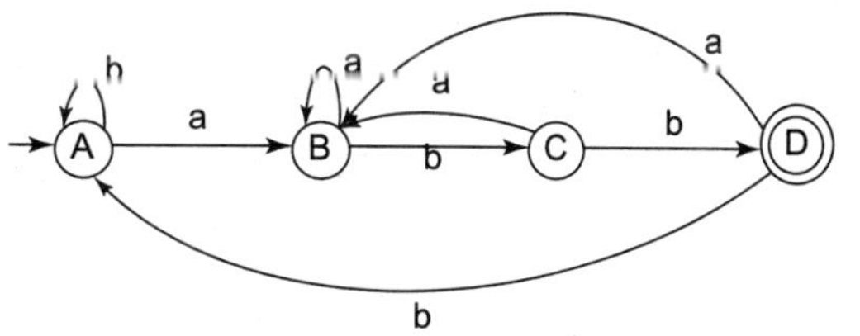

Figure 2.23 DFA for Example 2.19

The DFA according to the *Dtran* transitions is shown in Fig. 2.23.

Example 2.20 Design DFA corresponding to the given RE using the direct method

Regular expression: (a|b)* ab*#

Step 1: Syntax tree construction for the given regular expression.
The syntax tree for the given regular expression is shown in Fig. 2.24. The tree after adding position numbers is shown in Fig. 2.25. All the leaf nodes are given unique integer numbers.

The position numbers of alphabets in the expression are:

Expression:	(	a	|	b	)	*	a	b	*	#
Position Numbers:		1		2			3	4		5

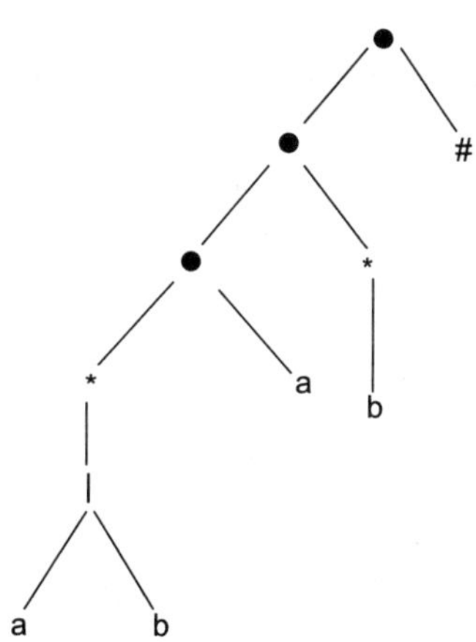

Figure 2.24 Syntax tree for RE, (alb)*ab*#

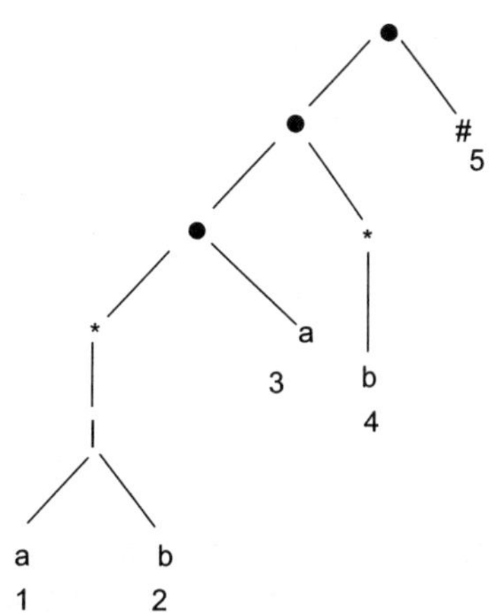

Figure 2.25 Syntax tree for RE, (alb)*ab* with position numbers

Step 2: Function computation: nullable, firstpos and lastpos.
The *nullable*, *firstpos* and *lastpos* values corresponding to all tree nodes are shown in Fig. 2.26.

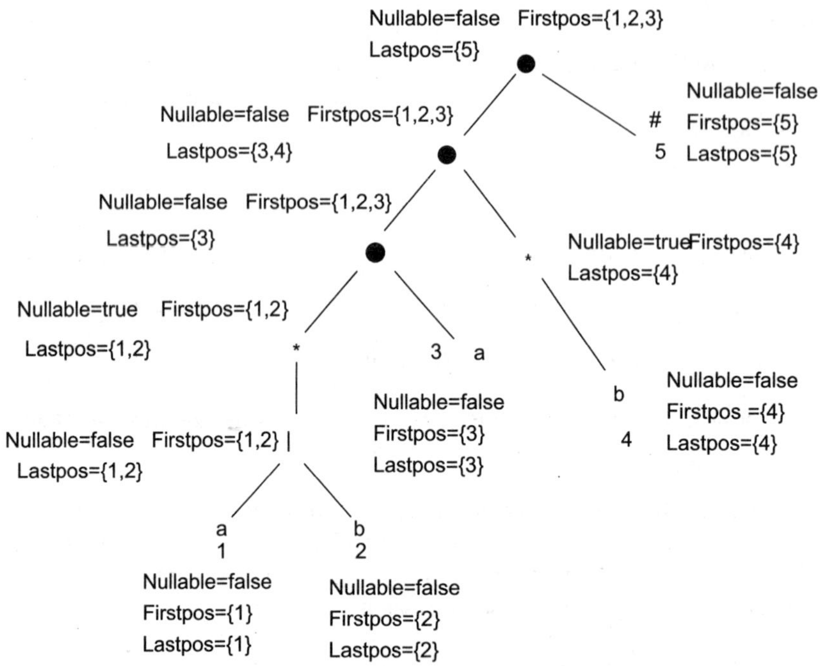

Figure 2.26 The nullable, firstpos and lastpos values for Example 2.20

Step 3: Computing followpos.

Applying Rule 1, for cat-node, for each position i in the *lastpos* of its left child, the *firstpos* of its right child will be in followpos(i). There are three cat-nodes. For the first cat-node (considering from bottom to top)

followpos(1)= {3}
followpos(2)= {3}
For the second cat-node
followpos(3)= {4}
For the third cat-node
followpos(3)= {5}
followpos(4)= {5}

Applying Rule 2, for the star-node, the *firstpos* of that node is in the *followpos* of all positions in the *lastpos* of that node. There are two star nodes. Considering from bottom to top and left to right.

For the first star-node
followpos(1)= {1,2}
followpos(2)= {1,2}
For the second star-node
followpos(4)= {4}

Node n	Followpos(n)
1	{1,2,3}
2	{1,2,3}
3	{4,5}
4	{4,5}
5	ø

Hence, the *followpos* of all the nodes of syntax tree are as shown in the table above.

Step 4: DFA construction.
Start with the *firstpos* of the root node and find the transition with each alphabet.

firstpos(n_0)= *firstpos*(root)= {1,2,3} = A

Finding transitions in *Dtran*
For *Dtran*[A,a] union *followpos*(i) where i is the position number of symbol a in A. Position numbers of symbol a are 1 and 3. Both 1 and 3 are in A. Hence
Dtran[A,a]= *followpos*(1) ∪ *followpos*(3)= {1,2,3,4,5}=B
Now, find the transition of symbol b from A.
Dtran[A,b]= *followpos*(2) = {1,2,3}=A

The next state is B
Dtran[B,a]= *followpos*(1) ∪ *followpos*(3)= {1,2,3,4,5}=B
Dtran[B,b]= *followpos*(2) ∪ *followpos*(4)={1,2,3,4,5}=B

The DFA according to the *Dtran* transitions is shown in Fig. 2.27.

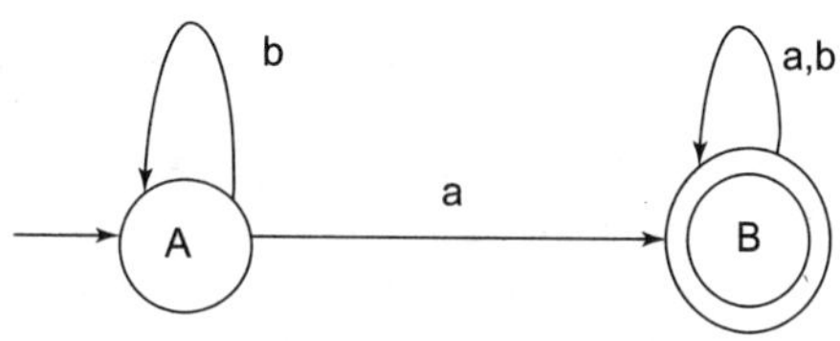

Figure 2.27 DFA for example 2.20

2.16 DFA Minimisation

The number of states of DFA can be minimised without changing the language being recognised. This DFA with minimum number of states is called the minimum-state DFA. If there is a DFA M, with a set of states S, and input symbol alphabet $\sum$, the starting state of the minimal DFA contains the original starting state and any group of accepting states. Assume that every state has a transition on every input symbol. If there is no transition from a state S to some input symbol a, a new 'dead state' d is introduced, with transitions from d to d on all inputs, and a transition is added from state S to d on input a.

The algorithm for DFA minimisation works by finding all groups of states that can be distinguished by some input string. Each group of states that cannot be distinguished is then merged into a single state. The algorithm maintains and refines a partition of the set of states. Each group of states within the partition consists of states that have not yet been distinguished from one another, and any pair of states chosen from different groups have been found distinguishable by some input. Next, distinguishable states and the algorithm for finding minimum DFA is described.

Distinguishable states

- String x distinguishes state s from state t, if exactly one of the states reached from s and t by following the path x is an accepting state.
- State s is distinguishable from state t, if there exists some string that distinguishes them.
- The empty string distinguishes an accepting state from a non-accepting state.

Algorithm for minimising the number of states of a DFA

1. Start with an initial partition Π with two groups: one group contains accepting states and other containing non-accepting states.
2. Apply the following procedure:
   for(each group G of Π)
   {
      Partition G into subgroups such that states s and t are in the same subgroup if for all input symbols a; state s and t have transitions on a, to states in the same group of Π
   }

3. Π new= Π and let Π final = Π; continue with Step 4. Otherwise, repeat Step 2 with Π new instead of Π.
4. Choose one state in each group of Π; for that group, the start state of D' is the representative of the group containing the start state of D. The accepting states of D' are the representatives of those groups that contain an accepting state of D, if:
   - s is the representative of G from Π
   - a transition from s on input a is t from group H
   - r is the representative of H; then in D' there is a transition from s to r on input a
5. If D' is a dead state, then remove d from D' and remove any states not reachable from the start state; any transitions to d from other states become undefined.

Example 2.21 DFA minimisation

Consider the DFA given in Fig. 2.28 for DFA minimisation. State 0 is the start state and state 4 is the final state, also referred to as the accepting state. The transition table corresponding to the DFA is shown in Table 2.10.

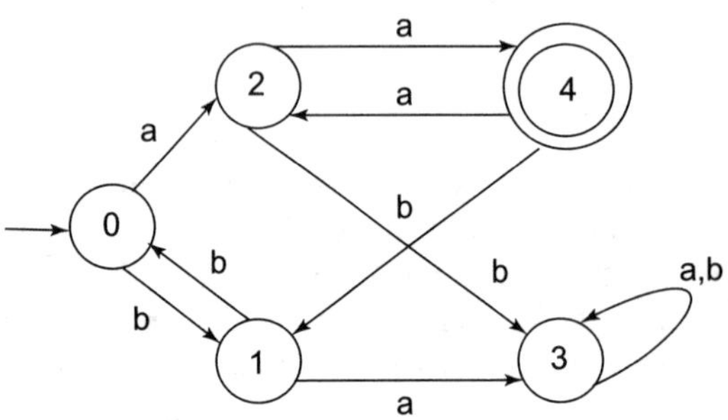

Figure 2.28 DFA for Example 2.21

Table 2.10 Transition table for DFA of Fig. 2.28

State	a	b
0	2	1
1	3	0
2	4	3
3	3	3
4	2	1

Let us create a partition having two groups: accepting state and non-accepting state.

G1={0,4} // Group contains accepting states
G2={1,2,3} // Group contains non-accepting states

Let us find the transition for group states for the input symbols. Group number of the state should be used instead of the state number in the transition table.

Considering G1, there is a transition from state 0 to state 2 on input symbol a. State 2 is in G2. So, in the transition table, (0,a)→G2. Also, there is a transition from state 0 to state 1 on input symbol b. State 1 is in G2. So, in the transition table (below, left) (0,b)→G2. Similarly, all the other entries are added as shown. As the transitions are the same for the states on each input symbol, mark G1 as done and add it to D'. Next, considering G2, the transitions will be as shown in the table below (right).

G1 states	a	b
0	G2	G2
4	G2	G2

G2 states	a	B
1	G2	G1
2	G1	G2
3	G2	G2

The transitions of all states are different for each input symbol. So, partition G2 into three groups containing {1}, {2} and {3}. Also, remove all the entries from D'; as G2 has now changed, there will be changes in G1 as well. Therefore, the new groups are

G1={0,4}
G21={1}
G22={2}
G23={3}

G1 states	a	B
0	G22	G21
4	G22	G21

Now, the only group with more than one element is G1. So, again process G1, as shown in the table above.

As states 0 and 4 have the same transitions, they will be in the same group. All the groups are processed. Hence, the minimum DFA will have states G1, G21, G22 and G23. The minimum DFA is shown in Fig. 2.29 and the transition table for minimum DFA is shown in Table 2.11.

Table 2.11 Minimum DFA for Example 2.21

State	a	b
G1	G22	G21
G21	G23	G1
G22	G1	G23
G23	G23	G23

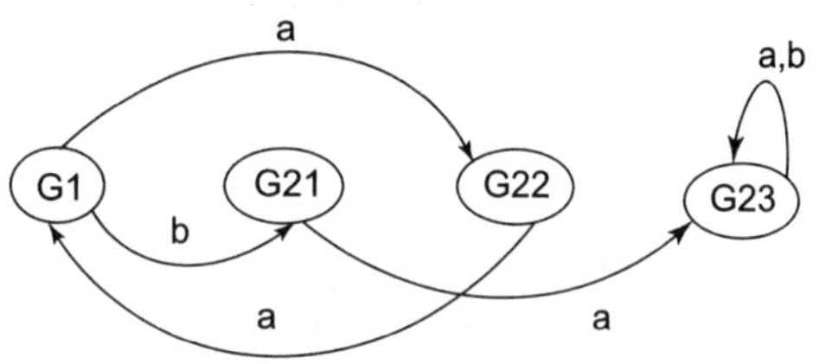

Figure 2.29 Minimum DFA for Example 2.21

Example 2.22 DFA minimisation: Find the states and transition table in minimum DFA
Consider the transition table given below (Table 2.12). * represents the final or accepting states and A is the start state.

Table 2.12 Transition table for Example 2.22

State	a	b
A	B	C
B	B	D
C	B	C
D	B	H
E	B	C
F	C	D
G	B	H
H*	B	D

Initially

G1= {H} // Accepting states
G2={A,B,C,D,E,F,G} // Non-accepting states

The transitions from G2 are as follows:

G2 states	a	B
A	G2	G2
B	G2	G2
C	G2	G2
D	G2	G1
E	G2	G2
F	G2	G2
G	G2	G1

A, B, C, E and F have the same transitions for input symbols. So, they can be in the same group. Also, D and G have the same transitions for input symbols. Hence, the new groups will be

G1={H}
G21={ A,B,C,E,F}
G22={D,G}

Now, consider transitions from G21. B and F have the same transitions for input symbols. So, they can be in the same group. Also, A, C and E have the same transitions for input symbols. Hence, the new groups will be

G21 states	a	b
A	G21	G21
B	G21	G22
C	G21	G21
E	G21	G21
F	G21	G22

G1={H}
G211={ B,F}
G212={A,C,E}
G22={D,G}

Now, consider transitions from G211.

As the transitions are not the same, partition the group into two. So, the new groups will be

G211 States	a	B
B	G211	G22
F	G212	G22

G1={H}
G2111={ B}
G2112={F}
G212={A,C,E}
G22={D,G}

Now, consider transitions from G212. As all the transitions are the same, A, C and E will remain in the same group. The groups will be

G212 states	a	B
A	G2111	G212
C	G2111	G212
E	G2111	G212

G1={H}
G2111={ B}
G2112={F}
G212={A,C,E}
G22={D,G}

Consider the transitions of G22.

As all the transitions are the same, D and G will remain in the same group. The final states of the DFA will be

G22 states	a	B
D	G2111	G1
G	G2111	G1

G1={H}
G2111={ B}
G2112={F}
G212={A,C,E}
G22={D,G}

The transition table for minimum DFA is shown below (Table 2.13).

Table 2.13 Transition table for minimum DFA of Example 2.22

State	a	b
G1	G2111	G22
G2111	G2111	G22
G2112	G212	G22
G212	G2111	G212
G22	G2111	G1

SUMMARY

- The lexical analyser is also called the scanner.
- The lexical analyser accepts the source program in high-level language and converts it into a stream of tokens.
- Input buffering is used to speed up input access.
- In the two-buffer scheme, two buffers hold the input. The buffer is divided into two N-character halves. Two pointers are used: the forward pointer (FP) and a lexeme_begin pointer (LP).
- For a set of strings in the input, the same token is produced as output. This set of strings is described by a rule called a pattern associated with the token.
- A lexeme is a sequence of characters in the source program that is matched by the pattern for a token.
- A string of characters that logically belongs together is called a token. Keywords, identifiers, constants, string literals, operators and symbols are examples of tokens.
- The lexical analyser needs to identify a finite set of valid tokens for a programming language.
- Regular expressions have the ability to express finite languages by defining a pattern for finite strings of symbols.
- All tokens are defined using regular expressions.
- Finite automaton is used to recognise regular expressions that specify tokens.
- There are two types of finite automata: deterministic finite automata (DFA) and non- deterministic finite automata (NFA).
- Regular expressions need to be converted to DFA. Method 1 (Thompson's subset construction): RE to NFA, then NFA to DFA. Method 2: Direct conversion from RE to DFA.

Exercises

Review Questions

Fill in the blanks with appropriate answers:

1. Concept of FSA is used in ________ phase of the compiler.
2. '/' in regular expression is an ________.
3. Regular expression that defines a set of all strings containing the substring 00 is ________.
4. ________ is a regular expression to search all the strings that contain the substring "cop".
5. ________ is considered as a sequence of characters in a token.
6. If NFA has n states, then after conversion from NFA to DFA, DFA can have a maximum of ________ number of states.
7. Finite automata recognise ________ language.
8. ________ function is used to find a set of positions at node ti that corresponds to the first symbol of the sub-expression rooted at n, during conversion of RE to DFA.
9. To speed up input access by the lexical analyser, the ________ method is used.
10. In int num = 2, int is a ________ for token ________, substring num is a ________ for token ________.

Answers: 1. Lexical analysis 2. Escape character 3. (0+1)*0(0+1)*0(0+1)* 4. .*cop.* 5. Lexeme 6. 2n 7. Regular 8. Firstpos 9. Input buffering 10. Lexeme, keyword, lexeme, identifier

State whether true or false:

1. In some programming languages, an identifier is permitted to be a letter followed by any number of letters or digits. If L denotes the set of letters and D denotes digits, then the regular expression $L\,(L \cup D)^*$ denotes an identifier.
2. The input string "ababbbbab" matches the pattern specified by the regular expression (ab + abb)* bbab.
3. The transitional function of a DFA is $Q\ X\ \Sigma \rightarrow Q$.
4. The transitional function of an NFA is $Q\ X\ \Sigma \rightarrow 2Q$.
5. Finite state machine cannot remember state transitions.
6. A regular language is produced by the union of two regular languages.
7. Every NDFA can be converted to a DFA.
8. ε-transitions do not add any extra capacity for recognising the formals.
9. DFAs, NFAs and ε-NFA s are equivalent.
10. In Thompson's subset construction method, RE is converted to DFA directly.

Answers: 1. True 2. False 3. True 4. True 5. True 6. True 7. False 8. True 9. True 10. False

Practice Questions

1. Explain the working of input buffering using the following methods: buffer pair and sentinels for the input statement, for(i=0;i<=10;i++). Assume that the value of n is 10 for buffer-1 and buffer-2.
2. Draw the transition diagram to recognise some of the given keywords of JAVA: case, catch, char, class, const, continue, final, finally, float, for, this, throw, throws, transient. Use Method 1, described in Section 2.10.

3. Draw the state transition diagram to accept string literals.
4. Draw the state transition diagram to accept symbols and operators.
5. Identifiers in Java follow the rule, "Start with a letter, underscore or $ sign, followed by zero or more letters, digits, underscore or $ sign". Write the regular expression to express the identifiers of Java. Also draw the transition diagram for the same.
6. Write a regular expression for the following:
   a. Non-negative decimal floating point numbers less than 10
   b. Negative decimal floating point numbers that can have a maximum of two digits after the decimal point
   c. Integer numbers. Comma (,) is allowed as a separator between groups of numbers to make integers easier to read. Numbers cannot begin or end with a comma.
   Also design a transition diagram for the same.
7. Write a regular expression for URLs. Special characters are allowed in the URL, but should not be mixed with genuine punctuation marks at the end of the URL in the text. For example, '.' or '?' or ')' or ';', etc.
8. Write a regular expression for accepting date and also draw the transition diagram. Consider the format of date as dd/mm/yy. Days should not extend beyond 31 and only 12 months must be allowed.
9. Find the total number of lexemes in the given C statement:
   printf("hello Word \n")   // print line
10. Draw the NFA for the transition table of Example 2.16. Also show the compute tree for input 0011.
11. Convert the regular expression to DFA using Thompson's subset construction for the following regular expressions:
    a. ab(a|b)b   b. a*(a|b)b   c. ab*(a|b)*
12. Convert the regular expressions given in Q10 to DFA using the direct method.
13. Find the minimum DFA for the DFA of Examples 2.19 and 2.20.
14. Explain how regular expression and deterministic finite automata are useful for lexical analysis.

Programming Questions

1. Implement the transition diagram of Example 2.13 in C language.
2. Write a lexical analyser by hand using the C language to recognise the following:
   a. All keywords in JAVA   b. Symbols and operators in JAVA
3. Write a lexical analyser that can accept identifiers of Java. Use the transition diagram of Q5 in the Practice Questions.

3 Syntax Analysis

Objectives

- To introduce the syntax analysis phase of the compiler
- To introduce the different parsing techniques
- To discuss the need for grammar in syntax analysis
- To discuss predictive and non-predictive top-down parsing
- To describe various bottom-up parsers
- To discuss how to handle ambiguous grammars

3.1 Introduction to Syntax Analysis

High-level programming languages are used to communicate an algorithm to the computer. Every programming language defines a set of rules, called the syntax of the language, that helps in developing well-formed programs. **Syntax** refers to the ways symbols may be combined to create well-formed sentences that are allowed in that language. It provides a structural description of the various expressions that make up legal strings in the language. Syntax deals with the form and structure of symbols in a language without giving any consideration to their meaning. The syntax of a programming language can be specified using grammars. The types of grammars and which type must be used for a given specification of language are discussed in Section 3.2.

The syntax analyser is also called the **parser**. The schematic of a syntax analyser is shown in Fig. 3.1. The lexical analyser provides tokenised input to the parser. The parser checks whether the tokens have been grouped according to the syntax of the programming language and then generates a tree representation, called the parse tree, as output. If the tokens are not grouped according to the language specification, the error handler is invoked. The parser also adds information about the various tokens in the symbol table.

The syntax analysis phase of compilation is a two-step process. In the first step, all valid constructs of a programming language are specified. Syntax validation is performed using context-free grammar

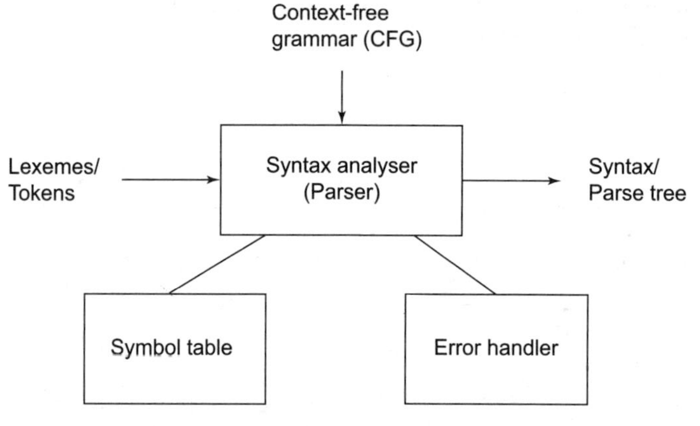

Figure 3.1 Syntax analyser (parser)

(CFG). In the second step, a suitable recogniser is used to determine whether a string of tokens generated by the analyser is a valid construct or not.

Types of parsers: Parsers can be broadly divided into two types: top-down and bottom-up. Figure 3.2 shows the types of parsers. Top-down parsers are further classified into predictive and non-predictive parsers. These can be recursive descent or non-recursive descent. The backtracking of non-predictive parsers is discussed in Section 3.6.1.

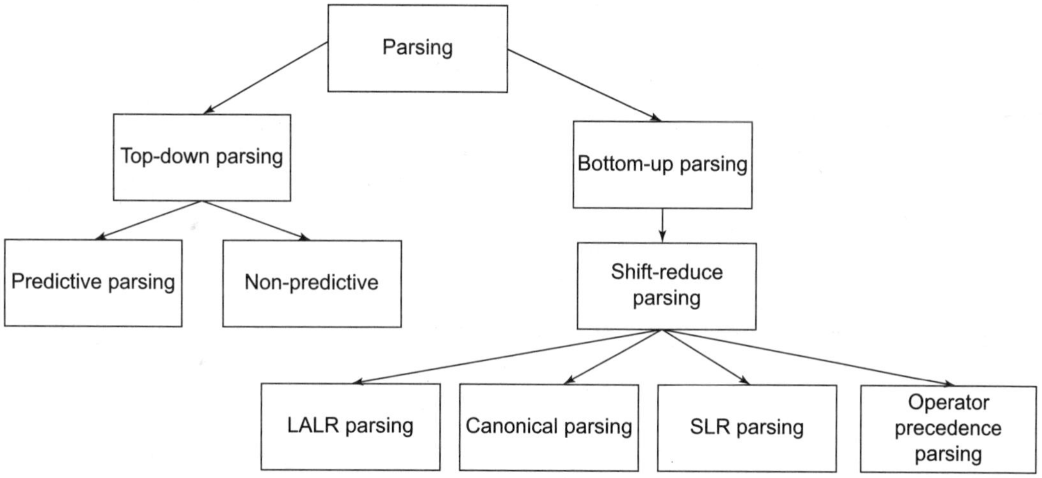

Figure 3.2 Types of parsers

Bottom-up parsers are shift-reduce parsers. The types of bottom-up parsers discussed are operator precedence, simple LR (SLR), complex LR (CLR) and LALR parsers (in LR, L stands for 'left to right scanning', while R stands for 'rightmost derivation'). SLR, CLR and LALR are types of bottom-up parsers that work only for sub-classes of CFG grammars, like LR. These sub-classes are expressive enough to describe most of the syntactic constructs in programming languages.

3.2 Types of Grammars

Grammar defines the syntactical rules of a language. According to Chomosky, the four types of grammer are type 0, type 1, type 2 and type 3. Table 3.1 shows the different types of grammars, and Fig. 3.3 shows the Chomosky hierarchy of grammars.

Table 3.1 Types of grammars, with details

Grammar type	Grammar accepted	Language accepted	Rules for grammar production	Example grammar	Automaton
0	Unrestricted grammar	Recursively enumerable language	Productions have no restrictions on the contents of the left and right sides.	S → ACaB Bc → acB CB → DD aD → Db	Turing machine

(Cont'd)

Table 3.1 (Continued)

Grammar type	Grammar accepted	Language accepted	Rules for grammar production	Example grammar	Automaton
1	Context-sensitive grammar	Context-sensitive language	Grammars can have one or more non-terminals on the left-hand side (LHS) while the right-hand side (RHS) can contain any number of terminals and non-terminals.	AB → AbBc A → bcA B → b	Linear bounded automata
2	Context-free grammar (CFG)	Context-free language	Grammars must have a single non-terminal on the LHS while the RHS can contain any number of terminals and non-terminals.	S → a S → ABb	Non-deterministic pushdown automata
3	Regular grammar	Regular language	Grammars must have a single non-terminal on the LHS while the RHS must consist of a single terminal or a single terminal followed by a single non-terminal.	S → a S → aA	Finite state automata

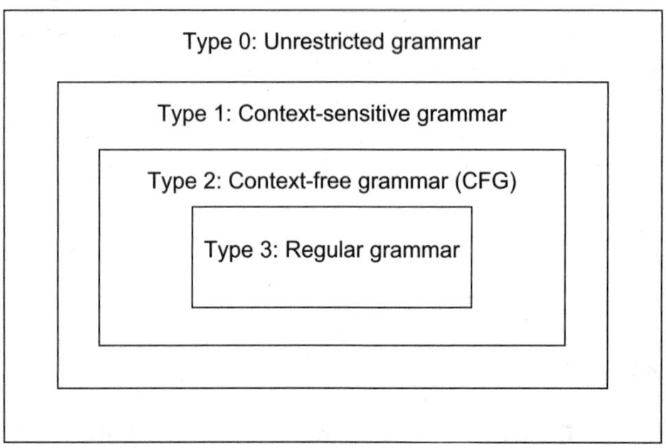

Figure 3.3 Chomosky hierarchy of grammars

3.3 Context-free Grammar

Context-free grammar specifies a context-free language that consists of terminals, non-terminals, start symbols and production rules.

- **Non-terminal symbols (V):** Non-terminals are syntactic variables that denote sets of strings. For notation purposes, capital letters are used to denote non-terminals.

- **Terminal symbols (T):** Terminals are the basic symbols or tokens from which strings can be formed. For notation purposes, lowercase letters are used to represent terminal symbols.
- **Productions (P):** The productions of a grammar specify the manner in which the terminals and non-terminals can be combined to form strings. Each production consists of a non-terminal on the LHS followed by an arrow, and a sequence of terminals and/or non-terminals on the RHS.
- **Start symbol (S):** The start symbol is the state from which the production begins.

Valid strings of grammar are derived from the start symbol by repeatedly replacing a non-terminal with the right side of a production rule. CFG is denoted as a set {V, T, P, S}, where V is the non-terminal or variable; T is the terminal; P is the set of productions; and S is the start symbol. For example, G = ({S}, {a, b}, P, S), where P contains production rules {S → aSa, S→ bSb, S → ε}.

Uses of CFG: The lexical analyser can be implemented using regular expressions, but regular expressions are not powerful enough to handle parsing. Many programming language constructs are inherently recursive. Such structures can be easily defined using CFG. For example
if E then S1 else S2
where S1 and S2 are statements and E is an expression. This form of conditional statement cannot be specified using the notation of regular expressions. On the other hand, using the syntactic variable *stmt* to denote the class of statements and *expr* to denote the class of expressions, we can denote the conditional statement using grammar production as
stmt → if *expr* then *stmt* else *stmt*

Sub-classes of CFG

- **LL(*k*) and LL(*) grammars:** Allow parsing by direct construction of a leftmost derivation and describe fewer languages.
- **Simple LR (SLR) and Look-Ahead LR grammars (LALR):** SLR and LALR are parsed using pushdown automata (PDA). LR parsing extends LL parsing to support a larger range of grammars.
- **Deterministic CFGs (LR(*k*)):** LR grammars allow parsing with deterministic PDA and describe deterministic context-free languages.
- **GLR parsing:** This was developed in the 1980s, but many new languages still use the LL, LALR or LR parser.

3.4 Derivation

String derivation is the process of checking the validity of a string against the grammar of the language. It can be carried out in two ways: leftmost derivation and rightmost derivation.

In **leftmost derivation**, at each step, the leftmost non-termination is considered for expansion by substituting its corresponding production in the derivation process. In **rightmost derivation**, the rightmost non-terminal is considered for expansion by substituting its corresponding production at every stage in the derivation process. Rightmost derivations are also called **canonical derivations**.

For example, consider the grammar for arithmetic expressions **(Grammar 3.1)**

E → E + E
E → E * E
E → E / E
E → E – E

E → (E)
E → id

Any string is a valid sentence of grammar if it can be derived using the production rules of the grammar. Let us consider a string (id + id), which can be derived as follows:

E → (E) → (E + E) → (id + E) → (id + id)

As the string can be derived beginning from the start state, it is a valid construct for the given grammar. The symbol → means 'derives in one step'. Often, we wish to say, 'derives in zero or more steps'. For this purpose, we use the symbol $\xrightarrow{*}$ (having * over the arrow →). Likewise, we use $\xrightarrow{+}$ to mean 'derives in one or more steps'.

Thus, for our example, we can write E $\xrightarrow{*}$ (id + id), indicating that (id + id) can be derived using E. The strings E, (E), (E + E), (id + E) and (id + id) are all sentential forms of the grammar.

As in the example, we have expanded the leftmost non-terminal in each step – it is a leftmost derivation. The rightmost derivation for the same example will be

E → (E) → (E + E) → (E + id) →(id + id)

The graphical representation of derivation is called the **parse tree**. The leaves of the parse tree are terminals and read from left to right; they constitute a sentential form, called the **frontier of the tree**. The parse tree for (id + id) is shown in Fig. 3.4. The parse trees for both leftmost derivation and rightmost derivation are the same. The order of computation of the tree, however, is different. The computation of the derivation tree for leftmost derivation is shown in Fig. 3.5 while that for rightmost derivation is shown in Fig. 3.6.

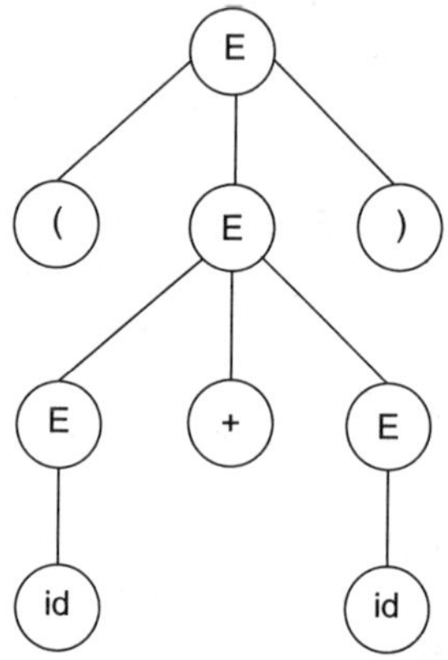

Figure 3.4 Parse tree for (id + id)

3.5 Ambiguous Grammar

A grammar that produces more than one parse tree for the same string is called an ambiguous grammar. In other words, an ambiguous grammar is one that produces more than one leftmost or more than one rightmost derivation for the same string. It is desirable in certain types of parsers that the grammar be unambiguous; otherwise, selection of an alternative to expand the non-terminal is not possible.

Let G = (V, T, P, S) be a CFG. We say that G is ambiguous if there is a string in T^* that has more than one parse tree. If every string in L (G) has at most one parse tree, G is said to be unambiguous.

Let us consider the grammar **(Grammar 3.2)**

E → E + E
E → E – E
E → (E)
E → id

The string id + id – id can be derived as follows using leftmost derivation:

E → E + E → id + E → id + E – E → id + id – E → id + id – id *Sequence 1* OR
E → E – E → E + E – E → id + E – E → id + id – E → id + id – id *Sequence 2*

As there exist two different derivation sequences for the same string, we obtain two different parse trees, as shown in Fig. 3.7 (a) and (b). The parse tree in Fig. 3.7 (a) assumes precedence of the + operator, while the parse tree in Fig. 3.7 (b) does not assume this precedence.

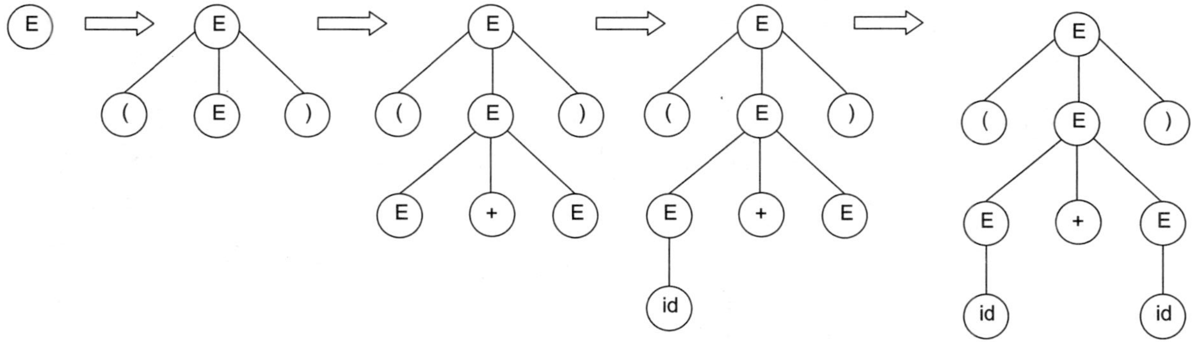

Figure 3.5 Leftmost derivation for (id + id)

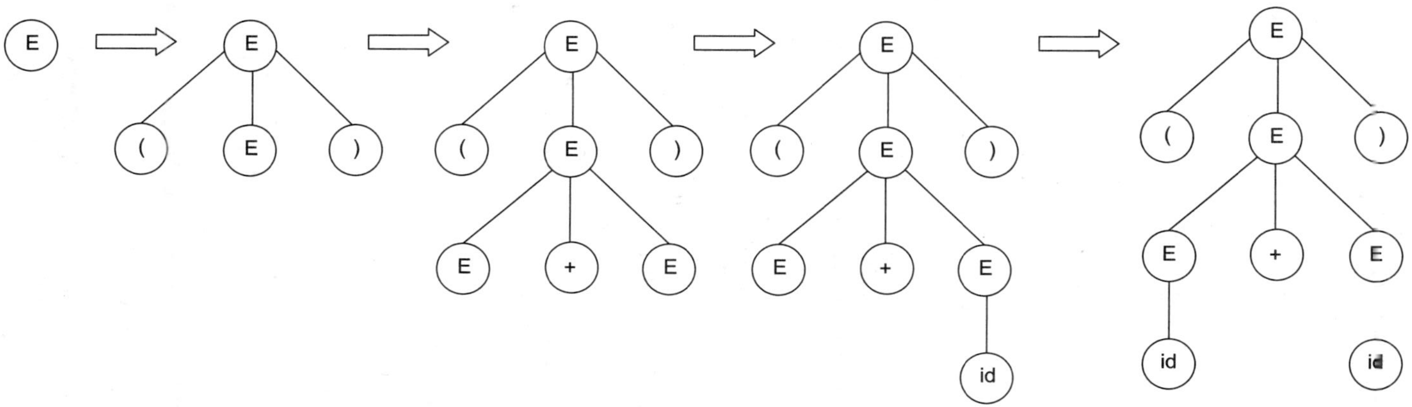

Figure 3.6 Rightmost derivation for (id + id)

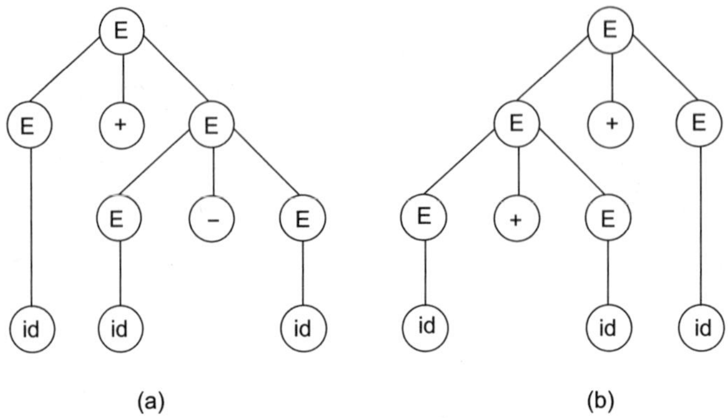

Figure 3.7 LMD parse tree for id + id – id

Removing ambiguity: Ambiguity in a CFG can usually be eliminated by rewriting the grammar. There is no fixed algorithm to remove ambiguity. The CFG must be examined to eliminate the ambiguity. In *Grammar 3.2*, there is no precedence of the + and – operators. Also, there is no grouping of the sequences of operators, for example, E + E + E can be E + (E + E) or (E + E) + E.

For *Grammar 3.2*, precedence rules must be applied to the operators in the grammar and associations must be specified to group the expression into right-associative or left-associative form. By introducing more variables, each representing expressions of the same 'binding strength', ambiguity can be resolved.

- **Factor:** A factor is an expression that cannot be broken apart by adjacent operators (+ or –). Factors, in our example, are identifiers and a parenthesized expression.
- **Term:** A term is an expression that cannot be broken by +. For example, a + a – b is the same as a + (a – b), and a – b + a is the same as (a – b) + a.
- **Expression:** The rest are expressions that can be broken apart with – or +.

Let us consider F for factors, T for terms and E for expressions. The grammar after rewriting will become

$E \rightarrow T \mid E + T$ **(Grammar 3.3)**

$T \rightarrow F \mid T - F$

$F \rightarrow id \mid (E)$

Grammar 3.3 is an unambiguous grammar. The only parse tree corresponding to the input string id + id – id is shown in Fig. 3.8.

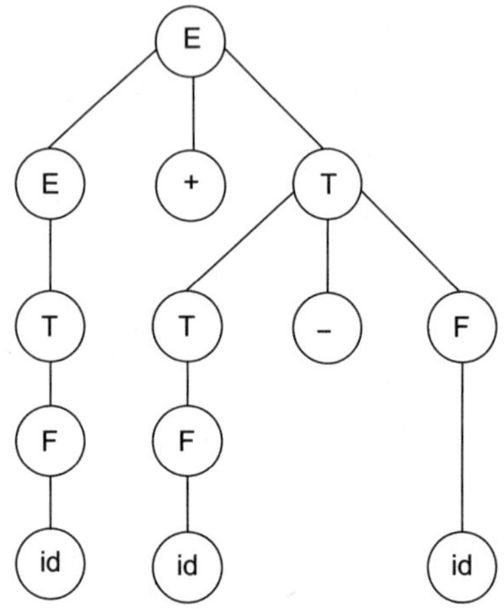

Figure 3.8 Parse tree corresponding to *Grammar 3.3*

3.6 Top-down Parsing

Top-down parsing attempts to find the leftmost derivation of the input string. It refers to the construction of the parse tree for an input string, with the start symbol as the root node and then expanding the non-terminals according to the grammar. Top-down parsing can be further classified as non-predictive and predictive.

3.6.1 Non-predictive Parsing

This form of top down parsing may involve backtracking and making repeated scans of the input. However, backtracking parsers are not used frequently. In natural language processing, backtracking is not very efficient.

During such parsing, the parser may encounter a situation where a non-terminal A is to be expanded, and there are multiple A productions, such as

$A \rightarrow X_1 \mid X_2 \mid X_3 \ldots\ldots\ldots\ldots\ldots\ldots\ldots \mid X_n$.

In such situations, the non-predictive parser selects any production rule of A, at random, for expansion of the non-terminal A. If the selected production rule leads to the input string, then the string is declared as a valid string of the grammar; otherwise, the parser backtracks to the non-terminal A and tries another production rule of non-terminal A. This is repeated until successful completion of the process or till it reports failure after trying all alternative productions. The selection of the production rule also affects the language being accepted by the grammar.

Example 3.1 **Consider the grammar and perform non-predictive parsing**

S → aAb **(Grammar 3.4)**

A → bc | d | e

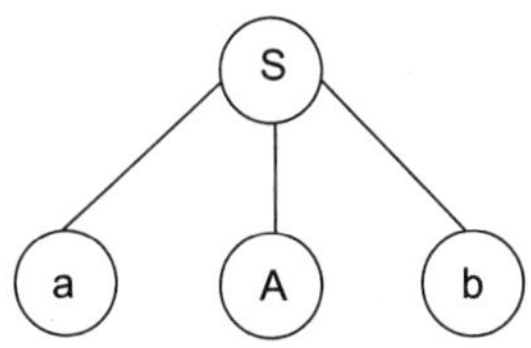

Consider the input string as "adb". Top-down parsing starts with S as the root node. As there is only one S production, S is expanded using S → aAb.

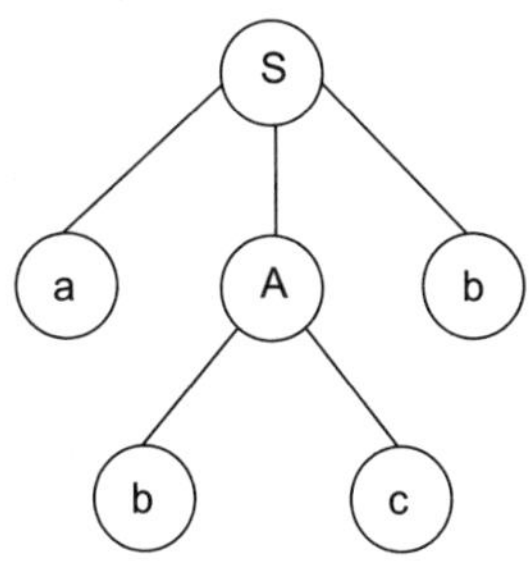

The input string is "adb". The first character in the input string is 'a' and it matches the leftmost 'a' in the parse tree. We proceed to the next input symbol and also proceed in the parse tree. Three alternative productions are available for expansion of the non-terminal A, A→bc | d | e. The non-predictive parser can expand using any of these three production rules. Let us assume that production rule A → bc is selected. The parse tree will be as shown on the right.

The next input symbol in the input string is 'd' (Fig. 3.9 (c)). However, the next symbol in the parse tree is 'b'. Hence, this is the point of failure and we must backtrack to the non-terminal A, as shown in Fig. 3.9 (a). After backtracking to A, another alternative production rule must be used for expansion, as shown in Fig. 3.9 (b).

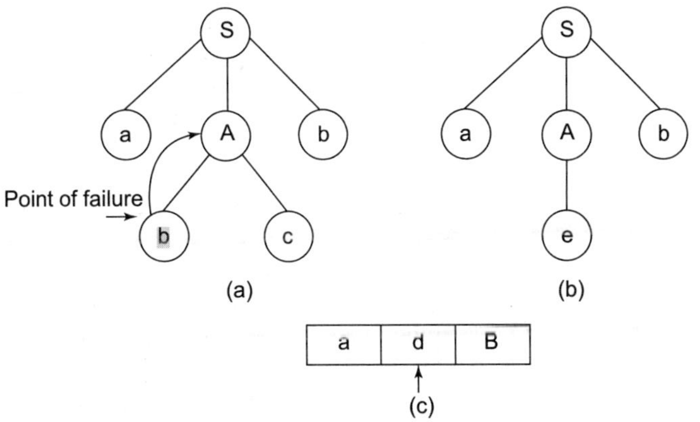

Figure 3.9 Non-predictive parsing for *Grammar 3.4*

Again, the input string contains 'd' and the next symbol in the parse tree is 'e'. Hence, the parser will backtrack to A and try another alternative (Fig. 3.10).

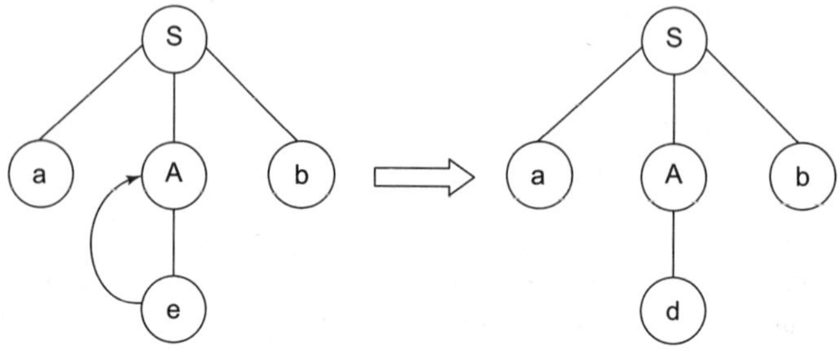

Figure 3.10 Non-predictive parsing for *Grammar 3.4*

Now, the parser accepts "adb" as a valid string of the grammar. Had the parser used A → d as the production rule for expansion in the earlier steps, the backtracking could have been avoided.

Example 3.2 Non-predictive parsing procedure for the given grammar
S → aAd
A → b | c

Initially the input pointer points to the first symbol 'a' and the tree contains only S (start symbol). For simplicity, the process of non-predictive parsing is shown in Table 3.2.

Table 3.2 Non-predictive parsing for *Grammar 3.5*

Input	LMD/Parse tree construction in stack	Action
a c d (↑ a)	S	S → aAd
a c d (↑ a)	aAd	Input 'a' matches 'a' in the LMD. Hence, proceed by advancing the input pointer and moving further in the parse tree.
a c d (↑ c)	Ad	A → b | c. Try the first production, A → b.
a c d (↑ c)	bd	The next input is 'c'. However, in the tree, we have 'b'. Hence, backtrack to A.
a c d (↑ c)	Ad	Backtrack to A and try another alternative, A → c.
a c d (↑ c)	cd	'c' matches. Advance the input pointer and proceed in the tree.
a b d (↑ d)	d	'd' matches, and hence, the string is valid.

3.6.2 Predictive Top-down Parsing

Non-predictive parsers may encounter the problem of backtracking. This problem can be solved if it can function as a deterministic recogniser, capable of predicting which alternatives must be used for expansion of the non-terminals.

Let us consider a non-terminal A, which has to be expanded next and there are multiple productions for A.

$A \rightarrow X_1 | X_2 | X_3 \ldots\ldots\ldots X_n$

The predictive parser determines which production of A must be expanded by looking at the next input symbol of the string. It finds out which X_i derives to a string with the terminal symbol that appears next in the string to be validated.

To accomplish this task, the predictive parser uses a look-ahead pointer, which points to the next input symbol. Look-ahead is the maximum number of tokens that a parser can use to decide the production rule that must be applied. To make the parser backtracking-free, the predictive parser adds constraints on the grammar and accepts only a class of grammar known as LL(*k*) grammar.

LL(*k*) grammars are CFGs for which there exists some positive integer *k* that allows a recursive descent parser to decide which production to use for the expansion of the non-terminal, by examining the next *k* tokens of input. LL(*k*) grammars exclude ambiguous and left-recursive grammars. Any CFG can be transformed into an equivalent grammar that has no left recursion, but removal of left recursion does not always yield an LL(*k*) grammar.

Here, the discussion is restricted to parsers with only one-symbol look-ahead, and thus, to LL(1) and LR(1) grammars. The main reason for the restriction is the considerable increase in cost (both time and space) that must be invested to obtain more look-ahead symbols in the parser generator. When dealing with LR grammars, not even the restriction to the LR(1) case is sufficient to obtain practical tables. Thus, we use an LR(1) parse algorithm, but control it with tables obtained through a modification of the LR(0) analyser.

Recursive predictive parsers: Recursive procedures are called for non-terminal symbols. These procedures follow a predictive approach. Transition diagrams can be used to represent recursive predictive parsers.

Transition diagrams can describe predictive parsers. In a predictive parser, one diagram corresponds to every non-terminal. Labels on edges can be terminals or non-terminals. A transition using a terminal means that it should take that particular transition if that token is the next input symbol. A transition on a non-terminal A is a call for the procedure for A. In other words, a predictive parsing program based on a transition diagram attempts to match terminal symbols against the input and make a potentially recursive procedure call whenever it has to follow an edge labelled a non-terminal.

For each non-terminal A, the following must be performed:

1. Create an initial and final state.
2. For each production $A \rightarrow X_1 X_2 \ldots X_n$, create a path from the initial to the final state, with edges labelled $X_1, X_2, \ldots, X_n$.

The parser begins from the start state. After some transitions, if it is in state s having an edge labelled with a terminal 'a' pointing to state t, and if the next input symbol is 'a', the parser moves the input cursor one position to the right and goes to state t. If, on the other hand, the edge is labelled by a non-terminal A, the parser goes to the start state for A, without moving the input cursor. If the final state of A is reached, it immediately goes to state t. If there is an edge from s to f labelled ε, then from state s, the parser goes to state t, without advancing the input.

The transition diagram is constructed and optimised. After optimisation, string validation can be carried out, as follows:

1. Start from the start state.
2. If an edge is labelled by a terminal, then move to the next state.
3. If an edge is labelled by a non-terminal, go to the DFA of the non-terminal and return to the DFA that was being processed, if the final state is reached.
4. Continue parsing in the DFA.
5. If the final state is reached, the string is successfully parsed.

It is inherently a recursive parser, so it consumes a lot of memory. Optimising it may not be simple as the complexity of the grammar increases. To remove this recursion, we use the LL parser, which is a table-driven parser.

Example 3.3 Transition diagram for the given grammar

Consider the following grammar:

E → T E'

E' → + T E' | ε

T → F T'

T' → * F T' | ε

F → (E) | id

The transition diagram is constructed for each non-terminal, as follows:

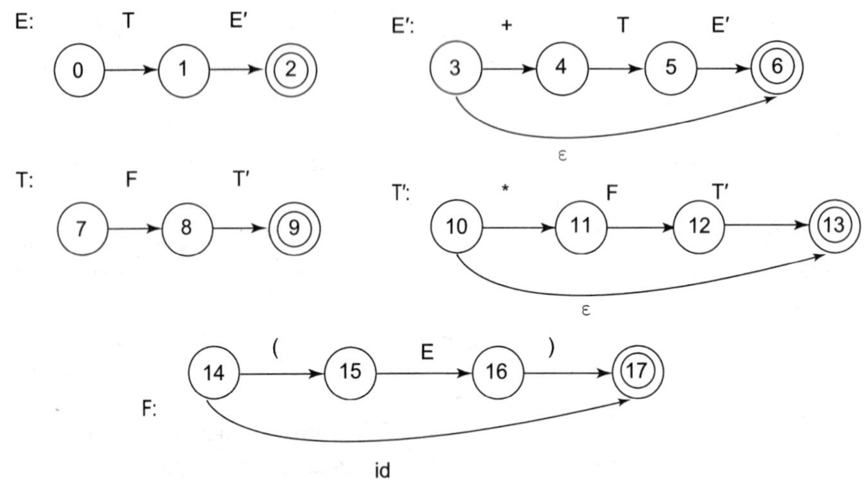

We can optimise the transition diagrams by reducing the number of states. The DFA of E' can be optimised by removing state 6 and adding a self-loop to E' as follows:

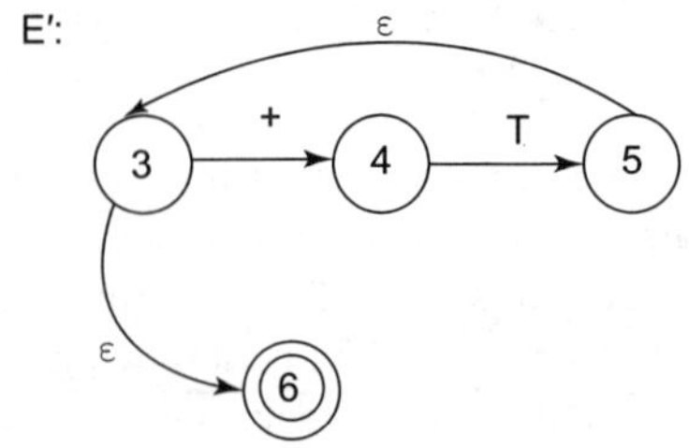

This can be further optimised as

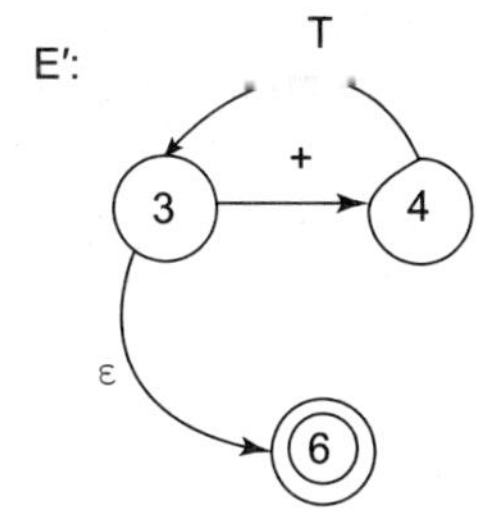

Combining with the DFA of E, we get

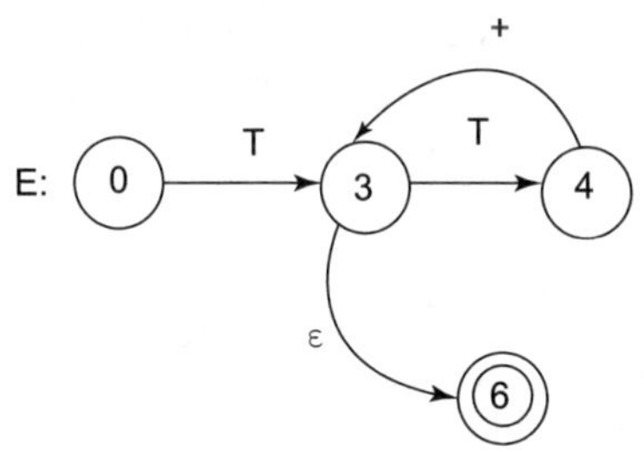

We can further optimise it to produce

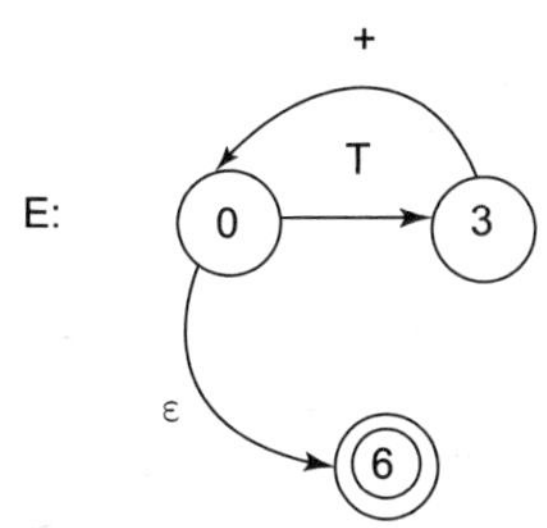

Similarly, we can optimise the DFA of T as follows:

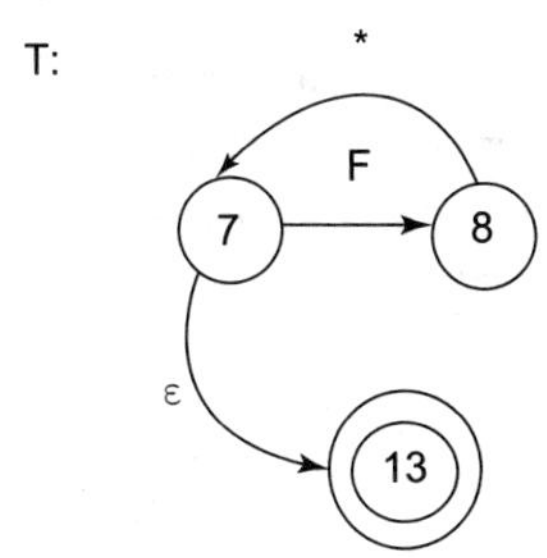

The DFA for F cannot be optimised.

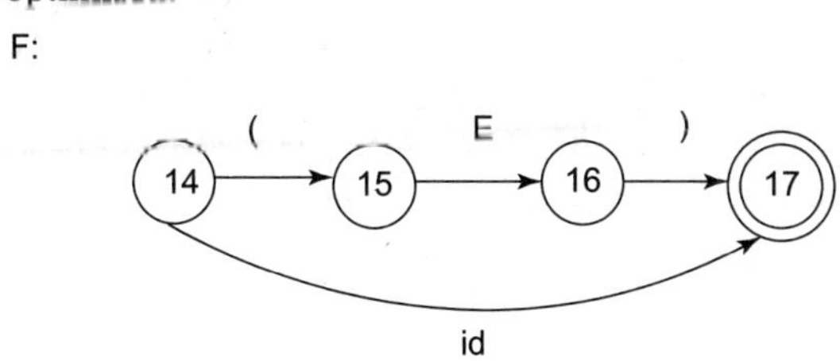

Let us consider a string (id * id). String validation will proceed as follows in the transition diagram:

1. We start from state 0, i.e., the non-terminal E. As per the optimised DFA of E, we can proceed through the edge labelled T. As it is a non-terminal, we call the DFA of T and continue in the DFA of T until the final state is reached. *(Call from E to T)*
2. In the DFA of T, we have an edge labelled F; so the DFA of F is called. *(Call from T to F)*. The symbol '(' is then parsed. Next, we encounter E, resulting in a call to the DFA of E. *(Call from F to E)*
3. From the DFA of E, jump to the DFA of T and to the DFA of F. We obtain the transition of the terminal id, so it is parsed, and we reach the final state 17 in the DFA of F. We then return to the previous DFA, which was T. We parse symbol * and again reach state 7. We further call the DFA of F.
4. The symbol id will be parsed and we reach the final state 17 of F, so we return to previous DFA of T and process ε, reaching the final state of T. We then return to the previous DFA of E.
5. We further return to all the previous DFAs with ε and we find that the string is valid for the given grammar.

Such recursive calls to DFAs can be implemented in a non-recursive way by using stacks.

Non-recursive predictive parser: It is possible to build a non-recursive predictive parser by maintaining a stack explicitly, rather than implicitly, through recursive calls. Non-recursive predictive parsing uses a parsing table to parse the input and generate a parse tree. For parsing the input, two data structures are used: buffer and stack. Both the stack and the input string buffer contain an end symbol $ to denote that the stack is empty and the input is consumed. The parser refers to the parsing table to take any decision on the input and stack element combination. The schematic for the same is shown in Fig. 3.11.

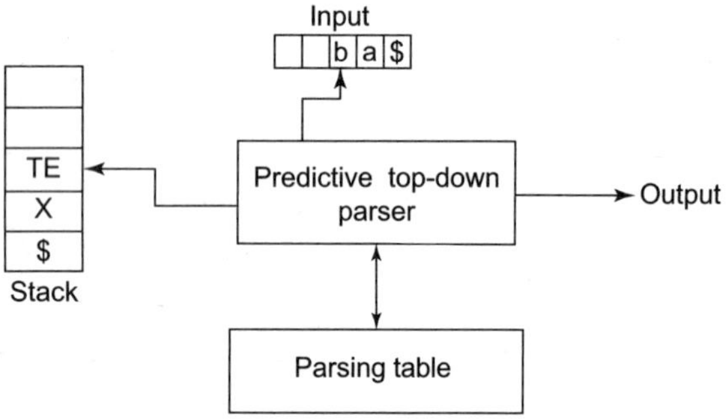

Figure 3.11 Predictive top-down parsing

The input contains a $ symbol followed by the string to be parsed, in reverse order. $ is used as an end marker. The stack contains a sequence of grammar symbols, followed by $, the bottom-of-stack marker. Initially the stack contains the start symbol of the grammar and $ as the bottom-of-stack marker. The parsing table is a two-dimensional array table [A, a], where A is a non-terminal, and a is a terminal or the symbol $.

The parser is controlled by the following procedure:

1. The program determines X, the symbol at the top of the stack, and a, the current input symbol.
2. These two symbols determine the action of the parser.

Backtracking is a technique that determines which production should be used by trying each production in turn. It is not limited to LL(k) grammars, but is not guaranteed to terminate unless the grammar is LL(k). Even when they terminate, parsers that use recursive descent with backtracking may require exponential time, whereas a predictive parser runs in linear time.

3.7 LL(1) – Predictive Top-down Parser

Need for predictive parser and computation of FIRST and FOLLOW: As discussed in the previous section, the problem of backtracking exists in non-predictive parsers as these parsers do not know which production must be used for expansion. To solve this problem, the compiler must know which production must be expanded by looking at the next input symbol of the string. That is, it must know the first character of the string that will be produced when a production rule is applied, and compare it to the current input string character, which would help in deciding which production rule to apply. This can be accomplished by computing FIRST.

Assume a grammar

S → AB
A → C | D
B → a
C → c
D → d

The input string is "ca". The parser starts with the start state S and uses the only available production rule. So, we get

S → AB

Now, as per LMD, the compiler needs to expand A using an appropriate production rule. If we already have FIRST for both the production rules of A, we get

FIRST (C) = {c} and FIRST (D) = {d}

The current input symbol is 'c'. So, the compiler knows that it must use the production A → C. After application of A → C and C → a, we get

S → AB → CB → cB

FIRST (B) = {a} and the next input symbol is also 'a'. So, we obtain the input string "ca". The parser can encounter one more problem, where a non-terminal can be replaced by ε to accept the string. Consider the grammar given below

A → cSa
S → b | ε

The input string is "ca". The parser starts with the start state A and uses the only available production rule. So, we get

S → cSa

Now, the parser checks for the second character of the input string, which is 'a'; the non-terminal to derive is S, but the parser cannot obtain any string derivable from B that contains 'a' as the first character. However, the grammar does contain a production rule, S → ε. If S → ε is applied, then the parser can accept the input "ca". This can be found if the parser knows that the character that follows B is the same as the current character in the input. So, the parser needs to find the FOLLOW information if the grammar contains ε.

Computation of FIRST: Let us consider a production rule of the format, A → aXY

FIRST (A) = FIRST (aXY)
= a if α is the terminal symbol **(Rule 3.1)**
= FIRST (α) if α is a non-terminal and FIRST (α) does not contain ε **(Rule 3.2)**
= FIRST (α) – ε ∪ FIRST (XY) if α is a non-terminal and FIRST (α) contains ε **(Rule 3.3)**

Computation of FOLLOW: If the given grammar contains ε, we need to find FIRST and FOLLOW. The FOLLOW of any non-terminal A that appears on the RHS of a production rule of grammar has the form S → α A B, where B is the last terminal or non-terminal of the production.

FOLLOW (A) = FIRST (B) if FIRST (B) does not contain ε **(Rule 3.4)**

= FIRST (B) – ε ∪ FOLLOW(S) otherwise if FIRST (B) contains ε **(Rule 3.5)**

The $ symbol is added to the FOLLOW set of start symbols. If there are more terminals or non-terminals after A and before B, the rules of FIRST are applicable. Thus, construction of predictive parsers requires prediction of the production rule to use for expansion of a non-terminal. FIRST and FOLLOW allow us to fill in the entries of a predictive parsing table. Sets of tokens yielded by the FOLLOW function can also be used as synchronising tokens during panic mode error recovery.

LL(1) parser: LL(1) is a table-driven non-recursive predictive parser, built using top-down pushdown automata. In LL(1), the first 'L' stands for left-to-right scanning of the input string, the second 'L' stands for leftmost derivation and (1) indicates the look-ahead of length one. LL(1) proceeds as follows:

1. Check whether the given grammar contains any unnecessary production rules. If yes, remove them.
2. Left recursion and/or left factoring are removed, if they exist in the given grammar.
3. Find FIRST and FOLLOW. If the new grammar contains ε, find both FIRST and FOLLOW; otherwise, find only FIRST.
4. Construct the parsing table. If the table contains multiple entries, it is not LL(1); otherwise, the grammar is considered as LL(1) grammar.

Removing unnecessary production rules: A non-terminal symbol X is productive, if there is a derivation $X \overset{*}{\rightarrow} w$ for some string w of terminal symbols. A non-terminal symbol X is called reachable if there is a derivation $S \overset{*}{\rightarrow} \alpha X \beta$ for some strings α, β of non-terminal and terminal symbols, where S denotes the grammar's start symbol.

A rule with an unproductive or unreachable symbol on its LHS can be deleted from the grammar without changing the language, along with the production rule containing such a symbol. For example, in the following grammar

S → A **(Grammar 3.7)**

A → a

B → b

b is unreachable because the non-terminal B does not appear on the right side of any production.

Hence, the production rule B → b can be removed as it is not required.

Left recursion: A grammar is left recursive if it has a non-terminal A such that there is a derivation $A \overset{+}{\rightarrow} A\alpha$, for some string a. Top-down parsing methods cannot handle left-recursive grammars, so there is a need for elimination of left-recursive production.

In general, any production of the form A →Aα | β can be replaced by a set of non–left-recursive productions. **(Rule 3.6)**

A → βA'

A' → α A' | ε

If more than one alternative is present on the RHS, the formula can be represented as

$A \rightarrow A\,\alpha_1 \mid A\,\alpha_2 \mid \ldots\ldots \mid \beta_1 \mid \beta_2 \ldots$

Then, the production rules can be rewritten as

A → β_1A'| β_2A'|
A' → α_1 A| α_2A|......| ε

For example, eliminate left recursion from the given grammar:

S → aA|Bc
A → A a |A c | b
B → b

The grammar contains left recursion in the production rule A → A a |A c | b. As per *Rule 3.1*, the production rule can be rewritten as

A → b A'
A → aA' | cA' | ε

Hence, the grammar after elimination of left recursion will be

S → aA | Bc
A → b A'
A → aA' | cA' | ε
B → b

Left factoring: This is a grammar transformation useful for producing grammar suitable for predictive parsing. If it is not clear which of the alternative productions should be used to expand a non-terminal A, we may be able to rewrite the A productions to defer the decision until we have seen enough of the input to make the right choice.
In general, a production of the form **(Rule 3.7)**

A → α β1 | α β2

can be replace by a set of non–left-factoring productions

A → α A'
A' → β1 | β2

Example 3.4 Eliminate left-factoring from the given grammars

(i) A → CD | Cd | Cb | Q | R

The grammar contains left recursion. As per *Rule 3.7*, the production rule can be re-written as

A → CA' | Q | R
A' → D | d | b

(ii) A → ab | ad | ε

As per *Rule 3.7*, the production rule can be rewritten as

A → a A' | ε
A' → b | D

Example 3.5 FIRST computation for the given grammar
Let us consider a grammar

S → Abc | ad

A → eS | Cr| ε
C → f | p | ε

FIRST is computed for all production rules/non-terminals, so that we can predict which alternative production to use for expansion of the non-terminal that might produce the next token in the input string.

FIRST (S) = FIRST (Abc) ∪ FIRST (ad)
FIRST (A) = FIRST (eS) ∪ FIRST (Cr) ∪ FIRST(ε)
FIRST (C) = FIRST (f) ∪ FIRST (p) ∪ FIRST (ε)
= {f}∪ {p} ∪ ε (Applying *Rule 3.1*)
= {f, p, ε}

Applying *Rule 3.1* to FIRST (eS), *Rule 3.3* to FIRST (Cr) and *Rule 3.1* to FIRST (ε), we get

FIRST (A) = {e} ∪ FIRST (Cr) ∪ ε.
= {e}∪ (FIRST(C) – ε ∪ FIRST(r)) ∪ ε
= {e}∪ ({f, p}∪{r}) ∪ ε
= {e, f, p, r, ε}

Applying *Rule 3.3* to FIRST (Abc) and *Rule 3.1* to FIRST (ad), we get

FIRST (S) = FIRST(Abc) ∪ {a}
= (FIRST (A) – ε U FIRST (bc)) ∪ {a}
= {e, f, p , r}∪ {b} ∪ {a}
= {a, b ε, f, p, r}

Non-terminal	FIRST
S	{a, b e, f, p, r}
A	{e, f, p, r, ε}
C	{f, p, ε}

Let us consider an input string "frbc" and trace the validity of the string. We show the use of FIRST for string validation.

- The look-ahead of LL(1) is one character. Hence, we know that the first input character is 'f'.
- In top-down parsing, we start with the start symbol to derive the input string.
- We start from S. Given the production rule S→ Abc | ad, there are two alternatives for expansion of S. FIRST (Abc) = {e, f, p, r} and FIRST (ad) = {a}. Hence, we must select production rule S → Abc for expanding S.
- After expansion, S → Abc. Now, A → es | Cr | ε. FIRST (es) = {e}, FIRST (Cr) = {f, p, r} and FIRST (ε) = {ε}. As per look-ahead, production rule A→Cr is used for expansion.
- After expansion, S → Abc → Crbc. Now, C → f | p | ε. As per look-ahead, we select the C → f production rule for expansion.
- After expansion, S → Abc → Crbc → frbc.
- As we can derive the given input string, starting from the start symbol, it is a valid string for the language specified by the grammar.

Later in this section, a stack-based procedure is described that makes the process easier. This process is a non-recursive predictive parsing procedure that takes place after we have the parsing table. We will also describe how the parsing table is constructed using FIRST, which can be directly used by the parser to validate the string.

Example 3.6 FOLLOW computation
Some example calculations for FOLLOW are shown in Table 3.3.

Table 3.3 Examples of FOLLOW computation

Example production rule	FOLLOW computation for corresponding example
Find FOLLOW of A if S → aAbC (S is the start symbol)	FOLLOW (A) = FIRST (bC) = {b} (as per *Rule 3.4*)
Find FOLLOW of C if S → aACB B → b (S is the start symbol)	FOLLOW (C) = FIRST (B) = {b} (as per *Rule 3.4*)
Find FOLLOW of C if S → aACB B → b | ε (S is the start symbol)	FOLLOW (C) = FIRST (B) − ε ∪ FOLLOW (S) Applying *Rule 3.5* = {b, ε} − ε ∪ FOLLOW(S) = {b, $}
Find FOLLOW of A if S → aACB C → c | d | ε B → b | ε (S is the start symbol) With FIRST (S) = {a} FIRST (C) = {c, d, ε} FIRST (B) = {b, ε} FOLLOW (S) = {$}	FOLLOW (A) = FIRST (CB) Now, FIRST (C) has ε, hence apply *Rule 3.3* of FIRST computation = FIRST (C) − ε ∪ FIRST (B) B is the last non-terminal of the rule and has ε, hence apply *Rule 3.5* of FOLLOW FOLLOW (A) = FIRST (C) − ε ∪ FIRST(B) − ε ∪ FOLLOW(S) = {c, d, ε} − ε ∪ {b, ε} − ε ∪ FOLLOW(S) = {c, d, b, $}

Example 3.7 FIRST and FOLLOW computation

Let us consider the given grammar

S → ABC| BCD|X b
A → bd | ε
B → CAX | ε
C → b | ec
D → Bc | ε
X → e | ε

Finding FIRST

FIRST (A) = {b, ε}
FIRST (C) = {b, e}
FIRST (X) = {x}
FIRST (B) = FIRST (CAX) | ε = FIRST (C) ∪ ε = {b, e, ε}
FIRST (D) = FIRST (Bc) ∪ FIRST (ε) = {b, e, ε} − ε ∪ FIRST (c) ∪ {ε} = {b, c, e, ε}
FIRST (X) = {e, ε}
FIRST (S) = FIRST (ABC) ∪ FIRST (BCD) ∪ FIRST (Xb) = {b, c, e, ε}

Finding FOLLOW

S does not exist on the RHS of any production rule. Hence
FOLLOW (S) = {$}
To find FOLLOW of A, the production rules that must be used are
S → ABC, B → CAX

FOLLOW (A) = FIRST (BC) ∪ FIRST (X)
= (FIRST (B) − ε ∪ FIRST (C)) ∪ FIRST (X) − ε ∪ FOLLOW (B)
= ({b, e} ∪ {b, e}) ∪{e}∪ FOLLOW (B)
= {b, e}∪ FOLLOW (B)

To find FOLLOW of B, the production rules that must be used are
S → ABC, D → Bc, S → BCD
FOLLOW (B) = FIRST (C) ∪ FIRST (c) ∪ FIRST (C)
= {b, e} ∪{c} ∪{b, e}
= {b, c, e}

To find FOLLOW of C, the production rules that must be used are
S → ABC, S → BCD, B → CAX
FOLLOW (C) = FOLLOW (S) ∪ FIRST (D) − ε ∪ FOLLOW (S) ∪ FIRST (AX)
= {$} ∪ {b, c, e }∪{$} ∪ {b, e, ε} − ε ∪ FOLLOW (B)
= {$} ∪ {b, c, e }∪{$} ∪ {b, e, ε} − ε ∪ {b, c, e}
= {b, c, e, $}

To find FOLLOW of D, the production rule that must be used is
S → BCD
FOLLOW (D) = FOLLOW (S) = {$}
To find FOLLOW of X, the production rules that must be used are
S → Xb, B → CAX
FOLLOW (X) = FIRST (b) ∪ FOLLOW (B)
= {b}∪{b, c, e}
= {b, c, e}

Also, FOLLOW(A) = {b, e} ∪ FOLLOW (B) = {b,e} ∪ {b,c,e} = {b,c,e}
The computed FIRST and FOLLOW are shown in the table on the right.

Non-terminal	FIRST	FOLLOW
S	{b, c, e, ε}	{$}
A	{b, ε}	{b, c, e}
B	{ b, e, ε}	{b, c, e}
C	{b, e}	{b, c, e, $}
D	{b, c, e, ε}	{ $ }
X	{e, ε}	{b, c, e}

Construction of parse table: The procedure to construct a predictive parsing table for a grammar G is as follows:

1. For each production of the form A→ α with α in FIRST (α), the parser will expand A by α, when the current input symbol is α.
2. Table [A, a] will contain A→ α for each terminal α in the FIRST (α).
3. If ε is in FIRST (α), then add an entry in table [A, b] containing production A → α, for each terminal b in FOLLOW (A).
4. If ε is in FIRST (α) and $ is in FOLLOW (A), add A→ α to the table at [A, $].

In other words, entry is made in the table at [A, a] for all a contained in FIRST (A). Production A→α is added in the table. If FIRST (A) contains ε, then the production that causes ε is added to the table at [A, b] for each terminal b contained in FOLLOW (A). Also, if FIRST (A) contains ε and FOLLOW (A) contains $, add thc production causing ε to the table at [A, $]. Each undefined entry in the table is an error. If while parsing the string an error entry is referred, the error handler must be invoked. If the parsing table does not contain multiple entries, the grammar is LL(1).

String validation though predictive parsing algorithm: The parsing table is referred to validate any input string. The validation process requires buffer and stack. The input string is placed in the buffer in reverse order, with $ as the initial symbol. The stack contains the start symbol followed by $. As it is LL(1), the look-ahead is one character in the input string. Table entries are searched for using production rules that must be used for expansion of the non-terminal. The first table entry to be searched is the table [start symbol, first input character]. The production rule available in the table is used to expand the start symbol. When the stack top contains the same terminal as the input string character, the terminal is popped from the stack and deleted from the buffer. This is called **match condition**, after which further characters in the input string are validated. If in the end only the $ symbol is left in the buffer and in the stack, the string is considered as a valid string for the given grammar. The predictive parsing algorithm is given below.

Algorithm: Predictive Parsing

```
{
Do
{
    Let X be the symbol at top of the stack and a the next input symbol
    {
        If X is a terminal or $
        {
            If X = a
            {
                Pop X from the stack and remove a from the input
            }
            Else
            {
                Invoke error routine        // terminal on stack and next input symbol do not match
            }
        }
        Else                                // X is non-terminal
        {
            If M [X ,a] = X →Y
            {
                Pop X from the stack;
                Push Y onto the stack top
            }
            Else
            {
                Invoke error routine
            }
        }
    }
} Until X = $                               //Stack is empty.
```

Example 3.8 Construction of LL(1) parsing table and string validation process of predictive parser (stack-based)

Consider the given grammar

S → PQr

P → aP | b | c

Q → q | rP

FIRST(S) = FIRST (PQr)

FIRST (P) = FIRST (aP) ∪ FIRST (b) ∪ FIRST (c)

= {a} ∪ {b} ∪ {c} = {a, b, c}

FIRST (Q) = FIRST(q) ∪ FIRST (rP)

= {q}∪ {r} = {q, r}

FIRST (S) = FIRST (PQr)

= FIRST (P) = {a, b, c}

The LL(1) parsing table for the given grammar is as follows:

	a	b	c	q	r
S	S→PQr	S→PQr	S→PQr		
P	P→aP	P→b	P→c		
Q				Q→q	Q→rP

FIRST (S) contains a, b and c. Hence, table entries must be made at [S, a] , [S, b] and [S, c]. At table [S, a], we must enter the production of S due to which terminal a appears in the FIRST (S). So, the table entry at [S, a] contains the production rule S → PQr. Similarly, the remaining table entries are filled. There is no ε production, so we compute only FIRST.

Validation for input string "acrbr": The input string is entered in the buffer in reverse order and the stack contains the start symbol S. Let us consider the first entry.

Buffer	Stack
$rbrca	S$

The action will be to refer the table entry at [S, a]. Table [S, a] has S → PQr, so S is expanded as PQr in the stack. Hence, the next entry will be

Buffer	Stack
$rbrca	PQr$

The action will be to refer the table entry at [P, a]. Table [P, a] has P → aP, so P is expanded as aP. Buffer and stack contents will be

Buffer	Stack
$rbrca	aPQr$

As the entries on the buffer and stack are the same, the symbol is deleted. Match of symbols indicates that the input symbol is accepted. The complete string validation process is shown in Table 3.4.

Table 3.4 String parsing using stack and buffer for Example 3.8

Sr.No.	Buffer	Stack	Action
1	$rbrca	S$	Table [S, a] has S → PQr
2	$rbrca	PQr$	Table[P, a] has P → aP
3	$rbrca	aPQr$	Match of 'a' in buffer and stack, so delete 'a' from buffer and pop 'a' from stack
4	$rbrc	PQr$	Table [P, c] has P → c
5	$rbrc	cQr$	Match of 'c' in buffer and stack, so delete 'c' from buffer and pop 'c' from stack
6	$rbr	Qr$	Table [Q, r] has Q → rP
7	$rbr	rPr$	Match of 'r' in buffer and stack, so delete 'r' from buffer and pop 'r' from stack
8	$rb	Pr$	Table [P, b] has P → b
9	$rb	br$	Match of 'b' in buffer and stack, so delete 'b' from buffer and pop 'b' from stack
10	$r	r$	Match of 'r' in buffer and stack, so delete 'r' from buffer and pop 'r' from stack
11	$	$	Valid string

Example 3.9 FOLLOW computation, building of LL(1) parse table using FIRST and FOLLOW information and validation of string

Let us consider the given grammar and the FIRST information computed in Example 3.2.

S → Abc | ad
A → eS | Cr| ε
C → f | p | ε

Assume S as the start symbol. We now compute the FOLLOW information. S appears on the RHS of production rule A→ eS. As there is nothing after S, the formula becomes

FOLLOW(S) = FIRST (ε) – ε ∪ FOLLOW (A)
= FOLLOW (A) ∪ {$} (We also add '$' to the start symbol)

Let us now compute FOLLOW (A). To do this, we find the production rules containing A on the RHS.

S → Abc
FOLLOW (A) = FIRST (bc) = {b}
Hence, FOLLOW (S) = {b, $}. To compute FOLLOW of C, we use production rule A → Cr
FOLLOW (C) = FIRST (r) = {r}

FIRST and FOLLOW information for the given grammar is given below:

Non-terminal	FIRST	FOLLOW
S	{a, b e, f, p, r}	{b, $}
A	{e, f, p, r, ε}	{b}
C	{f, p, ε}	{r}

The LL(1) parse table for the given grammar is shown in Table 3.5.

Table 3.5 LL(1) parsing table for Example 3.9

	a	b	c	d	e	f	p	r	$
S	S→ad	S→Abc			S→Abc	S→Abc	S→Abc	S→Abc	
A		A→ε			A→eS	A→Cr	A→Cr	A→Cr	
C						C→f	C→p	C→ε	

FIRST (A) contains ε. So, while making the entry in the parsing table, we refer to FOLLOW (A), which is {b}. A table entry is made at table [A, b] containing the production rule of A, due to which ε appears in the grammar. Hence, table [A, b] contains A → ε. Similarly, FIRST (C) contains ε. So, the table entry of table [A, b] contains C → ε.

After construction of the parsing table, the parser refers to the table entries to determine the validity of the input string. The validation process for input string "frbc" is shown in Table 3.6. Here, the ε production rule is not used. There may be strings that need ε production, which is handled by computing FOLLOW and making the appropriate table entry. Validation of string "erbcbc" (Table 3.7) is one such example.

Table 3.6 Validation process for string "frbc" for Example 3.9

Buffer	Stack	Action
$cbrf	S$	Table [S, f] has S → Abc
$cbrf	Abc$	Table [A, f] has A → Cr
$cbrf	Crbc$	Table [C, f] has C → f
$cbrf	frbc$	Match of 'f' in buffer and stack, so delete 'f' from buffer and pop 'f' from stack
$cbr	rbc$	Match of 'r' in buffer and stack, so delete 'r' from buffer and pop 'r' from stack
$cb	bc$	Match of 'b' in buffer and stack, so delete 'b' from buffer and pop 'b' from stack
$c	c$	Match of 'c' in buffer and stack, so delete 'c' from buffer and pop 'c' from stack
$	$	Valid string

Table 3.7 Validation of string "erbcbc" for Example 3.9

Buffer	Stack	Action
$cbcbre	S$	Table [S, e] has S → Abc
$cbcbre	Abc$	Table [A, e] has A → eS

(Cont'd)

Table 3.7 (Continued)

Buffer	Stack	Action
$cbcbre	eSbc$	Match of 'e' in buffer and stack, so delete 'e' from buffer and pop 'e' from stack
$cbcbr	Sbc$	Table [S, r] has S → Abc
$cbcbr	Abcbc$	Table [A, r] has A → Cr
$cbcbr	Crbcbc$	Table [C, r] has C → ε
$cbcbr	rbcbc$	Match of 'r' in buffer and stack, so delete 'r' from buffer and pop 'r' from stack
$cbcb	bcbc$	Match of 'b' in buffer and stack, so delete 'b' from buffer and pop 'b' from stack
$cbc	cbc$	Match of 'c' in buffer and stack, so delete 'c' from buffer and pop 'c' from stack
$cb	bc$	Match of 'b' in buffer and stack, so delete 'b' from buffer and pop 'b' from stack
$c	c$	Match of 'c' in buffer and stack, so delete 'c' from buffer and pop 'c' from stack
$	$	Valid string

Example 3.10 To find out if the given grammar is LL(1) or not

S → abBc | abDr
B → b
D → d

Left-factoring occurs in the production S → abBc | abDr. So, we first remove the left-factoring; the production rule becomes

S → abS'
S' → Bc | Dr

The grammar after removal of left-factoring is as follows:

S → abS'
S' → Bc | Dr
B → b
D → d

The grammar contains no ε, so we find only FIRST information.

FIRST (S) = FIRST (abS')
= FIRST (a)
= {a}

FIRST (S') = FIRST (Bc) ∪ FIRST (Dr)
= FIRST (B) ∪ FIRST (D)
= {b, d}

FIRST (B) = FIRST (b)
= {b}

FIRST (D) = FIRST (d)
= {d}

The parsing table for the given grammar is shown in Table 3.8.

Table 3.8 Parsing table for Example 3.10

	a	b	c	d	R	$
S'	S → abS'					
S		S' → Bc		S' → Dr		
A		B → b		D → d		
C						

As multiple entries are not present, the grammar is said to be LL(1) grammar.

Example 3.11 To find out if the given grammar is LL(1) or not

S → iEtSS' | a
S' → eS | ε
E → b

The grammar contains ε, hence we will compute FIRST and FOLLOW.

FIRST (E) = {b}
FIRST (S') = {e, ε}
FIRST (S) = {i, a}

To find the FOLLOW of S, we use the production rules S → iEtSS' and S' → eS. We also append $ to FOLLOW (S), as it is the start state.

FOLLOW (S) = FIRST (S') ∪ FOLLOW (S') ∪ {$}
= (FIRST (S') – ε ∪ FOLLOW (S)) ∪ FOLLOW (S') ∪ {$}
= {e} ∪ FOLLOW (S) ∪ {$}
= {e, $} (FOLLOW (S) is omitted as we are computing FOLLOW (S))

To find the FOLLOW of S', we use the production rule S → iEtSS'.

FOLLOW (S') = FOLLOW (S)
= {e, $}

To find the FOLLOW of E, we use the production rule S → iEtSS'.

FOLLOW (E) = FIRST (tSS') = {t}

Table 3.8 (a) Parsing table for Example 3.11

	i	t	a	e	$	b
S	S → iEtSS'		S→a			
S'				S'→ε S'→eS	S'→ ε	E → b
E						

As the table contains multiple entries, the grammar is not LL (1).

Example 3.12 To find out if the given grammar is LL(1) or not

Consider the given grammar

E → E + T | T

T → T * F | F

F → (E) | id

The grammar contains left-recursion in the productions E → E + T and T → T * F. After removing left–recursion, the grammar is as follows:

E → T E'

E' → + T E' | ε

T → F T'

T' → * F T' | ε

F → (E) | id

As the above grammar contains ε, we need to find FIRST and FOLLOW.

FIRST (F) = FIRST (E) ∪ FIRST (id)
= {(, id}

FIRST (T') = FIRST (*FT') ∪ FIRST (ε)
= { * , ε }

FIRST (T) = FIRST (FT)
= FIRST (F)
= {(, id }

FIRST (E') = FIRST (+TE') ∪ FIRST (ε)
= { +, ε }

FIRST (E) = FIRST (TE')
= FIRST (T)
= {(, id }

Non-terminal E exists on the RHS of production rule F → (E). Hence, FOLLOW (E) contains ')'and $, as it is the start state.

FOLLOW (E) = {), $}

To compute FOLLOW of E', we use production rules E → T E' and E' →+ T E'.

FOLLOW (E') = FOLLOW (E) ∪ FOLLOW (E') ∪ {$}
={), $}

To compute FOLLOW of T, we use production rules E → T E' and E'→+ T E'.

FOLLOW (T) = (FIRST (E') – ε ∪ FOLLOW (E)) ∪ (FIRST (E') – ε ∪ FOLLOW (E'))
= {+} ∪ {), $} ∪ {+} ∪ {$}
= {+,), $ }

To compute FOLLOW of T', we use production rules T → FT' and T' → *FT'.

FOLLOW (T') = FOLLOW (T) ∪ FOLLOW (T')
= {+ ,), $}

To compute FOLLOW of F, we use production rules T → FT' and T' → *FT'

FOLLOW (F) = (FIRST (T') – ε ∪ FOLLOW (T)) ∪ (FIRST (T') – ε ∪ FOLLOW (T'))
= {*} ∪ { + ,), $} ∪ {*} ∪ {+,), $}
= {*, +,), $ }

	FIRST	FOLLOIW
E	{(, id }	{), $}
E'	{+, ε}	{),$}
T	{(, id}	{+,), $}
T'	{* , ε }	{+,), $}
F	{(, id}	{*, +,), $}

Table 3.9 Parsing table for Example 3.12

	+	*	(	id	)	$
E			E→TE'	E→TE'		
E'	E'→+TE'				E'→ ε	E'→ ε
T			T →FT'	T →FT'		
T'	T'→ε	T'→*FT'			T'→ε	T'→ε
F			F →(E)	F→id		

Example 3.13 To find out if the given grammar is LL(1) or not

D → L:T
L → L, id | id
T → integer

We assume the colon and comma as terminal symbols. The grammar contains left recursion in the production rule, L→ L, id. The grammar after removing left recursion is

D → L : T
L → id L'
L' → , id L' | ε
T → integer

As the grammar contains ε, we need to find FIRST and FOLLOW.

FIRST (T) = FIRST (integer)
= {integer}

FIRST (L') = FIRST (id L') ∪ FIRST (ε)
= {id, ε}

FIRST (L) = FIRST (id L)
= {id}

FIRST (D) = FIRST (L : T)
= FIRST (L)
= {id}

D does not appear on the RHS of any production

FOLLOW (D) = {$}

To find FOLLOW of L, we use the production rule D → L : T

FOLLOW (L) = FIRST (: T) = {:}

To find the FOLLOW of L', we use production rules L → id L' and L → , id L

FOLLOW (L') = FOLLOW (L) U FOLLOW (L') = {:}
To find FOLLOW of T, we use the production rule D → L:T

FOLLOW (T) = FOLLOW (D) = {$}

Table 3.10 The parse table for Example 3.13

	:	id	,	integer	$
D		D→L : T			
L		L →id L'			
L'	L'→ ε		L→ , id L'		
T				T→integer	

As multiple entries are not present in the parsing table, the grammar is LL(1).

Example 3.14 Building an LL(1) parser for a subset of the English language. The tokens available in the language are given. Consider a grammar that can describe the language in CFG form, construct a parsing table and show validation of the example string.

Tokens given for language L:
Noun → championship | ball | toss
Verb → is | want | won | played
Pronoun → me | I | you
Proper-Noun → India | Australia | Steve | John
Determiner → the | a | an
Preposition → on | of
Grammar example:
S → NP VP
NP → Pronoun | Proper-Noun | Determiner Noun
VP → Verb NP
Let us represent the grammar words using letters
S → NP VP
NP → P | PN | D N
VP → V NP
N → championship | ball | toss
V → is | want | won | played
P → me | I | you
PN → India | Australia | Steve | John
D → the | a | an
String for validation: 'India won the championship'
FIRST (N) = {championship, ball, toss}
FIRST (V) = {is, want, won, played}
FIRST (P) = {me, I, you}
FIRST (PN) = {India, Australia, Steve, John}
FIRST (D) = {the, a, an}

Table 3.11 Parsing table for Example 3.14

	Championship	ball	toss	is	want	won	Played	me	I	you	India	Australia	Steve	John	the	a	an
S				S→ NP VP	S→ NP VP	S→ NP VP	S→ NP VP	S→ NP VP	S→ NP VP	S→ NP VP	S→ NP VP	S→ NP VP	S→ NP VP	S→ NP VP	S→ NP VP	S→ NP VP	S→ NP VP
NP								NP→P	NP→P	NP →P	NP →PN	NP →PN	NP →PN	NP →PN	NP →DN	NP →DN	NP → DN
VP				VP→ V NP	VP → V NP	VP →V NP	VP→ V NP										
N	N→ championship	N→ ball	N→ toss														
V				V→ is	V→ want	V→ won	V→ played										
P								P→me	P→I	P→you							
PN											PN→ India	PN→ Australia	PN→ Steve	PN→ John			
D															D→the	D→a	D→an

FIRST (NP) = FIRST (P) ∪ FIRST (PN) ∪ FIRST (D N)
= {me, I, you} ∪ {India, Australia, Steve, John} ∪ {the, a, an}
= {me, I, you, India, Australia, Steve, John, the, a, an}
FIRST (VP) = FIRST (V NP)
= {is, want, won, played }
FIRST(S) = FIRST (NP) ∪ FIRST (VP)
= {me, I, you, India, Australia, Steve, John, the, a, an} ∪ {is, want, won, played}
= {me, I, you, India, Australia, Steve, John, the, a, an, is, want, won, played}

Let us try to validate the string 'India won the championship'. The parsing is shown in Table 3.12.

Table 3.12 String parsing for Example 3.14

Buffer	Stack	Action
$ championship the won India	S$	Table [S, India] has S → NP VP
$ championship the won India	NP VP $	Table [NP, India] has NP → PN
$ championship the won India	PN VP$	Table [PN, India] has PN → India
$ championship the won India	India VP$	Match of 'India' in buffer and stack, so delete 'India' from buffer and pop 'India' from stack
$ championship the won	VP$	Table [VP, won] has VP →V NP
$ championship the won	V NP$	Table [V, won] has V → won
$ championship the won	Won NP $	Match of 'won' in buffer and stack, so delete 'won' from buffer and pop 'won' from stack
$ championship the	NP $	Table [NP, the] has NP →D N
$ championship the	D N $	Table [D, the] has D→the
$ championship the	the N $	Match of 'the' in buffer and stack, so delete 'the' from buffer and pop 'the' from stack
$ championship	N $	Table [N, championship] has N→ championship
$ championship	championship $	Match of 'championship' in buffer and stack, so delete 'championship' from buffer and pop 'championship' from stack
$	$	Valid string

3.8 Bottom-up Parsing

Bottom-up parsing can be defined as an attempt to reduce the input string w to the start symbol of a grammar by tracing the rightmost derivation of the string in reverse. This is equivalent to constructing a parse tree for the input string by starting with leaves and proceeding toward the root in a bottom-up manner. At each reduction step, a substring that matches the right side of any production of the grammar is replaced by the LHS non-terminal symbol of that production rule.

Example: Tracing RMD for the given grammar in reverse for bottom-up parsing. Consider the grammar

S → pQRv
Q → tR | q
R → Rup | r

The string "pqrupv" can be reduced to S as

pqrupv
pQrupv
pQRupv
pQRv
S

The input string "pqrupv" is scanned to find a substring that matches the right side of any production rule. Substrings q and p match. Let us select q and replace it with Q (as per production rule Q → q). Next, we replace r with R (as per production rule R → r). We now have the string "pQRupv", the substring "Rup" matches the right side of production rule R → Rup. So, we obtain "pQRv", which can in turn be reduced to S.

These reductions trace the rightmost derivation in reverse order as follows:

S → pQRv → pQRupv →pQrupv → pqrupv

3.8.1 Handle and Viable Prefix

The **handle** of a right sentential from γ is a production A → β with the position of β in γ in such a way that the replacement of β by A in γ will produce the previous sentential form in the RMD of γ. A **viable prefix** of a right sentential form is that prefix that contains a handle but no symbol to the right of the handle.

Example 3.15 To find the handle and viable prefix

Consider the given grammar

S → 0A1 | 0B
A → 0A | 0

The input sting is '00001'.

Handle information: To find the handle, derive the string using Right Most Derivation (RMD) in reverse. The RMD for the input string is: S → 0A1 → 00A1 → 000A1→ 00001. The handle information is given below:

RMD	Handle
00001$	A → 0 Following the third '0'
000A1$	A → 0A Following the second '0'
00A1$	A → 0A Following the first '0'
0A1$	A → 0A1 preceding '$'
S$	

Viable prefix: To find the viable prefix, use the shift-reduce method.

1. Initially, the stack contains '$' and the buffer contains a string ending with '$'. The first step is to shift.

2. If the stack top contains a handle, then reduce; otherwise, continue to shift till we obtain the handle on top of the stack.
3. If at the end we obtain the start symbol in the stack and '$' in the buffer, the string is accepted.

To find the viable prefix, we need to first find the handle and then use the shift-reduce method. The stack contents when we obtain the handle on top of the stack is called viable prefix.

Stack	**Action**	**Buffer**
$	Shift '0'	00001 $
$ 0	Shift '0'	0001 $
$ 00	Shift '0'	001 $
$ 000	Shift '0'	01 $
$ 0000	Reduce with A→ 0	1$
$ 000A	Reduce with A→ 0A	1$
$ 00A	Reduce with A→ 0A	1$
$ 0A	Shift '1'	1$
$0A1	Reduce with S→0A1	1$
$S	Accepted	$

Viable prefixes are stack entries corresponding to the reduce action. All the viable prefixes are listed below:

0000
000A
00A
0A1

Example 3.16 To find the handle and viable prefix

Consider the given grammar

S → a | ^ | (T)
T → T, S | S

The input string is "((a, a), a)".

Handle information: Perform RMD to derive the input string. The handle information is found when we track RMD in reverse. The RMD for the input string will be:

S→ (T) →(T, S) →(T, a) → (S, a) →((T), a) →((T, S),a)→ ((T, a), a) →((S, a), a) →
(a, a), a)

So we obtain the handle given below

RMD	**Handle**
((a, a), a) $	S→a Following the second opening '('
((S, a), a) $	T→S Following the second opening '('
((T, a), a) $	S→a Preceding the first closing ')'
((T, S),a) $	T→T, S Preceding the first closing ')'
((T), a) $	S→(T) Following the opening '('
(S, a) $	T→S Following the opening '('
(T, a) $	S→a Preceding the closing ')'
(T, S) $	T→T, S Preceding the closing ')'

(T) $ S→(T) Preceding the '$'
S $

Viable prefix: We use the shift-reduce method, as discussed in the previous example.

Stack	Action	Buffer
$	Shift '('	((a, a), a) $
$ (	Shift '('	(a, a), a) $
$ ((	Shift 'a'	a, a), a) $
$ ((a	Reduce with S→ a	, a), a) $
$ ((S	Reduce with T→S	,a), a) $
$ ((T	Shift ','	, a), a) $
$ ((T,	Shift a	a), a) $
$ ((T,a	Reduce with S→a	), a) $
$ ((T,S	Reduce with T→T,S	), a)$
$ ((T	Shift ')'	), a) $
$ ((T)	Reduce with S→(T)	, a) $
$ (S	Reduce with T→S	, a) $
$ (T	Shift ,	, a) $
$ (T,	Shift 'a'	a) $
$ (T,a	Reduce with S→a	) $
$ (T,S	Reduce with T→T,S	) $
$ (T	Shift ')'	) $
$ (T)	Reduce with S→(T)	$
$ S	Accepted	$

All the viable prefixes are listed below:

1) ((a
2) ((S
3) ((T,a
4) ((T,S
5) ((T)
6) (S
7) (T,a
8) (T,S
9) (T)

3.8.2 Shift-reduce Parsers

Shift-reduce parsers parse the input string using a parsing table and the shift-reduce parse method. It is a bottom-up parser, consisting of an input, an output, a stack, a driver program and a parsing table that has two parts: action and goto. The parsing program reads characters from an input buffer one at a time. Other types of parsers are discussed in the following sections.

Operator precedence parser: This is a simple shift-reduce parser, capable of parsing a subset of LR(1) grammars. These grammars have the property that there exists no ε in the RHS of the production rule and no two or more non-terminals are adjacent. The grammar in which there are no adjacent non-terminals on the right side of the production rule are operator grammars. These parsers are simple, and hence, numerous compilers use the operator precedence parsing technique for expressions. Often, these

parsers use recursive descent, for statements and higher-level constructs. Operator precedence parsers have been built for entire languages.
Let us consider a grammar

E → E S E | (E) | − E | id
S → + | − | * | / | ^

In the grammar, there are two consecutive non-terminals in the production rule E → E S E. Hence, the grammar is not operator grammar.

To convert the grammar to operator grammar, we substitute all productions of S in place of S in the production E→ E S E .

E → E + E | E − E | E * E | E / E | E ^ E | (E) | − E | id

Relations in operator precedence parser (D): Three disjoint precedence relations exist between certain pairs of terminals: <· , =, ·>. These precedence relations guide the selection of handles and have the following meaning:

Relation	Meaning
a<·b	a yields precedence to b (b has higher precedence than a)
a=b	a has the same precedence as b
a·>b	a takes precedence over b

The precedence relation between a pair of terminals can be determined in two ways.

Method 1: Based on the traditional notions of associativity and precedence of operators. For example, if * is to be given higher precedence than +, we make + <· *. To resolve ambiguity of the grammar, E→E+E | E − E | E*E | E/E | E↑E | (E) | −E | id using method 1 for a given string, we use relations. However, the unary minus sign (−) causes problems.

Method 2: Selecting operator precedence relations. This is done by the construction of an unambiguous grammar for the language that reflects the correct associativity and precedence in its parse trees. This is not difficult for expressions. For the other common source of ambiguity, the dangling else, grammar is a useful model. After unambiguous grammar is obtained, there is a mechanical method for constructing operator precedence relations from it. These relations may not be disjoint, and they may parse a language other than that generated by the grammar, but with the standard sort of arithmetic expressions, few problems are encountered in practice.

Using operator precedence relations: Precedence relations delimit the handle of a right sentential form, with <· indicating the left end, = appearing in the interior of the handle and ·> indicating the right end. Assume a right sentential form of an operator grammar that has no adjacent non-terminals on the right side of production. It implies that no right sentential form will have two adjacent non-terminals either. Then, the right sentential form is written as $\beta_0 a_1 \beta_1 \ldots a_n \beta_n$, where each β_i is either ε or a single non-terminal and each a_i is a single terminal. Also, only one of the relations <·, =, ·> holds between two terminals. Further, we usc $ to mark each end of thc string and define $ <·b and b ·> $ for all terminals b.

Steps to find the handle: The handle can be found using the following process:

1. Scan the string from the left until the first ·> is encountered.
2. Then scan backwards (to the remaining string before ·>) until a <· is encountered.

3. The handle contains everything to the left of the first ·> and to the right of <·.
4. After we obtain the handle, reduce it using the appropriate rule.
5. Continue the above steps until only $ and $ are left, indicating that the string is parsed and is valid for the given grammar.

Example 3.17 Operator precedence using operator precedence relation
Consider the grammar

E → E + E | E * E | (E) | id

The corresponding operator precedence relation table is as follows:

	id	**+**	*****	**$**
id		·>	·>	·>
+	<·	·>	<·	·>
*	<·	·>	·>	·>
$	<·	<·	<·	

Consider the initial right sentential form id + id * id. Using the operator precedence relations as per the steps:

1. Use $ to mark each end of the string, and define $ <·b and b ·> $ for all terminals b.
2. One of the relations <·, = , ·> holds between two terminals.

Thus, the string with the precedence relations inserted will be as follows:

$ <· id ·> + <· id ·> * <· id ·> $

Let us now find the handle and reduce the strings until the string is parsed, using the steps to find the handle, discussed in this section.

Step 1: Scan the string from the left until the first ·> is encountered.

- When we scan the string, we obtain the highlighted ·> as the first ·> relation.

  $ <· id ·> + <· id ·> * <· id ·>

Step 2: Then scan backwards (to the remaining string before ·>) until a <· is encountered.

- We scan backwards towards left from the highlighted ·>.

  $ <· id ·> + <· id ·> * <· id ·>

  We obtain the result as

  $ <· id ·> + <· id ·> * <· id ·>

Step 3: The handle contains everything to the left of the first ·> and to the right of <·.

- According to $ <· id ·> + <· id ·> * <· id ·>
  The handle is id.

Step 4: After we obtain the handle, reduce it using the appropriate rule.

- We must reduce it using E → id.
- So, we replace id with E, giving the equation as

  E + id * id, which can be represented as $ <· E <· + <· id ·> * <· id ·> $

Similarly, when we continue further, we obtain E + E * id, followed by E + E * E. Then, the non-terminals are deleted; $ + * $ will remain. Insert the operator relation and reduce. Inserting the precedence relations, we get

$ <· + <· * ·> $,

This indicates that the left end of the handle lies between + and * and the right end between * and $. These precedence relations indicate that in the right-sentential form E + E * E, the handle is E * E.

Algorithm for Parsing Operator Precedence

Input: An input string w and a table of precedence relations.
Output: If well-formed, with a placeholder non-terminal E labelling all interior nodes; otherwise, an error indication.

Method: Initially, the stack contains $ and the input buffer the string w$.

```
Set ip to point to the first symbol of w$;
Repeat forever
If $ is on top of the stack and ip points to $ then
          Return
Else begin
        Let a be the topmost terminal symbol on the stack and b be the symbol pointed to by ip;
          If a <· b or a = b then begin
               Push b onto the stack;                         // This is the shift operation
               Advance ip to the next input symbol;
End;
Else if a ·> b then
              Repeat
                   Pop the stack        // Reduce operation
            Until the top stack terminal is replaced by <· to the terminal most recently popped
        Else error( )
End
```

Example 3.18 Parsing an input string using the operator precedence parsing algorithm based on stack and buffer

Consider the grammar and relations used in Example 3.17. Let the input string to parse be id + id * id; the input after parsing using the operator precedence parsing algorithm based on stack and buffer is shown in Table 3.13.

Table 3.13 String parsing for Example 3.18 using operator precedence parsing algorithm

Stack	Input buffer	Precedence relation between stack top and input terminal
$	id + id * id$	$<·id (from the operator precedence relation table) Push id on stack and advance the input pointer
$id	+ id * id$	id·> + (from operator precedence relation table) Pop id. The top stack terminal is replaced by <·and reduced using E→id. Replace id on stack with E

(Cont'd)

Table 3.13 (Continued)

Stack	Input buffer	Precedence relation between stack top and input terminal
$<·E	+ id * id$	E<·+ (because E is non-terminal) Shift + on stack
$<·E+	id * id$	+ <· id. Shift id on stack
$<·E+ id	* id$	Pop id and reduce using E→id Replace id on stack with E
$<·E+<·E	* id$	Shift * on stack
$<·E+<·E*	id$	Shift id on stack
$<·E+<·E*id	$	Pop id and reduce using E→id Replace id on stack with E
$<·E+<·E*E	$	Reduce by E→E*E
$<·E+E	$	Reduce by E→E+E
$E	$	Valid string

Operator precedence relations from associativity and precedence: The rules are designed to select proper handles to reflect a given set of associativity and precedence rules for binary operators.

1. If operator θ1 has higher precedence than operator θ2, make θ1 ·> θ2 and θ2 <· θ1. These relations ensure that in an expression of the form E + E * E + E, the central E * E is the handle that will be reduced first.
2. If θ1 and θ2 are operators of equal precedence (they may in fact be the same operator), then
   - Make θ1 ·> θ2 and θ2 ·> θ1, if the operators are left associative
   - Make θ1 <· θ2 and θ2 <· θ1, if the operators are right associative

   These relations ensure that E – E + E will have handle E – E selected and E ^ E ^ E will have right E ^ E selected.
3. Make θ <· id and id ·> θ, θ <· (and (<· θ,) ·> θ and θ ·>), θ ·> $ and $ ·> θ, for all operators θ. Also
   (=),
   $ <· (,
   $ <· id,
   (<· (,
   id .> $,
) ·> $,
   (<· id,
   id ·>),
) ·>)

These rules ensure that both id and (E) will be reduced to E. Also, $ serves as both the left and the right end marker, causing handles to be found between $s wherever possible.

Example 3.19 Operator precedence relations for the given grammar and string parsing
Consider the grammar

E→E+E | E–E | E*E | E/E | E^E | (E) | –E | id

Input string "id * (id ^ id) – id / id" using the operator precedence relations is as shown below:

	+	–	*	/	^	**id**	(	)	**$**
+	·>	·>	<·	<·	<·	<·	<·	·>	·>
–	·>	·>	<·	<·	<·	<·	<·	·>	·>
*	·>	·>	·>	·>	<·	<·	<·	·>	·>
/	·>	·>	·>	·>	<·	<·	<·	·>	·>
^	·>	·>	·>	·>	<·	<·	<·	·>	·>
id	·>	·>	·>	·>	·>			·>	·>
(	<·	<·	<·	<·	<·	<·	<·		
)	·>	·>	·>	·>	·>			·>	·>
$	<·	<·	<·	<·	<·	<·	<·		

Precedence functions: Compilers using operator precedence parsers need not store the table of precedence relations. In most cases, the table is encoded by two precedence functions, f and g, which map terminal symbols to integers. Select f and g so that for symbols a and b

f(a) < g(b) whenever a <· b,
f(a) = g(b) whenever a = b,
f(a) > g(b) whenever a ·> b

Thus, the precedence relation between a and b is determined by a numerical comparison between f(a) and g(b).

Algorithm for Constructing Precedence Functions

Input: An operator precedence matrix.

Output: Precedence functions representing the input matrix or an indication that none exist.
Method:

1. Create symbols fa and ga for each a that is a terminal or $.
2. Partition the created symbols into as many groups as possible, in such a way that if a = b, then fa and gb are in the same group.
3. Create a directed graph whose nodes are the groups found in (2).
   a) For any a and b, if a <· b, place an edge from the group of gb to the group of fa.
   b) If a ·> b, place an edge from the group of fa to that of gb.
   Note: An edge or path from fa to gb means that f(a) must exceed g(b); a path from gb to fa means that g(b) must exceed f(a).
4. If the graph constructed in (3) has a cycle, then no precedence functions exist. If there are no cycles, let f(a) be the length of the longest path beginning at the group of fa; let g(b) be the length of the longest path from the group of gb.

Example 3.20 Derive the precedence function for the given grammar
Consider the grammar

E → E + E | E * E | (E) | id

The corresponding operator precedence relation is shown in the table on the right.

	id	+	*	$
id		·>	·>	·>
+	<·	·>	<·	·>
*	<·	·>	·>	·>
$	<·	<·	<·	

Let us create the precedence function using the algorithm for constructing precedence functions.

Step 1: Create symbols fa and ga for each a that is a terminal or $.

- There are four terminal symbols id, +, * and $.

  We create f symbols, f_{id}, f_+, f_* and $f_\$$, and g symbols, g_{id}, g_+, g_* and $g_\$$.

Step 2: Partition the created symbols into as many groups as possible, in such a way that if a = b, then fa and gb are in the same group.

- There are no symbols with = relation.

Step 3: Create a directed graph whose nodes are the groups found in (2).

a) For any a and b, if a <· b, place an edge from the group of gb to the group of fa.
   - Consider for example, + <· id , so we add an edge from g_{id} to f_+
   - Consider $ <· *, so we add an edge g_* to $f_\$$

   Similarly other edges are added for the <· relation.

b) If a ·> b, place an edge from the group of fa to that of gb.
   - Consider * ·> +, we add an edge from f_* to g_+
   - Consider id ·> $, we add an edge f_{id} to $g_\$$

   Similarly other edges are added for ·> relation. The complete graph with edges is shown in Fig. 3.12.

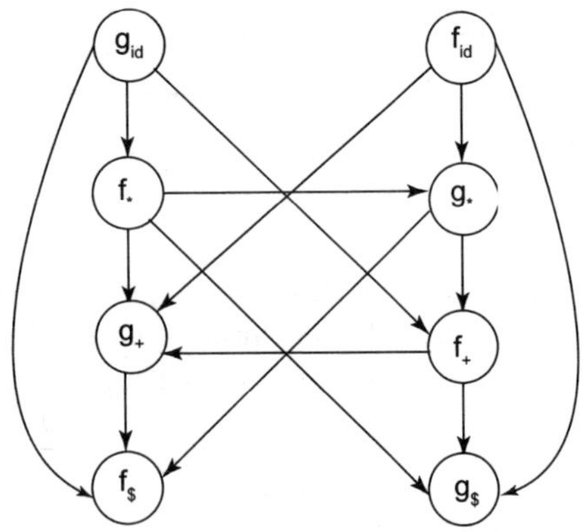

Figure 3.12 Graph for precedence relation

Step 4: If the graph constructed in (3) has a cycle, then no precedence functions exist. If there are no cycles, let f(a) be the length of the longest path beginning at the group of fa; let g(b) be the length of the longest path from the group of gb.

- There are no cycles in the graph shown in Fig. 3.12.
- For example, there is a path from g_{id} to f_* to g_* to f_+ to g_+ to $f_\$$= 5, the precedence function g representing id is 5.
- There is a path from fid to g_* to f_+ to $g_\$$ as the longest path = 4. Hence, precedence function of f contains 4 in id.
- The longest path starting from f_* is, f_* to g_* to f_+ to g_+ to $f_\$$ = 4. Hence, precedence function of f contains 4 in *.
- The longest path starting from f_* is, f_* to g_* to f_+ to g_+ to $f_\$$ = 4. Hence, precedence function of f contains 4 in *.

Similarly, we obtain the precedence functions represented in Table 3.14.

Table 3.14 Precedence function

	+	*	id	$
f	2	4	4	0
g	1	3	5	0

LR parsers: These are shift-reduce parsers, in which L stands for left-to-right scanning of the input program and R stands for rightmost derivation. The driver program for string parsing is the same for all LR parsers; only the parsing table changes from one parser to another. The string derivation process, also called string validation, is discussed in Section 3.9, after discussing the construction of the SLR parsing table.

All LL languages are LR languages, but there are more LR languages than LL languages. We will discuss the different LR parsers in the next few sections.

3.9 Simple LR Parser (SLR)

The SLR method involves the construction of a deterministic finite automata (DFA) from a grammar to recognise a viable prefix. We group items into sets, which give rise to the states of the SLR parser. The items can be viewed as the states of an NFA recognising viable prefixes. NFA can be converted to DFA, consisting of DFA states that are a collection of items. We can directly construct the DFA by finding the set of items called canonical collection of LR(0) items. The algorithm to find the DFA set of items requires computing the *closure* and *goto* functions, discussed in this section.

LR(0) items: An LR(0) item of a grammar G is a production of G with a dot at some position on the right side. The production rule, for example, A→ABC, can yield the following four items:

A→ .ABC
A→ A.BC (indicates viable prefix A)
A→ AB.C (indicates viable prefix AB)
A→ ABC. (indicates handle ABC)

The production A→ ε generates only one item, A→.

An item indicates how much of a production we have seen at a given point in the parsing process. Moving the dot represents how much of the production has been processed, i.e., a viable prefix (until the handle has been found). For example, in A→ .ABC, we hope to see a string derivable from ABC next on the input. A→ A.BC indicates that we have just seen a string derivable from A on the input and we are expecting to see a string derivable from BC.

A collection of sets of LR(0) items, also called canonical LR(0) items, provides the basis for the construction of SLR parsers. To find out the canonical LR(0) items for a grammar, we define an augmented grammar and apply the closure function. To find the DFA, we apply the *goto* function.

Augmented grammar: For a grammar G with start symbol S, the augmented grammar is G with a new production S'→S. This new production indicates to the parser when to stop parsing and announce the acceptance of the input. That is, acceptance occurs when the parser is about to reduce by S' → S.

Closure operation: If I is set of items for a grammar G, then *closure* (I) is the set of items constructed from I using the following rules:

1. Initially, every item in I is added to *closure* (I). **(Rule 1 of closure)**
2. If A → α.Bβ is in *closure* (I) and B → γ is a production, then add the item B → γ to I, if it is not already there. This rule is applied until no more new items can be added to *closure* (I). **(Rule 2 of closure)**

For example, consider a grammar

E → E + T | T **(Grammar 3.5)**
T → T * F | F
F → (E) | id

The augmented grammar will contain an extra production rule, E' → E. The augmented grammar will be
E' → E
E → E + T | T
T → T * F | F
F → (E) | id

All the possible LR(0) items for the augmented grammar are as follows:

E'→.E
E'→E.
E→.E+T
E→E.+T
E→E+.T
E→E+T.
E→.T
E→T.
T→.T*F
T→T.*F
T→T*.F
T→T*F.
T→.F
T→F.
F→.(E)
F→(.E)
F→(E.)
F→(E).
F→.id
F→id.

To form sets of LR(0) items, we use the function *closure.* Let us now find *closure* (E). As per *Rule 1 of closure*

E'→.E

As there is a non-terminal just after the dot in E'→.E, we must add the production rules of E with the dot as the leftmost symbol on the right side of the production rule, by *Rule 2 of closure.*

E→.E+T
E→. T

E productions are already present, so we must add T productions, as per *Rule 2 of closure.*

T→.T*F
T→.F

Adding the production rules of F

F→.(E)
F→.id

Hence, *closure* (*E*) =

{ E'→.E
E→.E+T
E→. T
T→.T*F
T→.F
F→.(E)
F→.id
}

***Goto* operation:** The second important function is *goto*. It can be represented as *goto*(I, X), where I is a set of items and X is a grammar symbol. *goto*(I, X) is defined as the closure of the set of all items [A → aX. b] such that [A → α.Xb] is in I. I is the set of items that are valid for some viable prefix γ, then *goto*(I, X) is the set of items that are valid for the viable prefix γ X.

For example

I={ E'→.E
E→.E+T
E→. T
T→.T*F
T→.F
F→.(E)
F→.id
}

Then *goto*(I,( ) will contain, F→(.E). We add productions of E, as per *Rule 2 of closure.*

E→.E+T
E→. T
T→.T*F
T→.F
F→.(E)
F→.id

Hence, *goto*(I,( ) =

{
F→(.E)
E→.E+T
E→. T
T→.T*F
T→.F
F→.(E)
F→.id
}

Construction of canonical collection of set of LR(0) items (C)

Procedure items (G')

```
Begin
        C := {closure([S' →.S])}
        Repeat
                For each set of items I in C and grammar symbol X
```

such that goto (I, X) is not empty and not in C do

Add goto(I, X) to C

until no more sets of items can be added to C

End

For example, the canonical collection of sets of LR(0) items for grammar (*Grammar 3.5*) are given below,

Note: If the dot has processed all the symbols and reached the end, dot processing will stop when the handle is reached.

I0: E'→.E
E→.E+T
E→. T
T→.T*F
T→.F
F→.(E)
F→.id

I1: E→ E.
E→E.+T

I2: E→T.
T→T.*F

I3: T→F.
Note: Will not be processed further as handle is reached (dot has processed all the symbols)

I4: F→(.E)
E→.E+T
E→. T
T→.T*F
T→.F
F→.(E)
F→.id

I5: F→id .
Note: Will not be processed further as handle is reached (dot has processed all the symbols)

I6: E→E+.T
T→.T*F
T→.F
F→.(E)
F→.id

I7: T→T*.F
F→.(E)
F→.id

I8: F→(E.)
E→E.+T

I9: E→E+T.
T→T.*F

I10: T→T*F.

I11: F→(E).

For every grammar G, the *goto* function of the canonical collection of sets of items defines a deterministic finite automaton that recognises the viable prefixes of G. We can visualise a non-deterministic finite automaton whose states are items themselves. The *goto* function for this set of items is shown as the transition diagram of a deterministic finite automaton D in Fig. 3.13.

The canonical collection of a set of LR(0) items can be found using **procedure items** as follows:

- Initially, C is null.
- We add the closure of a new rule of the form {*closure*([S' →.S])}. Hence, for *Grammar 3.5*, C = closure (E'→.E)

 = {
 E'→.E
 E→.E+T
 E→. T
 T→.T*F
 T→.F
 F→.(E)
 F→.id
 }

Call this *state I0.* Now, we will find *goto* (dot processing for each rule).

goto(I0,E)= closure({E'→E. , E→E.+T})
 = { E'→E.
 E→E.+T
 } = I1

goto(I0,T) = *closure* ({E→T. , T→T.*F })
 = { E→T.
 T→ T.*F
 } = I2

goto(I0,F) = *closure*({T→F.})
 = { T→F.} = I3

goto(I0,( ) = *closure*({F→(.E)})
 = {
 F→(.E)
 E→.E+T
 E→. T
 T→.T*F
 T→.F
 F→.(E)
 F→.id
 } = I4

goto(I0,id) = *closure*({F→id .})
 = { F→id .} = I5

- All the symbols of I0 have been processed. So, in the second iteration, we process I1.

 goto(I1,+) = *closure*({E→E+.T })
 = {
 E→E+.T

T→.T*F
T→.F
F→.(E)
F→.id
} = I6

- Processing I2
  goto(I2,*) = *closure*({T→T*.F })
  = {
  T→T*.F
  F→.(E)
  F→.id
  } = I7
- Process I3: Will not be processed further as handle is reached (dot has processed all the symbols)
- Process I4:
  goto(I4,E) = *closure*({F→(E.) ,E→E.+T})
  = { F→(E.)
  E→E.+T
  } = I8
  goto(I4,T) = *closure*({E→T. ,T→T.*F })
  = {
  E→T.
  T→T.*F
  } = I2
  The same state already exists in I2. Hence, *goto*(I4,T)= I2
  goto(I4,F) = *closure*({T→F.})
  = {
  T→F.
  } = I3 (already existing)
  goto(I4,() = I4
  goto(I4,id) = I5
- Productions in I5 are completely processed.
- Process I6, *goto*(I6,T) = *closure*({E→E+T. , T→T.*F})
  = { E→E+T.
  T→T.*F
  }
  goto(I6,F) = I3
  goto(I6,( ) = I6
  goto(I6,id) = I5
- Process I7
  goto(I7,F) = *closure*({T→T*F.})
  = {T→T*F.} = I10
- Process I8
  goto(I8,)) = *closure*({F→(E).})
  = { F→(E).}
- Process I9,
  goto(I9,*) = I7
- I10 and I 11 have been completely processed. So, we stop as no new state can be added to C.

The DFA for the above procedure is as shown in Fig. 3.13. The canonical set of items can be combined with the *goto* function for this set of items and directly written as states. The DFA along with LR(0) items represented inside the nodes is shown in Fig. 3.14. We use the representation of the form shown in Fig. 3.14 further in this chapter.

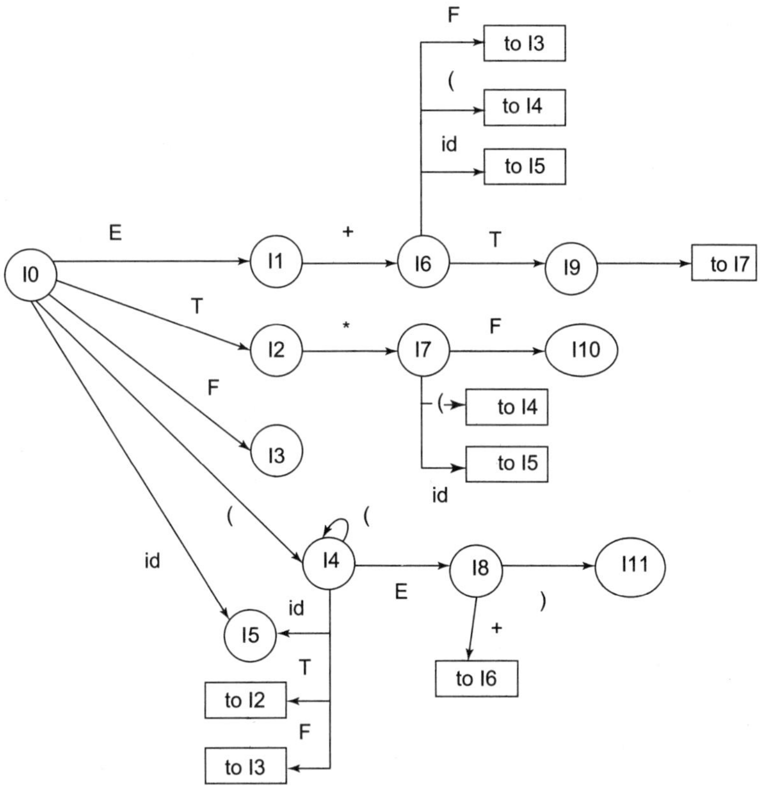

Figure 3.13 DFA representing *goto* transition

SLR parsing table construction: We will now discuss the construction of the SLR parsing table, which consists of two functions: *goto* and *action*. It requires us to know FOLLOW (A) for each non-terminal A of a grammar.

Given a grammar G, the main steps in constructing an SLR parse table are as follows:

1. Augment G to produce G'.
2. Construct C, the canonical collection of sets of items from G', by finding LR(0) items and applying the *closure* operation.

Construct the parsing table functions *action* and *goto* using C.

The method to construct a parsing table is as follows:

1. Construct C ={I0, I1 , . . . , In}, the collection of sets of LR(0) items for G.
2. State I is constructed from Ii. The parsing actions for state i are determined as follows:

   a) If A→ $\alpha.\alpha\beta$ is in Ii and *goto*(Ii, a) = Ij, then set *action*[i, a] to shift j, if a is a terminal.

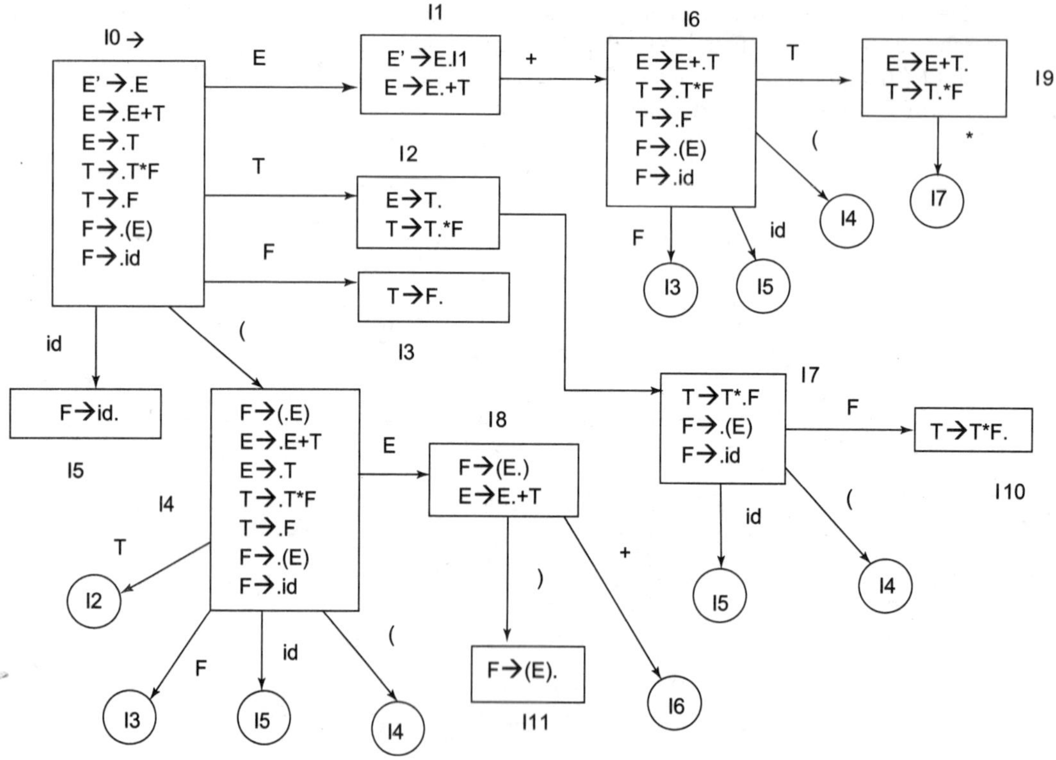

Figure.3.14 DFA with LR(0) items inside states

b) If A→α is in Ii, then set *action*[i, a] to reduce A → α for all α in FOLLOW (A). Here, A may not be S'.

c) If S → S' is in Ii, then set *action*[I,$] to accept.

If any conflicting actions are generated by the above rules, we say the grammar is not SLR(1). The algorithm fails to produce a parser in this case.

3. The *goto* transitions for state i are constructed for all non-terminals A using the rule: If *goto*(Ii, A) = I, then *goto*[i, A] = j.
4. All entries not defined by rules (2) and (3) are called errors.
5. The initial state of the parser is constructed from the set of items containing S' → .S

Example 3.21 Construction of SLR parsing table

Consider the grammar

S→Aa | bAc | Bc | bBa

A→ d

B→ d

The augmented grammar will be

S' → S *(New rule added)*

S →Aa

S →bAc
S →Bc
S →bBa
A →d
B →d

We construct the canonical sets of LR(0) items along with *goto* for the given grammar, in a finite automaton.

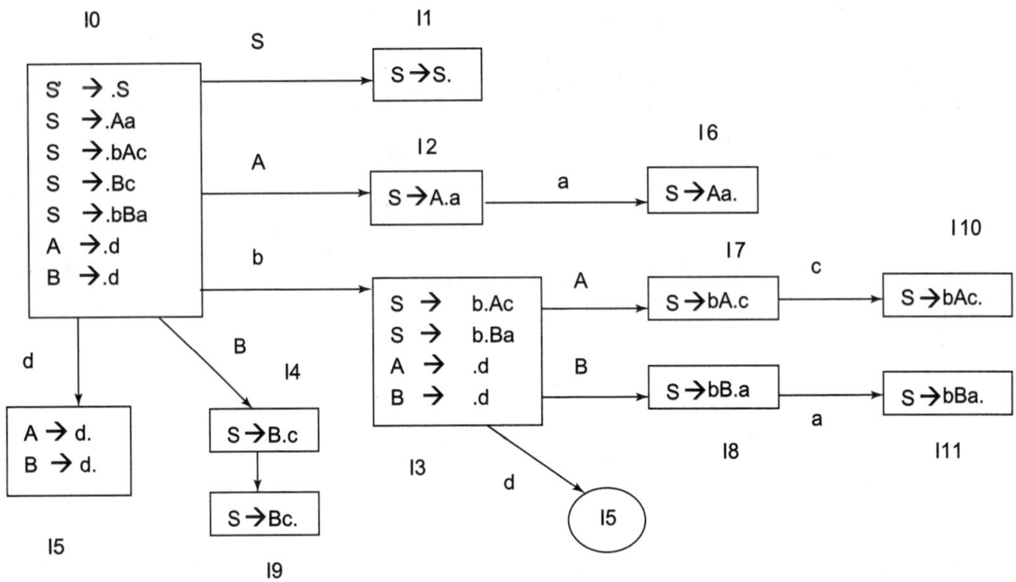

Figure 3.15 DFA for Example 3.21

The states represent the canonical collection of LR(0) items. FIRST and FOLLOW for the given grammar are as follows
FIRST (B) = {d}
FIRST (A) = {d}
FIRST (S) = {d. b}
FOLLOW (S) = {$}
FOLLOW (A) = {a, c}

FOLLOW (B) = {a, c}

The parsing table is constructed as follows:

1. There is a row corresponding to each state.
2. The *action* function is determined as follows:
   - For a transition from state I to state X, on terminal symbol a, shift entry is added. For transition *goto*(I,X) using a terminal symbol a, table entry is made at [I, a]=S_X (for all terminals a, where S is the shift entry).

(*Cont'd*)

- If dot processing is complete for a production in a state I, a reduce entry is made for the production that is terminated (say A→α.). It is represented by R followed by the production number of the completely processed production rule. This reduce entry is added to the table at [I, b], for all β are in the FOLLOW of A, which is the non-terminal on the LHS of the processed rule (for the rule A→α., the FOLLOW of A is considered).
- We add accept at table entry [1,$] as the new added production S'→S is completely processed in state I1. It is added to mark the acceptance of a string while parsing.

3. The *goto* entry is made if there is a transition from state I to another state X, with a non-terminal N. Table entry is made at [I,N] containing the state number X.

The parsing table for the grammar is shown in Table 3.15.

Table 3.15 SLR parsing table

State	ACTION					GOTO		
	a	b	c	d	$	S	A	B
0		S3		S5		1	2	4
1					Accept			
2	S6							
3				S5			7	8
4			S9					
5	R5,R6		R5,R6					
6					R1			
7			S10					
8	S11							
9					R3			
10					R2			
11					R4			

Let us consider some action entries. There is a transition from state I0 to state I3 on terminal symbol b, resulting in a table entry at [0,b] containing S3. Transition from I0 to I5 on terminal symbol d results in a table entry [0,d] containing S5. Transition from I2 to I6 on terminal symbol a results in a table entry [2,a] containing S6. Similarly, the remaining shift entries are added.

Let us consider an example for the reduce entry. State I5 contains items A→d. and B→d. Dot processing of both the production rules is complete as the dot has reached the end. So, we need to add a reduce entry. Let us assign numbers to production rules in G as follows:

S→Aa | bAc | Bc | bBa (Rule number 1, 2, 3 and 4)
A→ d (Rule number 5)
B→ d (Rule number 6)

So a reduce entry R5 has to be made corresponding to the production rule A→d and R6 has to be made corresponding to production rule B→d. The reduce entry is made in the row corresponding to the state (state I5 in our case). The column is found using FOLLOW. The reduce entry R5 corresponding to the production rule A→d is added to the table at [5,a] and [5,c] as FOLLOW(A)={a,c}. Similarly, R6 corresponding to production rule B→d is added to the table at [6,a] and [6,c] as FOLLOW(B)={a,c}. In state I6, the item is S→Aa. with the rule number 1. Table entry [6,$]=R1, as FOLLOW(S)={$}.

Sample goto entries: As in the automaton for the given grammar, there is transition from state I0 to state I1 on non-terminal S, adding 1 at table[0,S]. Transition I0→I2 on non-terminal A results in table entry [0,A] containing 2. Similarly, the remaining entries are added for *goto*.

As there are multiple entries in the parsing table, the grammar is not SLR(1). Every SLR(1) grammar is unambiguous, but there are many unambiguous grammars that are not SLR(1). The grammar given in the example is not ambiguous, but still reduce-reduce conflicts arise from the fact that the SLR parser construction method is not powerful enough. The canonical LR and LALR methods, discussed next, succeed on a larger collection of grammars. Still, there can be unambiguous grammars for which every LR parser construction method will produce a parsing *action* table with conflicts.

String parsing in LR parser: Stack implementation of shift-reduce parsing. The string parsing method is the same for all LR parsers. As all are the shift-reduce type of parsers. Two issues must be handled for implementation by the shift-reduce parser:

- To find the sub-string to be reduced in a right sentential form
- To determine what production to choose in case there are nultiple productions with that substring on the right side

One way to implement a shift-reduce parser is to use a stack to hold grammar symbols and an input buffer to hold the string w to be parsed. Initially, the stack contains the first state and thew buffer contains the string w followed by $, as shown on the right.

Stack	Buffer
0	w$

The parser proceeds until the input is accepted or the error routine is called.

In the parsing table, four entries are possible: shift, reduce, accept and error.

- **Shift:** For a shift action, *action*[S, ai]=S_n ,the next input symbol (ai) is shifted onto the top of the stack along with the next state n and the next input to be processed becomes ai+1
- **Reduce:** In a reduce action; the parser knows the right end of the handle is at the top of the stack. It must then locate the left end of the handle within the stack and decide with what non-terminal to replace the handle.
  For *action*[S,ai]= reduce A→β. The length L of the RHS of the rule is found.
  Length L= length(β). Twice L number of symbols is popped from the stack, making Sp the current top of the stack. Then, the LHS of the rule, i.e., A, is placed on the stack. Next, we push the entry of *goto*[Sp,A] onto the stack.
- **Accept:** The parser announces successful completion of parsing.
- **Error:** The parser discovers that a syntax error has occurred and invokes an error recovery routine.

For example, the *action* and *goto* entries for *Grammar 3.5* are shown in Table 3.16 and string parsing is shown in Table 3.17.

Table 3.16 SLR parsing table for *Grammar 3.5*

State	ACTION						GOTO		
	id	+	*	(	)	$	E	T	F
0	S5			S4			1	2	3
1		S6				Accept			
2		R2	S7		R2	R2			
3		R4	R4		R4	R4			
4	S5			S4			8	2	3
5		R6	R6		R6	R6			
6	S5			S4				9	3
7	S5			S4					10
8		S6			S11				
9		R1	S7		R1	R1			
10		R3	R3		R3	R3			
11		R5	R5		R5	R5			

Table 3.17 String parsing for input string id * id + id for *Grammar 3.5* using SLR parsing

Stack	Buffer	Action
0	id*id+id$	shift
0id5	*id+id$	Reduce by F→id
0F3	* id+ id$	Reduce by T→F
0T2	* id+ id$	shift
0T2*7	id+ id$	shift
0T2*7id5	+ id$	Reduce by F→id
0T2*7F10	+ id$	Reduce by T→T*F
0T2	+ id$	Reduce by E→T
0E1	+ id$	Shift
0E1+6	id$	Shift
0E1+6id5	$	Reduce by F→id
0E1+6F3	$	Reduce by T→F
0E1+6T9	$	Reduce by E→E+T
0E1	$	Accept

Example 3.22 Construct the SLR parsing table for the given grammar and show the string parsing for the given input string

Consider the grammar

S → AxB | Bc
A → yA | z
B → xB | ε

Non-terminal	FIRST	FOLLOW
S	y, z, x, c	$
A	y, z	x
B	x, ε	c,$

The input string w = "yzxx". FIRST and FOLLOW for the grammar is given on the right.

Collection of canonical sets of LR(0) items along with *goto* for the given grammar is represented in the deterministic finite automaton, as shown in Fig. 3.16. The production B→ ε, is represented by B→.

The parsing table is shown in Table 3.18 and string parsing in Table 3.19. The rules are allocated numbers, as follows:

S → AxB (1)
S → Bc (2)
A → yA (3)
A → z (4)
B → xB (5)
B → ε (6)

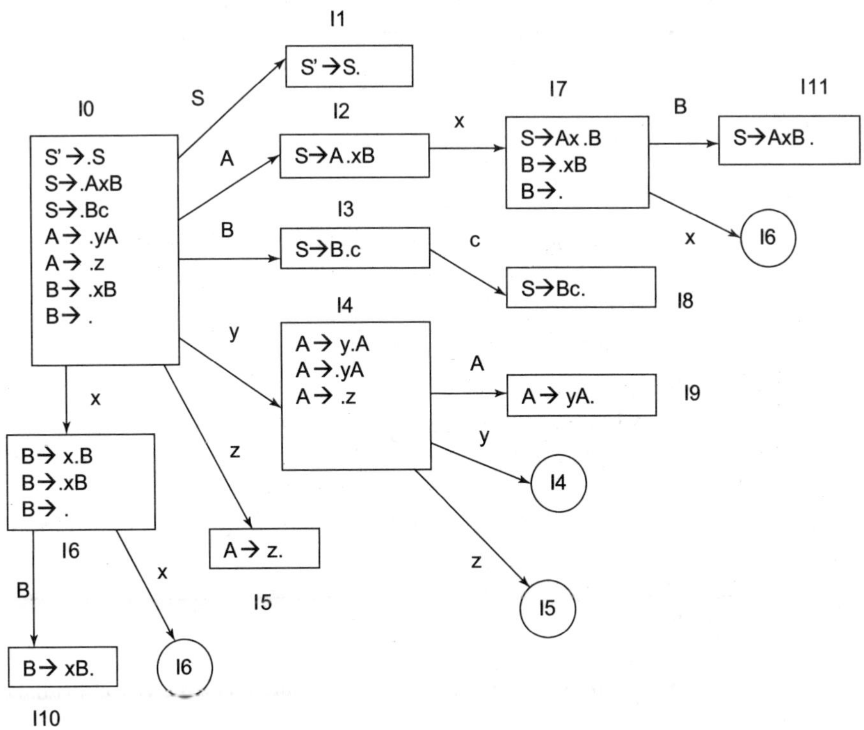

Figure 3.16 DFA for Example 3.22

Table 3.18 SLR parsing table for Example 3.22

State	ACTION					GOTO		
	x	y	z	c	$	S	A	B
0	S6	S4	S5	R6	R6	1	2	3
1					Accept			
2	S7							
3				S8				
4		S4	S5				9	
5	R4							
6	S6			R6	R6			10
7	S6			R6	R6			11
8					R2			
9	R3							
10				R5	R5			
11					R1			

Table 3.19 String parsing for w = "yzxx" for Example 3.22

Stack	Buffer	Action
0	yzxx$	Table[0, y] = S4. Shift y and cover with state 4.
0y4	zxx$	Table[4, z] = S5. Shift z and cover with state 5.
0y4z5	xx$	Table[5, x] = R4. Reduce with A→z. length(z) = L = 1. 2L = 2. Pop the top two symbols from stack z5 and place the LHS of rule A, stack contents = 0y4A; cover it by entry at [4, A] = 9, resulting in stack contents 0y4A9.
0y4A9	xx$	Table[9, x] = R3. Reduce with A→yA. length(yA) = L = 2. 2L = 4. Pop the top four symbols from stack y4A9 and place the LHS of rule A, stack contents = 0A; cover it by entry at [0, A] = 2, resulting in stack contents 0A2.
0A2	xx$	Table[2, x] = S7. Shift x and cover it with state 7.
0A2x7	x$	Table[7, x] = S6. Shift x and cover it with state 6.
0A2x7x6	$	Table[6, $] = R6. Reduce with B→ε length(ε) = L = 1. 2L = 2 Pop the top two symbols from stack x6 and place the LHS of rule B, stack contents = 0A2x7B; cover it by entry at [7, B] = 11, resulting in stack contents 0A2x7B11.

(Cont'd)

Table 3.19 (Continued)

Stack	Buffer	Action
0A2x7B11	$	Table[11, $] = R1. Reduce with S→AxB. length(yA) = L = 3. 2L = 6 Pop the top six symbols from stack A2x7B11 and place the LHS of rule S, stack contents = 0S; cover it by entry at [0, S] = 1, resulting in stack contents 0S1.
0S1	$	Table[1, $] = accept

Example 3.23 Construct the SLR parsing table for the given grammar and comment if the grammar is SLR. Also show the string parsing for the given input string.

Consider the grammar

X → iXYj | jY
Y → kY | mX | Z
Z → Zn | n

Non-terminal	FIRST	FOLLOW
X	i, j	k, m, n, j, $
Y	k, m, n	k, m, n, j, $
Z	n	k, m, n, j, $

FIRST and FOLLOW for the grammar are shown on the right. The collection of canonical sets of LR(0) items along with *goto* for the given grammar is represented in the deterministic finite automaton, as shown in Fig. 3.17. The parsing table is shown in Table 3.20. The rules are allocated numbers, as follows:

X→iXYj (1)
X→jY (2)
Y→ kY (3)
Y→ mX (4)
Y→ Z (5)
Z→ Zn (6)
Z→ n (7)

Table 3.20 Parsing table for Example 3.23

State	ACTION						GOTO		
	i	j	k	m	n	$	X	Y	Z
0	S2	S3					1		
1						Accept			
2	S2	S3					4		
3			S6	S7	S9			5	8
4			S6	S7	S9			10	8
5		R2	R2	R2	R2	R2			
6			S6	S7	S9			11	8

(Cont'd)

Table 3.20 (Continued)

State	ACTION						GOTO		
	i	j	k	m	n	$	X	Y	Z
7	S2	S3					12		
8		R5	R5	R5	S13, R5	R5			
9		R7	R7	R7	R7	R7			
10		S14							
11		R3	R3	R3	R3	R3			
12		R4	R4	R4	R4	R4			
13		R6	R6	R6	R6	R6			
14		R1	R1	R1	R1	R1			

As there are multiple entries in the table, it is not SLR, due to the existence of shift-reduce conflict. String parsing for the string "yzxx" is shown in Table 3.21. However, if the stack top contains state 8 and the buffer contains n, there will be shift-reduce conflict, as shown in string parsing for the string "ijnnj". Thus, we need to remove the shift-reduce conflict to consider solving the grammar using SLR parsing. The method for handling conflicts is discussed in Section 3.12.

Table 3.21 String parsing for w = "yzxx" for Example 3.23

Stack	Buffer	Action
0	jmjn$	Table[0, j] = S3. Shift j and cover with state 3.
0j3	mjn$	Table[3, m] = S7. Shift m and cover with state 7.
0j3m7	jn$	Table[7, j] = S3. Shift j and cover with state 3.
0j3m7j3	n$	Table[3, n] = S9. Shift n and cover with state 9.
0j3m7j3n9	$	Table[9, $] = R7. Reduce with Z→n length(n) = L = 1. 2L = 2 Pop the top two symbols from the stack and place the LHS of rule Z, resulting in stack contents 0j3m7j3Z8.
0j3m7j3Z8	$	Table[8, $] = R5. Reduce with Y→Z. length(Z) = L = 1. 2L = 2 Pop the top two symbols from the stack and place the LHS of rule Y, resulting in stack contents 0j3m7j3Y5.
0j3m7j3Y5	$	Table[5, $] = R2. Reduce with X→jY. length(jY) = L = 2. 2L = 4 Pop the top four symbols from the stack and place the LHS of rule X, resulting in stack contents 0j3m7X12.

(Cont'd)

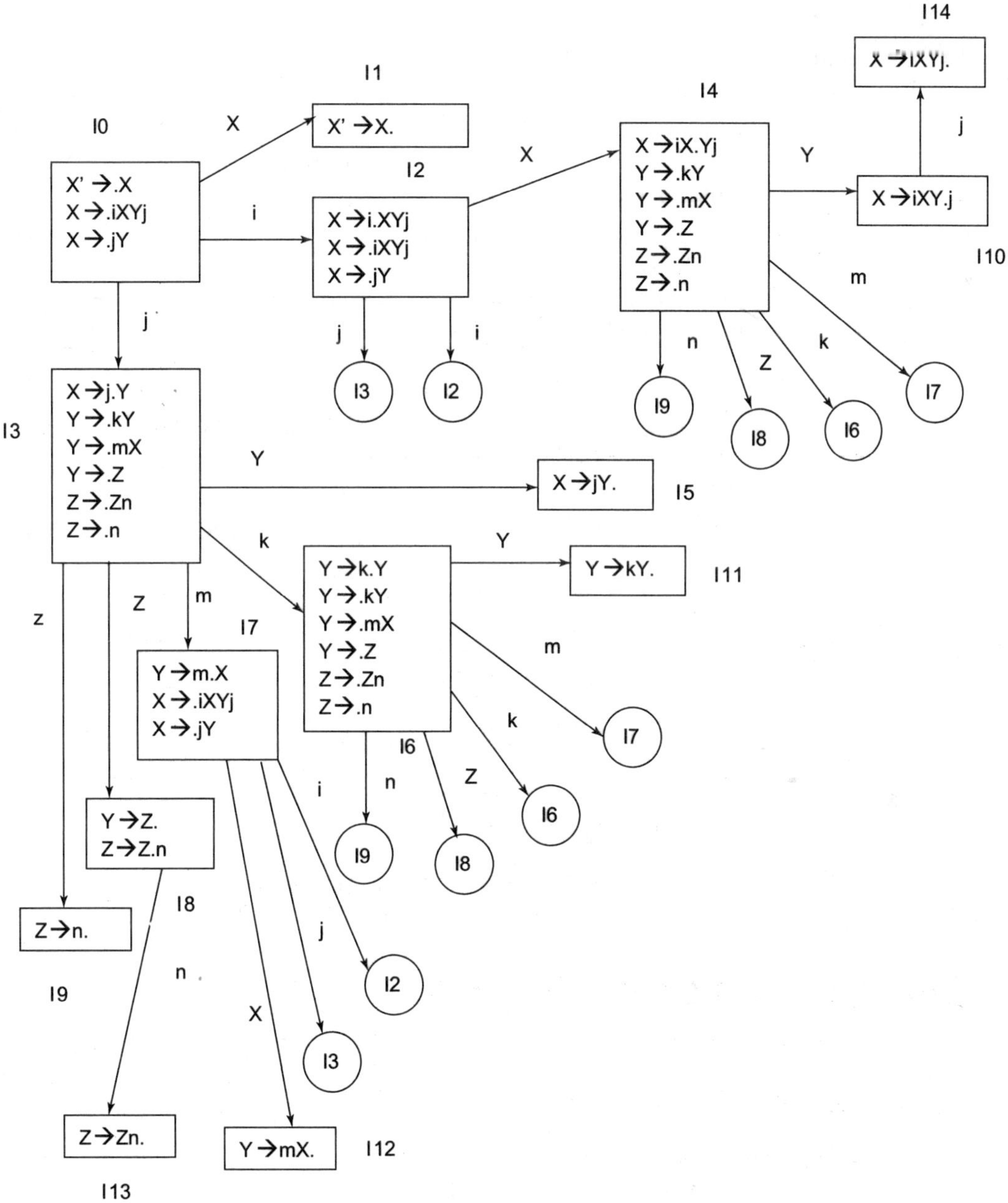

Figure 3.17 DFA for Example 3.23

Table 3.21 (Continued)

Stack	Buffer	Action
0j3m7X12	$	Table[12, $] = R4. Reduce with Y→mX. length(mX) = L = 2. 2L = 4 Pop the top four symbols from the stack and place the LHS of rule Y, resulting in stack contents 0j3Y5.
0j3Y5	$	Table[5, $] = R2. Reduce with X→jY. length(iXYj) = L = 4. 2L = 8 Pop the top eight symbols from the stack and place the LHS of rule X, resulting in stack contents 0X1.
0X1	$	Table[1, $] = accept

Table 3.22 String parsing for w = "ijnnj" for Example 3.23

Stack	Buffer	Action
0	ijnnj$	Table[0, i] = S2. Shift i and cover with state 2.
0i2	jnnj$	Table[2, j] = S3. Shift j and cover with state 3.
0i2j3	nnj$	Table[3, n] = S9. Shift n and cover with state 9.
0i2j3n9	nj$	Table[9, n] = R7.
0i2j3Z8	nj$	Table[8, n] = S13/ R7 Hence, there is a shift-reduce conflict.

3.10 Canonical LR Parser (CLR)

In the SLR method, LR(0) items were used. In canonical LR (CLR) parsing, extra information is incorporated into the state by redefining items to include a terminal symbol as a second component. These items are called LR(1) items. So, an LR(1) item is composed of two parts: the LR(0) item and the look-ahead of length one. When the parser looks ahead in the input buffer to decide whether reduction is to be carried out or not, information about the terminals will be available in the state of the parser itself. Using LR(1) items, we can produce a more powerful parser. Hence, CLR is the most powerful parser. The general form of an LR(1) item is given below:

[A →α.β, a]

where A →α.β is the production and a is the terminal or the right end marker $. An item of the form [A→ α., a] calls for reduction by A→ α only if the next input symbol is a. Thus, we must reduce by A→ α only on those input symbols for which [A→ α., a] is an LR(1) item in the state on top of the stack. The set of such 'a's will always be a subset of FOLLOW (A).

The *closure* and *goto* functions used in the SLR parser are modified to include LR(1) items instead of LR(0) items. The set of LR(1) item construction is carried out using the procedures *closure* and *goto*. The main routine is *items,* as given below:

Input: An augmented grammar G'
Output: The sets of LR(1) items valid for one or more viable prefixes of G'.

```
Procedure closure(I)
Begin
Repeat
        For each item of the form A→a.Bβ, a in I
            For each production B→γ in G' and each terminal b in FIRST(βa)
        Add B→ .γ, b to closure(I) until no more items can be added to I;
End;

Procedure goto(I, X)
Begin
        Let J be the set of items [A→X. β, a]
        such that [A→ Xβ, a] is in I
Return closure(J)
End;
Procedure items(G')
Begin
        C := {closure({S'→. S,$})};
        Repeat
            For each set of items I in C and each grammar symbol X
            such that goto(I , X) is not empty and not in C do
                Add goto(I , X) to C
        until no more sets of items can be added to C
End;
```

For example, let us consider the following grammar

S → ABd **(Grammar 3.6)**
A → Bb | c
B → d | eB

The construction of a set of LR(1) items is performed as follows.

Finding augmented grammar: Augmented grammar will be as follows:
S'→S
S → ABd
A → Bb
A→c
B → d
B→ eB

closure and *item* set construction along with *goto*.

closure ({S'→S,$}) = { S'→.S,$ // Add S productions
S → .ABd, $ // look-ahead will be FIRST($). Also add A productions
A → .Bb, d|e // look-ahead will be FIRST(Bd$)={d,e}. Also add B productions

A→.c, d|e // look-ahead will be FIRST(Bd$)={d,e}.
B → .d , b // look-ahead will be FIRST(bde)={b}.
B→ .eB , b // look-ahead will be FIRST(bde)={b}.
} = I

goto (I,X) = *closure*{A→ from aXβ,a | A→a.Xβ, a is in I})

That is, to find out *goto* from I on X, first identify all the items in I with a dot preceding X in the LR(0) section of the item.(i.e., over X), and then take this new set's *closure*. For example

goto(I, A) = *closure* ({S→ A.Bd,$ })
= { S→ A.Bd,$
B→.d , d
B→ .eB, d
}

The DFA containing all the sets of LR(1) *items* and *goto* is shown in Fig. 3.18.

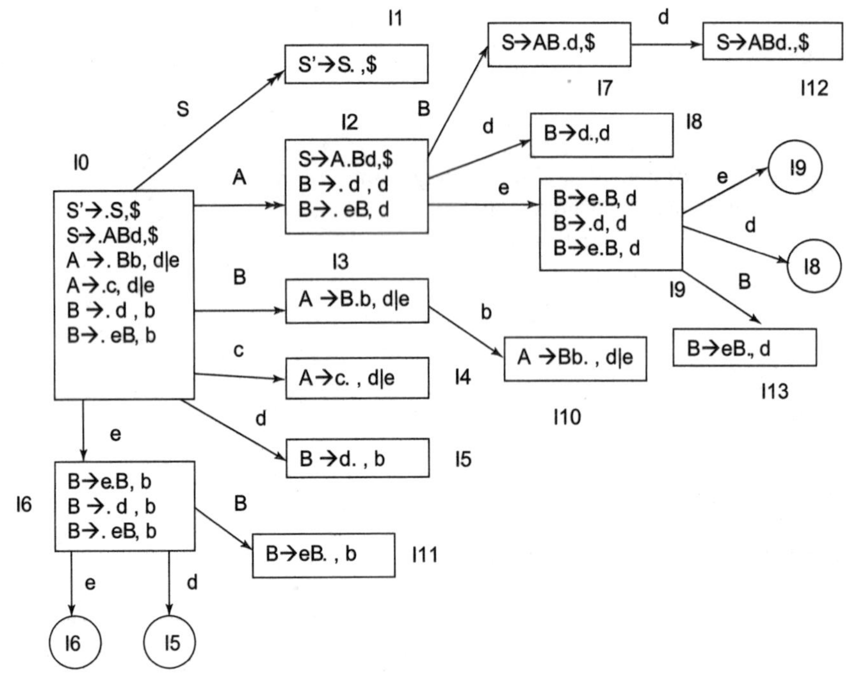

Figure 3.18 DFA for example

Construction of the canonical LR parsing table: The parsing table is constructed using the method described below.

Input: An augmented grammar G'.
Output: The canonical LR parsing table functions *action* and *goto* for G'

Method:

1. Construct C={I0,I1.........., In}, the collection of sets of LR(1) items for G'.
2. State I of the parser is constructed from Ii. The parsing actions for state I are determined as follows:
   a) If [A → α. a β, b] is in Ii, and *goto*(Ii, a) = Ij, then set *action*[i,a] to "shift j." Here, a is required to be a terminal.
   b) If [A → α., a] is in Ii, A ≠ S', then set *action*[i,a] to "reduce A → α."
   c) If [S'→S.,$] is in Ii, then set *action*[i ,$] to "accept."

   If a conflict results from these rules, the grammar is said not to be LR(1), and the algorithm is said to fail.
3. The *goto* transition for state i are determined as follows: If *goto*(Ii, A)= Ij, then *goto*[i,A]=j.
4. All entries not defined by rules (2) and (3) are "error".
5. The initial state of the parser is the one constructed from the set containing item [S'→.S, $].

Example 3.24 CLR parsing table construction

Consider *Grammar 3.6*

S → ABd
A → Bb | c
B → d | eB

Table 3.23 Parsing table for Example 3.24

State	Action					Goto		
	b	c	d	e	$	S	A	B
0		S4	S5	S6		1	2	3
1					Accept			
2			S8	S9				7
3	S10							
4			R3	R3				
5	R4							
6			S5	S6				9
7			S12					
8			R4					
9			S8	S9				
10			R2	R2				
11	R5							
12					R1			
13			R5					

Continuing the example, we will construct the parsing table for the DFA of Fig. 3.18.

- Transition from state I0 on S leads to state I1. Hence, the table entry at [0, S] = 1.
- Transition from state I0 on c leads to state I4. Hence, the table entry at [0, c] = S4.
- Production A→c. , d|e in state 4 causes a reduce entry, R3. These entries are made in the look-ahead symbols d and e. Hence, [4, d] = R3 and [4, e] = R3.

The complete CLR parsing table is shown in Table 3.23.

Example 3.25 CLR parsing table construction

Consider the given grammar

S→SA|Ba
A→Ab|c
B→aA|c

We add the production S'→.S, $ to the rules and start building state I0. S after the dot indicates that we need to add the production rules for non-terminal S. We also need to add a second parameter containing FIRST ($) as the look-ahead. So, the production rules added are:

I0= {
    S'→.S, $
    S→.SA, $
    S→.Ba,$
}

Again, due to production rule S→.SA, we must add S productions; but this time, the look-ahead will be FIRST (A$) = {c}. Adding the look-ahead symbol to the rules, we get

I0= {
    S'→.S, $
    S→.SA, $|c
    S→.Ba,$|c
}

Also, due to production S→.Ba, $|c, we must add the productions of non-terminal B. The look-ahead will be FIRST (a$c) = {a}. So, state I0 will be

I0= {
    S'→.S, $
    S→.SA, $|c
    S→.Ba,$|c
    B→.aA,a
    B→.c,a
}

The remaining LR(1) sets of items are found in a similar manner, the DFA for the given grammar having LR(1) set of items is shown in Fig. 3.19. Table 3.24 shows the CLR parsing table for the given grammar. As multiple entries are not presnt, it is a CLR grammar.

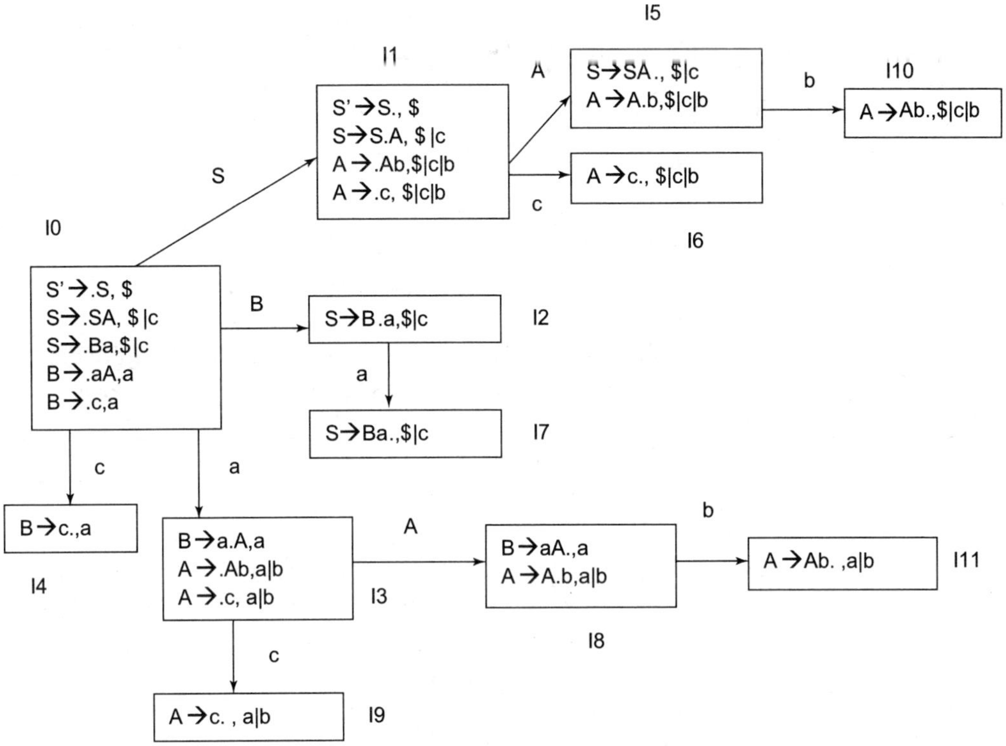

Figure 3.19 DFA for Example 3.25

Table 3.24 Parsing table for Example 3.25

State	Action				Goto		
	a	b	c	$	S	A	B
0	S3		S4		1		2
1			S6	Accept		5	
2	S7						
3			S9			8	
4	R6						
5		S10					
6		R4	R4	R4			
7			R2	R2			
8	R5	S11					
9	R4	R4					
10			R3	R3			
11	R3	R3					

Let us now give w = "acbba" as the input string and find out the result of string validation by the CLR parser, using the parsing table constructed. The string parsing is shown in Table 3.25.

Table 3.25 String parsing for CLR parser for w = "acbba" for Example 3.25

Stack	Buffer	Action
0	acbba$	Table[0, a] = S3. Shift a and cover with state 3.
0a3	cbba$	Table[3, c] = S9. Shift c and cover with state 9.
0a3c9	bba$	Table[9, b] = R4. Reduce with A→c. length(c) = L = 1. 2L = 2. Pop the top two symbols from stack c9 and place the LHS of rule A, stack contents = 0a3A; cover it by entry at [3, A] = 8, resulting in stack contents 0a3A8.
0a3A8	bba$	Table[8, b] = S11. Shift b and cover with state 11.
0a3A8b11	ba$	Table[11, b] = R3. Reduce with A→Ab. length(Ab) = L = 2. 2L = 4. Pop the top four symbols from the stack and place the LHS of rule A, stack contents = 0a3A; cover it by entry at [3, A] = 8, resulting in stack contents 0a3A8.
0a3A8	ba$	Table[8, b] = S6. Shift b and cover with state 11.
0a3A8b11	a$	Table[11, a] = R3. Reduce with A→Ab. length(Ab) = L = 2. 2L = 4. Pop the top four symbols from the stack and place the LHS of rule A, stack contents = 0a3A; cover it by entry at [3, A] = 8, resulting in stack contents 0a3A8.
0a3A8	a$	Table[8, a] = R5. Reduce with B→aA. length(aA) = L = 2. 2L = 4 Pop the top four symbols from the stack and place the LHS of rule B, stack contents = 0B; cover it by entry at [0, B] = 2, resulting in stack contents 0B2.
0B2	a$	Table[2,a] = S7. Shift a and cover it with state 2.
0B2a7	$	Table[7,$] = R2. Reduce with S→Ba. length(Ba) = L = 2. 2L = 4. Pop the top four symbols from the stack and place the LHS of rule s, stack contents = 0S; cover it by entry at [0, S] = 1, resulting in stack contents 0S1.
0S1	$	Accept. Hence, the string is declared as valid by the CLR parser.

3.11 LALR Parser

The parsing table of the CLR parser may grow very large. LALR parsing reduces the size of the CLR parsing table by merging the states with the same set of productions but with different look-aheads;

it still retains some of the power of the LR(1) look-aheads. LALR or Look-ahead LR parser is often used in practice because the tables obtained by it are considerably smaller than the canonical LR table. Most syntactic constructs of programming languages can be expressed conveniently by an LALR grammar.

The SLR and LALR tables for a grammar always have the same number of states. For the same language, the CLR parser produces a much larger number of states. SLR and LALR are much easier to construct; whereas, CLR parsers are costlier to construct.

LALR parsing table construction: An LALR(1) parsing table is built from the sets in the same way as canonical LR(1); the look-aheads determine where to place the reduce actions. If there are no states that can be merged, the LALR table will be identical to the corresponding LR(1) table and we gain nothing. However, there will be states that can be merged and the LALR table will have fewer rows than in LR.

The method to construct an LALR parsing table is given below.

Input: An augmented grammar G'
Output: LALR parsing table functions *action* and *goto*

Method:

1. Construct all canonical LR(1) states. C = $\{I_0, I_1, \ldots I_n\}$.
2. Merge those states that have same core (identical production rules) but different look-aheads. The states being merged must have the same number of items and the items the same core. The look-ahead on merged items is the union of the look-aheads of the states being merged.
3. The *action* and *goto* entries are constructed from LALR(1) states as for the canonical LR(1) parser. The *goto* table is constructed as follows:

   If J is the union of one or more sets of LR(1) items, that is, $J = I_1 \cup I_2 \cup \ldots I_k$, then the cores of *goto*(I1, X), *goto*(I2, X), . . . , *goto*(Ik, X) are the same, since $I_1, I_2, \ldots, I_k$ all have the same core. Let K be the union of all sets of items having the same core as *goto* (I1, X). Then, *goto*(J, X) = K.

Example 3.26 Combine the states of the CLR parser and show if the given grammar is LALR

Consider the grammar
S→aAd | bBd | aBe | bAe
A→c
B→c
The augmented grammar will be
S'→S, $
S→aAd, $
S→bBd, $
S→aBe, $
S→bAe, $
A→c
B→c

The CLR parsing table for the given grammar is shown in Table 3.26. States I_6 and I_9 have the same productions but different look-ahead characters. Hence, we can combine these two states; the merged parsing table called the LALR parsing table is shown in Table 3.27.

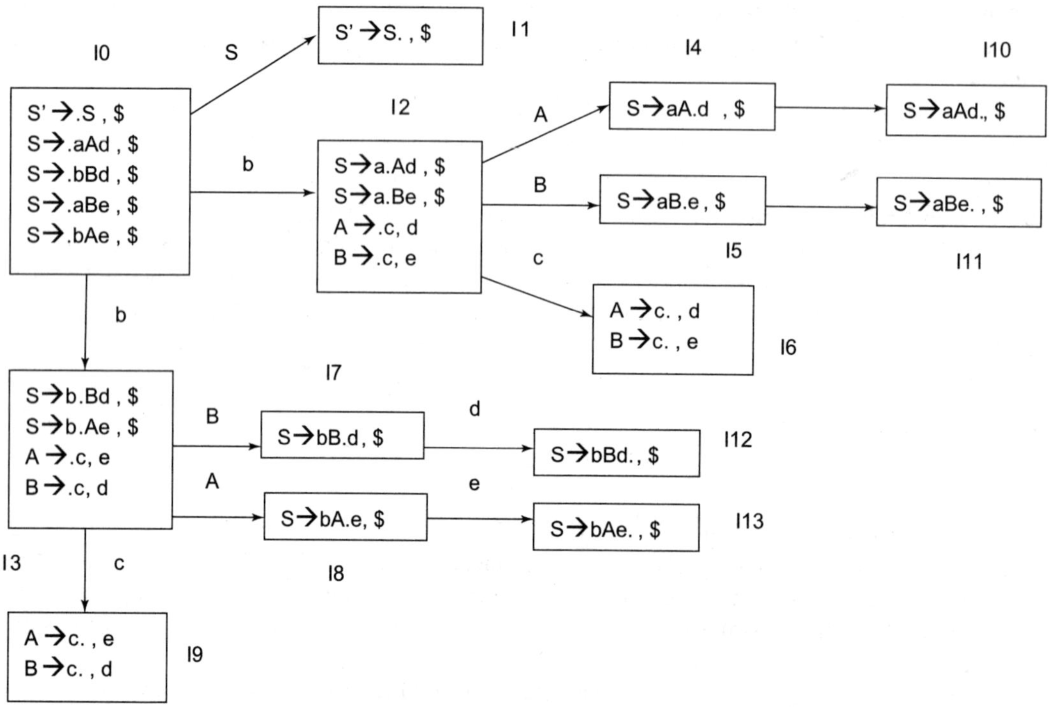

Figure 3.20 DFA for Example 3.26

Table 3.26 CLR parsing table for Example 3.26

State	a	b	c	d	e	$	S	A	B
I0	S2	S3					1		
I1						Accepted			
I2			S6					4	5
I3			S9					8	7
I4				S10					
I5					S11				
I6				R5	R6				
I7				S12					
I8					S13				
I9				R6	R5				

(Cont'd)

Table 3.26 (Continued)

State	a	b	c	d	e	$	S	A	B
I10						R1			
I11						R3			
I12						R2			
I13						R4			

Table 3.27 LALR parsing table for Example 3.26

State	a	b	c	d	e	$	S	A	B
0	S2	S3					1		
1						Accepted			
2			S69					4	5
3			S69					8	7
4				S10					
5					S11				
6-9				R5/R69	R6/R5				
7				S12					
8					S13				
10						R1			
11						R3			
12						R2			
13						R4			

As there are multiple entries, it is not LALR.

Example 3.27 LALR parser

Consider the given grammar

S→CC
C→cC | d

The augmented grammar will be
S'→S
S→C C
C→c C
C→d

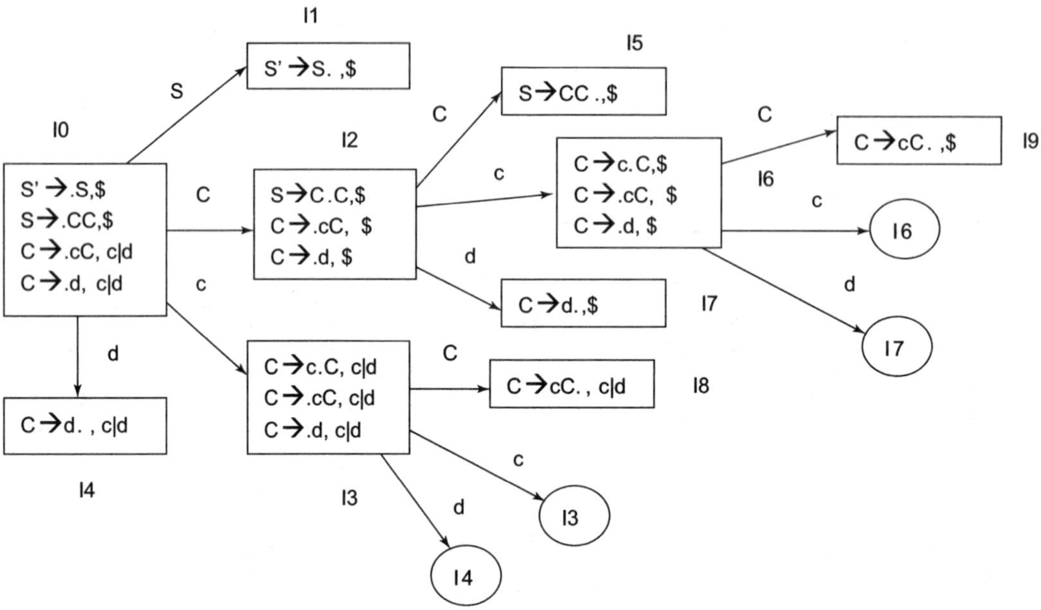

Figure 3.21 DFA for example

The CLR parsing table for the given grammar is shown in Table 3.28.

Table 3.28 The CLR parsing table for Example 3.27

State	Action			Goto	
	c	d	$	S	A
0	S3	S4		1	2
1			Accept		
2	S6	S7			5
3	S3	S4			8
4	R3	R3			
5			R1		
6	S6	S7			9
7			R3		
8	R2	R2			
9			R2		

States having the same productions but different look-aheads can be merged. Hence, we can merge state I_3–I_6, I_8–I_9 and I_4–I_7. The LALR parsing table after merging the states is shown in Table 3.29.

Table 3.29 LALR parsing table for Example 3.27

State	Action			Goto	
	c	d	$	S	A
0	S3 6	S4 7		1	2
1			Accept		
2	S3 6	S4 7			5
3 6	S3 6	S4 7			8 9
4 7	R3 6	R3 6	R36		
5			R1		
8 9	R2	R2	R2		

As multiple entries are not present in the parsing table shown in Table 3.29, the grammar is LALR.

Example 3.28 LALR parser

Consider the grammar

S→aBAc

B→Bbe | D

A→AeD| D

D→S|d

The DFA along with items in state and *goto* information is represented in Fig. 3.22. The CLR parsing table for the given grammar is shown in Table 3.30 and Table 3.31 shows the table after merging the states with the same production rules but different look-aheads, representing the LALR parsing table.

Table 3.30 CLR parsing table for Example 3.28

	a	b	c	d	e	$	S	B	A	D
0	S2						1			
1						Accept				
2	S7			S6			5	3		4
3	S13	S9		S12			11		8	10
4	R3			R3						
5	R6			R6						
6	R7			R7						
7	S7			S6			5	14		4
8			S15		S16					
9					S17					

(Cont'd)

Table 3.30 (Continued)

	a	b	c	d	e	$	S	B	A	D
10			R5							
11			R6							
12			R7							
13	S7			S6			5	18		4
14	S13	S9		S12			11		19	10
15						R1				
16	S13			S12			11			20
17	R2			R2						
18	S13			S12			11		21	10
19			S22		S16					
20			R4							
21			S23		S16					
22	R1			R1						
23			R1							

Table 3.31 LALR parser for Example 3.28

State	Action						Goto			
	a	b	c	d	e	$	S	B	A	D
0	S2-7-13						1			
1						Accept				
2-7-13	S2-7-13			R6-12			5-11	3-14-18		4
3-14-18	S2-7-13	S9		R6-12			5-11		8-19-21	10
4	R3-14-18			R3-14-18						
5-11	R6-12		R6-12	R6-12						
6-12	R6-12		R2-7-13	R6-12						
8-19-21			S15-22-23S		S16					
9					S17					
10			R5-11							
15-22-23	R1		R1	R1		R1				
16	S2-7-13			S6-12			5-11			
17	R2-7-13			R2-7-13						
20			R4							

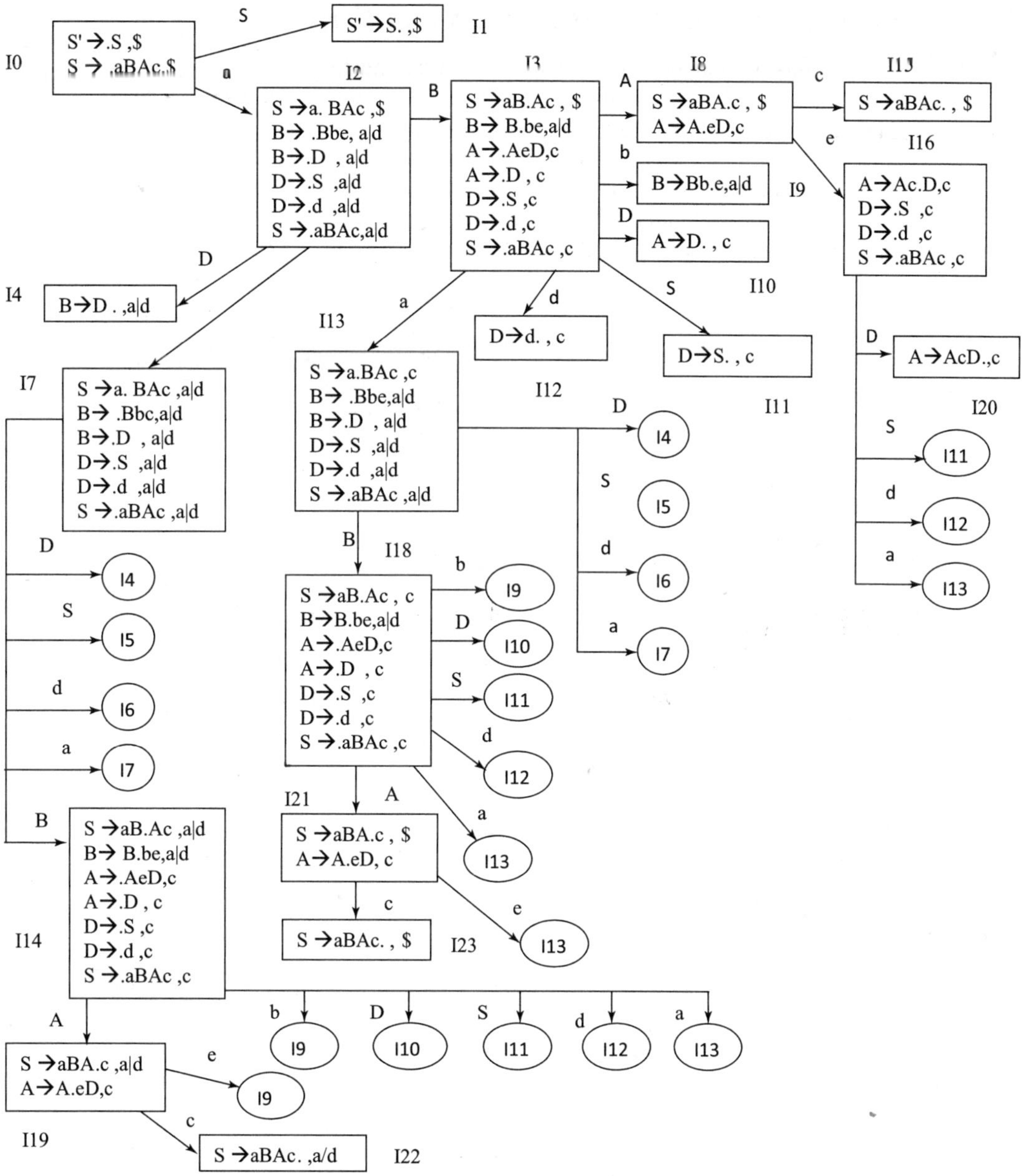

Figure 3.22 DFA for Example 3.28

3.12 Ambiguous Grammars in LR Parsing

There are no ambiguous grammars in LR. They will not belong to SLR, CLR or LALR, but some ambiguous grammars are useful for specifying language. They are often simpler, as well. To deal with ambiguous grammar, we use precedence and association of operators.

Example 3.29 Handling ambiguous grammars in SLR parsing
Let us consider an ambiguous grammar, $E \rightarrow E + E \mid E * E \mid (E) \mid a$
The DFA for the grammar is shown in Fig. 3.23 and the parse table in Table 3.32.

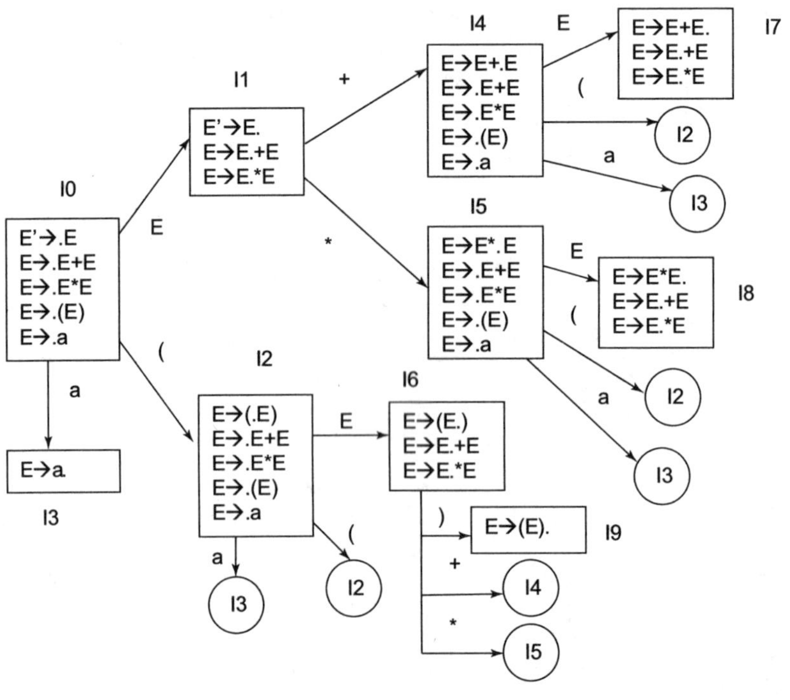

Figure 3.23 DFA for Example 3.29

Let us consider strings to find the conflicts and how we can resolve them.
Case 1: For string a + a + a

Stack	Buffer	Action
0	a+a+a$	Shift. [0, a] = S3
0a3	+a+a$	Reduce by E→a. [3, +] = R4
0E1	+a+a$	Shift. [1, +] = S4
0E1+4	a+a$	Shift. [4, a] = S3
0E1+4a3	+a$	Reduce by E→a. [3, +] = R4
0E1+4E7	+a$	[7, +] = S4, R1

Table 3.32 SLR parsing table for Example 3.29

Sate	Action						*goto*
	a	+	*	(	)	**$**	**E**
0	S3			S2			1
1		S4	S5			Accept	
2	S3			S2			6
3		R4	R4		R4	R4	
4	S3			S2			7
5	S3			S2			8
6		S4	S5		S9		
7		S4,R1	S5,R1		R1	R1	
8		S4,R2	S5,R2		R2	R2	
9		R3	R3		R3	R3	

For stack contents 0E1+4E7 and buffer contents +a$, there are two options: reduce by E→E+E or shift + onto the stack. For left association, we use reduce, and for right association, we use shift. We will use now the left association; hence the table entry [7, +] = R1.

Case 2: For string a * a * a

Stack	Buffer	Action
0	a*a*a$	Shift. [0, a] = S3
0a3	*a*a$	Reduce by E→a. [3, *] = R4
0E1	*a*a$	Shift. [1, *] = S5
0E1*5	a*a$	Shift. [5, a] = S3
0E1*5a3	*a$	Reduce by E→a. [3, *] = R4
0E1*5E8	*a$	[8, *] = S5, R2

For stack contents 0E1*5E8 and buffer contents *a$, there are two options: reduce by E→E*E or shift * onto the stack. For left association, we use reduce, and for right association, we use shift. We will now use the left association; hence the table entry [8,*] = R2.

Case 3: For string a + a * a

Stack	Buffer	Action
0	a+a*a$	Shift. [0, a] = S3
0a3	+a*a$	Reduce by E→a. [3, +] = R4
0E1	+a*a$	Shift. [1, +] = S5
0E1+4	a*a$	Shift. [4, a] = S3
0E1+4a3	*a$	Reduce by E→a. [3, *] = R4
0E1+4E7	*a$	[7, *] = S5, R1

For stack contents 0E1+4E7 and buffer contents *a$, there are two options: reduce by E→E+E or shift * onto the stack. For precedence of the + operator, we use reduce, and for precedence of the * operator, we use shift. We will now give precedence to * over +. Hence, the table entry at [7,*] = S5.
Case 4: For string a * a + a

Stack	Buffer	Action
0	a*a+a$	Shift. [0, a] = S3
0a3	*a+a$	Reduce by E→a. [3, *] = R4
0E1	*a+a$	Shift. [1, *] = S5
0E1*a5	a+a$	Shift. [5, a] = S3
0E1*a5a3	+a$	Reduce by E→a. [3, +] = R4
0E1*a5E8	+a$	[8, +] = S4, R2

For stack contents 0E1*a5E8 and buffer contents +a$, there are two options: reduce by E→E*E or shift + onto the stack. For precedence of the * operator, we use reduce, and for precedence of the + operator, we use shift. We will now give precedence to * over +. Hence, the table entry at [8,+] = R2.

After giving precedence to the * operator over the + operator and using left association, the parsing table without conflicts will be as shown (Table 3.33).

Table 3.33 Parsing table after conflict removal

Sate	Action						*goto*
	a	+	*	(	)	$	E
0	S3			S2			1
1		S4	S5			Accept	
2	S3			S2			6
3		R4	R4		R4	R4	
4	S3			S2			7
5	S3			S2			8
6		S4	S5		S9		
7		R1	S5		R1	R1	
8		R2	R2		R2	R2	
9		R3	R3		R3	R3	

3.13 Parser Conflicts

LR parsers are shift-reduce type of parsers. In general, ambiguous grammars cause conflicts, but there can be un-ambiguous grammars that may cause conflicts. Two types of conflicts can occur in LR parsers:

1. **Shift-reduce (SR) conflict:** Here, the parser cannot decide whether to shift or to reduce. If in an LR parsing table, there is an entry for shift as well as reduce in the same cell, then there is a conflict.

- *SR conflict exists in state I of the SLR parser* if
  - LR(0) items of I contain the production rule of the form $A \rightarrow \alpha.a\beta$ causing a shift-entry on [I, a], and
  - There is a production rule $B \rightarrow \gamma.$ that will cause a reduce entry and FOLLOW (B) contains terminal 'a', leading to a reduce entry at 'a'.
- *SR conflict exists in state I of the CLR parser* if
  - LR(1) items of I contain the production rule of the form $A \rightarrow \alpha.a\beta$, causing a shift entry on [I, a], and
  - There is a production rule $B \rightarrow \gamma.$ that will cause a reduce entry and which contains a terminal 'a' as the look-ahead character, leading to a reduce entry at 'a'.
- *SR conflict in the LALR parser*
  - The condition for conflict is the same as in the CLR parser, but a shift-reduce conflict cannot exist in a merged set unless the conflict was already present in one of the original LR(1) sets. When merging two sets, they must have the same core items (production rules). If the merged set has a configuration that shifts on a and another that reduces on a, both configurations must have been present in the original sets, and at least one of those sets must have had a conflict already.

    Suppose there is a conflict on look-ahead a because there is an item $[A \rightarrow \alpha., a]$ calling for a reduction by $A \rightarrow \alpha$, and there is another item $[B \rightarrow \beta.a\gamma, b]$ calling for a shift. Then, some set of items from which the union was formed contains item $[A \rightarrow \alpha., a]$ and since the cores of all these states are the same, it must have an item $[B \rightarrow \beta.a\gamma, c]$ for some c. However, this state has the same shift/reduce conflict on a, and the grammar was not LR(1). Thus, the merging of states with common cores can never produce a shift-reduce conflict that was not present in one of the original states.

2. **Reduce-reduce conflict:** Here, the parser knows it must reduce, but cannot decide which production to use.
   - *RR conflict exists in state I of the SLR parser* if
     - LR(0) items of I contain the production rule of the form $A \rightarrow \alpha.$, causing a reduce entry and another production $B \rightarrow \gamma.$, causes another reduce entry, with FOLLOW(A) $\cap$ FOLLOW(B) $\neq \varnothing$
   - *RR conflict exists in state I of the CLR parser* if
     - LR(1) items of I contain the production rule of the form $A \rightarrow \alpha.,b$ and $B \rightarrow \gamma., b$ where the look-ahead is not disjointed causing reduce entries in b.
   - *RR conflict in the LALR parser*
     - Reduce-reduce conflict can arise in an LALR parser after merging the states of CLR parser, even if there was no conflict in the CLR parser.
     - If the states of the CLR parser are:

       $A \rightarrow \alpha.\ , a$
       $B \rightarrow \gamma., b$
       and
       $A \rightarrow \alpha.\ , b$
       $B \rightarrow \gamma., a$

       Then, the merged state will be
       $A \rightarrow \alpha.\ , a|b$
       $B \rightarrow \gamma., a|b$
       Hence, there is a RR conflict.

3.14 Handling Ambiguous Grammars in LALR Parser

Let us consider the dangling ambiguity in the if-else construct.

stmt → if *expr* then *stmt*
  | if *expr* then *stmt* else *stmt*
  | other

Simplifying the representation, we get S→ iS | iSeS | o

This is an ambiguous grammar. Let us consider the Yacc tool that generates the LALR parser. We consider the Yacc program and show how it handles ambiguous grammars.
The Yacc program for if-else grammar is as follows:

```
%% S: 'i' S
     | 'i' S 'e' S
     | 'o';
%%
yylex() {
     int c;
     while ((c = getchar()) == ' ');      /* skip blanks */
     if (c == '\n') return 0; /* convenient for interactive use */
     return c;
     }

yyerror(char *s) {
     printf("%s\n", s);
     }
main()   {
     if (yyparse() == 0) printf("ok\n");
     }
```

Yacc informs the user that this grammar has one shift-reduce conflict. By default, Yacc resolves shift/reduce conflicts in favour of shift. However, we may not always prefer shift over reduce, So, in Yacc, we can specify the precedence. Example 3.30 shows how to give precedence to any operator.

Example 3.30 Giving precedence in Yacc to handle ambiguous grammars
Consider the grammar E→ E + E | E ∗ E | (E) | a. The Yacc program for ambiguous expression grammar will be

```
%%
E:    E '+' E
    | E '*' E
    | '(' E ')'
    | 'a'
    ;
%%
yylex() {
    int c;
```

```
        while ((c=getchar()) == ' ');
        if (c == '\n') return 0;
        return c;
}
yyerror(char *s) {
        printf("%s\n", s);
}
main() {
        if (yyparse() == 0) printf("ok\n");
}
```

There are four shift-reduce conflicts. Yacc provides a simple mechanism for specifying the associativity and precedence of tokens. The program after specifying precedence and associativity is as follows:

```
%left '+'
%left '*'
%%
E:      E '+' E
        | E '*' E
        | '(' E ')'
        | 'a'
        ;
%%
yylex() {
        int c;
        while ((c=getchar()) == ' ');
        if (c == '\n') return 0;
        return c;
}
yyerror(char *s) {
        printf("%s\n", s);
}
main() {
        if (yyparse() == 0) printf("ok\n");
}
```

3.15 Selection of Parsing Algorithm

The choice of parsing technique to use in a compiler depends on the economic and implementation view points. The cost of development of the compiler is one such factor. It depends on the experience with a particular technique and availability of a program to construct the parser. The parser should work deterministically under all circumstances and parse correct programs in a time linearly dependent upon program length, avoiding backtracking and the need to unravel parser actions.

LL and LR algorithms are special cases of deterministic techniques that recognise a syntactic error at the first symbol (t) that cannot be the continuation of a correct program; other algorithms may not discover the error until attempting to reduce the simple phrase in which t occurs. Moreover, LR(k) grammars comprise the largest class whose sentences can be parsed using deterministic pushdown automata.

The availability of a parser generator affects the choice between the LL and LR algorithms. If one has such a generator at one's disposal, then the technique it implements is given preference. If no parser generator is available, then an LL algorithm should be selected because the LL conditions are substantially easier to verify by hand. Also, a transparent method for obtaining the parser from the grammar exists for LL but not for LR algorithms.

By using this approach, recognisers for large grammars can be programmed relatively easily by hand. LR algorithms apply to a larger class of grammars than LL algorithms, because they postpone the decision about the applicable production until the reduction takes place. The main advantage of LR algorithms is that they permit more latitude in the representation of the grammar. However, this advantage may be neutralised if distinct structure connections that frustrate deferment of a parsing decision must be introduced.

3.16 Comparison of LR Parsers

The SLR parser is the most simple and easy to implement, but it is not powerful enough for most grammars, that is, SLR is too restrictive in recognition power. CLR is the most powerful parser, having linear parsing cost, but it is complex and computationally expensive in parser generation due to high time and space costs. The CLR parser produces large tables. LALR is a well-balanced parser and is considered powerful enough to cover most programming languages and efficient enough in practice, but it may contain reduce-reduce conflicts and thus lead to a lot of effort in grammar redesign. The LALR(1) parsing machine is smaller than the CLR parsers. Error detection is immediate in CLR but not in LALR. Errors are discovered when a slot in the *action* table is blank. Canonical LR(1) parsers detect and report error as soon as it is encountered. LALR(1) parsers may perform a few reductions after the error has been encountered, and then detect it, since LALR parsers are generated by state merging. Therefore, LR(1) detects error earlier. Though the time and space complexity in LALR and CLR is greater, efficient methods exist for parser construction.

3.17 Applications of the LR Parser

- LR parsing is generally used for the parsing process in compilers based on CFG.
- LR parsing can be used for parsing in natural languages. Besides this, LR parsers can be used as the index of approximate pattern matching in applications like information retrieval, speech recognition, etc.
- Error correction in natural language processing is possible because it has the ability to predict the next character in the sentence.
- Equation Solver can be implemented by taking equations as input, which the parser will parse.
- It can be used in database systems for query processing by parsing the input query.

3.18 LR Parser in Natural Language Processing

LR parsers are the most widely used because they are deterministic parsers that scan the input string and can detect errors at an early stage. However, standard LR parsers can handle only a subclass of

CFG, called LR grammars. Natural language processing may require more powerful grammatical structures that are not allowed by LR grammars. There may be some features such as prepositional phrase attachment which are inherently ambiguous, leading to a non-LR parsing table.

Generalised LR (GLR) parsing can be used for natural language grammars. The GLR parsing algorithm for CFGs, introduced by Tomita in 1986, is a polynomial-time implementation of non-deterministic LR parsing. It uses a graph-structured stack to represent the contents of the non-deterministic parser. It represents all the contents of the stack for all possible branches of computation in a single computation step. It can handle general CFGs while retaining the advantages of standard LR parsing. It has been specifically designed for practical parsing tasks in computational linguistics. GLR branches into multiple stacks for different parse options, eventually disregarding the rest and only keeping one.

Another extension of the LR parser is MLR. It can handle multiple defined entries using a dynamic programming method. When an input sentence is ambiguous, the MLR parser produces all possible parse trees without parsing any part of the input sentence more than once in the same way. The MLR parser and its parsing table generator have been implemented at Carnegie-Mellon University.

Summary

- The syntax analyser is also called the parser.
- Syntax refers to the ways symbols may be combined to create well-formed sentences that are allowed in that language.
- The syntax of a programming language can be specified using grammars.
- The syntax anlayser uses CFG.
- The parser accepts tokens from the lexical analyser and validates that the tokens have been grouped according to the syntax of the programming language. For valid syntax, the syntax tree is generated as output, while invalid syntax is reported as error.
- A grammar that produces more than one parse tree for the same string is said to be an ambiguous grammar.
- Parsing techniques: top-down and bottom-up.
- A non-predictive top-down parser is also called a backtracking parser. It cannot predict the production rule that must be applied during expansion of a non-terminal.
- In predictive top-down parsing, the production rule that must be used for expansion of the non-terminal can be predicted.
- LL(1) is a predictive top-down parser having a look-ahead of one.
- FIRST and FOLLOW information is needed for prediction in the LL(1) parser.
- Recursive predictive parsers require a lot of memory.
- Grammar with left recursion and/or left factoring is not LL(1).
- Grammar of the form $A \rightarrow \alpha | \beta$ is LL(1) if the following conditions are satisfied: FIRST(α) $\cap$ FIRST(β) = ϕ; and FIRST(α) $\cap$ FOLLOW(A) = ϕ and FIRST (β) $\cap$ FOLLOW(A) = ϕ.
- Operator precedence parser, SLR, CLR and LALR are bottom-up parsers.
- To handle ambiguous grammars, precedence and association rules are used.
- Shift-reduce and reduce-reduce conflicts can occur in LR parsers.
- The SLR parser is the most simple and easy-to-implement parser.
- CLR is the most powerful parser with linear parsing cost.
- Canonical LR(1) parsers detect and report the error as soon as it is encountered.
- All LL languages are LR languages, but there are more LR languages than LL languages.

Exercises

Review Questions

Fill in the blanks with appropriate answers:

1. The production rule S→aBbc is a type __________ grammar.
2. The top-down parser uses __________ type of derivation.
3. S → SS | (S) | b is not suitable for predictive parsing because the grammar is __________.
4. Shift-reduce parsers are __________ (top-down or bottom-up parsers).
5. In LL(1), the first L stands for __________, the second L stands for __________ and (1) is the __________.
6. Look-ahead LR is __________.
7. S-R conflict is present in LALR if and only if __________.
8. The maximum number of reduce moves required by a bottom-up parser for a grammar with no epsilon and unit production to parse a string with n tokens is __________.
9. The LALR parsing table is created by merging the states of the __________ parser.
10. Yacc is a __________.

Answers: 1. Type 2 2. Leftmost 3. Left-recursive 4. Bottom-up parser 5. Left to right scanning of input, RMD and look-ahead 6. LALR 7. LR parser for grammar has S-R conflict 8. N-1 9. SLR 10. Parser generator

State whether true or false:

1. The syntax analyser will create a parse tree representation as output.
2. Regular expressions are type 0 grammar.
3. LL(1) is a shift-reduce parser.
4. Regular expressions are closed under union, intersection and Kleene Star.
5. SLR and LALR generate the same number of states.
6. The recursive descent parser is a bottom-up parser.
7. Given grammar as LL(1),
   S → C C
   C → c C | d
8. SLR is more powerful than LALR.
9. PDA is used by the parser.
10. Left-recursive grammars are LL(1).

Answers: 1. True 2. True 3. False 4. True 5. True 6. False 7. True 8. False 9. True 10. False.

Practice Questions

1. Consider the given grammar and find the leftmost derivation and rightmost derivation for the string "cddbbbd".
   S→AAB | c
   A→Bb | ab | b
   B→cdA | d | Sa
2. Using a non-predictive backtracking parser, show if the strings "cda" and "acd" are valid for the given grammar.

A→BC | DC
B→ cd | c
C→a | b
D→e | f

3. Find FIRST and FOLLOW for the given grammar:
A→Bi | h
B→ejA | Ck | ε
C→m | n | Ap | ε
4. Construct the LL(1) parsing table for the grammar in Q3. Also show the string validation process for the input string "ejhpkii".
5. Construct the LL(1) parsing table for the given grammar:
P→PS
S→aU | ac | U
U→e | f
6. Construct the LL(1) parsing table for the given grammar:
E→RS
S→+E | ε
R→(E) | int A
A→*R | ε
7. Consider the LL(1) parsing table of Example 3.16. Show whether the following strings will be accepted by the grammar or not:
(i) Australia won the toss
(ii) won Steve played
8. Find the handle and viable prefix for the string "aabb" for the grammar
S→CC
C→aC | b
9. Generate the SLR, CLR and LALR parsing tables for the given grammar and comment on the size of parsing tables.
S' → S
S → L = R | R
L → *R | id
R → L
10. Generate the SLR and CLR parsing tables for the given grammar
A→XYZ
X→yX | zZ
Y→aZ
Z→bA | ZXc
11. Can any ambiguous grammar be SLR? Consider the ambiguous grammar given and find the type of conflicts that arise in the SLR parser. Also suggest how to remove the conflicts.
S→A
S→B
S→AB
A→aA
B→bB
A→c
B→c

12. Suggest data structures that can be used to implement LL and LR parsers.
13. Generate the CLR parsing table for
    S→id=E
    E→E*E
    E→(E)
    E→E+E
    E→id
    Is merging of states possible. If yes, merge the states and produce the LALR parsing table.
14. Generate the SLR parsing table for:
    A→ L=E
    E→(E) | E+E | L
    L→elist] | id
    elsit→elist,E | id[E

Programming Questions

1. Write a program to produce RMD for the input grammar and input string.
2. Write a program to find LR(0) items of a given grammar.
3. Write a program to generate the SLR parsing table for a specific grammar. Use suitable data structures to store the parsing table. Also assume an input string and show the string validation.
4. Take as input the states of the CLR parser. Find if the states of the parser can be merged. If yes, then merge the states and construct the LALR parsing table.
5. Consider a grammar and prove that the grammar is not LL(1), without constructing a parsing table.
6. Input: Parsing table for any grammar [States, Terminals and Non-Terminals]
   Process: Scan operation on the parsing table
   Output: To decide
   a. Number of positions in the parsing table [blank entries] which can be replaced by error entry.
   b. Write a method/function/subroutine which will be invoked for expression grammar, for the strings starting with OPERATOR. For example, +ab should be converted into a + b.
7. Input: Parsing table for any grammar [States, Terminals and Non-Terminals]
   Process: Scan operation on the parsing table
   Output: To decide
   a. Which rules of the grammar takes least time in reduction? [One or more rules may take the same time]
   b. Which rules of grammar are frequently used in string derivation?
   c. From the parsing table, find out the possible start symbols of a valid string.
   d. How many non-terminals in grammar have the same FOLLOW set or at least some component common in the FOLLOW set.
8. Input: Parsing table for any grammar [States, terminals and non-terminals]
   A string of characters
   Process: Perform string parsing using STACK
   Output: To decide
   a. Whether the given string is a palindrome using STACK contents
   b. Whether the given string is an ODD- or EVEN-sized palindrome

4 Syntax-directed Translation and Semantic Analysis

Objectives

- To introduce the semantic analysis phase of the compiler
- To discuss syntax-directed definitions and translations
- To determine semantic rules and their evaluation order
- To describe S-attributed and L-attributed definitions
- To discuss the construction of syntax trees and DAG
- To discuss types, type expressions, the type system and the type checker

4.1 Introduction to Semantic Analysis and Type Checking

A compiler should check the syntactic and semantic conventions of the source language. The semantics of the source code is verified after the syntax is checked. **Semantic analysis** validates the meaning of the code by checking that the sequence of tokens is meaningful and correct, is associated with the correct type and is consistent and correct in the way in which control structures and data types are used. The semantics of the language is validated with the help of semantic rules.

Semantic analysis is not always a separate phase in a compiler. It is usually combined with other phases like the parser. Implementing semantic actions is conceptually simpler in recursive descent parsing because these actions are simply added to the recursive procedures. Implementing semantic actions in a table-driven parser requires the addition of a third type of variable to the productions and the necessary software routines to process it. The translation of languages is guided by context-free grammars (CFGs). Semantic rules can be attached to grammar to perform type checking. These **semantic rules** are a collection of procedures called at appropriate times by the parser as the grammar requires. Semantic rules can be applied to the grammar by attaching attributes to the CFG. The application of semantic rules and translations are discussed in Sections 4.2 through 4.7.

After semantic analysis, some sort of representation of the program is produced: either object code or an intermediate representation. One-pass compilers will generate object code without using an intermediate representation; code generation is part of the semantic actions performed during parsing. Other compilers produce an intermediate representation during semantic analysis; most often, it will be an abstract syntax tree or quadruples.

Semantic analysis typically involves type checking, label checking, uniqueness checking, name-related checking and control flow checks. In **type checking**, data types are checked to ensure that they are used in consistence with their definition. A compiler must report an error if an operator is applied to incompatible operands. **Label checking** involves checking if the referenced labels exist in a program. In many situations, objects may need to be defined exactly once; this must be ensured by the compiler. Sometimes, the same name can appear two or more times. For example, a loop or block may have a name that appears at the beginning and end of the construct. The compiler must check that the same name is used in both places. In **flow control checking**, the control structures are validated. All these checks are called **static checks**.

Semantics can be static or dynamic. The **static semantics** of a language is related to the meaning of the program that can be checked at compile time. **Dynamic semantics** refers to the meaning of expressions, statements and other program units that can only be checked at run-time.

Most static checks can be implemented using simple techniques and can be folded into other activities. For example, as the information about a name is entered into a symbol table, it can be checked if the name is unique. Many compilers, like those of Pascal, combine static checking and intermediate code generation with parsing. However, for more complex languages, it may be convenient to have a separate type-checking pass between parsing and intermediate code generation. Figure 4.1 shows the position of type checking, and in the next section, type checking is described. Type checking and related concepts are discussed from Section 4.8.

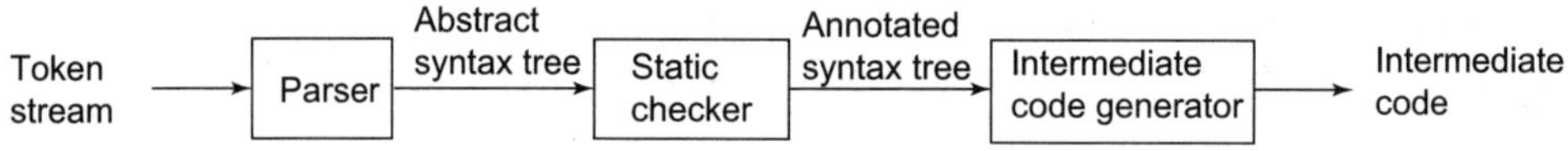

Figure 4.1 Position of type checking

4.2 Attributes and Specification of Semantic Rules

CFGs are used to specify the syntactic structure of the language, as seen in the syntax analysis phase. Semantic analysis can be performed by adding some information to the existing grammar. So, the CFG is extended by associating a set of attributes with the grammar symbols and a set of semantic rules with the production. Semantic rules specify how the attributed values of the grammar symbols of the production are manipulated.

Two notations are used to associate semantic rules with productions: syntax-directed definitions and translation schemes. **Syntax-directed definitions** are high-level specifications for translations; which hide many implementation details from the user. The user need not specify the order in which translation takes place. Whereas, **translation schemes** indicate the order in which semantic rules are to be evaluated.

Both in syntax-directed definitions and in translation schemes, the input token stream is parsed, the parse tree is built, and then the tree is traversed as needed to evaluate the semantic rules at the parse-tree nodes. The order is as follows:

Input string → Parse tree →Dependency graph → Evaluation order of semantic rules

Evaluation of the semantic rules comprises generating code, saving information in the symbol table, issuing error messages and translating the token stream.

Semantic rules set up dependencies between attributes that will be represented by a graph called the dependency graph. In a **dependency graph**, an evaluation order for the semantic rules is derived. Evaluation of the semantic rules defines the values of the attributes at the nodes in the parse tree for a given input string. A parse tree showing the values of the attributes at each node is called an **annotated parse tree** or **decorated parse tree**.

An attribute can represent a string, number, type or memory location. The value of an attribute at a parse-tree node is defined by a semantic rule associated with the production used at that node.

Some cases of syntax-directed definitions can be implemented without explicitly constructing a graph showing dependencies between attributes, in a single pass by evaluating semantic rules during parsing.

Attribute grammar: An attribute grammar is an extension of a CFG that is used to describe features of a programming language that cannot be described in Backus Normal Form (BNF) or can be described in BNF only with great difficulty. Attribute grammar is a special form of CFG where some additional information, called attribute, is appended to one or more non-terminals to provide context-sensitive information for performing semantic analysis or intermediate code generation or both. An attribute grammar is a syntax-directed definition in which the functions in semantic rules cannot have side effects. It provides semantics to CFG and can help specify the syntax and semantics of a programming language. Each attribute has a well-defined domain of values, such as integer, float, character, string, and expressions. Attribute grammar (when viewed as a parse tree) can pass values or information among the nodes of a tree.

Consider the statement

$$E \rightarrow E + T \; \{E.value = E.value + T.value\}$$

Grammar production is added to the information represented on the right side of the production rule inside { and }, that is, the semantic rule that specifies how the grammar should be interpreted. Here, the values of non-terminals E and T are added and the result is copied to the non-terminal E.

Semantic attributes may be assigned values from their domain at the time of parsing and evaluated at the time of assignment or conditions. Based on the way the attributes obtain their values, they can be broadly divided into two categories: synthesized attributes and inherited attributes.

Synthesized attributes: The attributes that obtain values from the attribute values of their child nodes are called synthesized attributes. Consider the following production:

$$E \rightarrow E + T$$

The parent node E obtains its value from its child nodes, E and T. Synthesized attributes do not take values from their parent nodes or any sibling nodes. In the parse tree, these attributes are passed up the tree. For example, consider the attribute grammar for evaluating the values of the expressions:

Production	**Semantic rules**
L → E	print(E.*val*)
E → E1 + T	E.*val* = E1.*val* + T.*val*
E → T	E.*val* = T.*val*
T → T * F	T.*val* = T1.*val* * F.*val*
T → F	T.*val* = F.*val*
F → *digit*	F.*val* = *digit.lexval*

The token *digit* has a synthesized attribute *lexval*, whose value is assumed to be supplied by the lexical analyser. The rule L→ E is only a procedure that prints the value of the arithmetic expression generated by E. This rule defines a dummy attribute for the non-terminal L.

The parse tree shown in Fig. 4.2 uses synthesized attributes to compute the values at each node. The attributes added to the parse tree make it an annotated parse tree. It takes as input an expression 5 + 3 and prints the value 8. The values are computed at any node based on the child nodes, from left to right and bottom to top. Consider the leftmost node, F. The value F.*val* is *digit.lexval*. The value of *digit* is 5, so F.*val* is 5.

Inherited attributes: In contrast to synthesized attributes, inherited attributes take values from parents and/or siblings. For example, if the production rule is S→ ABC, A can obtain values from S, B and C. B can take values from S, A and C. Likewise, C can take values from S, A and B. In

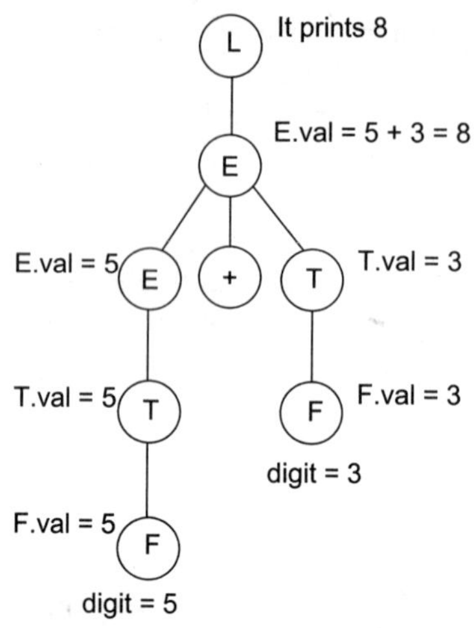

Figure 4.2 Annotated parse tree

the parse tree, these attributes are passed down. Inherited attributes are convenient for expressing the dependency of a programming language construct on the context in which it appears. A dependency graph is a directed graph that shows the interdependencies among the attributes. For example, consider the attribute grammar for evaluating the values of the following expressions:

Production	**Semantic rules**
D → TL	L.*type* = T.*type*
T → int	T.*type* = int
T → real	T.*type* = real

L → L, *id*	L.*type* = L.*type* // L depends on its left child
	enter(*id.entry*, L.*type*)

L → *id*	enter(*id.entry*, L.*type*)

The annotated parse tree for input string real "a, b, c" is shown in Fig. 4.3.

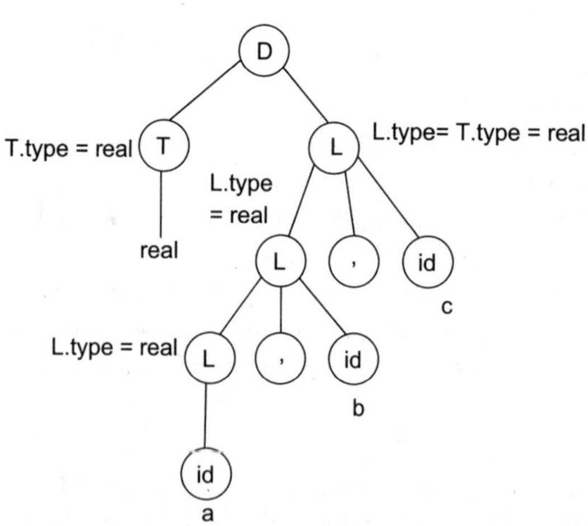

Figure 4.3 Parse tree with inherited attribute at each node labeled L

The semantic rule L.*type* = T.*type*, associated with production D → TL, sets inherited attribute L.*type* to the type in the declaration. The rules then pass this type down the parse tree using the inherited attribute L.*type*. Rules associated with the production for L call the procedure *addtype* to add the type of each identifier to its entry in the symbol table.

4.3 Syntax-directed Definition

Syntax-directed definition (SDD) specifies the values of attributes by associating semantic rules with the production. SDD is easy to read and specify. The grammar along with the set of rules constitute the syntax-directed definitions. These may be of two types: S-attributed and L-attributed. In a syntax-directed definition, terminals are assumed to have synthesized attributes only, as the definition does not provide any semantic rules for terminals. Values for the attributes of terminals are usually supplied by the lexical analyser, and the start symbol is assumed not to have any inherited attributes.

S-attributed definitions: SDDs that use only synthesized attributes are known as S-attributed definitions. If the translations are specified using S-attributed definitions, the semantic rules can be evaluated by the parser itself during parsing. These attributes are evaluated using S-attributed syntax-directed translations (SDTs) that have their semantic actions written after the production. Attributes in S-attributed SDTs are evaluated in bottom-up parsing, as the values of the parent nodes depend upon the values of the child nodes. A parse tree for an S-attributed definition is annotated by evaluating the semantic rules for the attributes at each node using the bottom-up approach.

L-attributed definitions: L-attributed definitions use both synthesized and inherited attributes with the restriction of not taking values from right siblings. In L-attributed SDTs, a non-terminal can obtain values from its parent, child and sibling nodes. Attributes in L-attributed SDTs are evaluated by depth-first and left-to-right parsing approach. A set of attribute equations is L-attributed if each equation can be processed at the point where it is written. Specifically:

- Synthesized attributes are allowed in L-attributed definitions.
- An attribute equation associated with production $A \rightarrow X_1 X_2 \ldots X_n$ defines an attribute of X_i. The RHS of that equation can use inherited attributes of A and inherited or synthesized attributes of $X_1, X_2, \ldots, X_{i-1}$.

If a definition is S-attributed, then it is also L-attributed, as the L-attributed definition encloses the S-attributed definitions, as shown in Fig. 4.4.

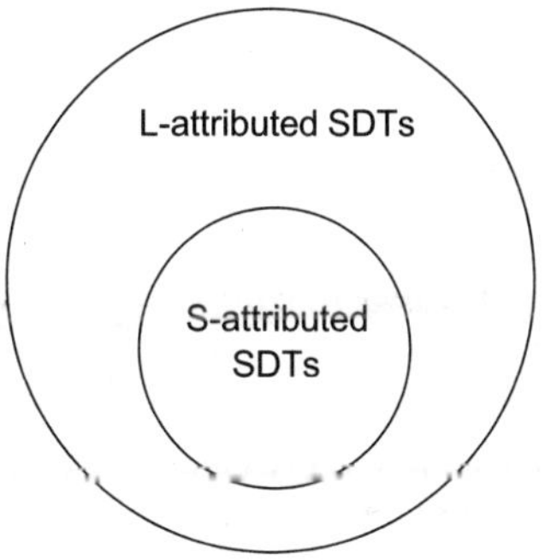

Figure 4.4 Relation between L-attributed and S-attributed SDTs

4.4 Syntax-directed Translation Scheme

The translation scheme for semantic analysis involves the addition of information to the symbol table and the verification of the values of each statement in the program. SDD specifies the values of attributes by associating semantic rules with the productions; whereas a syntax-directed translation scheme embeds program fragments (called semantic actions) within production bodies. The position of the action defines the order in which it is executed.

For SDT, the values of the attributes at the nodes are computed by visiting the nodes of the parse tree. The process of SDT involves two steps:

1. Construction of the syntax tree.
2. Computing values of attributes at each node by visiting the nodes of the syntax tree.

Semantic actions: Semantic actions are fragments of code that are embedded within production bodies by SDT. They are usually enclosed within curly braces ({ }). They can occur anywhere in a production but are found usually at the end of production.

Types of translations

- **L-attributed translation:** It performs translation during parsing itself. There is no need to explicitly construct the tree. 'L' in L-attribution means 'left to right'.
- **S-attributed translation:** It is performed in connection with bottom-up parsing. 'S' in S-attribution represents 'synthesized'.

SDD and SDT for infix to postfix computation are given below:

SDT Scheme	*SDD*	
E → E +T {print '+'}	E → E +T	{E.*code* = E.*code*‖T.*code*‖ '+'}
E → E −T {print '−'}	E → E −T	{E.*code* = E.*code*‖T.*code*‖ '−'}
E → T	E → T	{E.*code* = T.*code*}
T → 0 {print '0'}	T → 0	{T.*code* = '0'}
T → 1 {print '1'}	T → 1	{T.*code* = '1'}
...	...	
T → 9 {print '9'}	T → 9	{T.*code* = '9'}

Example 4.1 Synthesized attributes in SDD

L → E	{Print (E.*val*)}
E → E1 + T	{E.*val* = E1.*val* + T.*val*}
E → T	{E.*val* = T.*val*}
T → T1 * F	{T.*val* = T1.*val* * F.*val*}
T → F	{T.*val* = F.*val*}
F → *id*	{F.*val* = *id.lexval*}

The token *id* has a synthesized attribute *lexval*, whose value is assumed to be supplied by the lexical analyser. The rule associated with the production L → E, for a starting non-terminal, is a procedure that prints as output the value of the arithmetic expression generated by E. The annotated parse tree for input 3 * 2 + 5 is shown in Fig. 4.5. It prints as output the value 11. The parse tree is evaluated from bottom to top, as the values at each node are computed using the values of the child nodes.

Consider the production

T → T1 * F T.*val* = T1.*val* * F.*val* = 3 * 2 = 6

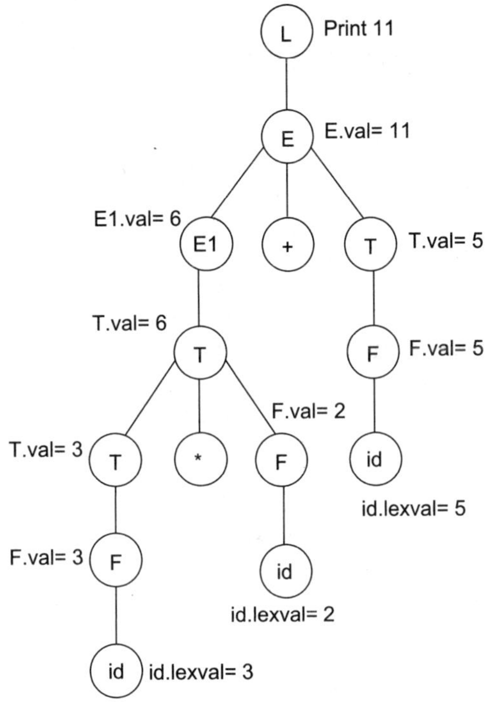

Figure 4.5 Annotated parse tree for input 3 * 2 + 5

Example 4.2 Inherited attributes in SDD

Consider a declaration generated by the non-terminal D in the SDD. It consists of the keyword `int` or `real`, followed by a list of identifiers. The non-terminal T has a synthesized attribute *type*, whose value is determined by the keyword in the declaration. The semantic rule L.*in* := T.*type*, associated with production D → TL, is an example of inherited attribute. The rules pass this type down the parse tree using the inherited attribute L.*in*. Rules associated with the productions for L call procedure *addtype* to add the type of each identifier to its entry in the symbol table. The grammar is given below and the parse tree is shown in Fig. 4.6.

D → T L	L.*in* = T.*type*
T → int	T.*type* = integer
T → real	T.*type* = real
L → L1, *id*	L1.*in* = L.*in*
	addtype(*id.entry*, L.*in*)
L → *id*	*addtype*(*id.entry*, L.*in*)

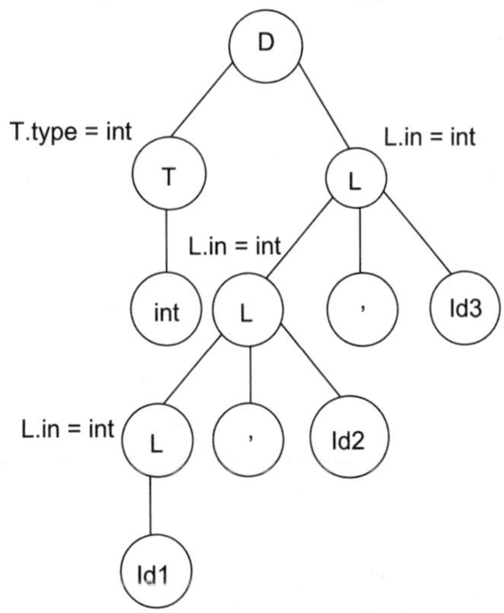

Figure 4.6 Annotated parse tree for the input int id1, id2, id3

The value of L.*in* at the three L-nodes gives the type of the identifiers id1, id2 and id3. These values are determined by computing the value of the attribute T.*type* at the left child of the root and then evaluating L.*in* top-down at the three L-nodes in the right subtree of the root. At each L-node, the procedure *addtype*, is called to insert into the symbol table the fact that the identifier at the right child of this node has type `int`.

4.5 Dependency Graph

Dependency graphs determine how attributes can be evaluated in parse trees. For each symbol X, the dependency graph has a node for each attribute associated with X. An edge from node A to node B means that the attribute of A is required to compute the attribute of B. The interdependencies among the inherited and synthesized attributes at the nodes in a parse tree can be depicted by a dependency graph. If an attribute b at a node in a parse tree depends on an attribute c, then the semantic rule for the b node must be evaluated after the semantic rule that defines c.

Before constructing a dependency graph for a parse tree, we place each semantic rule in the form b = f (c1, c2, c3 . . , cn), by introducing a dummy synthesized attribute b for each semantic rule that consists of a procedure call. The dependency graph for a given parse tree is constructed as follows:

For each node n, in the parse tree do
    For each attribute a of the grammar symbol at n do
        Construct a node in the dependency graph for a;
For each node n in the parse tree do
    For each semantic rule b = f(c1, c2, ... ck)
        associated with the production used at n do
For i := 1 to k do
    Construct an edge from the node for ci to the node for b;

For example, consider the production rule, A → BC, and semantic rule, A.a = f(B.b, C.c). A.a is a synthesized attribute that depends on attributes B.b and C.c. So, the dependency graph will have three nodes A.a, B.b and C.c, with an edge from B.b to A.a and from C.c to A.a.

Sample dependency graph for production rule A → B + C

The parse tree along with the dependency graph (shown in solid) for the production rules is shown in Fig. 4.7. The value at A is computed using the values at B and C.

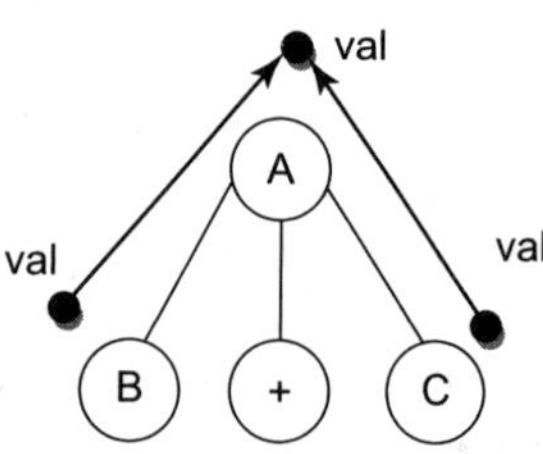

Figure 4.7 Dependency graph for A → B + C

4.6 Methods to Calculate Semantic Rules

Several methods have been proposed for calculating semantic rules:

- **Parse-tree method:** In this method, the evaluation order is found by applying a topological sort to the dependency graph constructed from the parse tree for each input. This method will fail to find an evaluation order only if the dependency graph for the particular parse tree under consideration has a cycle.
- **Rule-based method:** The semantic rules associated with the productions are analysed, either by hand or using a specialised tool. For each production, the order in which the attributes associated with that production are evaluated is predetermined at compiler construction time.
- **Oblivious method:** The evaluation order is chosen without considering the semantic rules. For example, if translation takes place during parsing, the order of evaluation is forced by the parsing

method, independent of the semantic rules. An oblivious evaluation order restricts the class of SDDs that can be implemented.

The rule-based and oblivious methods need not explicitly construct the dependency graph at compile time; so, they can be more efficient in their use of compile time and space.

An SDD is said to be circular if the dependency graph for some parse tree generated by its grammar has a cycle.

4.7 Evaluation Order of Semantic Rules

A topological sort of a directed acyclic graph is of the order ml, m2. . . . , mk of the nodes of the graph such that edges go from nodes earlier in the ordering to later nodes: that is, if there is an edge from mi → mj, then mi appears before mj in the order.

Any topological sort of a dependency graph gives a valid order in which thc semantic rules associated with the nodes in a parse tree can be evaluated. The parse tree is constructed for the input grammar, then the dependency graph is constructed and the topological sort of the dependency graph is obtained to find the evaluation order for the semantic rules. Evaluation of the semantic rules in this order yields the translation of the input string.

Sample dependency graph and evaluation order

Let us consider the parse tree of Fig. 4.3 and draw the dependency graph. The dependency graph along with the topological sort is shown in Fig. 4.8. The numbers represent the topological sequence.

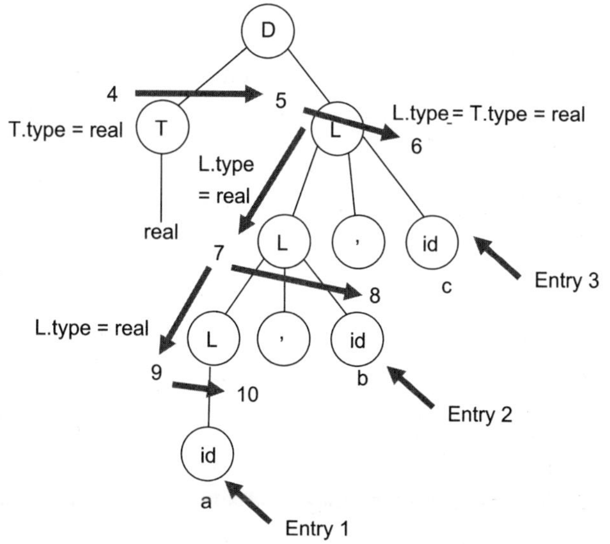

Figure 4.8 Dependency graph for parse tree of Fig. 4.3

From this topological sort, the following program is obtained. Notation 'an' or a_n, is used for the attribute associated with the node numbered 'n' in the dependency graph.

a4 = real;
a5 = a4;
addtype(*id.entry*, a5);
a7 = a5;
addtype(*id.entry*, a7);
a9 = a7;
addtype(*id.entry*, a9);

Evaluating these semantic rules stores the type in the symbol-table entry for each identifier.

4.8 Syntax Trees

SDDs can be used to specify the construction of syntax trees and other graphical representations of language constructs. The use of syntax trees as an intermediate representation allows translation to be decoupled from parsing. Transition routines invoked during parsing must work with two kinds of restrictions. First, a grammar that is suitable for parsing may not reflect the natural hierarchical structure of the constructs in the language. Second, the parsing method constrains the order in which nodes in a parse tree are considered. This order may not match the order in which information about a construct becomes available. For this reason, compilers for C usually construct syntax trees for declarations.

An (abstract) syntax tree is a condensed form of a parse tree that is useful for representing language constructs. The production, S → if B then S1 else S2, can be represented in a syntax tree as shown on the right. In the syntax tree, operators and keywords do not appear as leaf nodes. SDTs can be based on syntax trees as well as parse trees.

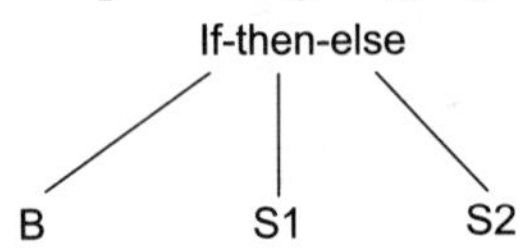

Construction of syntax trees for expressions: The construction of a syntax tree for an expression is similar to the translation of the expression into postfix form. The syntax tree for expressions has nodes for operators and operands. The children of an operator node are the roots of the nodes representing the sub-expressions constituting the operands of that operator.

Operator nodes are labelled as the operator along with the left and right children that point to the nodes of the operands. In this section, the following functions are used to create the nodes of syntax trees for expressions with binary operators. Each function returns a pointer to a newly created node.

- *mknode*(*op*, *left*, *right*) creates an operator node *op* and two fields containing pointers to the *left* and *right*.
- *mkleaf*(*id*, *entry*) creates an identifier node with label *id* and a field containing *entry*, a pointer to the symbol table entry for the identifier.
- *mkleaf*(*num*, *val*) creates a number node with label *num* and a field containing *val*, the value of the number.

SDD for constructing syntax trees: An S-attributed definition for constructing a syntax tree for an expression containing the operators + and – is given below:

Production rule	Semantic rule
E → E1 + T	E.*nptr* = *mknode*('+', E1.*nptr*, T.*nptr*)
E → E1 – T	E.*nptr* = *mknode*('–', E1.*nptr*, T.*nptr*)
E → T	E.*nptr* = T.*nptr*

T → (E)	T.*nptr* = E.*nptr*
T → *id*	T.*nptr* = *mkleaf*(*id*, *id.entry*)
T → *num*	T.*nptr* = *mkleaf*(*num*, *num.val*)

The synthesized attribute *nptr* for E and T keeps track of the pointers returned by the function calls. The semantic rules associated with the production T→ *id* and T→ *num* define the attribute T.*nptr* to be a pointer to a new leaf for an identifier and number, respectively. Attributes *id.entry* and *num.val* are the lexical values assumed to be returned by the lexical analyser with the tokens *id* and *num*. Production E → E1 + T causes E.*nptr* to make a node with the operator as '+' and to point to the previous E1.*nptr* and T.*nptr*. The parse tree created corresponding to the input string 5 − 2 + c is shown in Fig. 4.9 and its corresponding nodes are shown in Fig. 4.10.

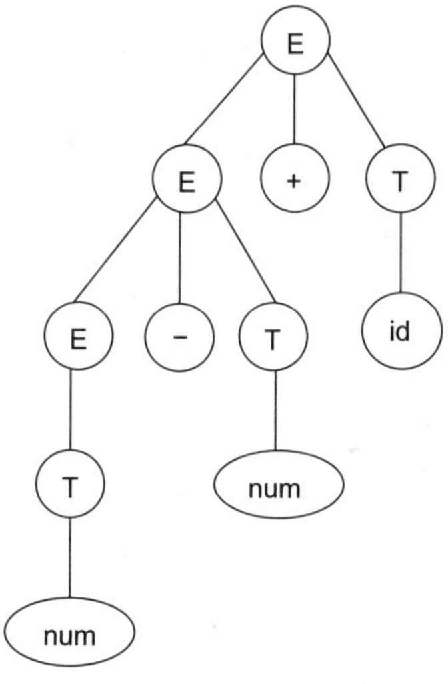

Figure 4.9 Parse tree for the input 5 − 2 + c

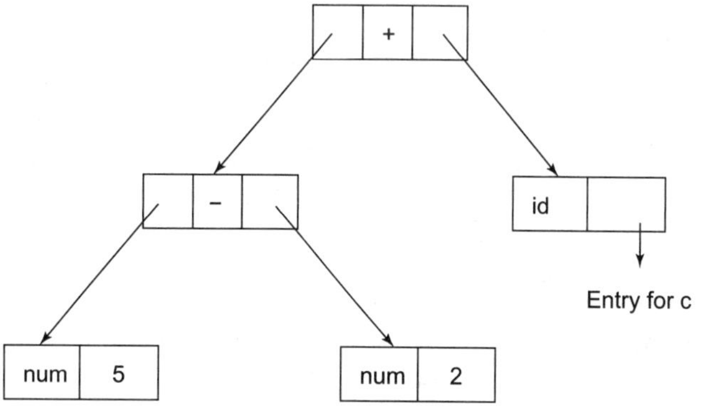

Figure 4.10 Syntax tree nodes for the input 5 − 2 + c

4.9 Directed Acyclic Graph Construction

A directed acyclic graph (DAG) for an expression identifies the common sub-expressions in the expression. DAG has a node for every sub-expression of the expression; an interior node represents an operator and its children represent its operands. The difference between DAG and the syntax tree is that a node in a DAG representing a common sub-expression has more than one parent; whereas in a syntax tree, the common sub-expression would be represented as a duplicated subtree. The DAG representation for the expression "a + (b − c) + (b − c) * d" is shown in Fig. 4.11.

The SDD for constructing syntax trees can be used for constructing DAGs, with some modifications:

- The function *makenode*, used to construct a node, must first check if an identical node already exists. For example, before constructing a new node with label *op* and fields with pointers *left* and *right*, *makenode*(*op*, *left*, *right*) can check whether such a node has already been constructed. If a node exists, *makenode*(*op*, *left*, *right*) will return a pointer to the previously constructed node; else a new node is created.
- The leaf-constructing function *mkleaf* also functions in a similar manner.

The sequence of instructions used to construct the DAG in Fig. 4.11 is given below:

P1 = *mkleaf*(*id*, a)
P2 = *mkleaf*(*id*, b)
P3 = *mkleaf*(*id*, c)
P4 = *makenode*('−', P2, P3)
P5 = *makenode*('+', P1, P4)
P6 = *mkleaf*(*id*, b)
P7 = *mkleaf*(*id*, c)
P8 = *makenode*('−', P6, P7)
P9 = *mkleaf*(*id*, d)
P10 = *makenode*('*', P8, P9)
P11 = *makenode*('+', P5, P10)

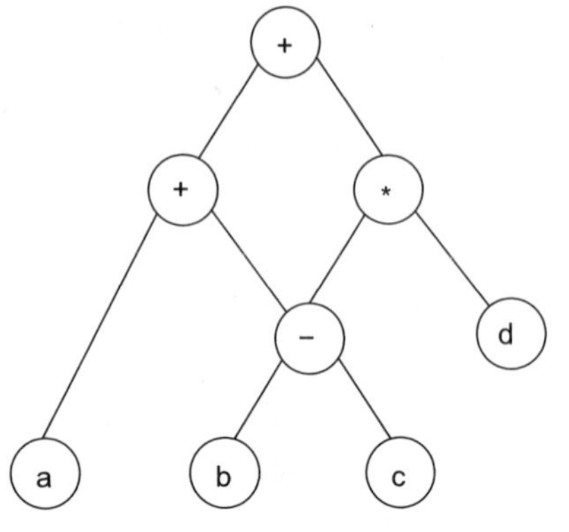

Figure 4.11 DAG for the input a + (b – c) + (b – c) * d

When the call *mkleaf*(*id*, b) is repeated on line 6, the node constructed by the previous call is returned, that is P6 = P2. Similarly, P7 = P3. Hence, the node returned on line 8 must be the same constructed by the call of *makenode* on line 4.

4.10 Type and Type Checking

In type checking, the data types of the variables used in the source program are checked to find out if they are consistent with their definition. Most programming languages require that the type of a token be declared before it is used. Types can be primitive or constructed. The different types in a programming language are as follows:

- Denotation type – the type is a set of values called a domain.
- Constructive type – the type is either primitive or constructed using simpler types.
- Abstraction-based type – the type is an interface consisting of a set of operations with well-defined and mutually consistent semantics.

For example, in the instruction `int` *a,* the variable *a* has type `int`; which is a primitive type. If further in the program there is an instruction *b=a,* then the type checker must check if the type of b is also `int` or any other compatible type like `float` or `double`.

Type checking can be static or dynamic. Static type checking is performed by the compiler at compile time; whereas, dynamic type checking is performed at run-time. In static type checking, the type information about the types of the variables is stored in the master symbol table, which can be referred by the type checker. After collecting type information, the types involved in each operation must be checked by the type checker. An operation can be semantically correct if the operands involved are of compatible type. In dynamic type checking, the compiler does not have the type information. It must determine the types at run-time and check if the correct types are being used.

4.10.1 Basic Types and Constructed Types

Basic or primitive types are atomic types that have no internal structure as far as the programmer is concerned. Some examples include integer, real, boolean, character or string, enumerated types, void, etc. Error is also included as a basic type.

Constructed types include arrays, records, sets and structures constructed from the basic types and/or other constructed types. Pointers and functions are also constructed types.

4.10.2 Type System and Type Checker

The type system is a set of rules for assigning type expressions to the syntactic constructs of a program. It enables the programmer to determine the appropriate use of operators in an expression. A sound type system eliminates run-time type checking for type errors. A type system also checks for the following:

- **Type equivalence**: Types of two values are the same. Type equivalence checks for name equivalence and structural equivalence.
  - *Name equivalence*: Two types are equivalent if they have the same name.
  - *Structural equivalence*: Two types are equivalent if they have the same structure. To test for structural equivalence, a compiler must encode the structure of a type in its representation.
- **Type compatibility**: When a value of a given type can be used in a given context.
- **Type inference**: Rules that determine the type of a language construct based on how it is used. Type inference specifies for each operator the mapping between the types of the operands and the type of the result.

A type checker verifies that the type of a construct matches that expected by its context. It is the implementation of the type system. The compiler must assign type expression to each component, determine the type expressions and confirm it to the type system. The type information gathered by a type checker may be required when code is generated. The role of the type checker is to verify the semantic contexts.

The type checker is designed for a language such that:

- It can identify the types that are available in the language.
- It can identify the language constructs that have types associated with them.
- It can identify the semantic rules for the language.

Type checkers are classified in terms of what they return:

- **Rude checker**: It only returns True or False. Such a type of checker may crash in an instance when variable look-up gives an error. It does not handle the error.
- **Error-reporting checker**: It returns OK or a message stating where the error is.
- **Annotating checker**: It returns a syntax tree annotated with more type information.

To build the back end of a compiler, the annotating type checker is used. The syntax tree obtained from the parser is annotated to include semantic rules.

Type conversions may be performed if needed. Explicit type conversion is carried out by the programmer. It is called **casting** or **type casting**. Whereas, implicit type conversion is performed automatically by the compiler. Implicit type conversion is also called **coercion**.

4.10.3 Type Expressions

This denotes the type of a language construct. It is either basic or constructed from other type expressions by applying an operator called a **type constructor**. Type expressions are formed based on the following rules:

- A basic type is a type expression. Other basic type expressions are 'type_error' to signal the presence of a type error and 'void' to signal the absence of a value.

- If the type expression has a name, then the type name is also a type expression.
- A type constructor applied to a type expression is a type expression. Constructors include:
  - **Arrays:** If T is a type expression and I is the index set, then *array (I, T)* denotes an array of elements of type T. I is often the range of integers. For example, consider array declaration in Java, `int` *num[ ]*= `new int[10]`. Here, array *num* is associated with type expression, *array(0..9, integer).*
  - **Products:** If T1 and T2 are type expressions, their Cartesian product, T1 x T2, is a type expression. For example, if the arguments of a function are integer, integer and real, then the type expression for the arguments is: integer x integer x real.
  - **Records or structure:** The fields in a record have names. These names should be included in the type expression of the record. For example, consider a record with n fields. For a record field with name R_{name} and type expression *Ti*, the type expression is given by $(R_{name} \times Ti)$. So the type expression for the record is, $((R_{name1} \times T1) \times (R_{name2} \times T2) \times \ldots\ldots (R_{name\ n} \times T_{n}))$
  - **Pointers:** If T is a type expression then *pointer* (*T*) denotes a pointer to an object of type T. For example, consider the pointer declaration in C, `int*ptr`; the type expression *pointer(integer)* is associated with *ptr*.
  - **Functions:** A function maps elements from its domain to its range. The type expression for a function is D → R, where D is the type expression for the domain of the function and R is the type expression for the range of the function. For example, the type expression of the mod operator is: integer x integer → integer, because it divides an integer by an integer and returns the integer remainder. The type expression for the domain of a function with no arguments is void. The type expression for the range of a function with no returned value is *void.* The type expression for a procedure with no arguments and no return value is *void → void.*

Type expressions may contain variables whose values are type expressions.

Representation of type expressions: A convenient way to represent a type expression is to use a graph. The syntax-directed approach can be used to construct a tree or a DAG for a type expression, with interior nodes for type constructors and leaves for basic types, type names and type variables.

Example 4.3 Type expression for structure

Consider the C source code given below that enters a record of students using structure and write the type expressions corresponding to the statements that involve types.

```
struct student
{
  char name[50];
  int roll;
  float marks;
} s;

void main()
{
  printf("Enter name: ");
  scanf("%s", s.name);
  printf("Enter roll number: ");
  scanf("%d", &s.roll);
```

```
  printf("Enter marks: ");
  scanf("%f", &s.marks);
}
```

Type expression for structure

```
struct student
{
  char name[50];
  int roll;
  float marks;
}
```

The type expression is given by $((R_{name1} \times T1) \times (R_{name2} \times T2) \times \ldots\ldots (R_{name\ n} \times Tn))$ for a record with n fields, where R_{name} denotes the field name and T denotes the type. So, the type expression for the given structure will be *((name x char) x (roll x int) x (marks x float))*. This type expression is attached to student.

Example 4.4 Type expression for function

Consider the C program to add two numbers using functions.

```
int main( ) {
  int num1, num2, res;
  printf("\nEnter the two numbers : ");
  scanf("%d %d", &num1, &num2);

  res = sum(num1, num2);       // function call to function sum having
                               two int parameters
  printf("\n Addition of two number is : %d ", res);
  return (0);
}

int sum(int num1, int num2) {
  int num3;
  num3 = num1 + num2;
  return (num3);
}
```

Type expressions

- Type expression associated with `main` function is *int.*
- Type expression associated with *num1*, *num2*, *res* is *int.*
- Type expression associated with function `sum` is *int* x *int* → *int*

Example 4.5 Type expression for the given statements

(a) Pointer to array of real numbers with array index ranging from 1 to 100.

Type expression will be: *pointer(Array(1....100 , real))*

(b) Function whose domain is the function having two characters as parameters and whose range is a pointer of integer.

Type expression will be: *char* x *char* → *pointer(int)*

4.10.4 Operator and Function Overloading

An **overloaded symbol** is one that has different meanings, depending on its context. Let us consider the addition operator. It can be overloaded, because + in an expression A + B can have different meanings when A and B are integers, real numbers, complex numbers or matrices. Moreover, in Java, the operator + can mean addition or string concatenation, depending on the types of its operands. Overloaded functions can be selected by observing the types of their arguments. Overloading is resolved when a unique meaning for an occurrence of an overloaded symbol is determined. The resolution of overloading is sometimes referred to as **operator identification**, because it determines which operation an operator symbol denotes.

For **function overloading**, the compiler must check that the type of each actual parameter is compatible with the type of the corresponding formal parameter. It must also check that the type of the returned value is compatible with the type of the function. The **type signature** of a function specifies the types of the formal parameters and the type of the return value.

Type checking rules for a set of possible types of an expression:

Production	Semantic rule
E' → E	E'.*type* = E.*type*
E → *id*	E.*type* = *lookup*(*id.entry*)
E → E1(E2)	E.*type* = |t| there exists an s in E2.*type* such that s→t is in E1.*type*

The type expression for function E → E1(E2) will be:

E.*type* = if E2.*type* = s and E1.*type* = s → t then t else type_error

The semantic rule for a function states that if s is one of the types of E2 and one of the types of El can map s to t, then t is one of the types of El(E2). A type mismatch during function application results in the set E.*type* becoming empty, a condition temporarily used to signal a type error.

4.10.5 Static and Dynamic Typing

Static typed programming languages are those in which variables need not be defined before they are used. This implies that static typing deals with the explicit declaration (or initialisation) of variables before they are used. Java is an example of a static typed language; C and C++ are also static typed languages. Note that in C (and C++), variables can be cast into other types, but they are not converted; you read them assuming that they are another type. Static typing does not imply that you have to declare all the variables first, before you use them; variables may be initialised anywhere, but developers must do so before they use the variables.

Dynamic typed programming languages are those in which variables must necessarily be defined before they are used. This implies that dynamic typed languages do not require the explicit declaration of the variables before they are used. Python is an example of a dynamic typed programming language, and so is PHP.

4.10.6 Encoding of Type Expressions

Type expressions can be encoded by using different encoding to basic types and constructed types. As there are only three type constructors, two bits can be used to encode a constructor, as follows:

Type constructor encoding	
Pointer	01
Array	10
Function	11

The basic types of C are encoded using four bits as:

Basic type	Encoding
Boolean	0000
Char	0001
Integer	0010
Real	0011

Restricted type expressions can be encoded as a sequence of bits. The rightmost four bits encode the basic type in a type expression. Moving from right to left, the next two bits indicate the constructor applied to the basic type, while the next two bits describe the constructor applied to that and so on. For example, the encoding corresponding to the given type expressions is as follows:

Type expression	Encoding
char	00 00 00 0001
function(char)	00 00 11 0001
pointer(function(char))	00 01 11 0001
array(pointer(function(char)))	10 01 11 0001

Example 4.6 Encoding of type expressions
Using the encoding of type expressions, encode the type expressions: int, function(int), pointer(int), pointer(array(int)).

Type expression	Encoding
int	00 00 00 0010
function(int)	00 00 11 0010
pointer(int)	00 00 01 0010
pointer(array(int))	00 01 10 0010

4.11 A Simple Type Checking System

The type checker implements a translation scheme that can synthesize the type expressions from the types of its sub-expressions. In this section, a type checker for a simple language is specified, in which the type checker can handle arrays, pointers, statements and functions. It is assumed that the type of each identifier must be declared before the identifier is used.

Following is the grammar of program P, which consists of a sequence of declarations D, followed by a single expression E.

P → D; S
D → D; D | *id* : T
T → char | integer | array[num] of T
S → S; S | *id* = E | if E then S | while E do S
E→ literal | num| *id* |E mod E | E[E] | E+E

Semantic rules are attached to the grammar to perform type checking. The grammar along with semantic rules is called **attribute grammar**. The translation scheme that saves the type of an identifier is as follows:

P → D; S	
D → D; D	
D → *id* : T	{ *addtype*(*id.entry* , T.*type*)}
T → char	{ T.*type* = char}
T → integer	{ T.*type* = int}
T → float	{ T.*type* = float}
T → array[num] of T1	{ T.*type* = array((1..num.*val*),T1.*type*) }

In the above language, there are three basic types: char, integer and float. Type_error is used to signal errors. *addtype* adds the type of the name to the symbol table. It is assumed that the lexical analyser adds the identifier name to the symbol table and the semantic analyser augments the name with T.*type* that the type checker identifies. The translation scheme for expressions is as follows:

E → literal	{E.*type* = char}
E → num	{ E.*type* = int}
E → *id*	{ E.*type* = *lookup*(*id.entry*)}
E → E1 mod E2	{ E.*type* = if E1.*type* = integer and E2.*type* = integer then integer else type_error}
E → E1[E2]	{ E.*type* = if E2.*type* = integer and E1.*type* = array(s, t) then t else type_error}
E → E1+E2	{ E.*type* = if E1.*type* = integer and E2.*type* = integer then integer else type_error}

Function *lookup(e)* is used to fetch the type saved in the symbol table entry pointed to by e. In an array reference E1[E2] , the index expression E2 must have a type integer. The result is the element type t obtained from the type array(s, t) of E1. The translation scheme for statements is as follows:

S → S; S	{S.*type* : = if S1.*type* = *void* and S1.*type* = *void* then *void* else type_error}
S → *id* = E	{S.*type*= if E.*type* = Boolean then S1.*type* else type_error}
S → if E then S1	{S.*type*= if E.*type* = Boolean then S1.*type* else type_error}
S → while E do S1	{S.*type* = if E.*type*= Boolean then S1.*type* else type_error}

Example 4.7 Type checking

Draw the syntax tree and apply type checking based on the translation scheme discussed in Section 4.11. Consider the code fragment

```
int a, b , c;
c = a + b;
b = c;
```

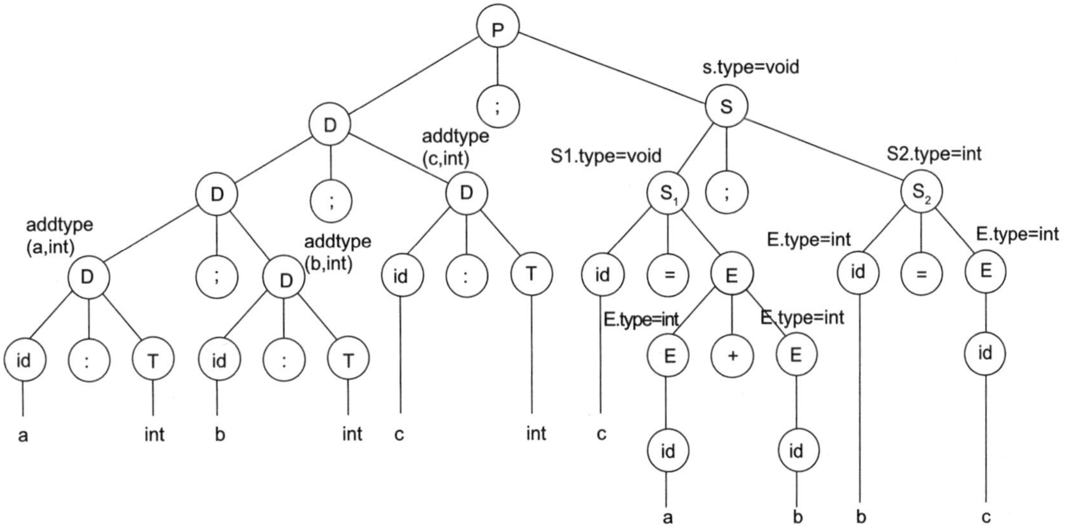

Figure 4.12 Annotated syntax tree for type checking

Figure 4.12 shows the annotated syntax tree. The type checker performs type checking based on the simple type checker discussed in Section 4.11. As no errors are reported, type checking is completed and the semantic analyser declares the input to be semantically correct. The function *addtype* adds the entry of the type corresponding to the identifier in the symbol table. The symbol table after type checking is shown in Table 4.1.

Table 4.1 Symbol table for Example 4.7

Name	Type
A	Int
B	Int
C	Int

Example 4.8 Type checking

Draw the syntax tree and apply type checking based on the translation scheme discussed in Section 4.11.

Consider the code fragment

```
int a;
char b;
a = b;
```

An error is reported, as according to the translation scheme, `char` cannot be assigned to `int`. Hence, the error routine must be invoked or type conversion can be applied in cases where it is possible.

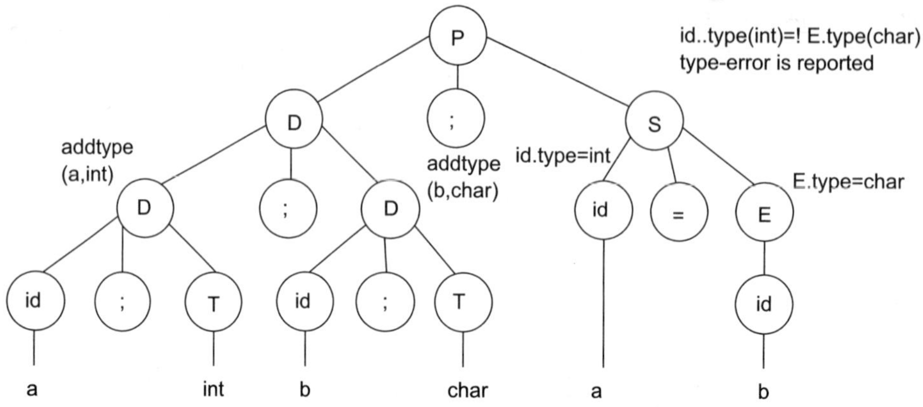

Figure 4.13 Annotated syntax tree for type checking (Example 4.8)

4.12 Type Conversion

The values of one type can be used in a context that expects another type using **type conversion** or **type casting**. The representation of integers and real numbers is different in a computer and different instructions are used for them. If in a computation, one variable is allotted as `real` and one as `int`, then the compiler may need to convert the type of a variable to evaluate the computation. The language determines when conversion is necessary.

4.12.1 Coercion

Conversion from one type to another can be either implicit or explicit. It is said to be implicit if it is to be done automatically by the compiler. Implicit type conversion is also called coercion. Conversion is said to be explicit if the programmer must write the code to cause the conversion. The coercion of expression is given as follows:

Statement	Semantic rule
E → num	E.*type* = integer
E → num. num	E.*type* = real
E → *id*	E.*type* = *lookup*(*id.entry*)
E → E1 op E2	E.*type* = if E1.*type* = int and E2 = int then int else if E1.*type* = int and E2.*type* = real then real else if E1.*type* = real and E2.*type* = int then real else if E1.*type* = real and E2.*type* = real then real else type_error

Example 4.9 Type conversion

Draw the syntax tree and perform type checking. Also perform type conversion if needed.

Consider the code fragment

```
int a;
real b, c;
b = c + a;
```

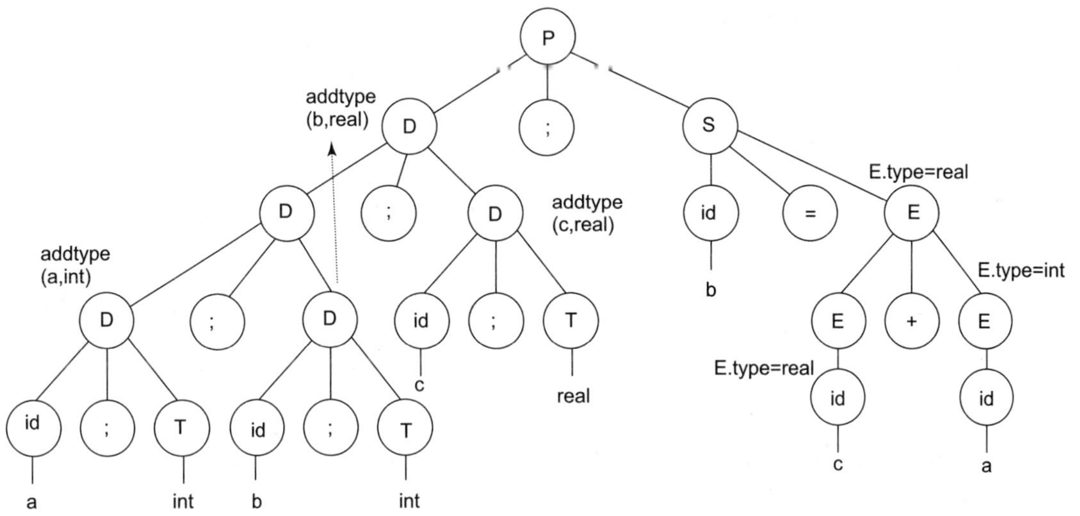

Figure 4.14 Syntax tree for type checking (Example 4.9)

The type of c is `real` and a is `int`. When expression c + a is evaluated, the type is changed to `real`. The type conversion rules are discussed in Section 4.10. Assume that if the type of b is also `int` then the type of b must also be changed to `real`. This will be done using inherited attributes.

4.13 Type Equivalence

Type equivalence can be specified in two ways:

- **Name equivalence:** Types are name equivalent when they have same name. Each name is a distinct type. Under **strict name equivalence**, aliases are not equivalent, and under **loose name equivalence**, aliases are equivalent.
- **Structural equivalence:** Types are structurally equivalent when they have same structure. That is, if they have same structure after substituting type expressions for type names. The rules for structural equivalence are given below, followed by the algorithm to find structural equivalence.

Rules for structural equivalence:

- s ≡ t if s and t have same basic type
- array(s1, s2) ≡ array(t1, t2) if s1 ≡ t1 and s2 ≡ t2
- pointer(s) ≡ pointer (t) if s ≡ t
- s1 → s2 ≡ t1 → t2 if s1 ≡ t1 and s2 ≡ t2

```
function sequiv(s, t): boolean
{ if (s ∧ t are of the same basic type) return true;
  if (s = array(s1, s2) ∧ t = array(t1,t2))
     return sequiv(s1, t1) ∧ sequiv(s2,t2);
  if (s = tuple(s1, s2) ∧ t = tuple(t1,t2))
     return sequiv(s1, t1)∧ sequiv(s2,t2);
  if (s = fcn(s1, s2) ∧ t = fcn(t1,t2))
     return sequiv(s1, t1)) ∧ sequiv(s2,t2);
```

```
    if (s = pointer(s1) ∧ t = pointer(t1))
        return sequiv(s1,t1);
}
```

In structural equivalence for records, the order of record fields affects the type equivalence. In some languages, the order does not matter, while in others, the order of record fields must be the same. For structural equivalence in arrays, the dimension of the arrays must be the same, the size of the arrays may be different.

C and C++ use structural equivalence except for structures and classes (where name equivalence is used). For arrays, size is ignored. That is, C uses name equivalence for structures, classes and union. Java uses structural equivalence for scalars. For arrays, it requires name equivalence for the component type, ignoring size. For classes, it uses name equivalence except that a subtype may be used where a parent type is expected.

Example 4.10 Structural equivalence and name equivalence

Assume the statements as follows:

```
Type T = array[1.....10] of integer;
var A,B :array[1.....10] of integer;
    C: array[1.....10] of integer;
    D: T;
    E:T;
```

The types that satisfy name equivalence are:

- Same type name in D and E.
- Declared together – A and B.

The types that satisfy structural equivalence are:

- Same structure means the same type, so A, B, C, D and E are structurally equivalent.

Example 4.11 Structural equivalence, order of fields of a structure

Find the types that are structurally equivalent.

```
T1 = Struct {
        a : integer;
        b : real;
        }
T2 = Struct {
        c : integer;
        d : real;
        }
T3 = Struct {
        b : real;
        a : integer;
        }
```

- T_1 and T_2 satisfy structural equivalence in all languages.
- T_3 is also structurally equivalent to T_1 and T_2 in most languages, but not in ML and ALGOL-68. As discussed in Section 4.11, for structural equivalence of records, the order of record fields affects the type equivalence. In some languages, the order does not matter, while in others, the order of record fields must be the same.

Example 4.12 Reason why C uses name equivalence for structures

Assume two structures are declared in a program.

```
Struct student
      {
         Name, Address: string
         Age: integer
      }
Struct school
      {
         Name, Address: string
         Age: integer
      }
```

They are structurally equivalent. Hence, it is not possible to distinguish between types that the programmer may think of as distinct, but which happen by coincidence to have the same internal structure. It is unlikely that the programmer intended to make these two types equivalent. This is why C uses name equivalence for structures. Hence, the given two structures are not type equivalent in C language.

Example 4.13 Are the given structures (records) equivalent in C language?

```
Struct T1 {
                int a;
          };
Struct T2 {
                int a;
          };
```

- T_1 and T_2 will be of different types in C as records are checked by name equivalence and these two structures have different names.

Example 4.14 Specify the equivalent types if name equivalence and structural equivalence are applied

Consider the given records as structures.

```
typedef struct{
      int data[100];
      int count;
      }stack;
```

```
typedef struct{
int data[100];
      int count;
      }set;
stack x,y;
set r,s;
```

- If name equivalence is used, then x and y have the same type. r and s also have the same type.
- If structural equivalence is used, then x, y, r and s have the same type.

Example 4.15 Find the arrays that are of equivalent types in C language

```
int n[10];
int p[20];
real a[10,20];
real b[10,20];
real c[20,30];
```

C uses structural equivalence for arrays. It is required that the dimension of the arrays be the same; the size of the arrays may be different. Hence, n and p are type equivalent. Also, a, b and c are type equivalent.

Summary

- A parse tree showing the values of the attributes at each node is called an annotated parse tree.
- An attribute grammar is an extension of a CFG that is used to describe the features of a programming language.
- The attributes that obtain values from the attribute values of their child nodes are called synthesized attributes.
- The attributes that obtain values from their parents and/or siblings are called inherited attributes.
- Syntax-directed definition (SDD) specifies the values of attributes by associating semantic rules with the production.
- SDDs that use only synthesized attributes are known as S-attributed definitions.
- Attributes in S-attributed SDTs are evaluated in bottom-up parsing.
- L-attributed definitions use both synthesized and inherited attributes with the restriction of not taking values from right siblings.
- Attributes in L-attributed SDTs are evaluated by depth-first and left-to-right parsing.
- If a definition is S-attributed, then it is also L-attributed.
- Semantic actions are fragments of code that are embedded within production bodies by SDT, enclosed within curly braces ({ }).
- Type expressions denote the type of a language construct. They are either basic or constructed from other type expressions.
- Two types are name equivalent if they have the same name and are structurally equivalent if they have the same structure.
- A type checker verifies that the type of a construct matches that expected by its context. It is an implementation of a type system.

- Static typed programming languages are those in which variables need not be defined before they are used.
- Dynamic typed programming languages are those in which variables must necessarily be defined before they are used.
- The type checker implements a translation scheme that can synthesize the type expressions from the types of its sub-expressions.
- C uses structural equivalence for arrays.

Exercises

Review Questions

Fill in the blanks with appropriate answers:

1. S-attributed grammar uses __________ parsers.
2. Type checking is done after __________ phase of the compiler.
3. Semantic rules set up dependencies between attributes that will be represented by a graph called __________.
4. An attribute grammar is an extension __________ grammar.
5. The evaluation order is found by applying a topological sort to the dependency graph constructed from the parse tree for each input in __________ method.
6. __________ and __________ are types of equivalence.
7. Explicit type conversion carried out by the programmer is called __________.

Answers: 1. Bottom-up 2. Syntax analysis 3. Dependency graph 4. CFG 5. Parse tree 6. Name and structure 7. Type casting

State whether true or false:

1. Dynamic languages have no variables types.
2. Coercion is conversion between compatible types.
3. SDT scheme embeds program fragments (also called semantic actions) within production bodies.
4. SDD is a CFG with attributes and rules.
5. In synthesized attribute, the value is computed from siblings and the parent.
6. Any topological sort of a dependency graph gives a valid order in which the semantic rules associated with the nodes in a parse tree can be evaluated.
7. Type inference specifies for each operator the mapping between the types of the operands and the type of the result.

Answers: 1. False 2. True 3. True 4. True 5. False 6. True 7. True

Practice Questions

1. Consider the attribute grammar given below. Draw the syntax tree and perform translation as per the translation scheme on the RHS of the production rule for the string 3 + 5 + 6 + 2.

E → E+E	{print +}
E → T	{print T.*val*}
T → *id*	{T.*val* = *id*.*val*}

2. Design a syntax-directed translation scheme for a new language as follows: basic types allowed are char and int. # denotes addition operation, $ denotes multiplication operation. Consider the input string as 3$5#2. Draw the annotated parse tree and print the result of computation.
3. Consider the given attribute grammar and draw the annotated parse tree for input expression 2 * 3 + 5.

L → E	{print(E.*val*)}
E → E1 + T	{E.*val* = E1.*val* + T.*val*}
E → T	{E.*val* = T.*val*}
T → T * F	{T.*val* = T1.*val* * F.*val*}
T → F	{T.*val* = F.*val*}
F → digit	{F.*val* = digit.lexval}

4. Consider the statements given below and write the type expressions corresponding to each:
   (a) float num[100]; (b) int twoD[10,20];
   (c) int *ptr [10]; (d) char conct(char a, char b)
5. Assume the language given in Q2. Also perform type checking for operands in the syntax-directed scheme. If both the operands are int, the result is int. If one operand is int and another is char, then error must be reported. Draw the annotated parse tree for the given code in the new language build:
   int a;
   char b, c;
   c = b + a;
6. In Q5, instead of reporting error, perform type conversion if one operand is int and another operand is char; change the type of the int operand to char. Also, if both the operands are char and the type of the result is int, then change the type of the result to char. Show the annotated parse tree for the code of Q5.

Programming Questions

1. Write a code to implement the SDTS designed in Q6 of the Practice Questions.
2. Implement the encoding of type expressions. The program must take as input the source code, convert it into type expressions and then encode the expressions.
3. Implement the SDTS for synthesized attributes discussed in the chapter.
4. Based on the translation scheme in Section 4.11, implement the type checker discussed in Example 4.7.

5 Intermediate Code Generation Using Syntax-directed Translations

Objectives

- To understand various representations of intermediate code
- To discuss the generation of three-address code for various language constructs using the syntax-directed translation scheme

5.1 Introduction to Intermediate Code Generation

The main aim of the compiler is to convert the source code written in high-level language to low-level language. Rather than converting the code directly to low-level language, many compilers convert the code to an intermediate representation. If the code is directly converted into machine language, there will be a need to develop optimisers and code generators for different languages and different target machines, respectively.

Let us consider that there are 10 source languages and 5 target machines. Then, the requirement will be 10 front ends, $10 \times 5 = 50$ optimisers and $10 \times 5 = 50$ code generators. Whereas, if an intermediate representation is used, the requirement is reduced to 10 front ends, 1 optimiser for machine-independent intermediate code and 5 code generators, one for each target machine. The **benefits** of using machine-independent intermediate code are as follows:

- It reduces the number of optimisers and code generators.
- It is easy to generate and translate code into the target program.
- It enhances portability. If a compiler translates the source language to its target machine language without having the option to generate intermediate code, then for each new machine, a full native compiler is required. This is because there can be some modifications in the compiler, according to the machine specifications.
- It is easy to optimise as compared to machine-dependent code.
- The representation of intermediate code can be directly executed using a program, which is referred to as the interpreter.

This chapter discusses how syntax-directed methods can be used to translate the source code into an intermediate form. Intermediate code generation can be integrated with the parser, if required.

5.2 Intermediate Code Representation

Intermediate codes are machine-independent codes, close to machine instructions. The given program in a source language is converted to an equivalent program in an intermediate language by the intermediate code generator. The designer of the compiler determines the intermediate language.

Various intermediate representations are discussed in this section. The intermediate representation can be selected based on the following:

- It should be easy to translate the source language to the intermediate representation.
- It should be easy to translate the intermediate representation to machine code.
- The intermediate representation should be suitable for optimisation.
- It should be neither too high level nor too low level.

General forms of intermediate representations are graphical representation and linear representation. **Graphical representations** can be parse trees, abstract syntax trees, DAG, etc. **Linear representations** are non-graphical like three-address code (TAC), static single assignment (SSA), etc.

Graphical representation: A syntax tree depicts the hierarchical structure of a source program. A DAG gives the same information but in a more compact way. It supports identification of common sub-expressions and promotes efficient code generation. A syntax tree and the DAG for the assignment statement a = b* c + b* c is shown in Fig. 5.1.

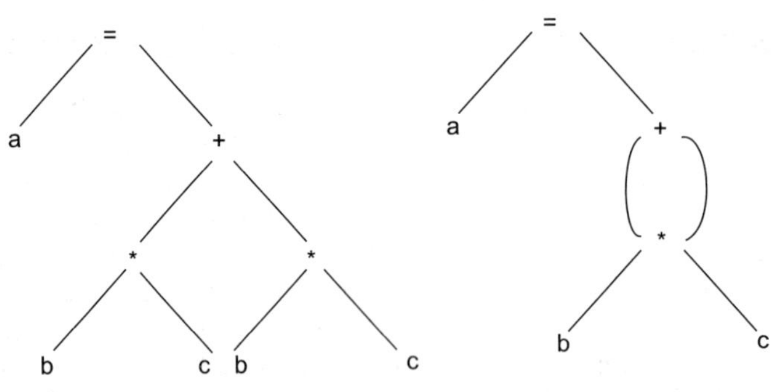

Figure 5.1 Graphical representation

Linear representation

- **Postfix notation:** This is a linearised representation of a syntax tree. It is a list of nodes of the tree in which a node appears immediately after its children. The postfix notation for the syntax tree in Fig. 5.1 (a) is a b c * b c * + =
- **Static single assignment (SSA):** This is a naming discipline used to explicitly encode information about both the flow of control and the flow of data values. A program is in SSA form if each definition [d] has a distinct name and each use [u] refers to a single definition (useful later on in UD-Chain computation).

For example, consider the code given below:

y = 1
y = 2
x = y

The SSA form will be

y1 = 1
y2 = 2
x1 = y2

- **Three-address code (TAC):** TAC instructions are of the form x = y op z, where x, y and z are names, constants or compiler-generated temporaries; op stands for any operator. TAC is a linearised representation of a syntax tree or a DAG in which explicit names correspond to the interior nodes of the graph. The syntax tree in Fig. 5.1 can be represented by the TAC sequence as follows:

  T1 = b * c
  T2 = T1 + T1
  a = T2

  The reason for the term 'three-address code' is that each statement usually contains three-addresses, two for the operands and one for the result. The concepts discussed in the chapter are based on TAC representation. During implementation of TAC, the programmer-defined name is replaced by a pointer to a symbol-table entry for that name. The common three-address statements are:

  - Assignment statements of the form x = y op z, where op is a binary arithmetic or logical operation.
  - Assignment instructions of the form x = op y, where op is a unary operation. Unary operations include unary minus, logical negation, shift operators and conversion operators that, for example, convert a fixed point number to a floating point number.
  - Copy statements of the form x = y, where the value of y is assigned to x.
  - The unconditional jump goto L. The three-address statement with label L is the next to be executed.
  - Conditional jumps such as if x relop y goto L, where relop is a relational operator.
  - Procedure calls, its parameters, call and return statements like param x and call p, n for procedure calls and return y, where y representing a returned value is optional. For example

    param x1
    param x2
    .
    .
    param xn
    call p, n
  - are generated as part of a call of the procedure p.
  - Indexed assignments of the form x = y[i] and x[i] = y.
  - Address and pointer assignments of the form x = &y, x = *y, and *x = y.

Representation of TACs: The data structures used to represent three-address code are quadruples, triples and indirect triples. Each representation is explained using the example A = −B * (C + D). The three-address code is as follows:

T1 = −B
T2 = C + D
T3 = T1* T2
A = T3

Quadruples: There are four fields: op, x, y and z in the three-address code as per the general format. All four fields are represented in quadruples. There are exceptions in unary operators, param and in conditional/unconditional jump. The quadruple representation of the assignment statement A = −B * (C + D) is shown below:

	op	x (operand1)	y (operand2)	z (result)
(1)	–	B		T1
(2)	+	C	D	T2
(3)	*	T1	T2	T3
(4)	=	A	T3	

Triples: In triples, only three fields are considered. The result field (z) is not considered. Results are referred by their positions. The triple representation of the example is as follows:

	op	x (operand1)	y (operand2)
(1)	–	B	
(2)	+	C	D
(3)	*	(1)	(2)
(4)	=	A	(3)

Indirect triples: Another representation uses an additional array to list the pointers to the triples in the desired order. This is called an indirect triple representation. When instructions are moved around during optimisations, quadruples are better than triples. Indirect triples solve this problem. Here, the triples are separated from their execution order. The indirect triple representation for the example is as follows:

(1)
(2)
(3)
(4)

	op	x (operand1)	y (operand2)
(1)	–	B	
(2)	+	C	D
(3)	*	(1)	(2)
(4)	=	A	(3)

The first column represents the order of execution. As the execution order here is the same as the order of the triples themselves, it is difficult to see the advantage of the use of indirect triples. Example 5.2 shows a case where the execution order is not the same as the order of the triple. With indirect triples, optimisation can change the execution order, rather than the triples themselves, so few references need be changed.

In this chapter, the three-address code is used to represent intermediate code and quadruple notation to represent the three-address code.

Example 5.1 Represent the expression a = (b + c) * −c in quadruple, triple and indirect triple representation

The three-address code for the given expression is as follows:

T1 = b + c

T2 = −c

T3 = T1* T2
a = T3

Representation in all three forms is given below.

Quadruple

	op	x (operand1)	y (operand2)	z (result)
(1)	+	b	c	T1
(2)	–	c		T2
(3)	*	T1	T2	T3
(4)	=	a	T3	

Triple

	op	x (operand1)	y (operand2)
(1)	–	b	c
(2)	–	c	
(3)	*	(1)	(2)
(4)	=	a	(3)

Indirect triple

		op	x (operand1)	y (operand2)
(1)	(1)	–	b	c
(2)	(2)	–	c	
(3)	(3)	*	(1)	(2)
(4)	(4)	=	a	(3)

Example 5.2 Optimisation can change the execution order, rather than the triples themselves, so few references need be changed in indirect triples

Consider the code

```
for i=1 to 10 do
begin
      a=b*c;
      d=i*2;
end
```

The three-address code for the above code fragment will be

```
i = 1
T1 = b * c
a = T1
T2 = i * 2
d = T2
i = i + 1
if i<10 goto (2)        // if statements start at (1)
```

The triple representation for the code will be

	op	x (operand1)	y (operand2)
(1)	=	1	i
(2)	*	b	c
(3)	=	(2)	a
(4)	*	2	i
(5)	=	(4)	d
(6)	+	1	i
(7)	LE	i	10
(8)	IFT	goto	(2)

Execution order: 12345678. There is scope for code optimisation in the given code fragment. Computation a = b * c can be moved out of the loop as it is not dependent on it. The optimised code will be

```
a = b * c;
for i = 1 to 10 do
begin
        d = i * 2;
end
```

The execution order is 23145678. It is needed to change the reference in (8); goto(2) becomes goto (4).

5.3 Syntax-directed Translation into Three-address Code – Principle

To translate any construct of a programming language, its syntax structure must be specified and semantic actions should be defined in the production rules of the grammar. The syntax-directed translation (SDT) scheme is used to generate the TAC. In SDT, the parsing process and parse trees are used to direct semantic analysis and the translation of the source program into TAC. Three-address code generation can also be carried out along with parsing; the evaluation is integrated with the generation of the parse tree. While generating three-address codes, temporary names are made up for the interior nodes of the syntax tree. The same temporary variables are used during three-address code generation. The attributes are associated with non-terminals and semantic action is associated with the production rule.

For example, the expressions represented by E have attributes E.*place* and E.*code*. E.*place* is the name that holds the value of E and E.*code* is a sequence of three-address statements evaluating E. For SDT, the values of the attributes at the nodes are computed by visiting the nodes of the parse tree. An SDT scheme to convert infix to postfix is given below:

Grammar	**Semantic rule**
E1 → E2 + T	E1.*string* = E1.*string* || T.*string* || '+'
E1 → T	E1.*string* = T.*string*

T1 → T2 * F	T1.*string* = T2.*string* || F.*string* || '*'
T → F	T.*string* = F.*string*
F → (E)	F.*string* = E.*string*
F → *num*	F.*string* = *num.string*

The annotated parse tree for the input string 2* 3 + 6 * 5 is shown in Fig. 5.2.

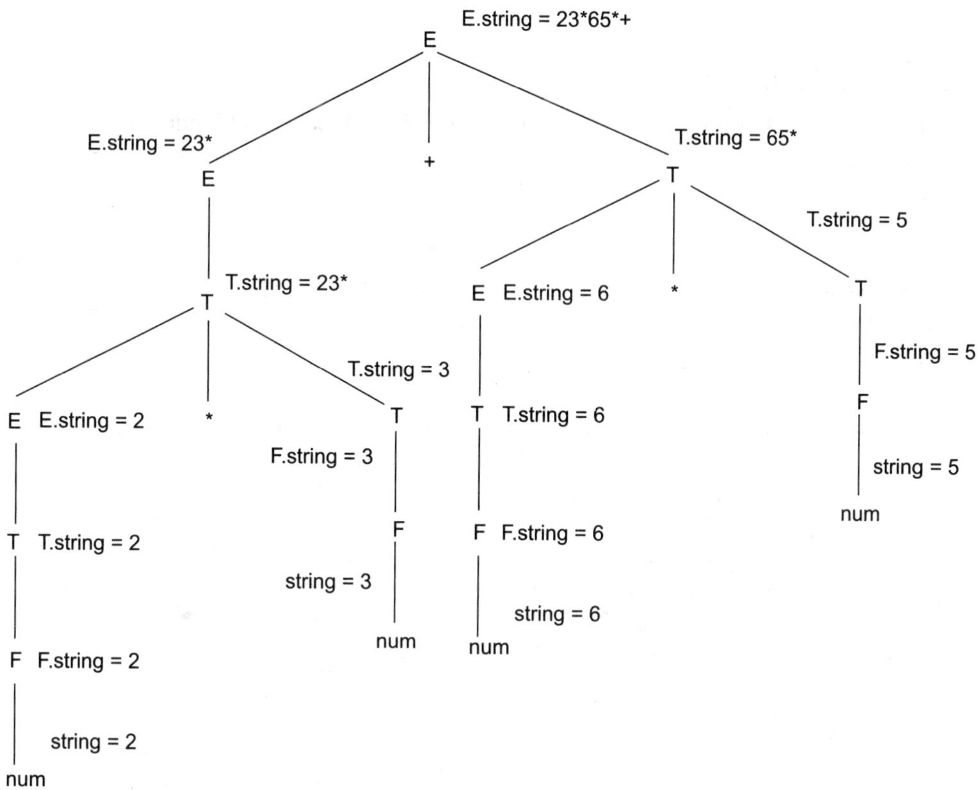

Figure 5.2 Annotated parse tree for infix to postfix

5.4 Syntax-directed Translation of Assignment Statement into Three-address Code

5.4.1 Assignment Statement

The assignment statement is the most fundamental construct of any programming language. A value is copied into or stored into the variable on the LHS of the "=" sign. Assignment statements may involve expressions that can be of type real, integer, array, record, etc. The values of names that are already stored in the symbol table by the scanner may be required. In this section, it is assumed that the lexeme for the name is represented by *id*. The function *lookup*(*id.name*) is used to check if there is an entry for the name. If yes, the pointer to the entry is returned; otherwise *nil* is returned to indicate that no entry is found for the name. The translation scheme for E→ *id* is as follows:

```
E → id     {  p = lookup(id.name);
              If p =! nil then
              E.place = E1.place
           }
```

It is assumed that the *lookup* function is implicit, and it is not written in the translation scheme. *id.place* has the pointer to *id* in the symbol table.

Grammar

A → *id* := E

E →E+E | E*E | E – E | (E) | *id*

SDT scheme: The translation scheme for the generation of the three-address code for the assignment statement is given in Table 5.1. The synthesized attribute A.*code* represents the three-address code for the assignment A.

The non-terminal E has three attributes:

- T is a variable that holds temporary values.
- E.*place* holds the value of E.
- E.*code* holds the sequence of the three-address statements evaluating E.

The function *newTemp* returns a sequence of distinct names *t1, t2, . . tn* in response to successive calls. The notation *gen*(x ':=' y '+' z) is used to generate the three-address statement starting at an index. Expressions that appear instead of variables like x, y and z are evaluated when passed to *gen*, and quoted operators or operands, like '+', are taken literally. In practice, three-address statements might be sent to an output file, rather than built up into the code attributes.

Table 5.1 Syntax-directed translation scheme for assignment statement

Production	Semantic rule
A →*id* = E	A.*code* = E.*code* || *gen*(*id.place* ' =' E.*place*)
E→ E1+E2	T= *newTemp*( ); E.*place* = T; E.*code* = E1.*code* || E2.*code* || *gen*(E.*place* ' =' E1.*place* '+' E2.*place*)
E→ E1*E2	T= *newTemp*( ); E.*place* = T; E.*code* = E1.*code* || E2.*code* || *gen*(E.*place* ' =' E1.*place* '*' E2.*place*)
E→ E1 – E2	T= *newTemp*( ); E.*place* = T; E.*code* = E1.*code* || E2.*code* || *gen*(E.*place* '=' E1.*place* '–' E2.*place*)
E→ –E1	T= *newTemp*( ); E.*place* = T; E.*code* = E1.*code* || *gen*(E.*place* ' =' '–' E1.*place*)
E→(E)	E.*place* = E1.*place* E.*code* = E1.*code*
E→*id*	E.*place* = *id.place* E.*code* = null

newTemp() function: *Returns a sequence of distinct variable names to use as temporary variables in the intermediate code.*
gen: *Generates the intermediate three-address code starting at an index. Index is maintained in the quadruple array.*

Example 5.3 SDT for assignment statement

Consider the assignment statement, P = (q + r) * (s + t).

The three-address code is generated as per the translation scheme of Table 5.1. Evaluating from left to right, bottom to top:

- Values of *ids* are the lexemes obtained from the scanner. Set *id.place* with the value of the lexeme.
- Translation of E→*id*, as per Table 5.1 is to set E.*place* as *id.place* and E.*code* as null.
- Going up the tree, E→E+E, a new temporary variable T1 is created and is saved in E.*place*. The code is generated starting at index 1000. The code to be generated is (E.*place* '=' E1.*place* '+' E2.*place*). The value of E1.*place* = q and E2.*place* = r. Hence, the code generated at index 1000 will be T1 = q + r.

The complete SDL of the assignment statement P = (q + r) * (s + t) is shown in Fig. 5.3. The three address-code generated is as follows:

1000 T1 = q + r
1001 T2 = s + t
1002 T3 = T1 * T2
1003 P = T3

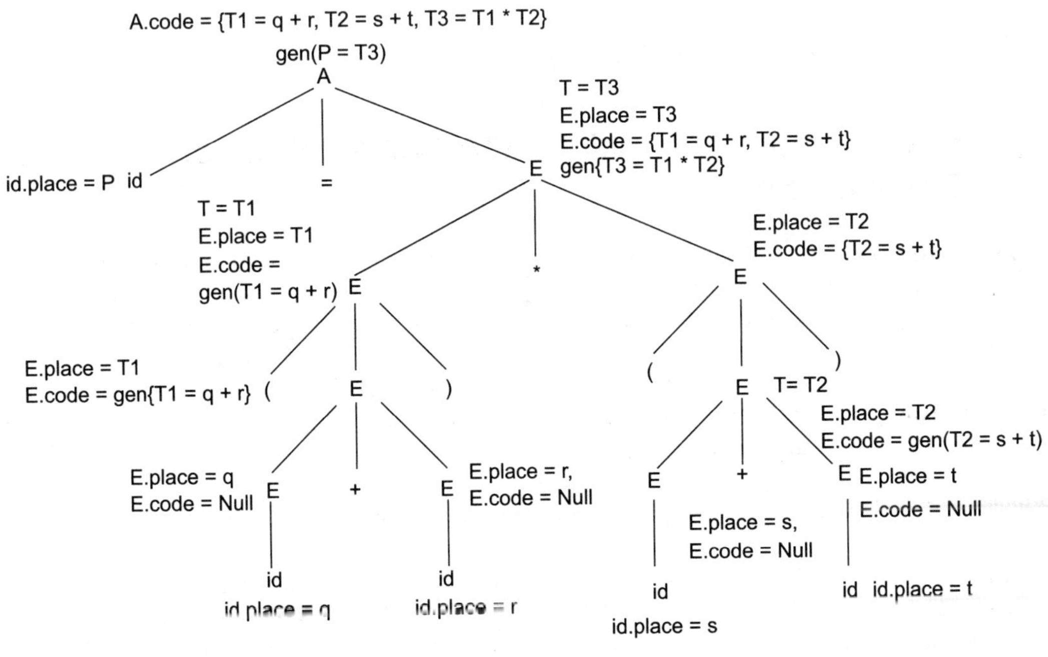

Figure 5.3 SDT for Example 5.3

Example 5.4 SDT for assignment statement

Consider the assignment statement, a= −b * c.

The three-address code is generated as per the translation scheme of Table 5.1. The SDT of the assignment statement a = − b*c, is shown in Fig. 5.4. Assuming the starting index of the quadruple array is 1000, the three address-code generated is as follows:

1000 T1= − b

1001 T2= T1 * c

1002 a=T2

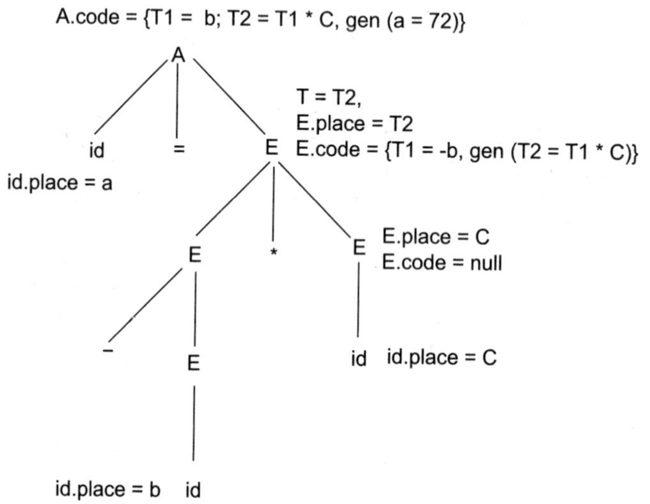

Figure 5.4 Annotated parse tree for Example 5.4

5.5 Syntax-directed Translation to TAC for Boolean Expressions

Boolean expressions: A Boolean expression in a programming language is an expression that produces a Boolean value: true or false. They are more often used as conditional expressions in statements that alter the flow of control, such as if-then, if-then-else, or while-do statements. A Boolean expression may be composed of a combination of Boolean constants and Boolean operators such as AND, OR and NOT. Boolean operators are applied to Boolean variables or relational expressions. Relational expressions are of the form *E1 relop E2*, where E1 and E2 are arithmetic expressions and relop is a relational operator such as AND, OR and NOT.

Grammar

E→E or E | E and E | not E | (E) | id relop id | true | false

Methods for translating Boolean expressions: Two methods can be used to represent the value of Boolean expressions.

- **Method 1:** Encode the true and false value to 0 and 1. This allows evaluation of Boolean expressions like arithmetic expressions.

- **Method 2:** In this method, the evaluation of Boolean expressions is by flow of control. The value of a Boolean expression is represented by the position reached in a program. Since this method is based on flow of control, it can be used to evaluate Boolean expressions in flow-of-control statements.

5.5.1 Method 1: Numerical Representation

True and false values are denoted by 0 and 1, respectively. The evaluation is from left to right, bottom-up, as in arithmetic expression evaluation. The translation scheme is given in Table 5.2. The variable *nextquad* is used in the scheme to keep track of the index of the quadruple.

> *nextquad: The variable nextquad is used to keep track of the index of the three-address code being generated. It holds the index of the next quadruple to follow. For example, if we have to write at index 'i', then i is nextquad.*

Table 5.2 Translation scheme for Boolean expressions (numerical method)

Production	Semantic rule

E→id1 relop id2	T = *newTemp*( );
	E.*place* = T;
	gen(if *id1.place* relop *id2.place* goto *nextquad*+3);
	gen(T = 0);
	gen (goto *nextquad*+2);
	gen (T = 1);

E→E1 or E2	T = *newTemp*( ); E.*place* = T; *gen* (T= E1.*place* or E2.*place*)
E→E1 and E2	T= *newTemp*( ); E.*place* = T; *gen* (T = E1.*place* and E2.*place*)
E→not E1	T= *newTemp*( ); E.*place* = T; *gen* (T = not E1.*place*)

Example 5.5 Three-address code for Boolean expressions
Consider the Boolean expression, A < B or C. The SDT of the expression is shown in Fig. 5.5. Evaluating from left to right, bottom to top:

- Values of *ids* are the lexemes obtained from the lexical analyser. Set *id.place* with the value of the lexeme.
- Translation of E→*id* is shown in Table 5.1. E.*place* is set as *id.place* and E.*code* is null.
- Going up the tree, E→E relop E, as in Table 5.2, a new temporary variable T1 is created and is saved in E.*place*. Four statements are generated as per the translation scheme. The code generation

starts at address 1000. This location is called *nextquad*. Hence, the goto contains *nextquad*+3 = 1000+3 = 1003.

- For E→E or E, as per Table 5.2, a new temporary variable T2 is created and is saved in E.*place* and code is generated at location 1004.

The TAC generated is as follows:
1000) if A<B goto 1003
1001) T1=0
1002) goto (1004)
1003) T1=1
1004) T2= T1 or C

If the condition A<B is true, then T1 is set to 1 by transferring the control to address 1003, else T1 is set to 0. After setting T1, it is ORed with C, by the statement at address 1004.

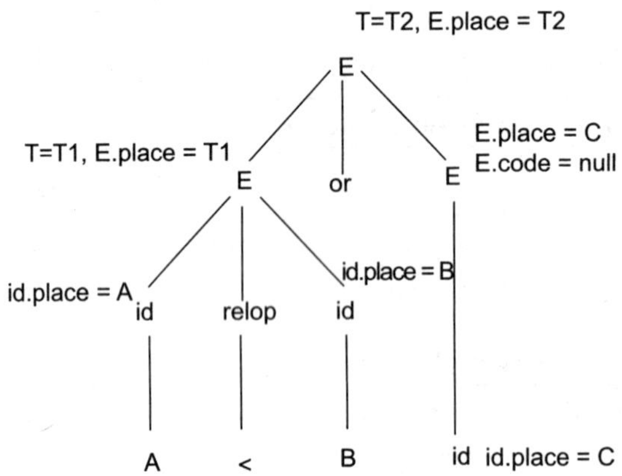

Figure 5.5 Annotated parse tree for Example 5.5

Example 5.6 Three-address code for Boolean expressions
Consider the Boolean expression, A>B and not(C>D or E>F) and the start of three-address code at an arbitrary location 'i'. The TAC generated is as follows if the code starts at an arbitrary index i:
i) if A> B goto i+3
i+1) T1 = 0
i+2) goto i + 4
i+3) T1 =1
i+4) if C < D goto i + 7
i+5) T2 = 0
i+6) goto i + 8
i+7) T2=1
i+8) if E>F goto i+11
i+9) T3=0
i+10) goto i+2

i+11) T3=1
i+12) T4=T2 or T3
i+13) T5=not T4
i+14) T6=T1 and T5

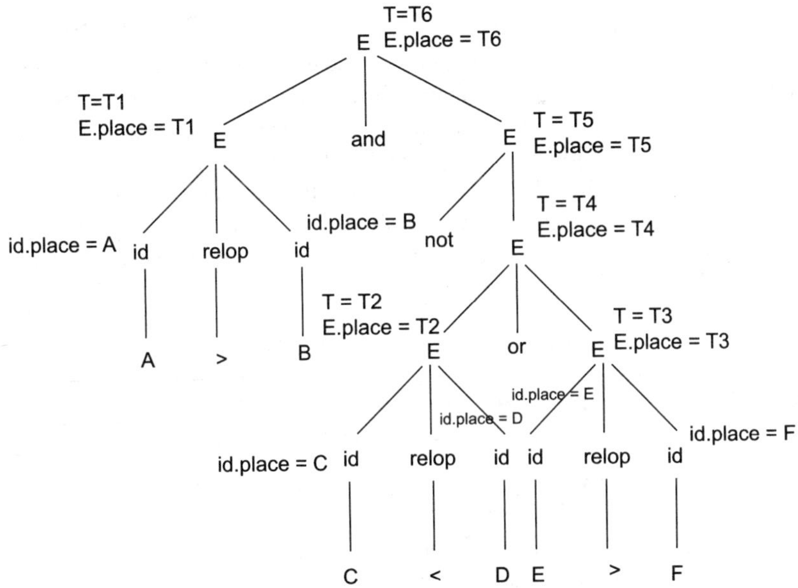

Figure 5.6 Annotated parse tree for Example 5.6

5.5.2 Method 2: Short Circuit Code

In this method, the TAC corresponding to the Boolean expression can be generated without evaluation of the entire expression. This style of evaluation is called short circuit or jumping code. It is possible to evaluate Boolean expressions without generating code for the Boolean operators, if the value of an expression is represented by a position in the code sequence. For example, if the expression is A<B or C<D, it is not necessary to evaluate the complete expression if A<B is true. If A<B is true then the value of the complete expression is also true. Let us consider the truth table of Boolean expressions and derive the translation scheme. However, before discussing the translation scheme, the concept of backpatching is described.

Backpatching: The easiest way to implement SDDs is to use two passes. In the first pass, construct a syntax tree for the input and then walk the tree in depth-first order, computing the translations given in the definition. The main problem in generating code for Boolean expressions and flow-of-control statements in a single pass is that during one single pass, the labels that control must go to at the time the jump statements are generated may be unknown. This problem can be solved by generating branching statements with the targets of the jumps temporarily left unspecified. These labels of jumps will be filled in when the proper targets can be determined. This filling in of labels is called backpatching.

To manipulate a list of labels, three functions can be used:

- *makelist*(i) creates a new list containing only i, an index into the array of quadruples. A pointer to the list is returned.
- *merge*(p1, p2) concatenates the lists pointed to by p1 and p2, and returns the pointer to the concatenated list.
- *backpatch*(p,i) inserts i as the target label for each of the statements on the list pointed to by p.

OR operator: The truth table for the OR operator is shown in Table 5.3. The expression is defined by the production E→E1 or E2. As per the explanation in Table 5.3, the value of the first expression must be false to start evaluation of the second expression. So, to begin execution of E2, it is required to remember where E2 starts; so, a nullable non-terminal M1 is introduced before E2. The false value of E is made the same as the true value of expression E2, and the true value of E is made the true value of both E1 and E2. The translation scheme is given in Table 5.4. The Boolean expression E is associated with two labels: E.*true* and E.*false*. E.*true* controls the flow if E is true, and E.*false* controls the flow if E is false.

Table 5.3 Truth table for OR operator

E1	E2	E1 or E2	Explanation
T	T	T	If the value of expression E1 is true then irrespective of the value of E2, the expression will evaluate to true. Hence, checking E2 if E1 is true is not required.
T	F	T	
F	T	T	If the value of expression E1 is false then evaluate the expression E2. If E2 is true then the answer is true, else false.
F	F	F	

Table 5.4 Translation scheme for OR operator

Production	Semantic rule
E→E1 or M1 E2	backpatch (E1.*false*, M.*quad*): E.*false* = E2.*false* E.*true* = *merge*(E1.*true*, E2.*true*);
M→ε	M.*quad* = *nextquad*

M→ε: M is appended before any statement S, to which the control can transfer during execution of the code. A nullable non-terminal M→ε is introduced to remember the start of statement S, by remembering the index in the quadruple array. The semantic action associated with M→ε, must remember nextquad just before the processing of statement S. Hence, M.quad = nextquad.

backpatch(p, i): i is inserted as the target label for each of the statements on the list pointed to by p.

AND operator: The truth table for the AND operator is shown in Table 5.5. The expression is defined by the production E→E1 and E2. As per the explanation in Table 5.5, the value of the first expression must be true to start evaluation of the second expression. So, to begin the execution of E2, the process should keep track of the start point of E2. A nullable non-terminal M1 is introduced before E2 to keep track of the start point of E2. For further execution, set the true value of E the same as the true value of expression E2, and set the false of E as the false value of both E1 and E2. The translation scheme is given in Table 5.6.

Table 5.5 Truth table for AND operator

E1	E2	E1 and E2	Explanation
T	T	T	If the value of expression E1 is true then evaluate the expression E2. If E2 is true then the answer is true, else false.
T	F	F	
F	T	F	If the value of expression E1 is false then irrespective of the value of E2, the expression will evaluate to false. Hence, it is not required to check E2 if E1 is true.
F	F	F	

Table 5.6 Translation scheme for AND operator

Production	Semantic rule
E→E1 and M1 E2	*backpatch* (E1.*true*, M.*quad*); E.*true* = E2.*true*; E.*false* = *merge*(E1.*false*, E2.*false*);
M→ε	M.*quad* = *nextquad*;

NOT operator: The truth table for the NOT operator is shown in Table 5.7. The expression is defined by the production E→not E1. If the value of expression E1 is true then the value of the expression becomes false, and if the value of E1 is false then the value of the expression becomes true. The translation scheme is given in Table 5.8.

Table 5.7 Truth table for NOT operator

E1	not E1
T	F
F	T

Table 5.8 Translation scheme for NOT operator

Production	Semantic rule
E→not E1	E.*true*=E1.*false*; E.*false*= E.*true*;

The translation scheme of other statements is given in Table 5.9.

Table 5.9 Translation scheme for other statements

Production	Semantic rule
E→*id*	E.*place* = *id.place*;
E→E1 relop E2	E.*true* = *makelist*(*nextquad*); E.*false* = *makelist*(*nextquad*+1); *gen* (if E1.*place* relop.val E2.*place* goto____); *gen*(goto ____);

(Cont'd)

Table 5.9 (Continued)

Production	Semantic rule
E→(E)	E.*true* = E1.*true*; E.*false* = E1.*false*;
A →*id* = E	A.*code* = E.*code* ‖ *gen*(*id.place* ‘ =’ E.*place*)

Example 5.7 Boolean expression using short circuit method

Consider the statement, not (a<b and (e > f or i < j)). The parse tree is annotated with the semantic actions generating the three-address code, as shown in Fig. 5.7. In the OR operation, there is *backpatch*(E1.*false*, M.*quad*) = *backpatch*(1003,1004). Hence, fill 1004 in the goto statement at address 1003. Also, in the AND operation, there is *backpatch*(E1.*true*, M.*quad*) = *backpatch*(1000,1002). The three-address code generated using the syntax-directed method is as follows:

1000) if a<b goto 1002
1001) goto__
1002) if e>f goto___
1003) goto 1004
1004) if i> j goto ___
1005) goto ___

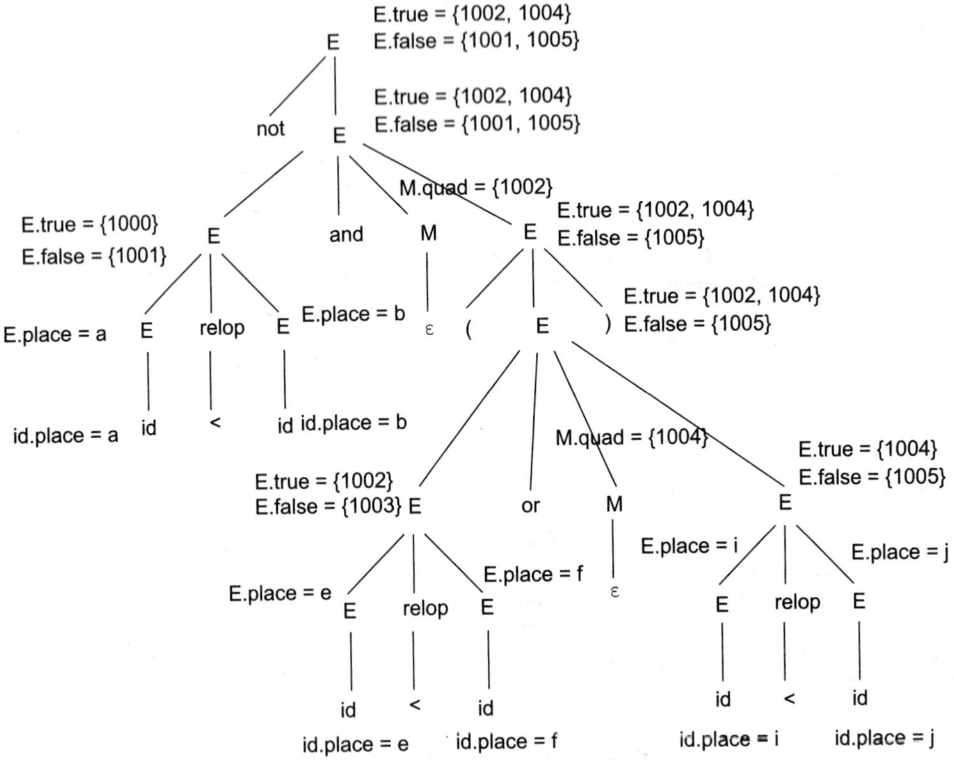

Figure 5.7 Annotated parse tree for three-address code generation of Boolean expression using short circuit method (Example 5.7)

Example 5.8 Boolean expression using short circuit method

Consider the statement, P < Q or (R < S and T < U). Figure 5.8 shows the annotated parse tree representing the translation of the given statement.

The three-address code generated is

1000 If P<Q goto ______.
1001 goto 1002
1002 If R<S goto 1004
1003 goto__.
1004 if T < U goto __.
1005 goto ____.

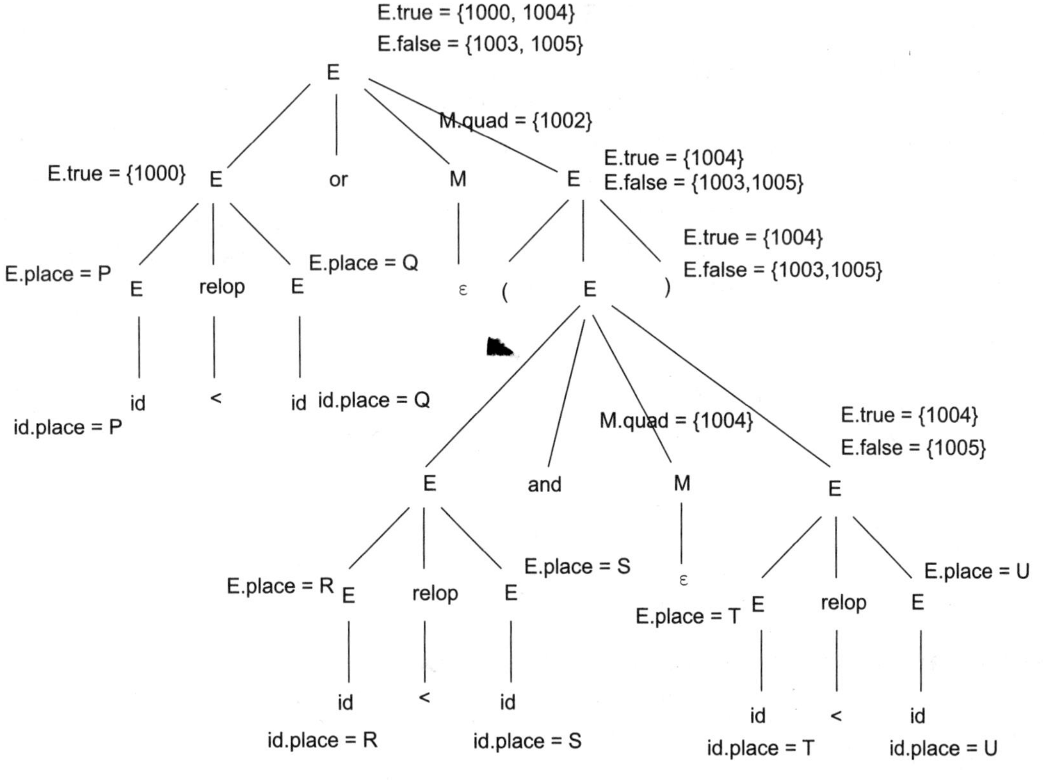

Figure 5.8 Annotated parse tree for three-address code generation of Boolean expression using short circuit method (Example 5.8)

5.6 Syntax-directed Translation into TAC for Programming Language Control Structures Using Backpatching

5.6.1 If-then Construct

The flow-of-control statement 'if-then' consists of a Boolean expression and a statement. The statement is executed only if the condition is true.

Grammar: if E then S1

SDL scheme: The statement S1 is executed only if the condition E is true. So, the translation scheme must transfer the control to S1 if E is true; if E is false, exit the loop and transfer the control to the next statement outside the loop. To transfer the control to S1, the index of the start of S1 must be remembered by introducing a nullable non-terminal M→ε, just before execution of S1. The flow of control is shown in Fig. 5.9, and the translation scheme is given in Table 5.10. along with the revised grammar.

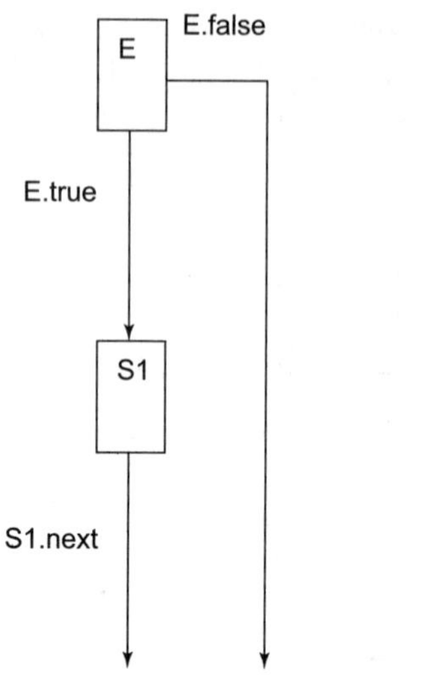

Figure 5.9 Flow of control of the if-then statement

Table 5.10 Translation scheme for flow-of-control statements

Production	Semantic rule
S→if E then M S1	*backpatch*(E.*true*,M.*quad*); S.*next* = *merge*(E.*false*,S1.*next*);
S→if E then M1 S1 N else M2 S2	*backpatch*(E.*true*,M1.*quad*); *backpatch*(E.*false*,M2.*quad*); S.*next* = *merge*(S1.*next*, *merge*(N.*next*, S2.*next*);
S→while M1 E do M2 S1	*backpatch*(S1.*next*, M1.*quad*); *backpatch*(E.*true*,M2.*quad*); S.*next* = E.*false*; *gen*('goto' M1.*quad*)
S→do M1 S1 while M2 E	*backpatch*(S1.*next*,M2.*quad*); *backpatch*(E.*true* = M1.*quad*); S.*next* = E.*false*;
M→ε	M.*quad* = *nextquad*;
N→ε	N.*next* = makelist(*nextquad*), *gen*(goto __)

Example 5.9 SDT of if-then statement into three-address code

Consider the flow-of-control statement, if (a > 10) then p = q + r. The annotated parse tree is shown in Fig. 5.10 and the three-address code generated is as follows:

1) if a>10 goto 3
2) goto__
3) T=q+r
4) p=T

5.6.2 If-then-else Construct

The flow-of-control statement 'if-then-else' consists of a Boolean expression and two sets of statements. If the condition is true then some set of statements/statement is executed, and if condition is false then another set of statements is executed.

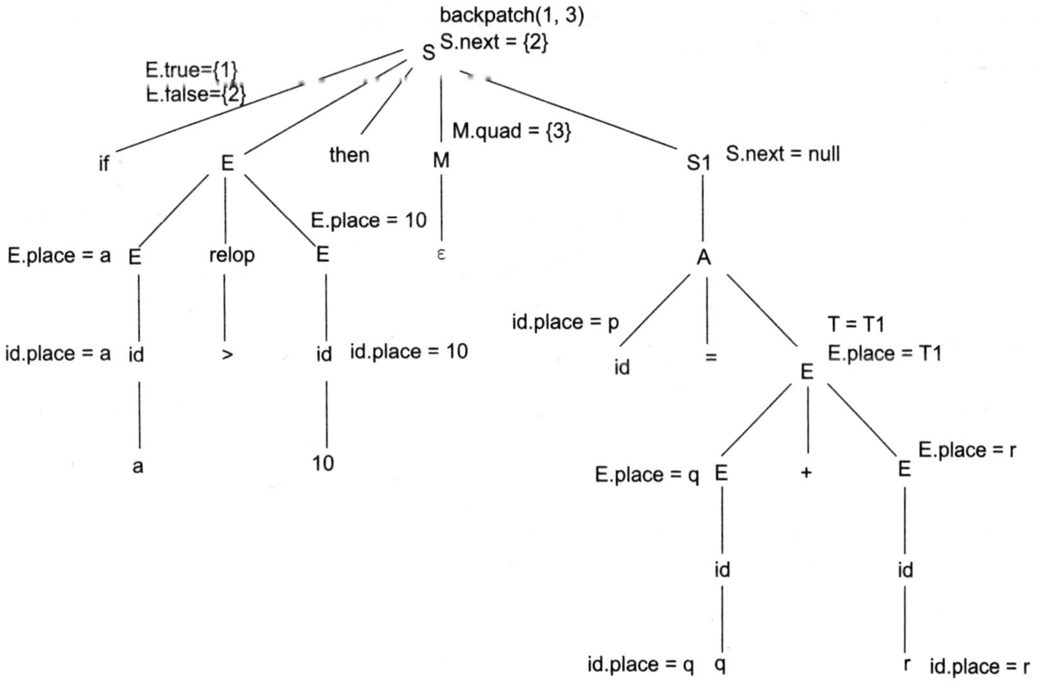

Figure 5.10 SDT for Example 5.9

Grammar: if E then S1 else S2

SDT scheme: Statement S1 is executed if the condition E is true. So, the translation scheme must transfer the control to S1 if E is true. Statement S2 is executed if condition E is false. To transfer the control to S1/S2, the index of the start of S1/S2 must be remembered by introducing a nullable non-terminal M→ε, just before execution of S1/S2. Use another marker non-terminal to introduce this jump after S1. Let N be this marker with production N→ε. N has attribute N.*next*, which will be a list consisting of the quadruple numbers of the statement goto__, that is generated by the semantic rule for N. So, the revised grammar will be S→ if E then M1 S1 N else M2 S2.

After the execution of statements, the control must be transferred to the next statement outside the loop. The flow of control is shown in Fig. 5.11, and the translation scheme is given in Table 5.10.

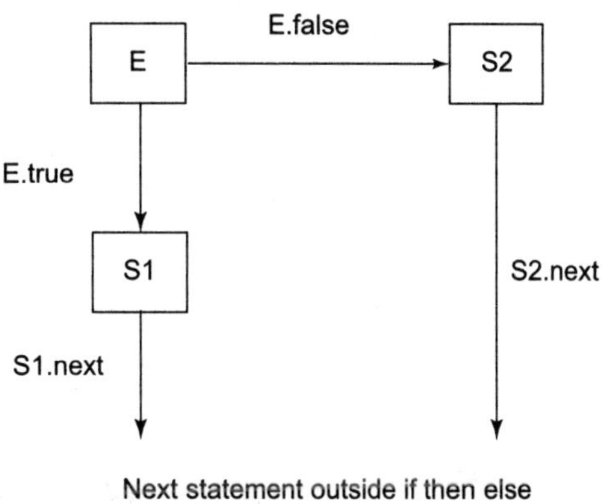

Figure 5.11 Flow of control of if-then-else statement

Example 5.10 SDT of if-then-else statement into three-address code

Consider the flow-of control statement:

if a>b then

x=x+1;

else

x=x+2;

The annotated parse tree is shown in Fig. 5.12 and the TAC generated is as follows:

100) if a>b goto <u>102</u>
101) goto <u>105</u>
102) T1=x+1
103) x=T1
104) goto ___
105) T2= x+2
106) x=T2

The translation scheme for E→E relop E is used from Table 5.9 and S→ A from Table 5.11.

Table 5.11 Translation scheme for other statements

Production	Semantic rule
S→begin L end	S.*next* = L.*next*;
S→A	S.*next* = nil;
L→L1; M S	*backpatch*(L1.*next*, M.*quad*); L.*next* = S.*next*;
L→S	L.*next* = S.*next*;
L →ε	L.*next* = S.*next*;

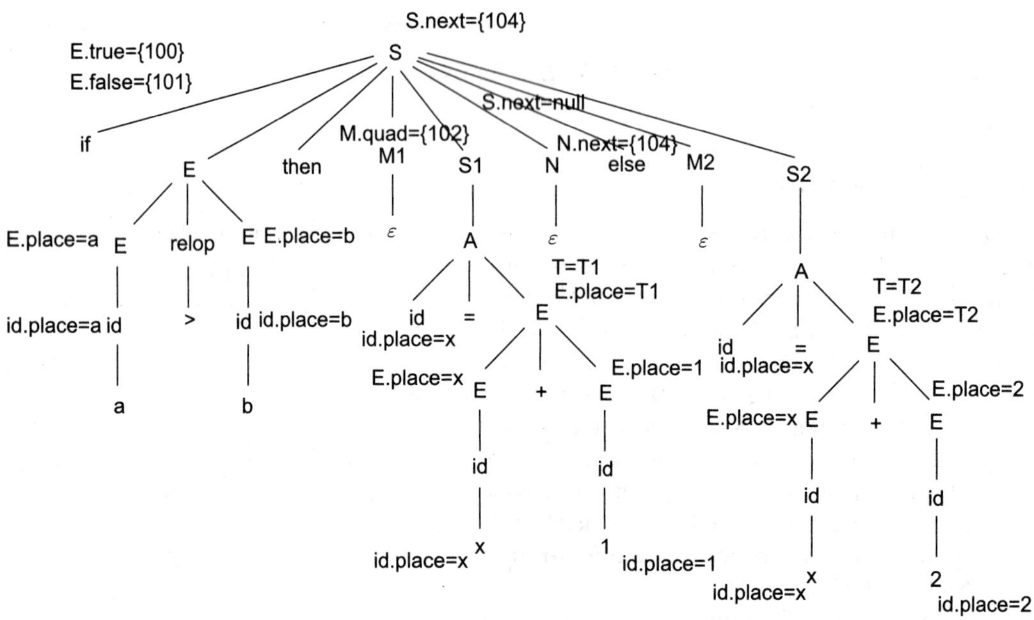

Figure 5.12 Translation into TAC for Example 5.10

Example 5.11 SDT of if-then-else statement

Consider the flow-of control statement:

if p<q then

```
        begin
                p=r+s;
                s=s+1;
        end
else
        p=t+u;
```

The annotated parse tree is shown in Fig. 5.13 and the TAC generated is as follows:

100) if p<q goto 102
101) goto 107
102) T1=r+s
103) p=T1
104) T2= s+1
105) s=T2
106) goto__
107)T3=t+u
108) p= T3

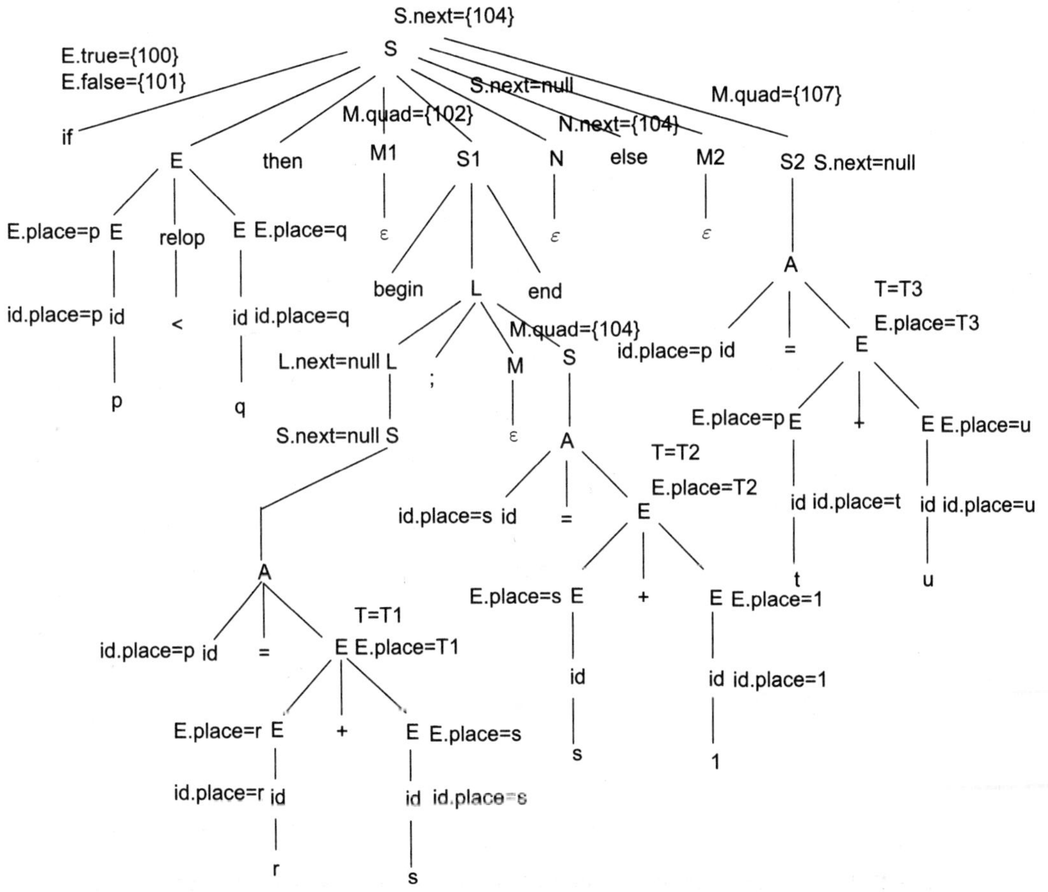

Figure 5.13 Annotated parse tree for TAC generation for if-then-else statement of Example 5.11

5.6.3 While Loop

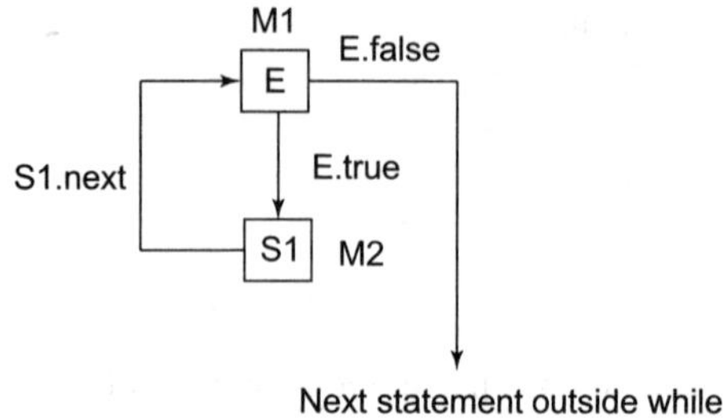

Figure 5.14 Flow of control in while loop

The flow-of-control statement 'while' consists of a Boolean expression and one set of statements. Statement S1 is executed till the condition E is true. The loop exits only when the condition of E becomes false.

Grammar: S → while E do S1

SDT scheme: Statement S1 is executed if the condition E is true. After the statement/set of statements is executed, the condition is checked again. So, the index of E and S1 must be remembered. The revised grammar will be S→ while M1 E do M2 S1. The flow of control is shown in Fig. 5.14, and the translation scheme is given in Table 5.10.

Example 5.12 SDT of while statement
Consider the flow-of control statement:

```
while(x>y) do
    a=b+c;
```

The annotated parse tree is shown in Fig. 5.15 and the TAC generated is as follows:

```
100) if x>y goto 102
101) goto __
102) T1=b+c
103) a=T1
104) goto 100
```

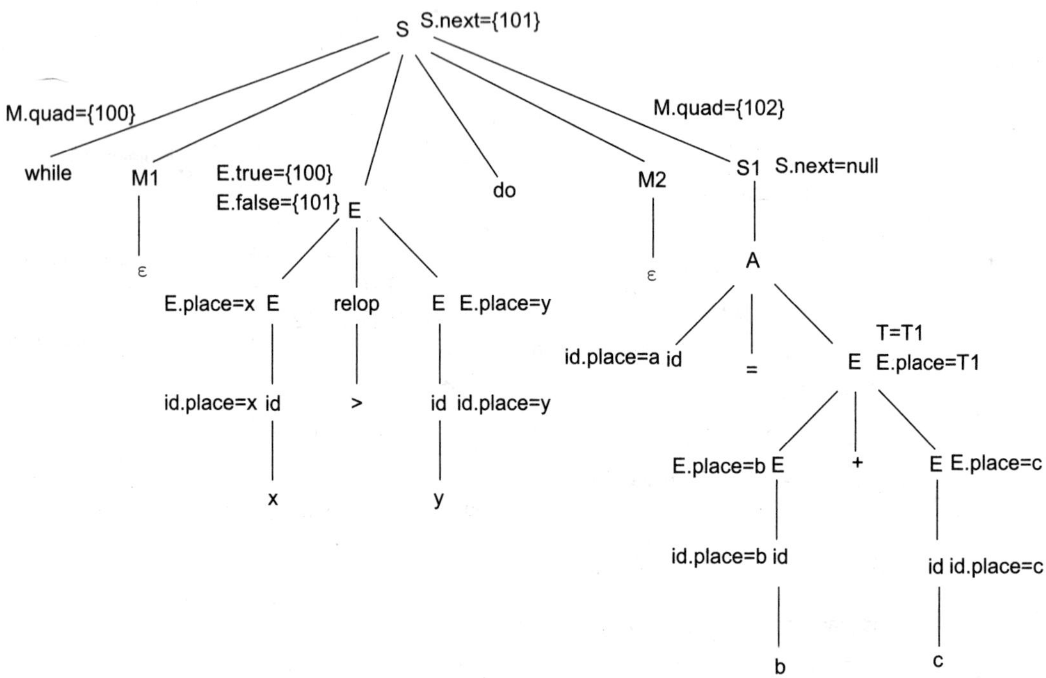

Figure 5.15 Annotated parse tree for TAC generation for while loop of Example 5.12

5.6.4 Do-while Loop

The flow-of-control statement 'do-while' consists of a Boolean expression and one set of statements. Statement S1 is executed at least once before the condition E is checked. The loop exits only when the condition of E becomes false.

Grammar: S→ do S while E

SDT scheme: Statement S1 is executed first without checking the condition. After the statement is executed, the condition E is checked. If the condition E is true then Statement S1 is executed again, else if E is false, then exit from the loop. The index of E and S1 are to be remembered, so introduce nullable non-terminals. The revised grammar becomes S→ do M1 S1 while M2 E. The flow of control is shown in Fig. 5.16, and the translation scheme is given in Table 5.10.

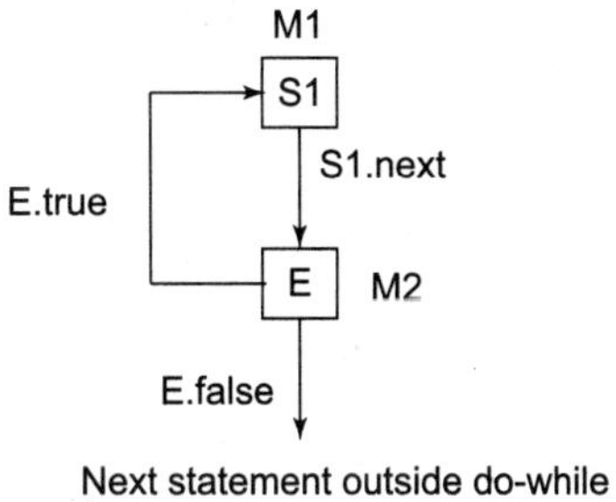

Figure 5.16 Flow of control in do-while loop

Example 5.13 SDT of do-while statement

Consider the flow-of control statement:

```
do
begin
    a=1;
    b=x*y;
end
while(p>=s)
```

The annotated parse tree is shown in Fig. 5.17 and the TAC generated is as follows

100) a=1
101) T1=x*y
102) b=T1
103) if p>=s goto <u>100</u>
104) goto __

5.6.5 For Loop

The for loop has three parts in the for statement. The first part is the initialisation. It is executed first, and only once. This step allows declaration and initialisation of loop control variables. Next is the condition. If it is true, the body of the loop is executed. If it is false, the body of the loop does not execute and the flow of control jumps to the next statement after the loop. After the body of the loop executes, the flow of control jumps back to the increment statement. This statement enables updating of loop control variables. The condition is now evaluated again. If it is true, the loop executes and the process repeats itself (body of loop, then increment step, and then the condition). When the condition becomes false, the for loop terminates.

Grammar: S→ for (A1; E ; A2) S1

SDT scheme: Statement S1 is executed if condition E is true. After the statement is executed, the condition E is checked again and the increment is applied. Initially, initialisation is carried out by A1. Non-terminals M1, M2 and M3 are introduced as follows:

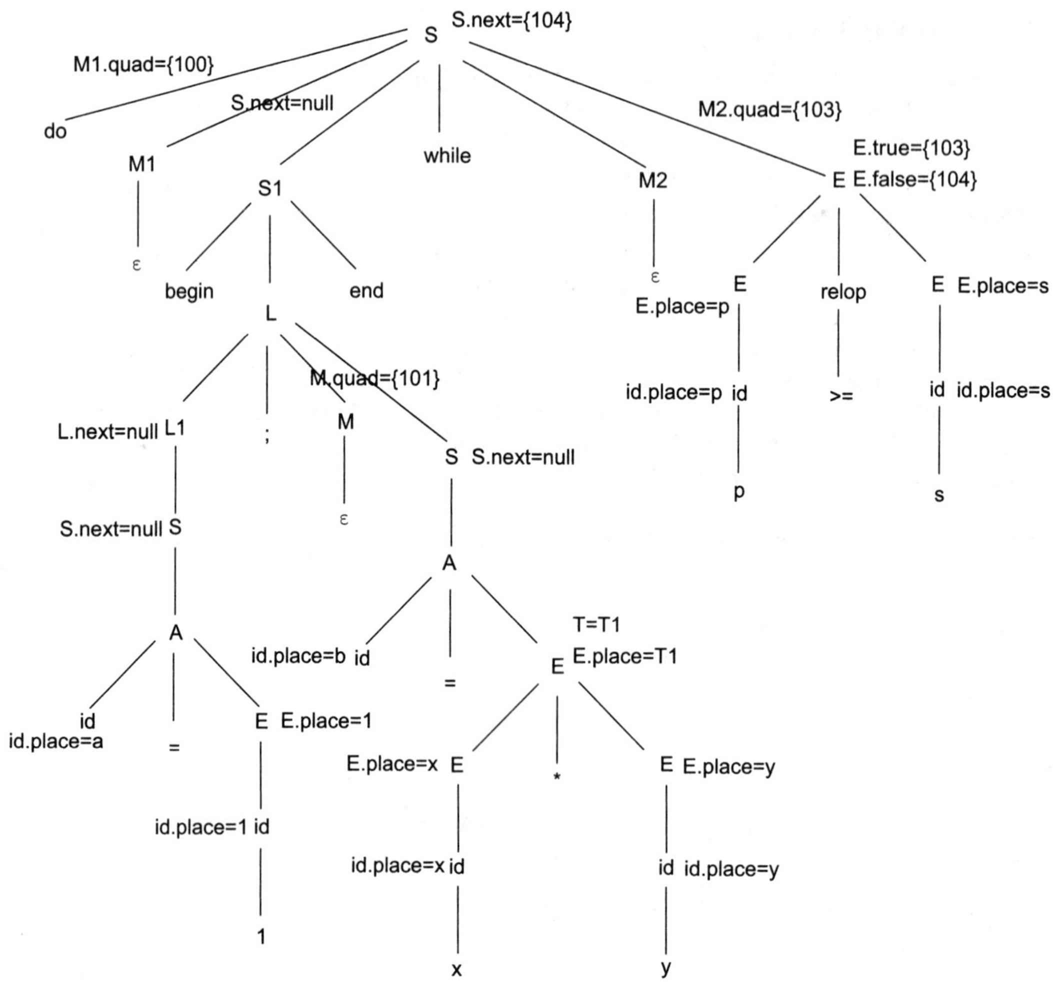

Figure 5.17 Annotated parse tree for TAC generation for do-while loop of Example 5.13

S→ for (A1; M1 E; M2 A2) M3 S1

The translation scheme is given in Table 5.12.

Table 5.12 Translation scheme for the for loop

Production	Semantic rule
S→ for (A1; M1 E ; M2A2)M3 S1	*backpatch*(E.*true*, M3.*quad*); *backpatch*(S1.*next*, M2.*quad*); *backpatch*(M3.*next*, M1.*quad*); S.*next*= E.*false*; *gen*('goto' M2.*quad*);

(Cont'd)

Table 5.12 (Continued)

Production	Semantic rule
M1→ε	M.*quad* = *nextquad*;
M2→ε	M.*quad* = *nextquad*;
M3→ε	M3.*next*= makelist(*nextquad*); *gen*(goto __); M3.*quad*=*nextquad*;

Example 5.14 SDT of the for loop
Consider the for statement:
for(i=1;i<=10;i=i+1)
    num=num+i
The annotated parse tree is shown in Fig. 5.18 and the TAC generated is as follows:
100) i=1
101) if i<=10 goto 106
102) goto___
103) T1=i+1
104) i=T1
105) goto 101
106) T2=num+i
107) num= T2
108) goto 103

5.6.6 Repeat-Until

The conditional expression appears at the end of the loop, so the statements in the loop are executed at least once before the condition is tested. If the condition is false, the flow of control jumps back to repeat, and the statement(s) in the loop execute again. This process repeats until the given condition becomes true.

Grammar: S→ repeat S until E

SDT scheme: Statement S1 is repeated until the condition E is false. The control of the program exits from the loop to the next statement, when the condition becomes true. It repeats until the statement/statements in the block are executed at least once as the conditional expression appears at the end of the loop. As a statement in the loop may be executed again after the condition check, the start of the loop statements must be remembered; so introduce a nullable non-terminal M before the statements inside the loop. Also, the expression E may be checked one or more times; so introduce M just before processing of the condition of the expression. To remember S1, add M1 before S1 and to remember E, M2 before E. The revised grammar becomes S→ repeat M1S1 until M2E. The SDTS for repeat-until is shown in Table 5.13. As shown in Fig 5.19, transfer of control to the Boolean expression E after execution of S1 must take place. Also, if the condition is false, the control transfers to the start of S1 and if E is true, the control transfers to the next statement after the loop.

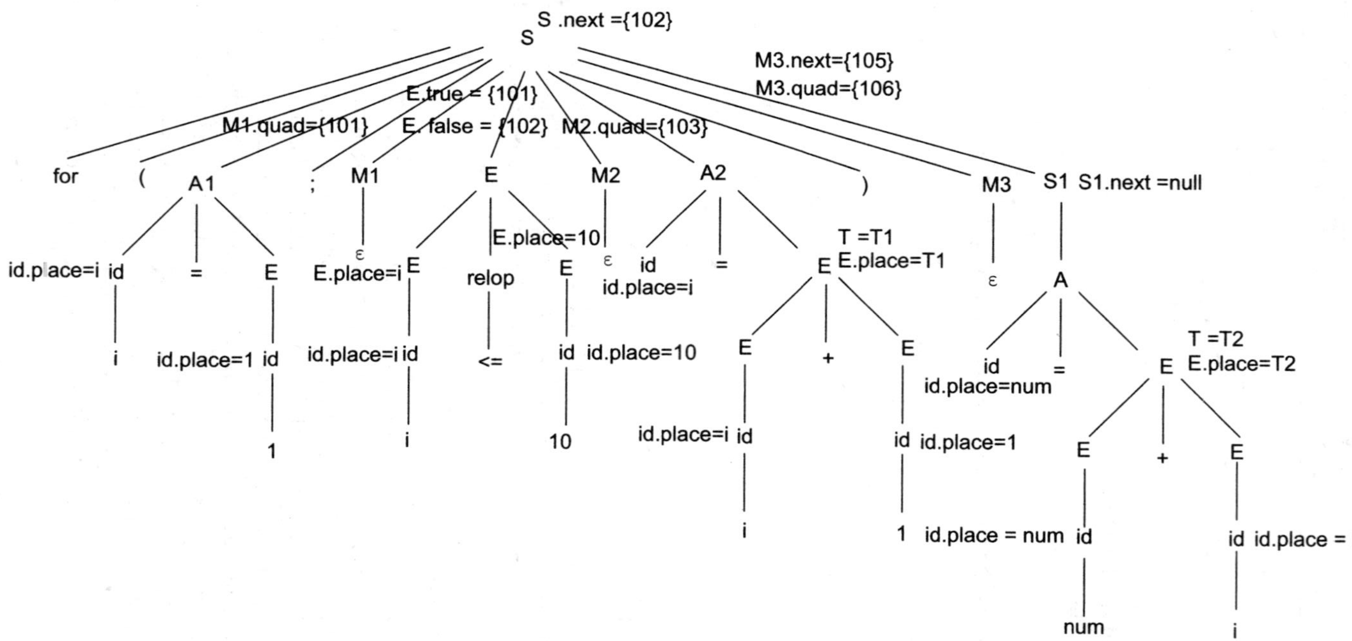

Figure 5.18 Annotated parse tree for TAC generation of for loop of Example 5.14

Table 5.13 Translation scheme for repeat until

Production	Semantic rule
S→Repeat M1 S1 until M2 E	*backpatch*(S1.*next* = M2.*quad*); *backpatch*(E.*false* = M1.*quad*); S.*next* = E.*true*;
M1→ε	M1.*quad* = *nextquad*;
M2→ε	M2.*quad* = *nextquad*;

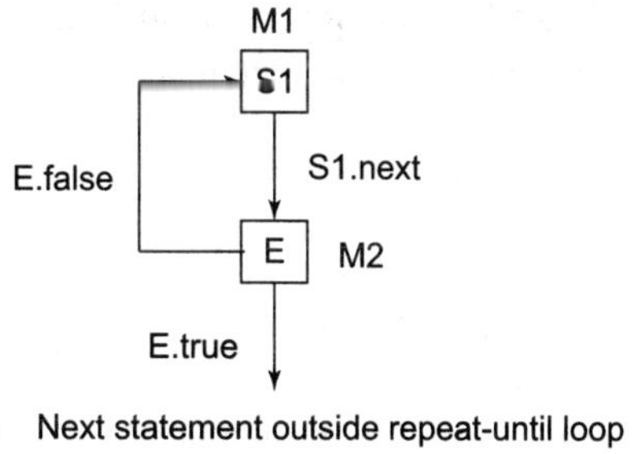

Figure 5.19 Flow of control in repeat-until loop

Example 5.15 SDT of repeat-until

Consider the repeat-until statement, repeat A = B + C until A < 10. Figure 5.20 shows the annotated parse tree representing the translation of the given statement. The TAC generated assuming the index starts at 100 is

100) T1= B+C
101) A = T1
102) if A < 10 goto___
103) goto 100

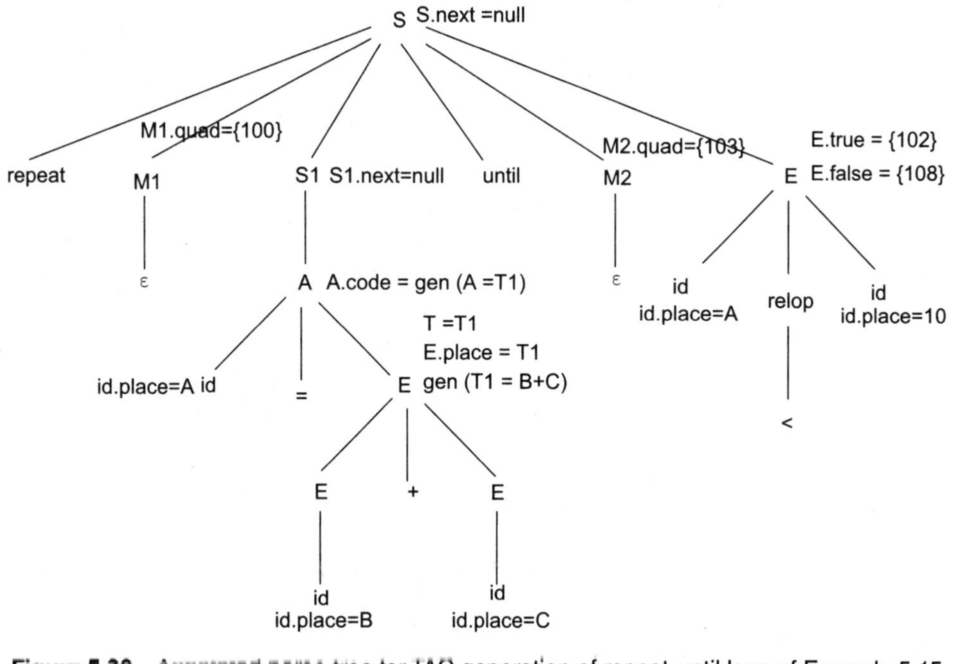

Figure 5.20 Annotated parse tree for TAC generation of repeat-until loop of Example 5.15

Example 5.16 SDT of repeat-until into TAC

Consider the repeat-until statement

```
repeat
        begin
            i = i+1;
            x = y+z;
        end
    until x < n ;
```

Figure 5.21 shows the annotated parse tree representing the translation of the given statement. The TAC generated assuming the index starts at 1 is as follows:

1) T1 = i + 1
2) i = T1
3) T2 = y+z
4) x = T2
5) if x < n goto ___
6) goto 1

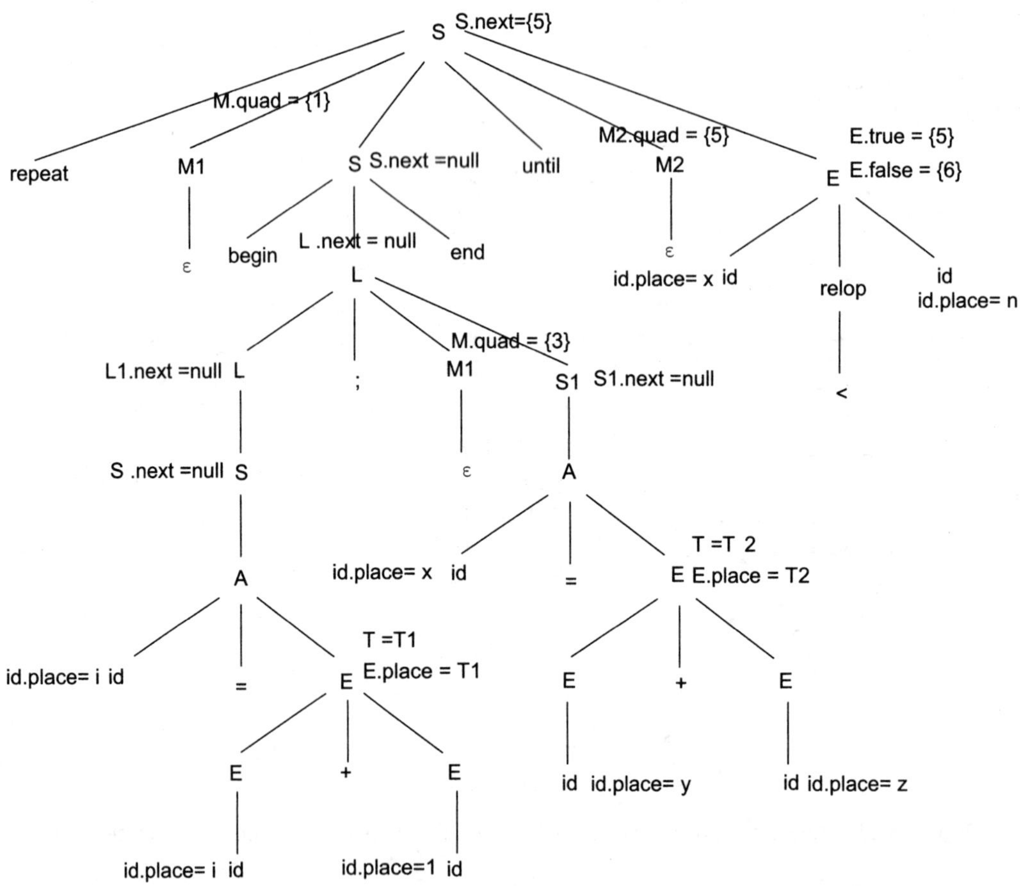

Figure 5.21 Annotated parse tree for TAC generation for repeat-until construct of Example 5.16

5.7 Syntax-directed Translation of Arrays to TAC

Arrays: Arrays can be single dimensional or multi-dimensional. Elements of the array can be accessed quickly if they are stored in a block of consecutive locations. If the width of each array element is w, then the ith element of array A begins at location $base + (i - low) \times w$, where low is the lower bound on the subscript and base is the relative address of the storage allocated for the array. That is, base is the relative address of A[low]. The expression can be partially evaluated at compile time if it is rewritten as $i \times w + (base - low \times w)$.

The sub-expression $c = base - low \times w$ can be evaluated when the declaration of the array is seen. Assume that c is saved in the symbol table entry for A. So, the relative address of A[i] is obtained by simply adding $i \times w$ to c.

Address calculation of multi-dimensional arrays: A two-dimensional array can be stored in one of two forms:

- Row-major (row-by-row)
- Column-major (column-by-column)

In the case of row-major form, the relative address of A[i1, i2] can be calculated by the formula base + ((i1 − low1) × n2 + i2 low2) × w, where low1 and low2 are the lower bounds on the values of i1 and i2, and n2 is the number of values that i2 can take. That is, if high2 is the upper bound on the value of i2, then n2 = high2 − low2 + 1. Assuming that i1 and i2 are the only values that are known at compile time, we can rewrite the above expression as

((i1 × n2) + i2) × w + (base − ((low1 × n2) + low2) × w)

The generalised expression for the relative address of A[i1, i2,…, ik] is

((. . . ((i1n2 + i2) n3 + i3) . . .) nk + ik) × w + base − ((. . .((low1n2 + low2)n3 + low3) . . .) nk + lowk) × w for all j, nj = highj − lowj + 1

Grammar

A→L=E
E→E+E | (E) | L
L→elist] | id
elist → elist, E | id [E

SDT scheme: To handle various dimensional limits nj of the array, group index expressions into an elist. The attribute NDIM of the elist is used to record the number of dimensions. The function *limit*(array, j) returns nj, the number of elements along the jth dimension of the array whose symbol-table entry is pointed to by array. An l-value L will have two attributes: L.*place* and L.*offset*. If L is a simple name, L.*place* will be a pointer to the symbol-table entry for that name, and L.*offset* will be null, indicating that the l-value is a simple name rather than an array reference. The SDT scheme for arrays is given in Table 5.14.

Table 5.14 Translation scheme for arrays

Production	Semantic rule

A→L=E	if (L.*offset* = null) then
	gen(L.*place* '=' E.*place*)
	else
	gen(L.*place*'['L.*offset*'] ' '=' E.*place*);

(Cont'd)

Table 5.14 (Continued)

Production	Semantic rule
E→E+E	T=*newTemp*( ); E.*place*=T; *gen*(E.*place* '=' E1.*place* '+' E2.*place*)
E→(E)	E.*place*= E1.*place*

E→ L	if (L.*offset* = null) then
	E.*place* = L.*place*
	else begin
	T = *newTemp*( );
	E.*place*=T;
	gen(T '=' L.*place* '[' L.*offset* ']');
	end

L→elist]	T= *newTemp*( ); U = *newTemp*( ); L.*place* = T; L.*offset* = U; *gen* (T '=' elist.Array-c) *gen* (U '=' w * elist.*place*); where c = [d2 * d3 *…dk + d3 * d4….dk+…..dk+1] * w.
L→ id	L.*place* = *id.place* L.*offset* = null

Elist → elist, E	T = *newTemp*();
	m= elist.*NDIM* + 1;
	gen (T= elist1.*place* '*' Limit(elist1.*array*,m));
	gen (T=T+E.*place*);
	elist.*array* = elist1.*array*;
	elist.*place*=T;
	elist.*NDIM* = m;

Elist → id [E	elist.*place* = E.*place*; elist.*array* = *id.place*; elist.*NDIM* = 1;

Example 5.17 SDT to generate TAC for the given array statement

Consider the array assignment statement, x = A[y,z]. Let the dimensions of array A be 10 × 20. Assume w as 4. The annotated parse tree for the assignment x = A[y,z] is shown in Fig. 5.22. The TAC generated is as follows:

1) T1 = y * 20
2) T1 = T1 + Z.
3) T2 = addr(A) − 84
4) T3 = 4 * T1
5) T4 = T2 [T3]
6) x = T4

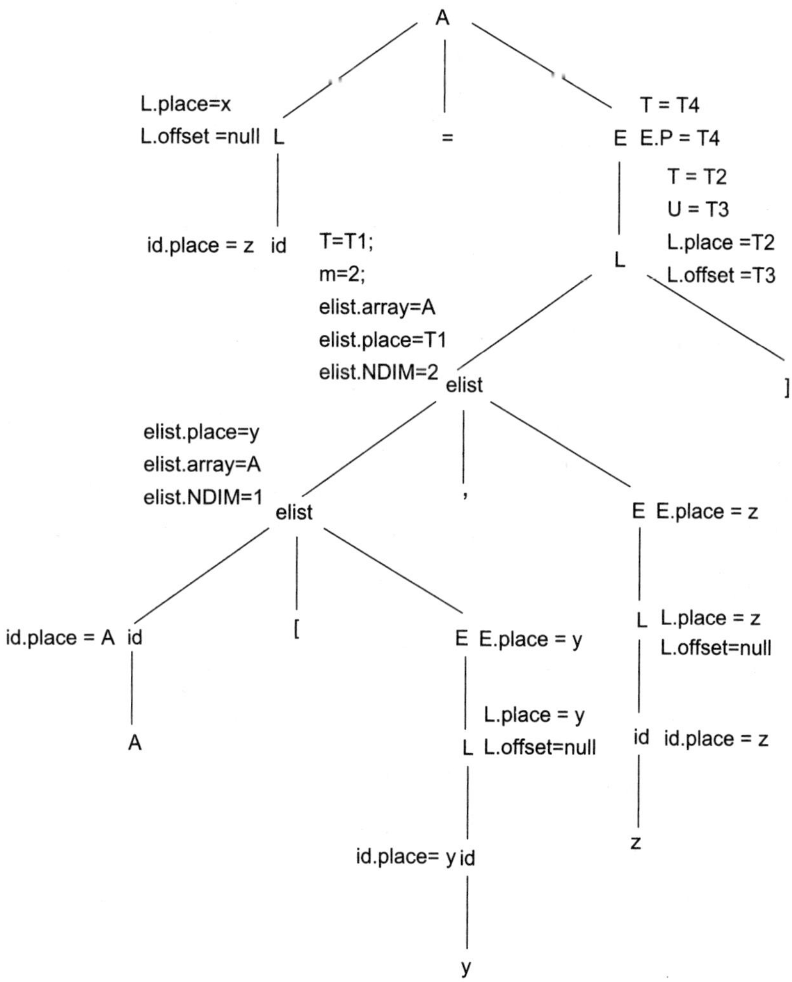

Figure 5.22 Annotated parse tree for generation of TAC for arrays

When generating code at index (1), call the function *limit*(A, 2). This will return the second dimension of the array, that is, 20. Hence, the code generated is T1 = y * 20. Also, when generating code at index (3), compute the value of c as C = (d2 +1)* w = (20 + 1)*4 = 84.

Example 5.18 SDT to generate TAC for the given array statement

Consider the array assignment statement, B [I, J, K] = A. The dimensions of array B are 10 × 20 × 30 and bpw is 4. The annotated parse tree for the array assignment is shown in Fig. 5.23. The TAC generated is as follows:

1) T1 = I * 20
2) T1 = T1 + J
3) T2 = T1 * 30
4) T2 = T2 + K
5) T3 = B – 2524

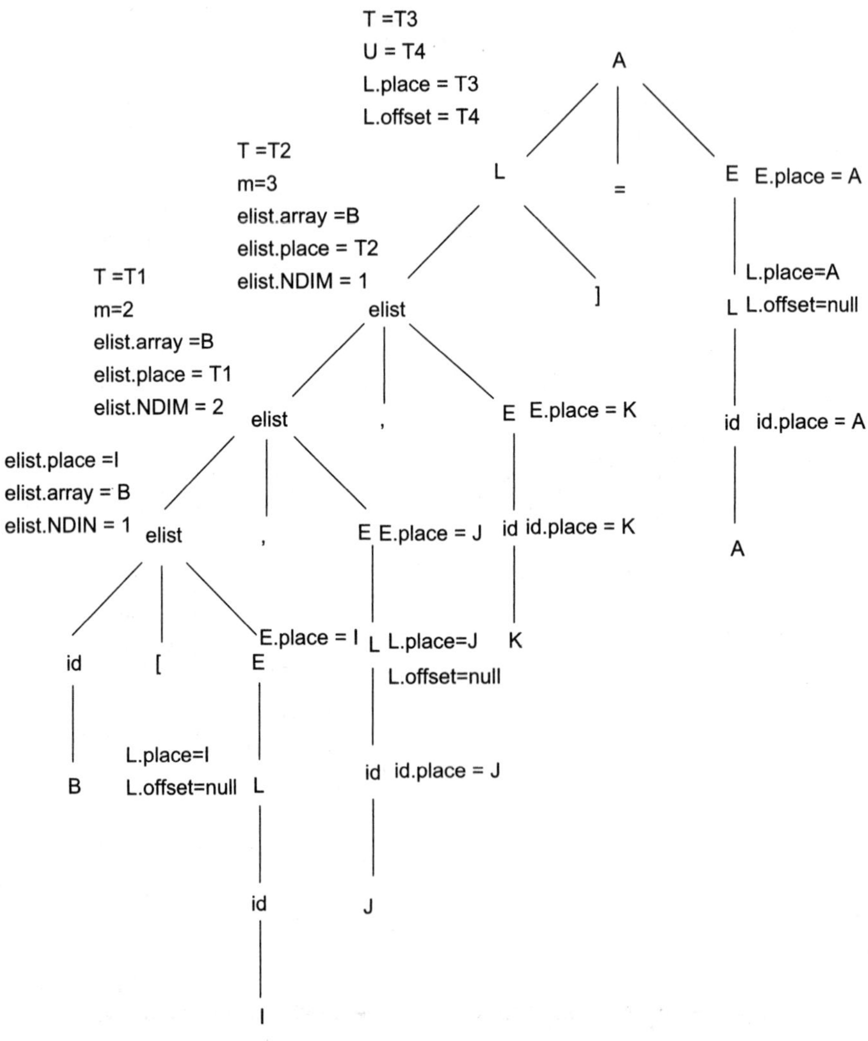

Figure 5.23 Annotated parse tree for generation of TAC for arrays

6) T4 = 4 *T2
7) T3[T4] =B

c = (d2 * d3 + d3 + 1) * w
= (20*30+30+1)*4
= (600 + 31)*4
= 631 * 4
= 2524

Example 5.19 SDT to generate TAC for the given array statement
Consider the array assignment statement, X [I, J] = Y [I, J] + Z[K]. Given the dimensions of array X and Y as 10 × 10, the dimension of Z is 10 and bpw is 2. The annotated parse tree for the array assignment is shown in Fig. 5.24.

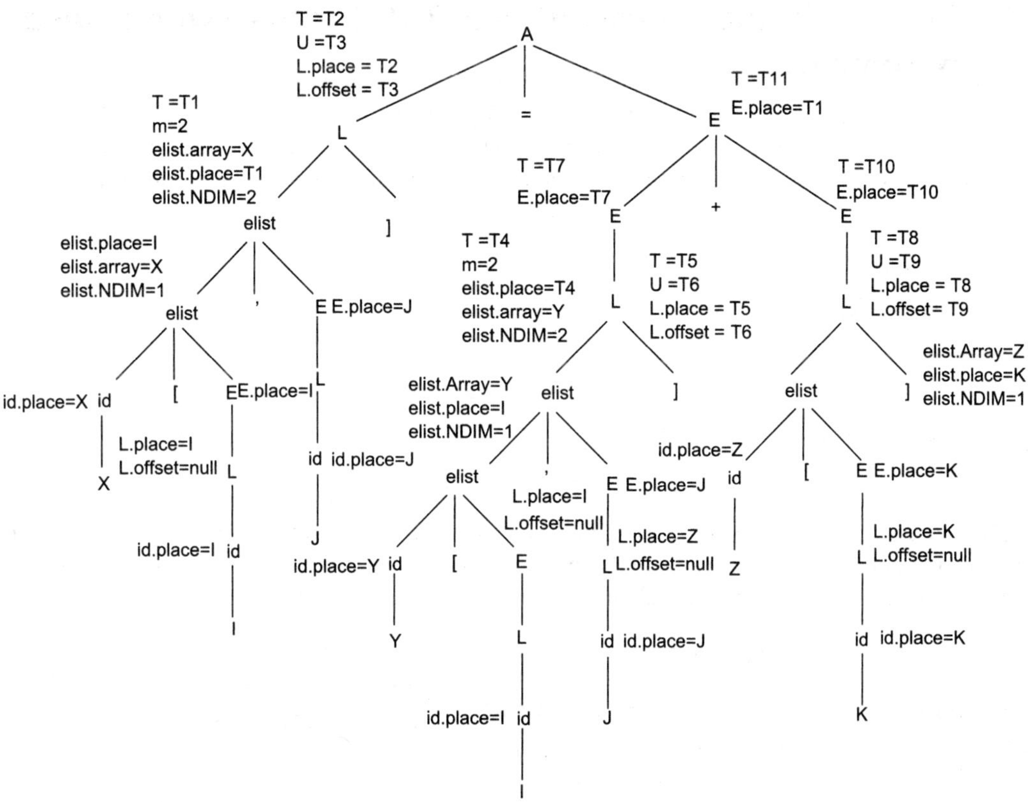

Figure 5.24 Annotated parse tree for generation of TAC for arrays

The TAC generated is as follows:

1) T1=I * 10
2) T1 = T1 + J
3) T2 = X-22
4) T3 = 2 * T1
5) T4 = I * 10
6) T4 = T4 + J
7) T5 = Y-22
8) T6 = 2 * T4
9) T7 = T5[T6]
10) T8 = Z – 22
11) T9 = 2 * K
12) T10 = T8[T9]
13) T11=T7+T10
14) T2[T3]=T11

C is computed as follows:

C = (10 + 1) * 2 = 22

5.8 Syntax-directed Translation to TAC for the Switch-Case Statement

While writing a program, if there is a need to check the value of a single variable, then the switch statement must be used. This statement is often faster than the nested if-else. Also, the syntax of the switch statement is cleaner and easy to understand. The syntax of switch-case is as follows:

```
switch E
begin
        case V1: S1
        case V2: S2
        :
        :
        :
        case Vn: Sn-1
        default: Sn
end
```

The expression E corresponding to switch is evaluated, followed by n constant values that the expression might take. After the value of the expression is evaluated, the value is searched for in the list of cases. The case that matches the evaluated value is executed.

Table 5.15 Translation scheme for switch-case

Production	Semantic rule

S→ Switch E N begin caselist end	*backpatch*(N.*next*, *nextquad*);
	for each entry in caselist.Q
	    gen(if E.*place*=caselist.Q.V goto caselist.Q.L;
	    if caselist.d ≠ null
	        gen(goto caselist.d)
	S.*next* = caselist.*next*;

caselist → case V : S	caselist.*next* =*makelist*(*nextquad*);
	caselist.*next* = *merge*(caselist.*next*, S.*next*);
	enter(caselist.Q,V.*place*,V.*next*);
	gen(goto__);

caselist → caselist case V : S	caselist.*next* = *makelist*(*nextquad*);
	caselist.*next* = *merge*(caselist.*next*, Caselist1.*next*, S.*next*);
	gen (goto__);
	Enter(caselist.Q,V.*place*,V.*next*);

caselist → caselist default M : S	caselist.*next* = *makelist*(*nextquad*) caselist.*next* = *merge*(caselist.*next*,caselist1.*next*, S.*next*); *gen*(goto__); caselist.d = M.*quad*;
V→id	V.*place* = *id.place*; V.*next* = *nextquad*;

(Cont'd)

Table 5.15 (Continued)

Production	Semantic rule
N→ε	N.*next* = *nextquad*; *gen*(goto__);
M→ε	M.*quad* = *nextquad*;

Example 5.20 To generateTAC for the given switch-case statement

Consider the switch-case statement

```
switch (a + b)
    begin
        case4: c = d + 1
        case5: c = d + 2
    default: c = d + 3
    end
```

The annotated parse tree for the array assignment is shown in Fig. 5.25. The TAC generated is as follows:

1) T1 = a + b
2) goto 12
3) T2= d + 1
4) c = T2
5) goto__
6) T3 = d + 2
7) c = T3
8) goto__.
9) T4 = d + 3
10) c = T4
11) goto __
12) If T1 = 4 goto 3
13) If T1 = 5 goto 6
14) goto 9

Caselist.Q

V	L
4	3
5	6

Example 5.21 To generate TAC for the given switch-case statement

```
switch (a+b)
begin
    case 5 : switch(p+q)
        begin
            case 0 : A = B+1
            case 1 : A = B + 3
        end
    case 3 : x= y – 1
    default: x=y + 1
end
```

Figure 5.25 Annotated parse tree for generation of TAC for switch-case

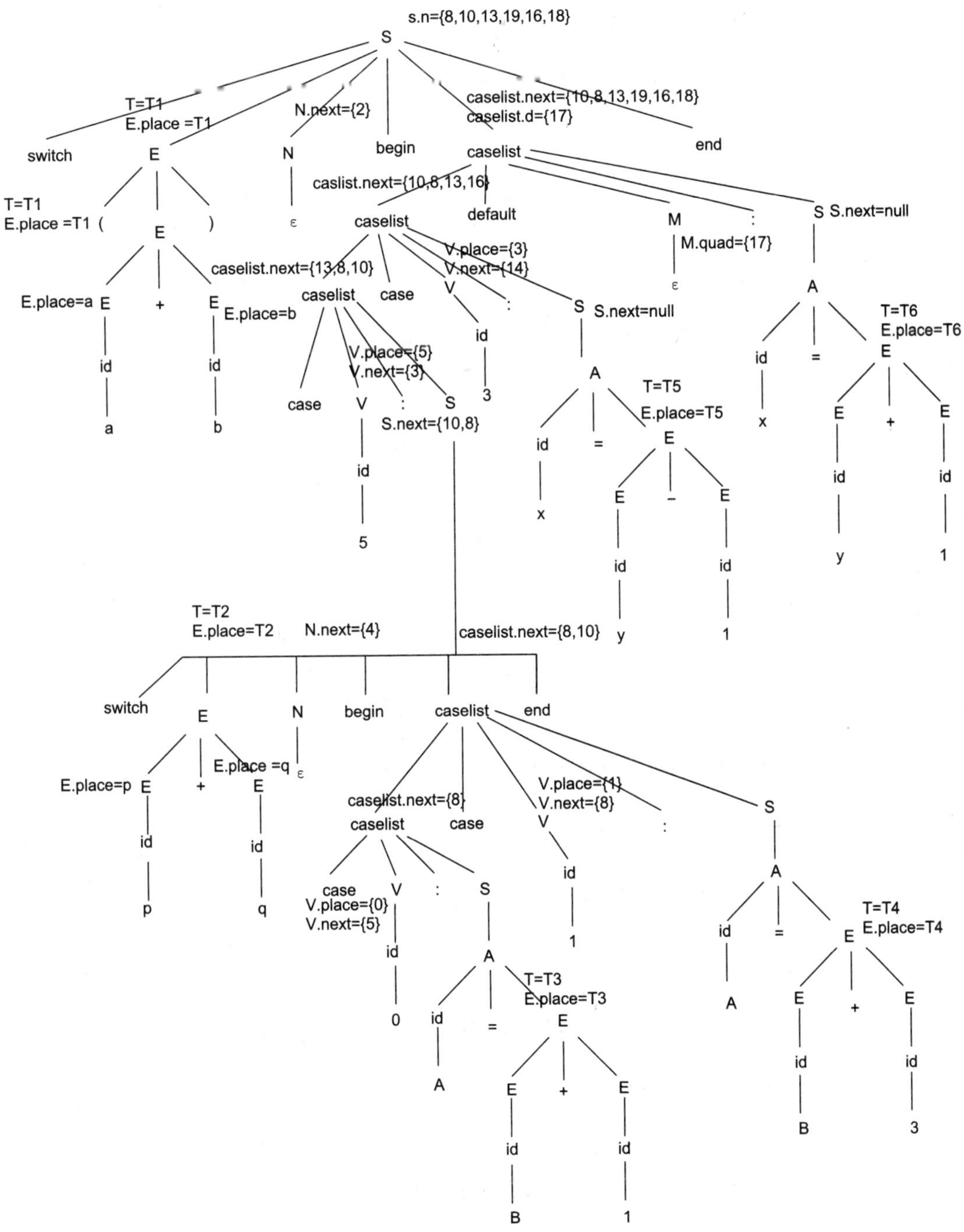

Figure 5.26 Annotated parse tree for generation of TAC for switch-case

The annotated parse tree for the array assignment is shown in Fig. 5.26. The TAC generated is as follows:

1) T1 = a + b
2) goto 25
3) T2=p +q
4) goto 11
5) T3 = B + 1
6) A=T3
7) goto__.
8) T4 = B+3
9) A = T4
10) goto __
11) If T2 = 0 goto 5
12) If T2 = 1 goto 8
13) goto__
14) T5 = y -1.
15) x = T5
16) goto__
17) T6 = y +1.
18) x = T6
19) goto__
20) If T1 = 5 goto 3
21) If T1 = 3 goto 14
22) goto 17

caselist.Q

V	L
0	5
1	8
5	3
3	14

5.9 Syntax-directed Translation to TAC for Procedures

The procedure is a frequently used programming construct. It is imperative for a compiler to generate good code for procedure calls and returns. When a procedure is called, a calling sequence must be executed, and after execution of the calling program is complete, the control must transfer to the program that called the procedure.

The translation for a call must include a calling sequence, a sequence of actions taken on entry to and exit from each procedure. When a procedure call occurs, space must be allocated for the activation record of the called procedure. The arguments of the called procedure must be evaluated and made available to the called procedure. Pointers must be established to enable the called procedure to access data in enclosing blocks. The state of the calling procedure must be saved so that it can resume execution after the call. This return address must be saved at a location.

Table 5.16 Translation scheme for procedure call

Production	**Semantic rule**
S→ call *id*(elist)	for each item p in queue do *gen* ('parameter' p); *gen* ('call' *id.place*);

(*Cont'd*)

Table 5.16 (Continued)

Production	Semantic rule
elist→ elist, E	append E, place at end of queue
elist→ E	initialise queue to contain only E.*place*

Example 5.22 Generate TAC for the given procedure call
Consider a procedure call statement
Call newProcedure (A + B, C, D − F);

The generated TAC is as follows and the annotated parse tree is shown in Fig. 5.27.

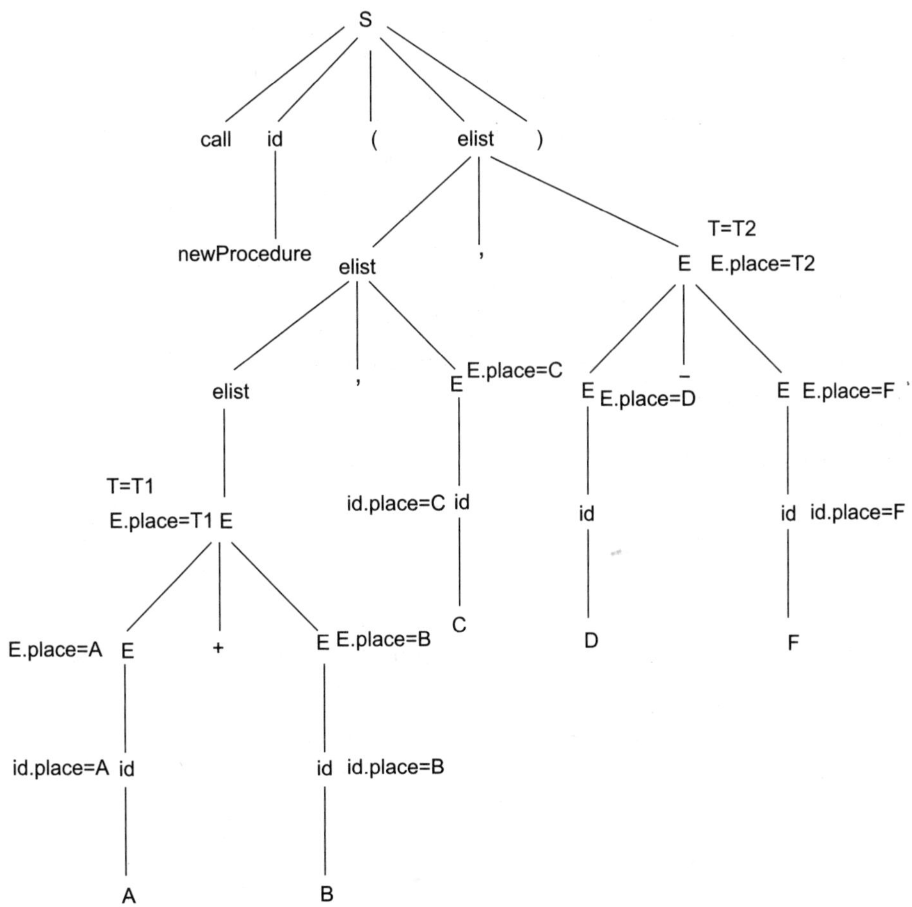

Figure 5.27 Annotated parse tree for generation of TAC for procedure call

1) T1 = A + B
2) T2 = D – F
3) Parameter T1
4) Parameter C
5) Parameter T2
6) call newProcedure

The queue created is

T1	C	T2

5.10 Syntax-directed Translation to TAC for Declarations

Declarative statements are used to declare the type of the variable used in the program. The variables are already entered by the scanner. During translation, add the type of the variable if the variable name is available in the symbol table.

Table 5.17 Translation scheme for declarative statements

Production	Semantic rule
D→ integer id	Enter (id.type=integer); D.attr = integer;
D→ real id	Enter (id.type=real); D.attr = real;
D→ D, id	Enter (id.*place*= D.attr); D.attr = D1.attr;

Example 5.23 Generate TAC for the given declarative statement
Consider the declarative statement
integer a, b;
The parse tree is shown in Fig. 5.28 along with the symbol table.

Name	Type
A	Integer
B	Integer

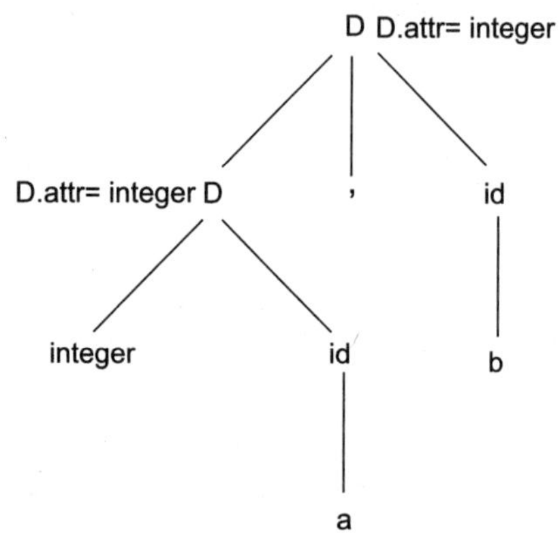

Figure 5.28 Annotated parse tree for declarative statement and symbol table

Example 5.24 Generate TAC for the given code fragment
for (i=1;i<50;i+1)
    if(i<10) then

```
        a=b+1
    else
        a=c+1
```

The TAC generated is as follows:

```
1)  i = 1
2)  if I < 50 then goto 7
3)  goto 2
4)  T1 = i + 1
5)  i = T1
6)  goto 2
7)  if i < 10 goto 9
8)  goto 12
9)  T2 = b + 1
10) a = T2
11) goto 4
12) T3 = c + 1
13) a = T3
14) goto 4
```

SUMMARY

- The use of intermediate code reduces the number of optimisers and code generators.
- Three-address code, single static assignment and graph representations can be used as intermediate representations.
- Data structures to represent TAC are quadruples, triples and indirect triples.
- E.*place* is the name that holds the value of E.
- E.*code* is a sequence of three-address statements evaluating E.
- The variable *nextquad* is used to keep track of the index of the three-address code being generated.
- Generating branching statements with the targets of the jumps temporarily left unspecified and then filling in the labels in the next pass is called *backpatch*ing.

EXERCISES

Review Questions

Fill in the blanks with appropriate answers:

1. S-attributed grammars have __________ attributes.
2. L-attributed grammars use __________ attributes.
3. A parse tree with the values of its attributes is called __________.
4. __________ is used as a tool to find the evaluation order of attributes at each node of the parse tree.
5. SDT is a sequence of steps: input String → Parse tree → __________ → Evaluate order of semantic rules.

Answers: 1. Synthesized 2. Synthesized and inherited 3. Annotated parse tree 4. Dependency graph 5. Dependency graph

State whether true or false:

1. If a grammar is L-attributed, then it must be S-attributed.
2. Attribute evaluation in S-attributed grammars can be incorporated conveniently in bottom-up parsing.
3. SDT hides implementation details and does not specify the order of evaluation of semantic actions.
4. SDTs are more efficient than SDD as they specify the order of evaluation of semantic actions.
5. If there are cycles in the graph, then there is no topological sort.
6. SDT can be implemented by building a parse tree and then performing actions in left-to-right, depth-first order.

Answers: 1. False 2. True 3. False 4. True 5. True 6. True.

Practice Questions

1. Represent the expression Z = (−A * B) + (C * D) + (E − F)/(C * D) in quadruple, triple and indirect triple notation. First give the TAC for the same.
2. Convert the expression in Q1 to postfix form using SDTS.
3. Generate TAC for the given assignment statements:
   (i) a = − b * (c + d)
   (ii) A = (B + C) * (−C)
   (iii) Z= − (a * b) + c
4. Generate TAC for the given Boolean expressions. Use the short circuit method.
   (i) A<B or C>D and not (E = F)
   (ii) A = B and not (C > D) or E
   (iii) not(p < q and r < s or not (t < v and r < q))
5. Generate TAC for the given control flow statements:

```
(i)  if (a < b or c > d) then
             x = y + z
     else
             x = y − z

(ii) if (x < y and y < = z ) then
             a= a + 1
     else
             a= a − 1

(iii) repeat x = y + z  until a  <  b
```

6. Write the SDTS, generate the parse tree and give the TAC for the given code fragment:

```
for(i=1; i<50;i+1)
   if (i<10) then
        a=b+1
   else
        a=c+1
```

7. Translate the following statement into intermediate code:
   A[ijk]=B[ij]+C[I + J K]
   where
   A is 3D array of size 10*10*10

B is 2D array of size 10*10
C is 1D array of size 30
Given that w = 2.

8. Translate the following code fragment into intermediate code:

```
switch (i + j)
{
    case1: x = y + z
    default: P = q + r
    case2: u = v + w
}
```

9. Write the SDTS for the switch statement and translate the following into TAC:

```
switch (x)
{
   case1: {a=b;break;}
   case2: {Switch (a)
             {case1: {b=2;break;}
             {case2: {b=a+2; break};
            }
   break;
default: {a=10;break}
```

10. Consider the given translation scheme and generate the parse tree and TAC for id + id * idSDTS:

E→E + E	{Print ' + '}
E→E * E	{Print ' * '}
E→id	{Print *id*.name(place)}
E→(E)	

11. Generate three-address code for while NOT(A>B or C>D).
12. Generate TAC using SDTS:

```
do
      if A = 0 then
            A = B+C*D
      else
      repeat
      A = A+1
      until A<5
      i=i+1;
while(i<10)
```

13. Generate TAC using SDTS:

```
if (L<=R AND C<D ) then
      i=1
      do
            A[I,J] = B[L + R,A[L,R]]
            i++
      while(i<=10 or i<C)
```

Assume the size of array A is 10 × 20 and array B is 10 × 20. Also, w = 2.

14. Generate the TAC using SDTS for A[I,J + 1]:= B[I,C[I,J]] + D[I,J+1] *E[I,J*2], where w = 4 and the size of arrays A, B, C, D and E is 10 × 20, 10 × 5, 5 × 5, 10 × 5 and 5 × 20, respectively.

6 Code Optimisation

Objectives

- To introduce the code optimisation phase of the compiler
- To discuss various machine-independent and machine-dependent code optimisation techniques

6.1 Introduction

The code generated by the compiler may not be very efficient, which provides scope for improvement of the target code. The application of transformation to the code for improvement of code quality or performance is called **optimisation**. Optimisation in code can lead to faster execution, reduced program size, improvement in terms of memory requirements for storage and execution of the code or reduce the requirement of any type of resource. Code optimisation should not modify the program objective, and after optimisation, the program should generate the same output for a given input, without introducing any new error. The optimisation applied must be worth the effort spent in performing the transformation. Compilers that apply transformations to improve the code are called **optimising compilers**.

Code optimisation can be broadly divided into machine-dependent and machine-independent optimisations. **Machine-dependent optimisations** depend on the target machine for which the object code is being generated. Register allocation, use of machine idioms and introducing parallelisation are some examples of machine-dependent optimisations. Optimisation techniques are best applied to intermediate code rather than to the generated code. Machine-independent optimisations are applied to intermediate code. **Machine-independent optimisations** are free from the architecture and properties of the underlying machine and apply transformations to the program. The part of the program that is executed more frequently is a good candidate for improvement; such frequently executing code is generally placed inside loops in the program. Hence, loop optimisations are the best machine-independent code optimisation techniques. The loop optimisation techniques discussed in this chapter are elimination of loop invariant computation, induction variable elimination, loop unrolling and loop jamming. Other machine-independent optimisations discussed are common sub-expression elimination, dead code elimination, constant propagation, copy propagation, function inlining and redundant code elimination.

Code optimisation can be applied in two steps: by first analysing the code to find the part on which the transformation must be applied, and then applying the appropriate transformation.

Need for code optimisation: The code written may be modified to run more efficiently. A program may be optimised so that it becomes smaller in size, consumes less memory, executes faster or performs fewer input/output operations. Optimisation can be performed by automatic optimisers or by programmers.

During **manual code optimisation**, knowledge of exactly how the optimisation should be done and what part of the program should be optimised is required. For various reasons (like slow input operations), 90% of the execution time of a program is spent executing only 10% of the code. Since optimisation takes additional time, apart from the time spent developing the program, the focus should be on optimising this time-critical 10% of code, rather than to try to optimise the whole program. These code fragments are known as **bottlenecks** and can be detected by special utilities, called **profilers**, which can measure the time taken by various parts of the program to execute.

An optimiser is a built-in unit of a compiler. Multiple complex optimisations at the level of machine code may cause a great slow-down in compilation. So, the optimisation phase in the compiler tries to find the part of the code on which to apply transformations and also determine the type of optimisations that must be applied. Modern processors can also optimise the execution order of code instructions.

Optimisation can be applied at different phases of compilation, with different scope of application like global, local, inter-procedural, etc. Source language optimisations are independent of the machine and carried out considering the language by exploiting constant bounds in loops and arrays, inhibiting code generation of unreachable code segments, unrolling loop bodies into equivalent sequential code, suppressing run-time checks that are redundant, etc., discussed in Section 6.2. Language design can have an impact on code quality based on named constants, operator assigns, case statements, protected loop indices, restricted jumps and gotos, etc. Operator assigns allow redundant computations to be identified easily. Case statements generate significantly better code than the equivalent if statements. Protected loop indices, which can be stored in registers, can often be guaranteed to be limited to a fixed range. Restricted jumps and gotos make flow analysis easier.

Code generation optimisations can be applied by careful allocation of registers, the use of instruction sets and hardware addressing modes and the exploitation of special hardware considerations. Good usage of registers is important, as it reduces the time it takes to go to memory to pick up information, thereby reducing the execution time.

6.2 Machine-independent Optimisation

Machine-independent optimisations perform code improvement by taking advantage of the control structure of the program and eliminating inefficiency in the intermediate code. These optimisations can be local or global. Local optimisations are performed within the basic blocks. Global optimisation is applied to control flow or can be inter-procedural. Various types of machine-independent optimisations are discussed in this section.

6.2.1 Common Sub-expression Elimination

The same sub-expressions can be evaluated many times in a program. Instead of computing the same values every time, these common sub-expressions can be eliminated and computation can be done once. Common sub-expressions can be local or global.

Any expression E is called a **common sub-expression** if E was previously computed and the value of E has not changed since the last computation of E.

Example 6.1 Common sub-expression elimination

```
a = b + c
d = e + f
g = b + c
h = e - f
```

The above instructions involve computation of $b+c$, common in both instructions; hence, the sub-expression $b+c$ in the second instruction can be replaced by a, as the value of $b+c$ has not changed since its last computation in $a = b+c$.

a = b + c
d = e + f
g = a
h = e − f

Example 6.2 Common sub-expression elimination
Now, let us consider an example where the value of the common sub-expression changes after its computation.

a = b + c
b = a − d
c = b + c
d = a − d

In this example, two sub-expressions appear to be common. Let us examine both one by one.

- Sub-expression *b+c* in instruction nos 1 and 3. The value of *b* changes in the second instruction, changing the value of *b+c* in the third instruction. The first and third instructions do not compute the same values, and hence, are not common sub-expressions.
- Sub-expression *a − d* in the second and fourth instructions compute the same value. Hence, the common sub-expression in instruction no. 4 can be eliminated.

The code after common sub-expression elimination will be:

a = b + c
b = a − d
c = b + c
d = b

Common sub-expression detection and elimination: Common sub-expressions can be detected by constructing a directed acyclic graph (DAG). The DAG for a basic block consists of nodes and edges with the following labels on nodes:

- Leaves are labelled with unique identifiers, either variables or constants. Leaves denote the initial values of names; hence, they are denoted with subscript 0. Further definition of the same variables use different subscripts to differentiate the initial and new values of names, i.e., nodes are optionally given a sequence of identifiers for labels.
- Interior nodes are labelled with an operator symbol.

Each node of the flow graph can be represented as a DAG, as a DAG is constructed for a single basic block in the local common sub-expression elimination.

DAG construction: For every three-address code (TAC) of the form X = Y op Z, search for nodes Y and Z. These could be leaf nodes or interior nodes of the DAG if their value is already evaluated.

Step 1:

- If nodes Y and Z exist, return the node and use them.
- If node Y or node Z does not exist, create a leaf node and return.
- If nodes Y and Z both do not exist, then create a leaf node named Y and a leaf node named Z and return both nodes.

Step 2:

- If nodes Y and Z exist, create a node labelled 'op', having Y as the left child and Z as the right child.
- If a node named op exists that has Y as the left child and Z as the right child, return this node.

For every **TAC of the form X = op Y,** search for node Y. This could be a leaf node or interior node of the DAG.

Step 1:

- If node Y exists, return the node and use it.
- If node Y does not exist, create a leaf node named Y and return it.

Step 2:

- If node Y is created, then create a node labelled 'op' having Y as the only child.
- If a node named op exists with Y as the only child, return this node.

Elimination of common sub-expression found with the help of DAG: After the DAG is constructed for a basic block, the nodes that have the same labels indicate the common sub-expressions. Such common sub-expressions can be eliminated from the basic block.

Array representation in DAG: Consider the array access given below.

x = a[i]
a[j] = y
z = a[i] (1)

a[i] would become a common sub-expression and can be optimised as

x:=a[i]
z:=x
a[j]:=y (2)

However, (1) and (2) compute different values for z in the case i=j and y!=a[i]. When processing an assignment to array a, kill all the nodes [ ] whose left argument is a plus or minus constant. This makes the node ineligible to be given an additional identifier label, preventing them from being recognised as a common sub-expression. Figure 6.1 shows the DAG representation and killed node. The sequence must be preserved in such cases.

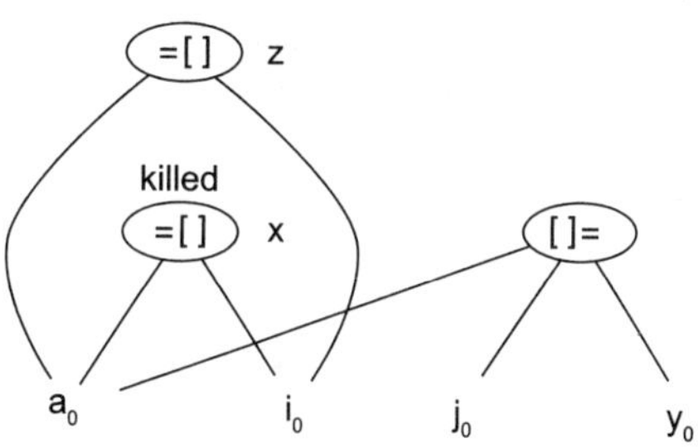

Figure 6.1 DAG representation of array

To re-assemble the DAG into a basic block and not use the order in which the nodes of the DAG were created, indicate in the DAG that certain independent nodes must be evaluated in a certain order. Let us introduce certain edges n→m in DAG that do not indicate that m is an argument of n, but rather that evaluation of n must follow evaluation of m in any computation of the DAG. The rules to be enforced are:

- Any evaluation of or assignment to an element of an array *a* must follow the previous assignment to an element of that array, if there is one.
- Any assignment to an element of an array *a* must follow the previous evaluation of *a*.

- Any use of any identifier must follow the previous procedure call or indirect assignment through a pointer, if there is one.
- Any procedure call or indirect assignment through a pointer must follow all previous evaluations of any identifier. That is, when reordering code, the uses of an array *a* may not cross each other, and no statement may cross a procedure call or an assignment through a pointer.

Also consider array access, as given below:

b = a + 12
x = b[i]
a[j] = y

Figure 6.2 shows the DAG representation for the same.

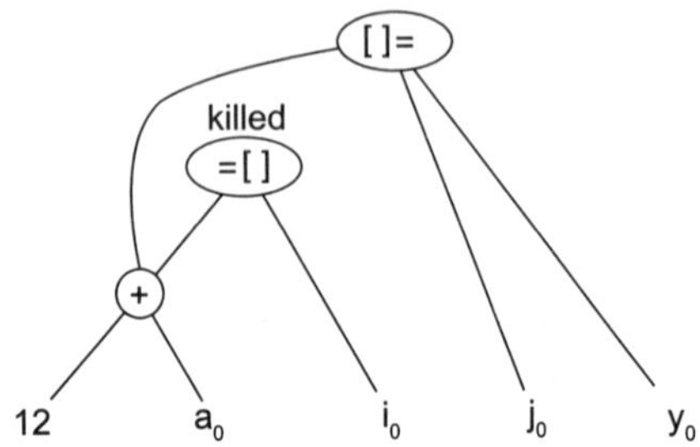

Figure 6.2 DAG representation of array

Example 6.3 Common sub-expression elimination with DAG construction
Consider the basic block

a = b + c
b = a – d
c = b + c
d = a – d

DAG construction

1. Consider instruction $a = b + c$. The RHS has variables *b* and *c*. As no such node exists, nodes *b* and *c* are created as initial nodes. New node '+' is created, having left child b_0 and C_0. The label of this node is *a*.
2. Consider instruction $b = a - d$. The RHS has variables *a* and *d*. Node *a* already exists (constructed in Step 1), node d_0 is constructed as it is the initial node. Node '–' is created with left child *a* and right child d_0. As this is the second occurrence of *b*, the node is named b_1.
3. Consider instruction $c = b + c$. Node b_1 is the left child and node C_0 is the right child of the node created, having symbol '+' and labeled as *c*, which is actually c_1.
4. Consider instruction $d = a - d$. Node – with right child *a* and left child *d* already exists, and hence, is named *d*.

The DAG constructed is shown in Fig. 6.3. As per the DAG, nodes that have two labels are b_1 and *d*, which is the common sub-expression. After common sub-expression elimination, the code is as follows:

a = b + c
b = a – d
c = b + c
d = b

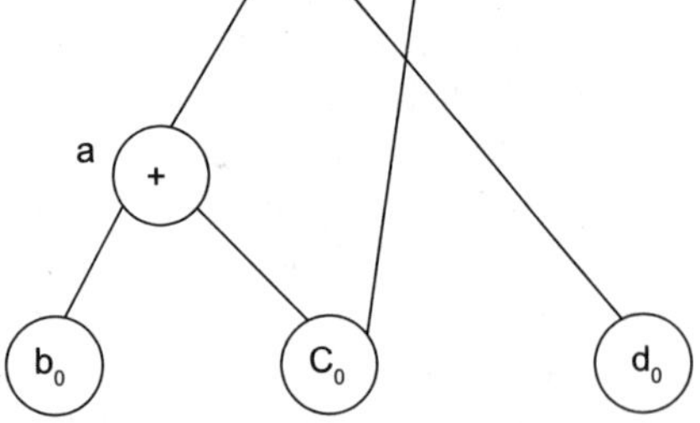

Figure 6.3 DAG for Example 6.3

Example 6.4 Common sub-expression elimination with DAG construction and to check if any other code optimisation can be applied

The TAC of a basic block is as follows:

```
t1 = b + c
t2 = d * e
t3 = b + c
t4 = t2 * t3
t5 = t4 * f
x = t1 – t5
```

Applying common sub-expression elimination, based on the algorithm discussed in Section 6.2.1, the DAG is as shown in Fig. 6.4. After common sub-expression elimination

```
t1 = b + c
t2 = d * e
t3 = t1
t4 = t2 * t3
t5 = t4 * f
x = t1– t5
```

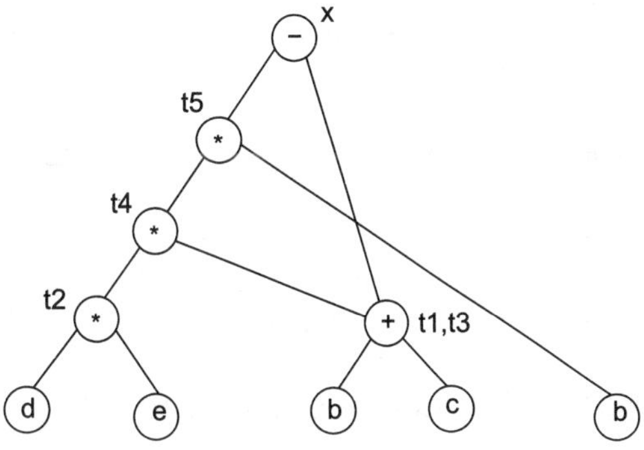

Figure 6.4 DAG for Example 6.4

This code can be further optimised; *t3 = t1* is a candidate for copy propagation. After optimisation, we get

```
t1 = b + c
t2 = d * e
t4 = t2 * t1
t5 = t4 * f
x = t1– t5
```

Example 6.5 Common sub-expression elimination with DAG construction involving arrays

Consider the following block of code:

```
t1 = 4 * i
t2 = a[t1]
t3 = 4 * i
t4 = b[t3]
t5 = t2 * t4
t6 = p + t5
p = t6
t7 = i + 1
i = t7
if i<20 goto(1)
```

The DAG for the basic block is shown in Fig. 6.5. It is constructed based on the algorithm discussed in Section 6.2.1.

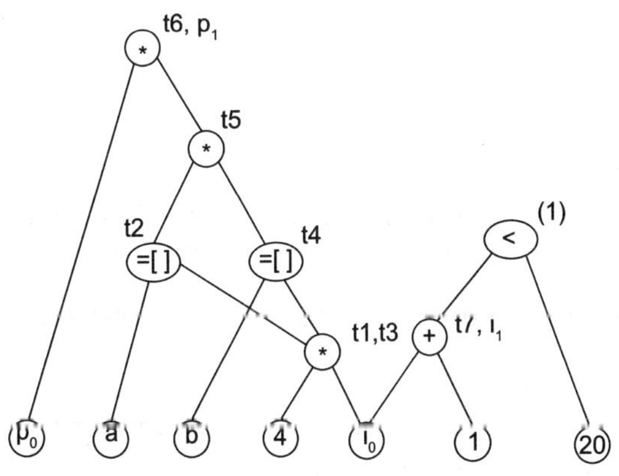

Figure 6.5 DAG for Example 6.5

6.2.2 Algebraic Simplification and Strength Reduction

Algebraic properties can be used for simplification of expressions. Some instructions can be simplified and some can be eliminated. Simplification can be applied repeatedly.

Expressions that can be eliminated:

- X = X + 0
- X = X * 1

Expressions that can be simplified:

- X + 0 ⇒ X
- X – 0 ⇒ X
- X * 1 ⇒ X
- X / 1 ⇒ X
- X * 0 ⇒ 0

Strength reduction involves replacing expensive operations:

- Y = Y^2 can be simplified as Y = Y * Y

6.2.3 Dead Code Elimination

Dead code comprises one or more statements of code in a program:

- That is never executed or is unreachable
- Whose output is never used after the last definition
- That affects only dead variables (written but not read)

Any dead code and assignments to dead variables must be eliminated. Removing such code does not affect the program results. Dead code elimination helps to reduce the program size by removing the code or variables that are never used; thereby, reducing the program execution time. Data flow analysis is performed to detect dead code. Dead code may be created in the program after application of other optimisations.

Example 6.6 Dead code elimination

Consider a block of code:

```
a = 1
b = 2
c = b + 3
d = x
e = x + c
```

In the above code, variables *a* and *d* are not used further, and hence, are dead code, which can be eliminated. Code after eliminating the dead code:

```
b = 2
c = b + 3
e = x + c
```

Partial dead code can also be present in the program. If a computed value is used only sometimes, when a condition becomes true, it is called **partial dead code**.

6.2.4 Copy Propagation

Copy propagation is a local optimisation technique. It is applied within a basic block. An instruction X=Y is a copy instruction where the value of X is copied to Y. For a copy instruction X=Y, all the subsequent uses of X can be replaced by Y, if the value of X is not changed in between.

Example 6.7 Copy propagation

```
a = b + c
p = a
q = p + r
```

After copy propagation, *p* is replaced by *a*.

```
a = b + c
p = a
q = a + r
```

Consider another example

```
a = b + c
p = a
i = b + a
p = i + 2
q = p + r
```

In the above example, *p* cannot be replaced by *a* as the value of *p* is changed by the instruction $p = i + 2$.

6.2.5 Constant Propagation

The constants assigned to a variable can be propagated through the flow graph and substituted on the use of the variable. Constant propagation can be local to a basic block or can be applied to the complete control flow graph.

Example 6.8 Constant propagation

```
a = 1;
b = a + 3;
```

Constant 1 is assigned to variable *a* in the instruction *a*=1; this constant can be propagated in further instructions. Use of variable *a* is replaced by constant value 1. After constant propagation, the code becomes

```
a = 1;
b = 1 + 3;
```

6.2.6 Constant Folding

In constant propagation, a variable is substituted by its assigned constant, whereas in constant folding, variables are found whose values can be computed at compilation time. **Constant folding** is used to evaluate expressions with constant operands at compile time rather than at run-time, improving performance and reducing code size.

The value of variables in the instructions involving only constants can be computed at compile time. In the three-address instruction of the form X = Y op Z, where Y and Z are constants, Y op Z can be computed at compile time. For example, X = 2 * 3 can be computed as X = 6. Instruction a = 2 + 3 in a basic block can be replaced by a = 5. Such expressions are generally not written by programmers but can be introduced by applying other optimisation techniques.

Example 6.9 Application of local optimisation techniques repeatedly until no further optimisation is possible

Let us consider the following basic block of code. Identify the type of optimisation that can be applied and then apply it until no further optimisation is possible.

```
a = 2
b = x^2
c = x
d = a + 5
e = b + c
f = c * c
g = d + e
h = e * f
```

1. Applying algebraic simplification to the instruction b = x^2

   a = 2
   b = x * x
   c = x
   d = a + 5
   e = b + c
   f = c * c
   g = d + e
   h = e * f

2. Apply constant propagation (*a*=2) and copy propagation (*c*=*x*)
   - Constant value of variable *a* is substituted at its use in the instruction *d* = *a* + 5. After constant propagation, *d* = 2 + 5.
   - Copy statement *c*=x is propagated by substituting the use of *c* with *x* in instruction *e*=*b*+*c* and *f*=*c***c*. After copy propagation, *e*=*b*+*x* and *f*=*x***x*.

   The code after constant propagation and copy propagation will be:

   a = 2
   b = x * x
   c = x
   d = 2 + 5
   e = b + x
   f = x * x
   g = d + e
   H = e * f

3. Apply constant folding on *d*=2+5 by computing the value at compile time rather than run-time. Instruction *d*=2+5 is substituted by *d*=7.

```
a = 2
b = x * x
c = x
d = 7
e = b + x
f = x * x
g = d + e
h = e * f
```

4. Apply constant propagation by prorogating the newly introduced constant *d*=7 as a result of constant folding applied in Step 3.

```
a = 2
b = x * x
c = x
d = 7
e = b + x
f = x * x
g = 7 + e
h = e * f
```

5. Common sub-expression elimination (CSE)
   - Sub-expression *x***x* is computed in *b*=*x***x* and *f*=*x***x*. Hence, redundant computations must be eliminated. After CSE, the code will be:

```
a = 2
b = x * x
c = x
d = 7
e = b + x
f = b
g = 7 + e
h = e * f
```

6. Constant folding is applied by replacing *f* with *b*

```
a = 2
b = x * x
c = x
d = 7
e = b + x
f = b
g = 7 + e
h = e * b
```

7. Dead code elimination
   - Dead variables are created during application of other optimisation techniques.
   - Variables that are not used after their last definition are dead variables and must be eliminated.
   - Variables *a*, *c*, *d* and *f* are not used after their definition and are dead variables.

After dead code elimination

b = x * x
e = b + x
g = 7 + e
h = e * b

After this step, no further optimisation is possible. Hence, this is the optimised code.

6.2.7 Function Inlining and Cloning

Function inlining involves replacing a function call with the body of the function. The overhead associated with calling and returning from a function by avoiding copying of parameters, return address, etc. can be eliminated by expanding the body of the function instead of the function call. Additional opportunities for optimisation may be exposed after application of function inlining. In function cloning, a special code is created for functions with different calling parameters.

6.2.8 Loop Optimisation

Loops in a program are the best candidates for machine-independent optimisations. Any optimisation is a two-step process of analysis and transformation. In loop optimisation, the two steps are to first find the loop in the program and then apply the appropriate loop optimisation technique. Loops in the high level language correspond to control structures such as while, for, if, if-else, if-else-then, etc. depending on the programming language used. The loop optimisation techniques are

1. Elimination of loop invariant computations
2. Induction variable elimination
3. Loop unveiling
4. Loop fission
5. Loop fusion
6. Loop peeling

Loop detection: Loop detection is a four-step process:

1. *Identification of leader statements*: Leader statements are identified by the following rules:
   Rule 1: The first instruction is considered the leader.
   Rule 2: The target of conditional or unconditional goto is a leader.
   Rule 3: The instruction that immediately follows a conditional goto is a leader.
2. *Identification of basic blocks*: A basic block consists of a leader and ends on the instruction just before the next leader, but not including the next leader.
3. *Detection of control flow in the program*: After the program is divided into basic blocks, the flow of the program is found by analysing the last statement of all the basic blocks. The flow can be directed to the next basic block or it may jump to another basic block if there is a conditional or unconditional goto statement. As output, a control flow graph (CFG) is constructed.

   A **control flow graph** is a directed graph of nodes with the nodes corresponding to basic blocks and the edges representing the flow of control in the program. An edge from node A to node B is added if the execution can flow from the last instruction of basic block A to the first instruction of basic block B. Figure 6.6 shows an example of a control flow graph, consisting of four basic blocks: B1, B2, B3 and B4. The control flow graph is constructed using the algorithm *CFG_Construction.*

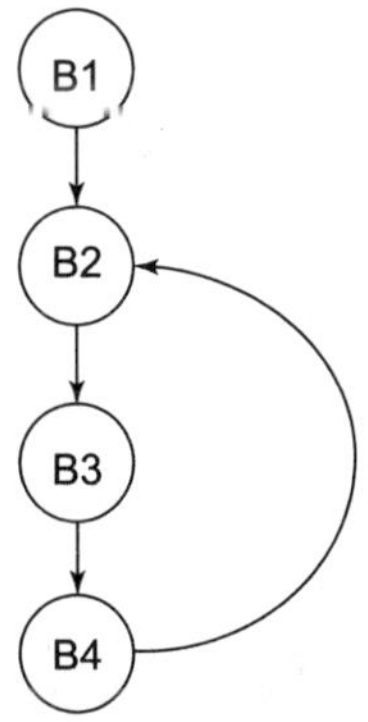

Figure 6.6 Control flow graph

Algorithm CFG_Construction

{

1. Identify the basic blocks.
2. Add a directed edge from Node A to Node B:
   a. Last instruction in basic block A is a conditional or unconditional goto that causes a jump to the first instruction in basic block B.
   b. Basic block B is next in sequence after block A, as per the instructions in the program.

}

4. *Loop identification*: A **loop** is a cycle that satisfies two conditions, namely, it has a single entry node and it is strongly connected. A loop exists in a program if and only if there are back edges in the program flow graph. To detect the back edge in the program flow graph, dominators must be found. The back edge is the edge in the program flow graph (PFG) where the head node dominates the tail node. The head node is the node of the flow graph to which the arrow points.

   Any node A *dominates* node B if every path from the initial node to node B goes through A. Also, every node dominates itself. For PFG of Fig. 6.6, the dominators of each node are as follows:

Node	Dominator
B1	B1
B2	B1, B2, B4
B3	B1, B2, B3
B4	B1, B2, B3, B4

   In Fig. 6.6, B4→B2 is the back edge, as the head node B2 dominates the tail node B4. Loop is detected by the back edge of the PFG. Loop of back edge A→B is the set of all nodes that can reach A without going through B, including A and B. For the definition, the loop of PFG, shown in Fig. 6.6, is B2-B3-B4-B2. Any program can contain one or more loops. Also, there can be smaller loops within larger loops, in which case, consider the bigger loop.

Example 6.10 Loop detection

Let us consider the algorithm for the addition of n numbers

```
int addition(int a[ ],n)
{
    int i, sum;
    sum=0;
    for(i=0; i<=n; i++)
    {
        sum=sum+a[i];
    }
    return sum;
}
```

The TAC corresponding to the algorithm for the addition of n numbers is as follows:

```
 1) sum=0
 2) i=0
 3) if i>n goto 12
 4) T1=addr(a)
 5) T2=i*4
 6) T3=T1[T2]
 7) T4=sum+T3
 8) sum=T4
 9) T5=i+1
10) i=T5
11) goto 3
12) return sum
```

Step 1: Let us find the leader statements in the TAC. As per the rules for identification of the leader statement.

1. The first instruction of the TAC is the leader as per Rule 1.
2. As per Rule 2, instructions 3 and 12 are leaders as they are the target of conditional and unconditional goto.
3. As per Rule 3, instruction 4 is the leader as it follows the conditional goto.

Step 2: The basic blocks of the TAC based on leader statements are shown in Fig. 6.7. For each leader, its basic block consists of that leader and all instructions up to but not including the next leader. Block B1 starts from the first leader and ends at Statement 2, which precedes the next leader statement at 3. Block B2 starts from the next leader Statement 3 and includes only one statement as the next leader is Statement 4, and preceding Statement 4 only Statement 3 is present. Block B3 starts from the next leader Statement 4 and ends at Statement 11, which precedes the next leader Statement 12. The last block contains only Statement 12.

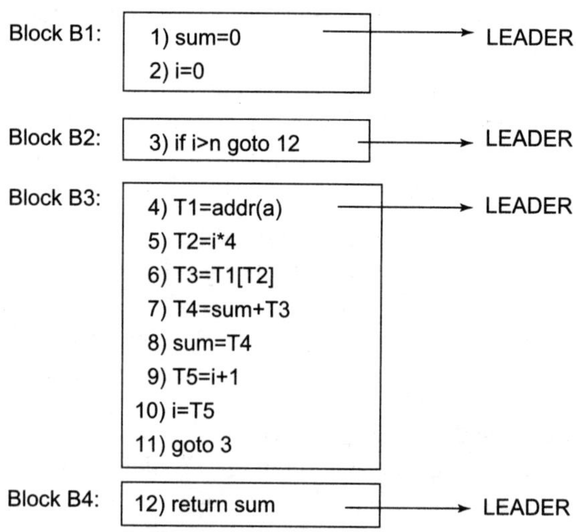

Figure 6.7 Leaders and basic blocks corresponding to Example 6.10

Step 3: The control flow graph is obtained by finding the flow of the program from one block to another block. Let us consider each block:

Block B1: Last statement in block B1 is i=0, after which the control flows to Statement 3, which is in block B2. So add the edge B1→B2.

Block B2: Last statement of B2 transfers the control to Statement 12 if the condition i>n is true, which is contained in block B4, adding the egde B2→B4. Also, if the condition is false, the control goes to Statement 4, contained in Block B3, adding the edge B2→B3.

Block B3: Last statement of B3 is goto 3, which transfers the control unconditionally to Statement 3, contained in Block B2, adding the edge B3→B2.

Block B4: Contains the last statement.

The PFG (Fig. 6.8(a)) shows the flow of the program indicated from the basic blocks. Another representation of PFG is shown in Fig. 6.8 (b).

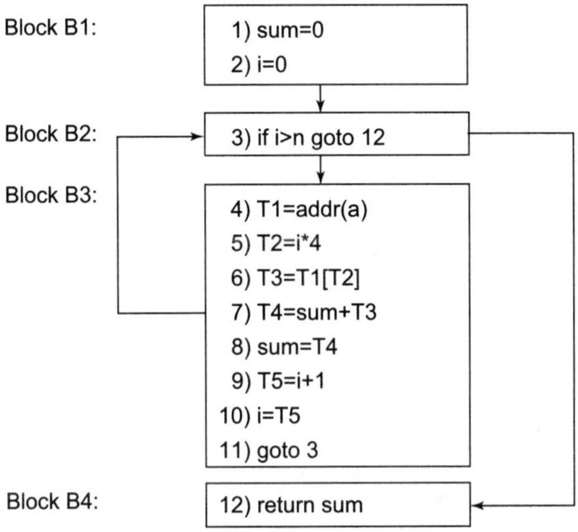

Figure 6.8(a) PFG for Example 6.10

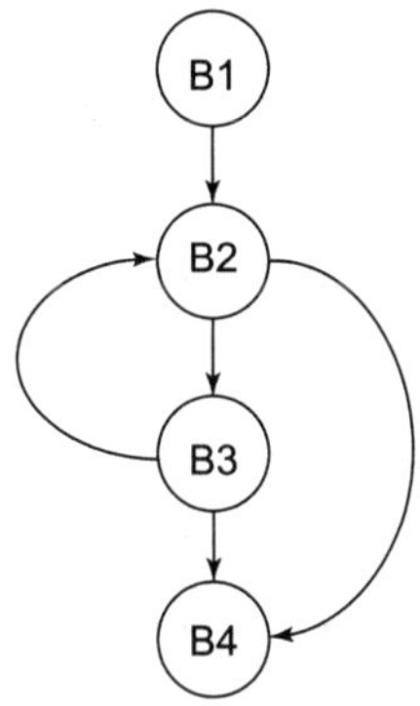

Figure 6.8(b) Another repre-sentaion of PFG (statements of the blocks are not written)

Step 4: Loop identification requires detection of back edges, which can be found by computing the dominators of each node of the PFG. The dominators for PFG in Fig. 6.8 are as follows:

Node	Dominator
B1	B1
B2	B1, B2
B3	B1, B2, B3
B4	B1, B2, B4

The back edge will be B3→ B2, as the head node B2 is contained in the dominator set of tail node B3. The loop containing the back edge for the example is B2→B3→B2.

1. Elimination of loop invariant computation: A loop invariant computation is one that computes the same value every time a loop is executed. A loop invariant computation must be found and moved out of the loop to optimise the program. The first step is to detect the loop, as discussed in Section 6.2.8 in the TAC, and then detect the loop invariant computation and its code motion.

To find the loop invariant computation, reaching definitions must be found. The variables that leave the block and enter the block must be found; these are referred to as **reaching definitions**. A three-address statement having a general form X=Y op Z is a loop invariant if:

Condition 1: Y and Z are constants. If Y and Z are constants, they will compute the same value every time the loop is executed.

Condition 2: All definitions of Y and Z are outside the loop.

To find reaching definitions, data flow equations must be found.

Data flow equations:

- IN (B): Set of all definitions which are reaching the start of Block B.
  IN (B) = U OUT (P) for predecessor P of B.

- OUT (B): Set of all definitions reaching the end of Block B.
  OUT (B) = IN (B)–KILL (B) U GEN (B)
- GEN (B): Set of all definitions generated in Block B.
- KILL (B): Set of all definitions outside Block B that define the same variables which are defined in Block B.

Continuing **Example 6.10**, GEN and KILL will be as follows:

Block	GEN	KILL
B1	{1, 2}	{8, 10}
B2	{3}	∅
B3	{4, 5, 6, 7, 8, 9, 10, 11}	∅
B4	{12}	∅

IN and OUT computation:

Block	Predecessor
B1	∅
B2	B1, B3
B3	B2
B4	B2

Initial computation:

Block	IN	OUT
B1	∅	{8, 10}
B2	∅	∅
B3	∅	∅
B4	∅	∅

First iteration:

Block	IN	OUT
B1	∅	{1, 2}
B2	{8, 10}	{3, 8, 10}
B3	∅	{4, 5, 6, 7, 8, 9, 10, 11}
B4	∅	{12}

Second iteration:

Block	IN	OUT
B1	∅	{1,2}
B2	{1, 2, 4, 5, 6, 7, 8, 9, 10, 11}	{1, 2, 3, 4, 5, 6, 7, 8, 9, 10, 11}
B3	{3, 8, 10}	{3, 4, 5, 6, 7, 8, 9, 10, 11}
B4	{3, 8, 10}	{3, 8, 10, 12}

Third iteration:

Block	IN	OUT
B1	∅	{1, 2}
B2	{1, 2, 3, 4, 5, 6, 7, 8, 9, 10, 11}	{1, 2, 3, 4, 5, 6, 7, 8, 9, 10, 11}
B3	{1, 2, 3, 4, 5, 6, 7, 8, 9, 10, 11}	{1, 2, 3, 4, 5, 6, 7, 8, 9, 10, 11}
B4	{1, 2, 3, 4, 5, 6, 7, 8, 9, 10, 11}	{1,2,3,4,5,6,7,8,9,10,11,12}

Fourth iteration:

Block	IN	OUT
B1	∅	{1,2}
B2	{1,2,3,4,5,6,7,8,9,10,11}	{1,2,3,4,5,6,7,8,9,10,11}
B3	{1,2,3,4,5,6,7,8,9,10,11}	{1,2,3,4,5,6,7,8,9,10,11}
B4	{1,2,3,4,5,6,7,8,9,10,11}	{1,2,3,4,5,6,7,8,9,10,11,12}

Reaching definition: Next, find the reaching definitions by computing the Use-Def Chain (UD-Chain) information. If the use of A in Block B is preceded by its definition inside the same block, then the UD-Chain of A contains only that statement. If the use of A in Block B is not preceded by the definition of A inside the block, then the UD-Chain for this use consists of all definitions of A contained in IN(B).

Steps to find UD-Chain:

1. Find the UD-Chain of operands on the RHS of all statements in the blocks contained in the loop.
2. If the UD-Chain of all operands contains a statement outside the loop, then it is loop invariant. If the statement is loop invariant, then it can be moved out of the loop to the pre-header if the conditions mentioned below are satisfied.

Continuing with **Example 6.10**, the loop detected was B2→B3→B2. UD-Chain is computed for all instructions of the blocks contained in the loop. First consider Block B2. There are no instructions for which UD-Chain can be computed. Now, consider Block B3.

- Instruction no. 5 → T2= i*4
  - 4 is a constant, so there will be no UD-Chain.

  - i is not defined in Block B3 before instruction (5). Hence, the UD-Chain for i will contain all the definitions of i contained in IN(B3).

    IN(B3)= {1,2,3,4,5,6,7,8,9,10,11}
    UD-Chain (i) = {2, 10}

    Instruction no. 10 is inside the loop, and hence, T2=i*4 is not a loop invariant computation. Any computation is loop invariant if all its definitions are outside the loop.
- Instruction no. 6 → T3 = T1[T2]
  - T1 is defined in the loop before instruction no. 6. UD-Chain (T1) = {4}.
  - T2 is defined in the loop before instruction no. 6. UD-Chain (T2) = {5}.

    Instruction nos 4 and 5 are inside the loop, and hence, T3 = T1[T2] is not a loop invariant computation.
- Instruction no. 7 → T4= sum + T3
  - sum is not defined in the block B3 before instruction (7). Hence, the UD-Chain for sum will contain all definitions of sum contained in IN(B3).

    IN(B3)= {1,2,3,4,5,6,7,8,9,10,11}
    UD-Chain (sum) = {1}

  - T3 is defined in the loop before instruction no. 7. UD-Chain (T1) = {6}. Instruction no. 6 is inside the loop, and hence, T4 = sum + T3 is not a loop invariant computation.
- Instruction no. 8 → sum= T4
  - T4 is defined in the loop before instruction no. 8. UD-Chain (T4) = {7}. Instruction no. 7 is inside the loop, and hence, sum=T4 is not a loop invariant computation.
- Instruction no. 9 → T5= i+1
  - 1 is a constant so there will be no UD-Chain.
  - i is not defined in Block B3 before instruction (5). Hence, the UD-Chain for i will contain all definitions of i contained in IN(B3).

    IN(B3)= {1,2,3,4,5,6,7,8,9,10,11}
    UD-Chain (i) = {2, 10}

    Instruction no. 10 is inside the loop, and hence, T5 = i+1 is not a loop invariant computation.
- Instruction no. 10 → i= T5
  - T5 is defined in the loop before instruction no. 10. UD-Chain (T1) = {9}. Instruction no. 9 is inside the loop, and hence, i = T5 is not a loop invariant computation.

For Example 6.10, there is no loop invariant computation that can be moved out of the loop. In further examples, we will consider blocks having loop invariant computation.

Conditions to move the loop invariant computation outside the loop

Condition (i): The block in which a loop invariant statement occurs should be a dominator of all exits of the loop.

Consider the control flow graph shown in Fig. 6.9. If instruction A=5 is loop invariant, to move it outside the loop, dom(B5) must contain B3. Dom(B5)= {B1,B2,B3,B4,B5}. Since the dominator of B5 contains B3, the loop invariant statement A=5 can be moved to the pre-header just before the loop starts. The loop in the flow graph is B2→B3→B4→B2. Figure 6.10 shows the flow graph after moving the loop invariant computation to the pre-header.

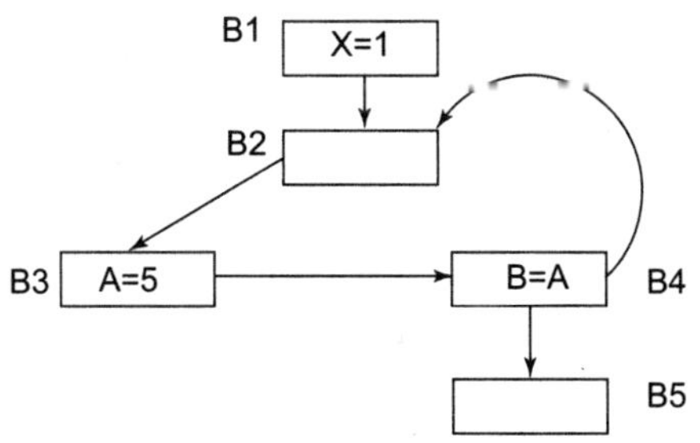

Figure 6.9 Control flow graph with A=5 as loop invariant instruction

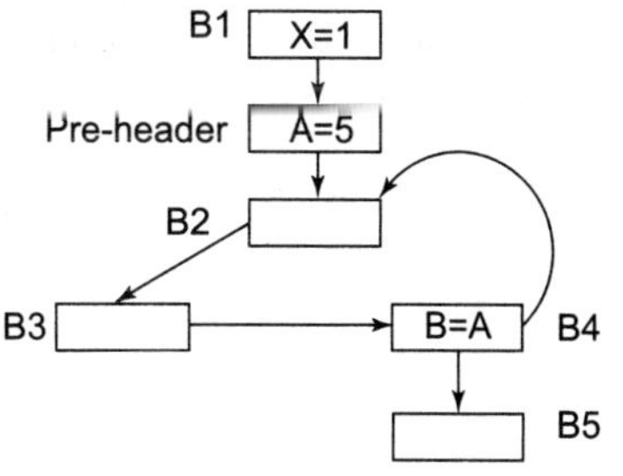

Figure 6.10 Control flow graph after moving loop invariant instruction to the pre-header

Condition (ii): A loop invariant computation which defines a variable A cannot be moved to the pre-header if there is another statement in the loop that defines A.

Let us consider the flow graph of Fig. 6.11 having A=2 as the loop invariant instruction. Instruction A=2 cannot be moved to the pre-header, outside the loop, as A=5 is inside the loop.

Condition (iii): Loop invariant computation, which states that A cannot be moved out of the loop if the use of A is reached by any definition of A.

A is used inside the loop by instruction X=A, which is reached by another definition of A (A=1), other than the loop invariant instruction A=2. Hence, A=2 cannot be moved to the pre-header.

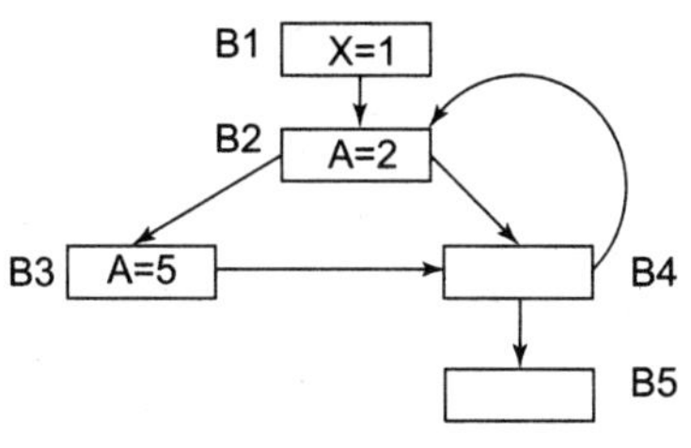

Figure 6.11 Control flow graph with A=2 as loop invariant instruction

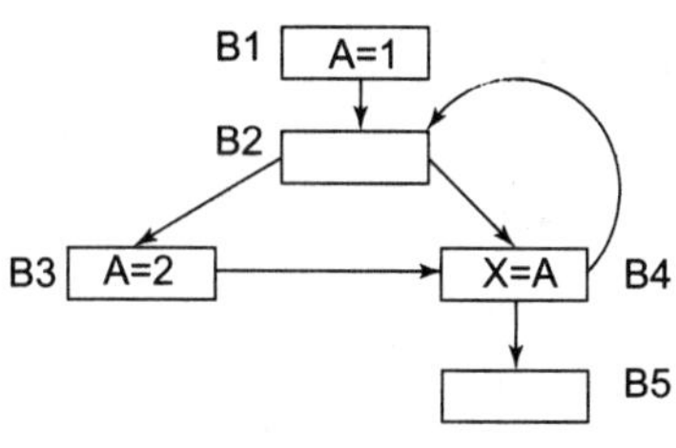

Figure 6.12 Control flow graph with A=2 as loop invariant instruction

Example 6.11 Constructing a control flow graph by finding leaders and basic blocks in the given TAC

Consider the following code:

```
count = 0;
result =0;
while (count ++ <20)
{
  increment = 2 * count ;
  result = increment;
}
```

The TAC corresponding to the above code will be

1. count = 0
2. result = 0
3. If count > 20 GOTO 8
4. count=count + 1
5. increment = 2 * count
6. result = result +increment
7. goto 3
8. end

Leader statements and corresponding blocks are given below:

1. count = 0 → leader ⎤ → B1
2. result = 0 ⎦
3. If count > 20 goto 8 → B2
4. count + 1 → leader ⎤
5. Increment = 2 * count
6. result = result +increment → B3
7. goto 3 ⎦
8. end → leader] → B4

Basic blocks and the control flow graph are as follows:

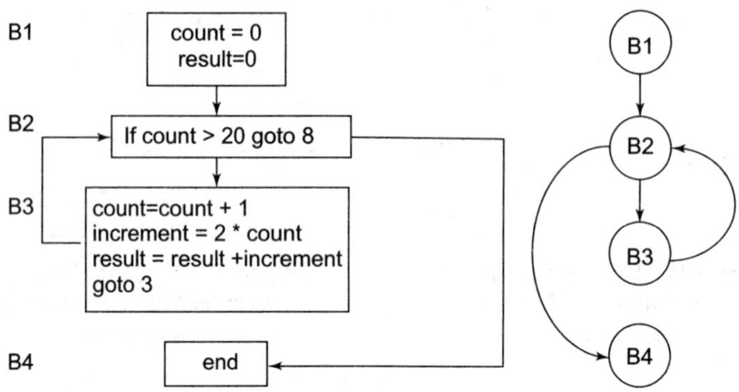

Example 6.12 Finding data flow equations for the given control flow graph

Find the predecessor nodes of all the blocks. The predecessor of any node is the incoming node to that block, also called the in-degree of the node.

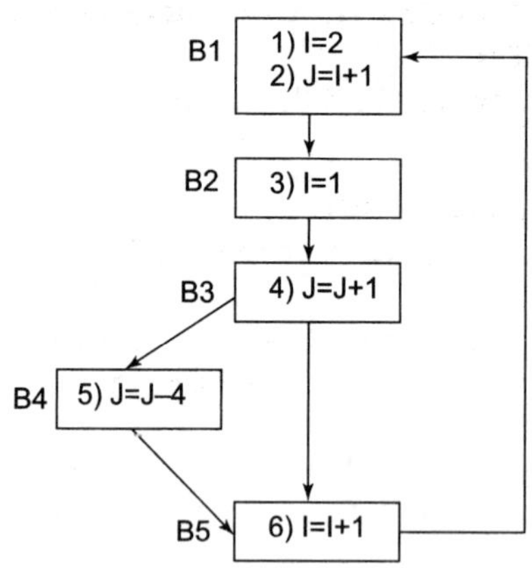

Node	**Predecessor**
B1	ϕ
B2	{B1, B5}
B3	{B2}
B4	{B3}
B5	{B3, B4}

GEN and KILL computation

- GEN for any block contains the instructions defined inside that block. The instruction number is used to represent the GEN set. Block B1 contains instruction nos 1 and 2, and hence, GEN(B1) ={1,2}.
- KILL is the set of all definitions outside Block B that defines the same variables which are defined in Block B. Block B1 defines variables I and J. Hence, KILL(B1) will contain the instruction number of all the statements that define I and J, resulting in KILL (B1)= {3,4,5,6}.
- The GEN and KILL set for all nodes in the flow graph are as follows:

Node	GEN	KILL
B1	{1,2}	{3,4,5,6}
B2	{3}	{1,6}
B3	{4}	{2,5}
B4	{5}	{2,4}
B5	*{6}*	*{1,3}*

Computing IN and OUT

Initially

IN= ϕ

OUT=GEN

Initial

Node	**IN**	**OUT**
B1	ϕ	{1,2 }
B2	ϕ	{3}
B3	ϕ	{4}
B4	ϕ	{5}
B5	ϕ	{6}

Computing IN and OUT using iterative solution

- IN(B) is the set of all definition reaching the start of Block B. It is the union of OUT of the predecessor of Block B.

  IN (B)= U OUT (P) for all predecessors P of B

- OUT (B) is the set of all definitions reaching the end of Block B.

  OUT (B)=IN (B)−KILL (B) U GEN (B)

First Iteration

Sample calculation:

IN(B2) = OUT(B1) U OUT(B5)

= {1,2 } U {6} = {1,2,6}

[*Note*: In the first iteration, refer OUT from the initial computation. In the second iteration, consider OUT from the previous iteration (iteration 1), and so on.]

OUT(B2) = IN(B2) – KILL(B2) U GEN(B2)
= {1,2,6}–{1,6} U {3} = {2} U {3} = {2,3}

[*Note*: In the first iteration, IN computed in the first iteration is considered, and so on.]

Similarly, IN and OUT for all blocks will be

First Iteration

Node	IN	OUT
B1	ϕ	{1,2 }
B2	{1,2,6}	{2,3}
B3	{3}	{3,4}
B4	{4}	{5}
B5	{4,5}	{4,5,6}

Second Iteration

Node	IN	OUT
B1	ϕ	{1,2 }
B2	{1,2,4,5,6}	{2,3,4,5}
B3	{2,3}	{3,4}
B4	{3,4}	{3,5}
B5	{3,4,5}	{4,5,6}

Third Iteration

Node	IN	OUT
B1	ϕ	{1,2 }
B2	{1,2,4,5,6}	{2,3,4,5}
B3	{2,3,4,5}	{3,4}
B4	{3,4}	{3,5}
B5	{3,4,5}	{4,5,6}

Fourth Iteration

Node	IN	OUT
B1	ϕ	{1,2}
B2	{1,2,4,5,6}	{2,3,4,5}
B3	{2,3,4,5}	{3,4}
B4	{3,4}	{3,5}
B5	{3,4,5}	{4,5,6}

Stop the computation as IN and OUT are the same in iterations 3 and 4. The In and OUT set for each block is as in iteration 4.

Example 6.13 Finding loop invariant computation and moving it to the pre-header, outside the loop in the given control flow graph

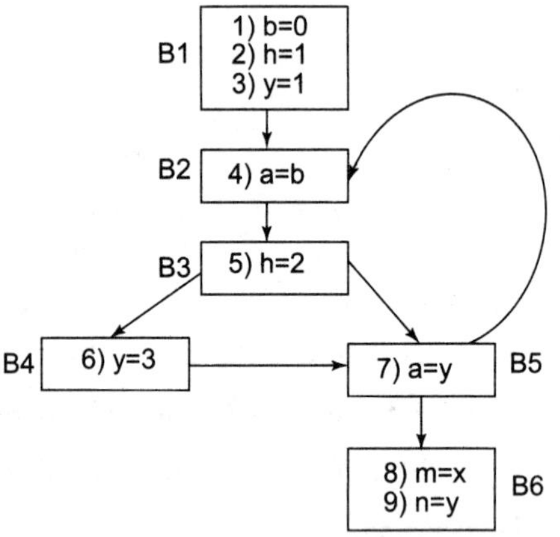

Computing Predecessor

Node	Predecessor
B1	ϕ
B2	{B1,B5}
B3	{B2}
B4	{B3}
B5	{B3,B4}
B6	{B5}

Computing GEN and KILL

Node	GEN	KILL
B1	{1,2,3}	{5,6}
B2	{4}	{7}
B3	{5}	{2}
B4	{6}	{3}
B5	{7}	{4}
B6	{8,9}	ϕ

Computing IN and OUT

Initially,

Node	IN	OUT
B1	ϕ	{1,2,3 }
B2	ϕ	{4}
B3	ϕ	{5}
B4	ϕ	{6}
B5	ϕ	{7}
B6	ϕ	{8,9}

First Iteration

Node	IN	OUT
B1	ϕ	{1,2 ,3}
B2	{1,2,3,7}	{1,2,3,4}
B3	{4}	{4,5}
B4	{5}	{5,6}
B5	{5,6}	{5,6,7}
B6	{7}	{7,8,9}

Second Iteration

Node	IN	OUT
B1	ϕ	{1,2,3}
B2	{1,2,3,5,6,7}	{1,2,3,4,5,6}
B3	{1,2,3,4,}	{1,2,3,4,5}
B4	{4,5}	{4,5,6}
B5	{4,5,6}	{5,6,7}
B6	{5,6,7}	{5,6,7,8,9}

Third Iteration

Node	IN	OUT
B1	ϕ	{1,2,3 }
B2	{1,2,3,4,5,6,7}	{1,2,3,4,5,6}
B3	{1,2,3,4,5,6}	{1,3,4,5,6}
B4	{1,3,4.5,6}	{1,4,5,6,7}
B5	{1,3,4,5,6,}	{1,3,5,6,7}
B6	{1,3,5,6,7}	{1,3,5,6,7,8,9}

Fourth Iteration

Node	IN	OUT
B1	ϕ	{1,2 ,3}
B2	{1,2,3,5,6,7,}	{1,2,3,4,5,6}
B3	{1,2,3,4,5,6}	{1,3,4,5,6}
B4	{1,3,4,5,6}	{1,4,5,6}
B5	{1,3,4,5,6}	{1,3,5,6,7}
B6	{1,3,5,6,7{	1,3,5,6,7,8,9}

Fifth Iteration

Node	IN	OUT
B1	ϕ	{1,2 ,3}
B2	{1,2,3,5,6,7}	{1,2,3,4,5,6}
B3	{1,2,3,4,5,6}	{1,3,4,5,6}
B4	{1,3,4,5,6}	{1,4,5,6}
B5	{1,3,4,5,6}	{1,3,5,6,7}
B6	{1,3,5,6,7}	{1,3,5,6,7,8,9}

Computing UD-Chain for Loop B2→B3→B4→B5→B2

- Considering the instructions of Block B2. IN(B2)={1,2,3,5,6,7}
  Instruction (4) a= b
  - Ud-Chain(b) = {1}
  - As 1 is outside the loop, **instruction (4) a=b is a loop invariant computation.**
- Considering the instructions of Block B3. IN(B3)= {1,2,3,4,5,6}
  Instruction (5) h=2
  - As h is assigned to a constant, **instruction (5) h=2 is a loop invariant computation.**
- Considering the instructions of Block B4. IN(B4)= {1,3,4,5,6}
  Instruction (6) y=3
  - As y is assigned to a constant, **instruction (6) y=3 is a loop invariant computation.**
- Considering the instructions of Block B5. IN(B5)= {1,3,4,5,6}
  Instruction (7) a=y
  - Ud-Chain(y)= {3,6}. Instruction 3 is outside the loop, instruction 6 is inside the loop. Hence, **instruction (7) a=y is not a loop invariant computation.**

Remove loop invariant instructions

1. Instruction a=b
   Condition (i): B2 should be in the dominator of B6. Dominator (B6) = {B1,B2,B3,B5,B6}. B2 is in the dominator of B6. Hence, condition (i) is satisfied.

Condition (ii): As the statement a=y is present in the loop, a=b cannot be moved to the pre-header.

2. Instruction h=2

   Condition (i): Block B3 is in the dominator of B6. Hence, condition (i) is satisfied.

   Condition (ii): There is no statement in the loop where 'h' is defined inside the loop. Hence, condition (ii) is satisfied.

   Condition (iii): There is no statement where 'h' is used, inside the loop. Hence, condition (iii) is satisfied.

   As all three conditions are satisfied, **the loop invariant computation h=2 can be moved out of the loop and inserted in the pre-header.**

3. Instruction y=3

   Condition (i): Block B4 is not in the dominator of Block B6. Condition (i) is not satisfied. Hence, instruction y=3 cannot be moved to the pre-header. The control flow graph after moving h=2 to the pre-header is shown in Fig. 6.13.

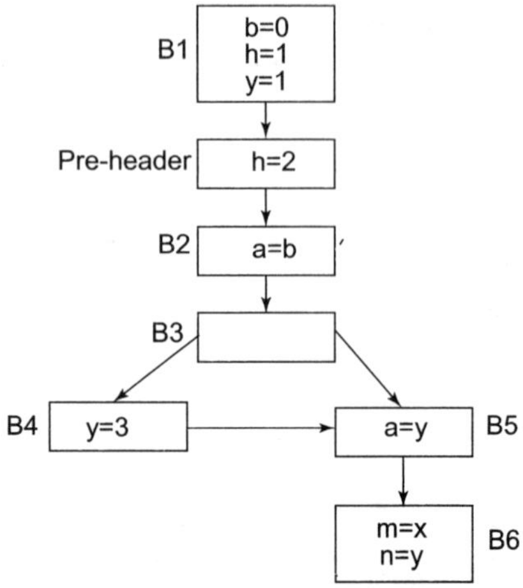

Figure 6.13 Control flow graph after moving loop invariant computation to pre-header for Example 6.13

2. Induction variable elimination: Induction variables are of two types: basic and derived. A **basic induction variable** is one that is increased or decreased by a fixed amount on every iteration of a loop having the general form I=I+C or I=I−C, where C is a constant.

A **derived induction variable** is one that is a linear function of another instruction variable. Such an induction variable J has the general form $J=C_1*I+C_{2,}$ where C1 and C2 = constant.

Steps for detecting and eliminating induction variables:

Step 1: Find all the basic induction variables in the loop as per its definition.

Step 2: Find all the derived induction variables. For each derived induction variable J, find the family of basic induction variable I to which J belongs.

Step 3: Consider each basic induction variable.

a) Create a new name temp.

b) Replace the assignment to J in the loop with J = TEMP.

c) Add the following statement to the pre-header.

   TEMP = C1 * I

   TEMP = TEMP + C2 (omit this Statement if C2 = 0)

d) After each assignment I=I+D, append the instruction TEMP =TEMP + C1 * D.

e) For each basic induction variable I of the form I relop X goto Y, replace such a test by

   i) TEMP P2 = C1 * X

   ii) TEMP2 = TEMP2 + C2 (omit if C2 =0)

e) For the instruction, If TEMP RELOP TEMP2 GOTO Y, delete all the assignment to I from the loop.

g) If there is no assignment to TEMP between the introduced statement I = TEMP and the use of I, replace all the use of I by TEMP and delete the statement I=TEMP.

Example 6.14 Elimination of induction variable

In the control flow graph shown in Fig. 6.14, detect the induction variables and eliminate them.

Step 1: The basic induction variable for the above loop B2 is I = I + 1, i.e., I is the basic induction variable.

Step 2: T1= 4*I is the additional induction variable. Comparing it with the general form, I = C1 I + C2, we get C1 = 4 , C2 = 0.

a) and b) Replace T1 = 4 * I by T1 = TEMP.

c) Add TEMP = 4 * I to the preheader.

d) After Statement No. 10, I=I +1, append a statement comparing it with the general form I = I+D; we get D=1, I=I. Append the following statement:

TEMP = TEMP + 4

e) For Statement no. 11, if I <= 20, goto B2, comparing it with general form. B RELOP X GOTO Y, we get, I=I, X=20, Y=B2. Replacing the statement with the following statements:

TEMP2 = 4* 20=80
IF TEMP<= TEMP GOTO B2

Now delete Statement no. 10, I= I+1, after applying the above steps. The control flow after applying the above changes is shown in Fig. 6.15.

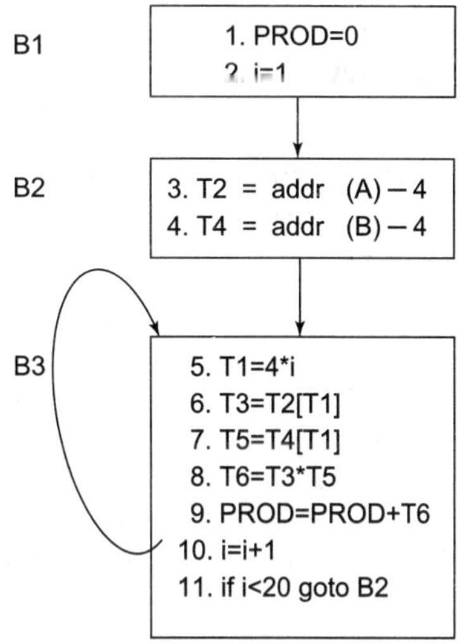

Figure 6.14 CFG for Example 6.14

Step 3: Replace T1 with TEMP and delete T1 = TEMP.

- In the instruction, IF TEMP <= TEMP2 GOTO B2, put the value of TEMP2=80 and delete TEMP=80.
- Put I=1 in TEMP 4*I and delete I=1.

After all the steps, the optimised code is as in Fig. 6.16

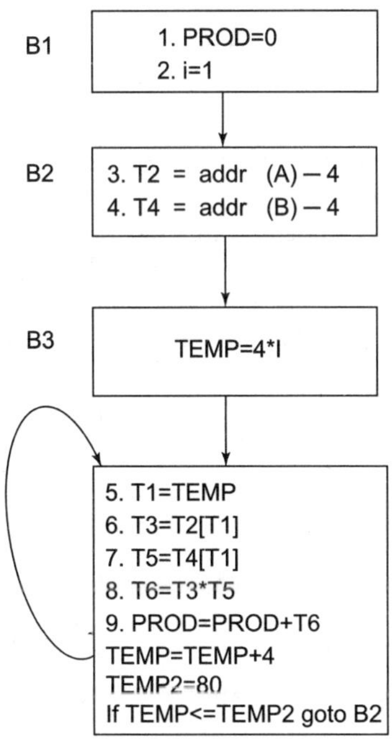

Figure 6.15 Intermediate result of applying induction variable elimination

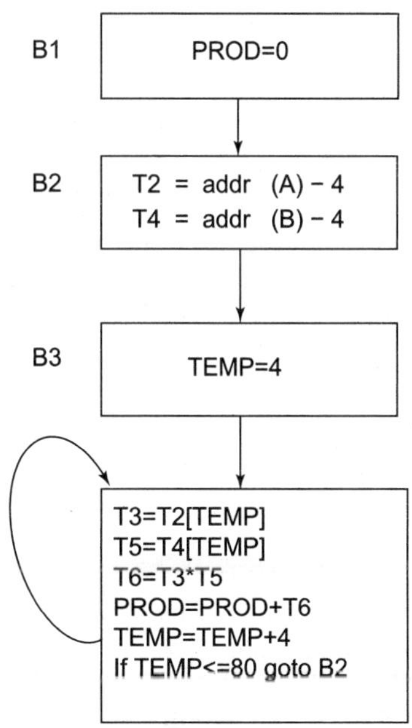

Figure 6.16 Result of induction variable elimination for Example 6.14

3. Loop unrolling: Loop unrolling refers to replication of the body of the loop to reduce the number of iterations. It increases the size of the code. It is an example of the space–time tradeoff, where increasing the size of the code reduces execution time.

Example 6.15 Loop unrolling

```
void example( )
{
      for(i=1;i<5;i++)
      {
      printf("Compiler /n");
      }
}
```

A loop with fewer number of iterations can be unrolled or unwinded to reduce the overhead of incrementing the loop variable and executing the loop. The unwinded loop for the above for-loop will be:

```
void example ( )
{
      printf("Compiler /n");
      printf("Compiler /n");
      printf("Compiler /n");
      printf("Compiler /n");
}
```

Example 6.16 Loop unrolling

```
for(i=1;i<=100;i++)
{
      A[i]=b[i]+2;
}
```

The `for` loop will be executed 100 times. However, if the body of the loop is replicated, then the number of times the loop is executed is reduced. If the body of the loop is replicated once, the loop is executed 50 times. It is possible to choose any divisor for the number of times the loop is executed; the body will be replicated that many times. Unrolling once, i.e., replicating the body to form two copies of itself, saves 50% of the possible execution time. If unrolling is done twice, the test will be executed 100/3 times; if unrolling is done three times, the test will be executed 100/4 times, and so on.
After replicating the body of the loop once, the loop will be:

```
for(i=1;i<=100;i+=2)
{
      A[i]=b[i]+2;
      A[i]=b[i]+2;
}
```

4. Loop fission: In loop fission, the loop is distributed or broken down into multiple smaller loops. It is also called loop splitting.

Example 6.17 Loop fission

```
for(i=0;i<=100;i++)
{
```

```
        A[i]=B[i];
        C[i]=C[i-1]+1;
}
After loop fission
for(i=0;i<=100;i++)
{
        A[i]=B[i];
}
for(i=0;i<=100;i++)
{
        C[i]=C[i-1]+1;
}
```

Example 6.18 Loop fission enables loop parallelisation

```
for(i=0;i<=100;i++)
{
        A[i]=0;
        B[i]=0;
        C[i]=0;
        D[i]=0;
        E[i]=0;
        F[i]=0;
        G[i]=0;
}
After loop fission
for(i=0;i<=100;i++)
{
        A[i]=0;
        B[i]=0;
        C[i]=0;
        D[i]=0;
}
for(i=0;i<=100;i++)
{
        E[i]=0;
        F[i]=0;
        G[i]=0;
}
```

5. Loop fusion: Also called loop jamming, this is a loop optimisation technique that merges the bodies of two loops. Two loops can be merged if they have the same indices and the same number of iterations. Also, the computations of one loop do not depend on those of the other loop that has to be merged. By merging loops, the loop overhead of one loop is reduced, resulting in faster execution and also reducing the size of the code.

Example 6.19 Loop fusion

```
for(i=0;i<=100;i++)
{
        A[i]=0;
}
for(i=0;i<=100;i++)
{
        B[i]=C[i]+2;
}
```

6. Loop peeling: In loop peeling, the first or first few iterations (or last or last few iterations) of the loop are split and moved outside the loop. This optimisation enforces initial memory alignment prior to loop vectorisation. It is a special case of loop fission.

Example 6.20 Loop peeling

Consider the loop

```
for(i=0;i<n;i++)
{
        A[i] = B[i] + C[i];
}
```

After loop peeling, the first iteration i = 0 is moved out of the loop and the loop starts from i = 1.

```
if(n>=1)
        A[0] = B[0] + C[0];
for(i=1;i<n;i++)
{
        A[i] = B[i] + C[i];
}
```

6.3 Machine-dependent Optimisation

Machine-dependent code optimisation takes advantage of the features of the target machine. It uses information about the limits and special features of the target machine to produce code that is shorter or which executes more quickly on the machine.

Machine-dependent code optimisation techniques:

- **Register allocation and assignment:** Modern computers are of LOAD-STORE type – these machines store operands in registers and data must be loaded from memory into a register, operated upon, and then stored again. Moreover, instructions involving register operands are shorter and faster than those involving operands stored in memory. Hence, efficient utilisation of the registers is necessary. This involves two sub-problems:
  - *Register allocation*, during which the set of variables that will reside in the registers at each point in the program are selected.
  - *Register assignment,* in which the register in which the variable will reside is selected.
- **Use of machine idioms:** Consider code intended for machines of the PDP-11 family. These computers have auto-increment and auto-decrement addressing modes. Hence, when code is

written for PDP-11, the auto-increment or decrement mode must be used instead of incrementing or decrementing the value in the program. The use of instructions in these modes reduces the code required for pushing and popping stacks. PDP-11 computers also have machine-level instructions to increment (INC) or decrement (DEC), by one, the values stored in memory. Whenever possible, the INC and DEC operations should be used instead of creating a constant with value 1 and adding or subtracting this constant from the value stored in memory.

- Instruction ordering or sequencing
- Introducing parallelisation
- Peephole optimisation

Some of the machine-dependent optimisation techniques will be discussed in Chapter 7.

6.3.1 Peephole Optimisation

The statement-by-statement code generation strategy often produces target codes that have redundant instructions and suboptimal constructs. A simple and effective technique to locally improve the target code is to apply peephole optimisation. The implementation of this technique is discussed after the code generation phase on the target code for its improvement; however, it can also be applied to intermediate code.

Peephole is a kind of optimisation technique that targets a small number of instructions by moving a small window over the target program. It finds the set of instructions that can be replaced by shorter or faster sets. In general, multiple passes are needed over the code. Each improvement may lead to additional improvements. The code in the peephole need not be contiguous.

The peephole optimiser is repeatedly passed over the modified assembly code, performing optimisations until no further changes are possible. Peephole optimisation leads to improvement in the performance, reduces the memory requirement and reduces the code size.

The common techniques applied in machine-dependent peephole optimisation are given below.

Removing redundant loads and stores:

(1) Load a, R0.
(2) Store R0, a.

Eliminate instruction (2) because whenever (2) is executed, (1) will ensure that the value of *a* is already in register R0.

If (2) had a label, it would not always be possible that (1) would be executed immediately before (2), so in such cases (2) cannot be removed.

Eliminating unreachable code: Another opportunity for peephole optimisation is the removal of unreachable instructions. An unlabelled instruction that immediately follows an unconditional jump may be removed. This operation can be repeated to eliminate a sequence of instructions.

For example, for debugging purposes, a large program may have within it certain segments that are executed only if the variable debug is 1. In C, the source code might look like:

```
#define debug 0
....

if (debug) {
          Print debugging information
}
```

In the intermediate representations, the if-statement may be translated as:

```
        if debug =1 goto L1
        goto L2
L1:     print debugging information
L2:                                   (a)
```

One obvious peephole optimisation is to eliminate jumps over jumps. Thus, no matter what the value of debug, (a) can be replaced by:

```
If debug ≠1 goto L2
Print debugging information
L2:                                   (b)
If debug ≠0 goto L2
Print debugging information
L2:                                   (c)
```

As the argument of the statement (c) evaluates to a constant true, it can be replaced by goto L2. Then, all the statements that print debugging information become unreachable and can be eliminated one at a time.

Eliminating multiple jumps: Redundant jumps can be eliminated. Consider the example

```
     if value = = 20 goto L1
     goto L2
L1:  print 20
L2:
```

The above code can be rewritten as given below after eliminating multiple jumps:

```
if value != 20 goto L2
print 20
L2:
```

Control flow optimisation: Jumps to jumps can be short circuited. Naive code generation often creates many jumps.

```
     goto L1
     ...
L1: goto L2
```

This can be replaced with

```
     goto L2
     ...
     L1: goto L2
```

Further optimisations are possible if no jumps to L1 exist. Similarly, optimisation is possible with conditional jumps:

```
     if (cond) goto L1
     ...
L1: goto L2
```

This can be replaced by

```
     if (cond) goto L2
     ...
L1: goto L2
```

Algebraic simplification: Eliminate identity operations like a=a+0, a=a*1.

Strength reduction: Reduction in strength replaces expensive operations with cheaper ones available on the target machine. Certain machine instructions are cheaper than others. For example, x^2 is cheaper to implement as x*x rather than using the exponential routine. Floating point division or multiplication by the power of 2 is cheaper to implement as a shift. Floating point division by a constant can be replaced by floating point multiplication by a constant, as it is cheaper.

Using machine idioms: The target machine may have hardwired instructions to implement specific operations efficiently. Detecting situations that permit the use of these instructions can reduce execution time significantly. For example, some machines have auto-increment and auto-decrement addressing modes. Using these modes can greatly improve the quality of the code. For example, an instruction like i=i+1 can be replaced by INC I in the machine code or by using the auto-increment addressing mode.
Note: Peephole optimisation can be applied to machine-independent code by finding and replacing a set of instructions with shorter or faster sets of instructions. This is performed by moving over a small window (peephole) of instructions. It is continued until no further optimisation is possible. The common techniques that can be used are constant folding, algebraic simplification, strength reduction, deletion of unnecessary operations, combine operation in which various operations can be combined in a single equivalent operation, and so on.

SUMMARY

- The application of transformation to code in order to improve its quality or performance is called code optimisation.
- Compilers that apply transformations to improve the code are called optimising compilers.
- Optimisation can be machine-dependent or machine-independent.
- Loop optimisation is a machine-independent optimisation technique.
- Examples of loop optimisation are elimination of loop invariable computation, induction variable elimination, loop unrolling, loop fission and fusion and loop peeling.
- Common-subexpression elimination, algebraic simplification, dead code elimination, copy propagation, constant propagation, constant folding, function inlining and cloning are all machine-independent optimisation techniques.
- If an expression E was previously computed and the value of E has not changed since the last computation of E, then such a computation is called common sub-expression.
- Function inlining involves replacing a function call with the body of the function.
- In loop optimisation, the two steps are to first find the loop in the program and then to apply the appropriate loop optimisation technique.
- Loop detection involves leader statement identification, identification of basic block, control flow in the program and loop identification.
- A loop is a cycle that satisfies two conditions, namely, it has a single entry node and it is strongly connected.
- Any node A dominates node B if every path from the initial node to node B goes through A. Also, every node dominates itself.
- The first instructions of the TAC, the target of conditional and unconditional goto and the instruction that follows conditional goto are leader statements.
- The set of all definitions reaching the start of block B is IN(B).
- The set of all definitions reaching the end of block B is OUT(B).

- The set of all definitions generated in block B is GEN(B).
- The set of all definitions outside block B that define the same variables which are defined in block B is KILL(B).
- Reaching definitions are found by computing the Use-Def Chain (UD-Chain).
- A basic induction variable is one that is increased or decreased by a fixed amount on every iteration of a loop.
- A derived induction variable is one that is a linear function of another instruction variable.

EXERCISES

Review Questions

Fill in the blanks with appropriate answers:

1. __________ type of optimisation depends on the target machine for which the object code is being generated.
2. __________ can measure the time taken by various parts of the program to execute.
3. Common sub-expressions can be detected by construction of __________.
4. If X^2 is replaced by X*X, then it is __________ type of optimisation.
5. Code that never gets executed is called __________.
6. A __________ is a directed graph of nodes with the nodes corresponding to basic blocks and the edges representing the flow of control in the program.
7. A loop exists in a program if and only if there are __________ types of edges in the program flow graph.
8. __________ refers to replication of the body of the loop to reduce the number of iterations.
9. The loop is broken down into multiple smaller loops in __________.
10. The loop optimisation technique that merges the bodies of two loops is __________.

Answers: 1. Machine dependent 2. Profilers 3. Directed Acyclic Graph (DAG) 4. Strength reduction 5. Dead code 6. Control flow graph 7. Back edges 8. Loop unrolling 9. Loop fission 10. Loop fusion

State whether true or false:

1. DAG is constructed for a single basic block in the local common sub-expression elimination.
2. Copy propagation is a global optimisation technique.
3. Constant propagation can be local or global.
4. Constant folding is used to evaluate the expressions with constant operands at compile time rather than at run-time.
5. OUT(B) is the set of all definitions reaching the start of block B.

Answers: 1. True 2. False 3. True 4. True 5. False

Practice Questions

1. Apply the appropriate loop optimisation techniques to the following code fragment:

```
for(int i=0; i<3; i++) {
    A[n+i] = i;
}
```

2. Use appropriate techniques of code optimisation to optimise the following code:

```
A=1
B=2
C=0
Whle(A<10)
{
    Avg=C/1;
    D= C*2;
    Temp= D + A/3;
    A=A+5;
}
```

3. Generate a three-address code. Find the dominators, back edges and program flow graph for the given code fragment:

```
while(c)
{
    b=3;
    x=y+1;
    y=2*z;
    if(a)
            x=y+z;
            z=1;
}
z=x;
```

4. Apply the invariant code motion for the given code fragment:

```
for(i=1 to N)
{
    x=x+2;
    for(j=1 to N)
    {
            a(i,j) = 1000*N + 10*I +j + x;
    }
    }
```

5. Find IN, OUT, GEN and KILL for the following program flow graph:

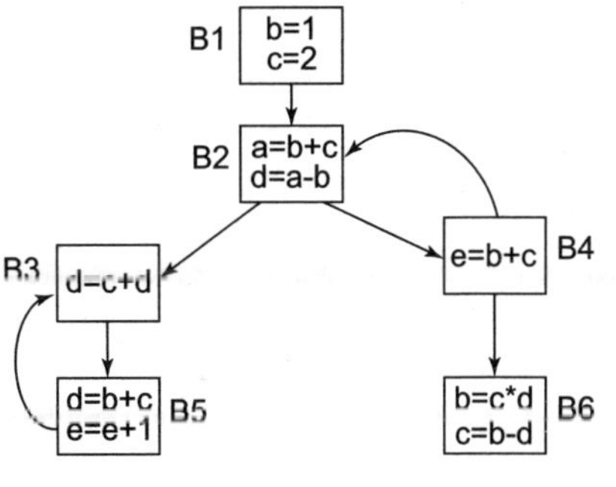

6. Compute the reaching definitions for the following:

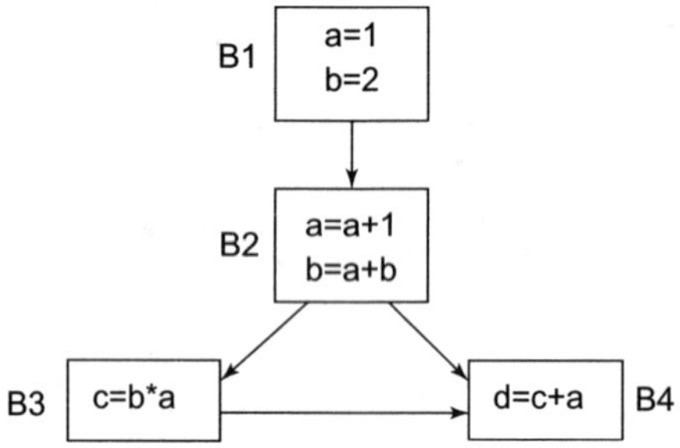

7. Compute the reaching definitions for the following:

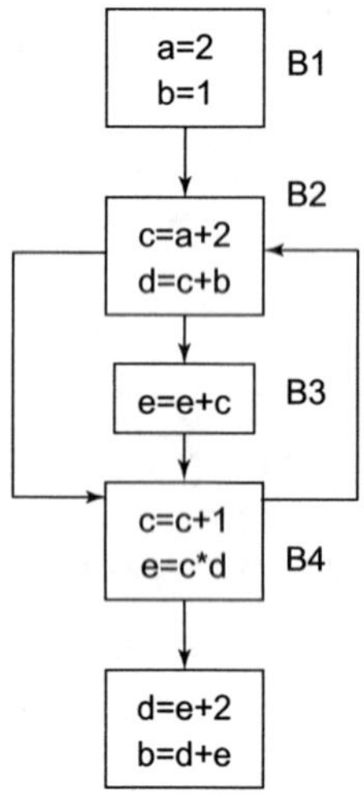

8. Remove the loop invariant computation in the following:

```
        a=0;
        b=1;
        c=2;
L2:     if (b>100) goto L3;
        a=a+1
        d=e+f
L1:     if (b>50) goto L3;
        c=a;
        g=10*d;
        h=g+c;
        b=b+2;
        goto L1;
        b=b+4;
        goto L2;
L3:     i=b;
```

9. Find the reading definitions for the following:

```
i=m-1;
j=n;
a= U1;
do
i=i+1;
j=j-1;
if e1 then
    a=U2
else
    i=U3
while e2
```

10. Generate the program flow graph for the following:

```
int func(int t)
{
    int x,y;
    x=t;
    y=t;
    while(a>100 and t>0)
    {
        y=y*x+t;
        x=x+1;
    }
}
```

11. Perform live variable analysis on the following:

```
int i,j,k;
i=45;
j=a+b;
if(a+i) >1000
    k=a+j
else
    k=b+j;
```

Programming Questions

1. Consider a three-address code and write a program to identify the leader statement and generate the program flow graph.
2. Given a program flow graph, write a program to find out the dominators and back edges.
3. Given a program flow graph, write a program to perform IN-OUT analysis.
4. Given a program flow graph, write a program to find out the live variable at the start and end of each block.
5. Consider a three-address code and write a program to find out the number of registers required for execution.

7 Code Generation

Objectives

- To introduce the code generation phase of compilation
- To discuss a simple code generator
- To describe how to determine the optimal order of evaluation of instructions
- To discuss the labelling algorithm and code generation using the *gencode* algorithm
- To discuss register allocation strategies
- To discuss code generation using dynamic programming

7.1 Introduction to Code Generation

Code generation is the final phase of the compilation process. The output of intermediate code generation is passed as input to the code generation phase. If there is an optimisation phase after the intermediate code generation phase, the optimised code is submitted as input to the code generation phase. The generated code must be correct and should use the resources of the target machine effectively.

The problem of generating optimal code is an un-decidable one. Heuristic techniques generate good, but not necessarily optimal, code. The choice of heuristic is important to generate code that is efficient and quick.

7.2 Problems in Code Generator Design

Problems in the design of a code generator are dependent on the target machine. However, the operating system, aspects such as memory management, instruction selection, register allocation and evaluation order, are inherited in most code generation problems. The general problems encountered in the design of code generators are discussed below.

Input: Input to the code generator consists of the intermediate representation of the source program produced by the front-end phases of compilation, along with the symbol table. It is assumed that the source program is scanned, parsed and translated into a reasonably detailed intermediate representation. The values of names appearing in the intermediate code can be represented by quantities that the target machine can directly manipulate. It is also assumed that the necessary type checking has been carried out and the semantic errors have already been detected and eliminated. In some compilers, semantic checking is performed together with code generation.

Target program: The output of the code generation phase is the target program. This target program may be absolute machine language, relocatable machine language or assembly language. The advantage of producing an absolute machine lang.age program as output is that it can be placed in a fixed memory location and be immediately executed. In a relocatable machine language program, subprograms are compiled separately and a set of these relocatable object modules are linked together and loaded for execution by a linking loader. Generating an assembly language program as output is easy. The output is fed to the assembler for code generation. In this chapter, assembly code is used as the target language.

Memory management: Mapping names in the source program to the addresses of data objects in run-time memory is carried out by the front-end phases and the code generator. Symbol table entries are created for names in the three-address form. The type in a declaration determines the amount of storage needed for the declared name. If machine code is being generated, labels in three-address statements must be converted to the addresses of instructions. This process is analogous to the backpatching technique.

Instruction selection: The instruction set of the target machine determines the difficulty of instruction selection. Uniformity and completeness of the instruction set, instruction execution speed and machine idioms are some important factors during instruction selection. If the efficiency of the target program is not a factor, instruction selection is straightforward.

For each type of three-address statement, a code skeleton is designed by the code generator. For example, every three-address statement of the form x = y + z, where x, y and z are statically allocated, can be translated into a sequence of code:

```
MDV y,R0    // Load y into register R0
ADD z,R0    // Add z to R0
MOV R0,x    //Store R0 in x
```

This kind of statement-by-statement code generation produces poor code. The quality of the generated code is determined by its speed and size.

Factors affecting code generation:

- Use cheaper instructions available in the instruction set. If it is required to execute x=x+1 and target machine support INC (increment instruction), then, loading the register, adding one to it and storing at location x can be avoided.
- The code sequence that performs better for a given three-address construct must be used. This may also require knowledge about the context in which that construct appears. Such selection is based on different factors, including system configuration and the architecture of the compiler. Thus, it can be categorised as an un-decidable problem.

Register allocation: The number of registers to be used for a given code sequence must be determined in order to efficiently utilise the available registers. Efficient use of registers is necessary for good code generation. The optimal number of registers for a computation is discussed in Section 7.6.2. Register allocation strategies are discussed in Section 7.7.

Choice of evaluation order: The order in which computations are performed can affect the efficiency and cost of the target code. Some computation orders require fewer registers to hold the intermediate result. The order in which the computation is performed affects the cost of the generated code. Hence, the optimal order of computation must be found. Example 7.2 elaborates this concept.

Approaches to code generation: The most important criterion for a code generator is the production of correct and executable code. A code generator must be designed in such a way that it is easy to implement, test and maintain. In Section 7.5, a simple code generation algorithm is discussed that uses information about subsequent uses of an operand to generate code for a register machine. It considers each statement in turn, keeping operands in registers as long as possible. The output of such a code generator can be improved by peephole optimisation techniques. Code generation is discussed after determining the optimal number of registers to be used in Sections 7.6.2 and 7.6.3.

7.3 Target Machine

Familiarity with the target machine and its instruction set is a prerequisite for designing a good code generator. In this chapter, the target machine computer is assumed to be a byte addressable machine, with four bytes to a word, and has n general purpose registers, R0, R1, . . . , Rn – 1. It has two address instructions of the form

Opcode source1 source2/destination

where, *source 1* has the first operand; *source 2* has the second operand and also acts as the destination for placing the result. Some of the opcodes available are MOV, ADD, SUB and DIV. Source and destination can be a memory location or a register. A memory location is denoted by M and the register by R followed by a number.

The **addressing modes** available in the machine are absolute, register, indexed and indirect. Address computation for operands and the costs corresponding to addressing modes are given in Table 7.1. Square brackets ([]) represent the contents. For example, [R] denotes the contents of register R. The immediate addressing mode allows the source to contain a constant value, and the added cost is 1.

Table 7.1 Addressing modes with address computation for operands and the corresponding cost

Addressing mode	Form	Address	Added cost
Absolute	M	M	1
Register	R	R	0
Indexed	c(R)	c+[R]	1
Indirect Register	*R	[R]	0
Indirect Indexed	*c(r)	[c+[R]]	1
Immediate	#const	–	1

7.4 Instruction Cost

The cost of an instruction is considered as the cost associated with the source and destination address modes (indicated as 'Added cost' in Table 7.1). This cost corresponds to the length (in words) of the instruction. Addressing modes involving only registers have 0 [zero] cost and those with a memory location cost 1 [one], because such operands have to be stored with the instruction. The instruction length should be minimised to reduce the space requirements.

In most machines, the time taken to fetch an instruction from memory exceeds the time spent executing the instruction. Therefore, by reducing the cost of the instruction, by reducing the instruction length, the execution time can be reduced. Example 7.1 shows the computation of instruction cost for some instructions.

Example 7.1 Find the instruction cost for the given instructions

a. MOV R0,R1

Cost = Added cost (from Table 7.1) + 1

The addressing mode of the instruction is register. Therefore

Cost = 0 +1 =1. // Added cost is 0 for register addressing mode

b. MOV R1,M
   The instruction moves the contents of register R1 to memory location M.
   Cost = 1+1=2 // Added cost of absolute instruction is 1
c. ADD #2,R1
   Source operand is a constant number 2, which is added to the contents of register R1, and the result is stored in R1.
   Cost = 1+1 = 2 //Added cost for immediate operand is 1
d. ADD 4(R1),*8(R2)
   Cost = 1+1+1 //Added cost for 4(R1) is 1, added cost for *8(R2) is 1
e. ADD 4(R1), R2
   ADD R2, R3
   MOV R3, A
   Total cost = 2 +1+ 2 = 5

7.5 Simple Code Generation

In this section, a simple code generation algorithm is discussed. The algorithm generates code for all the statements contained in the basic block. The instructions in the basic block are in the three-address format. The code generation algorithm uses descriptors to keep track of the register contents and addresses for names or variables.

A **register descriptor** keeps track of the contents of the register. It is maintained for all the registers in the machine. It is referred whenever a new register is required. Initially, the register descriptor shows all the registers as empty. As the code generation algorithm progresses, the register descriptors are updated.

An **address descriptor** keeps track of the location where the current value of a name can be found at run-time. This location can be a register or memory. This information can be stored in the symbol table and is used to determine the accessing method for a name.

7.5.1 Code Generation for a Three-address Statement of the form X = Y op Z

For every three-address statement of the form X=Y op Z, in the basic block, perform the following:

1. Invoke function *getreg()* to find the location in which the computation Y op Z should be performed. Let this location be L. It is usually a register, but it could also be a memory location.
2. For operand Y, consult its address descriptor to find the current location of Y.
   - If the value of Y is currently both in the memory as well as in the register, prefer the register to increase computation speed.
   - If the value of Y is currently not available in L, then generate an instruction: MOV Y,L.
3. (a) Generate the instruction op Z,L and (b) Update the address descriptor of X to indicate that X is in L. If L is in the register, then update its descriptor to indicate that it contains the value of X. Remove X from all other register descriptors.
4. If the current value of Y and/or Z is of no further use, then alter the register descriptor to indicate that those registers will not contain Y and/or Z after the execution of X = Y op Z.

Function *getreg()*: This returns a location L to hold the value of X for the three-address statement of the form X= Y op Z. This function uses a scheme based on the next-use information collected in the last section, as follows:

1. Search for the location containing Y. If Y is in the register and is of no further use after the execution of X= Y op Z, return register Y as the location L. Update the address descriptor of Y to indicate that Y is no longer in L.
2. Otherwise, search for an empty register, if there is one, and return it as location L.
3. If there is no empty register and if X is used later in the block, find a suitable occupied register R. Empty the register by transferring its value to a proper memory location M [MOV R, M] and return the register for L.
4. If X is not used and no suitable register is found, then a memory location is used.

Example 7.2 Code generation using the *getreg()* function
Consider the three-address code corresponding to the expression x = [(a+b) – (c+d)] + (c+d)], as given below:

t = a + b
u = c + d
v = t – u
w= v + u

Assume that there are two registers, R0 and R1. Initially, all the registers are empty. For the TAC t=a+b, there is no location where 'a' exists. Hence, a register R0 is returned as location L to store 'a' and instruction MOV a, R0 is generated. Next, the instruction generated is ADD b,R0. The register and address descriptors are updated accordingly. After applying the code generation algorithm to the TAC, the result is as is shown in Table 7.2.

Table 7.2 Instructions generated for the expression x = [(a+b) – (c+d)] + (c+d)]

Statement	L	Instruction generated	Cost	Register descriptor	Address descriptor
				All Registers Empty	
t = a + b	R0	MOV a,R0 ADD b,R0	2 2	R0 contains t	t is in R0
u = c + d	R1	MOV c,R1 ADD d,R1	2 2	R1 contains u R0 contains t	u is in R1 t is in R0
v = t – u	R0	SUB R1,R0	2	R0 contains v R1 contains u	v is in R0 u is in R1
w = v+u	R0	ADD R1,R0	1	R0 contains w R1 contains u	w is in R0 u is in R1
		Mov R0, x	2		x is in R0 and memory
			Total cost = 13		

The cost of the code generated is 13. This cost can be reduced by using more sophisticated techniques. One such technique is to sequence the order of the statements.

7.5.2 Reordering of Statements for Improved Cost of Generated Code

The cost of the generated code can be reduced by reordering the computing order. Example 7.3 shows the costs in the case of different computing sequences, with different orders for computation. In Section 7.6.1, the heuristics that help in finding the optimal order of computation is discussed.

Example 7.3 Improvement in cost by reordering computation order

Consider the TAC in the same sequence as given below

t = a − b
u = c * d
v = e + u
w = t + v

PART A: Computation order as it is given: t-u-v-w.

The code generated will be as shown in Table 7.3.

Table 7.3 Instructions generated for TAC of Example 7.3 (Part A)

Statement	L	Instruction generated	Cost	Register descriptor	Address descriptor
				All Registers Empty	
t = a − b	R0	MOV a , R0 SUB b , R0	2 2	R0 contains t	t is in R0
u = c * d	R1	MOV c , R1 MUL d , R1	2 2	R0 contains t R1 contains u	t is in R0 u is in R1
v = e + u		MOV R0 , t	2 2 1	R0 is empty R1 contains u	t is in mem u is in R1
	R0	MOV e , R0 ADD R1,R0		R0 contains v R1 will be empty because u is not used further	v is in R0
w = t + v	R1	MOV t , R1 ADD R0 , R1	2 1	R1 contains w	w is in R1
		MOV R1, x	2		X contains R1, which is the answer of the expression
			Total cost = 18		

PART B: Computation order u-v-t-w

u = c * d
v = e + u

t = a – b
w = t + v

Table 7.4 Instructions generated for TAC of Example 7.3 (Part B)

Statement	L	Instruction generated	Cost	Register descriptor	Address descriptor
				All Registers Empty	
u = c * d	R0	MOV c , R0 MUL d , R0	2 2	R0 contains u	u is in register R0
v = e + u	R1	MOV e , R1 ADD R0,R1	2 1	R1 contains v Register R0 will be empty because u is not used further	v is in R1
t = a – b	R0	MOV a , R0 SUB b , R0	2 2	R0 contains t R1 contains v	t is in R0 v is in R1
w = t + v	R0	ADD R1 , R0	1	Register R0 contains w R1 is empty because v is not used further	w is in R0
		MOV R0 , x	2		x contains the result of the expression
			Total cost = 14		

Thus, the cost is 18 for the sequence of computation t-u-v-w and 14 for the sequence u-v-t-w. Since 14 < 18, the sequence u-v-t-w is better than the computation sequence t-u-v-w. To find the optimal sequence for computation, the labelling algorithm can be used (discussed in Section 7.6).

7.5.3 Code Generation for a Three-address Statement of the Form X = Y

For a three-address statement of the form X=Y, perform the following steps:

1. If Y is in the register, change the register and address descriptors to record that the value of X is now available in the register holding the value of Y.
2. If Y is not used further, the register no longer holds the value of Y.
3. If Y is only in memory, use *getreg* to find a register in which to load Y and make that register the location of X.

Alternatively, instruction MOV Y, X can be generated, which would be preferable if the value of X is not used further in the block. Statements of the form X=Y will not be generated if the code generation phase is preceded by the code optimisation phase. Most, if not all, copy instructions will be eliminated if block improving and copy propagation algorithms are used. These algorithms are already discussed in Chapter 6.

Example 7.4 Code generation for TAC having a statement of the form X = Y
Consider the three-address code corresponding to the expression, as given below:

p = a − b
q = a − c
r = q
s = r + p

The code generated is shown in Table 7.5, assuming the result is stored in memory location x. The statement r=q is of the general form X=Y. After applying the algorithm described in Section 7.5.3, q is contained in register R1 as per the address descriptor in Sr. No.3. Hence, the register and address descriptors are updated in Sr. No. 4 to record that r is in register R1.

Table 7.5 Instructions generated for TAC of Example 7.4

Sr. No.	Statement	L	Instruction generated	Cost	Register descriptor	Address descriptor
1					All Registers Empty – R0, R1	
2	p = a − b	R0	MOV a,R0 SUB b,R0	2 2	R0 contains p	p is in R0
3	q = a − c	R1	MOV a,R1 SUB c,R1	2 2	R1 contains q R0 contains p	q is in R1 p is in R0
4	r = q				R1 contains r R0 contains p	r is in R1 p is in R0
5	s = r + p	R1	ADD R0,R1	1	R0 is empty R1 contains s	s is in R1
6			MOV R1, x	2		s is in R1 and memory
				Total cost = 11		

7.5.4 Generating Code for Array Assignment and Pointer

The code generated for array allocations of the type a=b[i] and a[i]=b, assuming b is statically allocated, is shown in Table 7.6, and the code generated for pointers is shown in Table 7.7.

Table 7.6 Code generated for array assignment statements

Statement	Assume i is in register Ri		Assume i is in memory	
	Instruction generated	Cost	Instruction generated	Cost
a=b[i]	MOV b(Ri),R	2	MOV Mi, R MOV b(R),R	4
a[i]=b	MOV b,a(Ri)	3	MOV Mi,R MOV b,a(R)	5

Table 7.7 Code generated for statements involving pointers

Statement	Assume i is in register Ri		Assume i is in memory	
	Instruction generated	Cost	Instruction generated	Cost
a=*p	MOV *Rp,a	2	MOV Mp, R MOV *R,R	3
*p=a	MOV a,*Rp	2	MOV Mp,R MOV a, *R	4

Example 7.5 Code generation for TAC containing array assignment
Consider the TAC given below:

x=a[i]
y=b[i]
z=x*y

The code generated as per the algorithm is shown in Table 7.8.

Table 7.8 Code generated for TAC in Example 7.5

Statement	L	Instruction generated	Register descriptor	Address descriptor
			All Registers Empty R0,R1,R2	
Assume i is stored in R0	R0	MOV i, R0	R0 contains i	i is in R0
x=a[i]	R1	MOV a(R0), R1	R0 contains i R1 contains x	i is in R0 x is in R1
y=b[i]	R2	MOV b(R0), R2	R0 contains i R1 contains x R2 contains y	i is in R0 x is in R1 y is in R2
z=x*y	R1	MUL R2,R1	R0 is empty R1 contains z R2 is empty	Z is in R1
		MOV R1,z		Z is in memory

For a machine that has the LD, MUL and ST instructions, the code generated will be

```
LD R1, i
MUL R1, R1, #4
LD R2, a(R1)
```

```
LD R1, b(R1)
MUL R1, R2, R1
ST z, R1
```

7.6 Code Generation Using DAG

As discussed in Section 7.5.2, different orders of computation generate different costs. To find the optimal sequence, construct a DAG representation of the basic block and then order the nodes. The advantage of using a DAG is that the order of the final computation sequence can be rearranged instead of starting from a linear sequence of three-address statements. One such heuristic to order nodes is discussed next.

7.6.1 Heuristic for Finding the Optimal Order of Nodes in DAG

The heuristic ordering for nodes is given in the algorithm below.
Node Listing Algorithm

```
{
  1. While unlisted interior nodes exist, execute step 2.
  2. Select an unlisted node n, all of whose parents have been listed
     a. List n
     b. While the leftmost child m of n has no unlisted parents and is not a leaf do
        i. List m
        ii. n := m
}
```

Order of computation is the reverse order of the listing of nodes.

Example 7.6 Optimal order of computation
Let us consider the TAC given below and convert it into DAG representation, as shown in Fig. 7.1.

```
t1=a+b
t2=t1−e
t3=c+d
t4=t2*t3
t5=t4+f
t6=g−t4
t7=t6*t5
```

After applying the node listing algorithm, the listing obtained is shown by numbers in the DAG of Fig. 7.2. Initially, the only node that has no unlisted parents is t7; it is given a listing of 1. The left child of t7 is t6, whose parent t7 is also listed, as 2. Similarly, the remaining nodes are listed. The order of computation is the reverse order of listing of nodes. Hence, the final order of computation must be 7654321, which corresponds to the following order of computation:

```
t3=c+d
t1−u+b
t2=t1−e
t4=t2*t3
t5=t4+f
t6=g−t4
t7=t6*t5
```

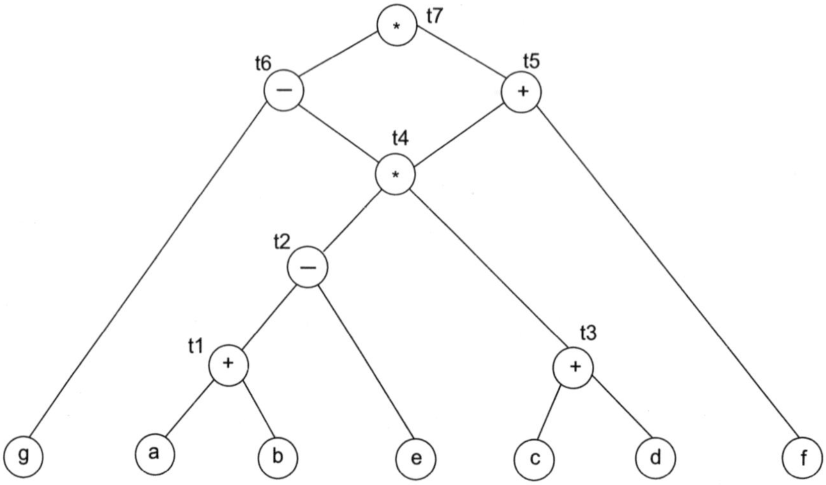

Figure 7.1 DAG corresponding to Example 7.6

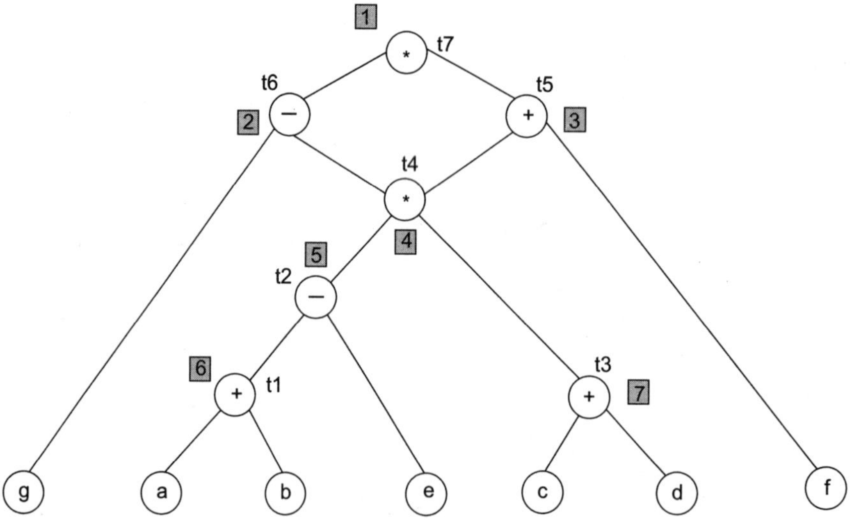

Figure 7.2 Node listing algorithm applied to DAG of Fig. 7.1

7.6.2 Labelling Algorithm

A simple algorithm to determine the optimal order in which to evaluate statements in a basic block when the DAG representation of the block is a tree is as follows. The optimal order means the order that generates the shortest instruction sequence, over all the instruction sequences that evaluate the tree. This algorithm has two parts:

- The first part labels each node of the tree, in bottom-up fashion, with an integer that denotes the number of registers required to evaluate the tree, with no storage of intermediate results.
- The second part of the algorithm is tree traversal, whose order is governed by the computed node labels. The output code is generated during tree traversal.

Labelling Algorithm

```
{
If n is a leaf mode then
      If n is the leftmost child of its parent then
            Label(n)=1
      Else
            Label(n)=0
      Else
            Label(n)=max[Label (ni)+(i−1)]   //for i=1 to k
                        // where n1, n2,........nk are the children of n.
}
```

For example, if L1=L2 →Label(n)=L1+1 and if L1≠L2 → Label (n)= max(L1,L2).

7.6.3 Code Generation From a Labelled Tree

The algorithm for code generation from a labelled tree takes as input a labelled tree T and produces as output a machine code sequence. The algorithm uses the recursive procedure *gencode(n)* to produce machine code, evaluating the subtree of T with root n into a register. The procedure uses a stack *rstack* to allocate registers. Initially, *rstack* contains all the available registers. When *gencode()* returns, it leaves the registers on *rstack* in the same order as it found them. The result is placed in the top register on *rstack.*

The function *swap(rstack*) interchanges the top two registers on *rstack*. The procedure *gencode( )* uses a stack *rstack* to allocate temporary memory locations. The statement *push*(*stack.*, X) pushes X onto the stack top. X := *pop(stack)* is used to pop the stack and assign the popped value to X.

The procedure *gencode()* has five cases. The subtrees for all cases are shown in Fig. 7.2. For case 0, where n is a leaf and the leftmost child of its parent, only a single load instruction is generated. For case 1, a parent has its left child as n1 and right child as n2; generate code to evaluate nl into register R=*top(rstack)* followed by the instruction *op name, R*. In case 2, n1 can be evaluated without stores but n2 is harder to evaluate than n1. For this case, swap the top two registers on *rstack*, then evaluate n2 into R = *top(rstack)*. Remove R from *rstack* and evaluate n1 into S = *top(rstack)*; where S was the register initially on top of *rstack* at the beginning of case 2. Then generate the instruction op R, S, which produces the value of n in register S. Another call to swap leaves *rstack* as it was when this call of *gencode()* began. Case 3 is similar to case 2 except that the left subtree is more complicated and is evaluated first. There is no need to swap registers here. In case 4, both subtrees require r or more registers to evaluate without stores. First evaluate the right subtree into the temporary T, then the left subtree, and finally the root.

Procedure gencode (n)

```
{
CASE0:
If n is a leaf node and the leftmost child of its parent then generate instruction
          mov name,RSTACK[top]
CASE1:
If n is an interior node with children n1 and n2 then
      If label(n2)= 0, then
            {
```

```
            Let name be the operand represented by n2;
            gencode(n1);
            generate op name, RSTACK[top]
            }
CASE2:
If n is an interior node with children n1 and n2
      if label (n2)>label (n1) and label(n1)<r then
            {
                  Swap top two registers of RSTACK gencode(n2)
                  R= pop (RSTACK)
                  gencode(n2)
                  generate OP R,RSTACK[top]
                  /* OP is the operator represented by n */
                  PUSH (R,RSTACK)
                  Swap top two registers of RSTACK
            }
CASE3:
If n is an interior node with children n1 and n2,
      Label (n2)<=Label(n1) and Label(n2)<r then
            {
                  gencode(n1)
                  R= pop (RSTACK)
                  gencode(n2)
                  generate OP RSTACK [top],R
                  PUSH (R,RSTACK)
            }
CASE4:
If n is an interior node with children n1 and n2,
      Label(n2)<=Label(n1), and Label(n1)>r and Label (n2)>r then
            {
                  gencode(n2)
                  T=pop (TSTACK)
                  generate MOV RSTACK [top],T
                  gencode(n1)
                  generate OP,T,RSTACK[top].
                  PUSH(T,TSTACK)
            }
  }
```

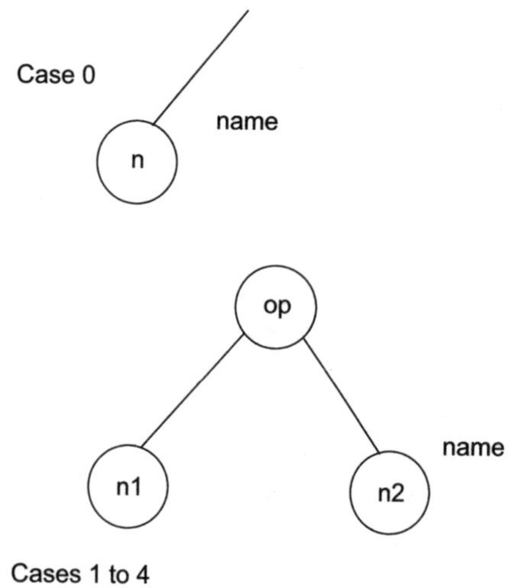

Figure 7.3 Subtree forms for cases 0 to 4

Example 7.7 Apply the labelling algorithm to the TAC by constructing DAG and then generate code using *gencode( )*

```
t1=a+b
t2=c+d
t3=e−t2
t4=t1−t3
```

The DAG after applying the labelling algorithm is shown in Fig. 7.3. The *gencode()* procedure applied is as in Table 7.9. The value of r is the number of registers indicated by the root node in the DAG. Here, r is 2. Let us assume R0 and R1 as the top two registers. The numbering in the 'Applied procedure' column of Table 7.9 gives the sequence of execution of instructions as per the procedure *gencode()*.

Table 7.9 *gencode()* on DAG of Figure 7.4

Call to *gencode()*	Condition satisfied and case	Applied procedure	RSTACK contains top two registers	Code generation

gencode(t4)	t4
	t1 t3
	(1) (2)
	n1=1, n2=2
	n2>n1, n1<r
	→ CASE2
		1) Swap top two registers
		2) Call *gencode (t3)*
		12) R = POP R1
		13) Call *gencode(t1)*
		17) Generate SUB R1,R0
		18) PUSH R1
		19) Swap top two registers
			R1,R0
			R1,R0
			R0
			R0
			R1,R0
			R0,R1
				MOV e, R1
				MOV c, R0
				ADD D, R0
				SUB R0,R1
				MOV a, R0
				ADD b, R0
				SUB R1,R0

gencode(t3)	t3
	e t2
	(1) (1)
	n1=1, n2=1
	n2<=n1, n2<r
	→ CASE3
		3) Call *gencode (e)*
		5) R=POP R1
		6) Call *gencode(t2)*
		10) Generate SUB R0,R1
		11) PUSH R1
			R1,R0
			R0
			R1,R0
				MOV e, R1
				MOV c, R0
				ADD D, R0
				SUB RO,R1

gencode(e)	Leaf node → Case 0	4) MOV e,R1	R1,R0	MOV e, R1
gencode(t2)	t2 c d (1) (0) n1=1, n2=0 n2=0 → CASE1	7) Call *gencode (c)* 9) Generate ADD D, R0	R0	MOV c, R0 ADD D, R0

(Cont'd)

Table 7.9 (Continued)

Call to *gencode()*	Condition satisfied and case	Applied procedure	RSTACK contains top two registers	Code generation
gencode(c)	Leaf node → Case 0	8) Generate MOV c, R0	R0	MOV c, R0
gencode(t1)	t1 a b (1) (0) n1=1, n2=0 n2=0 → CASE1	14) Call *gencode (a)* 16) Generate ADD b, R0	R0	MOV a, R0 ADD b, R0
gencode(a)	Leaf node → Case 0	15) Generate MOV a, R0	R0	MOV a, R0

The code generated is shown in the first row (highlighted), in Table 7.9. The code generated is given below:

```
MOV e, R1
MOV c, R0
ADD D, R0
SUB R0,R1
MOV a, R0
ADD b, R0
SUB R1,R0
```

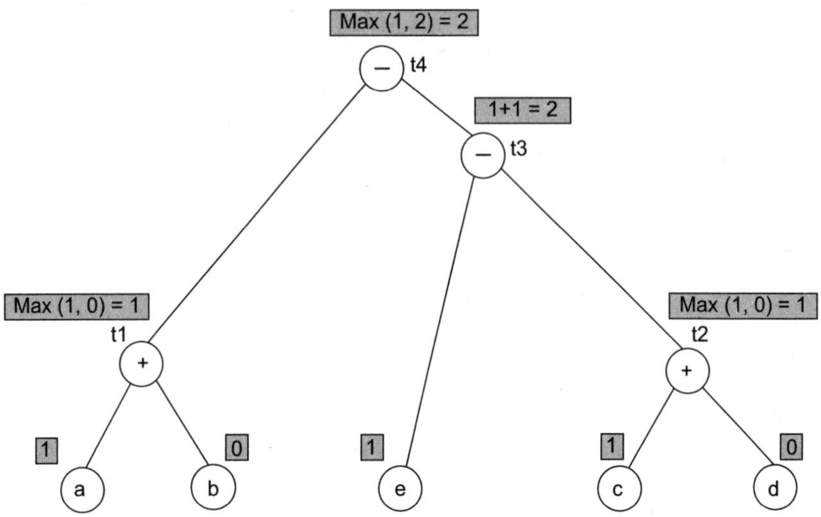

Figure 7.4 Labelling algorithm on DAG for TAC of Example 7.9

Example 7.8 Generate the code for the expression a=b−(c*d)+e/(f+g), using the *gencode()* algorithm

The TAC corresponding to the expression a=b−(c*d)+e/(f+g) is as follows:

T1=c*d
T2=b−T1
T3=f+g
T4=e/T3
a=T2+T4

The DAG and application of the labelling algorithm is as shown in Figure 7.5. Application of the *gencode()* procedure is as shown in Table 7.10. As the root has the value 3 (Fig. 7.5), the code generation algorithm using the *gencode()* procedure will require three registers. Let us assume the stack has its top three registers as R0, R1 and R2, where R0 is the stack top.

Table 7.10 *gencode()* procedure for Example 7.8

Call to *gencode()*	Applicable case of *gencode()*	Applied procedure	RSTACK contains top two registers	Code generation

gencode(a)	Case 3	1) Swap the top two registers
		2) Call *gencode (t2)*
		12) R = POP R1
		13) Call *gencode(t4)*
		22) Generate ADD R0,R1
		23) PUSH R1
			R1,R0,R2
			
			R0,R2
			R0,R2
			
			R1,R0,R2
				MOV b, R1
				MOV c, R0
				MUL d, R0
				SUB RO,R1
				MOV e, R0
				MOV f, R2
				ADD g, R2
				DIV R2,R0
				ADD R0,R1

gencode(t2)	Case 3	3) Call *gencode(b)*
		5) R=POP R1
		6) Call *gencode(t1)*
		10) Generate SUB R0,R1
		11) PUSH R1
			R1,R0,R2
			R0,R2
			
			R1,R0,R2
				MOV b, R1
				MOV c, R0
				MUL d, R0
				SUB RO,R1

gencode(b)	Case 0	4)Generate MOV b,R1	R1,R0,R2	MOV b, R1
gencode(t1)	Case 1	7) Call *gencode(c)* 9) Generate MUL D, R0	R0,R2	MOV c, R0 MUL d, R0
gencode(c)	Case 0	8) Generate MOV c, R0	R0,R2	MOV c, R0

gencode(t4)	Case 3	14) Call *gencode(e)*
		16) R=POP R0
		17) Generate (T3)
		20) Generate DIV R2,R0
		21)PUSH R0
			R0,R2
			R2
			R2
			
			R0,R2
				MOV e, R0
				MOV f, R2
				ADD g, R2
				DIV R2, R0

(Cont'd)

Table 7.10 (Continued)

Call to *gencode()*	**Applicable case of *gencode()***	**Applied procedure**	**RSTACK contains top two registers**	**Code generation**
gencode(e)	Case 0	15) Generate MOV e, R0	R0,R2	MOV e, R0
gencode(T3)	Case 1	18) *gencode(f)* 19) Generate ADD g, R2	R2	MOV f, R2 ADD g, R2
gencode(f)	Case 0	21) Generate MOV f,R2	R0,R2	MOV f, R2

The code generated is as follows:

```
MOV b, R0
MOV c, R1
MUL d, R1
SUB R1, R0
MOV e, R1
MOV f, R2
ADD g, R2
DIV R2, R1
ADD R1, R2
```

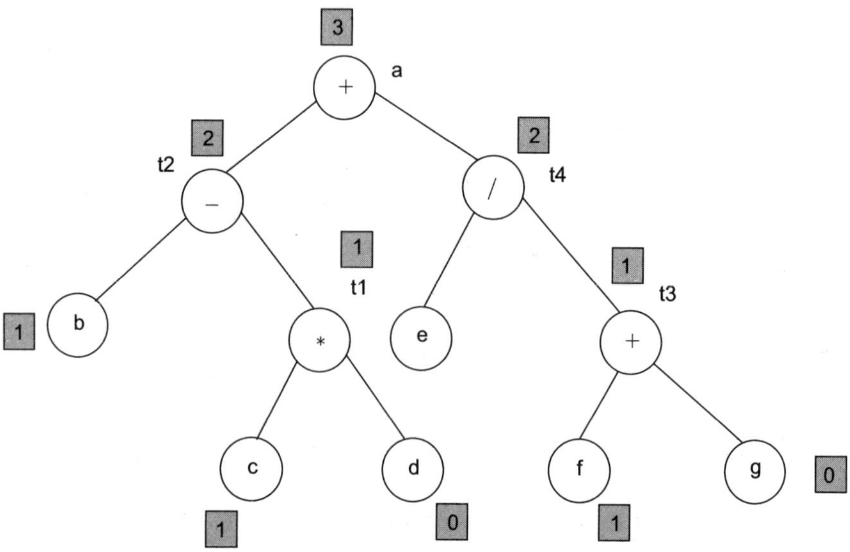

Figure 7.5 DAG with labelling algorithm applied for Example 7.8

Example 7.9 Apply *gencode()* to DAG, if there are common sub-expressions
If there are common sub-expressions, then there exist nodes that have more than one parent. In such cases, partition the DAG into a set of trees. The labelling algorithm and *gencode()* are then applied, starting from the root node. Let us consider the DAG shown in Fig. 7.6; the DAG is partitioned into subtrees as shown in Figure 7.7.

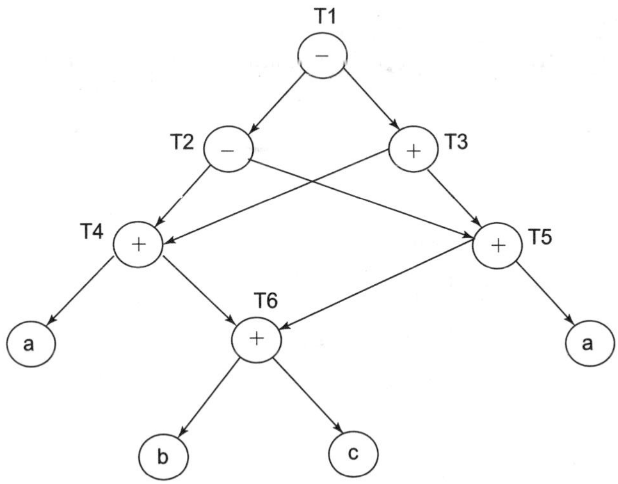

Figure 7.6 DAG containing common sub-expressions

Table 7.11 *gencode()* for Example 7.9

Call to *gencode()*	Applicable case of *gencode()*	Applied procedure	RSTACK contains top two registers	Code generation

gencode(T1)	Case 3	1) Call *gencode(T2)*
		18) R = POP R0
		19) Call *gencode(T3)*
		35) Generate SUB R1,R0
		37) PUSH R0
			R0,R1,R2
			R1,R2
			
			R0,R1,R2
				MOV a, R0
				MOV b, R1
				ADD c, R1
				ADD R1, R0
				ADD d, R1

				SUB R1,R0
				MOV a, R1
				MOV b, R2
				ADD c, R2
				ADD R2,R1
				ADD R2,R1
				SUB R1,R0

gencode(t2)	Case 3	2) Call *gencode(T4)*
		12) R=POP R0
		13) Call *gencode(T5)*
		16) Generate SUB R1,R0
		17) PUSH R0
			R0,R1,R2
			R1,R2
			
			R1,R2
			R0,R1,R2
				MOV a, R0
				MOV b, R1
				ADD c, R1
				ADD R1,R0
				ADD d, R1
				SUB R1,R0

(Cont'd)

Table 7.11 (Continued)

Call to *gencode()*	Applicable case of *gencode()*	Applied procedure	RSTACK contains top two registers	Code generation

gencode(T4)	Case 3	3) *gencode(a)*
		5) R=POP R0
		6) *gencode(T6)*
		10) Generate: ADD R1,R0
		11) PUSH R0
			R0,R1,R2
			R1,R2
			
			R0,R1,R2
				MOV a, R0
				MOV b,R1
				ADD c,R1
				ADD R1,R0

gencode(a)	Case 0	4) Generate MOV a, R0	R0,R1,R2	MOV a, R0
gencode(T6) (Condition 2)	Case 1	7) *gencode(b)* 9) Generate ADD c, R1	R1,R2	MOV b, R1 ADD c, R1
Gencode(b)	Case 0	8) Generate MOV b, R1	R1,R2	MOV b, R1

Gencode(T5)	Case 1	14) *gencode(T6)*
		15) Generate ADD d, R1
			R1,R2	MOV b, R1
				ADD c, R1
				ADD d, R1

gencode(T3)	Case 3	20) Call *gencode(T4)*
		30) R=POP R1
		31) Generate(T5)
		34) Generate ADD R2,R1
		35)PUSH R1
			R1,R2
			
			R2
			
			R0,R2
				MOV a, R1
				MOV b, R2
				ADD c, R2
				ADD R2, R1
				MOV b, R2
				ADD c, R2
				ADD d, R2
				ADD R2,R1

gencode(T4)	Case 3	21) Call *gencode(a)*
		23) R=POP R1
		24) Generate(T6)
		28) Generate ADD R2,R1
		29)PUSH R1
			R1,R2
			R2
			
			R1,R2
				MOV a, R1
				MOV b, R2
				ADD c, R2
				ADD R2,R1

gencode(a)	Case 0	22) Generate MOV a, R1	R1,R2	MOV a, R1
gencode(T6)	Case 1	25) *gencode(b)* 27) Generate ADD c, R1	R2	MOV b, R2 ADD c, R2
gencode(b)	Case 0	26) Generate MOV b, R2	R2	MOV b, R2

gencode(T5)	Case 1	32) *gencode(T6)*
		33) Generate ADD d, R2
			R2	MOV b, R2
				ADD c, R2
				ADD d, R2

The code generated is as follows:

```
MOV a, R0
MOV b, R1
ADD c, R1
ADD R1, R0
ADD d, R1
SUB R1,R0
MOV a, R1
MOV b, R2
ADD c, R2
ADD R2,R1
ADD R2,R1
SUB R1,R0
```

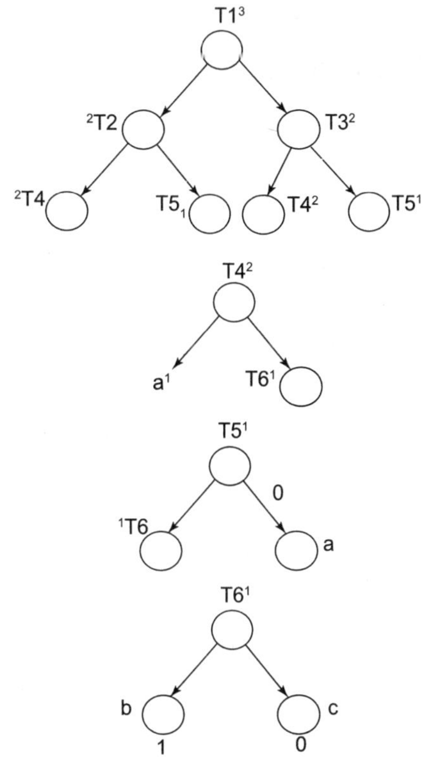

Figure 7.7 DAG partitioned into subtrees

7.7 Register Allocation

Register allocation is the process of assigning variables to registers and managing data transfer in and out of registers. There are an unlimited number of variables in the code, but on a physical machine, there are a small number of registers. Moreover, most machines have a set of registers, dedicated memory locations that can be accessed quickly, can have computations performed on them, and exist in small quantities. Using registers intelligently is a critical step in any compiler. A good register allocator can generate code orders of magnitude better than a poor register allocator. A simple code generator uses a simple strategy for allocation of register in Section 7.5. Also, in Section 7.6, the optimal number of registers to be used is determined and implemented. Next, register allocation strategies are discussed.

7.7.1 Global Register Allocation

The following strategies are adopted while performing global register allocation:

- The global register allocation has a strategy of storing the most frequently used variables in fixed registers throughout the loop.
- Another strategy is to assign some fixed number of global registers to hold the most active values in each inner loop.
- The registers that are not already allocated may be used to hold values local to one block.

7.7.2 Register Assignment for an Outer Loop

Consider that there are two loops. L1 is the outer loop and L2 is the inner loop. The following criteria should be adopted for register assignment for the outer loop:

- If a register A is allocated in loop L2, then it should not be allocated in L1–L2, where L1–L2 are the instructions inside loop L1 before the start of loop L2.

- If a register A is allocated in L1 and is not allocated in L2, then store A on entering L2 and load A while leaving L2.
- If a register A is allocated in L2 and not in L1, then load A on entering L2 and store A on exit, not from L2.

7.7.3 Register Allocation by Graph Colouring

When a register is required for a computation, but all the available registers are in use, the contents of one of the used registers must be stored into a memory location in order to free up a register. Graph colouring is a simple, systematic technique for allocating registers and managing register spills. Register allocation by graph colouring involves the following steps:

1. Perform liveliness analysis on the CFG, to find the live variables.
2. Construct an interference graph, consisting of all the variables of the program.
3. Use graph colouring to find the registers that the variables can use.

Liveliness analysis: A variable is live if it holds a value that may be used in the future. A variable v is live on a CFG edge if

- There exists a directed path from that edge to a use of v (node in use[v]), and
- That path does not go through any def of v (no nodes in def[v]).

The terminology that will be needed to perform liveliness analysis and the algorithm to detect live variables are discussed further.

A control flow graph has nodes with out-edges and in-edges. *pred[n]* is the set of all predecessors of a node, consisting of all nodes that have an in-edge to node n. *succ[n]* is the set of all successors of node n, consisting of nodes that are reached by out-edges from node n. *use[n]* comprises the variables that are used inside node n, while *def[n]* comprises the variables that are defined inside node n.

Liveliness Algorithm

```
{
// Initialize
For each node n in CFG
{
    in[n] = ∅;
    out[n] = ∅;
}
Repeat
{
    For each node n in CFG in reverse order
    {
    //Save current results
        in'[n] = in[n];
        out'[n] = out[n];
    // Solve to find data-flow equations
        out[n] = ∪ in[s];
        in[n] = use[n] ∪ (out[n] – def[n]);
    }
}
```

Until (in'[n]=in[n] and out'[n]=out[n] for all n)
}

The algorithm to find liveliness computes the out and in values in the reverse order of the nodes in the flow graph.

Interference graph construction: Two temporary variables interfere if they are live at the same time. Interfering variables cannot be assigned to the same register. The interference relation can be represented by an interference graph in which nodes correspond to variables and edges connect interfering variables.

1. Add one node corresponding to each variable of the program in the graph.
2. Add an undirected edge between two nodes if those nodes represent variables that are live at the same time. Intuitively, an edge between two variables states that these variables must be in different registers.

Graph colouring: No adjacent nodes can be of the same colour.

Example 7.10 Register allocation based on graph colouring in the given control flow graph

PART A: Liveliness Analysis

Consider the flow graph shown in Fig. 7.8. To perform liveliness analysis, find

- Successors of each node
- *use* and *def* for all nodes in reverse order
- Out and In values iteratively till the same values are obtained in two consecutive iterations

Steps 1 and 2: Node 1 consists of statement a=0.

- *use(node 1)*= ∅; as there is no variable used in the RHS of the expression
- *def(node 1)* = {a}; as a is defined in the statement a=0.

Similarly, *use* and *def* are found for all nodes in the CFG of Fig. 7.7. Successors, along with *use* and *def* are shown in Table 7.12.

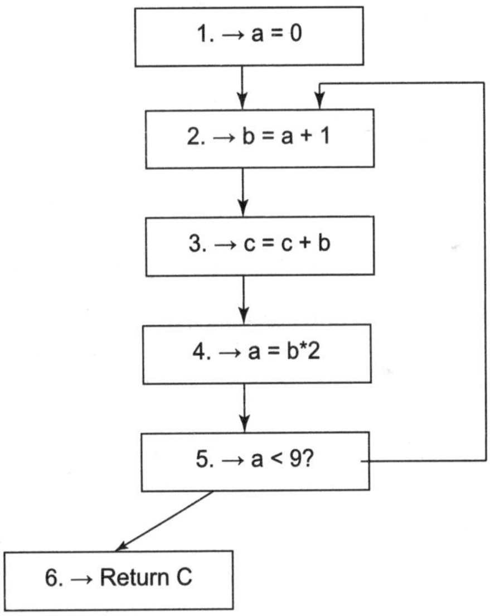

Figure 7.8 Control flow graph for Example 7.10

Table 7.12 Successor, *use* and *def* information of CFG in Fig. 7.8

Node	*succ()*	*use()*	*def()*
6	∅	c	∅
5	6,2	a	∅
4	5	b	a
3	4	b c	c
2	3	a	b
1	2	∅	a

Step 3: Initially, In and Out are ∅. Then

out[n] = ∪ in[s];

in[n] = use[n] ∪ (out[n] – def[n]);

where s is the successor of node n

Computation for some nodes, in the first iteration, first find Out and then In.

Node 6

- Out(node 6) will be ∅, as node 6 has no successors.
- In(node 6) = use[node 6] ∪ (out[node 6] – def[node 6]);

  $= \{c\} \cup (\varnothing - \varnothing)$

  $= \{\chi\}$

Node 5

- Out(node 5)= in[node 6] ∪ in[node 2] // Node 5 has two successors node 6 and node 2

  $= \{c\} \cup \{\varnothing\} = \{c\}$ // in[node 6] is computed in the same iteration (i.e., iteration1) as c and in[node 2] was computed in previous iteration as ∅
- In(node 5) = use[node 5] ∪ (out[node 5] – def[node 5]);

  $= \{a\} \cup (\chi - \varnothing)$

  $= \{a\} \cup \{\chi\} = \{\alpha\ \chi\}$

The complete computation of In and Out for the CFG in Fig. 7.8 is shown in Table 7.13.

Note: The most recent computed values of In and Out are considered.

Table 7.13 In and Out for all nodes of CFG in Fig. 7.8

Node	Initially		First iteration		Second iteration		Third iteration	
	Out	In	Out	In	Out	In	Out	In
6	∅	∅	∅	c	∅	c	∅	c
5	∅	∅	c	a c	a c	a c	a c	a c
4	∅	∅	a c	b c	a c	b c	a c	b c
3	∅	∅	b c	b c	b c	b c	b c	b c
2	∅	∅	b c	a c	b c	a c	b c	a c
1	∅	∅	a c	c	a c	c	a c	c

PART B: Inference Graph Construction

From the In and Out computation, the variables that can be live at the same time are {a c} and {b c}. So, an undirected edge is added from a to c and b to c. The inference graph for Example 7.10 is shown in Fig. 7.9.

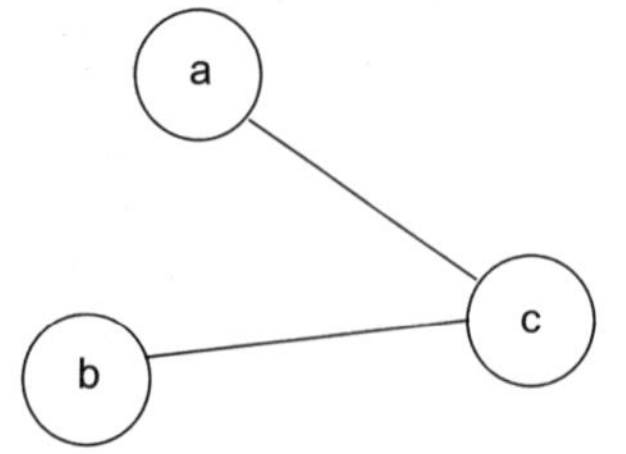

Figure 7.9 Interference graph for Example 7.10

PART C: Register Allocation

Register allocation is based on graph colouring, where a and b are not connected, and hence, can use the same colours as per the graph colouring algorithm. Variables a and b can use register R1 and c can use register R2.

Simplify-select process for graph colouring

Simplify Phase (Pruning):

1. Remove nodes with fewer than *k* neighbours, where *k* is the number of colours to offer.
2. Push the removed node on a stack and remove its edges from the graph.
3. If a point is reached where every node has *k* neighbours (or more), any node is chosen as a possible candidate. Once a candidate is chosen, the node is then removed from the graph and pushed onto the stack, just like the others, and the algorithm continues to the next node.

Select Phase (Assign): For all variables/nodes in the stack

1. Pop a node off the stack.
2. Re-insert the popped node into the graph, and assign it a colour. The colour must be different from that of all of its neighbours.

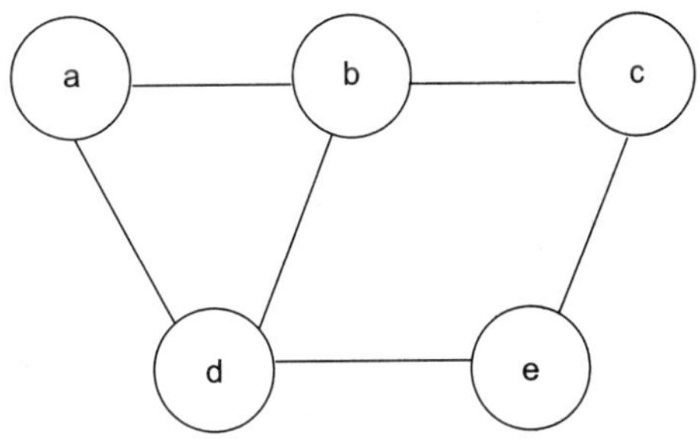

Figure 7.10 Interference graph

Example 7.11 Applying the simplify-select process of graph colouring to the interference graph

Let us consider the interference graph of Fig. 7.10 and apply the simplify and select process to find the registers to use for each variable.

Applying *simplify* assuming *k*=3,

Procedure	Graph	Stack
Since all nodes have fewer than *k* neighbours, select any node for removal. Let us remove node c from the graph and push it on the stack.	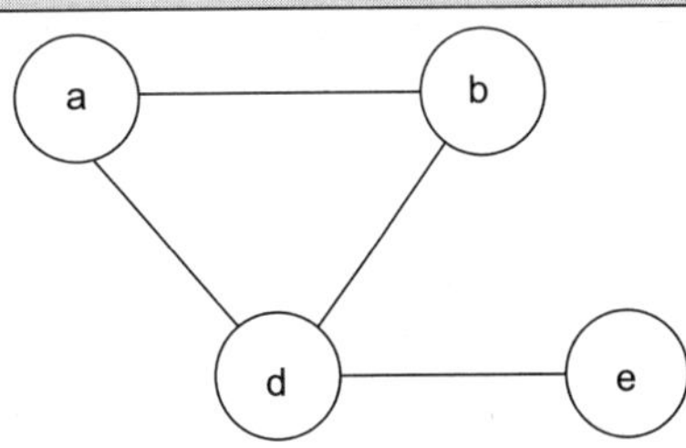	c
Remove a	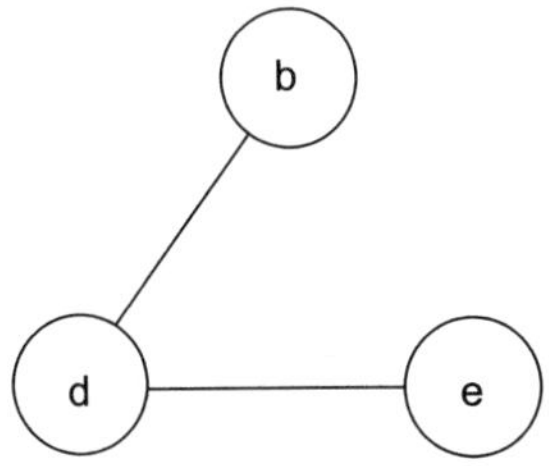	a c
Remove b	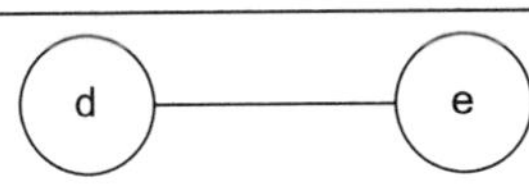	b a c
Remove d	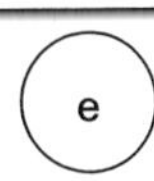	d b a c

(Cont'd)

Table (Continued)

Procedure	Graph	Stack
Remove e		e d b a c

Select process: In this step, pop the node from the stack, add to the graph with edges and allocate the colour.

Procedure	Graph	Stack
		e d b a c
Pop node e Add to graph. Colour the node. (e-RED)	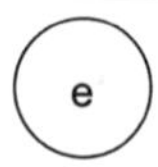 	d b a c
Pop node d. Add to graph with edges and colour. (e-RED, d- GREEN)	 	b a c
Pop node d. Add to graph with edges and colour. (e-RED, d- GREEN, b-RED)	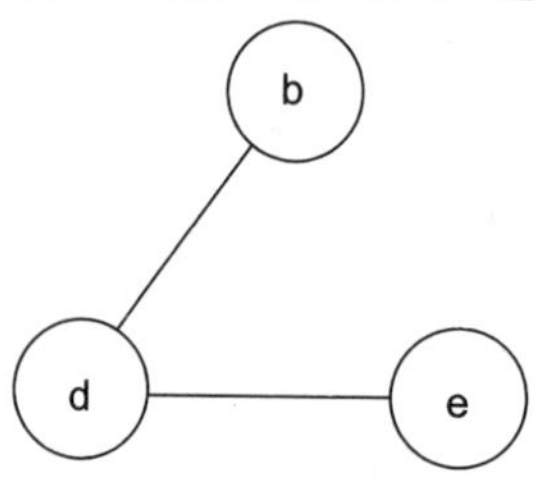 	a c
Pop node a and add to graph with edges and colour. (e-RED, d- GREEN, b-RED, a-BLUE)	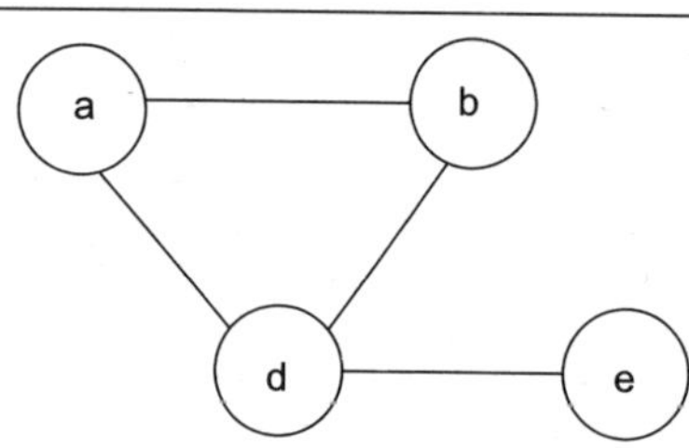 	c

(*Cont'd*)

Table (Continued)

Procedure	Graph	Stack
Pop node c and add to graph with edges and colour. (e-RED, d- GREEN, b-RED, a-BLUE, c- GREEN)	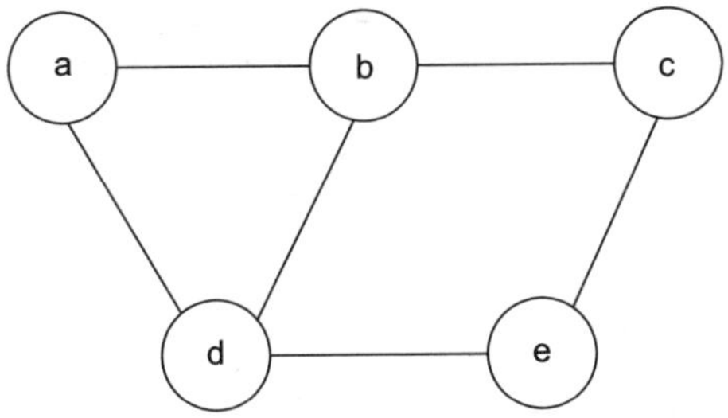	

After the procedure, each node is allocated the following colours: e-RED, d-GREEN, b-RED, a-BLUE, c-GREEN. These colours correspond to registers in the machine. Hence, register allocation will be as follows:

Variables e and b will use register R1, variables c and d will use register R2 and variable a will use register R3.

7.8 Code Generation by Dynamic Programming

The dynamic programming algorithm proceeds in three phases. Suppose the target machine has r registers, the three phases are as follows:

1. **Cost vector computation:** In the first phase, compute bottom-up for each node n of the expression tree T an array C of costs. The 0th component of the cost vector is the optimal cost of computing the subtree S into memory. The contiguous evaluation property ensures that an optimal program S can be generated by considering combinations of optimal programs only for the subtrees of the root of S. This restriction reduces the number of cases that need to be considered.

   To compute C[i] at node n, consider each machine instruction R:= E, whose expression E matches the sub-expression rooted at node n. By examining the cost vectors at the corresponding descendants of n, determine the costs of evaluating the operands of E. For those operands of E that are registers, consider all possible orders in which the corresponding subtrees of T can be evaluated into registers. The value C [i] is the minimum cost over all possible orders.

   The first component of the cost vector is the optimal cost of computing the subtree S, assuming there is one register. The second component of the cost vector is considered as the optimal cost of computing the subtree S, assuming there are two registers.
2. **Determination of the instruction sequence:** Traverse T, using the cost vectors to determine which subtrees of T must be computed into memory.
3. **Generation of target code:** Traverse each tree using the cast vectors and associated instructions to generate the final target code. The code for the subtrees computed into memory locations is generated first. These two phases can also be implemented to run in time linearly proportional to the size of the expression tree

Consider a machine having two registers, R0 and R1, and the following instructions.

$R_i = M_j$
$R_i = R_i \text{ op } R_j$

R_i=R_i op M_j
R_i =R_j
M_j= R_i

In these instructions, R_i is either R0 or R1, and M_j is a memory location.

Example 7.12 Apply dynamic programming code generation algorithm to the DAG in Fig. 7.11

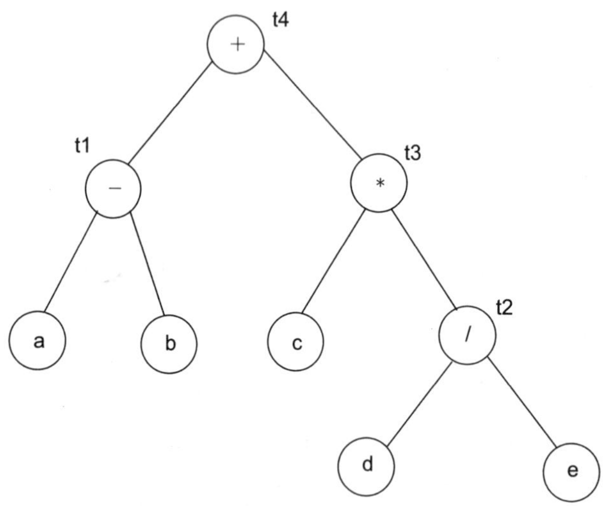

Figure 7.11 DAG for Example 7.12

The cost vector for some nodes is shown in Table 7.14; the last column shows the complete cost vector based on parts of costs calculated in the previous columns. The computation of cost vector is done in a bottom-up manner. The cost at the internal node is based on its storage and 1 is added to it. Figure 7.12 represents the cost vectors for all nodes and the application of code generation in a bottom-up manner.

Table 7.14 Cost vector computation for Example 7.12

Node	Instruction format	Cost vector C[1]	Cost vector C[2]	Cost vector C[0]-memory used	Cost vector (mem,1reg, 2regs)
a, b, c, d, e	Leaf node (All are in memory)	The cost of computing a into a register is 1, so load it into a register with the instruction R0 = a. C[1]=1	The cost of loading a into a register with two registers available is the same as that with one register available. C[2]=1	Already in memory. C[0]=0	**C=(0,1,1)**

(Cont'd)

Table 7.14 (Continued)

<table>
<tr><th>Node</th><th>Instruction format</th><th>Cost vector C[1]</th><th>Cost vector C[2]</th><th>Cost vector C[0]-memory used</th><th>Cost vector (mem,1reg, 2regs)</th></tr>
<tr><td rowspan="3">t1</td><td>$R_i=R_i-M$</td><td>If one register is available for a and t2 is in memory, C[1]=1+0+1=2</td><td>If two registers are available for a and b in memory, C[2]=1+0+1=2</td><td>-</td><td rowspan="3">C[1]=2

C[2]= min(2,3,3) =2

C[0]= Min(c[1],c[2])+1 =2+1=3

C=(3,2,2)</td></tr>
<tr><td rowspan="2">$R_i=R_i-R_j$</td><td rowspan="2">-</td><td>**CASE1:**
For the left child, two registers are available, one register for the right child (use C2 of a, C1 of b), then C[2]= 1+1+1=3</td><td></td></tr>
<tr><td>**CASE2:**
For the right child, two registers are available, one register for the left child (use C2 of b, C1 of a), C[2]= 1+1+1=3</td><td></td></tr>
<tr><td>t3</td><td>$R_i=R_i*M$</td><td>If one register is available for c and t2 should be in memory (use C1 of c and use C0 of t2), C[1]=1+3+1=5</td><td>If two registers are available for c and t2 is in memory. (use C2 of c and C0 of t2), C[2]=1+3+1=5</td><td>-</td><td>C[1]=5

C[2]= Min(5,4,4)=4

C[0]= Min(c[1],c[2])+1 =min(5,4)+1 =4+1=5
C=(5,5,4)</td></tr>
<tr><td></td><td>$R_i=R_i*R_j$</td><td>-</td><td>**CASE1:**
For the left child, two registers are available, one register for the right child (use C2 of c, C1 of t2), then C[2]= 1+2+1=4</td><td></td><td></td></tr>
</table>

(Cont'd)

Table 7.14 (Continued)

Node	Instruction format	Cost vector C[1]	Cost vector C[2]	Cost vector C[0]- memory used	Cost vector (mem,1reg, 2regs)
			CASE2: For the right child, two registers are available, one register for the left child (use C1 of c, C2 of t2) C[2]= 2+1+1=4		

The generated code will be

R0=c
R1=d
R1=R1/e
R0=R0+R1
R1=a
R1=R1−b
R1=R1+0

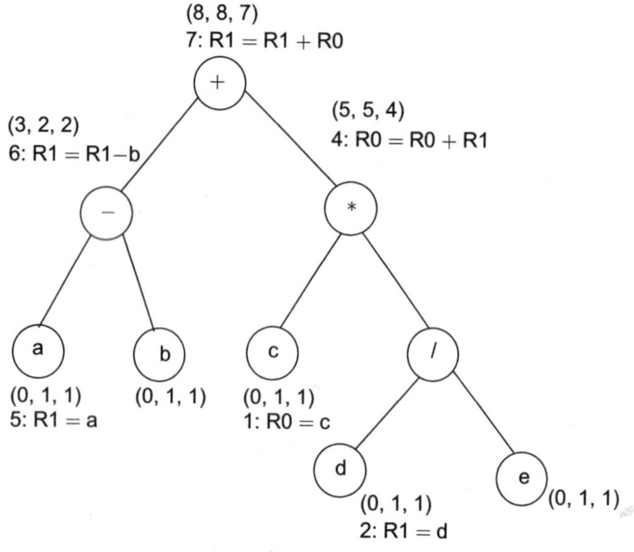

Figure 7.12 Application of cost vector, traversal and code generation for Example 7.12

SUMMARY

- In a simple code generator, a register descriptor keeps track of the contents of the register and an address descriptor keeps track of the location where the current value of a name can be found at run-time.
- Statements need to be reordered to improve the cost of the generated code.
- Some problems in the design of the code generator are input to the target program, memory management, instruction selection, register allocation, choice of evaluation order and approaches to code generation.
- The cost of an instruction can be computed as one plus cost associated with the source and destination addressing modes given by the added cost.

- Optimal order of computation is found by applying heuristic to DAG.
- Labelling algorithm is used to determine the optimal order in which to evaluate statements in a basic block and then code is generated using the procedure *gencode()*.
- Register allocation is the process of assigning variables to registers and managing data transfer in and out of registers.
- Register allocation by graph colouring involves liveliness analysis, inference graph construction and application of colouring.
- Cost vector computation, determination of the instruction sequence and generation of target code are the phases of code generation that use dynamic programming.

Exercises

Review Questions

Fill in the blanks with appropriate answers:

1. Cost of instruction ADD a, R1 will be ________.
2. Cost of instruction ADD R0,R1 will be ________.
3. Cost of instruction SUB 3(R0),*5(R1) is ________.
4. Code generation takes as input ________ and produces an equivalent target program as the output.
5. A variable is live at a point in a basic block, if its value can be used subsequently. Otherwise, it is ________ at that point.
6. ________ can be used to determine the names that are used inside the block and those computed outside the block.

Answers: 1. Two 2. One 3. Three 4. Intermediate representation of the source program 5. Dead 6. DAG

State whether true or false:

1. DAG is used to determine the common sub-expressions.
2. *getreg()* is used to return an empty register or an address location.

Answers: 1. True 2. True

Practice Questions

1. Generate code for the expression a=b(c*d)+e/(f+g), using the simple code generation algorithm.
2. Obtain the optimal order of execution of statements for the three-address code of the expression given in Q1 using the heuristic algorithm.
3. Construct the DAG and determine the register requirement for the computation of the expression: Z=(A+B)*(C–D)/E+D
4. Generate code for following block using *gencode()*.
   t1 = b + c
   t2 = b * c
   t3 = t2 * t1
   x =t3 * f
   Also find the register requirement using the labelling algorithm before applying *gencode()*.

5. Construct the DAG for the expression: a+a * (b–c) + (b–c) *d. Also calculate the number of registers required.
6. Generate the code for the given three-address code using the simple code generation algorithm. Find the most efficient order of computation.
   T1=x*y
   T2=z+x
   T3=w/T2
   T4=T1+T3
7. Generate the target code for the given program fragment:
```
main( )
{
    int i,j,a,b;
    i=a+5;
    j=i+b;
}
```
8. Generate code using *getreg()* function for the expression:
   Z= [a*(b+c)–b*(b+c)] + c* (a*(b+c)

Programming Questions

1. For a program flow graph, write a program to find out the live variable at the start and end of each block.
2. For a three-address statement, write a program to find out the number of registers required for execution.
3. Consider a TAC. Convert the TAC to DAG and write a program to implement the heuristic code generation algorithm.

8 Storage Management and Symbol Table

Objectives

- To introduce the run-time environments, storage management and the symbol table
- To discuss activation of procedures
- To discuss various storage allocation strategies
- To explain garbage collection
- To discuss parameter passing techniques
- To describe the data structures that can be used for symbol table implementation

8.1 Introduction to the Run-time Environment

The purpose of the compiler is to convert the source code to low-level language so that the code in the program can be executed by performing actions at run-time. A program contains the names of procedures, identifiers, etc. During execution, the same name in the source code can denote different data objects in the target machine. Hence, mapping of names with the actual memory location at run-time is required. For execution of a code, a **run-time environment** is required. This is a state of the target machine, which may include software libraries, environment variables, etc., to provide services to the processes running in the system. It deals with linkage of procedures and functions, parameter passing, interfaces to input/output devices, interfaces to the operating system, a mechanism for accessing variables and allocation and layout of storage. Various aspects to be handled in the run-time environment are memory organisation, activation record, procedure call and return and parameter passing.

The allocation and de-allocation of data objects during execution is managed by the **run-time support package**. It consists of routines loaded with the generated target code. The design of the run-time support package is influenced by the semantics of procedures.

8.2 Storage Organisation

Run-time storage memory can be subdivided as follows:

- Generated target code
- Data objects
- Counterpart of the control stack to keep track of procedure activations

The size of the generated target code is fixed at compile time, so the compiler can place it in a statically determined area, perhaps at the low end of memory. Similarly, the size of some of the data objects may also be known at compile time, and these too can be placed in a statically determined area, as in Fig. 8.1. One reason for statically allocating as many data objects as possible is that the addresses of these objects can be compiled into the target code.

When a call occurs, execution of current activation is interrupted and information about the status of the machine, such as the value of the program counter and machine registers, is saved on the stack before the control is passed to the calling program/procedure. When control returns from the call, this activation can be restarted after restoring the values of the relevant registers and setting the program counter to the point immediately after the call.

The data objects whose lifetimes are contained in that of an activation can be allocated on the **stack**, along with other information associated with the activation. A separate area of run-time memory, called the **heap**, holds all other information. Languages in which the lifetimes of activations cannot be represented by an activation tree, use the heap to store the activation information. The way in which data is allocated and de-allocated on a stack makes it cheaper to place data on the stack than on the heap. The sizes of the stack and the heap can change as the program executes. Stacks grow downwards, as memory addresses increase as we go down. *top* is used to point to the top of the stack. Mostly the value of *top* is stored in a register.

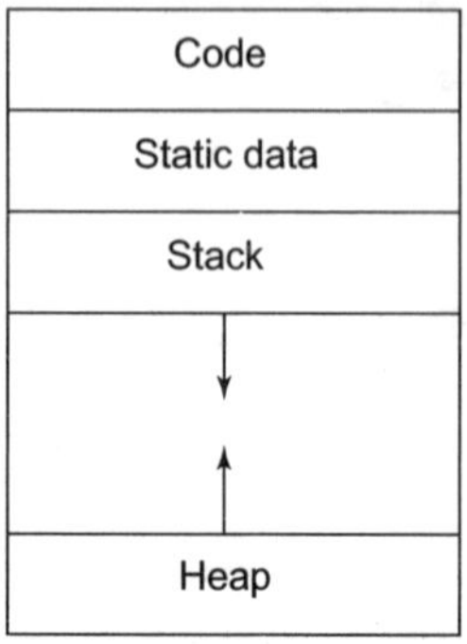

Figure 8.1 Typical subdivision of run-time memory into code and data areas

8.3 Activation of Procedures

A program is a sequence of instructions combined into a number of procedures. Instructions in a procedure are executed sequentially. A procedure has a start and an end delimiter and everything inside it is called the body of the procedure. The procedure identifier and the sequence of finite instructions inside it make up the body of the procedure.

Each execution of a procedure is referred to as an **activation of the procedure.** If the procedure is recursive, there will exist several activations for the procedure which may be alive at the same time. Each call of a procedure leads to an activation that may manipulate the data objects allocated for its use. The **lifetime of an activation** is the sequence of steps present in the execution of the procedure. If two procedures are called one after another, their activations will be non-overlapping. If a procedure is recursive, a new activation begins before an earlier activation of the same procedure has ended. An activation tree shows the way control enters and leaves activations.

The representation of a data object at run-time is determined by its type. Often, elementary data types, such as characters, integers and real numbers can be represented by equivalent data objects in the target machine. However, aggregates, such as arrays, strings and structures, are usually represented by collections of primitive objects.

8.3.1 Activation Tree

If the program control flows in a sequential manner, and a procedure is called, its control is transferred to the called procedure. When a called procedure is executed, it returns the control to the caller. This type of control flow makes it easier to represent a series of activations in the form of a tree, known as the **activation tree**. The activation tree represents the sequence of procedure calls that corresponds to pre-order traversal and the sequence of returns that corresponds to post-order traversal. The activation tree depends on the run-time behaviour of a program. It may be different for every program input. The activation tree is built such that:

- Each node represents an activation of a procedure.
- The root represents the activation of the main program.

- The node for "a" is the parent of the node for "b", if and only if, control flows from activation "a to b"
- The node for "a" is to the left of the node for "b", if and only if, the lifetime of "a" occurs before the lifetime of "b".

To understand this concept, consider a piece of code as an example:

```
int main( ) {
        .
        .
        A ( );
        .
        .
}
        A( ) {
                int b=B( );
                int c=C  ( );
                int a= b+c;
                return a;
        }

        B( ) {
                .
                .
                return r1;
        }

        C( ) {
                .
                .
                return r2;
        }
```

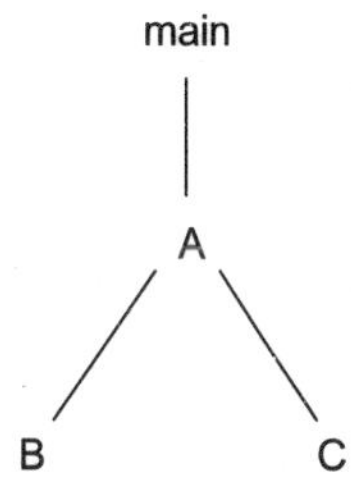

Figure 8.2 Activation tree

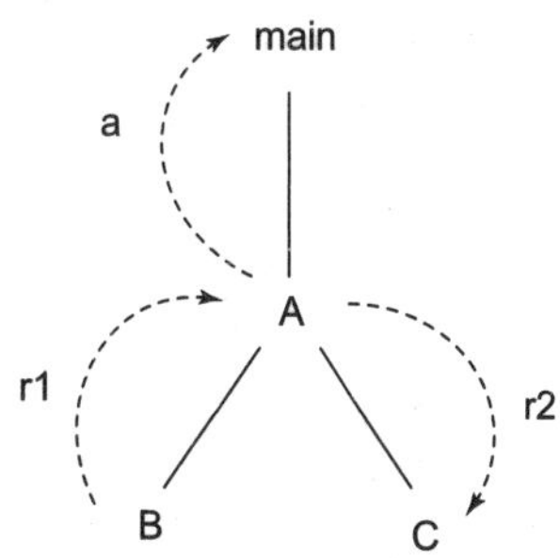

Figure 8.3 Activation tree with return

In this code there is a call to procedure A from the main program. Hence, after main is activated, procedure A will be activated. Inside procedure A, there is call to procedures B and C. First, B will be activated, and then C. The activation tree is shown in Fig. 8.2. The sequence of procedure calls and its activation corresponds to the pre-order traversal of the nodes in the tree. The pre-order traversal lists the nodes in the order: root, left child, right child. The pre-order traversal for the tree in Fig. 8.2 is A B C; it is the order of the activation of procedures.

Procedure B returns a value r1 to the calling procedure A. This returned value is accepted in variable b in procedure A. Also, procedure C returns a value r2 to the calling procedure A. This returned value is accepted in variable c in procedure A. A new value 'a' is computed in procedure A and returned to the main program. The sequence of return corresponds to the post-order traversal of tree nodes. The post-order traversal lists the nodes of the tree in the order: left child, right child, root. The returns are marked in Fig. 8.3. The post-order traversal and order of sequence of return for the example is r1, r2, a.

8.3.2 Control Stack

A stack representing procedure calls, returns and flow of control is called a **control stack** or **runtime stack.** The control stack is used to keep track of the live procedure activations, i.e., the procedures whose execution have not been completed. Space is allocated in the control stack for activation of each procedure, space is de-allocated for return and the record is popped off the stack. Hence, memory is required for activation of procedures. The information needed to manage a single procedure activation is called an **activation record**. The contents of the activation record are discussed in Section 8.3.3. When a procedure is called, an activation record is pushed onto the stack and as soon as the control returns to the caller function, the activation record is popped.

Note: For simplicity, only the name of the procedure is written, whose activation record will be present in the stack in the following example and in Example 8.1. That is, the procedure name is pushed on to the stack when it is called (activation begins) and it is popped when it returns (activation ends).

Next, memory allocation and de-allocation in the control stack is explained. Let us consider the example code discussed in Section 8.3.1:

- The program starts from main. Hence, main is allocated space in the stack.
- There is a call to procedure A. To activate procedure A, it is allocated space in the stack.
- Procedure A calls procedure B. The control stack till this point in execution is as is shown in Fig. 8.4.
- Procedure B executes and returns r1 to procedure A. Hence, B is popped off and space is de-allocated. Now, A calls procedure C and it is placed in the stack. The control stack till this point in execution is as is shown in Fig. 8.5.
- Procedure C is executed, returns r2 and is popped off the stack. Now, procedure A has values “b” and “c”; it computes “a” and returns to main. Hence, at this point only main is present in the stack. After execution of main, the program is complete and the stack is emptied.

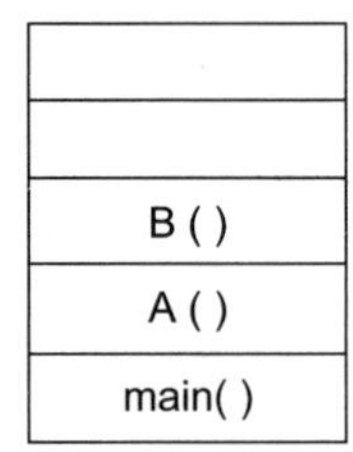

Figure 8.4 Control stack for procedure calls

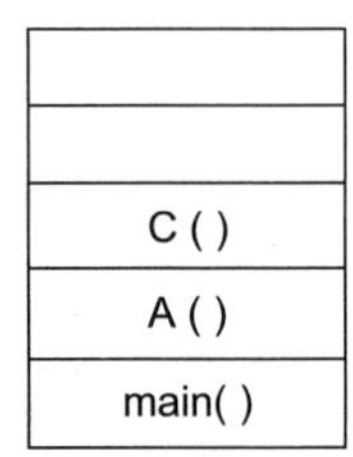

Figure 8.5 Control stack for procedure calls

Example 8.1 Activation tree and control stack for Fibonacci series

The program to compute the Fibonacci series is as follows:

```
int fib(int n)
{
    if (n <= 1)
        return n;
    else {
            a= fib(n-1);
            b= fib(n-2);
            return a+b;
          }
}
```

```
void main ( )
{
        int n=5;
        printf("%d", fib(n));
}
```

The algorithm is a recursive one that recursively calls the fib function. Let us assume that the input to the fib function is 5, that is, the value of n is 5, as indicated in main. Execution of the program starts from main. Inside main, there is a call to the fib function by passing an integer parameter 5. Hence, the fib function is activated after main. The value 5 is first checked for the condition 5<=1, which is false. So, the else part is executed, placing a call to fib(4), which calls fib(3), which calls fib(2), which calls fib(1). The control stack till this point is as is shown in Fig. 8.7 and the activation is as is shown in Fig. 8.6. The contents of the control stack can also be represented by dotted lines in the activation tree, as shown in Fig. 8.8. In this chapter, the stack notation of Fig. 8.7 is used.

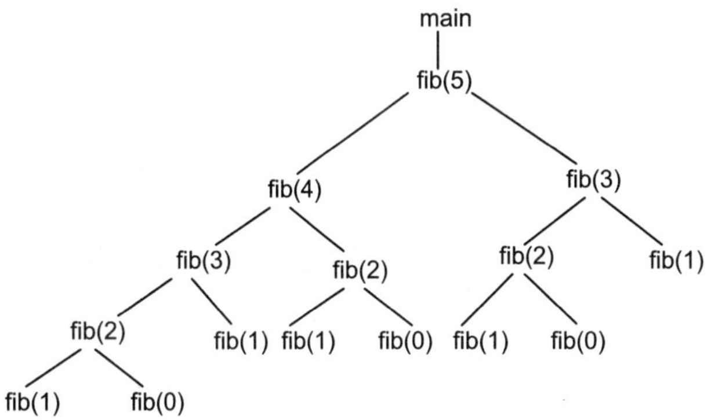

Figure 8.6 Activation tree for Fibonacci series with input integer as 5

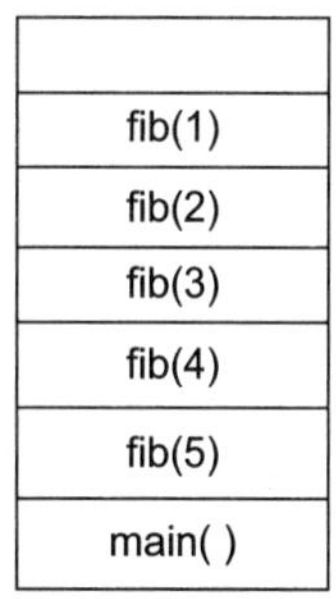

Figure 8.7 Control stack for Fibonacci series

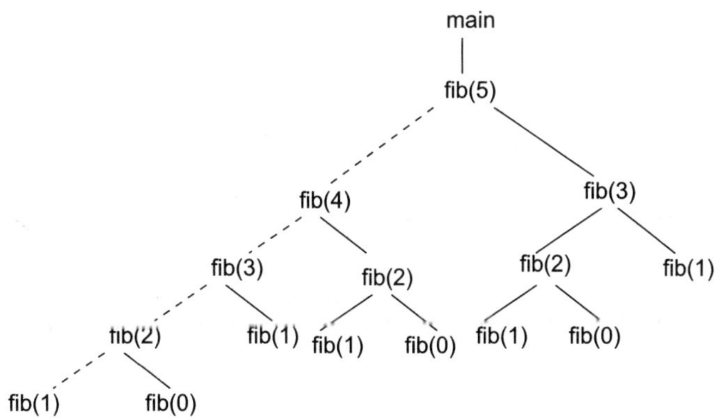

Figure 8.8 Control stack contents for Fibonacci series (marked by dotted lines)

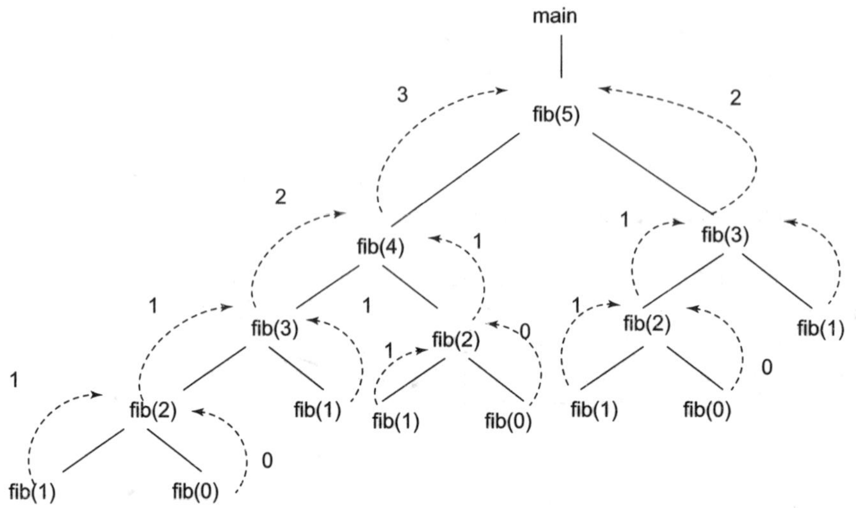

Figure 8.9 Activation tree with return for Fibonacci series generation

`fib(1)` will return value 1 to the calling procedure `fib(2)` and pop off the control stack. Now, `fib(2)` calls `fib(0)` and space is allocated for it on the stack. `fib(0)` returns 0 and is popped off the stack. `fib(2)` now has both the parameters; it adds 0 and 1 and returns the value 1 to its calling procedure `fib(3)`. Similarly, the procedure continues until the complete program is executed. The return of computation is shown in Fig. 8.9, producing the Fibonacci series 1 1 2 3 5.

8.3.3 Activation Record

Whenever a procedure is executed, its activation record (activation frame) is stored on the stack, also known as the control stack. When a procedure calls another procedure, the execution of the caller is suspended until the called procedure finishes execution. At this time, the activation record of the called procedure is stored on the stack. An activation record contains all the necessary information required to call a procedure. It may contain a collection of fields, as shown in Fig. 8.10. The purposes of fields in an activation record are as follows:

Return value
Actual parameters
Optional control link
Optional access link
Saved machine status
Local data
Temporaries

Figure 8.10 General activation record

- **Temporaries**: Stores temporary and intermediate values of an expression during its evaluation.
- **Local data**: Holds the data that is local to the execution of the procedure.
- **Machine status**: Holds information about the status of the machine just before the function call. It stores the values of machine registers, program counter, etc., before the procedure is called. These values are necessary to return to the caller program.
- **Access link** (optional): Refers to the non-local data held in other activation records.
- **Control link** (optional): Points to the activation record of the caller. That is, it stores the address of the activation record of the called procedure.

- **Actual parameters**: Stores the actual parameters, i.e., parameters that are used to send input to the called procedure.
- **Return value**: Used by the called procedure to return a value to calling procedure. It stores return values.

Example 8.2 Control stack representation for Fibonacci series

Let us continue with Example 8.1:

- The control stack containing the activation record when `fib(1)` is about to return for the first time is shown in Fig. 8.11.
- The control stack containing the activation record when `fib(1)` is about to return for the third time is shown in Fig. 8.12.
- The control stack containing the activation record when `fib(1)` is about to return for the fifth time is shown in Fig. 8.13.

fib(1), 1
fib(2), 2 , a=f(1), b=f(0)
fib(3), 3 , a=f(2), b=f(1)
fib(4), 4, a=f(3), b=f(2)
fib(5), 5, a=f(4), b=f(3)
main( )

Figure 8.11 Control stack for first return from `fib(1)`

fib(1), 1
fib(2), 2 , a=f(1), b=f(0)
fib(4), 4, a=f(3), b=f(2)
main( )

Figure 8.12 Control stack for third return from `fib(1)`

fib(1), 1
fib(3), 3 , a=f(2), b=f(1)
fib(5), 5, a=f(4), b=f(3)
main( )

Figure 8.13 Control stack for fifth return from `fib(1)`

8.4 Scope of Declaration

A declaration in a language is a syntactic construct that associates information with a name. A declaration is used to announce the existence of the entity in the program. It specifies the following:

- Name of the identifier
- Type of the entity, such as function, variable, constant and class, enumerations, type definitions, etc.
- Data type for variables and constants, or the type signature for functions
- Dimensions for arrays

For example, int i = 2; i is defined as an integer variable and is declared to have 2 as its value.

There may be independent declarations of the same name in different parts of a program. The scope rules of a language determine which declaration of a name applies when the name appears in the text of a program. The portion of the program to which a declaration applies is called the **scope of that declaration**. An occurrence of a name in a procedure is said to be local to the procedure if it is in the scope of a declaration within the procedure; otherwise, the occurrence is said to be non-local. The distinction between local and non-local names carries over to any syntactic construct that can have declarations within it.

At compile time, the symbol table can be used to find the declaration that applies to an occurrence of a name. That is, the symbol table is used for scope resolution. When a declaration is seen, a symbol table entry is created for it. Within the scope of the declaration, its corresponding entry is returned when the name in it is looked up. The symbol table is discussed in Section 8.8 and scope in the symbol table in Section 8.10.

Consider the code given below:

```
class Person
{
    public int age;

    public void student( )
    {
        age = 18;
    }

    public void teacher( )
    {
        int age;
        age = 40;
    }
}
```

Scope is an enclosing context or region that defines where a name can be used. In most languages, both scope and declaration space are defined by a statement block enclosed by braces. Scopes can be nested and overlap each other. If scope defines the visibility of a name and scopes are allowed to overlap, any name defined in an outer scope is visible to an inner scope, but not vice-versa.

In the above example code, the scope of variable *age* is the entire body of class *Person*, including the functions `student` and `teacher`. In function `student`, the use of *age* refers to the field named *age* and in the function `teacher`, the scopes for variable *age* overlap because there is also a local variable named *age* that is in the scope of the body of the function `teacher`. Within the scope of `teacher`, when variable *age* is referred, it is referring to the locally scoped entity named *age* and not the one in the outer scope. When this happens, the name declared in the outer scope is hidden by the inner scope.

Binding of names: Even if each name is declared once in a program, the same name may denote different data objects at run-time. The term **data object** corresponds to a storage location that holds the value. **Environment** refers to a function that maps a name to a storage location, and **state** refers to a function that maps a storage location to the value held, as shown in Fig. 8.14. An environment maps a name to an l-value, and a state maps the l-value to an r-value. An assignment changes the state, but not the environment.

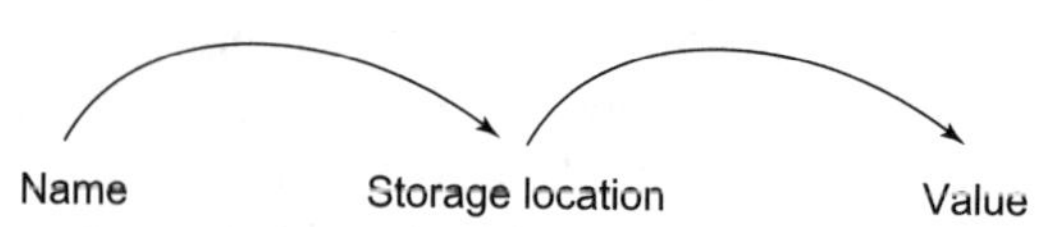

Figure 8.14 Mapping of name to value

For example, if variable *i* is stored at location 1000, it means the environment associates storage location s with a name x, that is, x is bound to s. If initially *i* =10, then location 1000 will hold the value 10. If later in the program, *i*=20, then the same storage location 1000 is used to store the value of *i*, which is then changed to 20.

Example 8.3 Scope of declaration
Consider the code fragment given below and show the scope of variables *a*, *b* and *y*.

```
A( )
{
        int a=1;
        B( )
        {
             int b;
             b=3;
             c=b+3;

             B1( )
             {
                  int y;
                  y=b+2;
             }
        }
        C( )
        {
        a=a+1;
        }
        z=a;
}
```

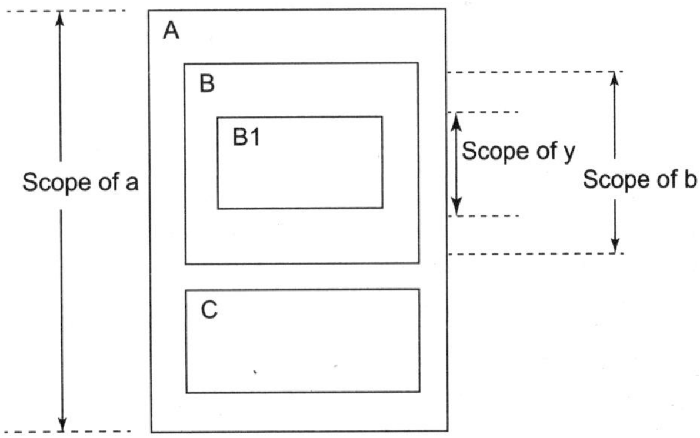

Figure 8.15 Scope of information

The scope information is shown in Fig. 8.15.

8.5 Storage Allocation Strategies

A different storage allocation strategy is used in each of the three data areas of storage organisation. These strategies can be broadly classified as static and dynamic allocation. **Static allocation** lays out storage for all data objects at compile time. In **dynamic storage allocation,** decisions are made only while the program is running. The following dynamic storage allocation strategies are discussed in this section:

- Stack allocation manages the run-time storage as a stack. Names local to a procedure are allocated space on a stack.
- Heap allocation allocates and de-allocates storage as needed at run-time from a data area known as heap. It is used for data that may live even after a procedure call returns.

These allocation strategies are applied to activation records.

8.5.1 Static Storage Allocation

In static allocation, names are bound to storage at compile time, so there is no need for a run-time support package. For any program, if memory is created at compile time, memory will be created in the static area. Also, if memory is allocated at compile time only, the same memory location will be used every time. That is, names are bound to the same storage locations every time a procedure is activated. When control returns to the calling procedure, the values of the locals are the same as they were when control left the last time. The data structures created are fixed and do not grow or shrink in size. FORTRAN uses static allocation. Memory can be statically allocated in C language also.

The amount of storage to be reserved for a name is determined based on the type of the name at compile time itself. The address of this storage consists of an offset from an end of the activation record for the procedure. The compiler must eventually decide where the activation records go, relative to the target code and to one another. Once this decision is made, the position of each activation record, and hence, of the storage for each name in the record is fixed. At compile time, the addresses can be filled at which the target code can find the data it operates on. Similarly, the addresses at which information is to be saved when a procedure call occurs is also known at compile time.

For example, global variables, file scope variables and variables qualified as static and defined inside functions can be declared ahead of time and can be static. The lifetime of such variables is the entire run-time of the program. It leads to efficient execution. However, if more static data space is allocated, then space may be wasted.

Limitations of static allocation

- Static allocation can be performed only if the size of the data object is known at compile time.
- Data structures cannot be created dynamically. That is, in static allocation, the allocation of memory at run-time is not possible. Memory is created at compile time and de-allocated after program completion.
- Recursive procedures are not supported by this type of allocation.

For example, consider a fragment of code:

```
main( ) {
        .
        .
        P1 ( );
        P2 ( );
        .
        .
        }
        P1( ) {
                int a;
                char c;
                .
                .
                }
```

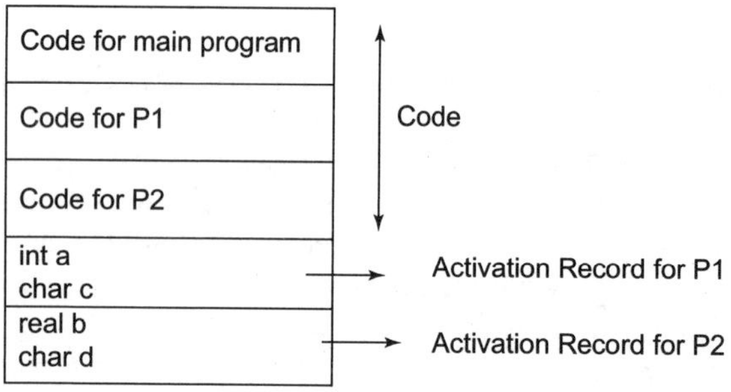

Figure 8.16 Static storage allocation for the local identifiers

```
P2( ) {
        real b;
        char d;
        .
        .
      }
```

The static storage allocation for the local identifiers is shown in Fig. 8.16.

8.5.2 Stack Storage Allocation

In stack allocation, storage is organised as a stack, and activation records are pushed and popped as activations begin and end, respectively. Storage for the locals in each call of a procedure is contained in the activation record for that call. Thus, locals are bound to fresh storage in each activation, because a new activation record is pushed onto the stack when a call is made. The values of locals are deleted when the activation ends; that is, the values are lost because the storage for locals disappears when the activation record is popped.

A form of stack allocation in which the sizes of all activation records are known at compile time is discussed first. Situations in which incomplete information about size is available at compile time are considered below.

Suppose register *top* marks the top of the stack. At run-time, an activation record can be allocated and de-allocated by incrementing and decrementing *top* by the size of the record. If procedure q has an activation record of size n, then *top* is incremented by n just before the target code of q is executed. When control returns from q, *top* is decremented by n. Hence, memory grows and shrinks on procedure calls and returns, respectively.

Memory allocation and de-allocation is partially predictable. It is a restricted strategy but simple and efficient. Allocation is hierarchical. Memory is freed in the opposite order of allocation. For example, if alloc(A), then alloc(B), then alloc(C), then memory must be freed in the order: free(C), then free(B), then free(A).

Calling sequences: Procedure calls are implemented by generating what are known as calling sequences in the target code. A **calling sequence** allocates an activation record and enters information into its fields. A **return sequence** restores the state of the machine so the calling procedure can continue execution.

Calling sequences and activation records differ, even for implementations of the same language. The code in a calling sequence is often divided between the calling procedure (the caller) and the procedure it calls (the callee). There is no exact division of run-time tasks between the caller and callee – the source language, target machine and the operating system impose requirements that may favour one solution over another.

In the design of calling sequences and activation records, the fields whose sizes are fixed early are placed in the middle. In general, the control link, access link, and machine status fields appear in the middle in the activation record, as shown in Fig. 8.17. The decision about whether or not to use control and access links is part of the design of the compiler, so these fields can be fixed at compiler construction time. If exactly the same amount of machine status information is saved for each activation, the same code can perform the saving and restoring for all activations.

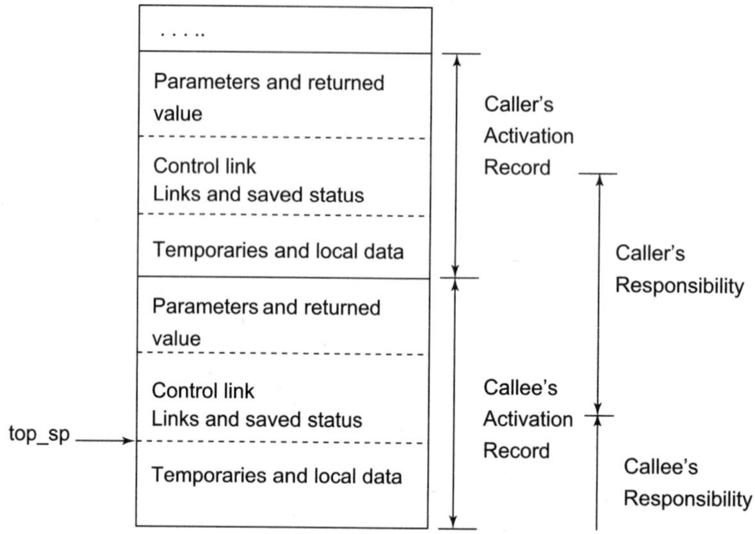

Figure 8.17 Division of task between caller and callee

The size of the temporaries field is fixed at compile time, but this may not be known to the front end. Hence, in the activation record, this field is shown after that for local data, where changes in its size will not affect the offsets of the data objects relative to the fields in the middle.

Each call has its own actual parameters, the caller usually evaluates actual parameters and communicates them to the activation record of the callee. In the stack, the activation record of the caller is just below that of the callee. The advantage of placing the fields for parameters and returned value next to the activation record of the caller is that the caller can then access these fields using offsets from the end of its own activation record, without knowing the complete layout of the record for the call.

Let us consider, for example, the register *top_sp* points to the end of the machine status field in an activation record. This position is known to the caller, so it can be made responsible for setting *top_sp* before control flows to the called procedure. The callee can access its temporaries and local data using offsets from *top_sp*. The call sequence is:

1. The caller evaluates actuals.
2. The caller stores a return address and the old value of *top_sp* into the callee's activation record. The caller then increments *top_sp* to the position shown in Fig. 8.17. That is, *top_sp* is moved past the caller's local data and temporaries and the callee's parameter and status fields.
3. The callee saves register values and other status information.
4. The callee initialises its local data and begins execution.

A possible return sequence is:

1. The callee places a return value next to the activation record of the caller.
2. Using the information in the status field, the callee restores *top_sp* and other registers and branches to a return address in the caller's code.
3. Although *top_sp* has been decremented, the caller can copy the returned value into its own activation record and use it to evaluate an expression.

Recursion in stack-based allocation: Let us consider the main program. It calls procedure Y, which in turn calls procedure X. Each call pushes another stack frame on top of the stack. Each stack frame has space for variables, parameters, return address, etc. On return from the procedure, the activation record is popped from the stack. Recursive calls can be handled in stack allocation.

Limitations of stack allocation: The stack allocation strategy cannot be used if either of the following is possible:

- The values of local names must be retained when an activation ends.
- A called activation outlives the caller. This possibility cannot occur for those languages where activation trees correctly depict the flow of control between procedures.

In each of the above cases, the de-allocation of activation records need not occur in a last-in first-out fashion, so storage cannot be organised as a stack.

8.5.3 Heap Storage Allocation

Heap allocation is used to dynamically allocate memory to the variables and claim it back when the variables are no longer required. Heap allocation allocates and de-allocates storage as needed at run-time from a data area known as heap. It is used for data that may live even after a procedure call returns. Heap allocation parcels out pieces of contiguous storage, as needed, for activation records or other objects. Pieces may be de-allocated in any order, so over time, the heap will consist of alternate areas that are free and in use.

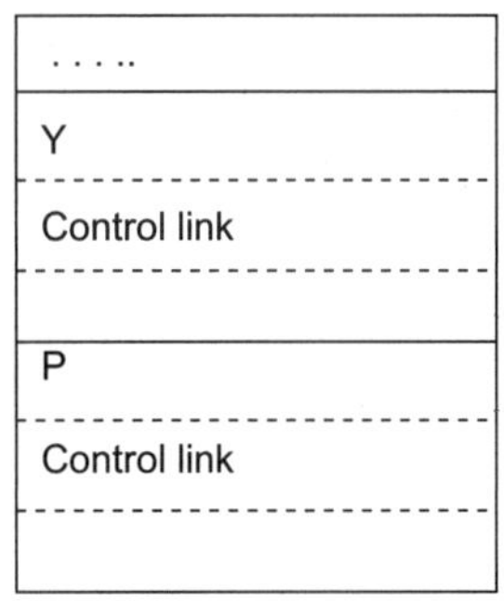

Figure 8.18 Activation record of Y and P in heap

The record for an activation of a procedure is retained when the activation ends. For example, procedure Y calls procedure P, it executes and returns. Then Procedure Y calls procedure Q. The stack after Y calls P is shown in Fig. 8.18 and the stack after P ends and Y calls Q is shown in Fig. 8.19. Even after the execution of P is completed, the activation record of P is retained. Therefore, Q cannot physically follow the activation record of Y. Now, if the retained activation record for P is de-allocated, there will be free space in the heap in between the activation records for Y and Q. It is left to the heap manager to make use of this space.

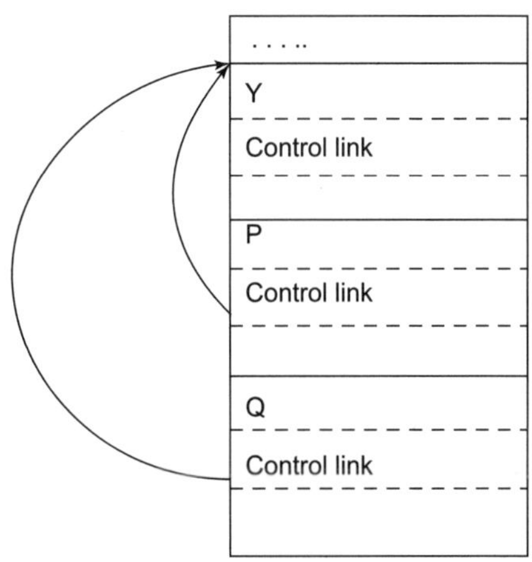

Figure 8.19 Activation record of Y, P and Q in heap

It is useful to handle small activation records or records of a predictable size as a special case, as follows:

1. For each size of interest, keep a linked list of free blocks of that size.
2. If possible, fill a request for size s with a block of size s', where s' is the smallest size greater than or equal to s. When the block is eventually de-allocated, it is returned to the freed list it came from.
3. For large blocks of storage, use the heap manager

This approach results in fast allocation and de-allocation of small amounts of storage, since taking and returning a block from a linked list are efficient operations. For large amounts of storage, the computation takes some time to use up the storage, so the time taken by the allocator is often negligible compared with the time taken to perform the computation. Memory allocation and de-allocation can be carried out at any time and at any place depending on the requirement of the user. Recursion is supported by heap allocation methods. However, this strategy may create free blocks in between and requires management of free blocks. It also requires a memory manager with garbage collection.

Typically, heap allocation schemes use a **free list** to keep track of the storage that is not in use.

Algorithms differ in how they manage the free list. Some of the heap allocation methods are discussed below:

- **Best fit**: In this method, the block that is closest to matching the needs of allocation is selected. For allocation, the whole list of free blocks must be checked to find the best fit free block. Excess space in the block is saved for later. Adjacent free blocks, if any, are merged during release operations.
- **First fit:** In this method, the first block that can accommodate the need of allocation is selected. The scanning process is stopped as soon as the first block that comes closest to matching the needs of allocation is encountered. Adjacent free blocks, if any, are merged during release operations.
- **Worst fit:** This selects the largest available free block.

Example 8.4 Free space allocation in heap using best fit, first fit and worst fit methods
Consider the heap memory shown in Fig. 8.20. The free space is indicated by shaded blocks.

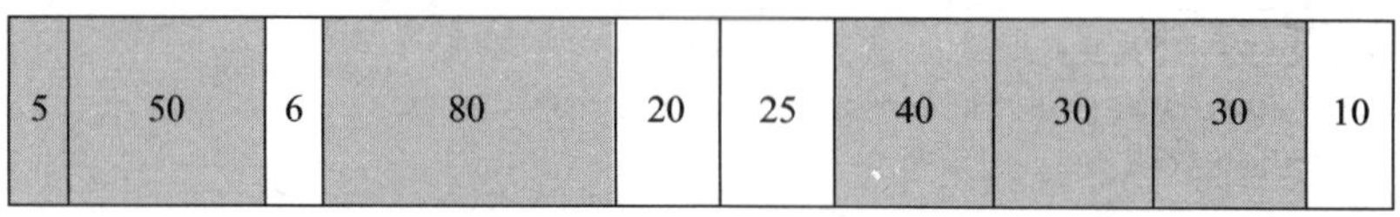

Figure 8.20 Heap memory

Consider there is a request for block allocation of size 36. In the best fit method, the closest possible match is for a block of size 40. The memory after allocation is shown in Fig. 8.21. Excessive memory of size 4 is added to the free list.

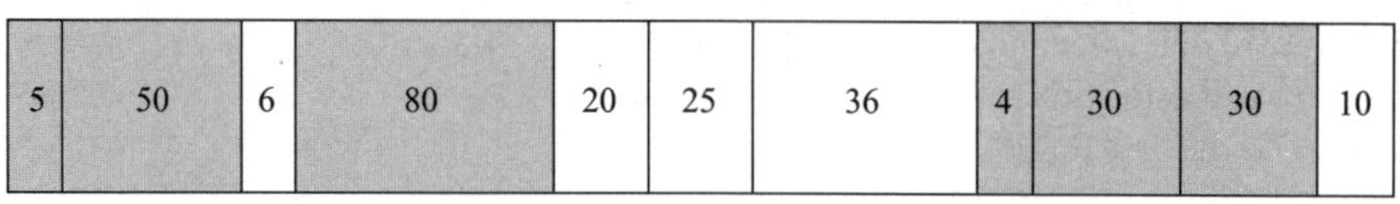

Figure 8.21 Heap memory after allocation using best fit method

Consider there is a request for block allocation of size 36 to the memory of Fig. 8.20. In the first fit method, the first block that can accommodate a block of size 36 is 50. The memory after allocation is shown in Fig. 8.22. Excessive memory of size 14 is added to the free list. In worst fit method, block 80 would have been selected.

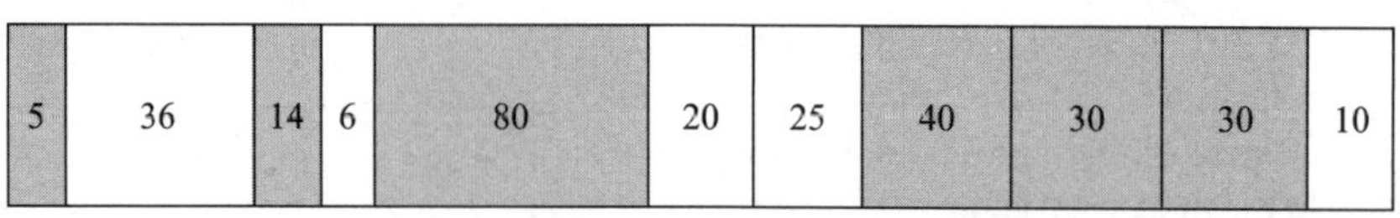

Figure 8.22 Heap memory after allocation using first fit method

8.6 Garbage Collection

Garbage collection is a form of automatic memory management. The garbage collector attempts to find and reclaim the memory occupied by objects that are no longer in use by the program. Garbage collectors may be classified as reference counters and trace-based methods. If nothing is done to reclaim heap storage after it is used, then eventually some programs may exhaust memory. Several partial solutions exist like explicit de-allocation, reference counting, tracing garbage collector, etc.

In **reference counting**, each heap object maintains an additional field containing the number of references to the object. The compiler must generate code that maintains this reference count correctly. When the count reaches 0, the object is de-allocated. The problem is that reference counting does not work well for circular data structures because reference counts in a cycle can remain positive even though the structure is unreachable.

A **mark-and-sweep collector** traverses the stack to find pointers in the heap and follows each of them, marking all reachable objects. It then sweeps through memory, collecting unmarked objects into a free list while leaving the marked objects in place. In this chapter, the trace-based garbage collection method called mark and sweep is discussed.

Mark and sweep collector: In the mark phase, all live nodes are traced by traversal while in the sweep phase, all un-reachable nodes are found by linear scan in the heap. It collects the garbage and adds the node to the free list. An extra mark bit is used for each node. Initially, the mark bit of all the nodes is set to zero. Then, in the mark phase, all reachable nodes are marked 1. Then, in the sweep phase, all mark bits are reset to zero and unreachable nodes are added to the free list. The algorithm for the mark and sweep phases is as follows:

```
Algorithm Mark{
list = all roots
while list= null do
{         pick V ∈ list
          list = list – {V}
          if mark(V) = 0
                    mark(V)=1;
          for each Vi referenced by V set mark(Vi)=1 and add Vi to list.
}
}
Algorithm Sweep{
For all object p in heap
{
          if mark(p) = 1
                    mark(p)=0;
          else
                    heap_release(p);
                    Add p to free list;
}
```

Example 8.5 Mark and sweep, trace-based garbage collector
Consider the memory blocks given in Fig. 8.23 with all mark bits set to 0 initially.

In the mark phase, reachable blocks are found starting from the root node and the mark bit is set to 1. The memory blocks after the mark phase are shown in Fig. 8.24. After the sweep phase, all the mark bits are set to 0 and other blocks are feed and added to the free list, as in Fig. 8.25.

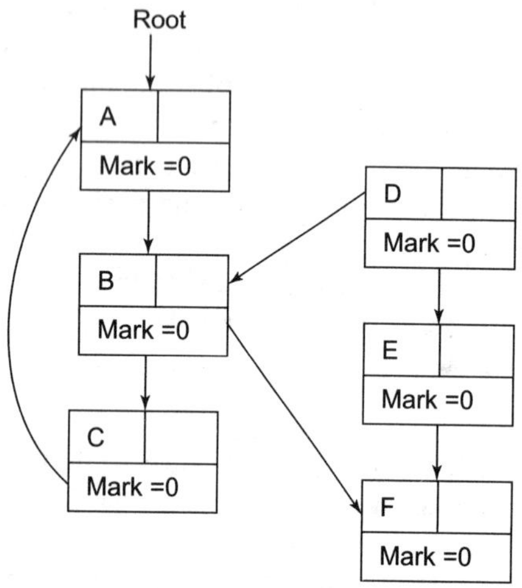

Figure 8.23 Initial memory blocks

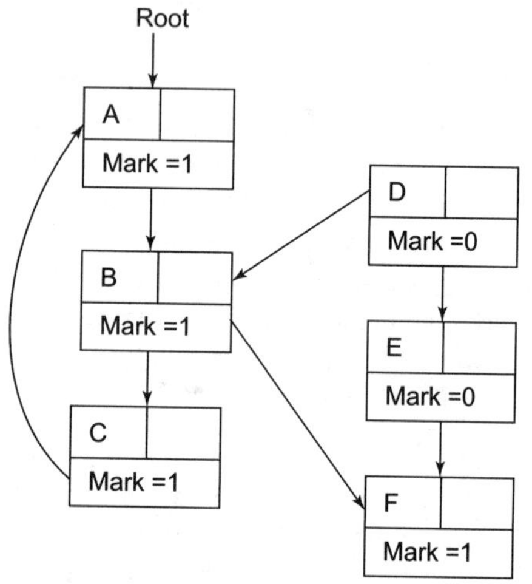

Figure 8.24 Memory blocks after the mark phase

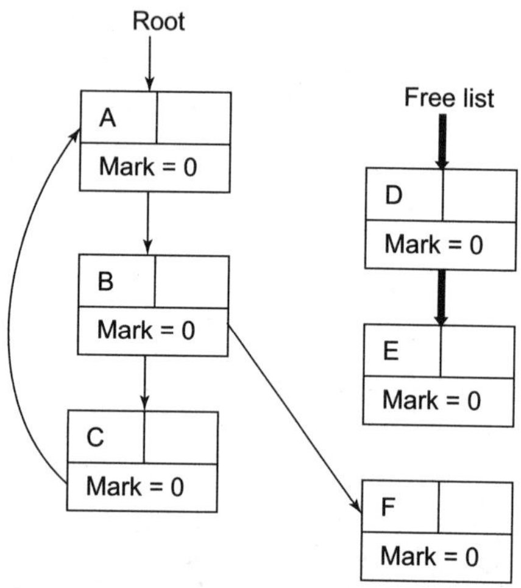

Figure 8.25 Memory blocks after the sweep phase

Example 8.6 Mark and sweep, trace-based garbage collector
Consider the nodes given in Fig. 8.26 (a). Apply the mark and sweep algorithms.

The algorithm starts with the root node. The mark bit of root node A is set to 1. Then, all the reachable nodes are set to 1. All the reachable nodes are shown in Fig. 8.26 (b) after the mark phase. Then, in the sweep phase, all the nodes whose bits are marked are reset to 0. Also, nodes that are not reachable are added to the free list (Fig. 8.26 (c)). These nodes are released from the heap.

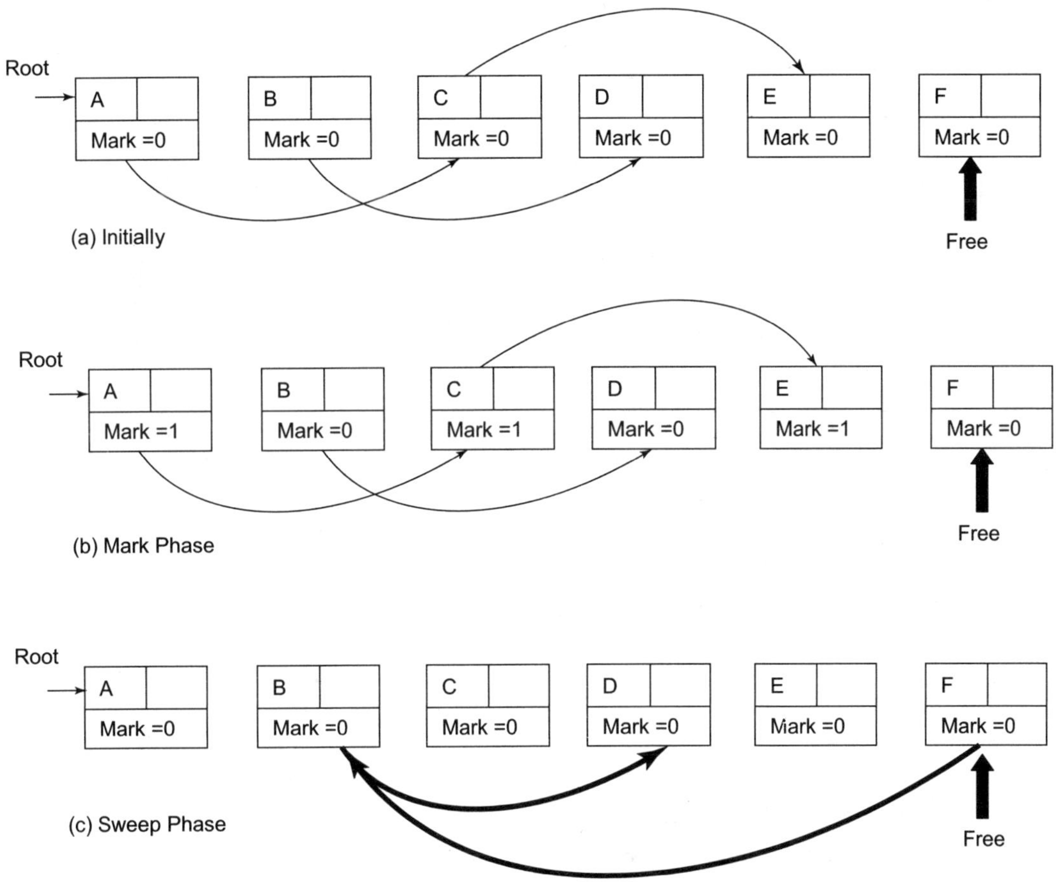

Figure 8.26 Mark and sweep (trace-based method) garbage collector

Example 8.7 Mark and sweep garbage collector

Consider the memory blocks given in Fig. 8.27. Apply the mark and sweep algorithms and state the blocks that will be contained in the free list after application of the mark and sweep phase.

After application of the mark phase, the marked bits of the blocks X, Y, P, Q, R are set to 1, when X is considered as the root. Block B is also marked as root, so blocks reachable from B are also processed and the mark bits of blocks B, C, D, T, V are set to 1.

After application of the sweep phase, all the marked bits of blocks marked in the mark phase are reset to 0 and unreachable states (states whose mark = 0 in after the mark phase) are de-allocated from memory and its name is added to the free list. Hence, the free list after application of sweep will contain blocks E, F, G, H, Z, U, S, A, W and U.

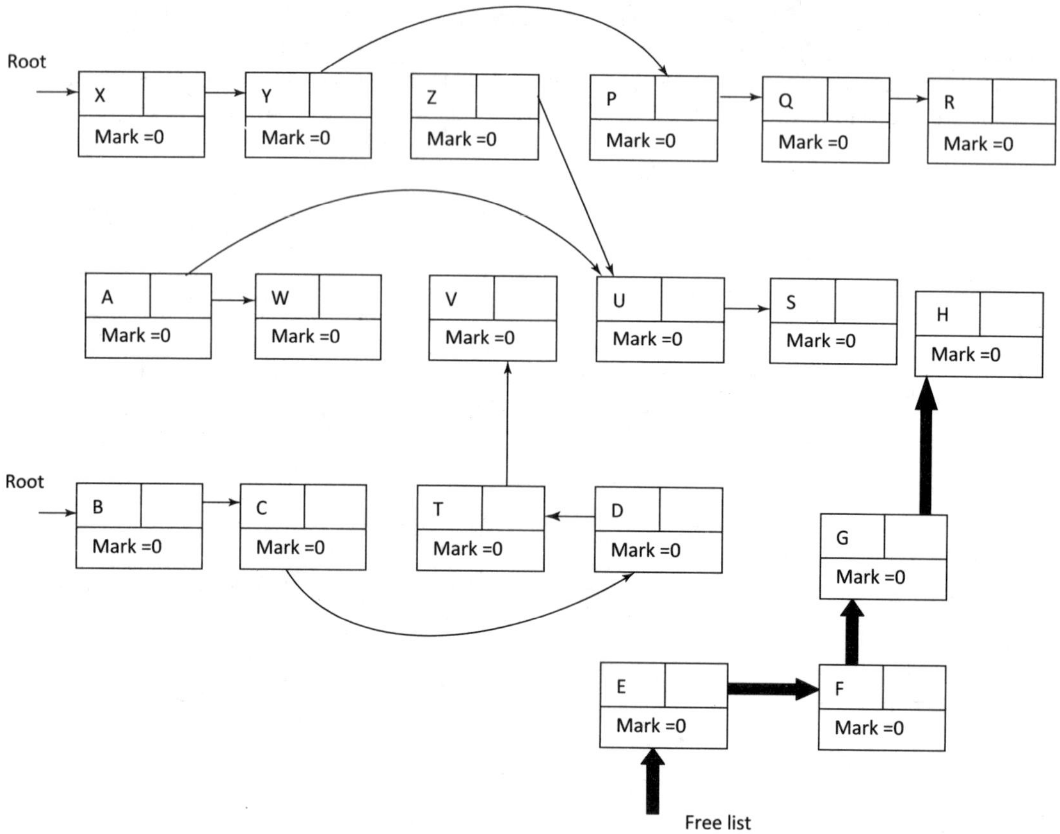

Figure 8.27 Initial memory blocks

8.7 Parameter Passing

The communication medium among procedures is known as parameter passing. The communication can involve non-local names and parameters. The values of the variables from a calling procedure are transferred to the called procedure.

Consider for example

```
P (exchange i, j: integer)
{
        int x;
        {
           x = a[i];
           a[i] = a[j];
           a[j] = x ;
        }
}
```

R-value: The value of an expression is called its r-value. The value contained in a single variable also becomes an r-value if it appears on the right side of the assignment operator. R-value can always be assigned to some other variable.

L-value: The location of the memory (address) where the expression is stored is known as the l-value of that expression. It always appears on the left side of the assignment operator.

Formal parameter: Variables that take the information passed by the caller procedure are called formal parameters. These variables are declared in the definition of the called function.

Actual parameter: Variables whose values and functions are passed to the called function are called actual parameters. Actual parameters are often called arguments.

Function P exchanges the values of a[i] and a[j]. Here, the array 'a' is non-local to the procedure exchange, and i and j are parameters. There are various parameter passing methods. It is important to know the parameter passing method a language (or compiler) uses, because the result of a program can depend on the method used. In the assignment statement, a[i]=a[j], expression a[j] represents a value and a[i] represents a storage location into which the value of a[j] is placed. The decision of whether to use the location or the value represented by an expression is determined by whether the expression appears on the left or right, respectively, of the assignment.

Different parameter passing methods are based on whether an actual parameter represents an r-value, l-value or the text of the actual parameter itself. Different ways of passing the parameters to the procedure are discussed below:

Call by value: In call by value, the calling procedure passes the r-value of the actual parameters and the compiler enters that in the called procedure's activation record. That is, prior to the call, the parameter is evaluated and its actual value is entered in a location private to the called procedure. Formal parameters hold the values passed by the calling procedure; thus, any changes made in the formal parameters do not affect the actual parameters. C and C++ use this method of passing parameters.
For example consider the C code

```
int add (int n)
{
    n= n+2;
    return n;
}
void main()
{
   int num1=10;
   int num2 = add(num1);
   printf("num1 value is: %d", num1);
   printf("\n num2 value is: %d", num2);
}
```

In the above code, n is a formal parameter and num 1 is the actual parameter. The value of the actual arguments are copied to the formal arguments, hence, any operation performed by the function on arguments does not affect the actual parameters. The output of the above code will be as follows.

Output:
num1 value is: 10
num2 value is: 12

Call by reference: In call by reference, the formal and actual parameters refer to the same memory location. The l-value of the actual parameters is copied to the activation record of the called function. Thus, the called function has the address of the actual parameters. If the actual parameters do not have an l-value, then it is evaluated in a new temporary location and the address of the location is passed. Any changes made in the formal parameters are reflected in the actual parameters.
For example, consider the C code

```
void add(*n)
{
      *n=*n+2;
}
void main()
{
    int num1=10;
    add(&num1);
    printf("num1 value is: %d", num1);
}
```

The output of the program will be num1 value is: 12

Call by copy restore: A hybrid between call by value and call by reference is the copy restore linkage. In call by copy restore, the compiler copies the values in the formal parameters when the procedure is called and copies them back in the actual parameters when control returns to the called function. The r-values are passed and on return the r-value of the formals are copied into the l-values of the actuals.

Call by name: In call by name the actual parameters are substituted for the formals in all the places the formals occur in the procedure. It is also referred as lazy evaluation because evaluation is performed on parameters only when needed.

The procedure is treated as if it were a macro; that is, its body is substituted for the call in the caller, with the actual parameters literally substituted for the formals. Such a literal substitution is called **macro-expansion**. The local names of the called procedure are kept distinct from the names of the calling procedure. We can think of each local of the called procedure being systematically renamed into a distinct new name before the macro-expansion is performed. The actual parameters are surrounded by parentheses, if necessary, to preserve their integrity.
Consider a swap procedure

```
swap(a, b){
        int a, b, temp;
        temp = a;
        a = b;
        b= temp;
}
```

It works well if the call is `swap(x,y)`. However, if the call is `swap(i, x[i])`, then

```
temp-i;
i=x[i];
x[i]=temp;
```

Call by name swaps sets i to x[i], as expected, but has the unexpected result of setting x[x[i0]] rather than x[i0], where i0 is the initial value of i. This phenomenon occurs because the location of x in the assignment x = temp of swap is not evaluated until needed, by which time the value of i has already changed. A correctly working version of swap apparently cannot be written if call by name is used.

8.8 Symbol Table

The compiler uses the symbol table to keep track of scope and binding information about names. The symbol table provides information about the identifier, the name of the identifier and attributes associated with the name and how to access this information. Symbol table names may be variables, parameters, constants, records, record fields, procedures, arrays and files. Different attributes can be associated with different names (Table 8.1). The symbol table is used by the analysis and synthesis phases to verify that the expressions and assignments are semantically correct by type checking, to verify that used identifiers have been defined and declared and to generate intermediate or target code.

Table 8.1 Attributes associated with name

Name	Attribute
Variable/Constant	Type, line number of declared variable, line number of referenced variable, scope information
Procedure	Number of parameters, parameters themselves, result type
Array	Number of dimensions, array bounds

A symbol table mechanism must allow us to add new entries and find existing entries efficiently. It is useful for a compiler to be able to grow the symbol table dynamically, if necessary, at compile time. If the size of the symbol table is fixed when the compiler is written, then the size chosen must be large enough to handle any source program that might be presented. Such a fixed size is likely to be too large for most, and inadequate for some, programs.

Symbol table entries: Each entry in the symbol table is for the declaration of a name. The format of entries may not be uniform, because the information saved about a name depends on the usage of the name. Each entry can be implemented as a record consisting of a sequence of consecutive words of memory. To keep symbol table records uniform, it may be convenient for some of the information about a name to be kept outside the table entry, with only a pointer to this information stored in the record.

Information is entered into the symbol table at various times. Identifiers and attributes are entered by the analysis phases. Let us consider the information entered by different phases of compilation and when are they accessed.

- Keywords are entered in the table initially, if at all.
- The lexical analyser looks up sequences of letters and digits in the symbol table to determine if a reserved keyword or a name has been collected. With this approach, keywords must be in the symbol table before lexical analysis begins. Alternatively, if the lexical analyser intercepts

reserved keywords, then they need not appear in the symbol table. If the language does not reserve keywords, then the keywords must be entered into the symbol table with a warning of their possible use as a keyword.

- The symbol table entry itself is made as soon as a name is seen in the input, by the lexical analyser.
- More often, one name may denote several different objects, perhaps even in the same block or procedure. For example, the C declarations

  ```
  int x;
  void x(int a, int b)
  ```

  The name 'x' is used as both an integer and as a function name; in such cases, the lexical analyser returns only the name to the parser, rather than a pointer to the symbol table entry. The record in the symbol table is created when the syntactic role played by this name is discovered. For the example, two symbol table entries for x would be created, one with x as an integer and one with x as a function.
- The symbol table is changed every time a name is encountered in the source; changes to the table occur if a new name is discovered or if new information about an existing name is discovered.
- In simple language with only global variables and implicit declarations, the scanner enters an identifier into a symbol table if it is not already there.
- In block-structured languages with scope and explicit declarations, the parser or semantic analyser enters identifiers and its attributes.

Information about the storage locations that will be bound to names at run-time is kept in the symbol table. If the target code is assembly language, the assembler handles the storage locations for the various names. The compiler needs to scan the symbol table, after generating assembly code for the program, and generate assembly language data definitions to be appended to the assembly language program for each name.

If machine code is to be generated by the compiler, then the compiler must determine the position of each data object relative to a fixed origin, such as the beginning of an activation record. The same applies to the block of data loaded as a module separate from the program.

Storage of names: In the symbol table, names can be stored in two ways. If there is a modest upper bound on the length of a name, then the characters in the name can be stored in the symbol table entry, as in Fig. 8.28.

Name										Attributes
i	n	t								
i										
r	e	a	d	a	r	r	a	y		

Figure 8.28 Fixed size space within a record

If there is no limit on the length of the name, then rather than allocating each symbol table entry the maximum possible amount of space to hold a lexeme, space can be utilised more efficiently by using pointers, as shown in Fig. 8.29. In the record for a name, place a pointer to a separate array of characters pointing to the first character of the lexeme. This indirect scheme keeps the size of the name field of the symbol table entry uniform for all records. However, occurrences of the same lexeme must be distinguished based on the scope of different declarations. Similarly, attribute information can also be maintained outside the record.

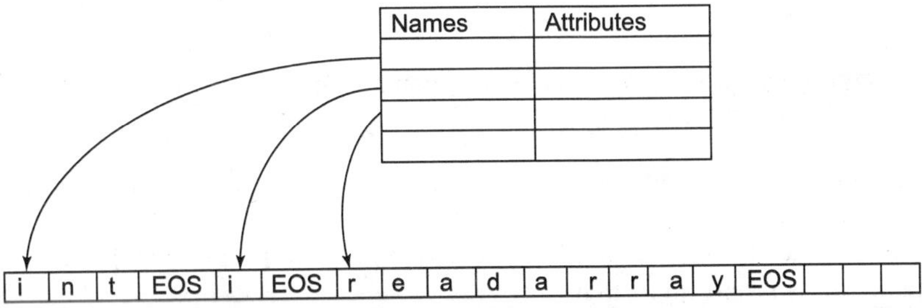

Figure 8.29 Pointer to names stored in separate array

Operations: Different operations can be performed on the symbol table:

- Insert – to insert a name in a symbol table and return a pointer to its entry
- Lookup/Search – to search for a name and return a pointer to its entry
- Free – to remove all entries and free the storage of a symbol table
- Allocate – to allocate a new empty symbol table

8.9 Data Structure for Symbol Table

Various organisations like linear list, binary trees and hash tables that can be used for symbol table implementation are discussed in this section. Linear lists are simple to implement but are poor in performance when the number of entries and the number of search operations are large, whereas hash tables have good performance but at the cost of increased programming effort and space overhead. Each scheme is evaluated on the basis of the time required to add n entries and make q inquiries. Both mechanisms can be adapted readily to handle the most closely nested scope rule.

8.9.1 Linear List

The simplest and easiest way to implement a data structure for a symbol table is a linear list of records. A single array or equivalently several arrays are used to store names and their associated information. The organisation using linear list is shown in Fig. 8.30. The operations that can be performed in a linear list are as follows:

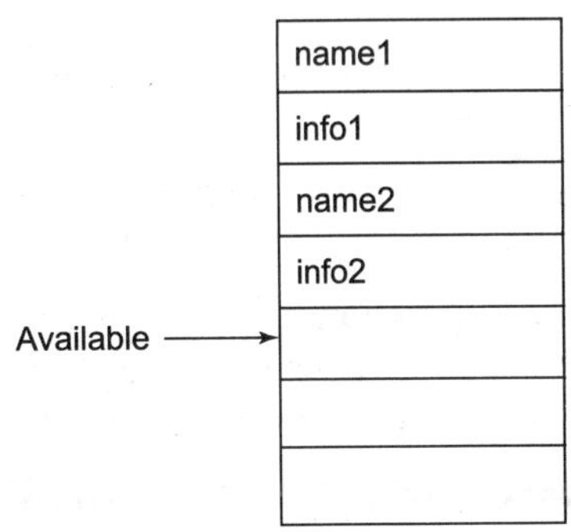

Figure 8.30 Linear list of records

Insert operation: New names can be added to the list in the order in which they are encountered. The table is first searched for the name that is to be added to check whether or not the name is already present in the table. If the name is not present, then a record is created and inserted at the location marked by the available pointer. This pointer is used mark the position in the array where the next entry to the symbol table will go. After the insert operation, the mark pointer is updated to point to the next position where a record can be inserted.

Lookup/Search operation: The search for a name is done backwards, starting from the end of the array to the beginning. When the name is located, the associated information can be found in the words that follow. If the beginning of the array is reached without finding the name, then it is not present in the table and error is reported.

Complexity: Let us consider that the symbol table contains n names. The steps necessary to insert a new name are as follows:

1. If the insertion is performed without checking whether the name is already in the table, then it is constant O(1).
2. If multiple entries for names are not allowed, then search the entire table for the name before insertion. This is proportional to n.
3. To find data about a name, on an average, search n/2 names so the cost of the search is also proportional to n.

Since insertion and search take time proportional to n, the total work for inserting n names and making q search inquiries is at most cn(n+q), where c is a constant representing the time necessary for a few machine operations.

8.9.2 Search Tree: Binary Search Tree

A binary tree consists of nodes containing links to two disjoint binary trees. The node at the top is called the **root** of the tree. The node referenced by the left link is called the **left subtree**, and the node referenced by the right link is called the **right subtree**. Nodes whose links are null are called **leaf nodes**. The **height** of a tree is the maximum number of links on any path from the root node to a leaf node. The symbol table record is represented by a node containing the name, information and two pointers pointing to the left and right subtrees, as shown in Fig. 8.31.

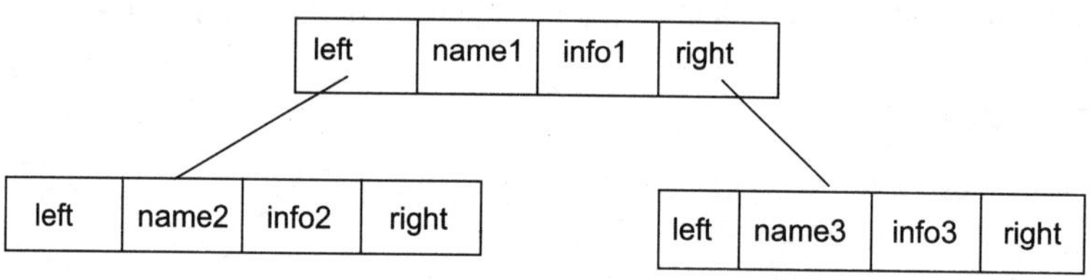

Figure 8.31 Organisation of the symbol table as search tree

Insert operation: To insert a new name in the symbol table organised as a binary search tree, search the binary tree for the name. If the name does not exist, then a new record is created and inserted following the alphabetical property.

Search operation: To search for a name in the binary search tree, the following rules are used:

- If the tree is empty, terminate the search as unsuccessful.
- If the name to be searched is the same as the name of the current node, then terminate the search as successful and return the corresponding information.

- If the search name alphabetically precedes the name in the current node, then search in the left subtree.
- If the search name occurs alphabetically after the name in the current node, then search in the right subtree.

Complexity: Time per operation (search, insert or delete) for n variables is O(log n). The time for n insert and q search operations is proportional to (n+q)log n. If there are a large number of records, this method outperforms the linear list organisation, but coding is relatively difficult.

8.9.3 Hash Table

Variations of the searching technique known as hashing have been implemented in many compilers. Here, consider a simple variant known as **open hashing**, where open refers to the property that there is no limit on the number of entries that can be made in the table. One such organisation is shown in Fig. 8.32. There is a hash table consisting of a fixed array of m pointers to table entries. Table entries are organised into m separate linked lists, called **buckets**. Each record in the symbol table appears on exactly one of these lists.

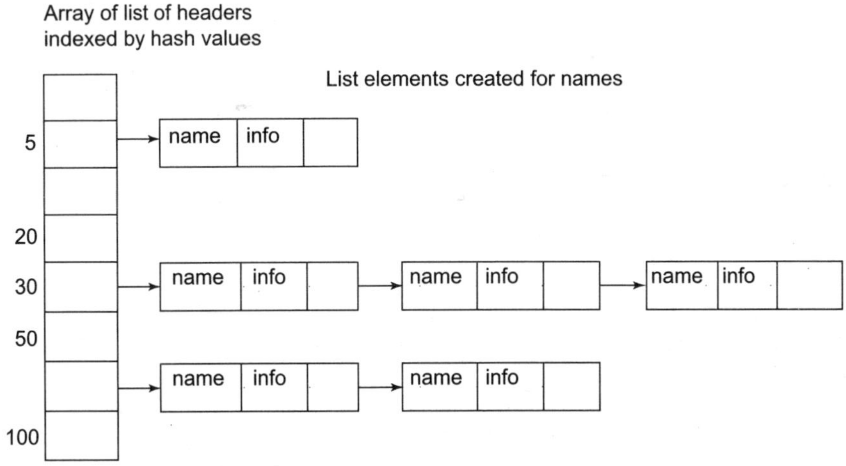

Figure 8.32 Sample hash table organisation

Insert operation: To insert string s in the symbol table, apply a hash function h to s, such that h(s) returns an integer between 0 and m – 1. If s is not in the list of h(s), then it is entered by creating a record for s that is linked at the front of the list numbered h(s). If s is in the list, then the name already exists and error is reported.

Search operation: To determine whether there is an entry for string s in the symbol table, apply a hash function h to s, such that h(s) returns an integer between 0 and m – 1. If s is in the symbol table, then it is on the list numbered h(s).

Complexity: Even this scheme gives us the capability of performing q search on n names in time proportional to n(n + e)/m, for any constant m of our choosing. Since m can be made as large as n, this method is generally more efficient than linear lists and is the method of choice for symbol table organisation.

The average list is n/m records long if there are n names in a table of size m. By choosing m so that n/m is bounded by a small constant, say 2, the time to access a table entry is essentially constant.

Example 8.8 Hash table if all the entries map to the same hash value
Consider a fragment of code

```
void f(int a, int b) {
        real x;
        while(z<10){
            int x, y;
        }
}
void a( ){
        f(p,q);
}
```

Let us assume that all the entries map to the same hash value 'k', then a list is created corresponding to the hash 'k', as shown in Fig. 8.33. In the organisation, an entry for scope management is added by attaching the level number.

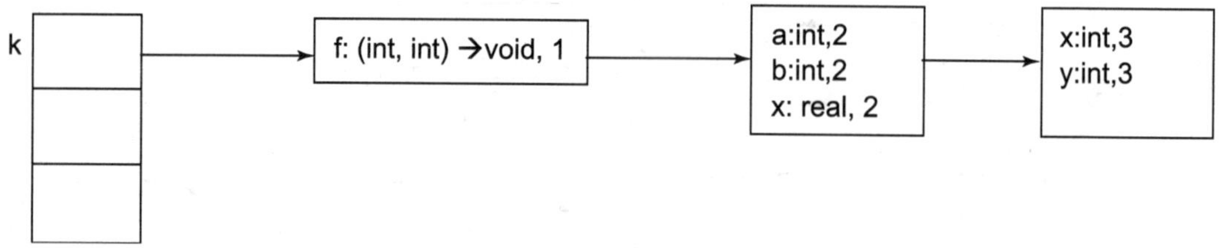

Figure 8.33 Hash table if all entries hash to hash value 'k'

8.10 Scope of Information in Symbol Table

The entries in the symbol table represent the declarations of names. When an occurrence of a name in the source text is looked up in the symbol table, the entry for the appropriate declaration of that name must be returned. The scope rules of the source language determine which declaration is appropriate. Lexical scope is a textual region in the program that can be a statement block, formal argument list, object body, function or method body, module body or whole program (multiple modules).

The most simple strategy is to maintain a separate symbol table for each scope. When a newly scanned name is searched, a match occurs only if the characters of the name match an entry character for character, and the associated number in the symbol table entry is the number of the procedure being processed. Most closely nested scope rules can be implemented in terms of the following operations on a name:

- Lookup: Find the most recently created entry
- Insert: Make a new entry
- Delete: Remove the most recently created entry

Generally, a compiler maintains two types of symbol tables:

- Global symbol table, accessed by all procedures
- Scope symbol table, created for each scope in the program

The scope information is maintained in these symbol tables. Another technique to represent scope of information in the symbol table is by specifying the **nesting depth**. The nesting depth of each procedure block is saved in the symbol table. The pair <procedure name, nesting depth> is used as the key to access information from the table.

The nesting depth of a procedure is the number obtained by starting with value one for main and adding one every time we go from an enclosing procedure to an enclosed procedure, that is, nested procedures. Variables can also be represented by the pair <nesting depth, static distance> in the symbol table. To find the static distance, calculate the difference between the static nesting level of the use of the variable and that of its definition. To access a non-local variable v with static distance d, the compiler sets up code to traverse d static links, then loads v at the known offset in that activation record.

Example 8.9 Scope information using different symbol tables

Consider the code below to represent the scope information. Also discuss how the search operation will proceed in the organisation.

```
int i;
void new1( ) {
      int a1;
      int a2;

            {
            int a3;          }   Inner Scope-1
            char a4;
            }
      int a5;

            {
            int a6;          }   Inner Scope-2
            }
}
void main( ) {
      int b1;
      int b2;

            {
            char b3;         }   Inner Scope-3
            char b4;
            }
      int b5;
}
```

The hierarchical structure of the symbol table is shown in Fig. 8.34.

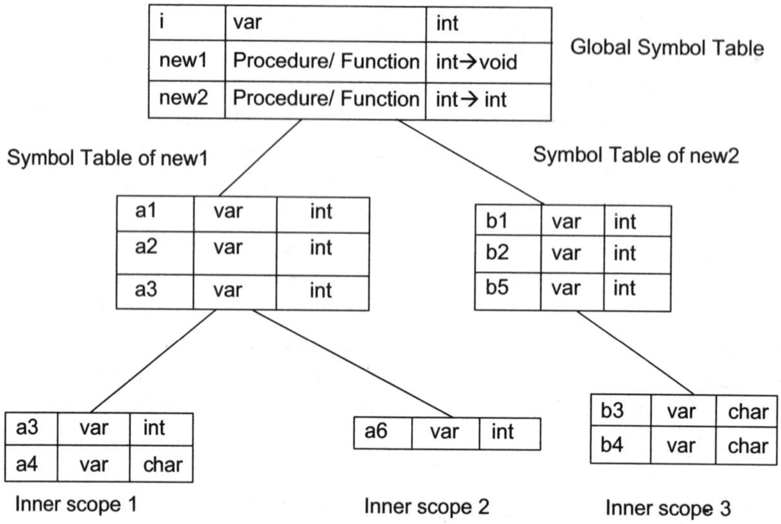

Figure 8.34 Use of global and scope symbol tables to represent scope information

To search the name, a search is first performed in the current symbol table, that is, the symbol table of current scope. If the name is found, the search is complete; else search in the parent symbol table until either the name is found or the global symbol table has been searched for that name. Consider, for example, that currently inner scope 2 is being processed. The search for 'i', will first start in the inner scope 2. If 'i' is not present in scope 2, go up in the hierarchy and search the symbol table of new1 for 'i'. It is not present. Going up in hierarchy, 'i' is found at the global system table.

Example 8.10 Scope information using different symbol tables

Consider the code below to represent the scope information

```
int a;
void P(int c) {
        float x,y;
        . . .
        {
        int i,j
        }
        . .
        {
        int x;
        }
}
int Q (int n) {
        char t;
        . . .
}
```

The global and scope symbol table in hierarchical fashion is shown in Fig. 8.35.

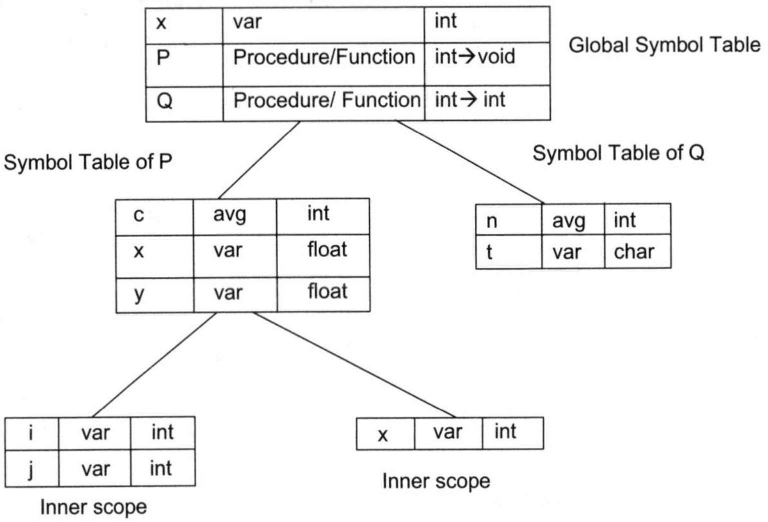

Figure 8.35 Hierarchical symbol table

Example 8.11 Scope information using nesting depth, static distance

Consider the code given below to find the nesting depth and static distance.

```
begin
      integer global, n;
      procedure square(n: integer);
      begin
            procedure shape;
            begin
                  print(global);
                  print(n);
            end;
            shape;      // call to shape
        end;

global := 3;
n := 100;
square(10);
end;
```

Procedure `square` has nesting depth=1.
Inside procedure `square`, n has static distance 0.

Procedure `shape` has nesting depth 2. So, inside `shape`, n has static distance 1, and global has static distance 2 (use the n defined in `square`). If procedure `shape` is not nested inside procedure `square`, then both procedures `square` and `shape` will have nesting depth as 1. Inside `shape`, both n and global will have static distance as 1.

Example 8.12 Symbol table contents with nesting depth information

Consider the code fragment given below

```
main()
{
        int x,y;
        int Z( ){
                char a,b;
                char R( ) {
                          int c;
                          }
                }
        int P( ){
                real s;
               }
}
```

Table 8.2 Symbol table along with nesting depth

x	var	int	1
y	var	int	1
Z	Procedure	int	1
P	Procedure	int	1
a	var	char	2
b	var	char	2
R	Procedure	char	2
c	var	int	3
s	var	real	2

The symbol table along with nesting depth is given in Table 8.2.

SUMMARY

- The allocation and de-allocation of data objects during execution is managed by the run-time support package. It consists of routines loaded with the generated target code. The design of the run-time support package is influenced by the semantics of procedures.
- Various aspects to be handled in the run-time environment are memory organisation, activation record, procedure call and return and parameter passing.
- An area of run-time memory is called a heap.
- Each execution of a procedure is referred to as an activation of the procedure.
- The lifetime of an activation is the sequence of steps present in the execution of the procedure.
- A series of activations can be represented in the form of a tree, known as the activation tree.
- The activation tree represents the sequence of procedure calls that corresponds to pre-order traversal and the sequence of returns that corresponds to post-order traversal.
- A stack representing procedure calls, returns and flow of control is called a control stack or run-time stack.
- The control stack is used to keep track of the procedures whose execution has not been completed.
- An activation record contains temporary data, local data, saved machine status, optional control link, actual parameters and return value.
- Declaration announces the existence of the entity in the program. It specifies name, type and data type for the entity.
- The portion of the program to which a declaration applies is called the scope of that declaration.
- Environment refers to a function that maps a name to a storage location, and state refers to a function that maps a storage location to the value held.
- Storage allocation can be static or dynamic.
- The garbage collector attempts to find and reclaim the memory occupied by objects that are no longer used by the program.

- Garbage collectors may be classified as reference counters and trace-based methods.
- The communication medium among procedures is known as parameter passing.
- The compiler uses the symbol table to keep track of scope and binding information about names.
- The symbol table provides information about the identifier, the name of the identifier and attributes associated with the name and how to access this information. Symbol table names may be variables, parameters, constants, records, record fields, procedures, arrays and files.
- Data structures like linear lists, binary trees and hash tables can be used for symbol table implementation.

EXERCISES

Review Questions

Fill in the blanks with appropriate answers:

1. Space is allocated in the __________ stack for activation of each procedure.
2. The information needed to manage a single procedure activation is called __________.
3. __________ is an enclosing context or region that defines where a name can be used.
4. __________ maps a name to an l-value, and __________ maps the l-value to an r-value.
5. In __________ storage allocation, storage for all data objects is done at compile time.
6. In __________ storage allocation, decisions are made only while the program is running.
7. __________ requires management of free blocks.
8. In __________ method, each heap object maintains an additional field containing the number of references to the object.
9. Mark and Sweep is a __________ based garbage collector.
10. Complexity per operation (search, insert or delete) for n variables in binary search tree is __________.

Answers: 1. Control 2. Activation record 3. Scope 4. Environment, state 5. Static allocation 6. Dynamic 7. Heap allocation 8. Reference counting 9. Trace-based 10. O(log n)

State whether true or false:

1. Memory is required for activation of procedures.
2. If scope defines the visibility of a name and scopes are allowed to overlap, any name defined in the outer scope is visible to the inner scope and that defined in the inner scope is visible to the outer scope.
3. Data structures cannot be created dynamically in static allocation.
4. Recursive procedures are supported by static allocation.
5. Recursive calls can be handled in stack allocation.
6. Reference counting does not work well for circular data structures.
7. In call by reference, the calling procedure passes the r-value of the actual parameters and the compiler enters that in the called procedure's activation record.

Answers: 1.True 2. False 3. True 4. False 5. True 6. True 7. False

Practice Questions

1. Write the C code for merge sort. Draw the activation tree when numbers 5 8 1 9 4 2 7 3 are to be sorted. Also show the intermediate control stacks having the activation records.

2. Write the C code for binary search. State the scope of variables and procedures. Add the details to the symbol table along with nesting depth.
3. State the problems of heap allocation and how can they be solved.
4. Apply free space allocation methods to the given memory blocks. Shaded blocks are free blocks. Show the blocks that will be utilised in different strategies if memory request is for a block of size 21.

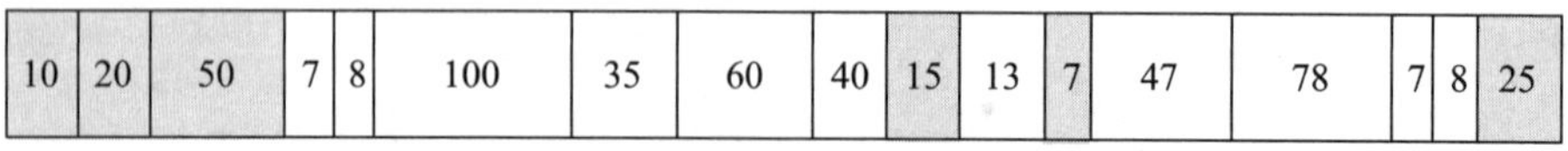

5. Consider the code fragment and build the symbol table with nesting depth and static distance.

```
main()
{
      int x,y;
      int A( ){

               char R( ) {
                          int c;
                          char a,b;
                          }
            }
      int B( ){
               real s;
               int p,q;

               int C( )
               {
               int s,t;
                       int D( )
                       {
                       int r;
                       }
               }
               }
}
```

Programming Questions

1. Consider an input program and build the symbol table as seen by the lexical analyser.
2. Consider an input program containing nested scope of procedures and variables. Build the symbol table along with nesting depth information.

9 Error Handling

OBJECTIVES

- To introduce the different types of errors
- To discuss the error handling techniques used during each phase of compilation

9.1 Introduction to Error Generation and Error Handling

A program written in a high-level language may have different types of errors. For example, logical errors, syntactic errors, semantic errors, etc. Errors may be classified broadly into compile-time errors and run-time errors. **Compile-time errors** are generated when the code does not comply with the syntactic and semantic rules of the language. The goal of the compiler is to ensure that the code is free of syntactic and semantic errors. Any violations of the rule that are detected at the compilation stage are called compilation errors.

When the program is compiled without any error, there is still a chance that it will fail at run-time. A **run-time error** occurs during the execution of a program and usually due to adverse system parameters or invalid input data. The **causes** of run-time errors are as follows:

- Insufficient memory to run an application or a memory conflict with another program
- Resource problems such as non-availability of file handlers
- Incompatible type-casting
- Referencing an invalid index in an array
- Using a null object, such as trying to invoke a method on an un-initialised variable
- Thread deadlocks
- Infinite loops

In this chapter, the compile-time errors that can be handled by the compiler are discussed. A compiler must perform the following tasks for error handling:

1. Detect error
2. Diagnose error
3. Error recovery

Generally, languages do not support error handling in design, that is, error-induced behaviour is not present in the language specification. Error handling is left to the compiler designer. A good compiler should assist in identifying and locating compile-time errors. A good error handler reports the presence of errors clearly and recovers accurately and quickly, in order to detect subsequent errors with minimal overhead of processing. The error diagnostic must be printed after the detection of error. Error must be reported along with the place in the source program where the error was detected. The common strategy is to print the line number of the error and point to the position where the error was detected. Error messages should point the errors in terms of the original source program rather than in some internal representation, which is unknown to the user. They must be useful and comprehensible to the user. These messages must be specific and localise the problem. The messages must not be redundant. It is possible that many messages appear owing to the same error. For example, if *a* is a simple variable that is not declared but used many times in the program, then all references to a will be flagged as erroneous use of the variable name. This can be achieved by setting a flag in the symbol table entry of a. This will enable us to detect and indicate all possible illegal uses of the identifier.

When an error is detected, a simple strategy would be to stop all activities and report the error. A better strategy would be to transform the error by applying an error correction strategy and then recover from it without stopping execution. There is no universally accepted recovery strategy, but there exist various error recovery strategies that can be applied depending on the compiler and type of error. Some of the types of compile-time errors are lexical errors, syntactic errors, semantic errors and logical errors.

9.2 Error Handling in Each Phase of Compilation

Errors can occur at every phase of compilation. However, after detecting an error, a phase must deal with it so that the compilation process can continue without interruption and enable further errors in the source program to be detected. After detecting and reporting an error, a phase can either repair it or pass it along to subsequent modules. If a phase attempts to repair the error, it should take care not to introduce other errors. If a phase transmits the error, the subsequent phases should be able to deal with the erroneous inputs passed to them.

Most errors are encountered in the early phases of the compiler. The syntax and semantic analysis phases handle a large fraction of the errors detectable by the compiler. The lexical phase can detect errors where the characters remaining in the input do not form any token of the language. Errors where the token stream violates the structure rules (syntax) of the language are determined by the syntax analysis phase. During semantic analysis, the compiler tries to detect constructs that have the right syntactic structure but are of no meaning to the operation involved. In the next sections, the types of errors that can occur in each phase of compilation and how these errors can be handled are discussed.

Error recovery strategies include panic mode error recovery, phrase level error recovery, production rules and global corrections. In panic mode error recovery, the compiler discards input symbols one at a time until one of a designated set of synchronizing tokens is found. In phrase level error recovery, local correction is applied on the remaining input. It replaces the remaining input with some string that allows the parser to continue. In error productions, the grammar productions are equipped to generate appropriate error diagnostics, while in global correction, a compiler would make as few changes as possible in processing an incorrect string algorithm for choosing the minimal sequence of changes to obtain globally a least-cost correction. Sections 9.3 through 9.5 discuss error handling in each phase of the compiler.

9.3 Error Handling in Lexical Analysis Phase

Few errors are discernible at the lexical level alone because a lexical analyser has a localised view of a source program, and the source program is input only to the lexical analyser. A character sequence that cannot be scanned into any valid token is a **lexical error**. Lexical errors are uncommon, but if they occur, they must be handled by the scanner. These errors can occur due to typing mistakes by the programmer. Some of the errors that must be detected during lexical analysis are:

- Numeric literals are too long
- Long identifiers

- Ill-formed numeric literals
- Misspelling of identifiers or keywords
- Missing operators
- Addition of an extraneous character
- Missing character that should be present

Most spelling errors may consist of one incorrect character, one missing character, one extra character or transposed adjacent characters. Mistakes in more than one character are very rare, but can exist.

For example, if 'els' is identified for the first time in the program, a lexical analyser cannot determine whether it is the misspelled keyword 'else' or an undeclared identifier. However, 'els' is a valid identifier; the lexical analyser must return the token for an identifier and let some other phase of the compiler handle any error. If a situation arises in which the lexical analyser is unable to proceed because none of the patterns for tokens match a prefix of the remaining input, then some error recovery strategy must be applied.

Missing operators are detected by their context. However, it is not always possible to detect missing operators because certain contexts tend to hide the absence of an operator. For example, A=B(C+D) is typed instead of A=B−(C+D). In this case, the missing operator '−' cannot be determined.

Error recovery by lexical analyser: The lexical analyser detects an error when it discovers that an input's prefix does not fit the specification of any token class. After detecting an error, the lexical analyser can invoke an error recovery routine. This can entail a variety of remedial actions.

The simplest recovery strategy is **panic mode recovery**. In this method, successive characters are deleted from the remaining input until the lexical analyser can find a well-formed token. However, this is likely to cause the parser to read a deletion error, which can cause severe difficulties in syntax analysis and the remaining phases. Also, this recovery technique may occasionally confuse the parser, but in an interactive computing environment, it may be quite adequate.

One way the parser can help the lexical analyser in improving its ability to recover from errors is to make its list of legitimate tokens (in the current context) available to the error recovery routine. The error recovery routine can then decide whether the remaining input's prefix matches one of these tokens closely enough to be treated as that token.

Other possible error recovery actions are:

- Deleting an extraneous character
- Inserting a missing character
- Replacing an incorrect character with the correct character
- Transposing two adjacent characters

Error transformations like these may be tried in an attempt to repair the input. The simplest such strategy is to check whether a prefix of the remaining input can be transformed into a valid lexeme by just a single error transformation. This strategy assumes most lexical errors are the result of a single error transformation, an assumption usually, but not always, borne out in practice. One way of finding the errors in a program is to compute the minimum number of error transformations required to transform the erroneous program into one that is syntactically well-formed. An erroneous program has k errors if the shortest sequence of error transformations that will map it into some valid program has length k. Minimum distance error correction is a convenient theoretical yardstick, but it is not generally used in practice because it is too costly to implement. However, a few experimental compilers have used the minimum distance criterion to make local corrections.

9.4 Error Handling in Syntax Analysis Phase

A syntax error is an error in the syntax of a sequence of characters or tokens acceptable to the programming language. Many parsers detect errors when they do not have a legal move from the correct configuration, which is determined by its state, stack content and current input symbol. Often, much of the error detection and recovery in a compiler is done in the syntax analysis phase, because many errors are syntactic in nature or are exposed when the stream of tokens coming from the lexical analyser disobeys the grammatical rules defining the programming language. Some examples of syntactic errors are as follows:

- An arithmetic expression with unbalanced parentheses
- Misplaced/Extra/Missing tokens such as semicolon, braces and punctuation symbols
- Use of a variable before it is initialised
- Value-returning function has no return statement

On discovering an error, the compiler can report it and stop or try to apply local correction on the remaining input. To recover from an error, a parser should ideally locate it, correct it and resume parsing.

One example of local correction is replacing the remaining input with some string that allows the parser to continue. For example, to replace a comma with a semicolon, to delete an extraneous semicolon, to insert a missing semicolon, etc. The choice of local correction is left to the compiler designer, such that the replacements do not lead to infinite loops. These may have difficulty in coping with situations in which the actual error has occurred before the detection point.

The chief concern while recovering from syntax errors is to attain a parser state from which the parser can safely resume parsing the input string. In this section, a few basic techniques for recovering from syntax errors are presented; their implementation is discussed in conjunction with the parsing methods in this chapter. The error handler in a parser should:

- Report the presence of errors clearly and accurately
- Recover from each error quickly enough to be able to detect subsequent errors
- Not significantly slow down the processing of correct programs
- Not add overheads to the processing of correct programs

Several parsing methods, such as the LL and LR methods, detect an error as soon as possible as they have the viable prefix property. This property detects an error as soon as the prefix of the input cannot be completed to form a string of the language.

The parser can use many general strategies to recover from a syntactic error. Four common error -recovery strategies can be implemented in the parser to deal with errors in the code:

- **Panic mode error recovery**: This is the simplest method to implement and is used by most parsing methods. On discovering an error, the compiler discards input symbols one at a time until one of a designated set of synchronizing tokens is found. The synchronizing tokens are usually delimiters, such as semicolon or end, whose role in the source program is clear. The compiler designer must select the synchronizing tokens appropriate for the source language. Panic mode correction often skips a considerable amount of input without checking it for additional errors. Moreover, it is guaranteed not to go into an infinite loop, and in situations where multiple errors in the same statement are rare, this method may be quite adequate.
- **Phrase level recovery**: On discovering an error, the parser may perform local correction on the remaining input; that is, it may replace the prefix of the remaining input by some string that

allows the parser to continue. A typical local correction would be to replace a comma with a semicolon, deletion of an extraneous semicolon, or insertion of a missing semicolon. The choice of the local correction is left to the compiler designer. These replacements should be such that they do not lead to infinite loops, as would be the case, for example, if insertion in input takes place ahead of the current input symbol. This type of replacement can correct any input string and has been used in several error-repairing compilers. The method was first used with top-down parsing. Its major drawback is the difficulty it has in coping with situations in which the actual error has occurred before the detection point.

- **Error productions**: If there is a good idea of the common errors that might be encountered, the grammar can be augmented for the language at hand with productions that generate the erroneous constructs. The grammar augmented by these error productions can be used to construct a parser. Erroneous productions include productions for common errors. A parser constructed from a grammar augmented by these error productions detects the anticipated errors, when an error production is used during parsing. The parser can then generate appropriate error diagnostics about the erroneous construct that has been recognised in the input.
- **Global correction**: A compiler must make as few changes as possible in processing an incorrect input string. There are algorithms for choosing the minimal sequence of changes to obtain a global least-cost correction. Given an incorrect input string x and grammar G, these algorithms will find a parse tree for the related string y, such that the number of insertions, deletions and changes of tokens required to transform x into y is as small as possible. Unfortunately, these methods are in general too costly to implement in terms of time and space, so these techniques are currently only of theoretical interest.
  The notion of least-cost correction does provide a yardstick for evaluating error recovery techniques, and it has been used for finding optimal replacement strings for phrase level recovery.

9.4.1 Error Recovery in Predictive LL Parser

LL error recovery refers to the stack of a table-driven parser as it makes explicit the terminals and non-terminals that the parser hopes to match with the remainder of the input. An error is detected during predictive parsing when the terminal on top of the stack does not match the next input symbol, or when non-terminal X is on top of the stack and a is the next input symbol, and parsing table entry $M[X, a]$ is empty.

Panic mode error recovery in LL parser: Panic mode error recovery is based on the idea of skipping symbols on the input until a token from a selected set of synchronizing tokens appears. It can be implemented using the synchronization set(s) as follows:

1. Pop items off the parse stack until a synchronization token is at the top of the stack.
2. Read the input symbols until the current look-ahead symbol matches the symbol at the top of the stack or until the end of the input is reached.
3. If the end of the input is reached, then error recovery has failed; otherwise, the error has been handled.

The effectiveness of panic mode error recovery depends on the choice of synchronizing set(s). The sets should be chosen such that the parser recovers quickly from errors that are likely to occur in practice and so that a minimal amount of input is ignored. Some heuristics for constructing synchronization set(s) are as follows:

1. Initially, place all symbols in FOLLOW(A) into the synchronization set for non-terminal A. Then, skip tokens until an element of FOLLOW(A) is seen in the input and pop A from the stack. By doing this, anything that could be generated from A is removed, and it is likely that parsing can continue successfully.
2. There is a hierarchical structure on constructs in a language. For example, expressions appear within statements, which appear within blocks, etc. Symbols that begin in the higher-level constructs can be added to the synchronization set of a lower-level construct. For example, keywords that begin statements can be added to the synchronization sets for the non-terminals that generate expressions.
3. Add the symbols in FIRST(A) to the synchronization set for non-terminal A. Then, it may be possible to resume parsing of A if a symbol in FIRST(A) appears in the input.
4. If a non-terminal can generate the empty string, then the production(s) deriving λ can be used as a default. That is, ε-productions are used as default for that non-terminal. This technique postpones some error detection without causing an error to be missed, by reducing the number of non-terminals that have to be considered during error recovery.
5. If a terminal on top of the stack cannot be matched to the input symbol, a simple idea is to pop the terminal, issue an informative message saying that the terminal was inserted into the input stream, and continue parsing. In effect, this approach takes the synchronization set of a token to consist of all other tokens.

Example 9.1 Panic mode error recovery

Consider the grammar given below

E→T E'
E'→+ T E' | ε
T→F T'
T'→* F T' | ε
F→(E) | id

FIRST and FOLLOW for the above grammar:

	FIRST	FOLLOIW
E	{(, id }	{), $}
E'	{+, ε}	{),$}
T	{(, id}	{+,), $}
T'	{* , ε }	{+,), $}
F	{(, id}	{*, +,), $}

The LL parsing table is shown in Table 9.1.

Table 9.1 LL parsing table

	+	*	(	id	)	$
E			E→TE'	E→TE'		
E'	E'→+TE'				E'→ ε	E'→ ε
T			T →FT'	T →FT'		
T'	T'→ε	T'→*FT'			T'→ε	T'→ε
F			F →(E)	F→id		

Table 9.2 Modified LL parsing table

	+	*	(	id	)	$
E			E→TE'	E→TE'	synch	synch
E'	E'→+TE'				E'→ ε	E'→ ε
T	Synch		T →FT'	T →FT'	synch	synch
T'	T'→ε	T'→*FT'			T'→ε	T'→ε
F			F →(E)	F→id		

FOLLOW of E contains) and $. Hence, synch is added to the {), $} entries of non-terminal E. FOLLOW(T) = {+,), $}, adding synch entries to terminals +,), $ for non-terminal T. Similarly, after adding the synchronizing tokens, the modified table is as is shown in Table 9.2. Note that the entries are to be added to the symbols in FIRST also. However, if the entries exist, then the synch entry is not made.

Error recovery after modifying the parse table is as follows:

- If the parsing table entry is blank, then the input symbol *a* is skipped.
- If the entry is synch, then the non-terminal on top of the stack is popped in an attempt to resume parsing.
- If a token on top of the stack does not match the input symbol, then we pop the token from the stack.

Error recovery for the input string "id *+ id" is shown in Table 9.3. The input string is entered in reverse in the input buffer.

Table 9.3 Error recovery in LL parsing using panic mode error recovery

Input	Stack	Action
$id +*id	E$	M[E,id] = E→TE'
$id +*id	TE'$	M[T,id] = T→FT'
$id +*id	FT'E'$	M[F,id] = F→id
$id +*id	id T'E'$	Pop 'id' from stack and move the input pointer further
$id +*	T'E'$	M[T,*] = T→*FT'
$id +*	*FT' E'$	Pop '*' from stack and move the input pointer further
$id +	FT' E'$	M[F,+] = synch Pop F
$id +	T' E'$	M[T',+] = T'→ε
$id +	E'$	M[E',+] = E'→+TE'
$id +	+TE'$	Pop '+' from stack and move the input pointer further
$id	TE'$	M[T,id] = T→ FT'

(Cont'd)

Table 9.3 (Continued)

Input	Stack	Action
$id	FT' E'$	M[F,id] = F→id
$id	id T' E'$	Pop 'id' from stack and move the input pointer further
$	T' E'$	M[T',$] = T'→ε
$	E'$	M[E',$] = E'→ε
$	$	Accept

Example 9.2 Panic mode error recovery

Consider the grammar

S→ AbS | e |ε

A→ a | cAd

FOLLOW(S) = {$}

FOLLOW(A)={b,d}

Table 9.4 LL parsing table

	a	b	c	d	e	$
S	S→ AbS	synch	S→ AbS	synch	S→ e	S→ ε
A	A→a	synch	A→cAd	synch	synch	synch

The parsing table is shown in Table 9.4. Let us consider an input string "aab". The string is not valid for the given grammar. Error recovery according to panic mode error recovery is shown in Table 9.5.

Table 9.5 Error recovery in LL parsing using panic mode error recovery

Input	Stack	Action
$baa	S$	M[S,a] = S→ AbS
$baa	AbS$	M[A,a] = A→a
$baa	abS$	Pop 'a' from stack and move the input pointer further
$ba	bS$	The token on top of the stack does not match the input symbol. Pop the token 'b' from the stack. ***Error Recovery Applied***
$ba	S$	M[S,a] = S→ AbS
$ba	AbS$	M[A,a] = A→a
$ba	abS$	Pop 'a' from stack and move the input pointer further
$b	bS$	Pop 'b' from stack and move the input pointer further
$	S$	M[S, $] = S→ ε
$	$	Accept

Phrase-level error recovery in LL parser: Phrase-level error recovery can be implemented by filling in the blank entries in the LL parsing table with error routines that are called when that entry in the table is accessed. These routines could change, insert or delete symbols on the input and issue appropriate warning messages. The routines could also manipulate the stack by popping or inserting symbols from/ to the stack. Such stack manipulation should ensure that there is no possibility of an infinite loop and that the corresponding derivation really represents a string in the language of the grammar. Checking that any recovery action eventually results in an input symbol being consumed is a good way to protect against such loops.

Example 9.3 Phrase level error recovery in LL parsing

Let us consider the grammar below and the LL(1) parsing table for the grammar, as shown in Table 9.6.

E→T E'
E'→+ T E' | ε
T→F T'
T'→* F T' | ε
F→ id

Table 9.6 LL parsing table

	id	+	*	$
E	$E \rightarrow TE_1$			
T	$T \rightarrow FT_1$			
F	$F \rightarrow id$			
E_1		$E_1 \rightarrow +TE_1$		$E_1 \rightarrow \varepsilon$
T_1		$T_1 \rightarrow \varepsilon$	$T_1 \rightarrow *FT_1$	$T_1 \rightarrow \varepsilon$

The modified table with error routines is shown in Table 9.7.

Table 9.7 Modified LL parsing table for phrase level error recovery

	id	+	*	$
E	$E \rightarrow TE_1$	e_1	e_1	e_1
T	$T \rightarrow FT_1$	e_1	e_1	e_1
F	$F \rightarrow id$	e_1	e_1	e_1
E_1	$E_1 \rightarrow \varepsilon$	$E_1 \rightarrow +TE_1$	$E_1 \rightarrow \varepsilon$	$E_1 \rightarrow \varepsilon$
T_1	$T_1 \rightarrow \varepsilon$	$T_1 \rightarrow \varepsilon$	$T_1 \rightarrow *FT_1$	$T_1 \rightarrow \varepsilon$
id	Pop			
+		Pop		
*			Pop	
$	e_2	e_2	e_2	Accept

Error routines e_1 and e_2 are given below. e_1 occurs when id is expected but there is an operator, and e_2 occurs when there are unwanted or erroneous characters in the input.

```
e1 {
Push an imaginary id into the stack
Issue error diagnostic missing id
}

e2{
Remove all remaining symbols from the input
}
```

Some error entries are blank. Appropriate error recovery routines may be added.

Let us trace the behaviour of the parser if the input string is "id id+ id". The input string is written in reverse order in the input buffer, as in Table 9.8.

Table 9.8 Error recovery in LL parsing using phrase level error recovery

Input	Stack	Action
\$ id +id id	E\$	M[E,id] = E → TE'
\$ id +id id	TE'\$	M[T,id] = T → FT'
\$ id +id id	FT'E'\$	M[F,id] = F → id
\$ id +id	id T'E'\$	Match of 'id'. Delete 'id' from buffer and pop 'id' from the stack
\$ id + id	T'E'\$	M[T',id] = T_1→ ε
\$ id + id	E'\$	M[E',id] = E'→ε
\$ id + id	\$	M[\$,id] = e_2
\$	\$	Accept

Example 9.4 Phrase level error recovery in LL parser

Let us consider the grammar below and the LL parsing table for the grammar (Table 9.9).

E→T E'
E'→+ T E' | ε
T→F T'
T'→* F T' | ε
F→(E) | id

Table 9.9 LL parsing table

	+	*	(	id	)	\$
E			E→TE'	E→TE'		
E'	E'→+TE'					E'→ ε
T			T →FT'	T →FT'		
T'	T'→ε	T'→*FT'				T'→ε
F			F →(E)	F→id		

The table with error entries that point to some error routine is shown in Table 9.10.

Table 9.10 LL parsing table with error routines

	+	*	(	id	)	\$
E	e_1	e_1	E→TE'	E→TE'	e_2	e_1
E'	E'→+TE'	e_1	E'→ ε	E'→ ε	E'→ ε	E'→ ε

(Cont'd)

Table 9.10 (Continued)

	+	*	(	id	)	$
T	e_1	e_1	T →FT'	T →FT'	e_2	e_1
T'	T'→ε	T'→*FT'	T'→ε	T'→ε	T'→ε	T'→ε
F	e_1	e_1	F →(E)	F→id	e_2	e_1
id				Pop		
+	Pop					
*		Pop				
(			Pop			
)					Pop	
$	e_3	e_3	e_3	e_3	e_3	Accept

e_1{
Push an imaginary id in the input string;
Issue diagnostic error message "missing operand"
}

e_2{
Remove the right parenthesis from the input;
Issue diagnostic error message "unbalanced right parenthesis"
}

e_3{
Remove all the remaining symbols from the input
Issue diagnostic error message "missing operator"
}

The error recovery for input string "id id + id" is shown in Table 9.11. The input string is written in reverse in the input buffer. Error recovery for input string "id + id(" is shown in Table 9.12.

Table 9.11 Phrase level error recovery for input string "id id + id"

Input	Stack	Action
$ id +id id	E$	M[E,id] = E →TE'
$ id +id id	TE'$	M[T,id] = T→FT'
$ id +id id	FT'E'$	M[F,id] = F→id'
$ id +id id	id T'E'$	Since match of 'id' in buffer and stack, pop 'id' from buffer
$ id +id	T'E'$	M[T,id] = T→ ε

(Cont'd)

Table 9.11 (Continued)

Input	Stack	Action
$ id +id	E'$	Table [E,id] = e_3
$	$	Accept

Table 9.12 Phrase level error recovery for input string "id + id"

Input	Stack	Action
$(id +id	E$	M[E,id] = E→TE'
$(id +id	TE'$	M[T,id] = T→FT'
$(id +id	FT'E'$	M[F,id] = F→id'
$(id +id	id T'E'$	Match of 'id'. Delete 'id' from buffer and pop 'id' from stack
$(id +	TE'$	M[T',+] = T'→ ε
$(id +	E'$	M[E,+] = E→+TE'
$(id +	+T'E'$	Match of '+'. Delete '+' from buffer and pop '+' from stack
$ (id	T'E'$	M[T',id] = T→ FT'
$ (id	FT'E'$	M[F,id] = F→id'
$ (id	id T'E'$	Match of 'id'. Delete 'id' from buffer and pop 'id' from stack
$ (	T'E'$	M[T',(] = T'→ ε
$ (	E'$	M[E,(] = E'→ε
$ (	$	M[$,(] = Call e_3
$	$	Accept

9.4.2 Errors in Shift-Reduce Parsers (LR Parser)

An LR parser will detect an error when it consults the parsing action table and finds a blank or error entry. Errors are not detected by consulting the *goto* table. An LR parser will detect an error as soon as there is no valid continuation for the portion of the input scanned thus far. A canonical LR parser will not make even a single reduction before announcing the error. SLR and LALR parsers may make several reductions before detecting an error, but they will never shift an erroneous input symbol onto the stack.

Panic mode error recovery in LR parser: This can be implemented as follows:

1. Scan down the stack until a state s with a goto on a particular non-terminal A is found.
2. Zero or more input symbols are then discarded until a symbol *a* is found that can legitimately follow A.
3. Stack the non-terminal A and the state GOTO(s, A) and resume normal parsing.
4. A situation might exist where there is more than one choice for the non-terminal A. Normally, these non-terminals would be representing major program pieces, for example, an expression, a statement or a block. If A is the non-terminal statement, *a* might be ; or }, which marks the end of a statement sequence. This method of error recovery attempts to eliminate the phrase containing the syntactic error.

5. The parser determines that a string derivable from A contains an error. Part of that string has already been processed, and the result of this processing is a sequence of states on top of the stack. The remainder of the string is still in the input, and the parser attempts to skip over the remainder of this string by looking for a symbol on the input that can legitimately follow A. By removing states from the stack, skipping over the input, and pushing GOTO(s, A) on the stack, the parser pretends that it has found an instance of A and resumes normal parsing.

Phrase level recovery in LR parser: Phrase level recovery is implemented by examining each error entry in the LR action table and deciding, on the basis of language usage, the most likely programmer error that would give rise to that error. An appropriate recovery procedure is constructed and executed when an error occurs. In designing specific error-handling routines for an LR parser, each blank entry is filled by an action field with a pointer to an error routine that will take the appropriate action when the error occurs. The actions may include insertion or deletion of symbols from the stack or the input or both, or alteration and transposition of input symbols. A safe strategy will assure that at least one input symbol will be removed or shifted eventually, or that the stack will eventually shrink if the end of the input has been reached. Popping a stack state that covers a non-terminal should be avoided because this modification eliminates from the stack a construct that has already been successfully parsed.

Example 9.5 Phrase level recovery in LR parser

Consider the expression grammar E → E + E | E * E | (E) | id. The LR parsing table without conflicts for the grammar is given in Table 9.13 and the table with error entries in Table 9.14. If any non-terminal has reduce entries, then that reduce entry is extended as default. This enables postponement of error detection until one or more reductions are made, but the error will still be caught before any shift takes place. Otherwise, error routines are pointed for each error.

Table 9.13 LR parsing table

	id	+	*	$	E
I0	S2				1
I1		S3	S4	Accept	
I2		R3	R3	R3	
I3	S2				5
I4	S2				6
I5		R1	S4	R1	
I6		R2	R2	R2	

Table 9.14 LR parsing table with error routines

	id	+	*	$	E
I0	S2	e_1	e_1	e_1	1
I1	e_2	S3	S4	Accept	

(Cont'd)

Table 9.14 (Continued)

	id	+	*	$	E
I2	R3	R3	R3	R3	
I3	S2	e_1	e_1	e_1	5
I4	S2	e_1	e_1	e_1	6
I5	R1	R1	S4	R1	
I6	R2	R2	R2	R2	

The error routines that are called on occurrence of the errors are

e_1{
Push an imaginary id onto the stack and cover it with state 2
}
e_2{
Push + onto stack and cover it with state 3
}

Let us consider an input string "id+*id" and trace the behaviour of the parser with erroneous input. Error occurs when table entry M[3,*] is accessed, which points to an error routine. The error routine e_1 pushes id on the stack and covers it with state 2. There was an error of missing id in the input string, which was recovered by error routine e_1. A message can be displayed stating that there is a missing id. Similarly, an error occurs if table entry M[1,id] is accessed. This error occurs because we are expecting an operator but id appears. Hence, the error recovery routine can push the + operator and cover it with state 3 or push the * operator and cover with state 4. The recovery is given in Table 9.15.

Table 9.15 Error recovery in LR parsing using phrase level error recovery

Stack	Input	Action
$0	id +*id$	M[0,id] = S2
$0id2	+*id$	M[2,+] = S3
$0 id2+3	*id$	M[3,*] = e_1
$0 id2+3id2	*id$	M[2,*] = R3
$0E1	*id$	M[1,*] = S4
$0E1*4	id$	M[4,id] = S2
$0E1*4id2	$	M[2,$] = R3
$0E1	$	Accept

Example 9.6 Phrase level error recovery in LR parsing

Consider the grammar given below and write the error routines to perform phrase level error recovery in LR parsing.

S→AxB | Bc
A→ yA | z
B→ xB | ε

The SLR parsing table for the given grammar is given in Table 9.16 and the modified parsing table showing only action entries in Table 9.17.

Table 9.16 SLR parsing table

State	Action					goto		
	x	y	z	c	$	S	A	B
0	S6	S4	S5	R6	R6	1	2	3
1					Accept			
2	S7							
3				S8				
4	S6	S4	S5	R6	S6		9	
5	R4							
6	S6			R6	R6			10
7	S6			R6	R6			11
8					R2			
9	R3							
10				R5	R5			
11					R1			

The error routines are as given below

e_1{
Delete current character from input
}
e_2{
Push x onto stack and cover it with state 7
}
e_3{
Push c onto stack and cover it with state 8
}

Table 9.17 Modified SLR parsing table (showing only action entries)

State	Action				
	x	y	z	c	$
0	S6	S4	S5	R6	R6
1	e_1	e_1	e_1	e_1	Accept

(Cont'd)

Table 9.17 (Continued)

State	Action				
	x	y	z	c	$
2	S7	e_2	e_2	e_2	e_2
3	e_3	e_3	e_3	S8	e_3
4	S6	S4	S5	R6	S6
5	R4	R4	R4	R4	R4
6	S6	R6	R6	R6	R6
7	S6	R6	R6	R6	R6
8	R2	R2	R2	R2	R2
9	R3	R3	R3	R3	R3
10	R5	R5	R5	R5	R5
11	R1	R1	R1	R1	R1

Example 9.7 Phrase level error recovery in LR parsing

Consider the grammar given below and write the error routines to perform phrase level error recovery in LR parsing.

E→ E+E | E*E | (E) | id

The SLR table is given in Table 9.18 and the modified SLR table for error detection and recovery in Table 9.19. The error routines are as follows:

e_1{
Push an imaginary id onto the stack and cover it with state 3
Issue diagnostics "missing operands"
}

This routine called from states 0, 2, 4 and 5, all of which expect the beginning of an operand, either an id or left parenthesis. Instead, an operator + or * or the end of the input is found.

e_2{
Remove the right parenthesis from the input.
Issue diagnostics "unbalanced parenthesis right parenthesis"
}

This routine is called from states 0, 1, 2, 4, 5 on finding the right parenthesis ")".

e_3{
Push + onto the stack and cover it with state 4
Issue diagnostics "missing operator"
}

This routine is called from states 1 or 6 when expecting an operator and an id or right parenthesis is found.

e_4{
Push right parenthesis onto the stack and cover it with state 9
Issue diagnostics "missing right parenthesis"
}

This routine is called from state 6 when the end of the input is found. State 6 expects an operator or right parenthesis.

Table 9.18 SLR parsing table

State	Action						goto
	id	+	*	(	)	$	E
0	S3			S2			1
1		S4	S5			Accept	
2	S3			S2			6
3		R4	R4		R4	R4	
4	S3			S2			7
5	S3			S2			8
6		S4	S5		S9		
7		R1	S5		R1	R1	
8		R2	R2		R2	R2	
9		R3	R3		R3	R3	

Table 9.19 Modified SLR parsing table

State	Action						goto
	id	+	*	(	)	$	E
0	S3	e_1	e_1	S2	e_2	e_1	1
1	e_3	S4	S5	e_3	e2	Accept	
2	S3	e_1	e_1	S2	e_2	e_1	6
3	R4	R4	R4	R4	R4	R4	
4	S3	e_1	e_1	S2	e_2	e_1	7
5	S3	e_1	e_1	S2	e_2	e_1	8
6	e_3	S4	S5	e_3	S9	e_4	
7	R1	R1	S5	R1	R1	R1	
8	R2	R2	R2	R2	R2	R2	
9	R3	R3	R3	R3	R3	R3	

The behaviour of the parser for input string "(id +id" is given in Table 9.20.

Table 9.20 Error recovery in LR parsing using phrase level error recovery

Stack	Input	Action
$0	(id+id$	M[0,( ] = S2
$0(2	id+id $	M[2,id] = S3
$0(2id3	+id$	M[3,+] = R4
$0 (2E6	+id$	M[6,+] = S4
$0(2E6+4	id$	M[4,id] = S3
$0(2E6+4id3	$	M[3,$] = R4
$0(2E6+4E7	$	M[7,$] = R3
$0(2E6	$	M[6,$] = e4
$0(2E6)9	$	M[9,$] = R3
$0E1	$	Accept

9.5 Error Handling in Semantic Analysis Phase

Semantic errors may be generated at compile time or at run-time. The programs may be syntactically correct but may have logical errors. Semantic errors may exist due to various sources of errors, some examples of which are given below:

- Type mismatch: Errors that have incompatible variable types, such as an operator applied to an incompatible operand(s). These types of errors can be detected by the compiler.
- Infinite loop: A loop that repeats indefinitely. For example, a loop variable that controls the execution of the loop always has the same value or is true for the loop to run every time.
- Array index is accessed that does not exist. It is a dynamic semantic error that can be detected at run-time, and is called Array Index Bounds Error.
- Misuse of reserved identifier
- Multiple declarations of variable in a scope
- Mismatch in actual and formal parameters
- Dangling else
- Use of a un-initialised variable
- Undeclared names: Recovery from an undeclared name is rather straightforward. The first time the undeclared name is encountered, an entry can be made in the symbol table for that name with an attribute that is appropriate to the current context. For example, if missing declaration error of *x* is encountered, then the error routine enters the appropriate attribute for *x*'s symbol table, depending on the current context of *x*. A flag is then set in the *x* symbol table record to indicate that an attribute has been added, and to recover from an error or not in response to the declaration of *x*.
- Code inside a loop that should have been placed outside the loop

Another type of error is the logical error. These errors may be due to use of wrong variable, wrong operation or operations in a different order. The code may be written completely differently from what was intended. For example, if the expression is mistakenly written as a=b*c, but the programmer intended to perform an addition operation. Such type of errors cannot be determined by the compiler. They need to be recognised and handled by programmer during testing.

SUMMARY

- Errors may be broadly classified as compile-time and run-time errors.
- Compile-time errors are generated when the code does not comply with the syntactic and semantic rules of the language.
- A run-time error occurs during the execution of a program and is usually due to adverse system parameters or invalid input data.
- Errors where the token stream violates the structure rules (syntax) of the language are determined by the syntax analysis phase.
- During semantic analysis, the compiler tries to detect constructs that have the right syntactic structure but which are of no meaning to the operation involved.
- Error recovery strategies include panic mode error recovery, phrase level error recovery, production rules and global corrections.
- The lexical analyser detects an error when it discovers that an input's prefix does not fit the specification of any token class.

EXERCISES

Review Questions

Fill in the blanks with appropriate answers:

1. Insufficient memory to run an application is a __________ error.
2. Referencing an invalid index in an array is a __________ error.
3. In __________ error recovery, local correction is applied on the remaining input, which replaces the remaining input with some string that allows the parser to continue.
4. Misspelling of identifiers or keywords can be detected in __________ phase of compilation.
5. In __________ error recovery, successive characters are deleted from the remaining input until a well-formed token is found.
6. Use of a variable before it is initialised can be detected in __________ phase of compilation.
7. __________ property used in parsers helps to detect an error as soon as the prefix of the input cannot be completed to form a string of the language.
8. If there is an error in the LL parser at table entry (T, +), phrase level error recovery will perform error recovery by __________.
9. Errors that have incompatible variable types are detected in __________ phase of compilation.

Answers: 1. Run-time 2. Run-time 3. Phrase level 4. Lexical analysis 5. Panic mode 6. Syntax analysis 7. Viable prefix 8. Pushing imaginary id onto stack and issue error message – missing id 9. Semantic analyser

State whether true or false:

1. Errors where the token stream violates the structure rules (syntax) of the language are determined by the syntax analysis phase.

2. Semantic errors may be generated only at compile time.
3. Multiple declarations of variables in a scope are detected by the semantic analyser.
4. Logical errors can be detected by the lexical anlayser.

Answers: 1. True 2. False 3. True 4. False

Practice Questions

1. Construct the LL parsing table for the given grammar and show the modified parsing table with error handing using phrase level error recovery.

   S→S + P| P
   P→P * Q | Q
   Q→Q–Z | Z
   Z→a | b

2. Apply phrase level error recovery for LL parsing using Table 9.7 for input string "id +* id id".
3. Perform phrase level error recovery for LR parser using Table 9.14 for input strings "id +* id)" and "id+)".
4. Find the errors in the following program and state the phase when the error can be discovered. Suggest an error recovery mechanism.

```
int a;
int funcNew( )
{
   int b;
   printf(b)
}
print(a1);
int funcNew1( )
{
int c;
char p;
a=c+p;
}
```

5. Suggest the type of error in the following code and how it can be detected.

```
int main()
{
  int i = 0;
  int n= 12;
while(i<n)
    {
        printf("loop ");
    }
}
```

Programming Questions

1. Maintain a list of legitimate tokens in the symbol table that corresponds to the key words of the language. Consider a source program as input and write a program that can detect lexical errors by applying the following error transformations:
   (a) Deleting an extraneous character (b) Inserting a missing character
   (c) Replacing an incorrect character with the correct character
   (d) Transposing two adjacent characters
   Use the token list created.
2. Consider an input program and detect the errors that can be identified at each phase of compilation.
3. Repeat program 2, with error recovery mechanism incorporated in the code.
4. Implement error recovery in LL parsing / LR parsing.

10 Compiler Construction Tools

Objectives

- To introduce various open source tools
- To introduce JFLAP
- To discuss Lex and Yacc
- To discuss JFlex and CUP
- To introduce the ANTLR tool

10.1 Introduction to Open Source Compiler Construction Tools

Writing a compiler by hand is a complex and time-consuming process. Writing the code for the entire compiler or for any phase of the compiler is a difficult task. Compiler construction tools can be used to design various phases of the compiler.

The most commonly used tools are the scanner and parser generators. The **scanner generator** generates lexical analysers from a regular expression description of the tokens of a language. The **parser generator** takes the grammatical description of a programming language and produces a syntax analyser. Syntax-directed translation engines produce a collection of routines that traverse a parse tree and generate the intermediate code. **Automatic code generators** take a collection of rules that define the translation of each operation of the intermediate language into the machine language for a target machine. A data flow analysis engine gathers information, that is, the values transmitted from one part of a program to each of the other parts – data flow analysis being a key part of code optimisation. Compiler construction toolkits provide an integrated set of routines for the construction of the phases of a compiler. The various tools discussed in this chapter are Lex/Flex, Yacc/Bison, JFlex, CUP, ANTLR and JFLAP. All the tools discussed in this chapter are open source and freeware; the source code is available for modification.

10.2 Java Formal Languages and Automata Package (JFLAP)

Java Formal Languages and Automata Package (JFLAP) is interactive software comprising graphical tools written in Java for experimenting with topics of formal languages and automata theory. JFLAP can be used for better understanding of topics like non-deterministic finite automata, non-deterministic pushdown automata, multi-tape Turing machines, types of grammars, parsing, etc. In addition, it allows us to create and simulate structures, such as programming a finite state machine, and experiment with proofs, such as converting a non-deterministic finite automaton (NFA) to a deterministic finite automaton (DFA). Figure 10.1 shows the start screen of JFLAP 7.0, displaying the various options available. A new redesigned version of JFLAP, known as JFLAP 8.0 BETA, is now available. Other details and tutorials can be accessed at http://www.jflap.org/

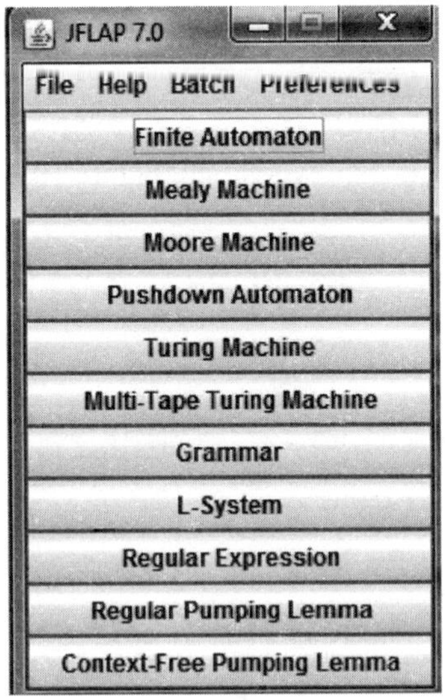

Figure 10.1 Start screen of JFLAP

Example 10.1: Conversion of regular expression to NFA using JFLAP

To convert a regular expression a*(a+b) to NFA, the steps to be followed in JFLAP are given below:

1. In the Start screen, select Regular Expression.
2. Enter the regular expression and select the Convert RE to NFA tab. Initially, the NFA with transition without breaking the RE is displayed, as shown in Fig. 10.2.

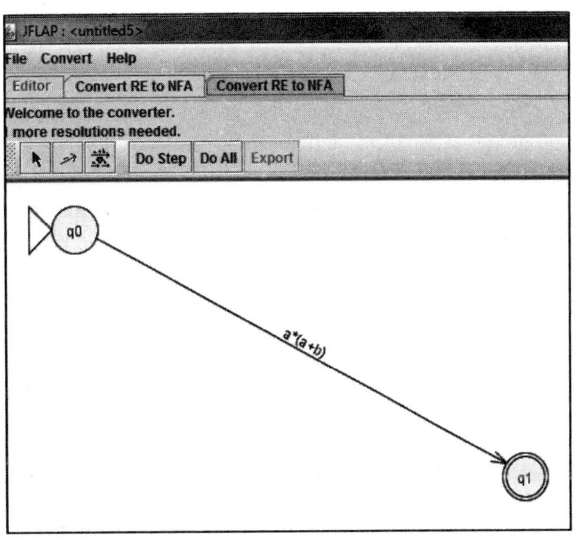

Figure 10.2 Select the Convert RE to NFA tab.

3. Now, to further break the sub-expression and enable conversion, click the (D)e-expressionify Transition button (third from left, to the immediate left of the Do Step button). Then, click

on the transition from 'q0' to 'q1'. It subdivides and adds the transition from q2→ q3 and q4→q5.

4. Add ε productions. In JFLAP, these are represented by the 'λ' transition.

Similarly, other transitions are (d)e-expressionified. Figure 10.3 shows the NFA for RE a*(a+b).

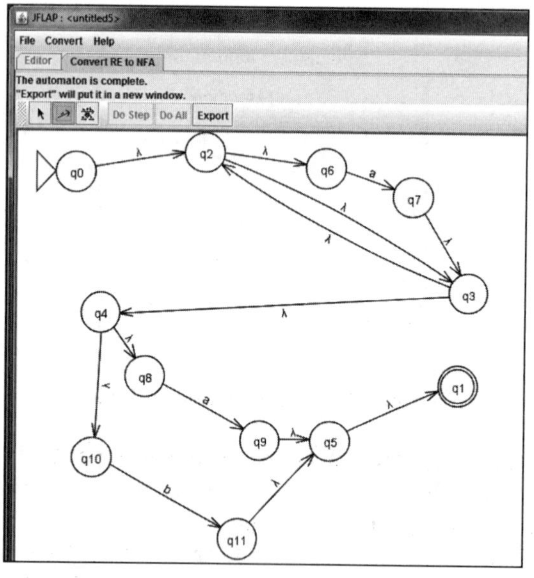

Figure 10.3 NFA for RE a*(a+b)

10.3 Scanner Generator: Lex

Lex is a tool that generates a lexical analyser for the C language; that is, it is a lexical analyser generator that helps in designing a lexical analyser for the C language. It produces a program which recognises regular expressions. These regular expressions are specified by the user in the source specifications given to Lex. The Lex written code recognises these expressions in an input stream and partitions it into strings matching the expressions. The Lex source file associates the regular expressions and the program fragments. As each expression appears in the input to the program written by Lex, the corresponding fragment is executed.

Lex can be used alone for simple transformations or for analysis and statistics gathering on a lexical level. Lex can also be used with a parser generator (like Yacc) to perform the lexical analysis phase. Lex generates a deterministic finite automaton from the regular expressions in the source. The automaton is interpreted, rather than compiled, in order to save space. The result is still a quick analyser. In particular, the time taken by a Lex program to recognise and partition an input stream is proportional to the length of the input. The number of Lex rules or the complexity of the rules is not important in determining speed, unless the rules which include forward context require a significant amount of rescanning. What does increase with the number and complexity of rules is the size of the finite automaton, and therefore, the size of the program generated by Lex.

Lex is not limited to sources that can be interpreted on the basis of a one-character look-ahead. For example, if there are two rules, one looking for ab and another for abcdefg, and the input stream is abcdefh, Lex will recognize ab and leave the input pointer just before cd. Such backup is more costly than the processing of simpler languages.

Lex accepts as input a '.l' file (lex source) that contains the user's expressions and actions specified and generates a program named yylex. The yylex program will recognise expressions in a stream and perform the specified actions for each expression as it is detected. Hence, yylex must be called from the main program, specified in the Lex file. To run a Lex program, execute the following steps on the console:

lex <pgm name>
cc lex.yy.c –ll
./a.out

'./a.out' runs the lexical analyser when required. The input can be specified on the console or given using the redirection operator as, ./a.out<input.txt. The schematic of Lex is shown in Fig. 10.4. The open source GNU version of Lex is called flex or the "fast lexical analyser".

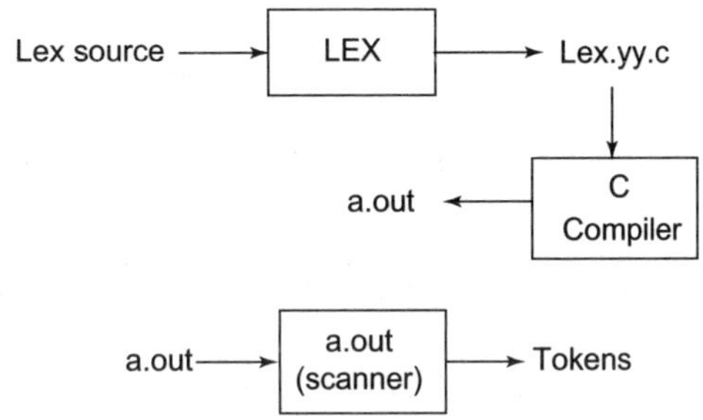

Figure 10.4 Overview of Lex

10.3.1 Lex Source File

The general format of the Lex source is given below:

{definitions}
%%
{rules}
%%
{user subroutines}

where the definitions and the user subroutines are often omitted. The second %% is optional, but the first is required to mark the beginning of the rules. The absolute minimum Lex program is thus

%%

(no definitions, no rules), which translates into a program that copies the input to the output unchanged.

Rules represent the user's control decisions. For example, consider an individual rule,

integer printf("found keyword INT"),

to search for the string integer in the input stream and print the message "found keyword INT" whenever it appears. In the example, the host procedural language is C and the C library function *printf* is used to print the string. The end of the expression is indicated by the first blank or tab character. If the action is merely a single C expression, it can be given on the right side of the line; if it is compound or occupies more than a line, it should be enclosed in braces.

Lex converts the rules into a program. Any source not intercepted by Lex is copied as it is into the generated program. These consist of three classes:

- Any line that is not part of a Lex rule or action and which begins with a blank or tab is copied into the Lex generated program. Such source input prior to the first %% delimiter will be external to any function in the code; if it appears immediately after the first %%, it appears in an appropriate place for declarations in the function written by Lex which contains the actions. So, the lines that begin with a blank or tab, and which contain a comment, are passed as it is to the generated program. This can be used to include comments in either the Lex source or the generated code. The comments should follow the host language convention.

- Anything included between lines and containing only %{ and %} is copied out as above. The delimiters are discarded.
- Anything after the third %% delimiter, regardless of the format, is copied out after the Lex output.

The definitions intended for Lex are provided before the first %% delimiter. Any line in this section not contained between %{ and %} is assumed to define Lex substitution strings. The format of such lines is *name* followed by *translation* and it causes the string given as a translation to be associated with the name. The name and the translation must be separated by at least one blank or tab, and the name must begin with a letter. The translation can then be called out by the {name} syntax in a rule.

Example 10.2 Lex code to delete all blanks or tabs at the end of lines from the input

```
%%
[ \t]+$    ;
```

The program contains a %% delimiter to mark the beginning of the rules, and only one rule. This rule contains a regular expression that matches one or more instances of the characters, blank or tab, just prior to the end of a line.

[ ] indicates the character class made of blank and tab; the + indicates 'one or more'. $ indicates 'end of line'. No action is specified; so the program generated by Lex (yylex) will ignore these characters. Everything else will be copied.

To change any remaining string of blanks or tabs to a single blank, add another rule:

```
%%
[ \t]+$ ;
[ \t]+  printf(" ");
```

The finite automaton generated for this source will scan for both rules at once, observing at the termination of the string of blanks or tabs whether or not there is a newline character.

10.3.2 Lex Regular Expressions

A regular expression specifies a set of strings to be matched. It contains characters that can be matched. In Table 10.1, the left column contains regular expressions and the right column contains actions.

Use of the Escape character: The operator characters are " \ [ ] ^ - ? . * + | ( ) $ / { } % <> and to use them as text characters, an escape character should be used. The quotation mark operator (") indicates that whatever is contained between a pair of quotes is to be taken as text characters.

For example, xyz"++" matches the string xyz++ when it appears. An operator character may also be turned into a text character by preceding it with \, as in xyz\+\+. Another use of the quotes is to insert a blank into an expression. Any blank character not contained within [ ] must be quoted. Several normal C escapes with \ are recognised: \n is newline, \t is tab and \b is backspace. To enter \ itself, use \\. As newline is illegal in an expression, \n must be used; it is not required to escape the tab and backspace. Every character but blank, tab, newline and the list above is always a text character.

Table 10.1 Regular expressions and corresponding actions

<table>
<tr><th>Regular expression</th><th>Action</th></tr>
<tr><td>\x</td><td>x, if x is a Lex operator</td></tr>
<tr><td>“xy”</td><td>xy, even if x or y is a Lex operator (except \)</td></tr>
<tr><td>[xy]</td><td>x or y</td></tr>
<tr><td>[x–z]</td><td>x, y, or z</td></tr>
<tr><td>[^x]</td><td>Any character but x</td></tr>
<tr><td>.</td><td>Any character but newline</td></tr>
<tr><td>^x</td><td>x at the beginning of a line</td></tr>
<tr><td><y>x</td><td>x when lex is in start condition y</td></tr>
<tr><td>x$</td><td>x at the end of a line</td></tr>
<tr><td>x?</td><td>Optional x</td></tr>
<tr><td>x*</td><td>0, 1, 2, ... instances of x</td></tr>
<tr><td>x+</td><td>1, 2, 3, ... instances of x</td></tr>
<tr><td>x{m,n}</td><td>m through n occurrences of x</td></tr>
<tr><td>xx|yy</td><td>Either xx or yy</td></tr>
<tr><td>x |</td><td>The action on x is the action for the next rule</td></tr>
<tr><td>(x)</td><td>x</td></tr>
<tr><td>x/y</td><td>x but only if followed by y</td></tr>
<tr><td>{xx}</td><td>The translation of xx from the definitions section</td></tr>
</table>

Classes of characters can be specified inside square brackets [ ]. For example, [abc] matches a single character, which may be a, b or c. Within square brackets, meanings of most operators are ignored. Only three special characters are allowed: \, – and ^. The – character indicates range. For example, [a–z0–9<>_], indicates the character class containing all the lowercase letters, digits, angle brackets and underscore. Ranges may be given in either order. Using “–” between any pair of characters which are not both uppercase letters, both lowercase letters or both digits is implementation dependent and will generate a warning message.

In character classes, the ^ operator must appear as the first character after the left bracket; it indicates that the resulting string is to be complemented. Thus, [^abc] matches all characters except a, b or c, including all special or control characters.

Repetitions and definitions: The {} operators specify either repetitions (if they enclose numbers) or definition expansion (if they enclose a name). For example, {digit} searches for a predefined string named digit and inserts it at that point in the expression. The definitions are given in the first part of the Lex input, before the rules. In contrast, a{1,5} searches for 1 to 5 occurrences of a.

When an expression is matched, Lex executes the corresponding action.

One of the simplest things that can be done is to ignore the input. Specifying a C null statement as an action causes this result. A frequent rule is

```
[ \t\n] ;
```

which causes the three spacing characters (blank, tab and newline) to be ignored.

Another way to avoid writing actions is the action character |, which indicates that the action for this rule is the action for the next rule.

Use of yytext and yyleng: In more complex actions, the user will often want to know the actual text that matched some expression, like [a–z]+. Lex leaves this text in an external character array named yytext. Thus, to print the name found, a rule like

```
[a-z]+   printf("%s", yytext);
```

will print the string in yytext.

The C function *printf* accepts a format argument and the data to be printed; in this case, the format is 'print string' (% indicating data conversion, and s indicating string type), and the data are the characters in yytext. So, this places only the matched string on the output. This action is so common that it may be written as ECHO.

```
[a-z]+   ECHO;
```

is the same as the above.

Lex also provides a count, yyleng, of the number of characters matched. For example, to count both the number of words and the number of characters in words in the input, the regular expression [a–zA–Z]+ {words++; chars += yyleng;} should be used. It counts the number of characters in the words recognised. The last character in the string matched can be accessed by yytext[yyleng – 1].

Use of yymore and yyless: Lex action may decide that a rule has not recognised the correct span of characters. Two routines are provided to aid in this situation. First, *yymore*() can be called to indicate that the next input expression recognised is to be tacked on to the end of this input. Normally, the next input string would overwrite the current entry in yytext. Second, *yyless*(n) may be called to indicate that not all the characters matched by the current successful expression are required right now. The argument n indicates the number of characters in yytext to be retained. Further characters previously matched are returned to the input.

Use of yywrap: *yywrap*(), is called whenever Lex reaches an end-of-file. If it returns 1, Lex continues with the normal wrap-up on end of input. Sometimes, it is necessary to take more input from a new source. In this case, the user should provide a *yywrap*() that arranges for new input and returns 0. This instructs Lex to continue processing. The default *yywrap*() always returns 1.

This routine is also a convenient place to print tables, summaries, etc. at the end of a program. It is not possible to write a normal rule which recognises end-of-file; the only access to this condition is through *yywrap*().

10.3.3 Ambiguous Source Rules

Lex can handle ambiguous specifications. When more than one expression matches the current input:

- The longest match is preferred.
- Among the rules that matched the same number of characters, the rule given first is preferred.

Thus, suppose the rules

```
integer  keyword action ...;
[a-z]+   identifier action ...;
```

are to be given in that order. If the input is integers, it is taken as an identifier, because [a–z]+ matches 8 characters while integer matches only 7. If the input is integer, both rules match 7 characters, and the keyword rule is selected because it was given first. Anything shorter (for example, int) will not match the expression integer, and so the identifier interpretation is used.

Lex normally partitions the input stream and does not search for all possible matches of each expression. This means that each character is accounted for once and only once. For example, suppose it is desired to count the occurrences of both 'she' and 'he' in an input text. Some Lex rules to do this might be

```
she s++;
he  h++;
\n  |
.   ;
```

where the last two rules ignore everything apart from 'he' and 'she'. Also '.' does not include newline. As 'she' includes 'he', Lex will normally not recognise the instances of 'he' included in 'she', as once it has passed a 'she', those characters are gone.

To override this 'he' action, REJECT can be used. It means 'go perform the next alternative'. It causes whatever rule was the second choice after the current rule to be executed. The position of the input pointer is adjusted accordingly. Suppose the user wants to count the included instances of 'he':

```
she {s++; REJECT;}
he  {h++; REJECT;}
\n  |
.   ;
```

After counting each expression, it is rejected; whenever appropriate, the other expression will then be counted.

In general, REJECT is useful whenever the purpose of Lex is not to partition the input stream but to detect all examples of some items in the input, and the instances of these items may overlap or include each other. Suppose a bigram table of the input is desired; normally the bigrams overlap, that is, the word 'the' is considered to contain both 'th' and 'he'. Assuming a two-dimensional array named bigram to be incremented, the appropriate source is

```
%%
[a-z][a-z] {
         bigram[yytext[0]][yytext[1]]++;
         REJECT;
         }
         .  ;
         \n ;
```

where REJECT is necessary to pick up a letter pair beginning at every character, rather than at every other character.

Example 10.3 Write a Lex code to count the words, lines, small letters, capital letters, digits and special characters in a text file

```
%{
#include<stdio.h>
int lines=0, words=0,s_letters=0,c_letters=0, num=0, spl_char=0,total=0;
%}
```

```
%%
\n { lines++; words++;}
[\t ' '] words++;
[A-Z] c_letters++;
[a-z] s_letters++;
[0-9] num++;
. spl_char++;
%%

main(void)
{
yyin= fopen("myfile.txt","r");
yylex();
total=s_letters+c_letters+num+spl_char;
printf(" This File contains ...");
printf("\n\t%d lines", lines);
printf("\n\t%d words",words);
printf("\n\t%d small letters", s_letters);
printf("\n\t%d capital letters",c_letters);
printf("\n\t%d digits", num);
printf("\n\t%d special characters",spl_char);
printf("\n\tIn total %d characters.\n",total);
}
 int yywrap()
{
return(1);
}
```

Example 10.4 Write a Lex specification to copy an input file while adding 3 to every positive number divisible by 7

```
%{
#include<stdio.h>
int k;
%}

%%

[0-9]+ {
          k = atoi(yytext);
          if (k%7 == 0)
               printf("%d", k+3);
          else
               printf("%d",k);
       }
main(void)
{
```

```
yylex();
}
 int yywrap()
{
return(1);
}
```

The rule [0–9]+ recognises strings of digits; atoi converts the digits to binary and stores the result in k. The operator % (remainder) is used to check whether k is divisible by 7; if it is, it is incremented by 3 as it is written out.

Example 10.5 Write a Lex code to display the histograms of the length of words

```
%{
#include<stdio.h>
int lengs[100];
%}
%%

[a-z]+   lengs[yyleng]++;
 .      |
\n      ;
%%

yywrap()
{
  int i;
  printf("Length  No. words\n");
  for(i=0; i<100; i++)
       if (lengs[i] > 0)
           printf("%d%d\n",i,lengs[i]);
       return(1);
}
```

This program accumulates the histogram, while producing no output. At the end of the input, it prints the table. The final statement return(1); indicates that Lex is to perform *yywrap*(). If *yywrap*() returns 0 (false), it implies that further input is available and the program is to continue reading and processing. To provide a *yywrap*() that never returns true causes an infinite loop.

Example 10.6 Write a Lex specification to eliminate comments from a C program

In a C program, comments will be associated only with '//' or '/*...*/'. So our aim is to detect the occurrences of these characters and ignore subsequent comments. The rules that used are given below:

- \/\/.* ; eliminates single-line comments, i.e., comments of the form ' //comment.. .. .. ;'.
- It simply looks on the '/' immediately followed by another '/' and ignores that line. The backslash (\) is used as an escape character. "." indicates any character and * indicates zero or more occurrences.
- \/*(.*\n)*.**\/ ; eliminates multiple comments, i.e., the code fragment lies within /*...*/

The Lex specification to perform the task is given below:

```
%{
#include<stdio.h>
%}
%%
\/\/.* ;
\/\*(.*\n)*.*\*\/ ;
%%
main()
{
yylex();
}
int yywrap()
{
return 1;
}
```

Example 10.7 Write a Lex specification to validate an e-mail id

```
%{
#include<stdio.h>
#include<stdlib.h>
int flag=0;
%}
%%
[a-z . 0-9]+@["gmail"| "yahoo" | "rediff" ]+ ".com"|".in" { flag=1; }
%%
int main()
{
yylex();
if(flag==1)
printf("Valid e-mail");
else
printf("In-valid e-mail ");
}
```

Example 10.8 Design a lexical analyser for C using Lex

The lexical analyser must recognise the following:

- Keywords: else, int, void, if, else, while, return, etc.
- Identifiers: An identifier is a sequence of letters and digits, starting with a letter.
- Integer: An integer number is a sequence of digits.

The underscore '_' counts as a letter. For each identifier, the lexer shall return the token IDENTIFIER, and for each integer number, it shall return the token CONSTANT.

```
%{
#include<stdio.h>
%}
```

```
OPERATOR [+\-*=/]
DIGIT [0-9]
LETTER [A-Za-z]
DOT [\.]
BRACE1 [<]
BRACE2 [>]

%%
#({LETTER})* {printf("\n Token is a Directive: %s",yytext);}
{BRACE1}({LETTER})*{DOT}({LETTER})*{BRACE2} {printf("\n Token is a
Header file: %s",yytext);}
'printf'|'while' {printf("\n Token is a Keyword: %s",yytext);}
\".*\" {printf("\n Token is a Printable statement: %s",yytext);}
void {printf("\n Token is a Null return type: %s",yytext);}
main {printf("\n Token is a main function: %s",yytext);}
int {printf("\n Token is a Datatype: %s",yytext);}
{OPERATOR} {printf("\n Token is an Operator: %s",yytext);}
{LETTER}({LETTER}|{DIGIT})* {printf("\n Token is an Identifier:
%s",yytext);}
({DIGIT})+ {printf("\n Token is a Digit: %s",yytext);}
[{|}|;|(|)|,|;|:] {printf("\n Token is a Puctuation Symbol: %s",yytext);}

%%
main()
{
        yylex();
}
```

Sample input (inputfile.txt):

```
#include<stdio.h>
void main()
{
int num;
num=num+1;
printf("%d",num);
while(num>1)
{
a=a+1;
}
}
```

Output:

Token is a Directive: #include
Token is a Header file: <stdio.h>
Token is a Null return type: void
Token is a main function: main
Token is a Puctuation Symbol: (

Token is a Puctuation Symbol:)
Token is a Puctuation Symbol: {
Token is a Datatype: int
Token is an Identifier: num
Token is a Puctuation Symbol: ;
Token is an Identifier: num
Token is an Operator: =
Token is an Identifier: num
Token is an Operator: +
Token is a Digit: 1
Token is a Puctuation Symbol: ;
Token is an Identifier: printf
Token is a Puctuation Symbol: (
Token is a Printable statement: "%d"
Token is a Puctuation Symbol: ,
Token is an Identifier: num
Token is a Puctuation Symbol:)
Token is a Puctuation Symbol: ;
Token is an Identifier: while
Token is a Puctuation Symbol: (
Token is an Identifier: num>
Token is a Digit: 1
Token is a Puctuation Symbol:)
Token is a Puctuation Symbol: {
Token is an Identifier: a
Token is an Operator: =
Token is an Identifier: a
Token is an Operator: +
Token is a Digit: 1
Token is a Puctuation Symbol: ;
Token is a Puctuation Symbol: }
Token is a Puctuation Symbol: }

Example 10.9 Write a Lex specification to recognise verbs and other constructs of a language by listing different verbs

```
%{
#include<stdio.h>
%}
%%
[\t ]+    /* ignore whitespace */ ;

is        |
am        |
are       |
were      |
was       |
```

```
be          |
being       |
been        |
do          |
does        |
did         |
will        |
would       |
should      |
can         |
could       |
has         |
have        |
had         |
go          { printf ("\"%s\" is a verb\n", yytext); }
[a-zA-Z]+{ printf ("\"%s\" is not a verb\n", yytext); }
.           |
\n          ECHO; /* which is the default anyway */
%%
main () {
yylex ();
}
```

Example 10.10 Write a Lex specification to accept: (i) a word list of verbs and nouns from the user; (ii) tokenise the input string to identify verbs or nouns; and (iii) make entries in the symbol table of the word and its type

The aim is to allow dynamic declaration of the parts of speech as the lexer is running, reading the words to declare from the input file. The declaration lines start with the name of a part of speech followed by the words to be declared. These lines, for example, declare four nouns and three verbs:

noun dog cat horse cow
verb chew eat lick

The table of words is a simple symbol table, a common structure in the Lex and Yacc applications. A C compiler, for example, stores the variable and structure names, labels, enumeration tags, and all other names used in the program in its symbol table. Each name is stored along with information describing the name. In a C compiler, the information is the type of symbol, declaration scope, variable type, etc. In our current example, the information is the part of speech.

Adding a symbol table changes the lexer quite substantially. Rather than adding separate patterns in the lexer for each word to match, there is a single pattern that matches any word and consults the symbol table to decide which part of speech is found. The names of the parts of speech (noun, verb, etc.) are now 'reserved words' as they introduce a declaration line. There is a separate Lex pattern for each reserved word. Symbol table maintenance routines are added. The following functions are created:

- *add_word*() inserts a new word into the symbol table
- *lookup_word*( ) looks up a word that is already present in the symbol table

A variable "state" is declared that keeps track of what is being done, whether words are being searched, or being declared. If words are being declared, the state remembers what kind of words are declared.

Whenever the name of a part of speech appears at the start of the line, set the state to declare that kind of word (VERB or NOUN in this example). Also, each time a "\n" is encountered, switch back to the normal lookup state.

enum is defined to record the types of individual words (VERB and NOUN in the example), and to declare a variable "state". To find the part of speech that appears at the start of the line, the caret sign '^' is used. It matches only at the beginning of an input line.

```
%{
enum {
        LOOKUP =0, /* default - looking rather than defining. */
        VERB,
        NOUN
     };
int state;
int add_word(int type, char *word);
int lookup_word(char *word);
%}

%%

\n    { state = LOOKUP; }   /* end of line, return to default state */
^verb { state = VERB; }
^noun { state = NOUN; }

[a-zA-Z]+ {
        if(state != LOOKUP) {
            /* define the current word */
            add_word(state, yytext);
          } else {
            switch(lookup_word(yytext)) {
            case VERB: printf("%s: verb\n", yytext); break;
            case NOUN: printf("%s: noun\n", yytext); break;
            default:
                  printf("%s: don't recognize\n", yytext);
                  break;
            }
        }
        }
.   /* ignore anything else */ ;

%%
main()
{
    yylex();
```

```
}

/* define a linked list of words and types */
struct word {
    char *word_name;
    int word_type;
    struct word *next;
};

struct word *word_list; /* first element in word list (Symbol Table) */
extern void *malloc() ;

int add_word(int type, char *word)
{
    struct word *wp;
    if(lookup_word(word) != LOOKUP) {
          printf("!!! warning: word %s already defined \n", word);
          return 0;
       }
    /* word not there, allocate a new entry and link it on the list */

    wp = (struct word *) malloc(sizeof(struct word));
    wp->next = word_list;

    /* have to copy the word itself as well */
    wp->word_name = (char *) malloc(strlen(word)+1);
    strcpy(wp->word_name, word);
    wp->word_type = type;
    word_list = wp;
    return 1;
}

int lookup_word(char *word)
{
    struct word *wp = word_list;
    /* search the list looking for the word */

    for(; wp; wp = wp->next) {
    if(strcmp(wp->word_name, word) == 0)

          return wp->word_type;
    }
    return LOOKUP;    /* not found */
}
```

10.4 Parser Generator: Yet Another Compiler-Compiler (Yacc)

Yet Another Compiler-Compiler (Yacc) is a parser generator. It is tool that imposes a structure on the input to a computer program, that is, to validate the syntax of a programming language. It is a Look Ahead Left-to-Right (LALR) parser generator, generating a parser, the part of a compiler that tries to make syntactic sense of the source code – specifically an LALR parser, based on an analytic grammar written in a notation similar to the Backus Normal Form (BNF).

Lex programs recognise only regular expressions; Yacc writes parsers that accept a large class of context-free grammars, but require a lower level analyser to recognise input tokens. Thus, a combination of Lex and Yacc is often used. When used as a preprocessor for a later parser generator, Lex is used to partition the input stream, and the parser generator assigns a structure to the resulting pieces.

The Yacc user prepares a specification for the input process; this includes rules describing the input structure, the code to be invoked when these rules are recognised, and a low-level routine to perform the basic input. The rules describing the syntax of the programming language are given as input to Yacc in a '.y' file. These rules are specified using CFG notation. Yacc produces y.tab.c as output, which is a C program describing *yyparse*(). Yacc generates a parser, and hence, needs the tokens from the lexical analyser. Yacc generates a function to control the input process. This function, called a parser, calls the user-supplied low-level input routine (the lexical analyser) to pick up the basic items (called tokens) from the input stream. These tokens are organised according to the input structure rules, called grammar rules; when one of these rules has been recognised, the user code supplied for this rule – an action – is invoked; actions have the ability to return values and make use of the values of other actions. The lexical analyser is generated using Lex. The header file generated by Yacc, called "*<programName>*.tab.h" is included in the input program to Lex having the '.l' extension. Here, *<programName>* is the name of the Yacc input file (file with .y extension). Figure 10.5 shows the flow of execution using the Yacc tool.

Lex writes is a program named *yylex*(), the name required by Yacc for its analyser, to use Lex with Yacc. Normally, the default main program on the Lex library calls this routine, but if Yacc is loaded, and its main program is used, Yacc will call *yylex*(). In this case, each Lex rule should end with

return(token);

where the appropriate token value is returned. An easy way to obtain access to Yacc's names for tokens is to compile the Lex output file as part of the Yacc output file by placing the line '# include "lex.yy.c"' in the last section of the Yacc input. The Yacc library (-ly) should be loaded before the Lex library, to obtain a main program which invokes the Yacc parser. Generation of the Lex and Yacc programs can be performed in either order.

For simplicity, it has been assumed that the file names are the same and the extensions are different. Different file names can be considered for Lex and Yacc. The GNU version of Yacc is called Bison. Flex, an automatic lexical analyser, is often used with Bison, to tokenise input data and provide Bison with tokens. In these examples, Flex and Bison have been used on the Ubuntu operating system for execution of the programs.

The steps to execute the Yacc code using Flex and Bison are as follows:

```
flex <pgm_name>.l
bison -d < pgm name>.y
gcc -c lex.yy.c <pgm name>.tab.c
gcc -o a.out lex.yy.o <pgm name>.tab.o -lfl
./a.out
```

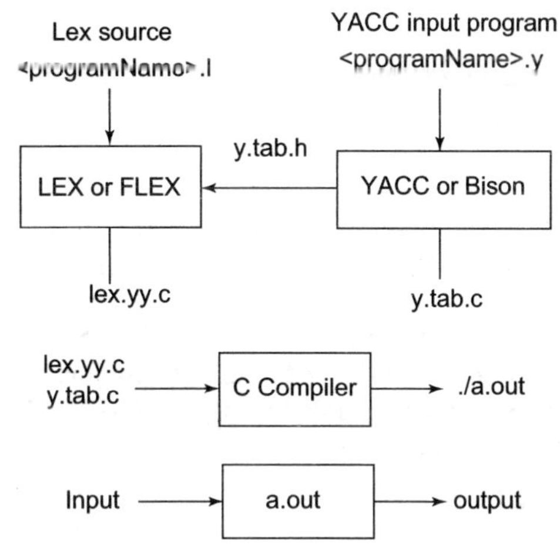

Figure 10.5 Generating a parser using Yacc/Bison and Lex/Flex

Specification file ('.y') format: Names refer to either tokens or non-terminal symbols. Yacc requires token names to be declared and it is desirable to include the lexical analyser as part of the specification file; it may be useful to include other programs as well. Thus, every specification file consists of three sections: the definitions, rules and programs. These sections are separated by a double percent '%%'. A full specification file has the following format:

```
definitions
%%
rules
%%
programs
```

The definition section contains information about tokens, data types and grammar rules. Any C code that must go directly into the output file is also included in the definition section. The rules section contains the grammar rules along with the actions to be performed if the rule is matched. These actions are specified as C code. The definition section may be empty. Moreover, if the programs section is omitted, the second %% mark may also be omitted; thus, the smallest legal Yacc specification is

```
%%
rules
```

Representing names: Names may be of arbitrary length and made up of letters, dots '.', underscores '_' and non-initial digits. Upper and lowercase letters are distinct. The names used in the body of a grammar rule may represent tokens or non-terminal symbols. Blanks, tabs and newlines are ignored. A literal consists of a character enclosed in single quotes. The escape character within literals is the backslash '\', and all the C escapes are recognised as follows:

'\n' newline
'\r' return
'\'' single quote

'\\' backslash
'\t' tab
'\b' backspace
'\f' form feed
'\xxx' "xxx" in octal

The null character ('\0' or 0) should never be used in grammar rules.

Names representing tokens must be declared; this is done by writing

%token name1 name2 . . .

in the declarations section. Every name not defined in the declarations section is assumed to represent a non-terminal symbol. Every non-terminal symbol must appear on the left side of at least one rule.

The tokens declared in the '.y' file must be accepted and returned by the lexical analyser.

Rules: A grammar rule has the form:

A : BODY ;

where, 'A' represents a non-terminal and BODY represents a sequence of zero or more names and literals. The colon and the semicolon are Yacc punctuations. It is possible that there are several grammar rules with the same left-hand side, so instead of writing the LHS non-terminal for every production, a vertical bar '|' can be used. In addition, the semicolon at the end of a rule can be dropped before a vertical bar. Thus, the grammar rules

```
A   :   B C D ;
A   :   E F ;
A   :   G ;
```

can be rewritten as

```
A   :   B C D
    |   E F
    |   G
    ;
```

If a non-terminal symbol matches the empty string; this is represented as

empty : ;

The non-terminal symbols are defined as rules. One non-terminal is called the start symbol. The parser is designed to recognise the start symbol. By default, the start symbol is taken to be the LHS of the first grammar rule in the rules section. It is possible to declare the start symbol explicitly in the declarations section using the *%start* keyword:

%start symbol

The end of the input to the parser is signalled by a special token, called the **end marker**. If the tokens up to, but not including, the end marker form a structure that matches the start symbol, the parser function returns to its caller after the end marker is seen; it accepts the input. If the end marker is seen in any other context, it is an error. It is the job of the user-supplied lexical analyser to return the end marker when appropriate. Usually, the end marker represents I/O status, such as 'end-of-file' or 'end-of-record'.

Actions for production rules: With each grammar rule, the user may associate the actions to be performed each time the rule is recognised in the input process. These actions may return values and may obtain the values returned by previous actions. Moreover, the lexical analyser can return values for tokens, if desired. An action is an arbitrary C statement, and as such can carry out input and output operations, call subprograms and alter external vectors and variables. An action is specified by one or more statements, enclosed in curly braces '{' and '}'. For example

```
A    :    b { printf("it is b"); }
```

is a grammar rule with the action to print some text.

The user may define other variables to be used by the actions. Declarations and definitions can appear in the declarations section, enclosed in the marks '%{' and '%}'. These declarations and definitions have global scope, so they are known to the action statements and the lexical analyser. For example

```
%{  int variable = 0;  %}
```

could be placed in the declarations section, making the variable accessible to all of the actions. The Yacc parser uses only names beginning with 'yy'; the user should avoid such names.

Pseudovariable: To facilitate easy communication between the actions and the parser, the action statements are altered slightly. The dollar sign '$' is used as a signal to Yacc in this context. To return a value, the action normally sets the pseudovariable '$$' to some value. For example, an action that does nothing but return the value 1 is

```
{$$ = 1;}
```

To obtain the values returned by previous actions and the lexical analyser, the action may use the pseudovariables $1, $2, . . ., which refer to the values returned by the components of the right side of a rule, reading from left to right. Thus, if the rule is

```
A    :    B C D ;
```

for example, then $1 has the value returned by B, $2 has the value returned by C, and $3 the value returned by D. By default, the value of a rule is the value of the first element in it ($1). Thus, grammar rules of the form

```
A    :    B ;
```

frequently need not have an explicit action.

In the examples above, all the actions appeared at the end of their rules. Sometimes, it is desirable to obtain control before a rule is fully parsed. Yacc permits an action to be written in the middle of a rule as well as at the end. This rule is assumed to return a value, accessible through the usual mechanism by the actions to the right of it. In turn, it may access the values returned by the symbols to its left. Thus, in the rule

```
A    :    B
              { $$ = 1; }
          C
              { x = $2;  y = $3; }
     ;
```

the effect is to set x to 1, and y to the value returned by C.

Parse tree construction: In many applications, the output is not obtained directly by the actions; rather, a data structure, such as a parse tree, is constructed in memory, and transformations are applied to it before the output is generated. Parse trees are particularly easy to construct, given the routines to build and maintain the tree structure desired. For example, suppose there is a C function node, written so that the call

node(L, n1, n2)

creates a node with label L and descendants n1 and n2, and returns the index of the newly created node. Then, the parse tree can be built by supplying actions such as:

```
expr  :     expr '+' expr
            { $$ = node( '+', $1, $3 ); }
```

in the specification.

Ambiguity and conflicts: A set of grammar rules is ambiguous if there is some input string that can be structured in two or more ways. For example, the grammar rule

expr : expr '–' expr

is a natural way of expressing the fact that one way of forming an arithmetic expression is to put two other expressions together with a minus sign between them. Unfortunately, this grammar rule does not completely specify the way that all complex inputs should be structured. For example, if the input is

expr − expr − expr

the rule allows this input to be structured as either

(expr − expr) − expr   or as   expr − (expr − expr)

The first is called left association, the second right association. Yacc detects such ambiguities when it is attempting to build the parser. It is instructive to consider the problem that confronts the parser when it is given an input such as

expr − expr − expr

When the parser has read the second expr, the input that it has seen: expr − expr, matches the right side of the grammar rule above. The parser could reduce the input by applying this rule; after applying the rule; the input is reduced to expr (left side of the rule). The parser would then read the final part of the input: − expr and again reduce. The effect of this is to take the left associative interpretation. Alternatively, when the parser has seen: expr – expr, it could defer the immediate application of the rule, and continue reading the input until it had seen expr − expr − expr. It could then apply the rule to the rightmost three symbols, reducing them to expr and leaving expr − expr. Now the rule can be reduced once more; the effect is to take the right associative interpretation. Thus, having read expr − expr, the parser can perform two legal actions: a shift or a reduction, and it has no way of deciding between them. This is called a shift-reduce conflict. It may also be that the parser has a choice between two legal reductions. This is called a reduce-reduce conflict. Note that there are never any shift-shift conflicts.

When there are shift-reduce or reduce-reduce conflicts, Yacc still produces a parser. It does this by selecting one of the valid steps wherever it has a choice. A rule describing which choice to make in a given situation is called a **disambiguating rule**. Yacc invokes two disambiguating rules by default:

Rule 1: In a shift-reduce conflict, the default is to perform the shift. The reductions are deferred whenever there is a choice, in favour of shifts.
Rule 2: In a reduce-reduce conflict, the default is to reduce by the earlier grammar rule (in the input sequence).

It gives the user rather crude control over the behaviour of the parser in this situation, but reduce-reduce conflicts should be avoided whenever possible.

Conflicts may arise due to the following reasons:

- Mistakes in input or logic
- The use of actions within rules, if the action must be performed before the parser can be sure which rule is being recognised

In these cases, the application of disambiguating rules is inappropriate, and leads to an incorrect parser. For this reason, Yacc always reports the number of shift-reduce and reduce-reduce conflicts resolved by Rule 1 and Rule 2. In general, whenever it is possible to apply disambiguating rules to produce a correct parser, it is also possible to rewrite the grammar rules so that the same inputs are read but there are no conflicts. Yacc will produce parsers even in the presence of conflicts. For example, consider a fragment from a programming language involving an if-then-else construction:

```
stat  :   IF '(' cond ')' stat
      |   IF '(' cond ')' stat ELSE stat
      ;
```

In these rules, IF and ELSE are tokens, cond is a non-terminal symbol describing conditional (logical) expressions, and stat is a non-terminal symbol describing statements. The first rule will be called the simple-if rule, and the second the if-else rule. These two rules form an ambiguous construction, as input of the form

```
IF ( C1 ) IF ( C2 ) S1 ELSE S2
```

can be structured according to these rules in two ways:

```
IF ( C1 ) {
     IF ( C2 ) S1
     }
ELSE S2
```

or

```
IF ( C1 ) {
     IF ( C2 ) S1
     ELSE S2
     }
```

The second interpretation is the one given in most programming languages having this construct. Each ELSE is associated with the last preceding "un-ELSE'd" IF. In this example, consider the situation where the parser has seen

```
IF ( C1 ) IF ( C2 ) S1
```

and is looking at the ELSE. It can immediately reduce by the simple-if rule to obtain

```
IF ( C1 ) stat
```

and then read the remaining input

ELSE S2

and reduce

IF (C1) stat ELSE S2

by the if-else rule. This leads to the first of the above groupings of the input.

On the other hand, the ELSE may be shifted, S2 read, and then the right hand portion of

IF (C1) IF (C2) S1 ELSE S2

can be reduced by the if-else rule to obtain

IF (C1) stat

which can be reduced by the simple-if rule. This leads to the second of the above groupings of the input, which is usually desired.

Once again, the parser can perform two valid actions – there is a shift-reduce conflict. The application of disambiguating Rule 1 tells the parser to shift in this case, which leads to the desired grouping.

This shift-reduce conflict arises only when there is a particular current input symbol, ELSE, and particular inputs already seen, such as

IF (C1) IF (C2) S1

In general, there may be many conflicts, and each one will be associated with an input symbol and a set of previously read inputs. The previously read inputs are characterised by the state of the parser. The conflict messages of Yacc are best understood by examining the verbose (-v) option output file.

Precedence: Arithmetic expressions can be naturally described by the notion of precedence levels for operators, together with information about left or right associativity. It turns out that ambiguous grammars with appropriate disambiguating rules can be used to create parsers that are faster and easier to write than parsers constructed from unambiguous grammars. The basic notion is to write grammar rules of the form

```
expr : expr OP expr
```

and

```
expr : UNARY expr
```

for all binary and unary operators desired. This creates a very ambiguous grammar, with many parsing conflicts. As disambiguating rules, the user specifies the precedence or binding strength of all the operators, and the associativity of the binary operators. This information is sufficient to allow Yacc to resolve the parsing conflicts in accordance with these rules, and construct a parser that realises the desired precedences and associativities.

These are attached to tokens in the declarations section. This is done by a series of lines beginning with a Yacc keyword: %left, %right, or %nonassoc, followed by a list of tokens. All of the tokens on the same line are assumed to have the same precedence level and associativity; the lines are listed in the order of increasing precedence or binding strength. Thus

```
%left '+' '-'
%left '*' '/'
```

describes the precedence and associativity of the four arithmetic operators. Plus and minus are left associative and have lower precedence than star and slash, which are also left associative.

The keyword %right is used to describe right associative operators, and the keyword %nonassoc to describe operators like .LT. in Fortran, that may not associate with themselves.

When this mechanism is used, unary operators must, in general, be given precedence. Sometimes, a unary operator and a binary operator have the same symbolic representation, but different precedence. An example is the unary and binary '–'; unary minus may be given the same strength as multiplication, or even higher, while binary minus has a lower strength than multiplication. The keyword %prec changes the precedence level associated with a particular grammar rule. %prec appears immediately after the body of the grammar rule, before the action or closing semicolon, and is followed by a token name or literal. It causes the precedence of the grammar rule to become that of the following token name or literal.

Precedences and associativities are used by Yacc to resolve parsing conflicts; they give rise to disambiguating rules. Formally, the rules work as follows:

- The precedences and associativities are recorded for those tokens and literals that have them.
- A precedence and associativity is associated with each grammar rule; it is the precedence and associativity of the last token or literal in the body of the rule. If the %prec construction is used, it overrides this default. Some grammar rules may have no precedence and associativity associated with them.
- When there is a reduce-reduce conflict or a shift-reduce conflict and either the input symbol or the grammar rule has no precedence and associativity, then the two disambiguating rules given at the beginning of the section are used, and the conflicts are reported.
- If there is a shift-reduce conflict, and both the grammar rule and the input character have precedence and associativity associated with them, then the conflict is resolved in favour of the action (shift or reduce) associated with the higher precedence. If the precedences are the same, then the associativity is used; left associative implies reduce, right associative implies shift, and non-associating implies error.

Conflicts resolved by precedence are not counted in the number of shift-reduce and reduce-reduce conflicts reported by Yacc. This means that mistakes in the specification of precedence may disguise errors in the input grammar.

Example 10.11 Precedence in Yacc

Write a Yacc code to give higher precedence to the + and – operators than * and /. All four operators are left associative. Show the precedence and association if the input is

a=b + c*d – e – f*g

Yacc file:

```
%right '='
%left '+' '–'
%left '*' '/'

%%

expr  :   expr '=' expr
      |   expr '+' expr
```

```
        | expr '–' expr
        | expr '*' expr
        | expr '/' expr
        | NAME
        ;
```

The input will be structured as follows:

a = (b + (((c*d) – e) – (f*g)))

Example 10.12 Unary minus to have the same precedence as multiplication
The rules might resemble:

```
%left '+' '–'
%left '*' '/'

%%

expr  :  expr '+' expr
      |  expr '–' expr
      |  expr '*' expr
      |  expr '/' expr
      |  '-' expr    %prec '*'
      |  NAME
      ;
```

A token declared by %left, %right, and %nonassoc need not, but may, be declared by %token as well.

Error handling in Yacc: Error handling is an extremely difficult area, and many of the problems are semantic ones. When an error is found, it may be necessary to reclaim parse tree storage, delete or alter symbol table entries, and, typically, set switches to avoid generating any further output. It is seldom acceptable to stop all processing when an error is found; it is more useful to continue scanning the input to find further syntax errors. This leads to the problem of getting the parser 'restarted' after an error. A general class of algorithms to do this involves discarding a number of tokens from the input string and attempting to adjust the parser so that input can continue.

To allow the user some control over this process, Yacc provides a simple, but reasonably general, feature. The token name 'error' is reserved for error handling. This name can be used in grammar rules; in effect, it suggests places where errors are expected and recovery might take place.

The parser pops its stack until it enters a state where the token 'error' is legal. It then behaves as if this token were the current look-ahead token, and performs the action encountered. The look-ahead token is then reset to the token that caused the error. If no special error rules have been specified, processing halts when an error is detected. In order to prevent a cascade of error messages, the parser, after detecting an error, remains in the error state until three tokens have been successfully read and shifted. If an error is detected when the parser is already in the error state, no message is given, and the input token is quietly deleted.

Example 10.13 Yacc program to validate the syntax of the while loop

Lex input file (p1.l)

```
%{
#include<stdio.h>
#include "p1.tab.h"
%}
DIGIT [0-9]
LETTER [A-Za-z]

%%
\while|int {return key;}
{LETTER}({LETTER}|{DIGIT})* {return id;}
\[+|>=|>|<|<=|==|!=] {return op;}
{DIGIT}+ {return dig;}
\( {return ob;}
\) {return cb;}
\{ {return oc;}
\} {return cc;}
\; {return sc;}
%%
```

Yacc input file (p1.y)

```
%{
#include<stdio.h>
%}
%token id op dig key ob cb oc cc sc
%%
start: s {printf("\n Valid while statement\n");}
s : key ob id op dig cb oc key id sc cc
%%
yyerror() {printf("\n Invalid\n");}
main()
{
       printf("\n Enter the Program Code:\n");
       yyparse();
}
```

Sample output:

cse@cse-Veriton-Series:~$ flex p1.l
cse@cse-Veriton-Series:~$ bison -d p1.y
cse@cse-Veriton-Series:~$ gcc -c lex.yy.c p1.tab.c
cse@cse-Veriton-Series:~$ gcc -o a.out lex.yy.o p1.tab.o -lfl
cse@cse-Veriton-Series:~$ ./a.out

Enter the Program Code:

while(num>0){int a;}

Valid while statement

Example 10.14 Yacc program to recognise nested IF control statements and display the levels of nesting

Yacc

```
%token IF RELOP S NUMBER ID
%{
 int count=0;
%}
%%
stmt : if_stmt { printf("No of nested if statements=%d\n",count); exit(0);}
 ;
if_stmt : IF '(' cond ')' if_stmt {count++;}
 | S;
 ;
cond : x RELOP x
 ;
x : ID
 | NUMBER
 ;
%%
int yyerror(char *msg)
{
 printf("Invalid Expression\n");
 exit(0);
}
main ()
{
 printf("Enter the statement");
 yyparse();
}
```

Lex

```
%{
 #include "y.tab.h"
%}
%%
"if" { return IF; }
[sS][0-9]* {return S;}
"<"|">"|"=="|"!="|"<="|">=" { return RELOP; }
[0-9]+ { return NUMBER; }
[a-zA-Z][a-zA-Z0-9_]* { return ID; }
\n { ; }
. { return yytext[0]; }
%%
```

Example 10.15 Yscc program to validate the syntax of for-loop

Lex file: for.l

```
alpha [A-Za-z]
digit [0-9]
%%
[\t \n]
for           return FOR;
{digit}+      return NUM;
{alpha}({alpha}|{digit})* return ID;
"<="          return LE;
">="          return GE;
"=="          return EQ;
"!="          return NE;
"||"          return OR;
"&&"          return AND;
.             return yytext[0];
%%
```

Yacc file: for.y

```
%{
#include <stdio.h>
#include <stdlib.h>
%}
%token ID NUM FOR LE GE EQ NE OR AND
%right "="
%left OR AND
%left '>' '<' LE GE EQ NE
%left '+' '-'
%left '*' '/'
%right UMINUS
%left '!'
%%

S       : ST {printf("Input accepted\n"); exit(0);}
ST      : FOR '(' E ';' E2 ';' E ')' DEF
        ;
DEF     : '{' BODY '}'
        | E';'
        | ST
        |
        ;
BODY    : BODY BODY
        | E ';'
        | ST
        |
```

```
    ;

E   : ID '=' E
    | E '+' E
    | E '-' E
    | E '*' E
    | E '/' E
    | E '<' E
    | E '>' E
    | E LE E
    | E GE E
    | E EQ E
    | E NE E
    | E OR E
    | E AND E
    | E '+' '+'
    | E '-' '-'
    | ID
    | NUM
    ;

E2  : E'<'E
    | E'>'E
    | E LE E
    | E GE E
    | E EQ E
    | E NE E
    | E OR E
    | E AND E
    ;
%%
```

Example 10.16 Yacc program to test the validity of a simple expression involving operators +, −, * and /

Yacc

```
%token NUMBER ID NL
%left '+' '-'
%left '*' '/'
%%
stmt : exp NL { printf("Valid Expression"); exit(0);}
 ;
exp : exp '+' exp
      | exp '-' exp
      | exp '*' exp
      | exp '/' exp
```

```
        | '(' exp ')'
        | ID
        | NUMBER
 ;
%%
int yyerror(char *msg)
{
 printf("Invalid Expression\n");
 exit(0);
}
main ()
{
 printf("Enter the expression\n");
 yyparse();
}
```

Lex

```
%{
 #include "y.tab.h"
%}
%%
[0-9]+ { return DIGIT; }
[a-zA-Z][a-zA-Z0-9_]* { return ID; }
\n { return NL ;}
. { return yytext[0]; }
%%
```

Example 10.17 **Yacc program to evaluate an arithmetic expression involving operators +, –, * and /**

Yacc

```
%token NUMBER ID NL
%left '+' '-'
%left '*' '/'
%%
stmt : exp NL { printf("Value = %d\n",$1); exit(0);}
 ;
exp : exp '+' exp { $$=$1+$3; }
          | exp '-' exp { $$=$1-$3; }
          | exp '*' exp { $$=$1*$3; }
          | exp '/' exp {
          if($3==0)
          {
            printf("Cannot divide by 0");
            exit(0);
          }
          else
```

```
            $$=$1/$3;
            }

            | '(' exp ')' { $$=$2; }

            | ID { $$=$1; }

            | NUMBER { $$=$1; }
            ;
%%
int yyerror(char *msg)
{
 printf("Invalid Expression\n");
 exit(0);
}
main ()
{
 printf("Enter the expression\n");
 yyparse();
}
```

Lex

```
%{
 #include "y.tab.h"
 extern int yylval;
%}
%%
[0-9]+ { yylval=atoi(yytext); return NUMBER; }
\n { return NL ;}
. { return yytext[0]; }
%%
```

Example 10.18 Yacc program to recognise a valid identifier

An identifier starts with a letter, followed by any number of letters or digits.

Yacc

```
%token DIGIT LETTER NL UND
%%
stmt : variable NL { printf("Valid Identifiers\n"); exit(0);}
 ;
variable : LETTER alphanumeric
 ;
alphanumeric: LETTER alphanumeric
       | DIGIT alphanumeric
       | UND alphanumeric
       | LETTER
```

```
        | DIGIT
        | UND
        ;
%%
int yyerror(char *msg)
{
 printf("Invalid Expression\n");
 exit(0);
}
main ()
{
 printf("Enter the variable name\n");
 yyparse();
}
```

Lex

```
%{
 #include "y.tab.h"
%}
%%
[a-zA-Z] { return LETTER ;}
[0-9] { return DIGIT ; }
[\n] { return NL ;}
[_] { return UND; }
. { return yytext[0]; }
%%
```

Example 10.19 Building an expression tree

```
%{
#include "y.tab.h"
static char findname (char *yytext) {return yytext [0];}
%}
%%
[0-9]+                  {yylval.a_number = atoi(yytext); return number;}
[A-Za-z][A-Za-z0-9]*    {yylval.a_variable = findname (yytext);
                        return variable;}
[ \t\n]                 ;
[-+*/( );]              return yytext[0];
.                       {ECHO; yyerror ("unexpected character");}
%%
int yywrap (void) {return 1;}

%{
#include <stdio.h>
enum treetype {operator_node, number_node, variable_node};
typedef struct tree {
```

```
    enum treetype nodetype;
    union {
       struct {struct tree *left, *right; char operator;} an_operator;
       int a_number;
       char a_variable;
    } body;
} tree;
static tree *make_operator (tree *l, char o, tree *r) {
  tree *result= (tree*) malloc (sizeof(tree));
  result->nodetype= operator_node;
  result->body.an_operator.left= l;
  result->body.an_operator.operator= o;
  result->body.an_operator.right= r;
  return result;
}
static tree *make_number (int n) {
  tree *result= (tree*) malloc (sizeof(tree));
  result->nodetype= number_node;
  result->body.a_number= n;
  return result;
}
static tree *make_variable (char v) {
  tree *result= (tree*) malloc (sizeof(tree));
  result->nodetype= variable_node;
  result->body.a_variable= v;
  return result;
}
static void printtree (tree *t, int level) {
#define step 4
  if (t)
    switch (t->nodetype)
    {
       case operator_node:
       printtree (t->body.an_operator.right, level+step);
       printf ("%*c%c\n", level, ' ', t->body.an_operator.operator);
       printtree (t->body.an_operator.left, level+step);
       break;
       case number_node:
       printf ("%*c%d\n", level, ' ', t->body.a_number);
       break;
       case variable_node:
       printf ("%*c%c\n", level, ' ', t->body.a_variable);
    }
}
%}
```

```
%union {
  int a_number;
  char a_variable;
  tree* a_tree;
 }
%start input
%token <a_number> number
%token <a_variable> variable
%type <a_tree> exp term factor
%%
input : exp ';'            {printtree ($1, 1);}
         ;
exp   : '+' term           {$$ = $2;}
      | '-' term           {$$ = make_operator (NULL, '~', $2);}
      | term               {$$ = $1;}
      | exp '+' term       {$$ = make_operator ($1, '+', $3);}
      | exp '-' term       {$$ = make_operator ($1, '-', $3);}
      ;
term    : factor           {$$ = $1;}
      | term '*' factor    {$$ = make_operator ($1, '*', $3);}
      | term '/' factor    {$$ = make_operator ($1, '/', $3);}
         ;
factor : number            {$$ = make_number ($1);}
      | variable           {$$ = make_variable ($1);}
      | '(' exp ')'        {$$ = $2;}
      ;
%%
void yyerror (char *s) {fprintf (stderr, "%s\n", s);}
int main (void) {return yyparse();}
```

10.5 JFlex and CUP

JFlex is a lexical analyser generator (scanner generator) for Java, written in Java. It takes as input a specification with a set of regular expressions and corresponding actions. It generates a program (lexer) that reads input, matches the input against the regular expressions in the specification file, and runs the corresponding action if a regular expression is matched. JFlex lexers are based on deterministic finite automata (DFAs). They are fast, without expensive backtracking. JFlex can work with the LALR parser generator CUP or the Java modification of Berkeley Yacc, BYacc/J. It can also be used with other parser generators like ANTLR or as a standalone tool.

JFLEX source file

{User code}
%%
{Options and declarations}
%%
{Lexical Rules}

In the user code section, the first part contains user code that is copied into the beginning of the source file of the generated lexer before the scanner class is declared. Package declarations and import statements are also included in this section. It is possible, but not considered as good Java programming style, to include our own helper class (such as token classes) in this section. It should get its own .java file instead.

The second part of the lexical specification, options and declarations contain options to customise the generated lexer (JFlex directives and Java code to include in different parts of the lexer), declarations of lexical states and macro definitions for use in the third section 'lexical rules' of the lexical specification file. Each JFlex directive must be situated at the beginning of a line and starts with the % character. Directives that have one or more parameters are described as follows: %class "classname" means that you start a line with %class followed by a space followed by the name of the class for the generated scanner.

Lexical rules contain a pattern and the corresponding action. The pattern is specified as a regular expression, and actions are snippets of Java code. Actions are triggered whenever a pattern is matched. JFlex regular expressions along with their meaning are given in Table 10.2.

Table 10.2 Regular expressions in JFlex

Pattern	Meaning
a	character a
"a"	character a (special characters also allowed)
abc	a followed by b followed by c
a|b	a or b
a*	zero or more repetitions of a
a+	one ot more repretiotns of a
a?	optional a
(a)	a itself
[abc]	any one character of a or b or c
[^abc]	any character . except a, b or c
.	any character . except newline

Class options and user class codes regard name, constructor, API and related parts of the generated scanner class. There are many options available; some of the class options and user class codes that can be included are as follows:

- %class "classname": JFlex gives the generated class the name "classname" and writes the generated code to a file "classname.java". If the -d command line option is not used, the code will be written to the directory where the specification file resides. If no %class directive is present in the specification, the generated class will get the name "yylex" and will be written to a file "yylex.java". There should be only one %class directive in a specification.
- %implements "interface 1"[, "interface 2", ..]: This makes the generated class implement the specified interfaces. If more than one %implements directive is present, all the specified interfaces will be implemented.

- %extends "classname": This makes the generated class a subclass of the class "classname". There should be only one %extends directive in a specification.
- %public: This makes the generated class public.
- %final: This makes the generated class final.
- %abstract: This makes the generated class abstract.
- %private: This makes all generated methods and fields of the class private. Exceptions are the constructor, user code in the specification, and, if %cup is present, the method next token. All occurrences of "public" (one space character before and after public) in the skeleton file are replaced by "private" (even if a user-specified skeleton is used). Access to the generated class is expected to be mediated by the user class code (see next switch).
- %{ ... %}: The code enclosed in %{ and %} is copied verbatim into the generated class. Here, you can define your own member variables and functions in the generated scanner. Like all options, both %{ and %} must start a line in the specification. If more than one class code directive %{...%} is present, the code is concatenated in the order of appearance in the specification.
- %init{ ... %init}: The code enclosed in %init{ and %init} is copied verbatim into the constructor of the generated class. Here, the member variables declared in the %{...%} directive can be initialised. If more than one initialise option is present, the code is concatenated in the order of appearance in the specification.
- %initthrow{ "exception1"[, "exception2", ...] %initthrow} or (on a single line) just %initthrow "exception1" [, "exception2", ...] : This causes the specified exceptions to be declared in the throws clause of the constructor. If more than one %initthrow{ ... %initthrow} directive is present in the specification, all specified exceptions will be declared.
- %scanerror "exception": This causes the generated scanner to throw an instance of the specified exception in case of an internal error (default is java.lang.Error). Note that this exception is only for internal scanner errors. With usual specifications, it should never occur (i.e., if there is an error fallback rule in the specification and only the documented scanner API is used).
- %include "filename": Replaces %include verbatim with the specified file. This feature is still experimental. It works, but error reporting can be strange if a syntax error occurs on the last token in the included file.

  Scanning methods can be customised. The name and return type of the method can be redefined and it is possible to declare exceptions that may be thrown in one of the actions of the specification. If no return type is specified, the scanning method will be declared as returning values of class yytoken. Scanning methods can be customized using the following:
- %function "name": It causes the scanning method to obtain the specified name. If no %function directive is present in the specification, the scanning method gets the name "yylex". This directive overrides settings of the %cup switch. The default name of the scanning method with the %cup switch is the next token. Overriding this name might lead to the generated scanner being implicitly declared as abstract, because it does not provide the method next token of the interface java cup. runtime.Scanner. It is possible to provide a dummy implementation of that method in the class code section, if you want to override the function name.
- %integer %int: Both cause the scanning method to be declared as of Java type int. Actions in the specification can then return int values as tokens. The default end-of-file value under this setting is YYEOF, which is a public static final int member of the generated class.
- %intwrap: It causes the scanning method to be declared as of the Java wrapper type int. Actions in the specification can then return int values as tokens. The default end-of-file value under this setting is null.

- %type "typename": It causes the scanning method to be declared as returning values of the specified type. Actions in the specification can then return values of typename as tokens. The default end of file value under this setting is null. If typename is not a subclass of java.lang. Object, you should specify another end of file value using the %eofval{ ... %eofval} directive or the <> rule. The %type directive overrides the settings of the %cup switch.
- %yylexthrow{ "exception1"[, "exception2", ...] %yylexthrow} or (on a single line) just %yylexthrow "exception1" [, "exception2", ...]: The exceptions listed inside %yylexthrow{ ... %yylexthrow} will be declared in the throws clause of the scanning method. If there is more than one %yylexthrow{ ... %yylexthrow} clause in the specification, all specified exceptions will be declared.

End of file: There is always a default value that the scanning method will return when the end of file has been reached. You may, however, define a specific value to return and a specific piece of code that should be executed when the end of file is reached. The default end-of-file values depend on the return type of the scanning method:

- For %integer, the scanning method will return the value YYEOF, which is a public static final int member of the generated class.
- For %intwrap, no specified type at all, or a user-defined type, declared using %type, the value is null.
- In CUP compatibility mode, using %cup, the value is new java cup.runtime. Symbol(sym.EOF).

User values and code to be executed at the end of file can be defined using these directives:

- %eofval{ ... %eofval}: The code included in %eofval{ ... %eofval} will be copied verbatim into the scanning method and will be executed each time the end of file is reached (this is possible when the scanning method is called again after the end of file has been reached). The code should return the value that indicates the end of file to the parser. There should be only one %eofval{ ... %eofval} clause in the specification. The %eofval{ ... %eofval} directive overrides the settings of the %cup switch and the %byaccj switch.
- %eof{ ... %eof}: The code included in %{eof ... %eof} will be executed exactly once, when the end of file is reached. The code is included inside a method void yy do eof() and should not return any value (use %eofval{...%eofval} or <> for this purpose). If more than one end-of-file code directive is present, the code will be concatenated in the order of appearance in the specification.

CUP compatibility: CUP is a parser generator. The generated scanner (generated by JFlex) can be interfaced with CUP. The %cup directive enables the CUP compatibility mode and is equivalent to the following set of directives:

```
%implements java_cup.runtime.Scanner
%function next_token
%type java_cup.runtime.Symbol
%eofval{ return new java_cup.runtime.Symbol(.EOF); %eofval}
%eofclose
```

The value of defaults to sym and can be changed with the %cupsym directive. In JLex compatibility mode (--jlex switch on the command line), %eofclose will not be turned on. %cupsym "classname" customizes the name of the CUP-generated class/interface containing the names of terminal tokens. The default is sym. %cupdebug creates a main function in the generated class that expects the name of an input file on the command line and then runs the scanner on this input file. It then prints the line, column, matched text, and CUP symbol name for each returned token to standard output.

Running JFlex

jflex <options> <inputfiles>

It is also possible to skip the start script in bin\ and include the file lib\JFlex.jar in your CLASSPATH environment variable instead. Then you run JFlex with:

java JFlex.Main <options> <inputfiles>

The input files and options are, in both cases, optional. If you do not provide a file name on the command line, JFlex will pop up a window to prompt you for one. Some of the main options available are:

- -d <directory> writes the generated file to the directory.
- --verbose or -v displays generation progress messages (enabled by default)
- --quiet or -q displays error messages only (no information about what JFlex is currently doing)
- --time displays time statistics about the code generation process (may not be very accurate)
- --version prints the version number
- --info prints system and JDK information (useful if you would like to report a problem)
- --pack uses the %pack code generation method by default
- --table uses the %table code generation method by default
- --switch use thes %switch code generation method by default
- --help or -h prints a help message explaining options and usage of JFlex

Example 10.20 Write the JFlex specification to search for the pattern (a|b)*abbb

```
%%
%class Search
%standalone
%line
%column
%%
(a|b)*abbb { System.out.println("*** found match [%s] at line %d, column
%d \n", yytext( ), yyline, yycolumn);}
\n { /* do nothing */}
. { /* do nothing */}
```

To run the code:
$ jflex search.flex
$ javac Search.java
$ java Search searchtest.txt

JFlex generates the Java file search.java since %class is specified. If %class is not included, then yylex.java will be created. Running the java file, for each match found, the text is printed along with its position within the input file.

Example 10.21 Write the JFlex specification to find whitespaces, digits, identifier and others

```
%%
%class Classify
%standalone
```

```
Digit = [0-9]
Letter = [a-zA-Z]
Whitespace = [ \t\n]+
%%
{Whitespace} {/* Do nothing! */}
{Digit}+ {System.out.printf("number [%s]\n", yytext());}
{Letter}({Letter}|{Digit})* {System.out.printf("word [%s]\n", yytext());}
. {System.out.printf("symbol [%s]\n", yytext());}
```

Example 10.22 Write the JFlex specification to add line numbers to the input file and print the input, line by line, with each line preceded with its line number

```
%%
%class LineCounter
%standalone
%{ int lineno = 1;
%}
line = .*\n
%%
{line} { System.out.printf("[%5d]: %s", lineno++, yytext()); }
```

Example 10.23 Write the JFlex specification to convert decimal to hexadecimal

```
%%
%class Dec2HexConvertor
%standalone
number = [0-9]+
%%
{number} {
int n = Integer.parseInt(yytext());
System.out.printf("%X (hex)", n);
}
```

Example 10.24 Write the JFlex specification to convert uppercase letters to lowercase

```
%%
%class Upper2Lower
%standalone
COMMENT = "/*" [^*] ~"*/" | "/*" "*"+ "/"
%%
[A-Z] { System.out.print(Character.toLowerCase( yytext().charAt(0)));
}
{COMMENT} { /* Do nothing */ }
```

Example 10.25 Calculator to evaluate the arithmetic expressions using JFlex and CUP

```
import java_cup.runtime.*;
parser code {:
   // Connect this parser to a scanner!
   scanner s;
```

```
   Parser(scanner s){ this.s=s; }
:}

/* define how to connect to the scanner! */
init with {: s.init(); :};
scan with {: return s.next_token(); :};

/* Terminals (tokens returned by the scanner). */
terminal         SEMI, PLUS, MINUS, TIMES, UMINUS, LPAREN, RPAREN;
terminal Integer  NUMBER;      // our scanner provides numbers as integers

/* Non terminals */
non terminal          expr_list;
non terminal Integer  expr;    // used to store evaluated subexpressions

/* Precedences */
precedence left PLUS, MINUS;
precedence left TIMES;
precedence left UMINUS;

/* The grammar rules */
expr_list ::= expr_list expr:e SEMI    {: System.out.println(e);:}
        | expr:e SEMI                  {: System.out.println(e);:}
;
expr    ::= expr:e1 PLUS  expr:e2      {: RESULT = e1+e2;        :}
        | expr:e1 MINUS expr:e2        {: RESULT = e1-e2;        :}
        | expr:e1 TIMES expr:e2        {: RESULT = e1*e2;        :}
        | MINUS expr:e                 {: RESULT = -e;           :}
          %prec UMINUS
        | LPAREN expr:e RPAREN         {: RESULT = e;            :}
        | NUMBER:n                     {: RESULT = n;            :}
        ;
```

Based on this file, a Java specification can be created with java -jar java-cup-11b.jar -interface -parser Parser calc.cup. Additionally, a scanner to produce tokens is needed, which can then process with the parser.

The scanner code is as follows:

```
import java_cup.runtime.*;
class Main {
   public static void main(String[] argv) throws Exception{
      System.out.println("Please type your arithmethic expression:");
      Parser p = new Parser(new scanner());
      p.parse();
   }
}
```

```
public class scanner {
 /* single lookahead character */
 protected static int next_char;

 /* SymbolFactory is used to generate Symbols */
 private SymbolFactory sf = new DefaultSymbolFactory();

 /* advance input by one character */
 protected static void advance() throws java.io.IOException  { next_char
 = System.in.read(); }

 /* initialize the scanner */
 public static void init() throws java.io.IOException       { advance();
}

 /* recognize and return the next complete token */
 public Symbol next_token() throws java.io.IOException
 {
   for (;;)
     switch (next_char)
           {
            case '0': case '1': case '2': case '3': case '4': case '5':
            case '6': case '7': case '8': case '9':
              /* parse a decimal integer */
              int i_val = 0;
              do {
                  i_val = i_val * 10 + (next_char - '0');
                  advance();
              } while (next_char >= '0' && next_char <= '9');
              return sf.newSymbol("NUMBER",sym.NUMBER, new Integer(i_
              val));

           case ';': advance(); return sf.newSymbol("SEMI",sym.SEMI);
           case '+': advance(); return sf.newSymbol("PLUS",sym.PLUS);
           case '-': advance(); return sf.newSymbol("MINUS",sym.MINUS);
           case '*': advance(); return sf.newSymbol("TIMES",sym.TIMES);
           case '(': advance(); return sf.newSymbol("LPAREN",sym.LPAREN);
           case ')': advance(); return sf.newSymbol("RPAREN",sym.RPAREN);
           case -1: return sf.newSymbol("EOF",sym.EOF);

           default:
              /* scanner  ignores everything else */
              advance();
              break;
           }
  }
};
```

Compiling all classes with javac -cp java-cup-11b-runtime.jar:. *.java creates the calculator, which can be called via java -cp ../../dist/java-cup-11b-runtime.jar:. Main

10.6 ANTLR

ANTLR (ANother Tool for Language Recognition) is a parser generator. The main advantage of ANTLR is productivity. Once the grammar is defined, ANTLR can generate multiple parsers in different languages. For example, a parser can be obtained in C# and one in Javascript to parse the same language in a desktop application and in a web application. The generated parser takes a piece of text and transforms it in an organised structure, such as an abstract syntax tree (AST). The steps to obtain an AST as given below:

1. Define a lexer and parser grammar.
2. Invoke ANTLR; it will generate a lexer and a parser in your target language (for example, Java, Python, C#, Javascript).
3. Use the generated lexer and parser. You can invoke them by passing the code to recognise and they can return an AST.

ANTLR can be downloaded in stand-alone mode. It can be installed as a plugin for IDEs like eclipse, Netbeans, etc. As an alternative, ANTLRWorks IDE can be downloaded and used.

Example 10.26 To write an ANTLR grammar to evaluate an arithmetic expression and generate the corresponding parse tree using ANTLRWorks IDE

The steps to be followed in the ANTLRWorks IDE are given below. Set the compiler and debugger preferences (in Antlrworks IDE):

- File → Preferences → Compiler
  Set the javac path: As per java in the PC (for example, C:\Program Files\Java\jdk1.7.0_03\bin)
- File → Preferences → Debugger
  Default Local Port: 49100 OR 49153, parser launch time-out: 10 sec

1. Create a grammar file.

Exp.g:

```
grammar Exp;
@header {
package test;
import java.util.HashMap;
}

@lexer::header {package test;}

@members {
/** Map variable name to Integer object holding value */
HashMap memory = new HashMap();
}

prog: stat+ ;
stat: expr NEWLINE {System.out.println($expr.value);}
    | ID '=' expr NEWLINE
      {memory.put($ID.text, new Integer($expr.value));}
    | NEWLINE
    ;
```

```
expr returns [int value]
    : e=multExpr {$value = $e.value;}
      (   ‘+’ e=multExpr {$value += $e.value;}
      |   ‘-’ e=multExpr {$value -= $e.value;}
      )*
    ;

multExpr returns [int value]
    : e=atom {$value = $e.value;} (‘*’ e=atom {$value *= $e.value;})*
    ;

atom returns [int value]
    : INT {$value = Integer.parseInt($INT.text);}
    | ID
      {
      Integer v = (Integer)memory.get($ID.text);
      if ( v!=null ) $value = v.intValue();
      else System.err.println(“undefined variable ”+$ID.text);
      }
    | ‘(‘ e=expr ‘)’ {$value = $e.value;}
    ;

ID  :  (‘a’..’z’|’A’..’Z’)+ ;
INT :  ‘0’..’9’+ ;
NEWLINE:’\r’? ‘\n’ ;
WS  :  (‘ ‘|’\t’)+ {skip();} ;
```

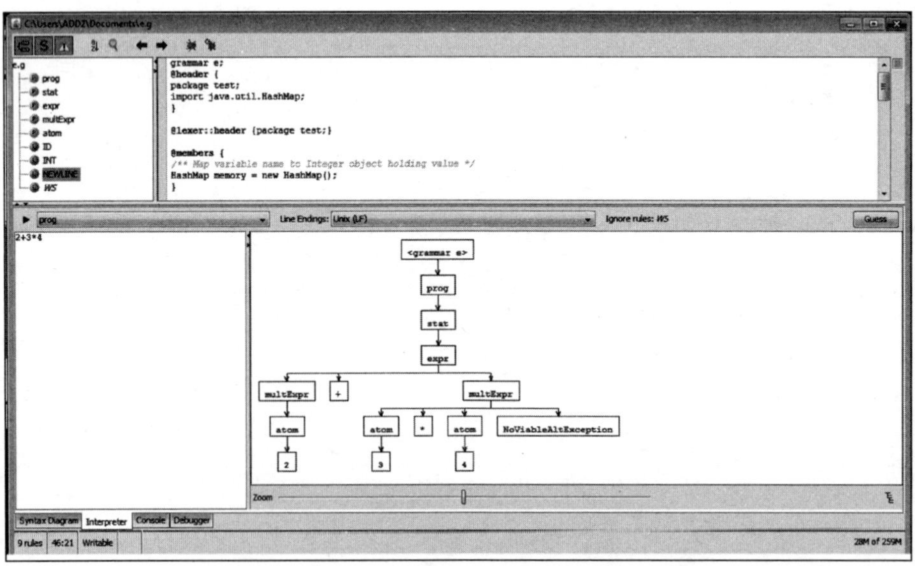

Figure 10.6 Parse tree generated for input “2+3*4”

2. Interpret.
   - In the Interpreter tab, enter the input: 2+3*4
   - Run (with prog).
   - The parse tree is generated, as shown in Fig. 10.6.
3. Debug.
   - Go to Run → Debug
   - Enter the input.
   - To see the output, press 
   - The parse tree with output is generated as shown in Fig. 10.7 (visible in the Output tab). The generated output is 14.

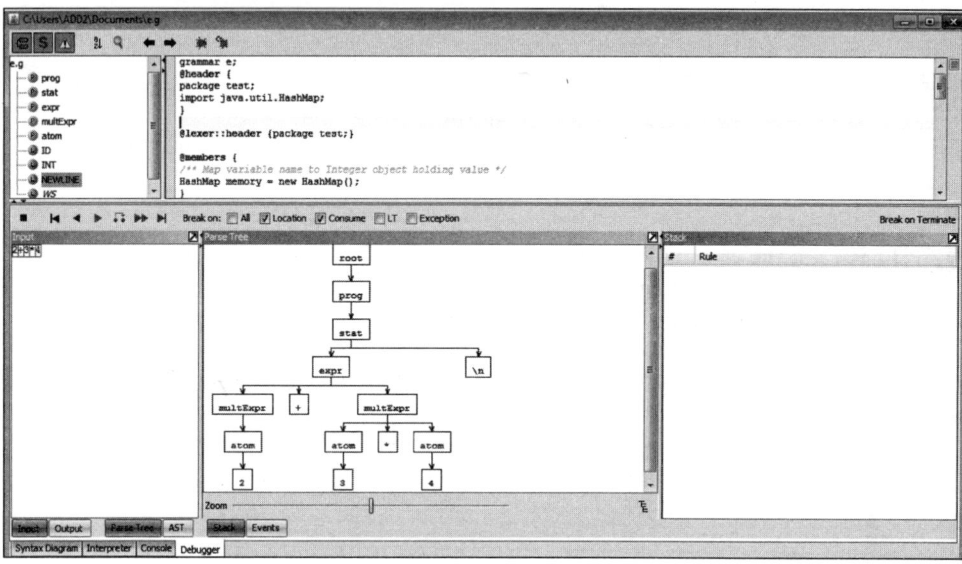

Figure 10.7 Parse tree with output (running step by step)

Example 10.27 To write a grammar in ANTLR for a simple calculator generating code in Java and run ANTLR from the command line

grammar SimpleCalc;

```
 tokens {
  PLUS     = '+' ;
  MINUS    = '-' ;
  MULT     = <*> ;
  DIV = </> ;
}
 @members {
   public static void main(String[] args) throws Exception {
   SimpleCalcLexer lex = new SimpleCalcLexer(new ANTLRFileStream(args[0]));
   CommonTokenStream tokens = new CommonTokenStream(lex);
   SimpleCalcParser parser = new SimpleCalcParser(tokens);
```

```
      try {
         parser.expr();
      } catch (RecognitionException e)   {
         e.printStackTrace();
      }
   }
}

/*PARSER RULES*/
 expr    : term ( ( PLUS | MINUS )  term )* ;
 term    : factor ( ( MULT | DIV ) factor )* ;
 factor  : NUMBER ;

/*LEXER RULES-*/
 NUMBER  : (DIGIT)+ ;
 WHITESPACE : ( ‹\t› | ‹ ‹ | ‹\r› | ‹\n›| ‹\u000C› )+ { $channel = HIDDEN;
 } ;
 fragment DIGIT  : '0'..'9' ;
```

To run ANTLR from the command line:
$ java -jar antlr-3.1.2.jar mygrammar.g
(after downloading jar file of antlr)

Example 10.28 To write a grammar in ANTLR for a simple calculator generating code in the C language

```
grammar SimpleCalc;
 options
{
  language=C;
}
 tokens
{
  PLUS    = '+' ;
  MINUS   = '-' ;
  MULT    = '*' ;
  DIV = '/' ;
}
@members
{
  #include "SimpleCalcLexer.h"
  int main(int argc, char * argv[])
 {
   pANTLR3_INPUT_STREAM     input;
   pSimplcCalcLexer   lex;
   pANTLR3_COMMON_TOKEN_STREAM    tokens;
   pSimpleCalcParser  parser;
```

```
    input = antlr3AsciiFileStreamNew      ((pANTLR3_UINT8)argv[1]);
    lex   = SimpleCalcLexerNew            (input);
    tokens = antlr3CommonTokenStreamSourceNew (ANTLR3_SIZE_HINT,
    TOKENSOURCE(lex));
    parser = SimpleCalcParserNew             (tokens);
    parser  ->expr(parser);

    // Must manually clean up
    //
    parser ->free(parser);
    tokens ->free(tokens);
    lex    ->free(lex);
    input  ->close(input);
    return 0;
  }
  }

/* PARSER RULES */
 expr   : term    ( ( PLUS | MINUS )  term )*
      ;
 term   : factor ( ( MULT | DIV  )  factor )*
      ;
 factor  : NUMBER
      ;

 /* LEXER RULES */
 NUMBER     : (DIGIT)+
      ;
 WHITESPACE  : ( '\t' | ' ' | '\r' | '\n'| '\u000C' )+
       {
         $channel = HIDDEN;
       }
       ;
 fragment
DIGIT   : '0'..'9'
       ;
```

Example 10.29 To write a grammar in ANTLR for a simple calculator generating code in the Python language

```
grammar SimpleCalc;
 options {
   language = Python;
}
 tokens {
   PLUS     = '+' ;
   MINUS    = '-' ;
   MULT     = '*' ;
```

```
  DIV = '/' ;
}
 @header {
import sys
import traceback
 from SimpleCalcLexer import SimpleCalcLexer
}
 @main {
def main(argv, otherArg=None):
  char_stream = ANTLRFileStream(sys.argv[1])
  lexer = SimpleCalcLexer(char_stream)
  tokens = CommonTokenStream(lexer)
  parser = SimpleCalcParser(tokens);
   try:
        parser.expr()
  except RecognitionException:
    traceback.print_stack()
}
 /*PARSER RULES */
 expr    : term ( ( PLUS | MINUS )  term )* ;
 term    : factor ( ( MULT | DIV ) factor )* ;
 factor  : NUMBER ;

/*LEXER RULES*/
 NUMBER  : (DIGIT)+ ;
 WHITESPACE : ( '\t' | ' ' | '\r' | '\n'| '\u000C' )+ { $channel = HIDDEN;
 } ;
 fragment DIGIT  : '0'..'9' ;
```

10.7 Other Tools and Techniques

JavaCC (Java Compiler Compiler) is an open-source parser generator for Java, including a scanner generator and parser generator. In addition to the parser generator itself, JavaCC provides other standard capabilities related to parser generation, such as tree building (via a tool called JJTree included with JavaCC), actions, debugging, etc. It is similar to Yacc in that it generates a parser from a formal grammar written in the EBNF notation and generates top-down parsers. It resolves choices based on the next k input tokens, and so can handle LL(k) grammars automatically, by using look-ahead specifications.

The basic technique in automatic code generation is template matching. The intermediate code statements are replaced by 'templates' that represent sequences of machine instructions in such a way that the assumptions about storage of variables match from template to template. The input specification for these systems contains description of the lexical and syntactic structure of the source language, output to be generated for each source language construct and description of the target machine. Another technique is to use dynamic programming. The language features can be integrated into automatically generated code generators that perform optimal instruction selection based on tree pattern matching combined with dynamic programming. Most of the information required to perform good code optimisation involves 'data flow analysis', the gathering of information about how values are transmitted from one part of a program to another. For information about the various data flow techniques, please see Chapter 6.

Summary

- Java Formal Languages and Automata Package (JFLAP) is an interactive tool written in Java for experimenting with formal languages and automata theory.
- Lex is a tool used to generate the lexical analyser.
- Lex generates the lexical analyser for C language, that is, it generates a lexical analyser which is a C program.
- Lex generates a deterministic finite automaton from the regular expressions in the source.
- Lex converts the set of rules specified in the '.l' file into a program. This program is the lexical analyser.
- The open source version of Lex is called Flex.
- Yacc is a tool for generation of the syntax analyser.
- Yacc is a Look Ahead Left-to-Right (LALR) parser generator.
- JFlex is a lexical analyser generator (scanner generator) for Java, written in Java.
- ANTLR (ANother Tool for Language Recognition) is a parser generator.
- JavaCC (Java Compiler Compiler) is an open-source parser generator for Java, including a scanner generator and parser generator.

Exercises

Programming Questions

1. Write a Lex specification to find floating point numbers, integers and strings in the given input file.
2. Write a Lex program to find the parameters given below in the question paper of an examination given as input:
   - Find the date of examination, semester, number of questions and number of words in the question paper.
3. Write a Lex code to find the total number of .txt, .doc, .png and .jpeg files. Consider the input to the lexical analyser is a file that contain file names with extensions.
4. Write a Lex and a Yacc code to generate a simple calculator.
5. Modify the code in Q3 and include syntax tree construction. After parsing, traverse the parse tree to generate the output.
6. Translate an HTML file with some HTML tags to a text file using Lex. Consider input from stdin. Discard all HTML tags and comments, and write the remaining text to stdout. The text output should simulate HTML characteristics such as list indent and paragraphs. Font characteristics such as bold and italic may not be simulated.

11 Functional Languages

Objectives

- To introduce the concept of functional languages
- To describe the basics of lambda calculus
- To discuss the compilation process in functional languages

11.1 Introduction to Functional Languages

Modern computing platforms undergo continuous change to enable improvement in performance. The use of multiple cores and processors for fast processing is very common in today's computers. Moreover, increasing computing demands bring in the scope for graphic processing units (GPUs) to support parallel processing and complex algorithm design. Parallel processing allows different parts or units of a program to be executed out-of-order or in partial order. However, this should not affect the final outcome and should provide proper concurrency. Hence, programmers are compelled to think about concurrency and provide proper concurrency control. Most regular programming languages make concurrency difficult to achieve. So, a language that abstracts programmers from concurrency control is required. Functional languages help in the development of constructs that ease concurrent development. Functional languages are not a replacement for procedural or object-oriented programming languages but provide a different paradigm altogether.

Functional languages use the functional programming paradigm, which takes advantage of functions which do not share memory and which have no side effects. Most of the functional languages abstract the developer from the concept of concurrency. In many cases, the programmer is unaware that processing is done in a concurrent manner. Hence, programmers need not worry about concurrency management but can instead focus on the programming logic. Many languages implement concurrent development by using the actor model.

Functional languages use a style of programming called **functional programming** which models computations as the evaluation of expressions or mathematical functions. It is a declarative programming paradigm, in which programming is carried out with expressions or declarations instead of statements. That is, in functional programming, programs are executed by evaluating expressions and avoiding changing-state and mutable data, whereas imperative programs are composed of statements which change the global state when executed.

Imperative programming results in change in state with the use of commands in the source code. Imperative programming does support functions in the sense of subroutines, but not in the mathematical sense. They can have side effects that may change the value of the program state. Functions without return values therefore make sense. Because of this, they lack referential transparency, i.e., the same language expression can result in different values at different times depending on the state of the executing program. In functional programs, the output value of a function depends only on the arguments that are passed to the function. So, for example, if a function f is called twice with the same value for an argument x, it produces the same result $f(x)$ each time. This is in contrast to procedures that depend on a local or global state, which may produce different results at different times when called with the same arguments but a different program state. Since, in functional programming, the changes in state do not depend on function inputs, it is easier to understand and predict the behaviour of a program. Hence, side effects are eliminated in functional programming.

Many programming languages support programming in both functional and imperative styles, but the syntax and facilities of a language are typically optimised for only one of these styles, and social factors like coding conventions and libraries often force the programmer towards one of the styles. Therefore, programming languages may be categorised as functional and imperative.

Functional programming has its origins in lambda calculus, a formal system developed in the 1930s to investigate computability. Many functional programming languages can be viewed as elaborations on lambda calculus. Another well-known declarative programming paradigm is logic programming, which is based on relations.

Data structures: Sequences, lists and trees are very common data structures in functional languages. Tuples and monads are other types of data structures available in most functional languages. **Tuples** are immutable sequences of objects. A **monad** is an abstract data type used to represent control flows or computations. The purpose of monads is to express input/output operations and changes in state without using language features that introduce side effects.

Examples of functional languages: Some of the prominent programming languages that support functional programming are Common, Lisp, Scheme, Clojure, Racket, Erlang, Haskell and F#. Programming in the functional style can also be accomplished in languages that are not specifically designed for functional programming, such as Perl, PHP, C++11 and C#.

Clojure is a modern dialect of the Lisp programming language that runs on the Java Virtual Machine, which is designed for concurrency. It is a dynamically typed programming language. An interesting case is that of Scala, which is frequently written in a functional style, but the presence of side effects and mutable state places it in a grey area between the imperative and functional languages. Scala is a language designed to integrate functional and object-oriented programming running on the Java Virtual Machine. It is a strongly typed programming language.

A new language that runs on the .Net CLR is an implementation of OCaml. It brings together functional programming and imperative object-oriented programming. It is a strongly typed programming language. JavaScript, one of the world's most widely distributed languages, has the properties of an untyped functional language, in addition to the imperative and object-oriented paradigms. Functional programming is also supported in some domain-specific programming languages like R (statistics). Domain-specific declarative languages like SQL and Lex/Yacc use some elements of functional programming. The Julia language also offers functional programming abilities.

11.2 Characteristics of Functional Languages

Functional programming is about writing pure functions, removing hidden inputs and outputs, so that as much of the code as possible just describes a relationship between inputs and outputs. In a functional language, the assignment of a value to a variable is binding, just as it would be in a mathematical function, and its value does not change. For example, if the value of a variable $x = 2$, then the value of x cannot change as we evaluate the problem at hand and it will always remain 2. Similarly, methods in a functional language are first class citizens and functional languages are not limited to just numerical value assignments. Consider for example, some variable $x = f(y)$. Then x will always be the same for a given y. The characteristics of functional languages are listed below:

- Functional languages are concise.
- They provide abstraction. To make a program structured, it is necessary to develop abstractions and split it into components which interface each other with those abstractions. Functional languages aid this by making it easy to create clean and simple abstractions. Higher-order functions can be created to abstract out a recurring piece of code.
- Many of the newer functional languages are multi-paradigm languages that run on virtual machines and bridge other object-oriented and imperative languages.
- Functional programming is known to provide better support for structured programming than imperative programming.
- Functional programming typically avoids using mutable state.
- Functional programs are often shorter and easier to understand than their imperative counterparts, leading to higher productivity.
- It eliminates side effects. Changes in state that do not depend on the function inputs can make it much easier to understand and predict the behaviour of a program, which is one of the key motivations for the development of functional programming.
- Function closure support
- Higher-order functions
- Use of recursion as a mechanism for flow control
- Focus on computation rather than how to compute
- Referential transparency
- Functional programming allows pattern matching to match a value or type.

11.3 Concepts in Functional Languages

The main concepts in functional languages are discussed in this section.

11.3.1 First Class Functions

Functional programming requires that functions are first class, which means that functions can be passed as arguments to other functions, returned from functions, stored in variables and data structures and built at run-time. Being first class also means that it is possible to define and manipulate functions from within other functions.

Special attention needs to be given to functions that reference local variables from their scope. If such a function escapes its block after being returned from it, the local variables must be retained in memory, as they might be needed later when the function is called. Often, it is difficult to determine statically when those resources can be released, so it is necessary to use automatic memory management.

Most languages support first class functions. The **properties** of first class functions are given below:

- A function is an instance of the Object type.
- You can store the function in a variable.
- You can pass the function as a parameter to another function.
- You can return the function from a function.
- You can store them in data structures such as hash tables, lists, etc.

For example, consider the code below that passes functions as arguments in Python:

```
import math
def find(x):
```

```
    return math.sqrt(x)

def compute(func):
            # storing the function in a variable
            val = func(25)
            print val

compute(find)
```

11.3.2 Pure Functions

Some functional languages allow expressions to yield actions in addition to return values. These actions are called side effects to emphasize that the return value is the most important outcome of a function. Pure functions are functions without side effects, like mathematical functions. For the same input, the functions always returns the same output. The result of any function call is fully determined by its arguments. Pure functions do not rely on global variables and do not have internal states. They do not print or write a file, that is, input-output is not supported. Pure functions are stateless and deterministic. Languages that prohibit side effects are called pure. Even though some functional languages are impure, they often contain a pure subset that is also useful as a programming language. It is usually beneficial to write a significant part of a functional program in a purely functional fashion and keep the code involving state and I/O to the minimum, as impure code is more prone to errors.

Example of pure functions:

```
def min(x, y):
  if x < y:
      return x
  else:
      return y
```

Properties of pure functions:

- **Immutable data:** Purely functional programs operate on immutable data. Instead of altering existing values, copies are created and the original value is preserved.
- **Referential transparency:** Pure computations yield the same value each time they are invoked.
- **Lazy evaluation:** Since pure computations are referentially transparent, they can be performed at any time and still yield the same result. This makes it possible to defer the computation of values until they are needed, that is, to compute them lazily. Lazy evaluation avoids unnecessary computations and allows infinite data structures to be defined and used.

Even though purely functional programming is very beneficial, the programmer might want to use features that are not available in pure programs, like efficient mutable arrays or input-output. This problem can be addressed using the following techniques:

- **Side effects in the language:** Some functional languages extend their purely functional core with side effects. The programmer must be careful not to use impure functions in places where only pure functions are expected.
- **Side effects through monads:** Another way of introducing side effects to a pure language is to simulate them using monads. While the language remains pure and referentially transparent, monads can provide implicit state by threading it inside them. The compiler does not even have to

know about the imperative features because the language itself remains pure. Allowing side effects only through monads and keeping the language pure makes it possible to have lazy evaluation that does not conflict with the effects of impure code. Even though lazy expressions can be evaluated in any order, the monad structure forces the effects to be executed in the correct order.

11.3.3 Higher-order Functions

Higher-order functions (HOFs) are those that take other functions as their arguments. The three most commonly used HOFs are map, filter and reduce.

Map: A basic example of an HOF is map, which takes a function and a list as its arguments, applies the function to all the elements of the list, and returns the list of its results. The function map applies a function to each element of a sequence: list, vector, hash map or dictionary and trees.

For instance, a function that subtracts 2 from all the elements of a list without using loops or recursion in Haskell is:

subtractTwoFromList l = map (\x → x – 2) l

Generalisation of this function to subtract any given number is:

subtractFromList l y = map (\x → x – y) l

The function given to map, then becomes a closure because \x → x – y references a local variable *y*, from outside its body.

Higher-order functions are very useful for refactoring code and reduce the amount of repetition. For example, most for-loops can be expressed using maps or folds. Custom iteration schemes, such as parallel loops, can be easily expressed using HOFs.

Higher-order functions can be simulated in object-oriented languages by functions that take function-objects, also called **functors**. Variables from the scope of the call can be bound inside the function-object, which acts as if it were a closure. This way of simulating HOFs is, however, very verbose and requires declaring a new class every time we want to use an HOF.
Consider another example in Haskell:

If a function f x = 3 * x + 1

Then, if "map fl [1, 2, 3]" is run, [4,7,10] is obtained as output.

Filter: Filter is used to apply a condition. For example,

list(filter (lambda x: x > 10, [1, 20, 3, 40, 4, 14, 8])) gives the output – [20, 40, 14].

Reduce or Fold: The function fold left is tail recursive; whereas the function fold right is not. This function is also known as reduce or inject. An example of fold left, foldl (\acc x → 10 * acc + x) 0 [1, 2, 3, 4, 5] gives –12345, while fold right can be written as foldr (\x acc → 10 * acc + x) 0 [1, 2, 3, 4, 5], giving 54321 as output.

11.3.4 Closure

Closure is a function that remembers the environment in which it was created. Technically, closures are dynamically allocated data structures containing a code pointer, pointing to a fixed piece of code computing a function result and an environment of bound variables. A closure is used to associate a function with a set of 'private' variables. Anonymous functions are a technique used to accomplish this in some languages

11.3.5 Currying

Currying is the decomposition of a function having multiple arguments in a chained sequence of functions into single arguments. The name currying comes from the mathematician Haskell Curry, who developed the concept of curried functions. Curried functions can take one argument at a time while an uncurried function must have all its arguments passed at once.

Let a function $f(x, y) = 10*x - 3*y$ be an uncurried function. It can only take two arguments at once. This function can be rewritten in a curried form as: $f(x)(y) = 10*x - 3*y$

Applying a value of $x = 4$, creates a function with parameter y:

- $g(y) = f(4) = 10*4 - 3*y$
- $g(3) = f(4)(3) = 10*4 - 3*3 = 31$

11.3.6 Lazy Evaluation

Lazy evaluation means that data structures are computed incrementally, as they are required. The parts that are never needed are never computed. Haskell uses lazy evaluation by default.

11.3.7 Recursion

Recursion is heavily used in functional programming as it is canonical and often the only way to iterate. Functional language implementations include tail call optimisation to ensure that recursion does not consume excessive memory.

11.4 Introduction to Lambda Notation/λ-calculus

There is a close association between functional development and mathematics. Lambda refers to lambda calculus or λ-calculus. **Lambda calculus** is a system designed to investigate function definition, function application and recursion.

Consider the function implemented as $f(x)=x^2$. In Haskell, it will be $f\ x = x\text{^}2$. Another way in Haskell is (\x → x^2). Notice that the function is just stated without naming it. This is the essence of lambda calculus. In lambda calculus notation, it can be expressed as $\lambda x.x^2$. This function can be applied on another variable or another function. For example, if the value 5 is applied to the function, output value 25 is obtained.

To compute a lambda expression is to transform it into a canonical form using a set of transformation rules/reductions. In brief, how to express functions in λ-calculus is exaplined in this section. λ-calculus can be called the smallest universal programming language of the world. It consists of a single transformation rule (variable substitution) and a single function definition scheme.

λ-calculus is universal in the sense that any computable function can be expressed and evaluated using this formalism. It is thus equivalent to Turing machines. However, λ-calculus emphasizes the use of transformation rules and does not care about the actual machine implementing them. It is an approach more related to software than to hardware. The central concept in λ-calculus is the "expression". A "name", also called a "variable", is an identifier which, for our purposes, can be any of the letters a, b, c, . . . An expression is defined recursively as follows:

<expression>:= name|<function> |<application>
<function> := λ<name> .<expression>
<application> :=<expression><expression>

An expression can be surrounded with parenthesis for clarity, that is, if E is an expression, (E) is the same expression. The only keywords used in the language are λ and the dot. In order to avoid cluttering expressions with parenthesis, adopt the convention that function application associates from the left, that is, the expression E1E2E3 … En is evaluated applying the expressions as follows:

(…((E1E2)E3)… En).

The simplest function abstraction that can be expressed in λ-calculus is the **identity function**, represented as λx.x. The name after the λ is the identifier of the argument of this function. The expression after the point (in this case, a single x) is called the 'body' of the definition. The identity function is denoted with *I* or |= (λx.x). The identity function applied to itself yields an identity function again.

Functions can be applied to expressions. For example, (λx.x)*y* is the identity function applied to *y*. Parenthesis are used for clarity in order to avoid ambiguity. Function applications are evaluated by substitution as given below,

$(\lambda x.x)y = [y/x]x \doteq (\lambda y.y)y = y$

where *[y/x]* indicates that all occurrences of *x* must be substituted by *y*.

The argument names in function definitions do not carry any meaning by themselves. They are just place holders. Therefore, (λz.z) ≡ (λy.y) ≡ (λt.t) ≡ (λu.u) where the symbol "≡" indicates that A is just a synonym of B.

11.4.1 Free and Bound Variables

In λ-calculus, all names are local to definitions. In the function λx.x*, x* is bound since its occurrence in the body of the definition is preceded by λx. A name not preceded by a λ is called a free variable.

For example,

- In (λx.xy) the variable *x* is bound and *y* is free.
- In (λx.x)(λy.yx) the *x* in the body of the first expression from the left is bound to the first λ. The *y* in the body of the second expression is bound to the second λ and the *x* is free. The *x* in the second expression is totally independent of the *x* in the first expression.

11.4.2 Substitution

In λ-calculus, names are not given to the functions. If a function has to be applied, then the whole function definition must be used. Moreover, substitutions should be performed carefully, so as to avoid mixing up the free occurrences of an identifier with bound ones.

For example, in the expression (λx.(λy.xy))*y*, the function to the left contains a bound *y*, whereas the *y* on the right is free. An incorrect substitution would mix the two identifiers with the erroneous result (λy.yy). Hence, renaming is used in such cases. The bound *y* is renamed as *t* to obtain (λx.(λt.xt))*y* = (λ*t.yt*).

11.4.3 Arithmetic Computations

Every programming language has the scope to perform arithmetical calculations. Hence, there is a need to represent numbers and perform operations on them. Numbers can be represented in lambda calculus by the 'Church numerals', starting from zero and writing "suc(zero)" to represent 1, "suc(suc(zero))" to represent 2, and so on.

Numbers defined using this technique are given in Table 11.1. The table shows the representation of only five numbers. Zero is defined as λs.(λz.z). This is a function of two arguments, *s* and *z*. It is abbreviated as λsz.z. It is understood here that *s* is the first argument to be substituted during the evaluation and *z* the second.

Table 11.1 Numbers in λ-calculus

Number	Representation in λ calculus
0	λsz.z
1	λsz.s(*z*)
2	λsz.s(*s*(*z*))
3	λsz.s(*s*(*s*(*z*)))
4	λsz.s(*s*(*s*(*s*(*z*))))

Successor function: Successor function is defined as *S* ≡ λwyx.y(*wyx*). Let us apply this successor function to our representation for zero, *S0* ≡ (λwyx.y(*wyx*))(λsz.z). In the body of the first expression, substitute all occurrences of *w* with (λsz.z) λyx.y((λsz.z)*yx*) = λyx.y((λz.z)*x*) = λyx.y(*x*) ≡ 1. That is, when successor function is applied to 0, the result is 1. Similarly, on application of successor function to 1 the result is 2, on 2 the result is 3, and so on.

S1 ≡ (λwyx.y(*wyx*))(λsz.s(*z*)) = λyx.y((λsz.s(*z*))*yx*) = λyx.y(*y*(*x*)) ≡ 2

Addition: Addition can be obtained immediately by noting that the body *sz* of our definition of the number 1, for example, can be interpreted as the application of the function *s* on *z*. To add, say 2 and 3, just apply the successor function two times to 3.

Let us try the following in order to compute 2+3:

2*S*3 ≡ (λsz.s(*sz*))(λwyx.y(*wyx*))(λuv.u(*u*(*uv*)))

The first expression on the right side is a 2, the second is the successor function, the third is a 3 (variables are renamed for clarity). The expression above reduces to

(λwyx.y((*wy*)*x*))((λwyx.y((*wy*)*x*))(λuv.u(*u*(*uv*)))) ≡ *SS*3 ≡ *S*4 = 5.

Multiplication: The multiplication of two numbers *x* and *y* can be computed using the following function: (λxyz.x(*yz*)). For example, the product of 2 by 2 will be (λxyz.x(*yz*))22, which reduces to (λz.2(2*z*)) =4.

11.4.4 Recursion

Recursive functions can be defined in λ-calculus using a function which calls a function *y* and then regenerates itself. For instance, consider the following function

Y: *Y* ≡ (λy.(λx.y(*xx*))(λx.y(*xx*)))

This function applied to a function R gives $YR = (\lambda x.R(xx))(\lambda x.R(xx)) = R((\lambda x.R(xx))(\lambda x.R(xx))))$. This states that $YR = R(YR)$, that is, the function R is evaluated using the recursive call YR as the first argument.

Assume, for example, to add the numbers from 0 to 3, the necessary operations are performed by the call $YR3 = R(YR)3 = Z30(3S(YR(P3)))$. Since 3 is not equal to zero, the evaluation reduces to $3S(YR2)$, that is, the sum of the numbers from 0 to 3 is equal to 3 plus the sum of the numbers from 0 to 2. Successive recursive evaluations of YR will lead to the correct final result. The final result will be $3S2S1S0$, that is, the number 6.

11.5 Basic Compilation

A functional compiler is a compiler for a functional programming language. When it comes to functional languages, the distinction between interpreter and compiler becomes blurred. Interpreters can perform compilation, and compilers for functional languages frequently provide an interactive interface in addition to simple compilation facilities. When a program written in a functional language is interpreted, the interpretation manages garbage collection, storage allocation, and other such issues. All this bookkeeping is the province of the run-time system, and it does not disappear simply because a program has to be compiled instead of interpreting it. In order to work, the compiled representation of a program written in a functional language must be coupled with a run-time system. It is a short step from providing each compiled representation with a run-time system to providing each with both a run-time system and its own, private interpreter. This code–runtime system–interpreter package is self-sufficient: it is directly executable. Such a package is, in fact, what some compilers for functional languages produce.

Other implementations offer the option of compiling a program to a bytecode representation for interpretation afterwards by a virtual machine. The same bytecode program can then be run on a variety of platforms, so long as its minimal platform – the virtual machine – is available to host it.

Run-time system: The run-time system is an essential part of compiling functional languages. It provides a common set of functionality necessary to all compiled programs. The two most critical services it provides are primitive operations and storage management. Primitive operations are what actually perform the computation specified by δ-rules. They also enable programs to interface with their environment by providing access to functionality related to the operating system. Storage management is essential, since space is allocated as needed and must be reclaimed in order to prevent excessive memory use.

The run-time system might also handle threading, bytecode interpretation and run-time linking of object code. As the run-time system oversees primitive operations and memory management, it also plays an important part in profiling the run-time behaviour of the compiled code. Every compiler for functional languages will contain a run-time system of some sort. A run-time system provides several distinct, important services. Storage management can become quite involved; primitive operations are a necessary part of producing working code. As each of these services can to some degree be dealt with independently of the others, the compiler's structure may not reflect a concept of a run-time system as such, but the basic services will nevertheless be in place and recognisable; they will simply not be grouped together.

Functional compilers perform conversion from source language to low-level language. The possible phases in a functional compiler are depicted in Fig. 11.1.

As in other types of languages the first compilation phase in a compiler for functional language is the lexical analysis, which breaks the source language into tokens. These tokens are passed to the parser for syntax analysis and a parse tree is given as output. Desugaring is applied after type checking is completed, followed by optimisation, intermediate code generation and finally, code generation. Functional languages use the notation of λ-calculus, as discussed in the previous section. λ-calculus is not a real machine; it defines an abstract machine that has useful operational semantics.

Most compilers for functional languages are multi-pass compilers that convert the functional code into successively more machine-like intermediate languages, until an imperative intermediate representation is obtained. Then, using machine code generation and register allocation, machine code is generated. Various challenges in the compilation of functional languages are:

- Type checking
- Memory management
- Polymorphism
- Higher order functions
- Lazy evaluation

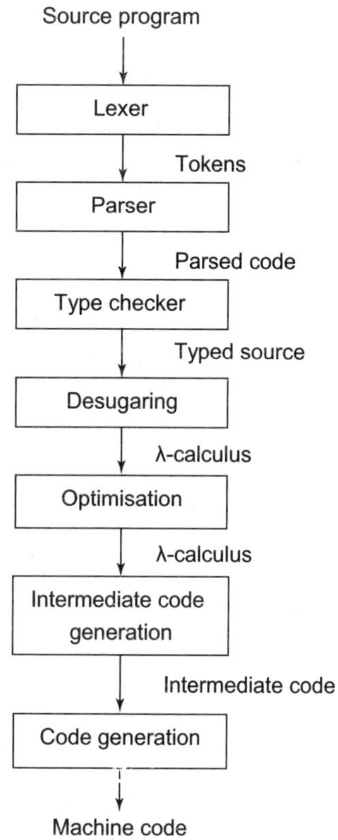

Figure 11.1 Compilation phases for functional compiler

Front end: The problems confronted by the front end are the same as in imperative languages. However, if it has been decided to implement the front end in the functional language then there is an advantage of the abstractions offered by functional languages in constructing the lexer and parser.

If generators for lexers and parsers are built using the functional language, it becomes easy to integrate lexing and parsing into a compiler written in the language itself. Other programs written in the language can then have ready access to a lexer and parser. In semantic analysis, type inference is taken for granted and the programmer can create new data types. Type inference can be treated as a pass in itself. It replaces type checking, as once the compiler has reconstructed a valid type for a term, the type has been checked. If the term cannot be assigned a valid type, type inference has failed: either the program is not well-typed, or the programmer must supply type annotations for some term that is valid but for which a type cannot be inferred.

Intermediate representations: Compilers for functional languages employ an intermediate representation called desugaring of lambda calculus. This makes it possible to represent a program written in a functional language using smaller and smaller subsets of the full language. Thus, source-to-source transformations are possible; where code in the source language can be transformed and rewritten in the source language in an altered form.

In the 1980s, it was popular to translate a functional language program into continuation passing style (CPS). In CPS, control flow and argument passing is made explicit. Every function is augmented with a further argument that serves as the continuation. The function is then called with another function that is to use the result of its computation as the continuation argument. Rather than returning the result x of evaluating the function to a caller, the function instead invokes continuation, with x as the continuation's argument. In compiling call-by-value languages, translation into CPS has been proven to enable more transformations than are possible in the source language.

However, since the translation to CPS is ultimately reversed during code generation, recent compilers have moved to carefully performing some of the transformations developed for use with CPS directly in the source representation. CPS is still used locally for some optimisations.

Graph representations of the program also play a bigger part in some compilers. Large classes of compilers build their back end around graph representations of the program. In such compilers, reduction is performed in terms of the graph. Such graph reduction machines make lazy evaluation feasible, since they provide an easy way to conceive of substitution in reduction without copying. If all terms are represented by a collection of linked nodes, rather than copying the term to each location in order to substitute it, make multiple links to the single original term.

Some compilers employ typed intermediate languages. This allows them to use the additional information provided by types throughout compilation. Instead of simply performing type checking to ensure the program is valid and subsequently ignoring types, the type of the terms becomes additional fodder for analysis and optimisation.

Middle end: Optimisation is the key to producing good code and a good compiler. It is the improvement of an existing compiler in the context of a particular language, set of intermediate representations and the back end. The optimisations that can be performed differ from compiler to compiler, but all compilers for functional languages confront a set of common problems due to the features that modern functional languages offer. These problems are partially addressed by enabling and performing specific kinds of optimisations and partially through the design of the back end. They can also be addressed through extensions to the language itself that allow the programmer to provide further information to the compiler.

Back end: The middle end uses analysis to optimise the representation of the program in preparation for translation to run on a von Neumann machine. The back end is responsible for effecting this translation. This translation consists in bridging the functional model of computation and the imperative model of computation. Conceptually, this is done by simulating functional computation-by-reduction in an imperative, von Neumann setting. This simulation is typically performed by an abstract machine. The abstract machine for a functional language should support the functional language and must be easy to map onto a real machine. The main goal of the back end of the abstract machine is code generation. A large variety of abstract machines have been proposed that can be classified as stack machines, fixed combinator machines and graph reduction machines.

- **Stack machines:** These work by compiling the low-level intermediate language into stack instructions. Stack machines represent the code as stack instructions. The instruction set is customised to the functional language. They might also use a variety of other stacks: environment, control flow and data. The environment stack stores environments of bindings mapping names to values. The control flow stack keeps track of the order of operations and is used to resume evaluation of an expression after a detour to evaluate one of its sub-expressions. The data stack is where data structures are allocated and stored and provides a way to access these structures, as well. The stack code can be optimised by application of peephole optimisations.
- **Fixed combinator machines:** These eliminate the need to maintain an environment by transforming the entire program into a fixed set of combinators applied to known arguments. The bindings that would have been provided by the environment are instead made explicit through

function application. The chosen set of combinators varies from machine to machine; a frequent subset of the chosen combinators are the S, K and I combinators, which are defined in terms of lambda calculus as

$$S = \lambda xyz.xz(yz) \; K = \lambda xy.x \; I = \lambda x.x$$

- **Graph reduction machines:** These conceive of the program as a graph of function, argument and application nodes. Reduction takes place in terms of the graph at application nodes; the result of evaluation replaces the application node. The final value of the program is obtained by reducing the graph to the root node.

11.6 Polymorphic Type Checking

The functional languages are based on lambda calculus and provide the programmer with a variety of higher-level abstractions such as algebraic data types, pattern matching and higher-order functions. New abstractions are not the only source of problems encountered when compiling functional languages. In functional language, it is required to perform a lowering process in lambda calculus. Functional languages are based on a model of computation fundamentally different from the von Neumann model at the root of the imperative languages. To compile a functional language, lambda calculus's computation-through-reduction must be modelled using the von Neumann computer that is the target platform.

Modern functional languages are founded not only on lambda calculus, but also on typed lambda calculi. Types are introduced into programming languages in order to make the language safer and easier to compile efficiently. Types make the language safer by making it much easier for the compiler to catch nonsensical operations, such as trying to add a string to a pointer and store the result in a structure. Programs, especially large, complex programs, written in type-safe languages are easier to debug than those written in non–type-safe languages.

Providing type information, however, can be burdensome on the programmer. It is desirable that the programmer need not explicitly specify the types involved in the program, but rather that the types be implicit in the values used and behaviours specified. This is done through type inference. Once all types have been inferred, type checking can proceed; once the program successfully passes type checking, the type information can be used in optimisation and code generation. To express that a given value is of a given type, write <value> : <Type>.

Polymorphism is the property of being of many types. It is informally divided into two kinds based on the polymorphism exhibited by a function: parametric polymorphism, where the function behaves uniformly across all types, and ad hoc polymorphism, where the behaviour of the function is specified separately for different types.

In **parametric polymorphism**, the parametric type of the function is best expressed by introducing a type variable. For example, if the notation [<type>] is used to represent a list of the given type, then a generic length function parameterized on the type of the list would have type $\forall\alpha.[\alpha] \rightarrow$ Int. * Parametric polymorphism is frequently achieved by exploiting some common property of the types involved.

Ad hoc polymorphism, on the other hand, requires separate definitions for all the types involved. The addition operator + is frequently ad hoc polymorphic. When given two integers, it returns an integer; when given two real numbers, it returns a real number; in some languages, when given two strings, it returns their concatenation, so that "to" + "day" returns "today". It is the nature of ad hoc polymorphism that the function will not be defined for all possible types and will not be uniformly defined even for those types to which it can be applied, as in the dual uses of + for both numerical addition and string concatenation.

A type is said to be polymorphic if it defines data structures holding values of other types and it encompasses operations which work independently of which particular values are held in the structure.

Polymorphism is desirable, but it also requires that all arguments be treated identically regardless of their type: no matter whether an argument is an integer or a list, it has to fit in the same argument box. For a function to be parametrically polymorphic, it must be able to accept any argument, regardless of the argument's type. Polymorphism forces a single, standardized representation of all arguments. Frequently, this takes the form of a pointer to heap-allocated structures with a common layout. Even arguments that could be directly represented, such as integers or floating point numbers, end up being allocated on the heap in order to look like all the other arguments. Such a representation is called a **boxed representation** because it can be thought of as placing every data type into a box, that makes them all look the same. To actually use the data, it must be unboxed and after use, it must be boxed again. This boxing can be expensive. The way to lessen this expense is to work at relaxing the constraint that required boxing in the first place by allowing functions to deal with unboxed arguments. Such arguments are cheaper to allocate and cheaper to work with and can lead to significant gains in efficiency. Enabling manipulation and use of unboxed arguments, and introducing an analysis that can discover when it is possible to substitute unboxed data for boxed data, is an important optimisation for languages with many polymorphic functions. Unboxed types can even be added directly to the language, which allows the programmer to directly manipulate them when efficiency is of particular concern.

11.7 Desugaring

Desugaring is the translation of the source code of a computer program into a more syntactically rigorous form. As a result, the language can be built to be consistent and having small programs. Higher-level features desugar to the same set of lower-level primitives, as given in Table 11.2. The examples are in Haskell language. Haskell's core language is very small, and most Haskell code desugars to either:

- Lambdas/Function application
- Algebraic data types/Case expressions
- Recursive let bindings
- Type classes and specialisation
- Foreign function calls

Table 11.2 Desugaring examples

High-level to lower-level primitive	Example construct	Result of desugaring
If statement desugars to case statement	if b then e1 else e2	case b of True → e1 False → e2
Lambdas of multiple arguments are equivalent to nested lambdas of single arguments	\x y z → e	\x → \y → \z → e

(Cont'd)

Table 11.2 (Continued)

High-level to lower-level primitive	Example construct	Result of desugaring
Functions are equivalent to lambdas	f x y z = e	f = \x y z → e which is equivalent to f = \x → \y → \z → e
Infix functions: Write functions of at least two arguments in infix form using backticks	x `f` y	f x y
Operators are just infix functions of two arguments that do not need backticks. You can write them in prefix form by surrounding them with parentheses	x + y	(+) x y
Parameters can be bound using operator-like names if you surround them with parentheses	let f (%) x y = x % y in f (*) 1 2	(\(%) x y → x % y) (*) 1 2 which is equivalent to 1 * 2
Partially apply operators to just one argument using a section	(1 +)	\x → 1 + x
Pattern matching on constructors desugars to case statements	f (Left l) = eL f (Right r) = eR	f x = case x of Left l → eL Right r → eR
Pattern matching on numeric or string literals desugars to equality tests	f 0 = e0 f 1 = e1	f x = if x == 0 then e0 else e1 which is equivalent to f x = case x == 0 of True → e0 False → e1
Map function	map f[]= [] map f (x:xs) = f x: map f xs	map = λ f . λ y s. case ys of nil → nil Cons x xs → Cons(f x) (map f xs)

Summary

- Functional languages abstract concurrency control. The programmer does not have to handle concurrency.
- Functional languages use the functional programming paradigm, which takes advantage of functions that do not share memory and which have no side effects.
- Functional languages use a style of programming called functional programming, which models computations as the evaluation of expressions or mathematical functions.
- Imperative programming results in change in state with the use of commands in the source code.
- Imperative programming does support functions in the sense of subroutines, but not in the mathematical sense.

- Programming languages may be categorised as functional and imperative.
- In a functional language, the assignment of a value to a variable is binding and its value does not change.
- Functional programming requires that functions are first class.
- First class functions can be passed as arguments to other functions, returned from functions, stored in variables and data structures and built at run-time.
- Pure functions are functions without side effects. For the same input, the functions always return the same output.
- Pure functions are stateless and deterministic.
- Currying is the decomposition of a function having multiple arguments in a chained sequence of functions into single arguments.
- Lambda calculus is a system designed to investigate function definition, function application and recursion.
- Functional compilation phases: lexical analysis, parsing, type checking, desugaring, optimisation, intermediate code generation and code generation.

Exercises

Review Questions

Fill in the blanks with appropriate answers:

1. ________ data structure used in functional programming has sequences of objects that do not change.
2. ________ means that data structures are computed incrementally, and the parts that are never needed are never computed.

Answers: 1. Tuple 2. Lazy evaluation

State whether true or false:

1. Functional language use the declarative programming paradigm.
2. In imperative programming, programs are executed by evaluating expressions and avoiding changing state and mutable data.
3. Haskell does not support functional programming.
4. Functional programming provides better support for structured programming.
5. Functional programming uses mutable state.
6. Referential transparency is provided by functional languages.
7. Pure functions rely on global variables.
8. Closures are dynamically allocated data structures.
9. For a function to be parametrically polymorphic, it must be able to accept any argument, regardless of the argument's type.
10. Desugaring is the translation of the source code of a computer program into a more syntactically rigorous form.

Answers: 1. True 2. False 3. False 4. True 5. False 6. True 7. False 8. True 9. True 10. True

12 Parallel Compilers and Scheduling

Objectives

- To introduce the concept of parallel programming
- To discuss dependency for parallelisation of programs
- To discuss NVCC for parallel compilation
- To discuss affine array indexes
- To discuss iteration spaces

12.1 Parallel Programming Concepts

The task of the processor is to execute a sequence of instructions. However, as the data increases, one single processor fails to offer efficiency. Hence, parallel processing is needed. In parallel processing, more than one processor is used. Parallel computing allows us to solve problems that do not fit on a single CPU or which cannot be solved in a reasonable time. Using parallel computing, larger problems can be solved faster. It involves solving a particular problem by dividing it into multiple independent sub-problems, creating multiple execution entities for them and then solving them independently through these execution entities onto different processors and establishing communication amongst them for any coordination if required in order accomplish the given task.

Parallel programs must be designed to take advantage of parallelism and should not add overhead to the program. Load balancing, efficient communication method, race conditions, deadlock, non-determinism and scaling limits due to inherent sequential parts in the code are some of the issues that must be taken care of while designing a parallel code. Efficient parallel programs result in minimal time for execution and are cost effective.

Parallelism can be expressed as functional or data parallelism. In **functional parallelism**, each processor works on their section of the problem, that is, each process performs a different function or executes different code sections that are independent. It is commonly programmed with message passing libraries. In **data parallelism,** each processor works on their section of the data. Each process does the same work on unique and independent pieces of data. It can be programmed at a high level with OpenMP, or at a lower level using a message passing library like MPI or with hybrid programming. A special case of data parallelism is called **task parallelism**. In this, each process performs the same function but does not communicate with each other, but only with a master process.

One of the most widely used classifications of parallel computers is given by Flynn. **Single instruction, single data (SISD)** is a non-parallel execution model. Only one instruction stream is executed by the CPU during any one clock cycle and only one data stream is used as input during any one clock cycle. **Single instruction, multiple data (SIMD)** is a parallel model, in which all processing units execute the same instruction at any given clock cycle and each processing unit can operate on a different data element. **Multiple instruction, single data (MISD)** is a parallel model, in which each processing unit operates on the data independently via separate instruction streams and a single data stream is fed into multiple processing units. **Multiple instruction, multiple data (MIMD)** is also a parallel model, in which every processor may be executing a different instruction stream and every processor may be working with a different data stream.

Another useful way to classify modern parallel computers is by their memory model:

- **Shared memory programming:** Shared memory systems have a single address space. Applications can be developed in which loop iterations (with no dependencies) are executed by different processors. Shared memory codes are mostly data parallel, that is, the same code is run on different sets of data.
- **Distributed memory programming:** Distributed memory systems have separate address spaces for each processor. It is composed of a collection of independent physically (and geographically) separated computers that do not share physical memory. Each processor has local memory that can be accessed faster than remote memory. The data must be manually decomposed and distributed across memory modules. The processors communicate using local and wide area networks.
- **Hybrid memory programming:** These are systems with multiple shared memory nodes or the memory may be shared at the node level, distributed above that.

Programming single-processor systems is relatively easy because they have a single thread of execution and a single address space. Programming shared memory systems can benefit from the single address space. Programming distributed memory systems is more difficult due to multiple address spaces and the need to access remote data. Programming hybrid memory systems is even more difficult, but gives the programmer much greater flexibility. Though numerous parallel programming languages are available, the dominant ones are MPI for distributed memory programming and OpenMP for shared memory programming.

12.2 Processes and Threads

In programming, there are two basic units of execution: processes and threads. Both execute a series of instructions and both are initiated by a program or the operating system.

A **process** is an instance of a program that is being executed. It contains the program code and its current activity. A process has a self-contained execution environment. That is, it has a complete, private set of basic run-time resources like memory space. Threads exist within a process and every process has at least one thread. Each process provides the resources needed to execute a program. Each process is started with a single thread, known as the primary thread. A process can have multiple threads in addition to the primary thread, for concurrent execution of instructions.

Each process has its own memory space. Running a single application may require more than one process. These processes communicate with each other by using inter process communication (IPC) resources, such as pipes and sockets. IPC resources can also be used for communication between processes on different systems.

A **thread** is the basic unit to which the operating system allocates processor time. A thread can execute any part of the process code, including parts currently being executed by another thread. An application can have one or more processes. A collection of worker threads that efficiently execute asynchronous callbacks on behalf of the application is called the **thread pool**. A thread can execute even the smallest sequence of programmed instructions that can be managed independently by an operating system. If multiple threads exist in a process, they share resources like memory, files, etc. This sharing of resources helps in efficient communication between threads.

On a single processor, multitasking takes place as the processor switches between different threads; it is known as **multithreading**. The switching happens so frequently that the threads or tasks are perceived to be running at the same time. Threads can truly be concurrent on a multiprocessor or multi-core system, with every processor or core executing the separate threads simultaneously. Threads may be considered lightweight processes, as they contain simple sets of instructions and can run within a larger process. Computers can run multiple threads and processes at the same time.

On a multiprocessor system, multiple processes can be executed in parallel. Multiple threads of control can exploit true parallelism, possible on multiprocessor systems. Threads have direct access to the data segment of its process but processes have their own copy of the data segment of the parent process. Changes to the main thread may affect the behaviour of the other threads of the process. However, changes to the parent process do not affect child processes. Processes are heavily dependent on the system resources available while threads require minimal amounts of resources; so a process is considered as heavyweight while a thread is termed a lightweight process.

12.3 Shared Memory and Message Passing

In a shared memory model, multiple processes operate on the same data by sharing memory. These cooperating processes can communicate through a message passing system, by means of exchanging messages. In shared memory systems, system calls are required only to establish the shared memory regions. Once shared memory is established, all access is treated as routine memory access, and no assistance from the kernel is required. Shared memory helps run processes concurrently but concurrent execution is not possible in message passing.

In the shared memory programming model, tasks share a common address space, which they read and write asynchronously. Various mechanisms such as locks and semaphores may be used to control access to the shared memory. An advantage of this model is that there is no need to explicitly specify the communication of data between tasks. However, it is difficult to understand and manage data locality. On shared memory platforms, the native compilers translate user program variables into actual memory addresses, which are global.

In the message passing model, a set of processors uses its own local memory during computation. Multiple tasks can reside on the same physical machine as well across an arbitrary number of machines. Processes exchange data through communications by sending and receiving messages. The message passing facility has two operations: send and receive. Data transfer usually requires cooperative operations to be performed by each process. For example, a send operation must have a matching receive operation. Message passing is useful for exchanging smaller amounts of data, because no conflicts need be avoided. Message passing is also easier to implement for inter-process communication.

From a programming perspective, message passing implementations commonly comprise a library of subroutines that are embedded in the source code. The programmer is responsible for determining all parallelism.

12.4 NVCC for Parallel Compilation

Computing is evolving from central processing on the CPU to co-processing on the CPU and GPU. Compute Unified Device Architecture (CUDA) is a parallel computing platform and programming model developed by NVIDIA for general computing on graphical processing units (GPUs). Computations can be speeded up significantly by harnessing the power of GPUs. In GPU-accelerated applications, the sequential part of the workload runs on the CPU, which is optimised for single-threaded performance, while the compute-intensive portion of the application runs on thousands of GPU cores in parallel. Hence, the CUDA program consists of different phases executed on:

- **The host (CPU):** Phases which exhibit little or no data parallelism run as ordinary processes. The C code is compiled with the host's C compiler.
- **The device (GPU):** Phases which exhibit high data parallelism are made to run on GPUs. C extended with keywords for labelling data parallel functions, called kernels, and their associated data structures, are used. The GPU code is further compiled by the NVCC.

The CUDA Toolkit from NVIDIA provides GPU-accelerated libraries, a compiler, development tools and the CUDA run-time required to develop GPU-accelerated applications. The CUDA platform is accessible to software developers through CUDA-accelerated libraries, compiler directives such as OpenACC and extensions to industry-standard programming languages including C, C++ and Fortran. CUDA C/C++ can be compiled with NVCC, Nvidia's LLVM-based C/C++ compiler. CUDA Fortran uses the PGI CUDA Fortran compiler from The Portland Group.

Source files for CUDA applications consist of a mixture of conventional C++ host code, plus GPU device functions. The CUDA compilation trajectory separates the device functions from the host code, compiles the device functions using NVIDIA compilers and assembler, compiles the host code using a C++ host compiler that is available, and afterwards embeds the compiled GPU functions as fat binary images in the host's object file. In the linking stage, specific CUDA run-time libraries are added for supporting remote SPMD procedure calling and for providing explicit GPU manipulation such as allocation of GPU memory buffers and host-GPU data transfer.

NVCC is the CUDA compiler driver. It hides the intricate details of CUDA compilation from developers. It accepts a range of conventional compiler options, such as for defining macros and include/library paths, and for steering the compilation process. All non-CUDA compilation steps are forwarded to a C++ host compiler that is supported by NVCC, which translates its options to the appropriate host compiler command line options.

The parallel portion of the application executes as a kernel. The entire GPU executes the kernel, which can have many threads. All threads are executed in parallel, running the same code. Each thread has a unique ID. The program must be written as a single-threaded program parameterized in terms of the thread ID. Use the thread ID to select a subset of the data for processing, and to make control flow decisions. Launch a number of threads, such that the ensemble of threads processes the whole data set. The kernel subdivides threads and they are grouped into blocks. Blocks are grouped into a grid and a kernel is executed as a grid of blocks of threads.

CUDA compilation trajectory: The input program is preprocessed for device compilation and is compiled to CUDA binary (cubin) and/or PTX intermediate code, which is placed in a fat binary file, that is, a computer executable program that has been expanded with code native to multiple instruction sets and which can run on multiple processor types. The file is larger than a normal binary file. The input program is preprocessed once again for host compilation and is synthesized to embed the fat binary and transform CUDA-specific C++ extensions into standard C++ constructs. Then the C++ host compiler compiles the synthesized host code with the embedded fat binary into a host object. The embedded fat binary is inspected by the CUDA run-time system whenever the device code is launched by the host program to obtain an appropriate fat binary image for the current GPU.

An NVCC compilation uses two types of architecture: a virtual intermediate architecture, plus a real GPU architecture to specify the intended processor to execute on. For such an NVCC command to be valid, the real architecture must be an implementation of the virtual architecture. The chosen virtual architecture is more of a statement on the GPU capabilities that the application requires: using the smallest virtual architecture still allows the widest range of actual architectures for the second NVCC stage. Conversely, specifying a virtual architecture that provides features unused by the application unnecessarily restricts the set of possible GPUs that can be specified in the second NVCC stage. The virtual architecture should be chosen as low as possible, thereby maximising the actual GPUs to run on and the real architecture should be chosen as high as possible.

The single instruction, multiple thread execution model is used. A set of 32 parallel threads execute together in the SIMT mode on a streaming multiprocessor (SM). This set of 32 parallel threads is called the **warp**. The SM hardware implements zero-overhead warp and thread scheduling. Threads can execute independently and converge when they branch independently. Each SM executes up to 1024 concurrent threads, as 32 SIMT warps of 32 threads.

Threads can access data in registers and local memory. Blocks of threads access shared memory and all blocks have a global memory. A thread block is a batch of threads that can cooperate with each other by synchronizing their execution, but two threads from two different blocks cannot cooperate.

There are separate file types, .c/.cpp, for host code and .cu for device/mixed code.

The compilation commands are as follows:

- Build release code, nvcc.cu [–o]
- Build debug CPU code, nvcc –g.cu
- Build debug GPU code, nvcc –G.cu
- Build optimised GPU code, nvcc –O.cu

Such jobs are self-contained, in the sense that they can be executed and completed by a batch of GPU threads entirely without intervention by the host process, thereby gaining optimal benefit from the parallel graphics hardware.

The GPU code is implemented as a collection of functions in a language that is essentially C++, but with some annotations for distinguishing them from the host code, plus annotations for distinguishing different types of data memory that exist on the GPU. Such functions may have parameters, and they can be called using a syntax that is very similar to regular C function calling, but slightly extended for being able to specify the matrix of GPU threads that must execute the called function. During its lifetime, the host process may dispatch many parallel GPU tasks.

Uses

- NVCC can be used for separate compilation. Prior to the 5.0 release, CUDA did not support separate compilation, so the CUDA code could not call device functions or access variables across files. Such compilation is referred to as whole program compilation. Starting with CUDA 5.0, separate compilation of device code is supported; though some code changes were required to achieve this.
- Cross-compilation
- Keeping intermediate phase files: NVCC stores intermediate results by default into temporary files that are deleted immediately before it completes the compilation process. The location of the temporary file directories used depends on the current platform.
- Printing code generation statistics

12.5 Dependency

Two statements can run in parallel if and only if there is no form of dependency between the two statements. Any program spends most of the time in the execution of loops. Loops are good candidates for parallelisation. Before parallelising the loop, find out if the loop can be parallelised, for which dependency analysis is performed. Different iterations of a loop can run on different processors in parallel if the iterations do not interfere with each other, that is, if there is no dependence between iterations.

Types of dependence

Flow dependence: Flow dependence occurs when one iteration writes a location that a later iteration reads. It introduces the read-after-write (RAW) hazard because the instruction that reads from the location in memory has to wait until it is written to by the previous instruction, or else the read instruction will read the wrong value. Consider, for example

```
for (i = 1; i < 4; i++)
{
    a[i] = b[i];
    c[i] = a[i - 1];
}
```

i = 1	i=2	i=3
W(a[1])	W(a[2])	W(a[3])
R(b[1])	R(b[2])	R(b[3])
W(c[1])	W(c[2])	W(c[3])
R(a[0])	R(a[1])	R(a[2])

Read(R) and Write (W) in different iterations are shown here along with the dependency.

Anti-dependence: When an iteration reads a location that a later iteration writes, it is called anti-dependence. This may lead to the hazard called write-after-read (WAR) because the instruction that writes the data into a memory location has to wait until that memory location has been read by the previous instruction, or else the reading instruction would read the wrong value. Consider, for example

```
for (i = 1; i < 4; i++)
{
    a[i-1] = b[i];
    c[i] = a[i];
}
```

i = 1	i=2	i=3
W(a[0])	W(a[1])	W(a[2])
R(b[1])	R(b[2])	R(b[3])
W(c[1])	W(c[2])	W(c[3])
R(a[1])	R(a[2])	R(a[3])

Read(R) and Write (W) in different iterations are shown here along with the dependency.

Output dependence: When an iteration writes a location that a later iteration writes, it is called output dependence. This introduces the write-after-write (WAW) hazard because the second instruction to write the value to a memory location needs to wait until the first instruction finishes writing data to the same memory location, or else when the memory location is read at a later time, it will contain the wrong value. Consider, for example

```
for (i = 1; i < 4; i++)
{
    a[i] = b[i];
    a[i+1] = c[i];
}
```

i = 1	i=2	i=3
W(a[1])	W(a[2])	W(a[3])
R(b[1])	R(b[2])	R(b[3])
W(a[2])	W(a[3])	W(a[4])
R(c[1])	R(c[2])	R(c[3])

Read(R) and Write (W) in different iterations are given above along with the dependency,

Loop-carried dependence: When a statement in one iteration of a loop depends on a statement in a different iteration of the same loop, a loop-carried dependence exists. A loop-carried dependence is present only if the statements occur in two different instances of a loop; otherwise, it a loop-independent dependence. Loop-carried dependences limit loop iteration parallelisation. Consider, for example

```
for (i = 1; i < 4; i++)
{
    b[i]=i;              //S1
    a[i] = b[i−1]+2;     //S2
}
```

In the above loop, there exists loop-carried dependence as the value of b[i−1] is needed from the previous loop. S2 of the current iteration depends on S1 of the previous iteration. However, if the second statement is replaced by a[i]=b[i]+2, statement S2 shows dependency on statement S1, but in the same iteration, making the dependency loop-independent.

12.6 Iteration Spaces

Iteration space represents each instance of a loop. It can defined by the following equation:

I = {[l1,...,ln]: LB1 <= l1 < UB1 && ... LBn <= ln < UBn};

The equation considers the upper bound (UB) and lower bound (LB) of all the loops. For example, consider the nested for-loop given below:

```
for (i=1; i<=10;i++)
        for(j=1; j<=5;j++)
                a[i,j] = a[i−1,j+1] +1;
```

The iteration space for the above code will be

I= {[i,j]: 1<=i<=10 && 1<=j<=5};

Iteration spaces can also be represented graphically in the form of graphs where each dynamic instance of a loop or, simply put, each iteration is represented as a point (or node) in a graph and dependencies are represented by directed arrows. Iteration space graphs (ISG) show the path that the code takes when traversing through the iterations of the loop.

Example 12.1 Represent the given loop using iteration space graph

```
for(i=1;i<=4;i++)
      a[i+1]=a[i];
```

Let us represent each iteration by a node and consider the read and write in each iteration.

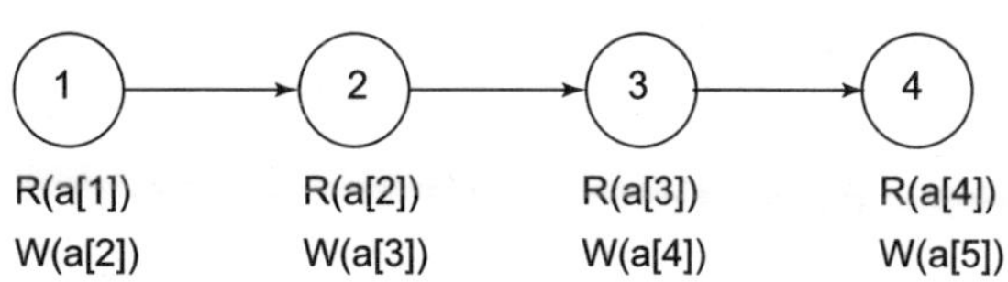

There is dependency from Write in the previous iteration to Read in the current iteration. Hence, dependency edges are marked as above. Now, consider the statement inside the loop is changed to a[i+2] = a[i]. Then, the dependency edge will be from node 1 to node 3, node 2 to node 4.

Example 12.2 Represent the given loop using iteration space graph

```
for(i=1;i<=4;i++)
        for(j=1;j<=4;j++)
                a[i+1][j−2] =a[i][j] + 2;
```

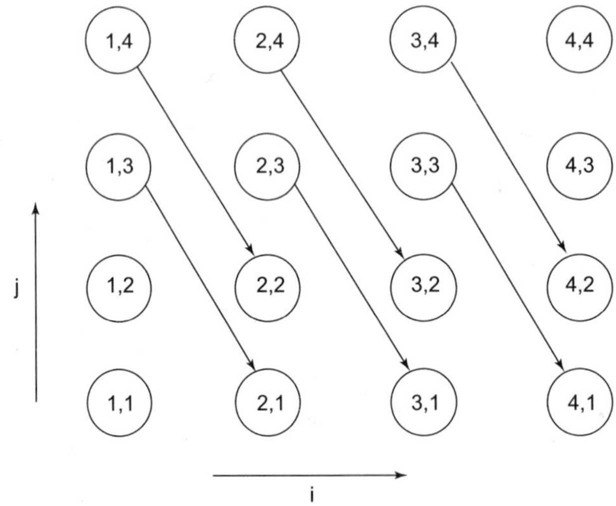

Figure 12.1 Iteration space graph

Consider i=1,j=3. There is dependency from a[i][j] to a[i+1][j−2]. Hence, there will be dependency from node (1,3) to (2,1). Other dependencies are as shown in Fig. 12.1. A compressed representation of the dependencies have also been devised, called distance and direction vectors. They capture the same dependencies as an iteration space. Distance vector captures the shape of dependencies, but not the particular source and sink; direction vector captures the direction of dependencies, but not the particular shape. The distance vector for the graph in Fig. 12.1 is computed as follows:
Consider a dependency from (1,3)→ (2,1)

Distance vector= (2−1,1−3)= (1,−2)

For the given graph, every dependency edge gives the same distance vector. Graphs may exist with more than one distance vector. Distance vector is a summary of dependencies but it loses the source and sink nodes. The direction of dependency can also be saved or only the direction vector can be saved.
For example
(2, −1) → (+, −)
(0, 1) → (0, +)
(0, −2) → (0, −)
'<' and '>' notation could be used instead of '+' and '−'

Loops without dependencies can be parallelised. Thus, the compiler needs to find the loops that can be parallelised. Hence, dependencies must be determined and the compiler may need to perform some loop transformations. Various loop transformation techniques are available. However, determine which loop transformations must be applied and in which order. The problem is undecidable in the worst case and may be NP-hard in the best case. The challenge is to find an order for the application of loop transformations that works for all applications. One approach is to identify important subsets of transformations and try to develop an integrated framework for those transformations. Frameworks are used in the compiler to abstract loops, memory access and data dependencies in loops. They also specify the effect of a sequence of loop transformations on the loop, its memory access and its data dependencies. Then generate code from the transformed loop.

Transformation frameworks: Transformations are carried out by the application of the following steps:

1. Represent the iteration space.
2. Represent the transformations.
3. Apply the transformations to the iteration space, dependencies and array access.
4. Test the legality of a transformation.

Given an iteration dependence graph, the graph is partitioned such that no data dependencies cross partitions and the locality is maximised. The criteria for parallelisation are that no loop-carried dependence is allowed and the loops inside a dependence-carrying loop are dependence free.

For example, the compiler analyses needed in C to obtain iteration space representation. This is done by performing loop analysis from AST or the control flow graph. The compiler also needs to perform pointer analysis and dependence analysis before the loop transformations.

Loop interchange

P := {[i,j] → [j,i]};

Loop interchange is also called loop permutation for the loop.

```
for(t1 = 0; t1 <= 49; t1++)
  for(t2 = 0; t2 <= 99; t2++)
  s1(t2,t1);
```

Interchanging two loops swaps the order of their entries in the distance/direction vectors. Legal interchanges are given below:

(0, +) → (+, 0)

(+, 0) → (0, +)

However, backwards dependencies are not allowed , so (+, –) → (–, +) is an illegal dependence, and loop interchange is not allowed.

Loop tiling: The basic idea is to strip-mine a loop into two loops, in such a way that the inner loop iterates within contiguous strips and the outer loop iterates strip by strip. Then, interchange the strip loop to the outside of the containing loops.

Other types of transformations are loop skewing, fusion and fission.

12.7 Affine Array Indexes

A function having one or more variables is affine or can preserve parallel relationships, if it can be expressed as the sum of a constant and constant multiples of the variables, as given below:

$$f = c_0 + \sum_{i=1}^{n} (c_i x_i)$$

Array subscript expressions are usually affine functions involving loop induction variables. Affine functions can be considered as linear functions.

Each array index is expressed as an affine expression of loop indexes and symbolic constants. Affine functions provide concise mapping from the iteration space to the data space, making it easy to determine which iterations map to the same data or same cache line.

Array access in a loop can be considered affine if the bounds of the loop are expressed as affine expressions of the surrounding loop variables and symbolic constants, and the index for each dimension of the array is also an affine expression of the surrounding loop variables and symbolic constants. For example, Z[i], Z[i + j + 1], Z[0], Z[i, i], and Z[2*i +1,3* j−10] are affine array accesses if i and j are loop index variables bounded by affine expressions. If n is a symbolic constant for a loop nest, then Z[S * n, n — j] is another example of an affine array access. However, Z[i * j] and Z[n * j] are not affine accesses.

Affine upper and lower bounds of a loop can be represented as a matrix-vector calculation. Once placed in the matrix-vector form, apply standard linear algebra to find pertinent information such as the dimensions of the data accessed and which iterations refer to the same data. Each affine array access can be described by two matrices and two vectors. The first matrix-vector pair is B and b that describe the iteration space for the access and the second pair is F and f, which represent the function(s) of the loop-index variables that produce the array index(es) used in the various dimensions of the array access.

Moreover, an array access in a loop nest can be represented by four-tuple T = (F,f,B,b). It maps a vector i within the bounds Bi +b >0 to the array element location Fi+f.

Array access X[i−1] can be expressed as affine expression

$$\begin{bmatrix} 1 & 0 \end{bmatrix} \begin{bmatrix} i \\ j \end{bmatrix} + \begin{bmatrix} -1 \end{bmatrix}$$

X[i,j] can be expressed as the affine expression

$$\begin{bmatrix} 1 & 0 \\ 0 & 1 \end{bmatrix} \begin{bmatrix} i \\ j \end{bmatrix} + \begin{bmatrix} 0 \\ 0 \end{bmatrix}$$

X[i,j+1] can be expressed as the affine expression

$$\begin{bmatrix} 1 & 0 \\ 0 & 1 \end{bmatrix} \begin{bmatrix} i \\ j \end{bmatrix} + \begin{bmatrix} 0 \\ 1 \end{bmatrix}$$

X[j,j+2] can be expressed as the affine expression

$$\begin{bmatrix} 0 & 1 \\ 0 & 1 \end{bmatrix} \begin{bmatrix} i \\ j \end{bmatrix} + \begin{bmatrix} 0 \\ 2 \end{bmatrix}$$

Dependencies between arrays can be checked if two static accesses A and A' are defined as

$$A = \langle F, f, B, b \rangle \text{ and } A' = \langle F', f', B', b' \rangle$$

A and A' are data dependent if $Bi \geq 0$; $B'i' \geq 0$ and $Fi + f = F'i' + f'$ and $i \neq i'$ for dependencies between instances of the same static access.

Summary

- Aspects to be handled while designing parallel code: load balancing, efficient communication method, race conditions, deadlock, non-determinism and scaling limits due to inherent sequential parts in the code.

- In functional parallelism, each process performs a different function or executes different code sections that are independent.
- In data parallelism, each processor runs the same program on unique and independent pieces of data.
- Flynn's classification of computers: SISD, SIMD, MISD, MIMD.
- A process is an instance of a program that is being executed. It contains the program code and its current activity.
- Compute Unified Device Architecture (CUDA) is a parallel computing platform and programming model developed by NVIDIA for general computing on graphical processing units (GPUs).
- CUDA programs consist of different phases executed on the host CPU and device (GPU).
- The GPU code is compiled by the NVCC.
- NVCC is the CUDA compiler driver.
- Two statements can run in parallel if and only if there is no form of dependency between them.
- Types of dependence: flow dependence, anti-dependence, output dependence, loop carried dependence.
- Iteration space represents each instance of a loop.

Exercises

Review Questions

Fill in the blanks with appropriate answers:

1. Processes communicate with each other using inter process communication (IPC) resources, such as ________ and ________.
2. A collection of worker threads that efficiently execute asynchronous callbacks on behalf of the application is called ________.
3. Processor switching between different threads is known as ________.
4. The input program to CUDA is preprocessed for device compilation and is compiled to ________.
5. An NVCC compilation uses two types of architecture: ________ and ________, to specify the intended processor to execute on.
6. The ________ execution model is used in NVCC.
7. The file type for host code is ________ and ________ for device code.
8. ________ graphs represent the path that the code takes when traversing through the iterations of the loop.

Answers: 1. Pipes and sockets 2. Thread pool 3. Multithreading 4. CUDA binary (cubin) and/or PTX intermediate code 5. A virtual intermediate architecture and a real GPU architecture 6. Single instruction, multiple thread 7. c/.cpp and .cu 8. Iteration space graphs (ISG)

State whether true or false:

1. Threads exist within a process.
2. An application can have one or more processes.
3. Processes are not dependent on the system resources.

Answers: 1. True 2. True 3. False

13 Programs on Compiler Design

OBJECTIVES

- To describe the implementation of regular expressions in Python
- To discuss the implementation of various aspects of different phases of the compiler

13.1 Regular Expressions in Python

Regular expressions are a powerful string manipulation tool. Most modern languages have library packages for regular expressions. The re module in Python provides support for regular expressions. Regular expressions can be used for:

- Searching a string (search and match)
- Replacing parts of a string (sub)
- Breaking strings into smaller pieces (split)

Patterns can be used to specify the regular expression. Table 13.1 shows some patterns along with their description.

Table 13.1 Patterns and their descriptions

Pattern	Description
^	Matches beginning of line.
$	Matches end of line.
.	Matches any single character except newline.
[...]	Matches any single character in brackets.
[^...]	Matches any single character not in brackets
re*	Matches 0 or more occurrences of the preceding expression.
re+	Matches 1 or more occurrences of the preceding expression.
re?	Matches 0 or 1 occurrence of the preceding expression.
?#...	Comment.
\w	Matches any alphanumeric character
\W	Matches any non-alphanumeric character
\s	Matches whitespace. Equivalent to [\t\n\r\f].
\A	Matches beginning of string.
\Z	Matches end of string. If a newline exists, it matches just before newline.
\z	Matches end of string.
\G	Matches the point where the last match finished.
\n, \t, etc.	Matches newlines, carriage returns, tabs, etc.

Before using regular expressions in the program, import the library using "import re". To run any Python code, we must save the file with a '.py' extension. After we have installed Python, navigate to it from the command line and type <programName>.py to run the Python code.

Example 13.1 Demonstrate the use of *re.match*

It searches for a match starting at the beginning. The syntax is as follows:
re.match(pattern, string, flags=0)

The term 'pattern' is the regular expression to be matched, while 'string' is the string, which would be searched to match the pattern at the beginning of the string; 'flags' can be used to specify different flags using the bitwise OR | . These are modifiers, which are listed in Table 13.2.

Table 13.2 Flags

Modifier	Description
re.I	Performs case-insensitive matching.
re.M	Makes $ match the end of a line (not just the end of the string) and makes ^ match the start of any line (not just the start of the string).
re.S	Makes a period dot match any character, including a newline.
re.U	Interprets letters according to the Unicode character set. This flag affects the behaviour of \w, \W, \b, \B.

This function attempts to match the re pattern to a string with optional flags. The *re.match* function returns a match object on success; none on failure. We use *groupnum* or the *groups* function of the match object to obtain matched expression.

Python code to identify whether the string is an e-mail address or not is given below:

```
import re
pat1 = "\w+@(\w+\.)+(com|org|net|edu)"
r1 = re.match(pat1,"abc@cs.edu")
if r1:
   print "Address : ", r1.group()
else:
   print "Nothing found!!"
```

Here, abc@cs.edu will be identified as an e-mail address. The *group()* function specifies the complete match.

Example 13.2 Demonstrate the use of *group()*

```
import re
line = "Cats are smarter than dogs"
     matchObj = re.match( '(.* ) are (.* ) .* ', line, re.M|re.I)
if matchObj:
     print "matchObj.group() :", matchObj.group()
     print "atchObj.group(1) :", matchObj.group(1)
     print "matchObj.group(2):", matchObj.group(2)
```

```
else:
    print "No match!!"
```

The output will be as follows:
matchObj.group() : Cats are smarter than dogs
matchObj.group(1) : Cats
matchObj.group(2) : smarter

Example 13.3 Demonstrate the use of *re.search()*
It searches for a pattern anywhere in a string.
Syntax: re.search(pattern, string, flags=0)

The term 'pattern' is the regular expression to be matched, while 'string' is the string that would be searched to match the 'pattern' anywhere in the string; 'flags' can specify different flags using the bitwise OR | . These are modifiers, which are listed in Table 13.2 .

It searches for the first occurrence of the re pattern within a string with optional flags. The *re.search()* function returns a match object on success; none on failure. We use *groupnum* or the *groups()* function of the match object to obtain the matched expression.

Python code to show the difference between *re.match* and *re.search*

```
import re
line = "Cats are smarter than dogs";
    matchObj = re.match( 'dogs', line, re.M|re.I)
if matchObj:
    print "match → matchObj.group() : ", matchObj.group()
else:       print "No match!!"
    searchObj = re.search( r'dogs', line, re.M|re.I)
if searchObj:
    print "search → searchObj.group() : ", searchObj.group()
else:       print "Nothing found!!"
```

The output will be as follows:
No match!!
search → searchObj.group() : dogs

Example 13.4 Demonstrate the use of *re.findall*
The *re.findall()* function is used to find all the matches in a string. It performs a global search of the whole input string. It returns a list of the matches or an empty list if no matches are found.
The syntax is as follows:

matchList = re.findall(pattern, input_str, flags=0)

Python code that uses *re.findall*

```
import re
regex = "[a-zA-Z]+ \d+"
matches = re.findall (regex, "June 24, August 9, Dec 12")
for match in matches:
print "Full match: %s" % (match)
```

Python code that uses *re.match*

```
import re
line="Todays date is 10/10/1999";
r1 = re.match(r'(.*) is ((\d+/\d+/\d+))',line)
if r1:
   p1=r1.group(2)
   print "Date: ", p1
else:
   print "Nothing found!!"
```

13.2 Programs for Different Phases of the Compiler

In this section, we present some programs for better understanding of the implementation of some phases. Programs on the LR parser and SDTS are provided. One way of implementation is suggested. There is a lot of scope for improvement and optimisation of these codes. Programs on LL parser, code optimisation, error handling, symbol table management, and so on, can be implemented as an exercise. We have suggested various implementations after each program.

Example 13.5 Program in C++ to find the augmented grammar and display all the states for the given grammar along with the parsing table

```
#include<iostream.h>
#include<conio.h>
#include<stdio.h>
#include<stdlib.h>
struct slr
{
 int no_rules;
 char a[4][7];
 int end;
}obj[7];

struct t
{
 int s;
 char c;
 int d;
}obj1[7];

void display(int nt)
{
 cout<<"\n\n Table:\n";
 for(int i=0;i<nt;i++)
 cout<<"( I"<<obj1[i].s<<" ,"<<obj1[i].c<<" ) = I"<<obj1[i].d<<"\n";
}

int find(int ind,char ter,int nt)
```

```
{
 for(int i=0;i<nt;i++)
 {
  if(obj1[i].s==ind && obj1[i].c==ter)
   return obj1[i].d;
  else ;
 }
 return -1;
}

void main()
{
 clrscr();
 int n,i,j,k,nt=0,no_t,no_nt,n1,a,t1[10][10];
 char temp,t[10][10],f[5][5];
 char arr[5][5];
 cout<<"\n Enter no. of productions:";
 cin>>n;

 //Struct initialization

 for(i=0;i<7;i++)
 {
  obj[i].no_rules=0;
  obj[i].end=0;
  for(j=0;j<n+1;j++)
   for(k=0;k<6;k++)
    obj[i].a[j][k]='0';
 }

 //Taking input
 cout<<"\n Enter the productions:\n";
 int j1=0;
 for(i=0;i<n;i++)
 {
  if(i==n-1) j1=1;
    else j1=0;
  for(j=j1;j<5;j++)
    cin>>arr[i][j];
 }
 //Display augmented grammar: I0

 obj[0].no_rules-n+1;
 for(i=0;i<obj[0].no_rules;i++)
 {
```

```
  if(i==n)
    {
      obj[0].a[i][0]=arr[i-1][1];
      obj[0].a[i][1]=arr[i-1][2];
      obj[0].a[i][2]=arr[i-1][3];
      obj[0].a[i][3]='.';
      obj[0].a[i][4]=arr[i-1][4];
    }
  else
  {
   for(j=0;j<6;j++)
   {
    if(i==0)
     {
      obj[0].a[i][0]='S';
      obj[0].a[i][1]='1';
      obj[0].a[i][2]='-';
      obj[0].a[i][3]='>';
      obj[0].a[i][4]='.';
      obj[0].a[i][5]='S';
     }
     else if(i>0 && j<3)
      obj[0].a[i][j]=arr[i-1][j];
     else if(i>0 && j==3)
      obj[0].a[i][j]='.';
     else
      obj[0].a[i][j]=arr[i-1][j-1];
   }
  }
}
//display I0:

cout<<"\n Augmented grammar: I0 \n";
for(i=0;i<obj[0].no_rules;i++)
{
 cout<<"\n";
 if(i==n)
 {
  for(j=0;j<n+2;j++)
   cout<<obj[0].a[i][j];
 }
 else
 {
  for(j=0;j<6;j++)
   cout<<obj[0].a[i][j];
```

```
  }
 }

 // Calculation of I1

 for(i=0;i<n+2;i++)
 {
  if(i<=3)
   obj[1].a[0][i]=obj[0].a[0][i];
  else
   {
    temp=obj[0].a[0][i];
    obj[1].a[0][i]=obj[0].a[0][i+1];
    obj[1].a[0][i+1]=temp;
   }
 }
 obj1[nt].s=0;
 obj1[nt].d=1;
 obj1[nt].c=obj[0].a[0][5];
 obj[1].no_rules=1;
 nt=nt+1;
 display(nt);
 obj[1].end=1;

 //display I1;

 cout<<"\n\n I1: ";
 for(i=0;i<obj[1].no_rules;i++)
 {
  cout<<"\n\n";
  for(j=0;j<n+3;j++)
   cout<<obj[1].a[i][j];
 }

 //calculation of I2

 for(i=0;i<n+1;i++)
 {
  if(i<3)
   obj[2].a[0][i]=obj[0].a[1][i];
  else
  {
   temp=obj[0].a[1][i];
   obj[2].a[0][i]=obj[0].a[1][i+1];
   obj[2].a[0][i+1]=temp;
```

```
 }
}
obj[2].a[0][n+2]=obj[0].a[1][n+2];
obj[2].no_rules+=1;

 // checking for '.' followed by non-terminal

 for(i=0;i<n+2;i++)
 {
  if(obj[2].a[0][i]=='.'  &&  (65<=obj[2].a[0][i+1]  &&  obj[2].a[0]
    [i+1]<=90))
  {
   for(j=1;j<n;j++)
   {
    obj[2].no_rules+=1;
    if(j==n-1)
     for(k=0;k<n+2;k++)
      obj[2].a[j][k]=obj[0].a[j+1][k];
    else
    {
     for(k=0;k<n+3;k++)
      obj[2].a[j][k]=obj[0].a[j+1][k];
    }
   }
  }
 }
 obj1[nt].s=0;
 obj1[nt].d=2;
 obj1[nt].c=obj[0].a[n-1][0];
 nt=nt+1;
 display(nt);
 getch();

//display I2

cout<<"\n\n I2:\n";
for(i=0;i<obj[2].no_rules;i++)
{
 cout<<"\n";
 if(i==obj[2].no_rules-1)
  for(j=0;j<n+2;j++)
   cout<<obj[2].a[i][j];
 else
  {
   for(j=0;j<n+3;j++)
    cout<<obj[2].a[i][j];
```

```
    }
  }

  // calculation of I3

  for(i=0;i<n+1;i++)
  {
   if(i<3)
    obj[3].a[0][i]=obj[0].a[2][i];
   else
   {
    temp=obj[0].a[2][i];
    obj[3].a[0][i]=obj[0].a[2][i+1];
    obj[3].a[0][i+1]=temp;
   }
  }
  obj[3].a[0][n+2]=obj[0].a[1][n+2];
  obj[3].no_rules+=1;

   // checking for '.' followed by non-terminal

   for(i=0;i<n+2;i++)
   {
    if(obj[3].a[0][i]=='.'  &&  (65<=obj[3].a[0][i+1]  &&  obj[3].a[0]
      [i+1]<=90))
    {
     for(j=1;j<n;j++)
     {
      obj[3].no_rules+=1;
      if(j==n-1)
       for(k=0;k<n+2;k++)
        obj[3].a[j][k]=obj[0].a[j+1][k];
      else
      {
       for(k=0;k<n+3;k++)
        obj[3].a[j][k]=obj[0].a[j+1][k];
      }
     }
    }
   }
   obj1[nt].s=0;
   obj1[nt].d=3;
   obj1[nt].c=obj[0].a[n-1][n+1];
   nt=nt+1;
   display(nt);
```

```
 getch();

 //display I3

 cout<<"\n\n I3:\n";
for(i=0;i<obj[3].no_rules;i++)
{
 cout<<"\n";
 if(i==obj[3].no_rules-1)
  for(j=0;j<n+2;j++)
   cout<<obj[3].a[i][j];
 else
  {
   for(j=0;j<n+3;j++)
    cout<<obj[3].a[i][j];
  }
}

//calculation of I4

for(i=0;i<n;i++)
 obj[4].a[0][i]=obj[0].a[n][i];
temp=obj[0].a[n][i];
obj[4].a[0][i]=obj[0].a[i][i+1];
obj[4].a[0][i+1]=temp;
obj[4].end=1;
obj[4].no_rules=1;
obj1[nt].s=0;
obj1[nt].d=4;
obj1[nt].c=obj[0].a[n][n+1];
nt=nt+1;
display(nt);
getch();

//display I4

cout<<"\n\n I4:\n\n";
for(i=0;i<n+2;i++)
 cout<<obj[4].a[0][i];

//calculation of I5

for(i=0;i<n+1;i++)
 obj[5].a[0][i]=obj[2].a[0][i];
temp=obj[2].a[0][i];
```

```
obj[5].a[0][i]=obj[2].a[0][i+1];
obj[5].a[0][i+1]=temp;
obj[5].end=1;
obj[5].no_rules=1;
obj1[nt].s=2;
obj1[nt].d=5;
obj1[nt].c=obj[0].a[n][0];
nt=nt+1;
display(nt);
getch();

//display I5

cout<<"\n\n I5:\n\n";
for(i=0;i<n+3;i++)
 cout<<obj[5].a[0][i];

//table entries

obj1[nt].s=2;
obj1[nt].d=3;
obj1[nt].c=obj[0].a[n-1][n+1];
nt=nt+1;
display(nt);
getch();
cout<<"\n";
obj1[nt].s=2;
obj1[nt].d=4;
obj1[nt].c=obj[0].a[n][n+1];
nt=nt+1;
display(nt);
cout<<"\n";
getch();

//calculation of I6

for(i=0;i<n+1;i++)
 obj[6].a[0][i]=obj[3].a[0][i];
temp=obj[3].a[0][i];
obj[6].a[0][i]=obj[3].a[0][i+1];
obj[6].a[0][i+1]=temp;
obj[6].end=1;
obj[6].no_rules=1;
obj1[nt].s=3;
obj1[nt].d=6;
```

```
obj1[nt].c=obj[0].a[n][0];
nt=nt+1;
display(nt);
getch();

//display I6

cout<<"\n\n I6:\n\n";
for(i=0;i<n+3;i++)
 cout<<obj[6].a[0][i];
cout<<"\n";

//table entries

obj1[nt].s=3;
obj1[nt].d=3;
obj1[nt].c=obj[0].a[n-1][n+1];
nt=nt+1;
display(nt);
getch();
cout<<"\n";
obj1[nt].s=3;
obj1[nt].d=4;
obj1[nt].c=obj[0].a[n][n+1];
nt=nt+1;
display(nt);

//-----------------------------------------------------

//getting input for table

cout<<"\n \n Enter no. of terminals:";
cin>>no_t;
cout<<"\n Enter the terminals:";
for(i=0;i<no_t;i++)
 cin>>t[0][i];
cout<<"\n\n Enter no. of non-terminals:";
cin>>no_nt;
n1=no_t+no nt;
k=0;
cout<<"\n Enter non-terminals";
for(i=no_t;i<n1;i++)
{
 cout<<"\n Enter non-terminal"<<k+1<<":";
 cin>>t[0][i];
```

```
  k=k+1;
  cout<<"\n Enter follow set for this non-terminal:";
  if(i!=no_t)
  {
   for(j=0;j<3;j++)
    cin>>f[i][j];
  }
  else
   cin>>f[i][0];
 }

 //creating table

 for(i=1;i<n+2;i++)
 {
  for(j=0;j<n1;j++)
  {
   a=find(i-1,t[0][j],nt);
   if(a==-1)
    t1[i][j]=0;
   else
    t1[i][j]=a;
  }
 }

 j=0;
 for(i=0;i<7;i++)
 {
  if(obj[i].end==1)
  {
   if(obj[i].a[0][0]=='S')
     t1[i+1][2]=1;
   else
    t1[i+1][j]=0;

    if(obj[i].a[0][0]=='A' && i==4)
     for(k=0;k<n;k++)
      t1[i+1][k]=3;
    else if(obj[i].a[0][0]=='A' && i==6)
     for(k=0;k<n;k++)
      t1[i+1][k]=2;
    else if(i>n+1)
      t1[i+1][j]=0;
    else ;
  }
```

```
  j++;
 }

 // displaying parsing table

 cout<<"\n\n Parsing table:\n\n";
 cout<<"  ";
 for(i=0;i<n1;i++)
  cout<<"  "<<t[0][i];
 for(i=1;i<n+2;i++)
 {
  cout<<"\n I"<<i-1;
  for(j=0;j<n1;j++)
  {
   if(i==n-1) break;
   if(j<n && t1[i][j]!=0)
    cout<<" S"<<t1[i][j];
   else if(j>=n && t1[i][j]!=0)
    cout<<"  "<<t1[i][j];
   else
    cout<<"  ";
  }
 }

 for(i=n+2;i<8;i++)
 {
  cout<<"\n I"<<i-1;
  for(j=0;j<n;j++)
  {
    if(t1[i][j]!=0 && i!=n+3)
     cout<<" R"<<t1[i][j];
    else if(i==n+3 && j==n-1)
     cout<<"   R"<<t1[i][j];
    else
    cout<<"  ";
  }
 }
getch();
}
```

Example 13.6 Program in Java to find the augmented grammar and display all the states for the given grammar

```
import java.util.ArrayList;
import java.util.scanner;
```

```
public class LRParser
{
static int STATE_NO=0;
static int n;
static state state[]= snew State[50];

public static void main(String args [])
{
String prod[]=new String[10];
Scanner in=new Scanner( System.in);
System.out.println("Enter no. of productions:");
n=in.nextInt( );
n++;
for(int i=1; i<n; i++)
prod[i]=in.next ( ):
System.out.println("Augmenting Given Grammer...\n");
prod[0]="P→"+prod[1].charAt (0):
int i=0;
String str;
do
{
    if(STATE_NO==0)
    {
        State s=new State(STATE_NO++);
        str=prod[0].substring (0,3) +","prod[0].substring(3,prod[0].
          length( ));
        s.prod.add(str);
        s.c=prod[0].charAt(3);
        s.parent=-1;
        GenerateState(s,prod);
        state[0]=s;
        Generategoto(s, prod);
    }
    else
    {
        GenerateState(state[i],prod);
        Generategoto(state[i],prod);
    }
    i++;
}
while(i<STATE_NO);

for(i=0;i<STATE_NO;i++)
{
    System.out.println("State I"+i+":");

    for(String str1:state[i].prod)
```

```
    {
        System.out.println(""+str1);
        System.out.println(" Goto : "+state[i].next):
        System.out.println("");
    }
}
static void GenerateState(State s, String prod[])
{
    int k=0;
    int i,j;
    char c;

    String p;
    String str;

        int x=0, size=s.prod.size();

        while(x<size)
        {
            p=s.prod.get (x);
            i=p.indexof('.');
            if(i+1<p.length())
            {
                c=p.charAt (i+1);
                for(j=1;j<n;j++)
                {
                    if(prod[j].charAt(0)==c)
                    {
                    Str=prod[j].substring(0,3)+"."+prod[j].substring(3,
                      prod [j].length());
                    if(!s.prod.contains(str))
                    s.prod.add(str);
                    }
                }
            }
            x++
            size=s.prod.size();
        }
}
static void Generategoto(State s, String prod[])
{
    int i,j,k;
    State ns;
    char c;
    char temp []=null;
    String t;
```

```
string look="";
boolean pres;

for(String p:s.prod)
{
    i=p.indexof('.');
    pres=false;
    if(i+1<p.length())
    {
        temp=p.tocharArray();
        c=temp [i];
        temp [i]=temp[i+1];
        temp [i+1]=c;
        t=new String(temp);
        c=p. charAt(i+1):
        if(!look.contains("" +c))
        {
            outer: for(k=0: k<STATE_NO; k++)
            {
                for(string pc:state[k].prod)
                if(pc.contains (t))
                {
                    pres=true;
                    look+=p.charAt (i+1)+""+k+" ";
                    break outer;
                }
            }
        }
        If(!pres && !look.contains (""+p.charAt (i+1)))
        {
            ns=new State(STATE_NO);
            ns.c=p.charAt(i+1);
            ns.parent=s.sid;
            ns.prod.add(t):
            look+=ns.c+""+STATE_NO+"";
            state[STATE_NO]=ns;
            STATE_NO++;
        }
        else
        if(!pres && look.contains("+ p.charAt (i+1)))
        {
            j=look.indexOf(p.charAt(i+1));
            int sindx=Integer.parseInt(""+look.charAt(j+1));
            if(!state[sindx].prod.contains(t))
            state [sindx]. prod.add(t);
        }
```

```
            }
        }
        s.next=look;
    }
}
class State
{
    int sid;
    char c;
    int parent;
    String next;
    ArrayList<String> prod;

    public State(int sid)
    {
        this.sid= sid;
        prod=new ArrayList();
    }
}
```

Output:

Enter no. of productions:
4
S→AB
A→aA
A→b
B→b
Augmenting Given Grammer.

State I0:
P→.S
S→.AB
A→.aA
A→,b
Goto:S1 A2 a3 b4

State Il:
P→.S
Goto:

State I2:
S→A.B
B→.b
Goto: B5 b6

State I3:
A→a.A
A-.aA
A→.b
Goto:A7 a3 b4

State I4:
A→b
Goto:

State I5:
S→AB
Goto:

State I6:
B→b.
Goto

State I7:
A→aA
Goto:

Example 13.7 Program in Java to perform syntax-directed translation for IF construct and to display the three-address code

The program prompts the user to enter the IF condition and the loop statements.

Sdts.java

```
package sdts;
import java.util.Scanner;
public class Sdts {
    public static void main(String[] args) {
        Scanner sc =new Scanner(System.in);
        String[] arr = new String[20];
        String[] str = new String[20];
        String[] t = new String[20];

        System.out.println("****SDTS for IF construct**** \n");
        System.out.println("Enter IF condition:");
        str[1]=sc.next();


        System.out.println("\n  Enter  Number  of  Statements  inside
          IF: ");
        int n=sc.nextInt();
        int s=0;
        int start=100;
        int addr=100;
```

```
        while(s<arr.length){
            System.out.println("Enter statements of IF loop");
            for(int i=2;i<=n+1;i++){
                str[i]=sc.next();
                t=str[i].split("=");
                arr[s]=((start)+""+"t"+i+"="+t[1]);
                s++;

                arr[s]=((start+1)+":"+t[0]+"=t"+i);
                s++;

                start =start +2;
            }
        arr[s]=((start)+":if("+str[1]+")goto"+(addr));s++;
        arr[s]=((start+1)+"goto"+""+(start+2));s++;
        arr[s]=((start+2)+"exit");
        break;
            }
        for(int i=0; i<=s;i++){
            System.out.println(""+arr[i]);
        }
        }
    }
```

Output:

```
****SDTS for IF construct****
Enter IF condition:
a<b
Enter Number of Statements inside IF:
3
Enter statements of IF loop
a=b+c
c=d+e
h=e+j
100t2=b+c
101:a=t2
102t3=d+e
103:c=t3
104t4=e+j
105:h=t4
106:if(a<b)goto100
107goto108
108exit
```

Example 13.8 Program in Java to detect leader statements and basic blocks in the given three-address code

Consider the input file 'file.txt' as given. Apply the rules of leader statement identification and print the statement number of the leader statements. Find the basic blocks and display the statements of the block. Also display the flow of the program by indicating the goto statements for each block.

Input file: 'file.txt'

```
f=1
i=2
if i<=x goto 8
f=f*i
t1=i+1
i=t1
goto 3
exit
```

Assumption: The statements are saved starting at 1 for f=1.

Leader.java

```
package leader;
import java.io.BufferedReader;
import java.io.FileNotFoundException;
import java.io.FileReader;
import java.io.IOException;
import java.util.ArrayList;
import java.util.Collections;

public class Leader {
    public static void main(String[] args) throws IOException,
    FileNotFoundException {
        // TODO code application logic here
        ArrayList<Integer> leaders=new ArrayList();
        BufferedReader br =new BufferedReader( new FileReader("file.
        txt"));
        int bcnt=1;
        String code[]=new String[50];
        String str;
        Block b[]=new Block[50];
        int i=1;
        int n;
        while((str=br.readLine())!=null) {
            System.out.println(i+":"+str);
            code[i++]=str;
                }
        n=i-1;
        leaders.add(1);
```

```
 int j,k;
 String t;
 int n1;

 for(i=1;i<=n;i++){
     if(code[i].contains("goto")){
         j=code[i].indexOf("goto");
         t=code[i].substring(j+5,code[i].length());
         n1=new Integer(t);
         if(!leaders.contains(n1))
         {
             leaders.add(n1);
          }
         if(!leaders.contains(i+1))
         {
             leaders.add(i+1);
         }
     }
 }

System.out.println("Leaders are:");
Collections.sort(leaders);
System.out.println(leaders);

int prev=1;
for(int l:leaders){
    if(l==1)
        continue;
    b[bcnt]=new Block();
    b[bcnt].s = prev;
    b[bcnt].e=l-1;
    for(i=prev;i<l;i++)
        b[bcnt].code.add(code[i]);
       prev=l;
       bcnt++;
    }
if(prev<=n){
    b[bcnt]=new Block();
    for(i=prev;i<l;i++)
        b[bcnt].code.add(code[i]);
    b[bcnt].s = prev;
    b[bcnt].e=n;
    bcnt++;
}
int flag;
for(i=1;i<bcnt-1;i++){
```

```
            flag=0;
            for(String s:b[i].code){
                if(s.contains("goto")){
                    flag=1;
                    j=s.indexOf("goto");
                    j+=5;
                    t=s.substring(j,s.length());
                    k=Integer.parseInt(t);
                    for(j=1;j<bcnt;j++){
                        if(b[j].s<=k && k<=b[j].e){
                            b[i].out +="block" +j+"";
                            if(s.contains("if")&&(i+1)<bcnt)
                                b[i].out+="block"+(i+1)+"";
                                break;
                        }
                    }

                }
            }

        if (flag==0)
            b[i].out+="block"+(i+1)+"";
    }

    System.out.println("\nBlocks are:");
    for(i=1;i<bcnt;i++)
    {
        System.out.println("BLOCK"+i+"");
        for(String t2:b[i].code)
            System.out.println(""+t2);
        System.out.println("goto");
        System.out.println(""+b[i].out);
        System.out.println("");

    }
}
}
class Block
{
int s,e;
ArrayList<String> code= new ArrayList();
String out="";
}
```

Output:

1:f=1

2:i=2

```
3:if i<=x goto 8
4:f=f*i
5:t1=i+1
6:i=t1
7:goto 3
8:exit
Leaders are:
[1, 3, 4, 8]

Blocks are:
BLOCK1
f=1
i=2
goto
block2

BLOCK2
if i<=x goto 8
goto
block4block3

BLOCK3
f=f*i
t1=i+1
i=t1
goto 3
goto
block2

BLOCK4
exit
goto
```

Exercises

Practice Questions

1. Implement LR parsing in Java.
2. Implement SDTS for various programming language constructs: while, for, if-else.
   Variation: Consider a file as input containing the complete loop; then extract the loop statements and perform intermediate code generation.
3. Write a program to find the leader statements and print the complete statements.
4. Find the basic block and display the program flow graph using proper representation.
5. Write a program for elimination of induction variables for a given input.

14 Solved GATE Questions

1. The process of assigning load addresses to various parts of the program and adjusting the code and data in the program to reflect the assigned addresses is called: (CS 2001)
(a) Assembly (b) Parsing (c) Relocation (d) Symbol resolution

Answer: (c). Relocation is the process of replacing symbolic references or names of libraries with actual usable addresses in memory before running a program. It is typically done by the linker during compilation (at compile time); it can also be done at run-time by a relocating loader. Compilers or assemblers typically generate the executable with zero as the lowermost starting address. Before execution of the object code, these addresses should be adjusted so that they denote the correct run-time addresses.

Relocation is typically performed in two steps: 1. Each object code has various sections such as code, data, .bss, etc. To combine all the objects into a single executable, the linker merges all sections of similar type into a single section of that type. The linker then assigns run-time addresses to each section and each symbol. At this point, the code (functions) and data (global variables) will have unique run-time addresses. 2. Each section refers to one or more symbols which should be modified so that they point to the correct run-time addresses.

2. Consider a program P that consists of two source modules, M1 and M2, contained in two different files. If M1 contains a reference to a function defined in M2, the reference will be resolved at: (CS 2004)
(a) Edit time (b) Compile time (c) Link time (d) Load time

Answer: (c). The compiler transforms source code into the target language. The target language is generally in binary form, known as object code. Typically, an object file can contain three kinds of symbols:

- Defined symbols, which allow it to be called by other modules
- Undefined symbols, which call the other modules where these symbols are defined
- Local symbols, used internally within the object file to facilitate relocation

When a program comprises multiple object files, the linker combines these files into a unified executable program, resolving the symbols as it goes along.

3. Match the following input (from the left column) to the compiler phase (in the right column) that processes it: (CS 2017)

(P) Syntax tree	(i) Code generator
(Q) Character stream	(ii) Syntax analyser
(R) Intermediate representation	(iii) Semantic analyser
(S) Token stream	(iv) Lexical analyser

(a) P→(ii), Q→ (iii), R→ (iv), S→(i) (b) P→(ii), Q→ (i), R→ (iii), S→(vi)
(c) P→(iii), Q→ (iv), R→ (i), S→(ii) (d) P→(i), Q→ (iv), R→ (ii), S→(iii)

Answer (c). Character stream is given as input to the Lexical analyser, and it produces Token stream. This is input to the Syntax analyser, which produces Syntax tree. This, in turn, is input to the next phase, Semantic analysis. Intermediate code is then given to the Code generator to produce the final output.

4. Which one of the following statements is FALSE? (CS 2018)
   (a) Context-free grammar can be used to specify both lexical and syntax rules.
   (b) Type checking is done before parsing.
   (c) High-level language programs can be translated to different intermediate representations.
   (d) Arguments to a function can be passed using the program stack.

   Answer: (b). Type checking is done in the semantic analysis phase and parsing in the syntax analysis phase. Syntax analysis precedes semantic analysis. So (b) is false.

Lexical Analysis

1. The number of tokens in the following C statement is: (GATE 2000)
   printf("i = %d, &i = %x", i, &i);
   (a) 3 (b) 26 (c) 10 (d) 21

   Answer: (c). In the C compiler, tokens can be identifiers, keywords, constants, operators, strings or other symbols. The tokens in the above statement are as follows:

Sr. No.	Token	Token type
1	Printf	Keyword
2	(	Symbol
3	"i-%d, &i= %x"	String
4	,	Symbol
5	i	Identifier
6	,	Symbol
7	&	Symbol
8	i	Symbol
9	)	Symbol
10	;	Symbol

   There are a total of 10 tokens; hence, option (c).

2. In a compiler, keywords of a language are recognised during: (CS 2011)
   (a) Parsing of the program (b) Code generation
   (c) Lexical analysis of the program (d) Data flow analysis

   Answer: (c). Keywords are a type of token, which is identified by the lexical analyser.

3. The lexical analysis for a modern computer language such as Java needs the power of which one of the following machine models in a necessary and sufficient sense? (CS 2011)
   (a) Finite state automata (b) Deterministic pushdown automata
   (c) Non-deterministic pushdown automata (d) Turing machine

   Answer: (a). In lexical analysis, the source program is divided into tokens. The tokens of a language constitute a regular set that can be specified using regular expression notation. For every regular expression, we can construct finite state automata that can recognise the token specified by the regular expression.

Parsing

1. Which of the following derivations does a top-down parser use while parsing an input string? The input is assumed to be scanned in left-to-right order. (CS 2000)
   (a) Leftmost derivation (b) Leftmost derivation traced in reverse
   (c) Rightmost derivation (d) Rightmost derivation traced in reverse

   Answer: (a)

2. Given the following expression grammar: (CS 2000)
   E → E * F | F + E | F
   F → F − F | id
   Which of the following is true?
   (a) * has higher precedence than +
   (b) − has higher precedence than *
   (c) + and − have the same precedence
   (d) + has higher precedence than *

   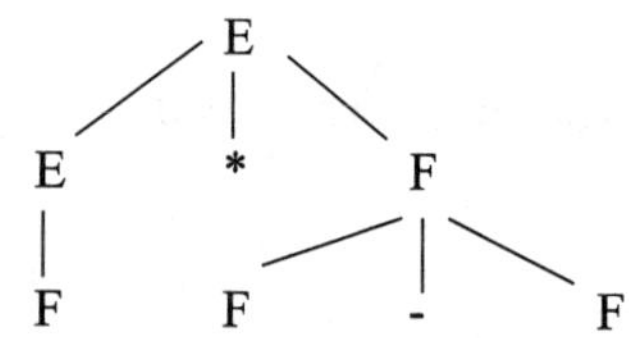

   Answer: (b). A production rule with higher precedence operator does not produce an expression with operator having lower precedence.
   Expression F → F − F will be evaluated before E →E * F. Hence − has higher precedence than *.

3. Which of the following derivations does a top-down parser use while parsing an input string? The input is assumed to be scanned in left-to-right order. (CS 2000)
   (a) Leftmost derivation (b) Leftmost derivation traced in reverse
   (c) Rightmost derivation (d) Rightmost derivation traced in reverse

   Answer: (a)

4. Which of the following statements is FALSE? (CS 2001)
   (a) An unambiguous grammar has same leftmost and rightmost derivations
   (b) An LL(1) parser is a top-down parser
   (c) LALR is more powerful than SLR
   (d) An ambiguous grammar can never be LR(*k*) for any *k*

   Answer: (a)

5. Which of the following suffices to convert an arbitrary CFG to an LL(1) grammar? (CS 2003)
   (a) Removing left recursion alone (b) Factoring the grammar alone
   (c) Removing left recursion and factoring the grammar (d) None of these

   Answer: (c)

6. Assume that the SLR parser for a grammar G has n1 states and the LALR parser for G has n2 states. The relationship between n1 and n2 is: (CS 2003)
   (a) n1 is necessarily less than n2 (b) n1 is necessarily equal to n2
   (c) n1 is necessarily greater than n2 (d) None of these

   Answer: (b)

7. In a bottom-up evaluation of a syntax-directed definition, inherited attributes can: (CS 2003)
   (a) Always be evaluated
   (b) Be evaluated only if the definition is L-attributed
   (c) Be evaluated only if the definition has synthesized attributes
   (d) Never be evaluated

Answer: (b). Syntax-directed definition is S-attributed if it has only synthesized attributes. It is L-attributed if it contains both synthesized and inherited attributes.

8. Consider the grammar shown below
S → i E t S S' | a
S' → e S | ε
E → b
In the predictive parse table M, of this grammar, the entries M[S', e] and M[S', $], respectively, are: (CS 2003)
(a) {S' → e S} and {S' → e} (b) {S' → e S} and {}
(c) {S' → ε} and {S' → ε} (d) {S' → e S, S'→ ε} and {S' → ε}

Answer: (d)

- FIRST of S' has e. Due to which M[S', e] will contain S' → e S.
- FIRST of S' also has ϵ, due to which S'→ ε entry will be made in M[S', FOLLOW(S')]

Hence, S'→ ε is added to M[S', e] and M[S', $].

Non-terminal	FIRST	FOLLOW
S	i, a	e, $
S'	e, ϵ	e, $
E	B	t

9. Consider the grammar shown below (CS 2003)
S → C C
C → c C | d
The grammar is:
(a) LL(1) (b) SLR(1) but not LL(1)
(c) LALR(1) but not SLR(1) (d) LR(1) but not LALR(1)

Answer: (a)

10. Which of the following grammar rules violate the requirements of an operator grammar? P, Q and R are non-terminals, and r, s and t are terminals. (CS 2004)
1. P → Q R 2. P → Q s R 3. P → ε 4. P → Q t R r
(a) 1 only (b) 1 and 3 only (c) 2 and 3 only (d) 3 and 4 only

Answer: (b). An operator precedence parser is a bottom-up parser that interprets an operator-precedence grammar. A grammar is considered as an operator precedence grammar if and only if:
1. There is no ε production
2. There are no two adjacent non-terminals on the RHS of the production rule.
These properties allow the terminals of the grammar to be described by a precedence relation.
- Production number 1 violates rule number 2
- Production number 3 violates rule number 1.

11. The grammar A → AA | (A) | ε is not suitable for predictive parsing because the grammar is: (CS 2005)
(a) Ambiguous (b) Left-recursive (c) Right-recursive (d) An operator grammar

Answer: (b)

12. Consider the grammar (CS 2005)
E → E + n | E × n | n
For a sentence n + n × n, the handles in the right-sentential form of the reduction are:
(a) n, E + n and E + n × n (b) n, E + n and E + E × n
(c) n, n + n and n + n × n (d) n, E + n and E × n

Answer: (d). To find the handle, we need to trace RMD in reverse.

RMD	HANDLE
E	
E x n	E → E x n
E + n x n	E → E + n, preceding x
n + n x n	E → n, preceding +

Hence, the handles are n, E + n and E x n

13. Consider the grammar (CS 2005)
S → (S) | a
Let the number of states in SLR(1), LR(1) and LALR(1) parsers for the grammer be n1, n2 and n3, respectively. Which of the following relationships holds good?
(a) n1 < n2 < n3 (b) n1 = n3 < n2 (c) n1 = n2 = n3 (d) n1 ≥ n3 ≥ n2
Answer: (b). States of LR(1) are merged to form LALR(1). So, the number of states in LALR(1) is less than in LR(1) (n3 < n2). SLR(1) and LALR(1) have the same number of states, i.e., (n1 = n3). Hence, option (b).

14. Consider the following grammar (CS 2006)
S → S * E
S → E
E → F + E
E → F
F → id.
Consider the following LR(0) items corresponding to the grammar above.
(i) S → S * .E (ii) E → F. + E (iii) E → F + .E
Given the items above, which two will appear in the same set in the canonical sets-of-items for the grammar?
(a) (i) and (ii) (b) (ii) and (iii) (c) (i) and (iii) (d) None of the above
Answer: (d). Constructing the SLR parsing diagram, we see that the above three productions do not appear in the same state.

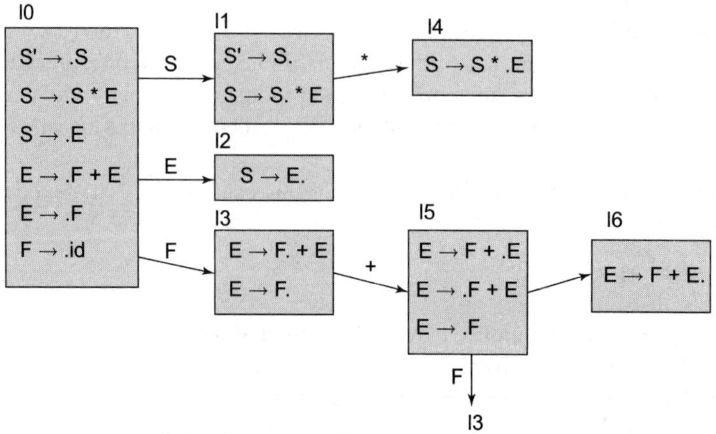

15. Consider the following grammar (CS 2006)
S → FR
R → S | ε
F → id
In the predictive parser table M of the grammar, the entries M[S, id] and M[R, $] correspond to:
(a) {S → FR} and {R → ε} (b) {S → FR} and { }
(c) {S → FR} and {R → *S} (d) {F → id} and {R → ε}

Answer: (a)

- id in FIRST of S will add the production rule S→FR at M[S, id]
- FIRST of R contains ϵ. So, we need to make an entry of R→ϵ in FOLLOW(R). Hence, M[R, $] will contain R→ ϵ

Non-terminal	FIRST	FOLLOW
S	id	$
R	s, ϵ	$
F	Id	s,$

16. Which one of the following is a top-down parser? (CS 2007)
(a) Recursive descent parser (b) Operator precedence parser
(c) An LR(*k*) parser (d) An LALR(*k*) parser

Answer: (a)

17. Consider the grammar with non-terminals N = {S,C,S1}, terminals T={a,b,i,t,e}, with S as the start symbol, and the following set of rules: (CS 2007)
S → iCtSS1|a
S1 →eS|ϵ
C → b
The grammar is NOT LL(1) because:
(a) It is left recursive (b) It is right recursive
(c) It is ambiguous (d) It is not context-free

Answer: (c)

- The grammar is not left recursive. Hence, (a) is incorrect.
- LL(1) is not affected by right recursion. Hence, (b) is incorrect.
- Grammar is context-free. Hence, (d) is incorrect.
- Option (c) is correct. We can obtain more than one parse tree for an input string using the given grammar.

18. Consider the following two statements: (CS 2007)
P: Every regular grammar is LL(1). Q: Every regular set has an LR(1) grammar.
Which of the following is TRUE?
(a) Both P and Q are true (b) P is true and Q is false
(c) P is false and Q is true (d) Both P and Q are false

Answer: (c). Statement P is false. Regular grammar can be ambiguous whereas LL(1) can parse only unambiguous grammar. Statement Q is true. For every regular set, we can have a regular grammar.

Common data for Q. 19 and 20. (CS 2007)
Solve the problems and choose the correct answers. Consider the CFG with {S, A, B}as the non-terminal alphabet, {a, b} as the terminal alphabet, S as the start symbol and the following set of production rules

s→bA	S→aB
A→a	B→b
A→aS	B→bS
A→bAA	B→aBB

19. Which of the following strings is generated by the grammar?
(a) aaaabb (b) aabbbb (c) aabbab (d) abbbba

Answer: (c)

20. For the correct answer string to Q. 19, how many derivation trees are possible?
(a) 1 (b) 2 (c) 3 (d) 4

Answer: (b)

21. Which of the following describes a handle (as applicable to LR parsing) appropriately? (CS 2008)
(a) It is the position in a sentential form where the next shift or reduce operation will occur.
(b) It is non-terminal whose production will be used for reduction in the next step.
(c) It is a production that may be used for reduction in a future step along with a position in the sentential form where the next shift or reduce operation will occur.
(d) It is the production p that will be used for reduction in the next step along with a position in the sentential form where the RHS of the production may be found.

Answer: (d)

22. An LALR(1) parser for a grammar G can have shift-reduce (S-R) conflicts if and only if: (CS 2008)
(a) The SLR(1) parser for G has S-R conflicts
(b) The LR(1) parser for G has S-R conflicts
(c) The LR(0) parser for G has S-R conflicts
(d) The LALR(1) parser for G has reduce-reduce conflicts

Answer: (b). LALR(1) states can be found by merging the LR(1) states of the LR(1) parser. The productions must be same but the look-ahead are different.

- LALR(1) must have the same items as LR(1); shift-reduce form will only take place if it is already present in the LR(1) states.
- Example: Consider two states of the LR(1) parser
  S→p.qR, x and S→p.qR, y
  R→r. , q R→r. , z
  It has an S-R conflict on q. Since, in the first rule, S→p.qR, x, the candidate for shift is q, and in the second production, R→r. , q, the production ends and has to be reduced using the look-ahead, which is q.
  After merging, the state becomes:
  S→p.qR, x|y
  R→r. ,q|z

As we can see, the S-R conflict is present now as it was present in LR(1).

- If there is no S-R conflict in the LR(1) state, it will never be reflected in the LALR(1) state obtained by combining the LR(1) states.
- Merging may introduce an R-R conflict, even if it was not present in LR(1), since union of look-aheads is considered.

23. Match all items in Group 1 with the correct options from those given in Group 2: (CS 2009)

Group 1	*Group 2*
P. Regular expression	1. Syntax analysis
Q. Pushdown automata	2. Code generation
R. Data flow analysis	3. Lexical analysis
S. Register allocation	4. Code optimisation

(a) P-4. Q-1, R-2, S-3 (b) P-3, Q-1, R-4, S-2
(c) P-3, Q-4, R-1, S-2 (d) P-2, Q-1, R-4, S-3

Answer: (b). Regular expressions are used in syntax analysis. Pushdown automata are used in syntax analysis. Data flow analysis is performed in code optimisation. Register allocation is done in code generation.

24. Which of the following statements are TRUE? (CS 2009)
    I. There exist parsing algorithms for some programming languages whose complexities are less than O(n3).
    II. A programming language which allows recursion can be implemented with static storage allocation.
    III. No L-attributed definition can be evaluated in the framework of bottom-up parsing.
    IV. Code improving transformations can be performed at both source language and intermediate code level.

(a) I and II (b) I and IV (c) III and IV (d) I, III and IV

Answer: (b)

25. The grammar S → aSa | bS | c is (CS 2010)

(a) LL(1) but not LR(1) (b) LR(1) but not LR(1)
(c) Both LL(1)and LR(1) (d) Neither LL(1) nor LR(1)

Answer: (c).
FIRST(aSa) = a
FIRST(bS) = b
FIRST(c) = c
Any grammar is LL(1) if FIRST of all the production rules for each non-terminal are disjoint.
FIRST(aSa)∩FIRST(bS)∩FIRST(c) = Ø. Hence, the grammar is LL(1).
As the grammar is LL(1), it will also be LR(1) as all LL(1) grammars are also LR(1).
So option (c) is correct.

26. For the grammar below, a partial LL(1) parsing table is also presented. Entries that need to be filled are indicated as E1, E2 and E3. ϵ is the empty string, $ indicates end of input, and | separates alternate right-hand sides of the productions. (CS 2012)

S → a A b B | b A A B | ε
A → S
B → S

	a	b	$
S	E1	E2	S → ε
A	A → S	A → S	error
B	B → S	B → S	E3

(A) FIRST(A) {a, b, ε} = FIRST(B)
FOLLOW(A) = {a, b}
FOLLOW(B) = {a, b, $}

(B) FIRST(A) = {a, b, $}
FIRST(B) = {a, b, ε}
FOLLOW(A) = {a, b}
FOLLOW(B) = {$}

(C) FIRST(A) {a, b, ε} = FIRST(B)
FOLLOW(A) = {a, b}
FOLLOW(B) = ∅

(D) FIRST(A) {a, b} = FIRST(B)
FOLLOW(A) = {a, b}
FOLLOW(B) = {a, b}

(a) A (b) B (c) C (d) D

Answer: (a).

Non-teminal	FIRST	FOLLOW
S	a,b, ϵ	a,b,$
A	a,b, ϵ	a,b
B	a,b, ϵ	a,b,$

27. Consider the data given in Q. 26. The appropriate entries for E1, E2 and E3 are: (CS 2012)

(a) E1: S → aAbB, A → S
E2: S → bAaB, B → S
E3: B → S

(b) E1: S → aAbB, S → ε
E2: S → bAaB, S → ε
E3: S → ε

(c) E1: S → aAbB, S → ε
E2: S → bAaB, S → ε
E3: B → S

(d) E1: A → S, S → ε
E2: B → S, S → ε
E3: B → S

Answer: (c). As we need to find entries E1 (Table[S,a]), E2 (Table[S,b]) and E3 (Table[B,$]) which are against the non-terminals S and B, we will deal with only those productions which have S and B on the LHS.

- Production rule S→aAbB will be added at Table[S,a] i.e., E1 for terminal a in the FIRST of S.
- For terminal b, production rule S→bAaB is added to Table[S, b], i.e., E2.
- FIRST of S also contains ϵ, due to which we also make an entry in all the terminals of FOLLOW. Hence, S→ ϵ will be added at E1 and E2.
- Production rule B →S will be added to the parsing table at position E3.

28. What is the maximum number of reduce moves that can be taken by a bottom-up parser for a grammar with no epsilon and unit production (i.e., of type A → ϵ and A →B) and no production of the form A→a, to parse a string with n tokens? (CS 2013)
(a) n/2 (b) n − 1 (c) 2n − 1 (d) 2^n

Answer: (b). The bottom-up parser reduces the input string to the start symbol of the grammar by tracing the RMD of the string in reverse. Let us consider a string with 5 tokens (n=5) and grammar without ϵ and unit production.
String: abcde

Grammar-1: S→aB
B→bcD
D→ de

RMD:

S	
aB	3. Reduce with S→aB
abcD	2. Reduce with B→bcD
abc**de**	1. Reduce with D→de

Here, the number of reduces = 3. Now, consider another grammar

Grammar-2: S→aB
B→bC
C→cD
D→ de

RMD:

S	
aB	4. Reduce with S→aB
abC	3. Reduce with B→bC
abcD	2. Reduce with C→cD
abc**de**	1. Reduce with D→de

Number of reduces = 4

We need to find the maximum number of reduces, which are from Grammar-2.

4 is maximum, which is 5 – 1, i.e., n – 1. By trying different grammars and different token lengths, we can obtain option (a), but that is not maximum. The maximum reduce we can get is n – 1.

29. Consider the following two sets of LR(1) items of an LR(1) grammar (CS 2013)

X →c.X, c/d	X→c.X, $
X → .cX, c/d	X → .cX, $
X →.d, c/d	X → .d, $

Which of the following statements related to merging of the two sets in the corresponding LALR parser is/are FALSE?

1. Cannot be merged since look-aheads are different.
2. Can be merged but will result in S-R conflict.
3. Can be merged but will result in R-R conflict.
4. Cannot be merged since goto on c will lead to two different sets.

(a) 1 only (b) 2 only (c) 1 and 4 only (d) 1, 2, 3 and 4

Answer: (d). All the statements are wrong. Hence, option (d).

Statement 1: Given LR(1) items. These are merged if they have same the productions but different look-aheads. Hence, the given statement is false. After merging, the state in LALR becomes:

X → c.X, c/d/$
X → .cX, c/d/$
X → .d, c/d/$

Statement 2: In the merged set, there is no shift-reduce conflict because the reduce action is not possible in the state. For a reduce action, the dot must be at the end of the production rule; for example, X→d, which is not present in the above state.

Statement 3: In the merged set, there is no reduce-reduce conflict because the reduce action is not possible in the above state.

Statement 4: This statement is also wrong, because goto is carried on non-terminal symbols and not on terminal symbols.

30. A canonical set of items is given below (CS 2014, Set-1)

S → L. > R
Q → R.

On input symbol <, the set has

(a) A shift-reduce conflict and a reduce-reduce conflict
(b) A shift-reduce conflict but not a reduce-reduce conflict
(c) A reduce-reduce conflict but not a shift-reduce conflict
(d) Neither a shift-reduce nor a reduce-reduce conflict

Answer: (d). The symbol in the question is ‘<’, which is not present in the given canonical set of items. Hence, it is neither a shift-reduce conflict nor a reduce-reduce conflict on symbol ‘<’. Hence, (d) is the correct option.

31. Consider the grammar defined by the following production rules, with two operators $*$ and $+$ (CS 2014, Set-2)

    $S \rightarrow T * P$
    $T \rightarrow U \mid T * U$
    $P \rightarrow Q + P \mid Q$
    $Q \rightarrow Id$
    $U \rightarrow Id$

    Which one of the following is TRUE?

    (a) + is left associative, while $*$ is right associative
    (b) + is right associative, while $*$ is left associative
    (c) Both + and $*$ are right associative
    (d) Both + and $*$ are left associative

    Answer: (b). Consider the production rule $P \rightarrow Q + P$. It has right recursion, so + is right associative. Now, consider the production rule $T \rightarrow T * U$. It is left recursive, so * is left associative.

32. Which one of the following is TRUE in any valid state in shift-reduce parsing? (CS 2015, Set-1)

    (a) Viable prefixes appear only at the bottom of the stack and not inside.
    (b) Viable prefixes appear only at the top of the stack and not inside.
    (c) The stack contains only a set of viable prefixes.
    (d) The stack never contains viable prefixes.

    Answer: (c)

33. In the context of abstract syntax tree (AST) and control flow graph (CFG), which one of the following is TRUE? (CS 2015, Set-2)

    (a) In both AST and CFG, let node N2 be the successor of node N1. In the input program, the code corresponding to N2 is present after the code corresponding to N1.
    (b) For any input program, neither AST nor CFG will contain a cycle.
    (c) The maximum number of successors of a node in an AST and a CFG depends on the input program.
    (d) Each node in AST and CFG corresponds to at most one statement in the input program.

    Answer: (c).

    - CFG may contain a cycle, due to which code corresponding to N2 can be present after the code corresponding to N1. Hence, option (a) is incorrect.
    - CFG may contain a cycle. Hence, option (b) is incorrect.
    - Single node contains a block of statements. Hence, option (d) is incorrect.
    - The maximum number of successors of a node in an AST and a CFG depends on the input program.

34. Match the following: (CS 2015, Set-2)

List-I	*List-II*
A. Lexical analysis	1. Graph colouring
B. Parsing	2. DFA minimisation
C. Register allocation	3. Post-order traversal
D. Expression evaluation	4. Production tree

	A	B	C	D
(a)	2	3	1	4
(b)	2	1	4	3
(c)	2	4	1	3
(d)	2	3	4	1

Answer: (c).

- Lexical analysis uses DFA.
- Register allocation is a variation of graph colouring.
- Parsing is construction of a production tree.
- Expressions can be evaluated by post-order traversal.

35. Among simple LR (SLR), canonical LR and look-ahead LR (LALR), which of the following pairs identify the method that is very easy to implement and the method that is the most powerful, in that order?(CS 2015, Set-2)

(a) SLR, LALR (b) Canonical LR, LALR
(c) SLR, canonical LR (d) LALR, canonical LR

Answer: (c)

- SLR is easy to implement.
- Canonical LR (CLR) is the most powerful parser.

36. Consider the following grammar G (CS 2015, Set-3)

S → F | H
F → p | c
H → d | c

where S, F and H are non-terminal symbols; p, d and c are terminal symbols. Which of the following statement(s) is/are correct?

S1: LL(1) can parse all strings that are generated using grammar G.
S2: LR(1) can parse all strings that are generated using grammar G.

(a) Only S1 (b) Only S2 (c) Both S1 and S2 (d) Neither S1 and S2

Answer: (d). The given grammar is ambiguous, and hence, cannot be LL(1) or LR(1).

37. Which one of the following grammars is free from left recursion? (CS 2016, Set-2)

(A) $S \rightarrow AB$
$A \rightarrow A\text{a} \mid \text{b}$
$B \rightarrow \text{c}$

(C) $S \rightarrow A\text{a} \mid B$
$A \rightarrow B\text{b} \mid S\text{c} \mid \varepsilon$
$B \rightarrow \text{d}$

(B) $S \rightarrow A\text{b} \mid B\text{b} \mid \text{c}$
$A \rightarrow B\text{d} \mid \varepsilon$
$B \rightarrow \text{e}$

(D) $S \rightarrow A\text{a} \mid B\text{b} \mid \text{c}$
$A \rightarrow B\text{d} \mid \varepsilon$
$B \rightarrow A\text{e} \mid \varepsilon$

(a) A (b) B (c) C (d) D

Answer: (b)

38. Which of the following statements about the parser is/are correct? (CS 2017)

I. Canonical LR is more powerful than SLR. II. SLR is more powerful than LALR.
III. SLR is more powerful than canonical LR.

(a) I only (b) II only (c) III only (d) II and III only

Answer: (a)

39. Consider the following grammar (CS 2017)

p → xQRS
Q → yz|z

R → w|∈
S → y
Which is FOLLOW(Q)?
(a) {R}   (b) {w}   (c) {w, y}   (d) {w, ∉}

Answer: (c).
FOLLOW(Q)= FIRST(RS) = FIRST(R)- ∈ FIRST(S)
= {w, ∈} − ∈ {y} = {w,y}

SDTS

1. Consider the translation scheme shown below (CS 2003)
   S → T R
   R → + T {print ('+');} R | ϵ
   T → num {print (num.val);}
   Here, num is a token that represents an integer and num.val represents the corresponding integer value. For an input string '9 + 5 + 2', this translation scheme will print:
   (a) 9 + 5 + 2   (b) 9 5 + 2 +
   (c) 9 5 2 + +   (d) + + 9 5 2

   Answer: (c). Construct the parse tree corresponding to '9 + 5 + 2'
   The tree is processed left to right, bottom to top:
   - T→num, will print 9
   - Next T→num, will print 5
   - Next T→num, will print 2
   - R → + T (Rightmost), will print +
   - Going upwards R → + T will print +

   String printed: 9 5 2 + +

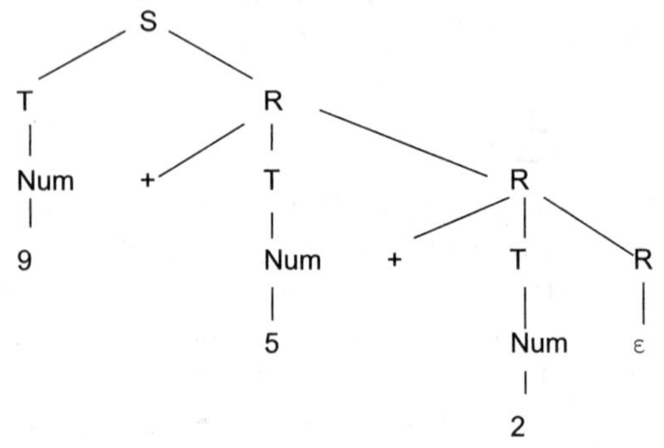

2. Consider the syntax-directed definition shown below (CS 2003)
   S → id : = E {gen (id.place = E.place;);}
   E → E1 + E2 {t = newtemp ( ); gen (t = El.place + E2.place;); E.place = t}
   E → id {E.place = id.place;}
   Here, gen is a function that generates the output code, and newtemp is a function that returns the name of a new temporary variable on every call. Assume that ti comprises the temporary variable names generated by newtemp. For the statement 'X: = Y + Z', the three-address code sequence generated by this definition is
   (a) X = Y + Z   (b) t1 = Y + Z; X = t1
   (c) t1 =Y; t2 = t1 + Z; X = t2   (d) t1 = Y; t2 = Z; t3 = t1 + t2; X = t3

   Answer: (b). Since E→ E+E is used only once, only one temporary variable must be generated.
3. Consider the grammar with the following translation rules and E as the start symbol (CS 2004)
   E → E1 # T { E.value = E1.value * T.value }
   | T{E.value = T.value }
   T → T1 & F { T.value = T1.value + F.value }
   | F{T.value = F.value }
   F → num{ F.value = num.value }
   Compute E.value for the root of the parse tree for the expression: 2 # 3 & 5 # 6 & 4.

(a) 200 (b) 180
(c) 160 (d) 40

Answer: (c).

The tree is processed left to right, bottom to top:

- The value 2 will be propagated up and E1.val =2
- T.val=T1.val+F.val = 3+ 5 = 8
- E.val for the left subtree will be= 2* 8 = 16
- Similary, T.val for the right subtree= 6 +4 = 10
- Root=16*10 = 160

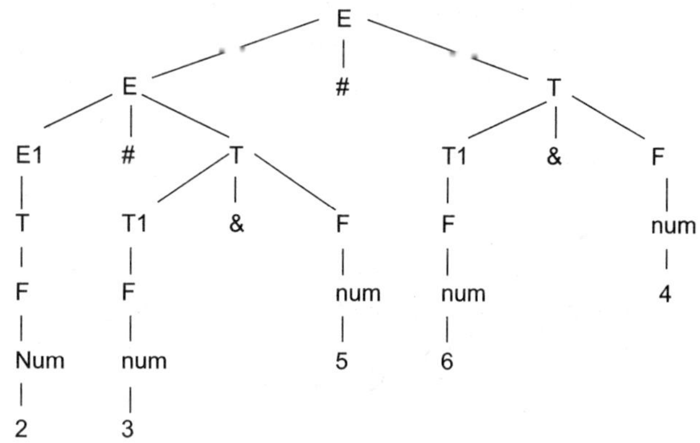

4. Consider the following expression grammar. The semantic rules for expression calculation are stated next to each grammar production.

E → number	E.val = number. val
| E '+' E	E(1).val = E(2).val + E(3).val
| E '×' E	E(1).val = E(2).val × E(3).val

The above grammar and the semantic rules are fed to a Yacc tool (which is an LALR (1) parser generator) for parsing and evaluating arithmetic expressions. Which one of the following is TRUE about the action of Yacc for the given grammar? (CS 2005)

(a) It detects and eliminates recursion. (b) It detects reduce-reduce conflict, and resolves it

(c) It detects shift-reduce conflict, and resolves the conflict in favour of a shift over a reduce action

(d) It detects shift-reduce conflict, and resolves the conflict in favour of a reduce over a shift action

Answer: (c)

5. Consider the following expression grammar. The semantic rules for expression calculation are stated next to each grammar production. (CS 2005)

E → number	E.val = number. val
| E '+' E	E(1).val = E(2).val + E(3).val
| E '×' E	E(1).val = E(2).val × E(3).val

Assume the conflicts in Q2 above are resolved and an LALR(1) parser is generated for parsing arithmetic expressions as per the given grammar. Consider an expression 3 × 2 + 1. What precedence and associativity properties does the generated parser realize?

(a) Equal precedence and left associativity; expression is evaluated to 7

(b) Equal precedence and right associativity; expression is evaluated to 9

(c) Precedence of '×' is higher than that of '+', and both operators are left associative; expression is evaluated to 7

(d) Precedence of '+' is higher than that of '×', and both operators are left associative; expression is evaluated to 9

Answer: (c)

6. Consider the following translation scheme.

S → ER

R → *E{print("*");}R | ϵ

E → F + E {print("*");} | F
F → (S) | id {print(id.value);}
Here, id is a token that represents an integer and id.value represents the corresponding integer value. For an input '2 * 3 + 4', this translation scheme prints: (CS 2006)

(a) 2 * 3 + 4 (b) 2 * +3 4 (c) 2 3 * 4 + (d) 2 3 4+*

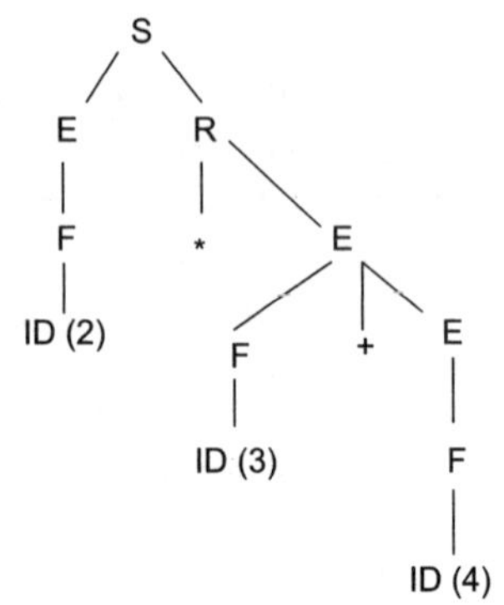

Answer: (d)

The tree is processed from left to right, bottom to top:

- When F→id is encountered first, it prints 2.
- E→ F, nothing is performed. Going from left to right.
- F→id, it prints 3, then 4 is printed.
- E→F+E prints +
- R→*E prints *

2 3 4 + * is printed.

7. Consider the following syntax-directed translation scheme (SDTS), with non-terminals {S, A} and terminals {a, b}}. (CS 2016, Set-1)

S → **a**A { print 1 }
S → **a** { print 2 }
S → **Sb** { print 1 }

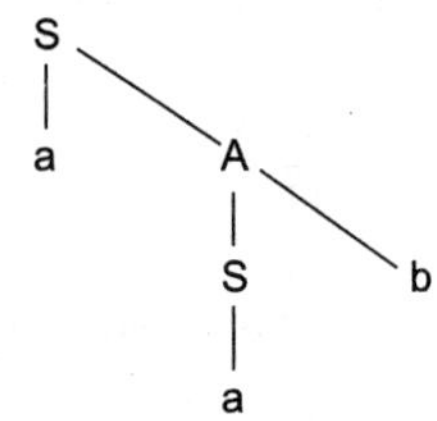

Using the above SDTS, the output printed by a bottom-up parser, for the input aab is

(a) 1 3 2 (b) 2 2 3 (c) 2 3 1 (d) Syntax Error

Answer: (c)

The tree is processed left to right, bottom to top:

- The bottom-most s→a will be processed first, which prints 2
- Next A→Sb will be processed, printing 3
- Last production to be processed is S→aA, which prints 1

Sequence printed: 2 3 1

Code Generation and Optimisation

1. In a simplified computer, the instructions are:

OP R_j, R_i - Performs R_j OP R_i and stores the result in register R_i.
OP m, R_i - Performs *val* OP R_i and stores the result in R_j *val* denotes the content of memory location m.
MOV m, R_i - Moves the content of memory location m to register R_i.
MOV R_i, m - Moves the content of register R_i to memory location m.

The computer has only two registers, and OP is either ADD or SUB. Consider the following basic block:

$t_1 = a + b$
$t_2 = c + d$
$t_3 = e - t_2$
$t_4 = t_1 - t_3$

Assume that all operands are initially in memory. The final value of the computation should be in memory. What is the minimum number of MOV instructions in the code generated for this basic block? (CS 2007)

(a) 2 (b) 3 (c) 5 (d) 6

Answer: (b)

2. Some code optimisations are carried out on the intermediate code because (CS 2008)
   (a) They enhance the portability of the compiler to other target processors
   (b) Program analysis is more accurate on intermediate code than on machine code
   (c) Information from data flow analysis cannot otherwise be used for optimisation
   (d) Information from the front end cannot otherwise be used for optimisation

   Answer: (a), (b)

3. Which one of the following is FALSE? (CS 2014, Set-1)
   (a) A basic block is a sequence of instructions where control enters the sequence at the beginning and exits at the end.
   (b) Available expression analysis can be used for common sub-expression elimination.
   (c) Live variable analysis can be used for dead code elimination.
   (d) $x = 4 * 5 => x = 20$ is an example of common sub-expression elimination

   Answer: (d)

4. One of the purposes of using intermediate code in compilers is to: (CS 2014, Set-3)
   (a) Make parsing and semantic analysis simpler. (b) Improve error recovery and error reporting.
   (c) Increase the chances of reusing the machine-independent code optimiser in other compilers.
   (d) Improve the register allocation.

   Answer: (c)

5. Consider the following C code segment

```
for(i = 0, i<n; i++)
{
    for(j=0; j<n; j++)
    {
        if(i%2)
        {
            x += (4*j + 5*i);
            y += (7 + 4*j);
        }
    }
}
```

   Which one of the following is FALSE? (CS 2006)
   (a) The code contains loop invariant computation
   (b) There is scope for common sub-expression elimination in this code
   (c) There is scope for strength reduction in this code
   (d) There is scope for dead code elimination in this code
   Answer: (d)

6. Consider the grammar rule E → E1 – E2 for arithmetic expressions. The code generated is targetted to a CPU having a single user register. The subtraction operation requires the first operand to be in the register. If E1 and E2 do not have any common sub-expression, in order to get the shortest possible code (CS 2004)
   (a) E1 should be evaluated first (b) E2 should be evaluated first
   (c) Evaluation of E1 and E2 should necessarily be interleaved
   (d) Order of evaluation of E1 and E2 is of no consequence

   Answer: (b)

7. Consider the intermediate code given below: (CS 2015, Set-2)

```
 1. i = 1
 2. j = 1
 3. t1 = 5 * i
 4. t2 = t1 + j
 5. t3 = 4 * t2
 6. t4 = t3
 7. a[t4] = –1
 8. j = j + 1
 9. if j <= 5 goto(3)
10. i = i + 1
11. if i < 5 goto(2)
```

   The number of nodes and edges in the control flow graph constructed for the above code are
   (a) 5 and 7 (b) 6 and 7 (c) 5 and 5 (d) 7 and 8

   Answer: (b)

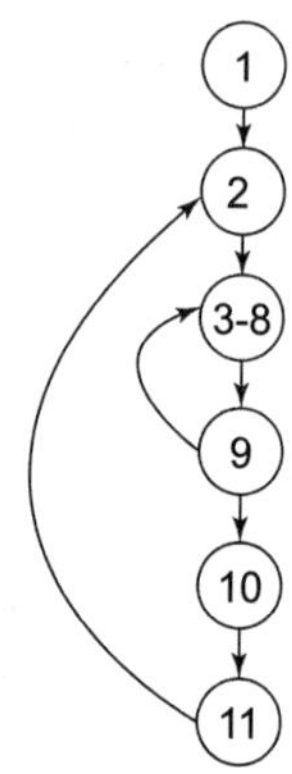

8. Consider the following code segment. (CS 2016, Set-1)

```
x = u – t;
y = x * v;
x = y + w;
y = t - z;
y = x * y;
```

   The minimum number of total variables required to convert the above code segment to static single assignment form is ________.

   Answer: 10. Static single assignment form (often abbreviated as SSA) is a property of an intermediate representation (IR), which requires that each variable is assigned exactly once, and every variable is defined before it is used. Converting the above code to SSA

```
x1 = u - t
y1 = x1 * v
x2 = y1 + w
y2 = t - z
y3 = x2 * y2
```

   Total variables used: 10 (x1, u, t, y1, v, x2, w, y2, z, y3)

Memory Allocation

1. Which of the following statements is FALSE? (CS 2003)

(a) In statically typed language, each variable in a program has a fixed type
(b) In up-typed languages, values do not have any types
(c) In dynamically typed languages, variables have no types
(d) In all statically typed languages, each variable in a program is associated with values of only a single type during execution of the program

Answer: (c)

2. Which of the following is NOT an advantage of using shared, dynamically linked libraries as opposed to using statically linked libraries? (CS 2003)
(a) Smaller sizes of executable (b) Smaller overall page fault rate in the system
(c) Faster program startup
(d) Existing programs need not be re-linked to take advantage of newer versions of libraries

Answer: (c)

3. Consider line number 3 of the following C program. (CS 2005)
```
int main (){                  | * Line 1 * |
int 1, N;                     | * line 2 * |
for (i=0, 1 < N, 1++);        | * Line 3 * |
}
```
Identify the compiler's response about this line while creating the object module:
(a) No compilation error (b) Only a lexical error
(c) Only syntactic errors (d) Both lexical and syntactic errors

Answer: (c)

4. Which of the following are TRUE? (CS 2008)
(i) A programming language option does not permit global variables of any kind and has no nesting of procedures/functions, but permits recursion to be implemented with static storage allocation
(ii) Multi-level access link (or display) arrangement is needed to arrange activation records only if the programming language being implemented has nesting of procedures/functions
(iii) Recursion in programming languages cannot be implemented with dynamic storage allocation
(iv) Nesting of procedures/functions and recursion require a dynamic heap allocation scheme and cannot be implemented with a stack-based allocation scheme for activation records
(v) Programming languages which permit a function to return a function as its result cannot be implemented with a stack-based storage allocation scheme for activation records
(a) (ii) and (v) only (b) (i), (iii) and (iv) only
(c) (i), (ii) and (v) (d) (ii), (iii) and (v) only

Answer: (b)

5. What data structure in a compiler is used for managing information about variables and their attributes? (CS 2010)
(a) Abstract syntax tree (b) Symbol table
(c) Semantic stack (d) Parse table

Answer: (b)

6. Which languages necessarily need heap allocation in the run-time environment? (CS 2010)
(a) Those that support recursion (b) Those that use dynamic scoping
(c) Those that allow dynamic data structure (c) Those that use global variables

Answer: (c)

Index

D

E

P

Q

R

U

V

W